"Every pastor has a favorite class from seminary or divinity school—a class that utterly changed their way of looking at the faith, a class that reaffirmed that ministry is a worthy calling, a delving into meaty and inspiring matters that merits every ounce of energy and creativity a person can possibly muster. For me, that class was Tom Long's class on the parables. This book is that class. It is one blessing after another, after another."

—Scott Black Johnston, pastor of Fifth Avenue Presbyterian Church

"Preacher, teacher, scholar, and disciple Tom Long offers readers a lifetime worth of fresh insights on parables we only thought we already knew well. Long provides a historical overview of biblical scholarship on parables, dives deep into the distinctiveness of each Gospel, and then explores the parables with energy, intelligence, imagination, and love. This book will be a helpful addition to preachers' and teachers' biblical reference library, but it is also worthy of being read devotionally. Either way, Long's words invite us to be surprised again by God's living Word."

—Jill Duffield, author of *Lent in Plain Sight*

"Every generation of preachers has a regularly visited bookshelf with volumes written by the finest minds of their times, promising to strike sparks they can coax into flame by the time Sunday morning comes around again. Tom Long's books have delivered on that promise for at least two generations now. With this new volume, he secures his legacy for generations to come—not only by offering his readers new ways of thinking about the purpose of the parables but also by nourishing us with his own powerful way of pointing to God's kingdom in our midst."

—Barbara Brown Taylor, author of *Always a Guest*

"This book is a literary revelation that intellectual reorientation is possible when one encounters a God with whom nothing is impossible. Tom Long, a major influential theological scholar who taught on the parables for over forty years, demonstrates that scholarship, ministry, and life are nonlinear but can be disrupted through the inbreaking of the kingdom of God from the parables. Long humbly admits his change in perspective on the parables after many years. He awakens to the fact that a parable is not solely a literary device but also a theological reality, a kingdom-of-God event that preachers should proclaim is 'at hand' yet not 'in' our hands. Parables are more than stories, metaphors, or ideas but are the power of the living God on earth as it is in heaven. Get this book into your hands to be reminded once again that the kingdom of God is at hand!"

—Luke A. Powery, Dean of Duke Divinity School Chapel

"In this volume, Tom Long does what trusted surf instructors do: show us how to ride the wave of a parable. He helps us glide along the unique contours of each one, feeling the structure, aims, surprises, and surprises-within-surprises. The jagged edges and pitfalls that tend to throw preachers off-balance are highlighted as well as many hidden gems. All the while Long keeps us focused on the Gospel writers' core themes, illumining them with his own unforgettable stories and illustrations. Ultimately, like a good parable, this book offers exhilarating glimpses of God's vision for humankind."

—Donyelle C. McCray, Associate Professor of Homiletics,
Yale Divinity School

"Be very afraid! While masquerading as a book about preaching and teaching the parables, this splendid volume shows how the parables do their work of unsettling, rearranging, and finally inviting. They preach themselves. Tom Long's extended conversation with Jesus' teaching has born fruit, thirty and sixty and a hundredfold. I, for one, am grateful."

—Beverly Roberts Gaventa, Helen H. P. Manson
Professor Emerita of New Testament Literature
and Exegesis, Princeton Theological Seminary

Proclaiming the Parables

Proclaiming the Parables

Preaching and Teaching the Kingdom of God

Thomas G. Long

First edition
Published by Westminster John Knox Press
Louisville, Kentucky

24 25 26 27 28 29 30 31 32 33—10 9 8 7 6 5 4 3 2 1

Book design by Sharon Adams
Cover design by Erika Lundbom
Cover art by Jorge Cocco. Used by permission

Library of Congress Cataloging-in-Publication Data

Names: Long, Thomas G., 1946- author.
Title: Proclaiming the parables : preaching and teaching the kingdom of God / Thomas G. Long.
Description: First edition. | Louisville, Kentucky : Westminster John Knox Press, [2024] | Includes index. | Summary: "A commentary on the major parables of Jesus written to strengthen and enliven preaching and teaching about the parables"-- Provided by publisher.
Identifiers: LCCN 2023050812 (print) | LCCN 2023050813 (ebook) | ISBN 9780664268619 (hardback) | ISBN 9781646983742 (ebook)
Subjects: LCSH: Jesus Christ--Parables--Study and teaching. | Kingdom of God--Study and teaching.
Classification: LCC BT377 .L66 2024 (print) | LCC BT377 (ebook) | DDC 226.8/06--dc23/eng/20231211
LC record available at https://lccn.loc.gov/2023050812
LC ebook record available at https://lccn.loc.gov/2023050813

PRINTED IN THE UNITED STATES OF AMERICA

⊗ The paper used in this publication meets the minimum requirements of the American National Standard for Information Sciences—Permanence of Paper for Printed Library Materials, ANSI Z39.48-1992

For my wife Kim, true companion in every way,
who in years of love and grace,
and in seasons of patience and forbearance,
has made real for me the promise that the "kingdom of God has drawn near."

Contents

Acknowledgments

I have taught courses on preaching the parables for over forty years, and across that span of time, debts build up—to students who pressed me with just the right questions, colleagues who supported my work and chipped in wise counsel, and the hosts of witnesses in the scholarly world who taught me, stretched me, and reassured me. I am grateful to all of them.

Most of all, though, I want to acknowledge the impact on my thinking by my friend, colleague, and now neighbor in retirement, Professor Steve Kraftchick. Steve and I taught courses together on the parables, both at Princeton Theological Seminary and at Candler School of Theology. Twice a week now, we toss our household trash into the back of my pickup and head out to the dumpster at the local volunteer fire department, twenty minutes each way. Our conversations in the truck during these trash runs have been wide-ranging, but rare would be the trip that I would not ask for his wisdom about one or another thorny parable. It would be hard to overstate the impact he has had on my thinking. He is not responsible, of course, for the places where this book, like the parabolic lost sheep, has gone astray, but more than once he has found my wandering argument and carried it home on his shoulders.

I also want to express my thanks to some particular colleagues in the company of scholars who are dedicated to doing serious exegetical work on the parables, especially Klyne Snodgrass, Amy-Jill Levine, Arland Hultgren, John Donahue, John Drury, Mary Ann Tolbert, Norman Perrin, John Dominic Crossan, and Ruben Zimmerman. There are others, but these especially seem like family. I have learned from all of them and quarreled, as siblings do, with each of them, but this book could not have happened without them.

I am indebted to the theological schools who have allowed me to teach about the parables through the decades: Erskine Theological Seminary, Columbia Theological Seminary, Princeton Theological Seminary, Candler School of Theology, Pacific School of Religion, Abilene Christian University, Luther Theological Seminary, and Yale Divinity School. I am also grateful to the wonderful and resourceful reference librarians at Candler School of Theology.

And, of course, I am indebted to my wife, Kim, who has given her unfailing love and support throughout this project and to whom this book is dedicated.

Thomas G. Long

Preface

"For the Jews . . . every second of time was the strait gate through which the Messiah might enter."

—Walter Benjamin, "Theses on the Philosophy of History"[1]

We are speaking of God here. Why are you surprised that you don't understand? If you do understand, then it is not God.

—Saint Augustine, "Sermon 67 on the New Testament"[2]

LIKE A THIEF IN THE NIGHT

"For you yourselves know very well," wrote the apostle Paul to the Thessalonians, "that the day of the Lord will come like a thief in the night."[3] In a much more modest way, the core idea of this book came just as swiftly, just as unexpectedly, and just as nocturnally.

As a newly retired professor from Candler School of Theology, I was spending a semester as a visiting professor at Yale Divinity School. My course, "Preaching the Parables of Jesus," was an old friend. I had taught some version of it nearly every year over a four-decade career of seminary teaching, and each time I taught it, I opened the course with a lecture or two about the power of parables and the promise of embodying that power in sermons. I would often quote Clarence Jordan, founder of Koinonia Farms in Georgia, who once quipped, "When Jesus delivered his parables, he lit a stick of dynamite [and] covered it with a story."[4] Jesus' parables, I assured my students, were powerful stuff.

But at Yale, having just given this lecture about the explosive power of the parables, as I was walking back to my campus apartment, suddenly the obvious hit me like a thunderclap: the students in this course were going to create sermons on the parables, and because they were bright and able students, the sermons would surely be good as well (and, as it turned out, they were). But these sermons would probably be no more powerful than any other sermons the students had crafted. And as for my own sermons on Jesus' parables? Frankly, as I thought about my preaching over the years, my sermons on parables were just sermons, too, no more or less punch in them than my sermons on prophetic oracles, healing stories, psalms, or any other kinds of texts. If I was teaching that the parables are so powerful, I had to ask myself, where is the power drain when it comes to our preaching on them?

I fretted about this for days, and then one night, about 2:00 a.m., I sat bolt upright in the bed, not so much with an answer to my question but with a light suddenly shining on a new and unexpected path. I rushed to my desk, turned on the laptop, and by dawn I had hammered out pages of notes.

James Loder, who was one of my teachers in graduate school, once guided our seminar through a discussion about how intellectual problems are resolved. As much as academics might like to imagine that a careful linear and logical process leads from problem to resolution, the fact is that many insights arise suddenly, seemingly gratuitously, in the midst of messy conflict and struggle. He gave us a homey example about a college student who was trying energetically to solve the challenging, three-dimensional, plastic puzzle Rubik's cube. For days in his dorm room, the student twisted the cube this way and that to no avail. Finally, well past midnight one night, the student, weary, discouraged, and frustrated, flung the cube across his room and fell exhausted into a deep sleep. That night, he had a dream in which he rose from his bed, walked across the room, picked up the puzzle, and, with a few quick twists, solved it. When he awoke that morning, he picked up the cube and was amazed to discover that from that moment on he could solve Rubik's Cube every time.

It felt like that to me, the insight about parables and power that came in the darkness of night, like a gift freely given. I saw clearly mistakes I had made for years in teaching the parables, and I saw a new way forward. In simple form (and this will be explored more fully in chapter 1), the insight I gained that night was this:

I already knew, of course, that all parables are literary devices (in the major parables, usually a narrative) set in comparison to the kingdom of God. All parables say, implicitly or explicitly, "The kingdom of God is like *this*." That sets out two big questions for students of parables to explore, two paths to follow: What is the kingdom of God? And, how does a parable "work" as a figure of speech to disclose that kingdom? In other words, there was a theological path to travel and a literary and rhetorical one.

For well over a century, since the groundbreaking work of Adolf Jülicher in the late nineteenth century, modern parables scholarship has expended most of its energy on the second path, the literary and rhetorical route. Vigorous arguments have been waged about literary form, about whether this or that parable is an allegory, a simile, an example, or a metaphor, and significant advances in parables theory have occurred around deciding which of these literary types best defines the genre "parable." Some scholars, of course, have explored the theological path (and again, this will be discussed more fully in chapter 1), but most of the traffic has been on the literary corridor.

I had followed the pack down the literary critical road. I spent much time in class scrutinizing how the gears, levers, and pulleys of a particular parable worked to generate its impact on hearers. I still think it is important to examine the inner workings of each of the parables (and the commentaries on individual parables in this book will include much of that sort of analysis), but I had assumed that the lauded power of Jesus' parables sprung from their literary dynamics, how, for example, the parables as metaphors overturned hearers' expectations and refreshed their imaginations in surprising ways. I had come perilously close to the view that parables scholar John Donahue criticizes in *The Gospel in Parable*: "The impression arises that at times salvation comes from metaphor alone!"[5]

The insight I had in the middle of that night was that the true power of the parables lies down the other path, not primarily in their literary form, but in the kingdom of God to which they refer. Yes, parables are potent literary devices. They would not have enchanted readers over the centuries if they were not. But their deepest purpose is to disclose the kingdom of God, which, as I will argue, is not an idea, not even just a complex symbol with generative and centrifugal force, but an event: the inbreaking of the life of God into life and history. I began to see parables not merely as creative figures of speech, but as GPS devices taking hearers to those places where the event of God is happening all around us. The parables take us to the places where the prayer "thy kingdom come, thy will be done on earth as it is in heaven" is even now being answered.

I do not claim this insight as a field-changing one by any means, and I do not imagine that others have not come to similar views before I have. But it was revolutionary for me, and this reorientation of perspective led me on a five-year journey to rethink the possibilities of Jesus' parables for preaching. The fruit of that journey is this book.

Thomas G. Long
Feast of the Epiphany, 2023

1

Jesus' Parables on the Playground of the Scholars

The real sin against the Holy Spirit is refusing to recognize, with "theological" joy, some concrete liberation that is taking place before one's very eyes.

—Jean Luis Segundo[1]

Entering the *basileia* [kingdom] is not an autonomous human action that transfers the disciple into another world, but rather an incorporation of [the disciple] into God's powerful invasion of this world.

—Joel Marcus[2]

THE TWO ROADS

"When you come to a fork in the road, take it," the Yankees' famed catcher Yogi Berra is alleged to have said.[3] Over a century ago, scholars interested in Jesus' parables came to a fork in the road, and many of them took it, mostly in one direction and not the other, with dramatic and not altogether beneficial consequences.

First, picture the fork. A parable is a literary performance in which a story, example, or image from our world of experience or imagination is compared to God's kingdom.[4] To put it even more simply, a parable brings two things together and lays them down, side by side: on the one side, something literary (usually a story) and, on the other side, something theological, the kingdom of God. That is the fork in the road, and to understand parables and how they work, we need to travel down both paths, the literary one and the theological one. For the most part, however, modern parables scholarship has chosen to traffic the literary path more than the theological one.

BANISHING ALLEGORY

The first modern scholar to hijack the bus and insist that it travel down the literary road was the enormously influential late nineteenth-century biblical professor at the University of Marburg, Adolf Jülicher. His massive two-volume treatment of Jesus' parables, *Die Gleichnisreden Jesu,* first published in 1888 and 1889, dominated parables scholarship for nearly a century.

Jülicher argued that what a parable *is*, in terms of literary form, governs to a great extent what it can *mean* and that, sadly, for eighteen centuries churchly interpreters made a huge, basic mistake: they misunderstood what a parable *is*. They thought parables are allegories, but they are not, insisted Jülicher; they're similes.

Jülicher began his study with a 120-page survey of the history of the interpretation of the parables from the patristic period up to the nineteenth century, and he found that history to be a garden overrun with toxic weeds. What the church got so wrong, Jülicher said, was that it saw parables as literary allegories, which are codes in which every detail stands for something outside the story. As C. H. Dodd describes the allegorical approach, "Each term [of a parable] was a cryptogram for an idea, so that the whole had to be de-coded term-by-term."[5] When the parables are defined as allegories, Jülicher railed, then the meanings of those parables can be known only by cracking their codes. Small wonder the interpretation of those parables degenerates into a confused mess.

As an aside, I confess that I was once in the thrall of Jülicher's and Dodd's antiallegorical prejudice. When I first began to teach about preaching the parables, I would chuckle in class over Dodd's scoffing description of Augustine's treatment of the Parable of the Good Samaritan. As Dodd presented it, Augustine advanced an enormously complex interpretation of the parable, in which every element of the narrative allegorically stood for something else. The man going down the road to Jericho was Adam, the robbers were the devil and his minions, the Samaritan was Christ, the inn was the church, and the innkeeper was the apostle Paul, just to mention a few of the allegorical decodings Augustine gave to this story. How could anyone, I wondered to my students, construe the parable so bizarrely?

Then years later I actually read a sermon of Augustine in which he employs this interpretation. The sermon is not on the parable at all, but on Psalm 126, one of the "psalms of ascent." Augustine understood this to be a psalm that pilgrims would chant as they climbed the steps of the temple in Jerusalem, as they ascended to the place of worship. Near the end of this sermon, Augustine, remembering the parable about the man who did not ascend to Jerusalem but rather went down the road from Jerusalem to Jericho, said (probably improvising brilliantly, as was his custom), "Remember: do not love to descend instead of to ascend, but reflect upon your ascent: because he who descended from Jerusalem to Jericho fell among thieves."

With that, the eloquent preacher was off and running. His congregation now rhetorically descending away from the holy city and having fallen among thieves, Augustine exulted that the Samaritan depicted Christ, who, unlike the priest and the Levite, did not pass us by in our fallenness:

> The Samaritan as He passed by slighted us not: He healed us, He raised us upon His beast, upon His flesh; He led us to the inn, that is, the church; He entrusted us to the keeper of the inn, that is, to the Apostle Paul; He gave this innkeeper two coins whereby we might be healed: the love of God, and the love of our neighbor. The Apostle spent even more on us. All apostles are permitted to receive, as Christ's soldiers, pay from Christ's followers, but that Apostle nevertheless toiled with his own hands and excused the followers the debt they owed him. All this has already happened: if we have descended and have been wounded, let us ascend, let us sing and make progress, in order that we may arrive![6]

Jülicher misunderstood. Dodd misunderstood. I misunderstood. Augustine was not mechanistically decoding allegorical cryptograms; he was preaching! Augustine was exercising what New Testament scholar Mary Ford calls "personal allegorical interpretation" or, perhaps better in our context, "homiletical allegory," in which the speaker is not arguing that one must understand the two coins in the parable to be implanted codes for the love of God and the love of neighbor, but rhetorically and artistically describing them that way is a creative and legitimate way to allow the parable to connect with our lives. Ford states,

> Allegorical interpretation provides a way to apply the text to oneself, by seeing, for example, that I am acting like the elder brother or the prodigal son. None of this implies that the text originally had these implications. It does imply that Scripture is expected to be practical, to provide models of reality in patterns of events so as to indicate a way of understanding, a course of action, a reason for hope, as well as insight into some aspect of the spiritual life.[7]

Ford goes on to claim that the bias against allegory shown, for example, by C. H. Dodd came in part because Dodd had a too restrictive definition of allegory. For Dodd and others like him, the structure of allegory was simply $x = a$. So, if the father of the Prodigal Son is x and God is a, then the only proper way to read the Parable of the Prodigal Son would be to see the father of the prodigal as a piece of code, a cryptogram, that equals God. However, most biblical narrative, Ford argues, typically manifests a different structure, something more like typology, in which *x* is to *y* as *a* is to *b*. Under this logic, the way the father in the parable (*x*) mercifully welcomes home the prodigal son (*y*) is like the way God (*a*) welcomes repentant sinners (*b*). She says,

> Once it is realized that most of the New Testament parables are situational allegories with the structure indicated above, then it is clear that the evangelists did not intend these parables to be cryptograms. Dodd, and others, only believed this because the cryptogram is the only type of allegory with which they were familiar. Most of the biblical critics' objections to the allegorical interpretations of the parables given by the evangelists (indeed, most of their reasons for rejecting allegory in general) disappear when an adequate understanding of allegory is brought to these texts.[8]

Jülicher, however, believed he had caught centuries of interpreters in the sin of misconstruing parables as allegories, secret codes able to be cracked only by spiritual virtuosi. For Jülicher, though, Jesus was not an enigmatic teacher, and parables aren't allegories at all but *similes*. In a simile, something is compared to something else, A is like B, as in "Amanda is like a bird." The goal of a simile is to reveal something about a complex subject (in this case, Amanda) by comparing that subject to something simpler, something that is known (in this case, a bird), Unlike allegories, similes have only one point of comparison, a single overlap, a focused *tertium comparationis*. So, if I say, "Amanda is like a bird," because this is a simile, I mean to say that Amanda is like a bird, not in a hundred different ways but in one, and only one, way.

Now, as it turns out, what I mean to say is that Amanda *sings* like a bird. But how do we know that I mean that Amanda sings like a bird and not that she is frail like a bird or eats like a bird or that, God forbid, is flighty like a bird? Listeners figure this out from the context. If my friend says, "Oh my, Amanda's solo at the concert last night was amazing!" and I reply, "Yes, Amanda is like a bird," then the context makes it clear that we are talking about singing and nothing else.

For Jülicher, Jesus' parables were similes, in which the kingdom of God, a complex and inherently ambiguous reality, is compared to something everyone can see and know clearly, like a mustard seed or a lost sheep. Since parables are similes, each parable teaches one and only one idea, one point per parable, to make everything clear and simple.

How did Jülicher come to the conclusion that Jesus' parables are similes and not allegories? Who gets to say that Jesus' parables are similes and not sonnets or rap songs or Zen-like koans or jokes? Jesus never introduces a parable, "Hey folks, don't take this allegorically, but . . . ," and, as a matter of fact, several of the parables we have in the New Testament practically scream that they are in fact full allegories. So where did Jülicher get his confidence that centuries of allegorical interpretation of the parables were off base and that the whole idea of allegory ought to be scrapped in favor of simile?

Significantly, Jülicher's prejudice against allegory comes not primarily from the evidence, from the actual parables found in the Synoptic Gospels, but rather from Jülicher's own view of the historical Jesus. The real Jesus, the Jesus of history, the Jesus behind the Gospel, Jülicher believed, was a preacher and a teacher who was heard by people gladly, clearly, and with deep understanding. (In the Gospels, of course, Jesus is not always heard gladly, was misunderstood a lot of the time, even by his disciples, and sometimes ticked off his hearers so much they wanted to kill him. But Jülicher didn't let that stand in the way of the "historical Jesus" he held in his imagination.) Perhaps the early church saw Jesus as a teller of parables that were hidden, secret communication in which the true meanings could be known only by insiders and spiritual elites who could break the allegorical codes, but that was the early church serving its own purposes and not Jülicher's "real" Jesus.

He was scandalized by the fact that, while everybody for centuries seemed to agree that the parables were allegories, no two interpreters could seem to agree on what any of the parables meant, which implied that Jesus was a mysterious and confusing teacher. The result was a veritable Babylonian captivity of the parables[9] or, perhaps better, a Tower of Babel of competing and conflicting interpretations. "It is positively alarming," said another parables scholar, Joachim Jeremias, "to read in [Jülicher] the story of the centuries of distortion and ill-usage which the parables have suffered through allegorical interpretation."[10]

Speak in allegories? Not the historical Jesus! Not my Jesus! Jülicher thundered. His Jesus would never have intentionally created mysterious parabolic puzzles that had to be decoded by bewildered listeners. No, this Jesus would have created simple and accessible pictures that could be readily grasped by all. In short, he would obviously have told parables that were simple similes.

THE SINS OF ADOLF JÜLICHER

Jülicher was an accomplished and meticulous scholar, and he argued his case so decisively, so thoroughly, and so well, the field was silenced before his logic. When he died in 1938, his obituary in the *Journal for Biblical Literature* could still boast that he had inaugurated "a change in the interpretation of the parables that will never be reversed."[11]

Not so. As a later parables scholar, Norman Perrin, liked to say, "Today's assured results are tomorrow's abandoned hypotheses."[12] Hardly any contemporary interpreters of parables stand with Jülicher now on the idea that Jesus' parables were all similes. If Jülicher has not been entirely reversed, he has certainly been thoroughly revised, and we need to make at least three objections to Jülicher's views on parables as we chart our own path forward:

1. First, Jülicher wouldn't allow Jesus fully to be a Jewish teacher. Jülicher looked to Greek thought, to Aristotle's *Rhetoric,* to make the distinction between simile, on the one hand, and metaphor (which in extended form would be allegory), on the other. What's the difference? When the poet says of Achilles, "And like a lion he rushed on," that's a simile. One single point is being made about a complex subject, Achilles, namely, that the way he rushed on was lion-like. But when the poet says of Achilles, "A lion rushed on," that's a metaphor.[13] Now Achilles *is* a lion, and the implications of that can be endless. The distinction was important to Jülicher because the simile is clear, the metaphor ambiguous. Since the historical Jesus, as Jülicher pictured him, was a master of clarity, then he must have been a maker of similes, not oblique metaphors.

But Jesus was not a Greek orator. He was a rabbi, and rabbis used all manner of lively figures of speech in their teaching—riddles, proverbs, similes and similitudes, and yes, metaphors and allegories. Sometimes the rabbis wanted to reveal things, and sometimes they wanted to conceal. In fact, the earliest biblical testimony about why Jesus spoke in parables, namely, Mark 4:10–12, does not portray Jesus as a clear teacher at all but as one who spoke in parables to conceal, so that his hearers "may indeed hear but not understand." The Hebrew word for all these striking rabbinical figures of speech, *mashal,* the antecedent of "parable" in the New Testament, has allegory well within its compass.

Jülicher's picture of the "historical Jesus" was suspiciously non-Jewish (in fact this Jesus sounded more like a nineteenth-century German professor than a first-century Jewish rabbi). His refusal to let Jesus be a Jew and to entertain that he, like other rabbis, might have spun some allegories and mysterious sayings among his parables turned out to be at least a category mistake, if not an expression of the subtle (and sometimes not so subtle) anti-Semitism of German idealism.

Jülicher's insistence that parables were similes also runs aground on the evidence, the actual body of parables in the New Testament. Yes, many of the parables look somewhat similar in terms of literary form: lots of stories about homey settings in real life. But when they are placed under a microscope, they turn out to show wide literary variation. No single literary category can contain all of the parables attributed to Jesus. Once Jülicher, or any other student of parables, makes an a priori decision that a parable must be a simile, or any other literary genre, and nothing else, then the question becomes what happens when the New Testament embarrasses the interpreter by including parables that don't fit the definition? These outlier parables either have to be rejected as corruptions of the pure parabolic form fostered by the early church, or they have to be subdued by radically reinterpreting them in nonallegorical ways. For example, when Matthew includes the Parable of the Wicked Tenants (Matt. 21:33–45), which is inescapably an allegory, or when we find in Mark 4:13–20 an undeniably allegorical interpretation of the Parable of the Sower, any interpreter following Jülicher's lead is condemned to build a firewall between these allegorical texts and the "true" parables Jesus first uttered. The allegories we have are then deemed inferior to the originals we don't have and tossed out as distortions of Jesus' real intent.

2. At least as damning were the simplistic moral lessons that Jülicher heard Jesus teaching in the parables. Since, for Jülicher, parables are similes, each parable is a clear-glass jar with a single idea inside, and because Jülicher was a classic nineteenth-century liberal, it is not surprising that the ideas he found in those glass jars were ideas compatible with those of his own age and his own ideology. As Robert Stein has observed, in Jülicher's hands Jesus turns out to be a typical nineteenth-century "apostle of progress," and "the main point of Jesus's parables was always a general tenet of nineteenth-century liberalism."[14]

The so-called clear points Jülicher heard in Jesus' parables were often incredibly gaseous and banal, fortune-cookie-like moralisms. For example, the one point of the Parable of the Rich Fool is that even the richest person is dependent upon God, and the point of the Parable of the Unjust Steward is that wise use of the present is the condition of a happy future. The lesson of the Parable of the Talents? Reward is earned only by performance.[15]

People who say things like that don't get crucified; they get tenure.

3. It is Jülicher's third sin, however, that most sets this book in motion. When Jülicher hit the fork in the road and decided to go down the literary and rhetorical path to understand Jesus' parables, the next century of parables scholarship followed after him. Even though most contemporary parables scholars reject Jülicher's claim that all parables must be understood as similes, they still travel mainly the literary path, trying to figure out, if the parables aren't necessarily similes, then what literary forms are they? Are they narrated metaphors? Expanded symbols? Realistic tales designed to raise political consciousness? The tacit assumption remains: once we determine the true literary structure and character of the parables, we can name their meanings and how they work to generate those meanings. That was Jülicher's agenda, and he has largely influenced the direction of the guild.

THE NEXT NEW THING: THE SBL PARABLES SEMINAR

As Jülicher's consensus that parables are similes began to unravel in the mid-twentieth century, a formidable new venture in parables interpretation emerged in the Parables Seminar of the Society of Biblical Literature. This seminar was formed in the early 1970s and operated for five years in connection with the annual meeting of the Society of Biblical Literature, the major North American guild of Bible scholars.

All of the biblical scholars who founded the Parables Seminar had already been doing innovative research on the parables of Jesus, but in the early 1970s they felt a collective energy gathering around their work. The Parables Seminar would be an opportunity for them to test their ideas over against each other, flint and steel. The result was that they changed the direction of academic parables study for at least a generation.

The ringleader of the seminar was Robert Funk, then a religion professor at Vanderbilt, who later founded the controversial Jesus Seminar. In addition to Funk, the Parables Seminar was populated with luminaries in the world of parables scholarship, such as John Dominic Crossan, Dan Via, Norman Perrin, and Amos Wilder; they eventually brought to the table Bernard Brandon Scott, Krister Stendahl, Eta Linnemann, Paul Ricoeur, Sallie McFague, and others.

The way the seminar was conducted was that a cluster, ten or twelve, of these principal scholars would gather around a long table placed in the center of a large meeting room. They would respond to each other's papers with lively and vigorous debate about approaches and methods in parables research, all along dismantling the old approaches and bringing in exciting new possibilities. As they did so, one or two hundred silent observers would surround the table, fishbowl style.

I was a brand-new doctoral student when the seminar began, and I took my place eagerly in the fishbowl year after year, the wind of excitement ruffling through my hair. These parables scholars were approaching biblical texts in bold and fresh ways, and they were producing essays so experimental and venturesome they were difficult to place in the established journals like the *Journal for Biblical Literature*. So they published them in a periodical they birthed for their own purposes, *Semeia*, a journal so unpolished in format, avant garde in content, and "hot off the press" that it looked like it had been printed on a mimeograph machine in the basement of the New School for Social Research.

This seminar not only introduced me to cutting-edge New Testament scholarship and advanced hermeneutical theories; it also stimulated me to teach an ever-evolving course on "Preaching the Parables of Jesus" almost every year of my more than forty years as a seminary teacher. The SBL Parables Seminar changed my thinking, changed my teaching, and changed my preaching.

Two aspects of the seminar's work I found particularly energizing:

1. First, this group of mavericks, following the lead of Joachim Jeremias at Göttingen, boldly and scandalously played taps over the once seemingly impregnable parables work of Jülicher, the Mount Everest of parables scholars, and then danced on the grave. Jülicher thought he had found the historical Jesus, a teacher of universally valid moral truths. The Parables Seminar, however, unmasked Jülicher's Jesus as a bland and boring bloviator of nineteenth-century ethical bromides. The Parables Seminar participants were not seduced by Jülicher's insistence that Jesus' parables were simple similes. The seminar members saw the parables, rather, as generative and powerful metaphors, sometimes quite complex and mysterious.

2. That leads to the second development of the Parables Seminar that engaged my imagination. The scholars in the seminar were tapped into the amazing rhetorical power of Jesus' parables. Most of the members of the seminar had been influenced by Ernst Fuchs's understanding of Jesus' parabolic speech. Jesus did not use parables, Fuchs insisted, to teach ideas or moral principles. No, Jesus used parabolic language to *cause things to happen*, to create a change in the world and in those who hear. The parables of Jesus, said Fuchs, are not mere teaching devices, but language events.[16]

The seminar members wanted to know how the parables worked as revolutionary speech, and to do so they were willing to stand bravely at a busy and dangerous interdisciplinary intersection. They broadly engaged linguistics, folklore studies, psychology, contemporary literary criticism, structuralism, social anthropology, and more, in attempting to understand how these language events took place. And in doing so they plumbed not only the rhetorical structure of Jesus' parables but also how those rhetorical structures managed to exercise life-changing power in those who heard the parables.

Crossan, for example, could say things like, "Jesus was not crucified for parables but for ways of acting which resulted from the experience of God presented in the parables. . . . [P]arables are the cause not effect of Jesus' other words and deeds."[17] In other words, Jesus wasn't killed because he spoke in parables; he was killed because he *believed* parables, saw the world parabolically, and acted according to the powerful vision generated by parables.

Parables, the seminar participants said, were literary devices with transformational, even destabilizing, power. To quote Crossan again: "Myth establishes the world. Apologue [that is, moral fable] defends the world. Action investigates the world. Satire attacks the world. *Parable subverts the world.*"[18]

Seminar participant Amos Wilder, a Harvard professor and an expert on early Christian rhetoric, claimed Jesus' parables stimulated shocking transformations in hearers: "The hearer not only learns about [the kingdom of God], he participates in it. He is invaded by it. Here lies the power and fatefulness of art. Jesus' speech had the character not of instruction and ideas but of compelling imagination, of spell, of mythical shock and transformation."[19]

Another seminar participant, Sallie McFague, is even more dramatic regarding the power of Jesus' parabolic art: "If the parable 'works,' the spectators become participants, not because they want to necessarily or simply have 'gotten the point,' but because they have, for the moment, 'lost control.' . . . The secure, familiar everydayness of the story of their own lives has been torn apart; they have seen another story."[20]

Powerful stuff there.

LOSING FAITH

But in recent years, I have had some second thoughts, not only about Jülicher and Dodd, but also about the Parables Seminar and some of the seminar's major directions. Doubts arose for me about the seminar's ideas concerning what parables are and what they do, and about some of the hermeneutical and pedagogical decisions those ideas prompted me to make. As I indicated in the preface, my doubts came to a head when, after years of making claims for the intrinsic power of the parable form, I compared that claim with actual performance: my students' sermons on parables, my own sermons, and the sermons of others. If the parables are so powerful, I wondered, why does that impressive power seem to drain away in the gap between parable and sermon?

Slowly I began to realize that the seminar's whole approach to parabolic speech was highly hyperbolic. They talked of the hearers of parables being "invaded" by the kingdom, that the parables create "spell, . . . shock, and transformation." Under the sway of parabolic narratives, hearers "lose control" and have their lives "torn apart."

But if someone were to run on stage at the Super Bowl halftime show, steal the mic from, say, Eminem or Snoop Dog or Rihanna, and, before security muscled them off, were to recite to the startled crowd one of Jesus' parables, maybe the Mustard Bush or the Seed Growing Secretly, the crowd would probably be confused, perhaps intrigued, but would almost surely not experience mythical shock, transformation, a loss of control, and their lives being torn apart.

Responding to this tendency in contemporary parables research to exaggerate the parables' rhetorical effect, and to McFague's claims in particular, Mary Ann Tolbert says,

> This kind of inflated language about the parables grants to them a power to which very few individuals or societies, much less literary texts, have ever held. . . . That these stories qua stories . . . have the inevitable ability to force hearers to lose control of themselves is rather unbelievable. It would be difficult to document cases of people who in reading a parable . . . experienced in that moment their lives being "torn apart." . . . [W]e must beware making exaggerated claims of power for the parable stories qua stories.[21]

But hyperbolic speech in academic scholarship can be handled. Just turn the volume down and glean what we can from more humble claims. But even when the claims of some in the Parables Seminar are softened, an underlying assumption that undergirded the seminar began to look more and more questionable, namely, that the parables themselves *as literary devices* are the redemptive change agents, and that redemption is accomplished by what the parable triggers in the existential awareness of the hearer.

Yes, Jesus' parables, rightfully understood, are engaging, imaginative, surprising, often provocative speech acts, and like poetry, parables have their undeniable appeal and effects. And they often have twists, unexpected features, and plot turns that cause hearers to stop and reimagine the possibilities. But the real power of the parables is not in the naked parables as performance art or in the recesses of the metaphorical process alone, but somewhere else.

The main power of parables is in their capacity to point to what God is doing in the world, that is, to the kingdom of God. The power is not in the trope, but in the referent. As theologian Austin Farrer said, "Christ does not save us by acting a parable of divine love; he acts the parable of divine love by saving us. That is the Christian faith."[22] In other words, Christ saves us, and by saving us enacts the true parable of divine love. It is not a parable, however vivid and full of divine wisdom, that saves us, but Christ.

DOUBLING BACK TO THE THEOLOGICAL PATH

When we recognize that the true power of parables is in their referent, the kingdom of God and what God is doing in the world, we are beckoned back to the fork in the road, called to travel not only the literary path but also that other, more theological, path. Ironically, we can perhaps allow Robert Funk, the originator of the Parables Seminar, to guide us back up the literary path and to lead us over the bridge to the theological one.

I will look at three claims about parables made by Funk. First, he, along with Dodd, Wilder, and many others, understands Jesus' parables to be "realistic."

Unlike the otherworldly pictures of saints singing praises in heaven, such as those found in the book of Revelation, the parables are about recognizable moments in everyday life, such as shepherding sheep, planting seeds, or attending a banquet. This "everydayness" of parables is important to Funk because, as he says, quoting Wilder: "Jesus . . . shows that for him [human] destiny is at stake in . . . ordinary creaturely existence, domestic, economic, and social."[23] People hear one of Jesus' parables, Funk states, and they respond, "Yes, that's how it is,"[24] and parables do not direct attention "away from mundane existence but toward it."[25]

Second, Funk acknowledges that there is some quality about parables that signals to hearers that there is more here than meets the eye or, perhaps better, more than meets the ear. "When Jesus speaks of a lost sheep, a mustard seed, or a banquet, or some other commonplace," Funk writes, "the auditor senses without prompting that more is involved than a pleasant or amusing anecdote."[26]

So far so good. Parables are about everyday, mundane realities but tease the hearers with the possibility that they are about more than what lies on the surface. But it is Funk's third claim that gets really interesting. Yes, the parables of Jesus are everyday narratives, but every one of them, Funk says, has some kind of joker in the deck. Every parable, as Peter Hawkins cleverly says, is "a curve ball."[27] All parables, says Funk, have "an unexpected 'turn' in them which looks through the commonplace to a new view of reality."[28] It may be some strange and unexpected development in the plot, like a corrupt judge who surprisingly ends up granting justice to a widow, or maybe an exaggeration, like an over-the-top, hundredfold harvest, but there is something in every parable that strikes the hearers that "the everyday world is surprisingly and oddly disfigured."[29] Paul Ricoeur calls this characteristic of the parables "extravagance."[30]

Funk seems unsure what to do with this insight that parables turn everyday reality upside down and inside out. On the one hand, he seems to think that parables, by presenting a topsy-turvy world, all by themselves shock hearers into a choice: Do you want to live in the everyday world as you normally see it, or do you want to open up a new future by living in the new, upside-down world portrayed by the parable? But to understand parables this way would mean only that they operate like all other imaginative fiction, presenting an alternative reality to readers that allows them to imagine themselves leaving where they are, to live in that new reality. That's powerful, but is it the deepest power of parables?

On the other hand, here and there Funk senses that, taken alone, this view of parables is too weak. To underscore an earlier point, a parable may contain an unexpected plot twist when a woman who has lost one of her coins throws a wildly extravagant party for her neighbors when she finds it, but no reasonable hearers are going to be thrown by this into an existential crisis in which they have "to choose between two worlds."[31]

Funk seems to recognize a deeper, more theological truth: that the real shock generated by parables is in the transference between what happens in the parable and a vision of the life of God.[32] The shocking surprise in the Parable of the Lost Coin is not that a woman loses all sense of proportion and throws an over-the-top party when she recovers one little coin, but that this unreasonable celebration of the least and the lost is also true of God. That's a radically different matter. Suppose (and this is a safe assumption) there are people who see the world like those who grumbled that Jesus "welcomes sinners and eats with them" (Luke 15:2), the people to whom Jesus first told the Parable of the Lost Coin. Now, if they (we?) encounter through this parable the disclosure that, like that woman in the story, God is ready to throw a lavish and festive party, one where the saints lift high their glasses, sing noisy songs of joy, and swing exuberantly from the chandeliers, whenever one lost sinner is found, then that's genuinely an "oddly disfigured" world to be reckoned with. There's the true shock and awe, and the parable forces the choice: my world or God's world?

WHAT IS THE KINGDOM OF GOD?

If, as we are claiming, the greatest power of parables is in their referent, the kingdom of God, what do we mean when we say "the kingdom of God"? To ask that question in a study of parables is, at best, ironic, at worst, foolish. The parables insist that we define the kingdom indirectly. What is the kingdom? Well, it's like a man who had two sons, it's like a woman mixing yeast into flour. One cannot speak straightforwardly about the mystery of God's kingdom. Indirection is necessary, and that's why there are parables in the first place.

If the kingdom of God could be described full flush—say as a list of principles, or a collection of big ideas, or as a series of scenes like those in a travelogue of Aruba—then once we had derived this description from the parables, we could throw the parables away. But when Jesus wants to talk about the kingdom, he looks off into the distance and asks, "What is the kingdom of God like, and to what should I compare it?" Then he tells a parable.

In one of his sermons, Frederick Buechner remembered standing at night on the bridge of a freighter somewhere in the middle of the Atlantic Ocean and conversing with one of the ship's officers. The officer's duty that night was to scan the horizon, being on the lookout for the lights of other ships. The officer told Buechner that the way to see the lights of ships on the horizon was not to look directly at the horizon, but indirectly, at the sky just above the horizon. "I discovered," said Buechner, "that he was right. This is the way to do it. Since then, I have learned that it is also the way to see other things."[33]

Indeed, that is the way to view the kingdom of God, indirectly, looking just above the horizon, where the parables give us not dictionary definitions but comparisons: the kingdom is like this, and it's like that. But this is not to say that the concept of God's kingdom is a black hole, completely mysterious and beyond conceptualization. Like a journalist interviewing eyewitnesses to an event and gradually getting a sense of what happened, just so, Jesus, in forty or so parables, gives us multiple testimonies about what the kingdom is like, and together they begin to reveal the whole.

There is reciprocity here. The way we interpret the parables shapes what we understand of God's kingdom, and then what we understand of God's kingdom repays the favor, governing how we interpret the parables.

Perhaps a good place to begin trying to say what we mean by the "kingdom of God" is to start midstream with the impressive work of Norman Perrin, a notable New Testament scholar and a participant in the Parables Seminar, one who in many ways broke ranks to travel the theological path and to give sustained and influential attention to the theological character of the kingdom of God.

In his first major monograph on the subject of the kingdom, published in 1963, before the advent of the Parables Seminar, Perrin presented the kingdom of God in Jesus' teaching as a big theological idea or, maybe we could even say, a doctrine.[34] God's kingdom was not a place, not a national possession; it was a statement, a claim, made in faith and hope, that one day God would establish full sovereignty over creation and the redeemed.[35] The kingdom of God was, for Perrin, an "apocalyptic concept," namely, the idea of "God's decisive intervention in history and human experience" and the implications concerning "the final state of the redeemed to which that intervention leads."[36] The function of the parables, then, is to fill in the concept, to flesh out the definition, to indicate what this hoped-for reality is going to be like.

In defining the kingdom this way, Perrin was taking on earlier modern scholarship about the kingdom of God. Nineteenth-century theologian Albert Ritschl, for example, understood the kingdom in purely ethical terms. Jesus had won freedom for individuals, through works of love, to establish a just and loving human society, to bring in the kingdom of God on earth.[37] Another nineteenth-century theologian, Johannes Weiss, however, took a position diametrically opposed to Ritschl. Jesus, said Weiss, wasn't interested in ethics or politics at all. To the contrary, the kingdom of God is a reality that only God, not human effort, can bring, and it involved the expectation that the drama of history was soon coming to a close and that God would establish dominion over all creation, destroying all of God's enemies, establishing Jesus as the royal Son of Man.[38] Alas, it didn't happen. This expectation for an imminent kingdom was not fulfilled in Jesus' lifetime, and Weiss decided that Jesus' mythological concept of the kingdom was a failed hope and irrelevant to modern people.

Perrin, though, didn't like Ritschl's idea of an ethical kingdom, nor did he favor Weiss's notion of a failed apocalypse. For Perrin, the kingdom of God was "apocalyptic concept," a claim that God's reign was already present but was to be fully realized in the future. People "can now experience the eschatological forgiveness of God and the manifestation of his eschatological powers," said Perrin, "and in the light of this, they are called upon to accept the responsibilities and privileges revealed in the eschatological Law."[39]

Ten years later, though, as Perrin actively participated in the Parables Seminar, he changed course. The notion of the kingdom of God as an "apocalyptic concept," an idea, was now, in his view, too static. He turned to literary theorist Philip Wheelwright to make the case that the kingdom of God was not a doctrine or a concept but rather a dynamic symbol that evokes a myth.[40] "[T]he teaching of Jesus has been bedeviled by the fact that scholars have thought of the Kingdom of God as a conception rather than a symbol,"[41] Perrin said, scolding his earlier self as well as other scholars.

Wheelwright defined a symbol as something that is given, something people can perceive, but that stands for something that cannot be fully perceived. A symbol stands for something else, something that cannot be fully described apart from the symbol itself. But not all symbols are alike, and Wheelwright named two different kinds: "steno symbols" and "tensive symbols."

Steno symbols have a one-to-one relationship to what they represent, for example, a red, octagonal road sign inscribed with the single word "Stop." When it comes to Stop, public safety pretty much depends upon the willingness of interpreters to forgo all hermeneutical cleverness and creativity in favor of just accepting the plain sense of the text, the one-to-one relationship between the stop sign and the behavior of putting on the brakes. This is the case even if the interpreter of that stop sign happens to be a Volvo-driving assistant professor of English approaching the intersection fresh from teaching a Jane Austen seminar. Pedestrians in the crosswalk are counting on him obediently to apply the brakes instead of searching the text for irony, ambiguity, unreliable narration, and the like.

A tensive symbol, on the other hand, doesn't have a one-to-one relation to what it symbolizes, but instead generates many meanings, and they "can neither be exhausted nor adequately expressed by any one referent."[42] Perrin now saw parables as tensive symbols, churning out endless meanings related to the myth of God's reign. He said,

> I argued that the Kingdom of God was a *tensive* symbol in the message of Jesus, that it was . . . a symbol of cultural range, a symbol having meaning for people in cultural continuity with ancient Israel and its myth of God acting as king, a cultural continuity in which Jesus surely stood. On the lips of Jesus the symbol evoked the ancient myth, and the claim of his message was that the reality mediated by the myth was to be experienced dramatically by his hearers.[43]

The myth of God's reign is what religion professor Stephen Crites would call a "sacred story."[44] Sacred stories are the most significant stories a culture has, since they point to the deepest values and understandings of that culture. But sacred stories cannot be told directly. No one can gather the children around a campfire and tell them a sacred story. They can only be told indirectly through smaller, everyday stories, which Crites called "mundane stories," and the parables are just such mundane stories.[45] For Perrin, parables are indeed mundane stories, and they function as tensive symbols to generate multiple meanings about the big, untellable sacred story, the myth of God's reign, and thereby to make that myth existentially present for the hearer.[46]

At the risk of shallowing this out, we can say that Perrin now understood the kingdom of God as a myth-based, open-ended symbol, something like our own culturally grounded, open-ended myth "the American dream," which is one of our culture's sacred stories. What is the American dream? "Tell me the story of the American dream, Mother." It can't be told straightforwardly; it resists definition, even as it perpetually generates itself in our imagination, by telling smaller mundane stories, like the one about mother and son who left Vietnam after the fall of Saigon on a thirty-foot-long fishing boat with forty others. They ended up in America with nothing. The mother worked as a seamstress, and money was a struggle. But they prevailed, and now the son is a successful businessman.[47] The American dream is like that. That's the way parables work too, Perrin claimed. "The kingdom of heaven" is like someone scattering seed on the ground—this smaller mundane story acting as a tensive symbol and centrifugally throwing out meanings related to the unspeakable myth of the kingdom of God.

So we now have two ways to think about the kingdom of God. Maybe it's a concept, or maybe it's a tensive mythic symbol. Actually, I think Perrin was closer to the truth early on, in his 1967 book *Rediscovering the Teaching of Jesus*, where he wrote a description of the kingdom of God not as a concept or a symbol, but as the activity of God: "The kingdom of God is the power of God expressed in deeds; it is that which God does wherein it becomes evident that he is king. It is not a place or community ruled by God; it is not even the abstract idea of reign or kingship of God. It is quite concretely the activity of God as king."[48]

The kingdom of God, in other words, is not an idea, not even a tensive symbol. It's an *event.* God is acting in the world, and acting in ways that demonstrate God's kingly rule. Parables are not first and foremost language events; they may be that, but what is important about them is that they take us to another and greater event: the places in our lives and world where God is acting. Those inbreakings of God we call glimpses of the "kingdom of God."

The theologian Christopher Morse is helpful here. In his *The Difference Heaven Makes: Rehearing the Gospel as News*[49] he explores the idea of heaven in the New Testament and finds that heaven is not primarily a place where the redeemed go after death but the place from which God comes to earth. If heaven is a symbol for the life of God, then the primary traffic is not that we go to heaven but that heaven comes to us.

Whatever comes from God is said to come from heaven," Morse says.[50] God speaks from heaven, acts from heaven. He remembers a song from his childhood: "Life is like a mountain railroad," and Christians are on that train, traveling to heaven.[51] But the song had it backwards. The traffic is not from here to there, but from there to here. Like waves crashing on the beach, God keeps adventing into our life and history, not only revealing God's life but also "overtaking what is passing away on earth."[52] Whenever God's kingdom advents, it brings with it the end of all temporary human kingdoms, no matter how strong or permanent they may seem. As God's life is constantly revealed among us, what is also disclosed is that, as Paul said, "the present form of this world is passing away" (1 Cor. 7:31). The inbreaking of God's kingdom is a perpetual revolution.

When God's life advents into ours, what results is not simply illumination or spiritual insight. Something actually happens. Morse quotes approvingly Barth's statement that "there is no Word of God without a physical event."[53] The world is changed when God advents. Using a line from Emily Dickinson, Morse says that God's advent is "invisible as Music, But positive as Sound."[54]

Morse ends his book with this provocative statement. People of faith are "called to be *on* hand for that which is *at* hand. But not *in* hand."[55] The kingdom of heaven comes "like a thief in the night" (1 Thess. 5:2). As Jesus said, "Keep awake—for you don't know when the master of the house will come" (Mark 13:35). God's kingdom is always "at hand." But it is not "in hand"; that is to say, it is not under our control, and it cannot be captured, institutionalized, and turned into one more rival kingdom on the earth.

The kingdom of God is "at hand" but not "in hand." This means that when God's life breaks into our lives, it makes a difference in this world, but it does not belong to this world. As Jesus, on trial, said to Pontius Pilate, "My kingdom is not from this world. If my kingdom were from this world, my followers would be fighting to keep me from being handed over to the Jews. But as it is, my kingdom is not from here" (John 18:36). The fact that the kingdom of God is not "in hand," and is subject to neither being defeated by nor being managed by the Pilates (or the pastors or the popes) of this world, exposes the grievous blasphemy of Governor Kevin Stitt of Oklahoma, who prayed when he was reelected in 2022,

> Father, we just claim Oklahoma for you. Every square inch, we claim it for you in the name of Jesus. Father, we can do nothing apart from you. We don't battle against flesh and blood but against principalities and darkness. And Father, we just come against that, we just loose your will over our state right now in the name of Jesus. We just thank you and we claim Oklahoma for you as the authority that I have as governor and the spiritual authority and the physical authority that you give me. I claim Oklahoma for you that we will be a light to our country and to the world. We thank you that your will was done on Tuesday and Father, that you will have your way with our state, with our education system, with everything within the walls behind me. Lord, we pray that you will root out corruption and bring the right people into this building.[56]

We are called to be "on hand" for God's kingdom, which is always "at hand," but is never in our little hands to claim as territory, even in Oklahoma.

What if we wanted to be on hand for that which is at hand, but not in hand? That is what the parables ask. They are like GPS devices that take us to the places where God is breaking in and open our eyes. There's the real power in what God is doing in the world. The kingdom of God is an event, and the parables take us to the feast so that we can marvel and participate.

Preaching the parables now becomes exciting, because we do not stand in the pulpit to explain the inner workings of the Prodigal Son or the Wheat and the Weeds. Our task is not to explain the parables but to *proclaim* them. We allow the parable to disclose where God is at work in the world, and with amazement we are privileged to announce this event. Preaching is not explanation, but exclamation and proclamation. There is where the power of the parables lies, the power I missed in so much preaching on the parables. All Christian preaching is an echo of Jesus' first sermon: "The time is now, God's life is breaking in. Turn around, look, and believe!" (paraphrase of Mark 1:14).

My wife and I live on the Chesapeake Bay in rural Maryland. There is a small church down the lane from our house, and for many years this was our church. On a good Sunday, there would be about twenty of us in worship. This congregation was so few in number, we had no educational program, no youth group, no committees, no choir, only Sunday worship and a tiny group of saints trying the best we could to show hospitality and grace to each other and to the rare visitor. The outreach mission was modest: serving meals at the Salvation Army overnight shelter in town and gathering socks and bath items for the residents.

The church had a long-standing and cherished practice of leaving the building open all the time for anyone who wished to come in and pray. When the church's insurance company cracked down and insisted that the church building be locked during the week, the congregation had no choice but to comply. So they installed a padlock and put the key under a rock beside the door with the word "key" painted on it.

Every summer, on an August Saturday, the church would hold its annual Peach Festival. The women of the congregation would stay up all night on Friday baking gorgeous peach pies and peach pound cakes. The men would set up folding chairs and wooden tables and churn gallons of fresh peach ice cream.

People would come in large numbers from all over the county to the festival, eager to consume peach fritters; to eat crabcake sandwiches, a local delicacy, and delicious chicken salad prepared according to a recipe handed down through the generations; to consume gallons of ice cream; to wander the booths set up by dozens of local craft artisans; and, of course, to purchase bushels of ripe and juicy peaches.

One year, I was behind the counter dishing up peach ice cream in what we euphemistically called our "fellowship hall," actually a rough cinderblock building set apart about a hundred feet from the wooden frame sanctuary. Between the church and the fellowship hall was the church cemetery, and wooden picnic tables had been placed on the green spaces between the graves. Two vans from the residential center for adults with intellectual disabilities had just arrived, and as the residents flocked eagerly to the line for ice cream, the staff of the center asked us to be generous with the portions, and we were.

At one point our pastor came over to me and said, "Come, look." Something about her face and voice made me immediately take off my apron, hand the ice cream scoop to another volunteer, and follow the pastor outside to the cemetery. There, sitting at the wooden tables set among the tombs and shaded by live oak trees, were a couple dozen folks quietly eating peach ice cream. They were rich, poor, and very poor; Black, Asian, Hispanic, and white; young and old; men and women; oystermen in bib overalls and women in faded-flower-print dresses; people able and infirmed; children, the stain of ice cream around their mouths, playing hide-and-seek among the gravestones; the living and the dead.

"Do you see what I see?" the pastor asked.

"I think I do," I said. "Yes, I do."

What she saw, and what I saw, was a glimpse of the beloved community, the peaceable kingdom of God breaking through and making itself known.

It would have been foolish to try to preserve the moment, to "make three dwellings" as Peter had wanted to do to hold the power of the transfiguration of Jesus. It would have been a blasphemy to erect a tent and to invite people to come in to see God's kingdom. They wouldn't have seen anything anyway. There was no holy glow over the scene; all that the naked eye could see was a group of miscellaneous people under the trees eating ice cream. Only to eyes focused by the promises of the gospel was this a revelation, and it was not ours to hold. The pastor and I were "on hand" for that which is "at hand," but it was by no means "in hand." This was gift and fleeting glimpse, the kingdom showing itself for a transitory moment, revealing the hope of a greater feast of glory to come, in which "people will come from east and west, from north and south, and take their places at the banquet in the kingdom of God" (adapted from Luke 3:29).

The next morning, the festival now over for the year, we gathered for worship as usual. The pastor had invited a young man in the congregation, a diesel engine mechanic who worked on bulldozers and earth-moving machinery, to read the Gospel lesson for the day. He was considering a call to ministry, and the pastor decided that giving him a role in worship would be a good way to encourage that sense of call.

When the time came, he got up from the pew and walked to the pulpit. He wore his Sunday best: boots, a western shirt with a bolo tie, and a black cowboy hat. When he stood behind the pulpit, he took off his hat reverently, and opened the Bible to the lectionary reading for the day in the Gospel of Luke. His voice was halting as he voiced the ancient promise. As I listened to him read, I realized that only the Spirit could have chosen that text for this day. He read, "Do not be afraid, little flock, for it is your Father's good pleasure to give you the kingdom" (Luke 12:32).

A WORD ABOUT TERMINOLOGY

Readers will have already noticed my decision to retain the traditional New Testament terminology "kingdom of God" and "kingdom of heaven." I am not unaware of the problems and controversies around such language, but none of the substitutions that have been advocated in recent years accomplishes, in my view, what the original language achieves.

Three significant claims are embraced by "kingdom of God" language. First, the kingdom of God is a revolutionary event initiated by God, not a political or philosophical innovation generated out of the human prospect. As Karl Barth once observed, without angels, the messengers of God, speaking

God's revelation, that revelation "would be hopelessly confused with some earthly circumstance, whether in the form of a sublime idea or a golden calf."[57]

Second, the kingdom of God, as God's activity in the world, creates an event, a troubling of the water in human life and history, a toppling of some proud earthly reign. "The kingdom of the world has become the kingdom of our Lord and of his Messiah" (Rev. 11:15). God's kingdom cannot be contained by any one moment in history, nor identified completely with it, but God's kingdom can be perceived and experienced in pivotal individual and societal events. As Jesus announced, "The time is now, the kingdom has drawn near" (Mark 1:14, adapted).

Third, as an event perceived in time and space, the event of the kingdom of God is perceived by some and generates a response. It creates a community of participants, "citizens" of the kingdom as it were, who are drawn into relationship with each other and who seek to adopt practices, customs, ways of speaking and living congruent with what God is doing in the world.

Language such as "the reign of God" or "the sovereignty of God" gets at the first claim, perhaps, but only weakly at the second and not at all at the third. As for "the commonwealth of God" or the popular suggestion of "the kin-dom of God," advocates of these phrases almost always underscore the first word in the term, "commonwealth" and "kin-dom," which gets at the third aspect nicely, the communal, but underplays the first and the second. Moreover, attempts to picture "kin-dom" type communities in actual practice, defined apart from God's calling, sustaining, ruling, and judging presence and activity, tend to ignore the historical evidence that such communities dedicated to inclusion soon display their instincts to neglect ongoing repentance and gravitate toward rigidity and intolerance.

For those who might object that kingdom language is obsolete, a constellation of dead metaphors, no longer accessible or meaningful to the modern democratic world, which is mostly far removed from monarchs and monarchies, I invite you to sit on the sofa with me and my granddaughters as we watch the *Frozen* movies. The dramatic events around Queens Anna and Elsa in the Kingdom of Arendelle are not only accessible to them but enchanting. If preschoolers can imagine and delight in a lively kingdom, perhaps biblical scholars and preachers can too.

2

Decisions Preachers Make

Keep awake therefore, for you know neither the day nor the hour.

—Matthew 25:13

Tell my brothers to be always watching unto prayer, and when the good old ship of Zion comes along, to be ready to step aboard.

—Harriet Tubman[1]

Maybe I see schizophrenia because the idea of a world with wandering prophets is particularly threatening; maybe the idea of a world riddled with psychopaths wandering around acting out of faulty brain chemistry is somehow less frightening than a world of prophets acting out God's will.

—Psychologist Elizabeth Simonsen, on Flannery O'Connor's "The Violent Bear It Away"[2]

When a preacher or a teacher chooses to present a parable, this sets in motion a domino chain reaction of other decisions. While we would love to imagine that these choices are like the buffet at Golden Corral, a nearly endless array of tasty options, in truth we are not at a tantalizing buffet at all but on a battlefield. Every one of these decisions is contested, and the choices we make will go a long way to governing what we are able to hear in the parable.

Here are four decisions any interpreter of the parables must make.

1. WHAT IS A PARABLE?

In the last chapter we advanced a simple definition of a New Testament parable: a parable is a literary performance in which a story, example, or image from our world of experience or imagination is compared to God's kingdom. Even though this definition is quite modest, it does have at least three significant implications:

First, our definition claims that a parable is a "literary performance," which is another way of saying that parables do not lie docilely on the page but demand an interaction with those who read and hear them. When I look up my favorite recipe for Three-Cheese Lasagna, I am grateful for the list of ingredients and cooking instructions, but I do not expect this recipe to jump off the page and demand that I change my life. Not so with parables. Just to read them is to "perform" them, to release their drama in which all who hear are involved. Klyne Snodgrass is correct when he states, "A parable's ultimate aim is to awaken insight. Stimulate the conscience, *and* move to action."[3]

Second, our definition recognizes that parables come in a variety of literary forms. There really isn't any tight literary genre called "parable"; rather, parables cover a cluster of genres. The New Testament word for "parable" is the Septuagint's rendering of the Hebrew *mashal*, a word that includes riddles, proverbs, stories, allegories, and more. Any attempt to force all of Jesus' parables into the same shoe box will mangle many parables that don't fit neatly into the container.

Third, in a parable some literary figure of speech is compared to God's kingdom, and, as we claimed in the last chapter, the kingdom of God involves the inbreaking of the life of God into history and life. Parables are not word games, like Wordle or the daily crossword puzzle, which can be "solved" by staying completely inside the puzzle. All of Jesus' parables, implicitly or explicitly, say, "The kingdom of God is like *this*." To wrestle with a parable is to be guided (or pushed) to the brink of mystery, to those places in life where God's reign is revealed. Parables move with centrifugal force, moving out from themselves to God's active presence. Parables are not done with us until we have allowed the parable to move us from where we are to those places where God's activity is erupting in the world and we have exclaimed with surprise, "Oh, now I see!"

The world of parables scholarship is, of course, awash with definitions of parables, many of them sexier and more appealing than the rather simple definition we have advanced. But more often than not, these definitions turn out to be like MG sports cars in the 1950s and 1960s, dazzling but prone to breaking down on the highway.

Take, for example, a definition that has won many fans, inside the academy and out, namely, C. H. Dodd's memorable statement: "At its simplest, the parable is a metaphor or simile drawn from nature or common life, arresting the hearer by its vividness or strangeness, and leaving the mind in sufficient doubt to its precise application to tease the mind into active thought."[4]

Nice. Parables are vivid and strange, and they tease us into active thinking. But we can quickly see, however, that this sports car of a definition may take us a long way, but it won't take us home. First, when Dodd claims that parables are metaphors or similes, what he doesn't say is that he is fencing off any figure of speech that is *not* a metaphor or a simile—especially allegory, which, as we saw in the last chapter, is a literary form that was important to the early church but which parables scholars since Jülicher, including Dodd, have been trying to eradicate like smallpox. So, when Dodd hits an inconvenient parable like the Parable of the Wicked Tenants (Mark 12:1–8), which is so clearly not simply a metaphor or a simile but an allegory, he has to twist himself into a pretzel to get to the weird place where he can see this parable, which involves exaggerated violence, a vineyard owner sending his "beloved son" into the blood-soaked terrain of the vineyard, and the murder of the owner's son, whose body is thrown out of the vineyard, as "natural and realistic in every way."[5]

John Dominic Crossan, in his exploration of the definition of a parable, narrows the range even more. He begins by declaring that understanding Jesus' parables as "poetic metaphor' is "a definite step in the right direction."[6] But not all metaphors work the same way, so Crossan needs to make a further distinction. Some metaphors, Crossan says, are merely teaching devices that an instructor might use with a pupil to illustrate a concept. In these cases, the teacher is employing a metaphor to illustrate useful information *outside* the metaphor. So, if the metaphor works and the student grasps this information, then the metaphor has served its purpose and can be thrown away. There are, however, other metaphors that are not about information outside of them but are referring to a world "so new or so alien to consciousness that [their] referent can only be grasped within the metaphor itself."[7] This is not a metaphor pointing to something outside; this is metaphor as essential, metaphor as an arena of discovery in which its meaning can "only be received *after* one has participated through the metaphor in its new and alien referential world."[8] In this case, the metaphor is not a classroom teaching tool; it's the classroom itself.[9] Jesus' parables, at least the ones that count, claims Crossan, are this latter sort of metaphor.

Crossan deserves (and has received from others) a longer response, but I will simply point out that the parables of Jesus we actually have in the New Testament seem to slide along a scale from mysteriously provocative ("so new or so alien to consciousness") to more straightforward and didactic expressions. Crossan knows this, of course, and his solution is simply to take the parables off the map that don't pass his metaphoric test. But a good definition of parables ought, it seems to me, to be a basket big enough to hold the parables actually given to us in the New Testament, not a filter to screen out what is unacceptable to the interpreter.

2. WHICH PARABLE TO PREACH OR TEACH?

Before the advent of modern historical biblical criticism, this question did not exist. But along with such criticism came the discovery that the parables we have in the New Testament are not, word for word, the parables spoken by Jesus. A full description of the textual issues involved is beyond our scope, but suffice it to say, many if not all of the parables in Matthew, Mark, and Luke show signs that they have been modified by the process of transmission through the decades between Jesus' ministry and the composition of the Gospels and by the editorial hand of the Gospel writers themselves. It may even be that some of the parables in the New Testament are entirely creations of the early church or the Gospel writers, composed in the spirit of what they understood of Jesus. We can still say, "Hear now Jesus' Parable of the Sower," but it would be more accurate to say, "This is, at least to some extent, the early church's preaching of Jesus' Parable of the Sower."

That would be merely an interesting thought, were it not for one other gift of modern biblical scholarship: the development of tools to peel back the layers and to reconstruct something close to Jesus' original parables. In the 1940s, Joachim Jeremias developed a list of what he called "laws of transformation," ways that the early church typically changed Jesus' parables,[10] and Jeremias and those who came after have used these "laws" as tools to boil the parables we have down to something like the parables that Jesus would have originally spoken.

For example, Jeremias said that the Gospel authors tended to embellish stories. So in Luke's "Parable of the Pounds" (or, as we will call it later, the Parable of the Minas [Luke 19:11–27] servants are each given a mina, a sum of money that amounts to a few month's wages, but in Matthew's similar parable (Matt. 25:14–30), each servant is given at least one talent, which is a lot more money, about fifteen years of wages. In Matthew's parable, there are only three servants involved, but in Luke's ten servants make an appearance. So, based on the principle of embellishment, Jeremias confidently states, "Luke, then, has increased the number of the servants, while Matthew has immensely magnified the amounts involved."[11]

Another of Jeremias's "laws of transformation" is that the early church often changed Jesus' parables to fit new circumstances in the life of the church. For example, by the time the Gospels were written, several decades had gone by since Jesus' death, and there was anxiety over the fact that Jesus had not yet returned as he promised. This later concern of the church about the delay of Jesus makes its way into some of the parables,[12] as when, in the Parable of the Ten Bridesmaids, "the bridegroom was delayed" (Matt. 25:5). For Jeremias, it was Matthew's church, not Jesus, that worried about a delayed Lord and talked about a delayed bridegroom.

Jeremias developed ten of these "laws of transformation," and they were immensely useful in recovering the original parables of Jesus. If the early church changed Jesus' parables in these ten ways, then logically all we have to do is reverse engineer the parables to disclose the originals. The ability to do this poses a serious challenge to preachers and teachers: do we present the parable we have in the Bible or the parable we think Jesus originally spoke? No longer is the question "which parable?" simply a matter of whether we present the Parable of the Good Samaritan or the Parable of the Wedding Banquet. If we present, say, the Parable of the Wedding Banquet, now the question is whether we preach Matthew's version or a reconstructed "original" version? Do we preach and teach the Scripture we have in the Bible, or do we concentrate on what we think Jesus *really* said?

Parables scholars have divided over this issue. Some, like Jeremias and Crossan, attempt to recover the parables of the historical Jesus, but others, like John Drury and John Donahue, focus on the parables in their canonical context.

In my view, the preferred choice is to go with Drury and Donahue and to preach and teach the parables as they appear in the biblical canon, in Matthew, Mark, and Luke, for three reasons:

1. Theologically, the parables as they appear in the canon are the church's Scripture, the Scripture we have been given, as opposed to the speculative proto-Scripture we imagine we can construct.

2. The scholars who do attempt to recover the parables as Jesus actually told them have had, at best, mixed results. When they get around to saying what this or that parable was when Jesus spoke it, and before it was altered by the church, they are notoriously all over the map. If Jeremias's "laws of transformation" (and other attempts like his) were truly sharp scalpels to separate out the originals, then why do the scholars differ so widely on their reconstructions of the parables?

Part of the reason is that Jeremias's so-called laws of transformation aren't really laws at all. At most they are probabilities. Imagine a historic Presbyterian church in North Carolina that desires to restore its 1850 building to the "original." They hire a restoration architect, but unfortunately there are no photographs, paintings, or drawings of the original building. So the architect is going to have to do a lot of guesswork, but it will be educated guesswork.

She knows, for example, that there was a trend in Presbyterian churches in the 1930s through the 1960s to remove center pulpits and to install split chancels, with a pulpit on one side and a lectern on the other. This would be an architectural version of a "law of transformation," and since this Presbyterian church does, in fact, have just such a split chancel, what the architect has to do is to get rid of it. So she removes the present chancel and restores the center pulpit, using furniture characteristic of the mid-nineteenth century.

"I have restored the original," she confidently tells the church officers. But has she? What if this church was one of the (few) Presbyterian buildings to have a split chancel in 1850? What if the architect is correct, the split chancel was added later, but the original building had the pulpit in the corner or on the side wall? She would have restored an "original" building that never was. My point is that smart people can use sound and logical principles to restore originals and be badly wrong. So it is with the parables.

3. There is often, among those scholars who are eager to strip away the churchly accretions and to recover the original parables of Jesus, an assumption, basically mistaken in my view, that the Gospel writers did damage to Jesus' original message. Either they misunderstood what Jesus said or, for reasons of ideology and self-preservation, intentionally distorted Jesus' message. The Gospel writers, in other words, weren't faithful transmitters of the gospel, but manglers of it. This view seems both cynical and historically improbable. Yes, they preached the parables to their own context, but that preaching showed natural, and mostly healthy, evolution from Jesus' preaching, not sabotage.

This is not to say that efforts to distinguish between the parables we have in the Gospels and what those parables may have been in the mouth of Jesus are not useful. To be able to say, for example, that behind Matthew's Parable of the Wedding Banquet (Matt. 22:1–14) there was likely a simpler, less allegorical parable that Jesus spoke allows us to plot the homiletical trajectory of that parable. That is, we make an educated guess about what Jesus' original parable was like, and then we see what that parable became when it was preached to Matthew's community. Plot that forward on the graph, and we might see where the parable may be heading in our own preaching. The parables as recorded in the Gospels were preaching, and they want to be preaching again.

Another implication of our counsel to preach the canonical parables is the further encouragement to preach the parables in the literary and theological context where they are found, that is, to preach a Matthew parable as it is set in Matthew, not in Mark or Luke, and so on. That is why, in this book, even when the same parable appears in more than one Gospel, we treat each version separately, hoping to provide nuanced readings of these parables as they appear in the contexts of the Gospels in which they appear.

This is especially important because the several dozen little stories that we call parables, scattered around like Easter eggs in Matthew, Mark, and Luke, are not literary clones. Luke's parables and Matthew's parables, for example, all point to the kingdom of God, but Luke tends to see that kingdom manifested in joy, hospitality, and justice, while Matthew emphasizes wisdom and righteousness. Luke wants his readers to experience the crisis that the kingdom is precipitating right now, in the middle of our lives, so he has five parables in which, as we shall see, a character in the middle of a crisis draws in the hearers of the parable by engaging in a soliloquy, asking, "What shall I do?" Matthew tends to be less interested in anguished self-examination over against following the ancient path of wisdom. So Matthew's parables tend to be more straightforward, saying things like, "OK, there were these ten bridesmaids. Five of them were wise, and five of them were fools. Any questions?"

Imagine that musician and songwriter Beyoncé, the poet Ocean Vuong, the dancer and choreographer Twyla Tharp, the former host of "Prairie Home Companion" Garrison Keillor, and a geological engineer from Cleveland take a trip together in a van to the Grand Canyon. As each of them approaches the rim, all of them are astounded by the vast canyon stretching out before them. In their amazement, Beyoncé begins to compose the lyrics to a song, Vuong a poem, Tharp a dance, Keillor a homey story about someone from Lake Wobegon standing on the rim of the canyon, and the engineer writes in his journal, "This is Lake Erie without the water!" That's like Matthew, Mark, and Luke. Each has his vocabulary, each has his own style, each has his own medium, but they are all pointing breathlessly at the vastness of God's kingdom.

A full spectrum of proclamation needs all of the Gospel emphases, and thus needs to honor the context of each parable. To approach all parables as if they were versions of the same oyster is like saying that we ought to approach "American Idol" and "Meet the Press" the same because they are both television shows. Indeed, the field of parables interpretation is littered with the wreckage of people who tried and failed to come up with some master strategy for interpreting and understanding all the parables.

As a warning flare about what can happen when preachers and other interpreters of the parables try to jackhammer the parables out of their context in the Gospels, I want to briefly examine William Herzog II's *Parables as Subversive Speech: Jesus as Pedagogue of the Oppressed.*[13] This work represents a trend in parables interpretation to see Jesus' parables in the context of an imagined society of Galilean politics and economics.

Herzog is persuaded that "to make sense of specific parables, interpreters need to entertain some larger idea of who Jesus was and what his public activity was about."[14] Fair enough, but what Herzog means to say, of course, is that the context of the Gospels and their pictures of Jesus are unreliable. The parables need some other context, and Herzog intends to find one, namely, the identity and public activity of a reconstructed "historical Jesus." Once he gets that picture of Jesus in place, then he can transfer the parables to this assembled Jesus and imagine what a specific parable would mean coming from his mouth.

This is a neat trick, something like ventriloquism, but where will we get this "larger idea of who Jesus was"? Herzog has read Albert Schweitzer's *The Quest of the Historical Jesus*, and his big takeaway is that, when it comes to Jesus, historians don't follow the customary path. Instead of painstakingly collecting facts and then making historical judgments, a Jesus historian "begins with a theory, not with facts."[15] Aha! To Herzog's mind, Jesus scholars dream up probable Jesuses of their own imagining, and then take the "facts" about Jesus out of the basket one by one and see if they can insert them into this imagined framework. Inspired by this move, Herzog sets out to concoct his own good theory about Jesus' identity and then to see if he can fit the parables into its cubby holes.

We can see Herzog's boat being swept out to sea here, but let's continue with him for a while. Since Jesus scholars make this all up anyway, Herzog proposes to fashion his needed "larger idea of who Jesus was" by viewing him through the lens of the remarkable twentieth-century Brazilian Marxist educator Paulo Freire. If this seems crazy on its face, Herzog honestly admits that he is conducting a highly speculative experiment (sort of like *Honey, I Shrunk the Kids*).

Jesus was no Freire and Freire was no Jesus; Herzog knows that. The differences are too great. One man was a first-century rabbi, the other a twentieth-century university professor; one was shaped by the Torah, the other by Karl Marx; and so on. But despite their differences, there are significant overlaps, Herzog insists, between Jesus and Freire. Both men worked "with the illiterate, the marginalized, and the poor, with peasants and villagers in the countryside," both "were considered politically subversive, and both suffered political consequences because of their work." The same could be said, by the way, of Dorothy Day, Oscar Romero, Martin Luther King Jr., and Francis of Assisi. We're going with Freire here, and the reason is yet one more quality that Herzog believes Jesus and Freire have in common: pedagogy. They both aimed through creative teaching to raise the political and social consciousness of their learners.

Now that we have Jesus imagined as a Freire-like figure, we can download the parables into the mouth of this mashup Jesus. What might the parables sound like when we do? Jesus would quite naturally speak in highly politicized speech, coded language designed to slip unnoticed past the oppressive rulers. Forget Jesus the eschatological Jewish prophet who announced the inbreaking of God's reign; think rather of Jesus the raiser of political consciousness. "The parable, then," declares Herzog, "was not primarily a vehicle to communicate theology or ethics but a codification designed to stimulate social analysis."

The untethering is now complete. The parables aren't about the inbreaking of the reign of God's righteousness and peace; they are about social analysis. We can admit that Herzog's experimental Jesus bears, to be sure, a few similarities to the pictures of him in Mark, Matthew, and Luke. After all, it is from the Gospel writers that we learn that Jesus' preaching was indeed threatening to the political establishment and that Jesus suffered the consequences. But this atheological Jesus who glided around Galilee using coded God-talk purely as a device to raise the political awareness of Galilean peasants about the brute facts of Roman imperialism is finally a creature of Herzog's fantasy.

We get an on-the-scene portrait of how Herzog conceives the impact of one parable, the Parable of the Sower, in a 2012 essay in *Review and Expositor*, "Sowing Discord: The Parable of the Sower (Mark 4:1–9)."[16] Herzog imagines that Jesus told this parable to the people of a tiny Galilean hamlet, and then departed, leaving behind to his peasant audience the task of mulling over the parable's implications. Later, at the request of the villagers, the local storyteller, the griot, recites Jesus' parable, and this retelling generates, Paulo Freire–style, heated and homespun political discussion. The part of the story about the birds eating up the seed on the hard path gets one of the villagers, Miriam, up on a soap box. "Sounds like birds coming down and devouring our seeds." After pausing for a moment, she asks, "Whose scorched-earth policies take our harvest before it can be accounted for? It seems like every harvest just withers away before we get a loaf of bread out of it."[17] "And the thorns," adds Joseph, another villager, "remind us of the master's class who chokes us every year at harvest."[18]

When the peasants hear about the great harvest at the end of the parable, they decide that it doesn't matter because their economic oppressors would just take it away from them anyway. "The master got the lion's share, that's for sure," said James, speaking about the local elite, a Herodian, who controlled their village. "We sow the seed, worry the crop along, and bring in the harvest before the master and his retainers swoop down and devour the harvest of our hard-earned work."[19]

To hear Herzog's village peasants spouting anachronistic liberationist slogans underscores how far away Herzog has wandered from the Markan setting and how his depictions of the villagers run perilously close to the wacky, jargon-spouting, Roman-hating "People's Front of Judea" bused in from the set of Monty Python's *Life of Brian*. Unfortunately, what gets most oppressed in this fanciful drama is the Markan parable itself, which is both flattened and distorted. The eschatological import of the parable gets washed away in favor of a clumsy lesson on Galilean land reform. What we get is a heavy dose of Herzog's contemporary politics, a light salting of the truly amazing Paulo Freire, and almost nothing of Mark or of the Jewish eschatological prophet known as Jesus of Nazareth.

It is one thing to say that we can hear this parable speaking to the plight of oppressed peasants in Galilee. It does have such implications, just as it can speak to the conditions of poverty and hopelessness in Buenos Aires and Chicago today. But to say that agricultural reform in the Roman Empire is the only horizon of this parable is to fail to see the sky. Jesus' teachings and ministry do indeed put Roman cruelty on the griddle, but Mark's Jesus also has other fish, and bigger fish, to fry than even the Roman Empire. In Mark, this parable is about the breaking in of the kingdom of God, which overturns every form of death and oppression, including, but not limited to, economic duress in ancient Palestine.

It is essential in preaching to recognize the political and social implications of Jesus' parables, but Herzog seems to think that the parables are only coded, atheological expressions of immediate political conditions. Burning away the eschatological framework of Jesus in Mark turns him into merely a local activist whose goals look a whole lot like the small span of our own watered-down, suburbanized self-righteous politics. It is but one more way to attempt to domesticate the wild and unmanageable claims of this and all Jesus' other parables.

3. TO EXPLAIN OR TO PROCLAIM

As listener-friendly as parables may seem, they still have many elements that are strange to our ears. For example, few contemporary hearers have attended weddings where the bridesmaids run around at midnight fretting because the groom is so far a no-show, or a wedding where the wedding party frets about their oil lamps. Few contemporary listeners have seen a king burn down a whole city because some people blew off his son's wedding party. Not only are there culturally strange and narratively odd bits in the parables like those, which need to be elucidated, but the parables themselves come across somewhat like puzzles needing to be solved.

An almost irresistible temptation arises for preachers to *explain* parables rather than to *proclaim* them. If we can explain what it meant that the prodigal son "came to himself," or make it clear how enormous was that batch of flour that the woman supplied with yeast, or demystify the allegorical code in the Parable of the Wicked Tenants, or lay out plank by plank the correct answer to Jesus' question, "Which of these three . . . was a neighbor to the man who fell into the hands of the robbers?" (Luke 10:36), then we can sit down in the pulpit chair with the satisfaction of a high school student who has just solved a quadratic equation. After all, Mark says that Jesus explained the parables to his disciples (Mark 4:34); shouldn't we do the same?

I do think that many good sermons on the parables will of necessity include some teaching, some explaining. For instance, as we will discuss later in regard to the Parable of the Minas (or Pounds, Luke 19:11–27), hearers will need some kind of scorecard to know the players. They will need to be taught, probably, what a "mina" is as a unit of money, and they may well need to hear the story that may lurk in the background of this parable, the story of Archelaus, the son of Herod who tried to talk Caesar into making him a king, but we should not stop with these explanations.

The problem with substituting explanation for proclamation is twofold. First, there is plenty of evidence that when Jesus spoke parables they landed with a punch. The crowds not only heard Jesus' parables; they were moved to follow the one who had spoken the parables (Matt. 19:1–2). One of Jesus' parables so irritated the Pharisees that they broke out in jeers of public ridicule (Luke 16:14), and another parable caused such a stir that Jesus came within a hair of being arrested on the spot (Mark 12:12). Somehow people shouting, "Lock him up!" after Jesus told a parable seems quite different from a parishioner pausing at the church door to say, "I really appreciated how you explained that business about the seed and those different soils. Never thought of it that way before."

Second, we have been making the case that the purpose of parables is not merely to *talk about* the kingdom of God but instead to take us to those places all around us where the inbreaking of God's kingdom can be perceived and *experienced*. The parables are to take us to places where, as we said in the previous chapter, we can be "*on* hand for [the kingdom] which is *at* hand but not *in* hand." The kingdom of God is not an idea but an *event*, and so should be preaching on the parables.

4. THE KINGDOM OF GOD, NOW OR IN THE FUTURE?

Jesus inaugurated his ministry with a stunning announcement: "The time is fulfilled, and the kingdom of God has come near; repent, and believe in the good news" (Mark 1:14). The NRSV doesn't put an exclamation point after Jesus' proclamation, but I am not sure why not. How could Jesus have walked into a Galilean village with the news that the long-awaited reign of God was knocking on the door, that the angel army of liberation was at long last on the outskirts of history, ready to liberate the death camp, without his voice rising in urgency?

But the question is, How near is the kingdom of God? C. H. Dodd, in his groundbreaking work on Jesus' parables, famously argued that, in Jesus, the kingdom had already arrived. He called this "realized eschatology," the claim that "the Kingdom of God is realized in experience."[20] How can this be, given the fact that the world still rocks on, broken and unredeemed? For Dodd, the church celebrates the coming of God's kingdom every time it gathers at the Eucharist:

> Above all, in the Sacrament of the Eucharist the Church recapitulates the historic crisis in which Christ lived, died and rose again, and finds in it the "efficacious sign" of eternal life in the Kingdom of God. In its origin and in its governing ideas it may be described as a sacrament of realized eschatology. The Church prays, "The Kingdom come"; "Come, Lord Jesus." As it prays, it remembers that the Lord did come, and with him came the Kingdom of God.[21]

But as powerful as the Eucharist is, surely when Jesus said, "There will be signs in the sun, the moon, and the stars and on the earth distress among nations confused by the roaring of the sea and the waves. People will faint from fear and foreboding of what is coming upon the world, for the powers of the heavens will be shaken. Then they will see 'the Son of Man coming in a cloud' with power and great glory" (Luke 21:25–27), he meant more than Christians gathered around the Lord's table. What is implied here is a redemption of the whole cosmos, a public shaking of the powers and acknowledgment of the glory of Christ, who reigns as king.

The book of Revelation looks forward to the time when there will be "a new heaven and a new earth; for the first heaven and the first earth had passed away" (Rev. 21:1). This coming time will be one of the banishment of all that claws at and oppresses human life. A loud voice from the throne of God proclaims:

> "See, the home of God is among mortals.
> He will dwell with them;
> they will be his peoples,
> and God himself will be with them and be their God;
> he will wipe every tear from their eyes.
> Death will be no more;
> mourning and crying and pain will be no more,
> for the first things have passed away."
>
> Rev. 21:3–4

When will these things be? As anyone who has stood at graveside to grieve someone loved well knows, we have not come to the time when death is no more. No wonder the book of Revelation, at its close, hears Jesus saying, "Surely I am coming soon," and then prays the anguished, heartfelt prayer, "Amen. Come, Lord Jesus!" (Rev. 21:20).

So from this perspective the kingdom of God is in the future, and the church cries out for Christ to come and be all in all, healing and redeeming the creation, freeing it from the power of death. But earlier in Revelation, when John, on the Lord's day, was carried by the Spirit into heaven, he heard the heavenly chorus singing an unceasing song, "Holy, holy, holy, the Lord God the Almighty, who was and is and is to come" (Rev. 4:8). Past, present, and future are gathered up in God, and already the chorus can proclaim that the kingdom of God has fully come: "The kingdom of the world has become the kingdom of our Lord and of his Messiah, and he will reign forever and ever" (Rev. 11:15).

For the parables preacher, the question is quite practical: when Jesus says in his parables, "The kingdom of God is like . . . ," are we to preach about a kingdom that is here now, or a kingdom that is to come in the future? The answer is complicated, but put simply, we are to preach both.

It is worth noting that the question of time is not only a theological issue, but has become a major concern for contemporary science as well. Philosopher of science Craig Callender writes in *Scientific American*, "Time is an especially hot topic right now in physics."[22] Most people naively assume that time is flowing from past through the present to the future. The past is fixed, over and done, and cannot be changed; the present is what we are experiencing now; and the future is wide open, a field of unlimited possibilities. "Yet as natural as this way of thinking is," writes Callender, "you will not find it reflected in science. The equations of physics do not tell us which events are occurring right now—they are like a map without the 'you are here" symbol."[23] Callender goes on to say that "many in theoretical physics have come to believe that time fundamentally does not even exist."[24]

Scientists disagree, of course, about what time is, or whether there is such a thing as time at all, but there is widespread agreement that, in an Einsteinian universe, time is fluid and malleable. Here's a homespun example: Imagine a train moving down the track. On this train is a boxcar with an open side, exposed to the outside. On this boxcar is a light projector, positioned exactly in the middle of the boxcar, with two lenses, one pointing forward and the other pointing backward. Standing beside this projector is a woman with her fingers grasping the "On" switch. Beside the track is another woman, watching the train go by. At the precise moment that the boxcar passes this second woman beside the track, the woman on the boxcar flips the switch and light projects toward the forward wall of the boxcar and also toward the back wall. The question is, does the light hit the front wall first, or the back wall first, or both at exactly the same time?

The commonsense answer is that, since the projector is in the middle of the boxcar, it hits the front and the back walls simultaneously. And that's true, but only for the woman on the train. Since she's on the train, she is moving with the train and with the projector, and for her, the light hits front and back walls at exactly the same time. But not so for the woman on the ground watching the train go by. For her, the front wall of the boxcar is moving away from the light, and the back wall is moving toward the light, so the light hits the back wall first. We're talking millionths of a nanosecond, and no human being could actually perceive this, of course, but the point remains: for the woman on the train and the woman on the ground, the same event is different in terms of time.

Two events—the light striking the front wall and striking the back wall—can be both simultaneous and not simultaneous. What is future for the woman on the ground, the light hitting the front wall, is already past for the woman standing on the train.

As theoretical physicist Brian Greene says of a similar example, "In other words, things that are simultaneous from the viewpoint of some observers will not be simultaneous from the viewpoint of others, if the two groups are in relative motion."[25] Another way to say this is that, for contemporary science, time is not some stable, universal reality. Time depends upon where one stands.

Now back to theology. Theologians, as well, recognize the instability of the concept of time. In his *Confessions*, Augustine famously said, "What then is time? If no one asks me, I know; if I want to explain it to a questioner, I do not know."[26] As he wrestled theologically and personally with the nature of time, Augustine came to two large insights. The first is that time is a creature of God; God is not a creature of time. Augustine noted that some people ask, "What was God doing before the creation of the world?" But the question is meaningless, concluded Augustine. It's foolish to ask what God was doing "then," when, since God created time, before God created time "there was not any 'then.'"[27] The key insight is that God doesn't exist "in time," as if God were simply one more time-bound creature as we are. God is time-less.

The second insight of Augustine on time is that, for human beings, time is a perceptual, existential, one might say psychological, experience. How do human beings experience time? There is the past, which cannot be changed, but it also exists only as a person remembers it in the present. And there is the future, which also doesn't exist except as anticipated in the present. So as time is perceived, there is only the present: the present as experienced in the moment, the past present in memory, and the future present in anticipation. But what is the "present"? As soon as one tries to get a footing on the present, it slips into the past. To live in time is to be constantly anxious, with nowhere firm to stand. Our only security is somehow to be delivered from the tyranny of disintegrating time and to be gathered into the timeless, the eternal. "For

Thou hast made us for Thyself," Augustine said of God, "and our hearts are restless until they rest in Thee."[28]

Now we are getting close to what we wish to say about the kingdom of God and time. In an even more profound way than theoretical physics, in theology the same event can have a different frame of time depending upon where one stands. What is true always in eternity can be, for us, coming true in history. God's kingdom, like God, has no time. God is eternal, beyond all time. When the book of Revelation speaks of God "who was and is and is to come," the idea is not that God is past, present, and future all wrapped into one. The point, rather, is that "who was and is and is to come" is the way we time-bound creatures have to talk when pointing to the God who is not bound at all by time.

So is the kingdom already here and fulfilled? Yes, in the sense that God is eternally king, beyond all past, present, and future. No, in the sense that we creatures perceive our lives and our history as flowing from the past through the present to the future. For us, we catch glimpses of God's kingdom here and there in our present experience, and the parables point to those moments. And for us, we remember those glimpses; thus we have a faithful past and a testimony to speak. We anticipate a day to come when what we have momentarily glimpsed here and there will become a cosmic and public reality for all to see, and the Son of Man will come as king of all reality, with "power and great glory" (Luke 21:27). But because God is not tied to our perceptual experience of past, present, and future, we must also confess that what we expect, what we anticipate in faith, what we hope for, is already and eternally true.

Theologian Herbert McCabe came up with a fine image to describe the life of the Trinity, which is timeless and eternal, and the relationship of the eternal Trinitarian life to the unfolding historical, time-shaped lives we live. He said,

> The story of Jesus is nothing other than the triune life of God projected onto our history, or enacted sacramentally in our history, so that it becomes story. . . . Now imagine a film projected not on a screen but on a rubbish dump. The story of Jesus—which in its full extent is the entire Bible—is the projection of the trinitarian life of God on the rubbish dump we have made of the world. . . . Watching, so to speak, the story of Jesus, we are watching the processions of the Trinity.[29]

An implication of McCabe's image is that the kingdom of God is without time, because the Trinity is eternal, not embedded in time. But since we are embedded in time, the Gospel story of Jesus comes to us precisely as *story*, a plot unfolding in time. And for us, we proclaim a kingdom of God that shows itself here and there in the present and fully at the end of the story, in the future.

The poet Christian Wiman, who has served as the editor of *Poetry* magazine and as a professor at Yale Divinity School, was raised as a Christian in a small-town Texas home, but lost his faith as a teenager. In his thirties, soon after he was married, he was diagnosed with a rare form of cancer, and, in the shock of this life-threatening event, returned to the Christian faith as "the only framework he knows that seems adequate to the extremes of joy and fear he has undergone."[30]

Some have scoffed, of course, that if Wiman hadn't been desperately ill, he wouldn't have reached out to God. Writing about that in *The New Yorker*, Adam Kirsch says,

> Yet why should the immediate cause of the call invalidate the call? "To admit that there may be some psychological need informing your return to faith does not preclude or diminish the spiritual imperative," [Wiman] insists, "any more than acknowledging the chemical aspects of sexual attraction lessens the mystery of enduring human love." Faith, like love, can be clinically described and analyzed from the outside, but it can be known only from the inside. That is why there is something so pitiable about the spectacle of those debates in which a celebrity atheist takes on a clergyman, and always wins. To argue for faith, at least in the twenty-first century, is already to lose the argument. What believers can give nonbelievers is an account of what it means to live in faith—not a polemic but a description, a confession, a kind of poem.[31]

After a long year battling his illness, Wiman and his family received the gift of a summer off, when the family could spend time together and recoup. Wiman describes that time:

> When our girls were just two years old, we spent a summer in Seattle, where I had lived for a while many years earlier. It was the first break I had managed to take from my editing job in a decade, and it was only eight months after I had undergone a bone marrow transplant. Time had a texture that summer, an hourly reality that we could taste and see. The girls went to a wonderful little daycare in the mornings so that my wife and I could write, and then we all came together in the afternoons to do something fun in the city. We had the same nightly ritual that we do now. I'd read to the girls and tuck them in before my wife took over, and the last thing I'd say every night was "I love you," and they would always reply promptly, "I love you too, Daddy."
>
> But one night after my declaration, Fiona was silent. She just kept staring at the ceiling.
>
> "Do you love me too, Fiona?" I asked, foolishly. A long moment passed.
>
> "No, Daddy, I don't."
>
> "Oh, Fiona sweetie, I bet you do," I said. Nothing.

> "Well," I said finally, "I love you, Finn, and I'll see you in the morning."
>
> And then as I started to get up, I felt her small hand on my arm and she said dreamily, without looking at me, like a little Lauren Bacall, "I will love you in the summertime, Daddy. I will love you . . . in the summertime."
>
> I have told this to a couple of people who thought it was heartbreaking, but I was so proud, I thought my heart would burst. I will love you in the summertime. What a piercing poetic thing to say—at two years old. And for weeks I thought about it. A year later . . . I even wrote a poem about it. I will love you in the summertime. Which is to say, given the charmed life we were living there in Seattle and all the grace and grief that my wife and I felt ourselves moving through at every second: I will love you in the time where there is time for everything, which is now and always. I will love you in the time when time is no more.
>
> Now, do I think that's what my Athena-eyed and mysteriously interior two-year-old daughter meant by that expression? No, I do not. But do I think that sometimes life and language break each other open to change, that a rupture in one can be a rapture in the other, that sometimes there are, as it were, words underneath the words—even the very Word underneath the words?
>
> Yes, I do.[32]

So there we are, we have an eternal God who, in Christ, loves us in the time when "there is time for everything, which is now and always . . . in the time when time is no more." The kingdom of God is a timeless, eternal kingdom. But we do not yet live in timelessness. We live time-bound. We are born, we live, and we die. History unfolds from episode to episode. We preach the kingdom of God because we believe there are weep holes in history and life when God's eternal kingdom shines through. The parables, with their everyday stories containing unexpected twists, say, "The kingdom of God is like this," and by doing so take us to those weep holes to see for ourselves.

Theologian Katherine Sonderegger, commenting on the conclusion of Wittgenstein's *Tractatus Logico-Philosophicus,* stated, "What we cannot speak about we must pass over in silence. What cannot be said, however, can be shown. They can manifest themselves, and we can point to them even as we cannot utter them or find them within the facts."[33] The kingdom of God manifests itself, reveals itself, in a town hall meeting here, in a hospital room there, in a broken relationship healed over here, and an unexpected and improbable manifestation of justice over there. The parables take us to those places of manifestation.

But preachers cannot "pass over in silence." We must speak, frail though our words be, and what we speak will be *news*, good news: "The time is fulfilled, and the kingdom of God has come near; repent, and believe."

If this seems too much for us. If the parables are too opaque and the gospel too elusive. If we stand in the pulpit embarrassed because we do not think we have what we are there to give, God's life-giving Word, we should be comforted by the words of Markus Barth: "The best Easter sermon that I have heard or read in the United States during the past ten years," he wrote,

> was an honest expression of the preacher's complete bafflement by the Resurrection stories. . . . It was a confession of lack of understanding; it revealed want of appropriation, and failure of communication. It was a cry for help and enlightenment: Here it is said that Thou art risen. But where are you now? How can we believe? Help our unbelief!—This preacher did more than take the Resurrection seriously. He could not stand up to it; like John of Patmos he just fell down.[34]

After all, the gospel we are sent to proclaim is to be *on* hand for God's kingdom, which is *at* hand, but also a kingdom that is not *in* hand, not even our hands.

3

Mark's Parables

Background

> Jesus is the Messiah, but in the eyes of the world, until the Resurrection, He is despised, suffering, and mortal. His divine glory is patent only to the narrowest circle of the elect. . . . In this way the Gospel of Mark was written as a book of secret epiphanies.
>
> —Martin Dibelius, *From Tradition to Gospel*[1]

> If only Jesus would come down from the cross so we might believe . . . ! Who of us is really prepared to accept that by remaining there he shows the way to liberation, to acknowledge that in this moment the powers are overthrown and the kingdom is come in power and glory?
>
> —Ched Myers, *Binding the Strong Man*[2]

MORE THAN MEETS THE EYE

At first glance, when Jesus begins to teach in parables in the Gospel of Mark, he seems to tell all the wrong stories. Mark's Gospel opens with a rapid pace and a fiery urgency. By comparison, most of the parables in Mark seem far too gentle, too mild, too domesticated.

The ministry of Jesus in Mark arrives like a Category 5 hurricane. John the Baptist is the weather siren, the urgent alarm interrupting the normal programming: "Warning! Get ready! Prepare the way of the Lord!" Then quickly the wind picks up, and the first drops of rain begin to fall, as Jesus is baptized and tempted. Lightning strikes and the ground shakes as Jesus inaugurates his ministry by thundering, "The time is now! The kingdom is at hand. Turn around. Believe the news of God's victory" (from Mark 1:14).

Then the wind begins to rattle the trees, and lightning flashes split the air all around. Jesus moves quickly and with purpose. He heals powerfully—a man with a demon, a leper, a paralytic, a man with a withered hand, a little girl, a deaf man, crowds of the afflicted—he teaches boldly, he calls disciples, he feeds thousands, he challenges the religious authorities, and when a darkened rival storm whips up ominously on the sea, he commands it to shut up and be still.

What interests Mark about Jesus is his forceful impact—his dramatic deeds, his bold words—not his personality. Think of the often-self-flattering "Who is our pastor?" bios that grace some church webpages today "My wife, Kristen, and I are foodies with a special fondness for Thai," say these sketches. "*The Princess Bride* is my favorite movie of all time, and I am passionate about the poetry of Mary Oliver. Kristen and I enjoy hiking in the mountains, walking Marley our beautiful Welsh Corgi, bingeing on Netflix, sipping a glass of Pinot Noir while listening to Springsteen, and watching football. Go Packers!"

Mark is not like this. He focuses on Jesus, to be sure, not on his temperament, hobbies, preferences, or whims—the stuff of contemporary biography—but on his actions and how they embody what God is doing in the world, on his deeds as God's agent in the battle against the demonic. As Adela Yarbro Collins says,

> Mark focuses on Jesus and his identity, not in the interest of establishing his character or essence, but in order to write a particular kind of history, which may be called a narration of the course of the eschatological events. . . . The gospel is not only "the good news that God was present in Jesus for our salvation"; it is the good news that God has acted and is acting in history to fulfill the promises of Scripture and to inaugurate the new age. The gospel begins with a reference to Jesus Christ (the Son of God), not out of interest in his character, but to present him as God's agent.[3]

In Mark, Jesus is no gentle sage waltzing around Galilee issuing witty and comforting *bon mots* about being the best persons we can be. The stakes are higher; the cosmos, including all humanity, is more desperate. Jesus has come to rescue; he is a savior. He has come to liberate the concentration camp. He is a soldier (a rough image, but accurate), a fiery-eyed apocalyptic warrior come to do battle with Satan and the powers of death. When he engages in combat with disease, blind ignorance, the wild forces of nature, and the religious elites, he is more than simply an advocate for peace and justice; he is the strong one of God, in pitched battle with the demonic powers of darkness.

At one point in Mark, Jesus encounters a man with a demon, an "unclean spirit," who thrashes around a cemetery night and day howling and bruising himself with rocks. Mark tells us that "no one could bind him" (5:3), and this statement about binding has a double meaning. In the ordinary sense, the man himself—this wretched, convulsing man—could not be secured; no chains were strong enough to bind him. But this story operates on the cosmic level, as well, and no earthly force was able to bind the evil that held this man captive. Satan, the "strong one," had coiled himself around the tormented man in a death grip. So this is no simple healing story. This is apocalyptic warfare, divine strength against demonic might. Jesus has come from God to do battle, to bind up the strong and evil one who cannot be bound, and then to plunder his house (3:24–27). And that is exactly what Jesus does as he breaks into Satan's chamber of horrors and rescues a life.

In Mark, Jesus "assumes awesome powers for himself," say the authors of *Mark as Story*, "pardoning sins, interpreting laws, appointing twelve to share the authority, exorcising demons, healing, commanding nature, prophesying, entering Jerusalem royally, and occupying the temple."[4] The first time he opens his mouth to preach in the synagogue, people are astounded not by the artistry or soft eloquence of his words but by their *power*. He spoke "with authority," not with footnotes like the scribes (1:21–22). He shows this authoritative power when a sudden storm on the Sea of Galilee threatens to swamp the boat carrying him and his disciples. We sometimes speak of this story as "Jesus stilling the storm" (4:35–41), but "stilling" is not a strong enough word. The storm is not a low-pressure front on the Weather Channel; it's a demonic maelstrom whipping up the strong winds and high seas of chaos. Jesus doesn't gently calm this storm; he shouts into its fury and rebukes it, just as he will later rebuke Peter for slipping over to the dark side and identifying with Satan (8:33). To put it in proper theological language, Jesus denounces the hell out of the storm, literally.

The point is, the Jesus portrayed in Mark is a force to be reckoned with. He is about the business of destroying the reign of Satan in all its guises. Even when he is teaching or feeding people, he is still on the attack. Every deed he performs is an exorcism of sorts, a plundering of the household of the demonic, including his engagements with the scribes and Pharisees. "[I]t is clear," writes Ched Myers of Mark's Gospel, "that there is more to Jesus' struggle with the scribal order than 'meets the eye.' This is a showdown with the Satanic order."[5]

We are not alone, of course, in these observations about Mark, that Jesus springs onto the scene as an apocalyptic warrior, the divine "strong man." Many commentators have noted this. But what is often overlooked is how, when the Jesus of Mark starts speaking in parables, the mood changes to one of gentleness, and we are puzzled. Given that the opening chapters of Mark tell the fast-paced story of Jesus unbinding those who are hopelessly bound and tossing demons out of every desperate back alley in Galilee, one would expect that the parables he speaks would be forceful too, with imagery more like the book of Revelation: swords, breastplates, trumpet blasts, dramatic conflict, and apocalyptic battle. But no, surprisingly, when he begins to speak in parables, the Jesus of Mark tells farm stories. When Jesus pauses midskirmish and preaches a parable-filled sermon (4:1–34), we are amazed that the parables he tells are not combat stories at all but gentle tales about seeds and soil.

When we scrutinize this seeming contradiction more closely, though, a pattern floats to the surface, and we can see a significant theological design at work in Mark. Closely read, Mark is actually telling two parallel stories in his Gospel, and the parables embody and express them both. The story that first catches our attention is the one we have just described, the dramatic story of the strong man of God, who has come to destroy Satan's reign and to rescue humanity. But when we look more closely, we notice in the latticework another story being unfolded: the story of an anguished servant who accomplishes God's mission by suffering and dying on a cross.

Mark's story of Jesus is like a 3D movie. Put on the 3D glasses, and you see Jesus springing off the screen as the apocalyptic warrior, slaying dragons and vanquishing demons. Take them off, though, and the screen goes blurry, and the story turns sad and tragic. Jesus barely gets his ministry going before the Pharisees conspire with the Herodians to put out a contract on him (3:6). Jesus' own mother and brothers are worried about him and want him to come back to his family (3:31–35). His disciples never fully comprehend what he is about. They don't even understand the very first parable he tells (4:13). Even after he has done great works, people ask him to leave town (5:17). The skepticism about him and the disbelief in his own home synagogue are so deadening, the power drains from him (6:1–6). As he gets closer to Jerusalem, he begins to talk frequently about his coming suffering and death. And when the forces of evil finally surround him, it results in his death, and not a peaceful death, not a death with dignity, but a spit- and rage-filled lynching. Jesus dies with an exclamation of God-forsakenness, a loud cry of pain, the violent expulsion of a final breath, and an unanswered prayer (15:33–37).

So what are we really watching here? What is this movie truly about, the strong Jesus who cleans out the demonic nest of vipers, or the weak Jesus who dies in ignominy on a cross?

Both, of course. In the beginning, Mark hands us a pair of 3D glasses, so that we can see Jesus at work in all of his power. But in the middle of the Gospel, Mark takes away our glasses, and the story of Jesus becomes a journey to Golgotha, "the place of a skull." When we put this together, we realize that Mark is depicting Jesus as the triumphant Messiah, but ironically, as one who enacts his messianic role through suffering and dying. It is the mystery of the Gospel of Mark that the Jesus we see on the narrative surface never completely discloses the fullness of who he is at the depths. Sometimes on the surface we see him in power, but he is on the way to the cross. Other times, we see him in weakness—betrayed, arrested, tried, mocked, and crucified, unwilling to save even himself—even as he promises that one day we will see him as the savior, sitting at the right hand of Power. The parables in Mark, the stories of seeds and soils, as we shall see, are fashioned to embody this multifaceted, twisting irony.

STRONG MESSIAH, HIDDEN MESSIAH, SUFFERING MESSIAH

A key strategy that Mark employs to tell his double narrative—the mighty Jesus and the crucified Jesus—is to blend three seemingly incompatible images into the person of Jesus: the strong Messiah, the hidden Messiah, and the suffering Messiah.

Strong Messiah. Jesus is the strong Messiah who performs mighty deeds of power. Rooted deep in the Judaism of the day was an expectation of a coming Messiah who would destroy the enemies of Israel and restore the fortunes of God's people. A good place to glimpse this hope is in the *Psalms of Solomon*, written a century or so before Mark's Gospel and included in the Septuagint.

Here the psalmist describes how God raised up David as a wise and just king over Israel and blessed his offspring so that his kingdom would never come to an end. But, as the story goes, things went awry. Israel decayed from within and was assailed from without. "But, for our sins," the psalmist laments, "sinners rose up against us." Dragged down by their own sins and the sins of foreigners, Israel went from victory to defeat, from pride to shame and captivity.

What Israel needed was a fresh start, so the psalmist cries out to God to raise up a new king, a truly everlasting king and Messiah, one who would be "the son of David" (*Psalms of Solomon* 17). This new king would defeat all of Israel's foes, restore righteousness to Jerusalem, rid the city of the wicked, make Israel a holy people once more, and reign in an enduring kingdom of justice and peace. As Adela Yarbro Collins says, "The expectation reflected in . . . the *Psalms of Solomon* was that the Messiah of Israel would be a successful military leader, who would throw off the foreign yoke and then rule as an autonomous king."[6]

Is the Jesus of Mark this expected messianic son of David? Yes, but in an unanticipated way. When Mark begins his Gospel by announcing "the beginning of the good news of Jesus the Messiah (Christ)," it naturally sets up great expectations in his readers. Mark's Messiah, however, is strong but in a way that differs from the nationalistic hero of the *Psalms of Solomon*, and this difference may have been a source of keen disappointment for some early followers of Jesus. Jesus is strong, but he commands no troops. He is the Son of David, but he marches across no earthly battlefield to defeat the despised Romans. He is in fact handed over to be crucified by a Roman official, and on his way to death he is openly mocked by Roman soldiers. His combat is instead cosmic; the enemies he battles are the powers of evil and death. Jesus is the expected strong Messiah, Mark proclaims to his readers, but get ready to adjust your preconceptions of what the Messiah will be and do.

Hidden Messiah. To the picture of Jesus as a strong and triumphant Messiah, Mark adds a second image: Jesus as the hidden Messiah. Curiously, at least at first, the Jesus of Mark does not want people to know his full identity. On numerous occasions in the first half of Mark, when Jesus has performed a mighty deed, he orders his disciples and others not to tell anyone about it (see 1:44; 3:12; 5:43; 7:36; 9:9). He says that he speaks in parables not to make things clear but to ensure that outsiders "may indeed look but not perceive" (4:12). On the Mount of Transfiguration, Peter, James, and John see Jesus transfigured, his clothes shining with blazing light, and hear the divine voice announcing, "This is my Son, the Beloved; listen to him" (9:1–8).

But as quickly as the vision comes, it goes.[7] On the way down the mountain, Jesus "ordered them to tell no one about what they had seen, until after the Son of Man had risen from the dead" (9:9). His identity will ultimately be revealed, but it must wait until the appointed time.

Mark seems to be drawing this theme of the hidden Messiah from the "Son of Man" traditions, which appear significantly in Daniel and Ezekiel. Since Daniel especially is a key source for Mark, let's take a brief detour into the book of Daniel.

The first six chapters of Daniel are a collection of folktales about four exemplary Jewish lads who, in the time of the exile, managed to make good in the Babylonian royal court, all the while remaining obedient and strictly observant Jews. No small feat. The four friends are pictured as perfect, ideal in every way—physically flawless, handsome, well-educated, and capable—so much so that the Babylonian royal staff, greatly impressed, selected them to be schooled in Chaldean culture and groomed to be attendants at the king's court.

The first step in this cultural education involved changing their names. Back home they were called Daniel, Hananiah, Mishael, and Azariah, names that were something of an embarrassment in Babylon. Those were distinctly Jewish names, with religious significations to boot. So the king's chief of staff quickly fixed that problem by renaming them Belteshazzar, Shadrach, Meshach, and Abednego, also religious-sounding names but this time referring to Babylonian gods. This was something like bringing four young men named Muhammed, Kareem, Zayed, and El Nayaan to a Christian community in America and renaming them Christopher, Peter, James, and John.

The narrator was not impressed with this renaming. He keeps calling Daniel by his Hebrew name. Indeed, the palace might try to change the Jewish boys' names, but it could not dislodge their identities or their loyalty to the God of Israel. The four young men walked a tightrope that many others have walked: they worked in high places in an alien land, but they continued to worship their God and refused to bow the knee to the golden statue of Babylon. Indeed, that's the point of this portion of the book of Daniel, to portray Daniel and his friends as heroic role models for other Jews who must live in unfamiliar and sometimes hostile cultures.

The book of Daniel was probably written during the time of the Seleucid King Antiochus IV, who tried to Hellenize the Jews and to deprive them of their Jewish traditions and practices.

One of the first tales told about Daniel's adventures in the palace is a bit of burlesque comedy. King Nebuchadnezzar, like Nancy Reagan consulting an astrologer, employed a coterie of wizards, magicians, necromancers, and sorcerers to help him divine important decisions in the affairs of the empire. The only problem was that these conjurers and so-called wise men were actually flimflam artists, fools, jacklegs, and liars. Every time they would proffer a forecast or an augury to the king, it would blow up in their faces. Soon Nebuchadnezzar learned increasingly to ignore his paid soothsayers and to turn more and more to Daniel and his friends, whom the king discovered were "ten times better than all of the magicians and enchanters in his whole kingdom" (Dan. 1:20).

When, as it happened, King Nebuchadnezzar rose from sleep with the memory of a particularly troubling and vexing dream, he needed to know what this dream meant. He called his usual Keystone Cops band of enchanters, who pranced onto the scene flattering the king and promising to unlock the secrets of his shadowy dream. "Not so fast," responded Nebuchadnezzar. "If you guys are *really* wizards, you'll have to prove it by doing more than just interpreting my dream. Anybody can fake *that*. No, first, tell me the content of the dream itself. What, exactly, did I dream?"

Then one of the enchanters, trying to fake his way out of a bad spot, came up with a clever idea. "Oh, dear king," he cooed, "we'll tell you what your dream is, no worries. But first, why don't you whisper what it was that you dreamed to one of your servants." Pretty smart. There are always leaks in any administration, and the wizards were confident they could pry the content of the dream loose from some lowly servant. But the king was not fooled.

"I can tell," Nebuchadnezzar growled, "that you're trying to buy some time. Well, stop it. What did I dream? Spit it out!"

Of course they couldn't. "We specialize in interpretations," they whined, "not the actual dream. Only you and the gods can know that." This threw the king into a violent rage, and he not only fired the entire staff of snake charmers; he also decreed (this being ancient Babylon) that they all be executed.

Daniel now walked onto the stage, and not only did he persuade the king to postpone the death sentences of his terrified pseudosages; he also told Nebuchadnezzar exactly what he had dreamed, scene by scene, and then interpreted the whole thing masterfully. As a result, Daniel was lavished with gifts, and he and his four Jewish friends were promoted to high positions in the empire.

This rich and rollicking tale is important to readers of the Gospel of Mark because it establishes Daniel as an amazing seer and a man in touch with dreams. In Daniel 7 this pays off when Daniel has his own strange and terrifying dream. Significantly, chapter 7 marks a major turning point in the book of Daniel. We leave behind the charming and often amusing stories of the four faithful Jewish boys who trusted God and outsmarted the mighty Babylonians, and we arrive in the strikingly different world of apocalyptic prophecy. Daniel 1–6 is a set of folk tales; Daniel 7–12 is a series of apocalyptic visions concerning cosmic history, similar to the ones found in the New Testament book of Revelation.

In Daniel's dream, four horrifying beasts crawl up out of the sea. The first was lionlike with eagles' wings, the second like a devouring bear with three tusks, the third like a leopard with four heads. Pretty terrible, but nothing like the fourth beast, which had iron teeth, ten horns, and a foul and arrogant mouth. An eleventh horn suddenly grew out of its head, one that had "eyes like human eyes." It roared around the earth, devouring and breaking everything in its path into pieces (Dan. 7:1–8).

But there's more to Daniel's dream. As the four beasts are rampaging across the earth causing destruction and suffering, suddenly "thrones were set in place" and "the Ancient One," the Ancient of Days, takes his throne. This new and powerful figure puts the fourth beast to death and pulls the fangs from the other three. And then comes the final scene of the dream, one that is echoed in Mark and is key to our understanding of Mark:

> I saw one like a human being [like a Son of Man]
> coming with the clouds of heaven.
> And he came to the Ancient One
> and was presented before him.
> To him was given dominion
> and glory and kingship,
> that all peoples, nations, and languages
> should serve him.
> His dominion is an everlasting dominion
> that shall not pass away,
> and his kingship is one
> that shall never be destroyed.
> Dan. 7:13–14

Daniel's menagerie of four beasts has historical referents. For example, most scholars identify the fourth and worst beast with the rule of Alexander the Great and the line of rulers that followed him. This "one like a Son of Man" confronts these tyrants of history, but in another sense is lifted above historical circumstance. We have here in Daniel 7 a vision of God, the Ancient of Days, putting an ultimate end to the bloodbaths of history and the oppressions of tyrants and then designating a figure known as the Son of Man to an everlasting kingship of glory. Morna Hooker, who has closely examined the Son of Man language in Mark, concludes that Jesus was deeply influenced by Daniel 7 and actually chose this title as a self-designation.[8]

The Son of Man figure is developed further in a portion of the book of *Enoch* called the *Similitudes of Enoch*. Did Mark know the *Similitudes*? Scholars are not sure, since the dating of the *Similitudes* is uncertain, and it may, in fact, postdate Mark. But, even if Mark did not know the *Similitudes* in written form, he was almost surely familiar with the oral traditions that eventually found expression in the *Similitudes*.[9]

In the *Similitudes*, the full identity of the Son of Man remains hidden until the last day, the day of reckoning. This does not mean that the Son of Man is not active in the meantime. According to the *Similitudes*, the Son of Man supports the righteous and keeps them from falling; he is a light to the Gentiles; and he is the hope of those who are troubled of heart (*1 Enoch* 48:4). But the Son of Man does all these things in a concealed way; his full identity remains hidden until judgment day. Until then, only a few chosen and righteous ones know who he is:

> For from the beginning the Son of Man was hidden,
> And the Most High preserved him in the presence of His might,
> and revealed him to the elect.
>
> *1 Enoch* 62:7[10]

On the last day, though, all will be revealed. Everyone "shall see and recognize how [the Son of Man] sits on the throne of his glory, and righteousness is judged before him, and no lying word is spoken before him" (*1 Enoch* 62:3).[11] When the great day of reckoning comes, the righteous will be overjoyed, but the powerful of the earth will be unpleasantly surprised, their wickedness exposed by the searchlight of the Son of Man. For the righteous, the appearance of the Son of Man is good news, indeed. They will behold their savior and be "clothed with garments of glory" (*1 Enoch* 62:13–15). But when kings and other high and mighty ones, who were oblivious to how the Son of Man was at work in the world, suddenly look up and see the Son of Man sitting on the throne of his glory, they will look at each other with terror and fall on their faces begging for mercy (*1 Enoch* 62:3–9).

In Mark, Jesus speaks of himself as the Son of Man, and he tells his disciples that his full identity will be disclosed at the end:

> But in those days, after that suffering,
> the sun will be darkened,
> and the moon will not give its light,
> and the stars will be falling from heaven,
> and the powers in the heavens will be shaken.
> Then they will see "the Son of Man coming in clouds" with great power and glory. Then he will send out the angels, and gather his elect from the four winds, from the ends of the earth to the ends of heaven.
>
> Mark 13:24–27

On another occasion in Mark, when Jesus is arrested and taken to stand before the priests, elders, and the scribes, the high priest interrogates him, asking, "Are you the Messiah?" Jesus answers, "I am; and 'you will see the Son of Man seated at the right hand of the Power'" and "'coming with the clouds of heaven'" (Mark 14:62). Like the Son of Man in *Enoch*, Jesus performs deeds of healing and mercy throughout his ministry, but only at the end of all things is he fully revealed in power and glory.

These first two images of Jesus—the strong Messiah who moves around Galilee performing deeds of power and the secret, hidden Messiah—are, of course, in tension. Mark allows this tension to play out in part by showing how Jesus, try as he might to keep people quiet about who he was and what he did, couldn't always pull it off. The good news about Jesus and the mighty deeds he performs keeps spilling over the top. After Jesus healed a man who was deaf and had a speech impediment, Mark (wryly?) comments, "Then Jesus ordered them to tell no one; but the more he ordered them, the more zealously they proclaimed it" (7:36).

Even though the identity of Jesus as the Son of Man is largely concealed in Mark, the hiddenness is not airtight. The disciples, even if they do not fully comprehend, are let in on "the secret of the kingdom of God" (4:11), and they are allowed to glimpse in advance the power and glory of Jesus at the transfiguration (9:2–8). There is also another group of characters in Mark who know immediately who Jesus is: the demons. The demons are apocalyptic figures—they, in effect, wear the 3D glasses—and see at the deep level of cosmic encounter. They know from the outset that Jesus is the messianic Son.

In fact, early in his Gospel, Mark tells his readers that Jesus healed the sick and cast out demons, but to keep his identity secret, he had to forbid the demons from speaking, "because they knew him" (1:34). When the demon-possessed man in the tombs encountered Jesus, he was immediately exposed as a deeply divided person. Part of the man was a distressed human being, a man in desperate need, and he ran to Jesus and bowed down in the posture of worship. But the other part of the man, the chaotic spirit within, became a crazed prophet, shouting at the top of his voice, "What have you to do with me Jesus, Son of the Most High God?" (5:6–7). The malicious spirit may have been evil, but the demon indeed knew who Jesus was, and its screeched sermon was theologically right on target.

Suffering Messiah. To the images of Jesus as the strong Messiah and the hidden Messiah, Mark added a third, and shocking, image: Jesus as the suffering Messiah. In Jewish tradition, the prophets experience rejection, suffer, and are sometimes even killed—but not the Messiah. As soon as Peter has confessed, "You are the Messiah" (8:29), Jesus makes it clear to the disciples that he is to remain the hidden Messiah ("he sternly ordered them not to tell anyone," 8:30), and offends them by asserting that he is also to be the suffering Messiah ("Then he began to teach them that the Son of Man must undergo great suffering," 9:31). As Collins says, "The combination of the prophetic motifs of suffering, rejection, and even death with the royal messianic role . . . was very unusual. That this was so is indicated by the reaction of Peter and Jesus' strong correction of his attitude (8:32–33)."[12]

In Mark, then, Jesus is the Son of Man, but he suffers; he is the Messiah, but he dies on a cross. When Jesus in great anguish cries out from the cross and breathes his last, a Roman soldier, a centurion, seeing how he died, says, "Truly this man was God's Son!" (15:39). Perhaps this was a confession of faith on the part of the soldier, but the great Markan scholar Don Juel claims that the centurion's statement should be read ironically. Juel would shock his students by speaking the centurion's words about Jesus dying on the cross in a tone of sarcastic scorn: "Oh, sure, *this* was God's Son."[13]

Was the centurion's remark a discernment or a scoff? Perhaps we are to hear it as both, a double entendre. Indeed, a main theological challenge that Mark places before his readers is to see how these messianic images—strength, hiddenness, suffering—could interplay in the single figure of Jesus. On one occasion, when Jesus was under arrest and vulnerable, he told his accusers that he was the Son of Man who would one day come in power and glory. On another occasion, when his disciples were talking about his glory, Jesus told them, "For the Son of Man came not to be served but to serve, and to give his life a ransom for many." One cannot understand the gospel, as Mark presents it, and even more important, one cannot see the world with gospel discernment, without grasping how the same Jesus could say and be both of these things.

So Jesus is the strong and saving Messiah. But if he were only this, we would expect Mark's Gospel to look like an *Avengers* movie, with the forces of good roaring to tumultuous victory. Instead, Jesus moves not to Armageddon but toward the cross. Jesus is also the hidden Messiah, whose final victory will be revealed at the end of all things. But if he were only this, Mark's Gospel would end with a radiant and risen Christ anticipating a coming victory in the clouds. Instead, we have a muted, ambiguous ending with frightened women fleeing the tomb of Jesus in terror, and instead of this world being vanquished and utterly replaced by God's kingdom, we have an unfinished plot: the risen Christ and his disciples still at work in this world. Mark presents an apocalyptic and victorious Jesus, but because Jesus is also a suffering Messiah, Jesus fulfills the messianic role in ways that defy all expectation. The centerpiece of Mark is Jesus' tragic and pain-filled death on a cross. But make no mistake; it is here that one sees God's kingdom breaking through in ironic power. The theme of Mark's Gospel is God's ultimate triumph over all the powers of death and evil; but make no mistake, this victory is glimpsed in the dying Messiah.

One theologian has suggested that if we really understand Mark's muted story of God's victory, we cannot easily sing Handel's triumphant "Hallelujah Chorus" on Easter. Perhaps this is so, especially if we have in mind the thunderous, tympani-driven, cymbal-crashing version of the Mormon Tabernacle Choir. But if we consider instead a quite different version of Handel's *Messiah*, the one recorded by the Viennese *Concentus Musicus*, we are perhaps closer to Mark's vision. Here, the victory of God in Christ is celebrated, but the proclamation is modest, even tentative. When the chorus sings "The glory of the Lord is risen upon thee," the word "thee" is immediately softened, pulled back, as if the ensemble can hardly believe that God's glory is upon *them.* And when the singers come to the climax of the oratorio, the grand "Hallelujah Chorus," the hesitant style conveys the truth that human beings can only dimly see and longingly hope that God is even now wresting victory from suffering, chaos, and captivity. As music critic Porter Anderson said,

> [The performance] rolls up into perhaps the most haunting "Hallelujah!" you'll ever hear—resignation, exhaustion, radiant surrender. . . . It's almost as if this formidable choral ensemble were in a dream, sometimes sitting bolt upright with the memory of a fine thought—"King of Kings"—then drifting again, as human distraction and preoccupation drag them back to a pianissimo of heartbreaking faith. They do rally, of course, to the closing cadence. But listen for the quick fade. Something here aches, longs, needs.[14]

In Mark too, something aches, longs, and needs, namely, the world and all humanity. It is a world that needs to be rescued, saved, from the power of death. The triumph of God is enacted in the heartaches, longings, and needs of the suffering and captive people.

THE MARKAN KALEIDOSCOPE

In her discussion of the phrase "the Son of Man" in Mark, Morna Hooker makes a summary statement that, in effect, lays out a crisp schematic of Mark's Christology.[15] For Mark, she says, Jesus had "the prophetic calling," like the Old Testament prophets before him, and his vocation was to fulfill "the mission of God's obedient people." In carrying out that mission, Jesus' life disclosed both "the possibility of suffering for those who were faithful to [God's] will" and the "promise of final vindication." Jesus "called others to share in that calling with him." After stumbling over Mark's enigmas, wandering around his labyrinths, and puzzling over his peekaboo style in revealing Jesus, one sometimes wishes that Mark had just taken a deep breath and composed, like Morna Hooker, a clear, linear description of Jesus' role and mission. But if he had, he would have been Morna Hooker, not Mark.

So instead, we get in Mark a flashing array of complex, often competing, images for Jesus. It is tempting to think of Mark as a master narrator, deftly interlacing his themes of Jesus' power, hiddenness, and suffering into an intricate, mystery-laden plot that transforms the theological vision of careful readers. Perhaps. Or maybe power, hiddenness, and suffering are simply theological fragments of glass that tumble over each other in Mark's kaleidoscope. He turns it this way, and we see this facet of Jesus. Another turn, and we see something else. Yet another turn, and the image shifts once more. Regardless, the ultimate effect of Mark's Gospel is that we are called to ponder the meaning of a Messiah who saves the world by giving up his life, and whose glory and power can be glimpsed now and then by the eyes of faith, even as they remain hidden and obscure to the world.

When we recognize Mark's intricate theological pattern and the multifaceted and ironic character of Mark's Jesus, the parables in Mark begin to open up and to reveal the mysterious and ironic ways God's kingdom breaks into life and history.

4

Mark

The Parables

Do you not understand this parable? Then how will you understand all of the parables?

—Mark 4:13

In their certainty of victory, Christians who were gathered for the Lord's Supper heard the alarmed questions of Satan and death, "Who is he that robs us of our power?" They answered with the exultant shout of victory, "Here is Christ, the crucified!"

—Eberhard Arnold[1]

In the fourth chapter of Mark, Jesus opens his mouth to preach, and what comes forth is a sermon in parables. The entire Gospel of Mark includes only five full parables,[2] and three of them are in this one sermon: the Sower, the Growing Seed, and the Mustard Seed. In the first three chapters of Mark, Jesus has roared onto the scene as God's strong man, engaging in a full-tilt assault on the demonic, healing the fevered sick, and casting out demons right and left. Given this dramatic introduction of Jesus, these farm and garden parables about seeds and soils come as a surprise, an emphatic change of tone, an unexpected swath of agricultural gentleness.

However, when we take into account Mark's grand and ironic theological theme—that Jesus is the strong man of God who nonetheless ultimately displays his strength in apparent weakness by giving his life on the cross, that despite all appearances the crucified Jesus crying out in pain on the cross is indeed the long-expected Messiah, the Son of Man who reigns in power at the right hand of God—these farmers' tales begin to make a strange sort of sense.

In all of them, something amazing and surprising happens despite appearances, despite seeming failure, hiddenness, and insignificance.

Mark wants us to know that once Jesus got started speaking in parables, in a way he never stopped. Mark announces at the beginning of this parables sermon that Jesus would "teach them many things in parables" (Mark 4:2), and so he does. Then at the end of that discourse, Mark doubles down, saying, "He did not speak to them except in parables" (4:34). That's hyperbole, of course, but it scores an excellent point. Jesus' proclamation of the kingdom was inextricably parabolic. These parables flow from Jesus' mouth not because he thought this was a clever idea for a sermon series, but because he lived parabolically, he performed his ministry parabolically, he saw the kingdom of God and all of life parabolically. Jesus in Mark spoke in parables for the same reason that Benjamin Franklin spoke in proverbs; that's the way he conceived of reality. In this opening volley of Jesus' preaching in parables, we come close to the nuclear reactor of the Markan Jesus' vision of God's kingdom.

THE PARABLE OF THE SOWER (MARK 4:1–20)

When Jesus begins preaching in parables in Mark 4, it comes at a slight bend in the road in the Jesus story. So far in Mark, we have mainly watched Jesus in action—calling, healing, casting out demons—but now we sit down with the crowd beside the sea for a different kind of action: teaching. We know that Jesus has already been preaching in Galilean synagogues (1:39), and that he has even taught before by the Sea of Galilee (2:13), but on those occasions the reader did not get to hear Jesus' actual words. Now, Mark announces, it is time for all of us to go to class and expressly hear what Jesus has to teach.

The Parable of the Sower is the first parable in Jesus' sermon in Mark 4. Technically speaking, this is not the very first parable mentioned in Mark. We learned earlier that Jesus pulled a few parables out of his quiver to defend himself against the charge of being an agent of Beelzebul (3:22–27). Also, depending on the way one defines things, Jesus may have spun a couple of miniature parables back in Mark 2, when he called himself a physician who cares for the sick, not the well (2:17), and when he brushed back the Pharisees' grousing that his disciples don't fast by countering with the image that wedding guests don't usually fast when the groom is around to celebrate (2:19–20). But those earlier parables are quick images and brief figures of speech more than they are the full-plotted narratives that characterize most of Jesus' parables.

Even if the Parable of the Sower is not the first parable in Mark, it is surely the signature parable. "It is *the* parable about parables," writes Klyne Snodgrass.[3] It is this parable that underscores Jesus as a preacher of parables, and it is this parable that provokes the disciples to ask Jesus why he speaks in parables at all (4:10–13). Jesus warns the disciples that if they don't grasp *this* one, it spells trouble for their understanding *any* of the parables (4:13).

The Parable of the Sower proper gets going in 4:3, and despite the fact that this is where many scholars begin their analysis, to start here is to miss batting practice, pitching warmups, and the national anthem. In chapter 2 we discussed decisions preachers of the parables must make, and we argued for focusing on the canonical settings of the parables, in this case the parable as it appears in Mark. This means refusing to pry the bare text of the parable out of its context, but taking as significant the whole setting Mark provides (versions of this parable appear in Matthew and Luke, and those versions and their respective settings are somewhat different. Both will be treated in later chapters). Mark tells us where Jesus spoke this parable, who heard it, and the conversation that resulted from it, and those details are important in understanding how Mark wishes us to receive this parable.

Places, Everyone!

If we look, then, at the whole context, we immediately notice that, before Jesus speaks a single word, there is a complicated but important bit of choreography. Like a movie director calling out to the cast, "Places, everyone!" Mark has to get Jesus and his hearers into their proper positions for this drama.

It takes two steps. First, Jesus takes up a position seaside: "Again he began to teach beside the sea" (4:1). With the word "again," Mark signals that this was not the first time that Jesus has been beside the sea. In fact, Mark is hardly three chapters old at this point, yet we have already been beside the sea with Jesus four times. First, it was beside the sea that he called four of his disciples: Simon, Andrew, James, and John (1:16–17). Second, "Jesus went again by the sea" (once more the word "again"), where he taught the crowd and called Levi to be a disciple (2:13–14). Then, in 3:7–12, we make another seaside journey with Jesus and the disciples, where a great crowd from a wide geographical area gathers because they had heard "all that he was doing," especially the acts of healing. Now, for a fourth time we find Jesus beside the sea.

By telling us, "Here he is again by the sea," Mark alerts his readers that these seaside stories are to be read as a set[4] and that there is something significant about the seaside location itself. Why is the seaside important? First, the seaside is obviously the border where the land meets the sea, and for Mark that is symbolically significant. As Markan scholar Elizabeth Struthers Malbon has said, "Mark presupposes the connotation of the sea as chaos, threat, danger in opposition to the land as order, promise, security." Where the land meets the sea signifies where ordinary life meets the demonic. When Jesus is beside the sea in Mark, he is not in a lovely retreat setting but walking along the battle front—the border between order and chaos, between the land, where humanity lives, and the sea, where the demonic prevails.

Second, the seaside is important because of what Jesus does there. He calls his disciples there; he teaches there; he heals the sick there; and he confronts demons there—in sum, a microcosm of his entire ministry. Jesus is no retiring general, directing the troops from a command tent behind the lines. He does his work on the front lines, "beside the sea." The totality of his ministry occurs on the border where the mundane world and the demonic domain collide.

The seaside setting also connects to Mark's two intertwined main narratives: the story of the strong man of God who has come to destroy Satan's reign, and the story of the suffering servant who rescues humanity by dying on a cross. Want to see the strong Jesus? Watch him at the sea. At the sea, Jesus will silence the storm (4:35–42), permit demons in the form of swine to rush down a seaside hill and crash to their death in the waves (5:1–13), and respond to the desperate plea of a synagogue leader to save his dying daughter, which results in the raising of the child from the dead (5:21–43). He will even disclose his authority over the chaos by walking on the sea (6:47–52). Want to see the suffering Jesus? Walk with him across the land. There he will finally be betrayed, rejected by the religious authorities, handed over to Pilate, mocked by soldiers, and crucified.

Indeed, the last time Jesus performed ministry by the sea (3:7–11), he had two congregations, one from each sovereignty. On the one hand, there was the crowd, pressing in on Jesus because of his reputation as a great healer; on the other hand, there were the "unclean spirits." The crowd saw only one side of Jesus' identity; he is a healer. The demons, however, perceive the bigger picture. They already knew that Jesus was more than a mere medicine man, and they served as a kind of Greek chorus chanting the deeper truth of the drama, the truth that Jesus did not yet want revealed: "You are the Son of God!"

Thus the Parable of the Sower opens with Jesus once again in a location that is both familiar and powerfully symbolic: beside the sea. But that's just step one. No sooner does Mark get everyone in place than he waves his hands and moves everybody around. The second movement seems at first simply logistical. The crowd is too large (the size of the throng shows how Jesus is, at this point, on an upward arc with the people), Jesus needs some elbow room, so he moves to a better vantage point by getting into a boat on the sea. Simple enough. But there is more going on here than at first meets the eye. Mark could have narrated this much more efficiently without this game of musical chairs. Why not just get down to the action, start the story with Jesus already positioned in the boat and the crowd already waiting to be instructed on the land? Why all the shifting around?

Because the shifting around is important, and Mark wants us to notice it. Mark wants us to pay attention to the fact that Jesus ends up not only *at* the sea but *on* the sea, teaching, and that the crowd ends up on the land, listening. The physical positions of Jesus and the crowd are a living enactment of the very parable Jesus is about to tell. The parable is a story about a farmer who sows seed on the land, *gēs* (γῆς and variants). That is exactly what Jesus is doing, casting his words to the hearers, who are pictured as "beside the sea on the land (γῆς)" (4:1). Jesus himself is the sower, and the crowd is identified with the earth upon which the seed is sown.

Also, Jesus is sitting down to teach, which is the position of authority, and he is sitting in a boat.[5] Oddly, though, Mark doesn't actually say Jesus is "sitting in a boat." What he says is more graphic, startling, and improbable: Jesus is seated *on the sea, en tē thalassē* (ἐν τῇ θαλάσσῃ). If Mark weren't so serious, it could be funny. This is Mark giving us those 3D glasses and saying, "Do you see what I see? This is not just a guy sitting on a boat and telling stories. This is Jesus sitting in authority on the chaotic sea. Even now he is Lord over the unruly powers." Herod might think that he is the authority on the land, but Jesus is in charge where no other human being can claim control, on the sea. Mark 4 is a self-contained vignette of Jesus at work seaside, and it begins as it will end, with Jesus in command of the unruly sea. Jesus begins by sitting in authority *on* the sea, and he will end this episode by commanding the disorderly waves and winds of the stormy sea (4:35–41).

Listen to This!

Now that the preacher and the hearers are finally in place, Jesus begins to teach. But he doesn't just teach; he teaches in *parables.* The *way* he teaches matches *what* he teaches. Jesus is not teaching mere facts that can be grasped and mastered—such as, salt is composed of equal portions of sodium and chlorine. He is disclosing "the secret [or better, 'the mystery'] of the kingdom of God" (4:11), and like the kingdom itself, parables are both luminescent and shrouded in mystery; they conceal and reveal.

The first word out of Jesus' mouth is a command: "Listen!" (4:3). This is a little word with a big echo. It is far more than the "Can you hear me now?" of the old Verizon commercial or "Listen up, children!" from a kindergarten teacher. This "Listen!" is the "Hear, O Israel" of the Shema (Deut. 6:4); the psalmist's, "O that today you would listen to his voice!" (Ps. 95:8); the divine command announced by the prophet Isaiah, "Listen, and hear my voice; Pay attention and hear my speech" (from Isa. 49:1); and, perhaps most directly, the cry in 2 Esdras:

> [And God] said, "Hear me, O Israel, and give heed to my words, O descendants of Jacob. For I sow my law in you, and it shall bring forth fruit in you, and you shall be glorified through it forever." But though our ancestors received the law, they did not keep it and did not observe the statutes; yet the fruit of the law did not perish—for it could not, because it was yours. Yet those who received it perished, because they did not keep what had been sown in them. (2 Esdras 9:30–33)

This "Listen!" is Jesus' command to the hearers to open themselves up to Jesus and to the word he is giving them, to become receptive, porous, deeply attentive.

It is perhaps a touch amusing to realize that immediately after Jesus says, "Listen!" (ἀκούετε), the very next word he utters is, "Look!" (ἰδοὺ). This double command is vaguely suggestive of the railroad crossing warning "Stop! Look! And Listen!" Does Jesus want us to listen or to look, to hear something or to see something? The King James Version and a few other older translations try to gather up both commands ("Hearken; Behold"), but that reads awkwardly. Most contemporary translations smooth things out by filtering out the "Look!" part and having Jesus simply say, "Listen!" That makes a kind of sense. If one is forced to choose between the two commands, listening is definitely the highest card on the table, as evidenced by the fact that the term appears ten times in this one chapter of Mark (vv. 3, 9, 12, 15, 16, 18, 20, 23, 24, 33).[6]

But what if we leave both commands in place? It's a little awkward syntactically, but if we hold "Listen!" and "Look!" together, we gain at least three insights. First, saying, "Listen! Look!" captures the truth that what we are supposed to hear comes, in the deepest sense, by observing what happens, namely, the actions in the parable. We are going to see something happen in this parable, and what we see will open us up to the truth we are to hear in our hearts. Second, the joining of "Listen!" to "Look!" alerts us to the fact that the way we are to attend to the parable is also the way we are to attend to Jesus. We are not only to listen to Jesus but to watch him as well. As he moves through Galilee and on to Jerusalem, we will truly see who he is. Third, the double command to "Listen!" and "Look!" promises that, if we truly listen to Jesus' teaching in this parable, it will open our eyes to see life in a new way. What Jesus offers in this parable, and in all the parables, is not a set of maxims that we can cross-stitch on a pillow, but a way of perceiving reality. "If you will open your ears," Jesus says, "I will open your eyes."

A Sower Goes Out to Sow

The parable is about a sower who goes out to sow seed. This sowing is depicted in four short scenes; each scene describes where the seed fell and then what happened to it:[7]

Scene	Where the Seed Fell	What Happened to It
1	on the path	the birds came and ate it up
2	on rocky ground	it sprang up quickly in the shallow soil, but because it had no deep roots, it was scorched by the sun and withered away
3	among thorns	the thorns grew up and choked it; no yield
4	into good soil	grew, increased, and yielded 30–60–100–fold

The picture is of a sower who casts seed broadly, throwing it everywhere—the hard path, the field of rocks, the thorn patch—and all in vain. Only at the end does the seed fall on productive soil, yielding an unexpectedly abundant harvest.

We need to pause here long enough to warn about a couple of rabbit trails that a few commentators would have us travel. First, some are eager to reassure us that this farmer, tossing seed every which way, is not as foolish as he looks, but is really using farming methods that are perfectly normal in the ancient world. The renowned parables scholar Joachim Jeremias, for example, urges us not to become too dismayed by the fact that this sower appears to be promiscuously tossing seed everywhere—hard ground, rocky ground, thorny ground. In ancient Palestine, Jeremias reminds us, farmers sowed first and plowed afterwards. So this farmer isn't wasting seed. No, he *intentionally* throws seed on the path, the thorn patch, and the rocks, because he knows he is going to plow the seed under afterwards. "What appears to the western mind as bad farming," Jeremias says soothingly, "is simply customary usage under Palestinian conditions."[8]

Really? Frankly, this view stretches credulity to the breaking point (intentionally sowing seed on hard ground with hungry birds circling overhead?), but more important, it ignores the details of the parable itself. If our sower intended to plow up those thorns, rocks, and hard ground later, it must have slipped his mind, because the parable never mentions it, and, according to the tale, all of that seed perished.

Similarly, a number of scholars shrug their shoulders over the size of the harvest, "thirty and sixty and a hundredfold." That's not so impressive, they say, but actually a rather ordinary yield in ancient Palestine.[9] Over against this minimizing view, Robert K. McIver, in his essay "One Hundred-Fold Yield—Miraculous or Mundane?,"[10] argues that pooh-poohing a hundredfold yield as "average" is the result both of misreading ancient agricultural data and being taken in by exaggerated descriptions of harvests in "tall tales told by travelers." In the ancient Mediterranean world, McIver says, a fourfold or fivefold yield was more the norm. In modern Israel, he reports, there are records of thirtyfold harvests, but only "using sophisticated farming machinery . . . [and] only in good years."[11] McIver concludes that "even the grain that gave a yield of thirty-fold in the parable of the sower was giving a crop that was not only exceptional, it was miraculous in first-century Palestine."

Probably the best argument against the view that the harvest in the parable is no great shakes, however, is not found in historical references to Mediterranean agricultural statistics but in the way Jesus tells the story. When we allow ourselves to be gathered into its inner rhythms and cadences of the parable, it becomes apparent that "brought forth grain, growing up and increasing and yielding thirty and sixty and a hundredfold" is clearly a narrative crescendo. If a woman from rural Louisiana were to say of her life, "I was married by my sixteenth birthday, and the babies started coming right off. Ten months and we had our first, and the next year another baby, and, Lord knows, the third year still another," it would be tin-eared to look up birth rates in rural Louisiana to point out that families with three children were not all that unusual. As a storyteller, she is plainly communicating that she was a young bride and that her babies came fast and furiously.

Likewise, when Jesus says that, after repeated sowing failures, some seed at last found purchase in good soil and grew and increased, thirty and sixty and a hundredfold, any apt listener to folktales knows instantly that we are invited to be amazed by abundance and that Jesus is not using all this dynamic and picturesque language merely to say, "And the harvest was, well, meh." One is reminded of Frederick Buechner's observation that reading the Bible so flatly is like "reading *Moby Dick* as a whaling manual."[12]

"Sensitive readers are good companions in appreciating a good story," writes Don Juel. When we read this parable as a good story, he goes on to say, "The farmer seems a bit careless with his seed. . . . He throws seed everywhere, apparently confident there will be a harvest in spite of the losses."[13]

Yes, the losses. This is a story of *loss*, and repeated failure is indeed a key reality to experience in this parable. The farmer sows, and the seed is lost, sows again and loses again, and sows a third time, only to receive a yield of nothing. The parable is a theater of loss. If we wished, we could point for support to the "rule of three" in folk tales. Often such tales have three persons or events. The first two are negative, but the third upsets the pattern by being positive. In the story "The Three Little Pigs," the first pig builds a house of straw (bad), the second a house of sticks (still bad), but the third builds a house of bricks, and even the ravenous wolf cannot blow it down (good). In "Cinderella" we have three sisters, two of them evil, but the third becomes a princess. In another parable we have a priest, a Levite, and then a good Samaritan. In the Parable of the Sower, however, the third sowing, into the thorns, doesn't break the pattern but confirms it. Failure, failure, and failure yet again mean failure confirmed.

But we don't actually have to know about the folklore "rule of three" to feel the loss in this parable. Again, just follow the story as it leads us in a repeated pattern of waste, adversity, and hopelessness. It is only with the fourth sowing, the one performed when hope of a harvest is all but gone, that the seed falls on good soil, and the harvest is abundant. This is not a parable about "if at first you don't succeed, try, try again." This is a parable about a situation of utter hopelessness into which an abundant harvest arrives as a complete surprise, a moment of astonishment.

On Hand for the Kingdom

If the parables, as we have said, help us to be *on hand* for the kingdom that is *at hand*, but not *in hand*, where is this parable taking us? Where is the kingdom of God appearing among us? Where does this parable point to the kingdom at hand? This parable calls us to look for the advent of the kingdom, the inbreaking of the life of God, in places of utter failure and grinding hopelessness.

This parable has no Joel Osteen–type message, that "God wants to bless you real good, so expect that blessing and don't worry about a thing." No, this is a parable about the places where one worries about everything, where life has been trampled down, where hope has been ground into dust, where the seed has yielded nothing time and again, and nothing more is expected. It is a parable of surprise, something like the claim of the country priest in Bernanos's great book, *The Diary of a Country Priest*, who looks out at the world and hears nothing but the cries of brutalized and distressed humanity. But then he sees in this sea of distress the surprise of the kingdom: "And yet I feel that such distress, distress that has forgotten even its name, that has ceased to reason or to hope, that lays its tortured head at random, will awaken one day on the shoulder of Jesus Christ."[14]

In one of his seminars, the pastoral theologian Seward Hiltner told of the 1950s-style mental hospital where the back ward was reserved for patients whom the psychiatric staff viewed as hopelessly untreatable. These patients were fed and kept safe, but they were otherwise largely abandoned, allowed to exist as they were, some mute and catatonic, some curled into fetal balls, all unresponsive to the presence of others. As it happened, a group of women from a nearby church asked the hospital administrator if they could have permission to visit patients who did not have family who regularly came to see them. Almost cynically, the administrator directed them to the untouchables in the back ward.

Innocently unaware that they had been dispatched to a circle of hell, the women began to visit these abandoned people, bringing plates of brownies, gifts of clothing, blankets, vases of flowers, and good cheer. Gradually, amazingly, the patients, said Hiltner, began to unfurl toward the touch of kindness. The mute began to speak, the frozen warmed to human touch and friendship, the unresponsive chanced an occasional smile and, miraculously, began to tell stories of their memories and hopes. The church women, unaware that they had been cast into a place of utter despair, may have taken this in stride, but the medical staff, who had long since forsaken any thought of healing, were astonished to see this kingdom harvest—thirtyfold, sixtyfold, a hundredfold. Listen! Look!

The Parable of the Sower sharpens our vision to see where God is adventing into life in places where hope seems futile. In the early 1990s, Atlanta philanthropist Tom Cousins was disturbed by an op-ed piece he read in the *New York Times* reporting that 70 percent of the prisoners in the New York state prison system came from just eight urban neighborhoods. Curious, Cousins examined the situation in his own state, only to be astonished to discover that a majority of prisoners in Georgia came from just one neighborhood, East Lake Meadows in Atlanta.

East Lake Meadows was a complex of 650 public-housing apartments, marked by graffiti and broken windows and riddled with crime, drugs, and roving gangs. The dropout rate in the public school was 70 percent, and the local police labeled the area "Atlanta's War Zone." Many reformers had brought programs of improvement to East Lake Meadows, but it was hard ground, rocky ground, and thorny ground, a place of repeated social and personal failure for its residents.

Cousins decided that East Lake Meadows was worth sowing some more seed. He formed a foundation and established partnerships with other philanthropists and with public agencies. He brought in people with experience in solving community problems and recruited capable and committed teachers and administrators for the schools. The residents were deeply suspicious of his efforts. They'd been taken advantage of so often by outsiders, condescended to by self-proclaimed "saviors." They had seen do-gooders fail time and again in East Lake Meadows' unfruitful environment. Cousins listened to the residents, sat silently but attentively as they raged their mistrust at him and all outsiders. When they finished pouring their bowls of wrath on him, he responded by asking them to become partners with him, to become key planners and decision-makers in a process of renewal.

Today East Lake (as it is now called) is by no means perfect, but it is a nationally recognized model for community revitalization. Mixed-income apartments are nestled among thriving shops and restaurants. Violent crime is down over 95 percent, and almost all of the eighth-graders in the East Lake school meet or exceed state reading levels. Look at East Lake sociologically, and one sees a successful project in community renewal. But look again at East Lake, this time through the lens of the Parable of the Sower, and one sees the green shoots of an improbable harvest, the adventing of God's kingdom, the God whose repeatedly trampled gospel finds at last a bit of good soil, bringing forth justice and new life, thirty, sixty, and a hundredfold.[15]

And the Disciples Said, "Huh?"

After Jesus speaks the Parable of the Sower, Mark shifts the scene. Suddenly we are no longer at seaside with Jesus in the boat. We are instead in a more private location where Jesus, his disciples, and other intimates have gathered. Mark is a bit vague and imprecise about this shift, because it looks as if, starting at 4:26,[16] Mark, without explicitly saying so, abruptly shifts again and has Jesus back out in public, resuming his parabolic teaching to the crowds. If we keep reading Mark, though, we'll soon discover that this public-private shift is not unusual. On several occasions in Mark, the disciples get a chance to ask Jesus privately about something that happened in public that they (and presumably the readers of the Gospel too) find hard to understand (see 7:17; 9:28; 10:10; 13:3). The private exchange in Mark 4 is simply the first of these sidebar conversations. The emphasis falls on the distinction between what Jesus says in public, to those on the "outside," and what he says in private, to those on the "inside."

This private conversation has two parts. First, the disciples and Jesus discuss why Jesus speaks in parables at all, and we will come back to that later. In the second part of the private conversation, Jesus explains the Parable of the Sower to the uncomprehending disciples. The disciples have apparently shrugged their shoulders and said, "Huh?" to the Sower, and a perhaps disappointed Jesus has responded that understanding this parable is important, that there is something about this parable that is a key to everything. "Do you not understand this parable?" he says. "Then how will you understand all of the parables?" (4:13).

The actual explanation Jesus gives (4:14–20) employs vocabulary that likely comes from a time later than Jesus' ministry, and most scholars think that the explanation of the parable represents an early church interpretation, or maybe even the outline of a Christian sermon, on the parable. The hard experiences of the sower in the parable, trying over and again to sow the seed, reflect, many commentators say, the difficult task of the early Christian preachers and evangelists.[17]

Our commitment, though, is to read this explanation as a part of the flow of the Markan narrative; viewed this way, the interpretation reflects how Mark wishes us to hear this parable. Close readers may be bothered by what seems to be some confusion of terms in the interpretation. It starts off with the sower sowing "the word" (4:14). The first type of hearers of that word, those who are "on the path," don't really have a chance to hear deeply, because "Satan immediately comes and takes away the word that is sown in them." So far, so good. However, by the time we get to the second kind of soil pictured in the parable, the "rocky ground," the images have shifted. Now it seems as though it is not the word that is sown but the hearers themselves ("And these are the ones sown on rocky ground, when they hear the word," 4:16). Trying to make perfectly consistent and logical sense out of the elements featured in the parable's interpretation can lead to frustration.

Instead of fretting over the mixed images here, though, it is more productive to follow the main contours of the parable's interpretation. Taken that way, we have, in broad strokes, four kingdom sowings, and we have four results:

Sowing	**Result**
1	The word sometimes lies on the hard surface of the hearers' lives, allowing Satan a chance to quickly swoop down and snatch it away. The yield: Zero.
2	The word sometimes lands in a rocky place. People hear the word with joy, but lacking any root, they fall away when trouble comes. The yield: Zero.
3	The word sometimes lands in a thorn patch. The word is heard, but soon enough worldly cares, wealth, and other distractions choke the word. Yield: Zero.
4	The word sometimes lands on the good soil. The word is heard and accepted. Yield: Abundance. Thirty, sixty, and a hundredfold.

Where is this interpretation taking us? We should be careful, because by force of habit and the weight of scores of sermons we have heard (or preached), we might be tempted to see this as an invitation to ask, "We have four kinds of soil, three bad and one good. So, what kind of soil am I? Am I good soil, or one of the bad soils?" But this misses Mark's focus. Mark is not interested here in self-interrogation about what kind of soil we might be toward our moral self-improvement. He would be dismayed if, after hearing this parable and its interpretation, we would respond, "You know, these days I'm feeling kind of like rocky soil in my spiritual life. I wonder if there is something I can do to turn myself into fertile soil." We will get to this approach soon enough when we come to Matthew's retelling of the same parable; moral inquiry is on Matthew's agenda. But right now we are in Mark's world, and his focus is not soil analysis but the astonishing harvest, one that happens over against all odds. Mark wants us to face harsh facts about life and the human prospect and then to be gobsmacked by that startling, overflowing, and victorious harvest.

Most of us are attuned to hear the Scripture asking us to roll up our sleeves and get to work doing God's work. Form a committee, write a check, march in the streets, work for better legislation. In Mark, though, that will come only later, much later. Right here—at this parable—we are not being asked to establish a charity or organize a precinct, much less attempt to practice alchemy by turning ourselves from poor fill dirt into potting soil. Jesus commands only this: Listen! Look! Sit there on the land with the rest of the crowd, and watch what happens when the sower goes out to sow.

Let's not kid ourselves. There is some pretty unpromising soil out there—hard patches, rocks, and thorns. When the vulnerable seed of the gospel is tossed onto the world's landscape, the results are as tragic as they are inevitable. Zero. What else could be expected? The world, as the old hymn proclaims, is full of "dangers, toils and snares." This is not a parable about how to make things better. This is a parable about the tough truth of how things are. By the time we have watched the sower waste seed prodigiously and fail each time, we are forced to confess that the world is a pitiful wasteland and that only God can bring forth a crop in this barrenness. And that, beyond all our amazement, is what happens. The astonishing thing about the Parable of the Sower is not that there are bad soils and crop failures. No surprise there. Watch CNN for an hour, and you will know this is true. The staggering thing, the truly mind-blowing event in the parable, is that there is a harvest at all, much less the unexpected bumper crop that at the end spills over the top.

This parable of repeated failure followed by unexpected abundance is like telling a story that goes like this: There once was a boy born to an impoverished family in Pittsburgh. His father abandoned the family when the boy was two months old and was soon imprisoned for murder. His mother became addicted to cocaine and was too addled, defeated, and distracted to provide any parental care. The boy himself wandered the streets of his crime-infested neighborhood, dropped out of school at age thirteen, and was arrested for stealing a car at age fifteen. Then he became a famed neurosurgeon who pioneered new techniques in spinal surgery and established a medical clinic for the indigent in Bangladesh.

What? Talk about a surprise ending. No wonder the disciples who heard the Parable of the Sower couldn't make heads or tails of it. Nothing about the parable prepares the hearer for the final lavish scene. But as we keep reading in Mark, the fog begins to clear a bit. As we go deeper into that Gospel, we realize that this parable is not merely the story of a farmer and his perilous experiences with the seed; it is also the story of Jesus and his ministry.

What happens to the sower in this story is what is going to happen to Jesus in the rest of Mark. Jesus not only told this parable; he lived this parable. He *is* this parable. That's why he began the parable, "Listen! Look!" Listen to the parable, and then watch me live it out. This is why he told the disciples that if they did not understand this one, they wouldn't understand any of the parables. This parable is the key to the whole Gospel of Mark, the key to understanding Jesus.

Like the farmer in the parable, Jesus sows the word, and although there is an occasional green shoot here or a promising sprig there, he ultimately fails time and again. What about that beaten path where the word lies on the surface only to get snatched up by the birds before it stands a chance? Jesus will hit some hard ground himself when he engages stubborn Pharisees and tries to do ministry in his own resistant hometown (see 6:1–6; 7:1–13; 8:11–13). What about the word that falls on rocky ground? Things look promising at first, but the plants that spring up have little root, and when trouble or persecution comes, as it always does, the once-promising but rootless faithful will "fall away" (σκανδαλίζονται, 4:16–17). That happens to Jesus too. Even his own disciples will finally "fall away," *skandalisthēsesthe* (σκανδαλισθήσεσθε, 14:27). And what about that thorn patch where worldly cares and the lust for wealth choke out the word? Well, Jesus will preach the demanding gospel to a rich man, but, sure enough, the man's money will choke out the word and send the man slinking away grieving (10:17–22).[18]

Now we see why the Parable of the Sower is the key parable, the parable that unlocks all of the other parables. Captured in the parable is the story of the ministry of Jesus; it is the whole Gospel of Mark in miniature. Jesus comes to Galilee sowing the word in every direction, but it falls in one unfruitful place after another. The enormous waste of energy and seed mounts until, at the end, the Sower himself is crucified. This is the way of God in the world. Do you not understand this parable? Then how will you understand all the parables?

But what about the good soil? Jesus says the good soil produces those "who hear the word and accept it and bear fruit" (4:20). Admittedly, it is difficult to find much good soil in Mark's story of Jesus, so overshadowed it is by resistance, rejection, and betrayal. But a few green shoots can be seen: a demon-possessed man in the country of the Gerasenes who was healed by Jesus and ended up proclaiming "how much Jesus had done for him" (5:1–20), a woman with a blood hemorrhage who dared to touch Jesus' cloak and whose faith made her well (5:24–34), a blind man named Bartimaeus who also had faith that made him well (10:46), a woman who "did what she could" by pouring costly ointment on Jesus' head, thereby symbolically anointing him for burial (14:3–9). These and a few others are the firstfruits of the great harvest, but we can hardly say that we yet see the surprising harvest, thirtyfold, sixtyfold, a hundredfold.

The abundant harvest will come, of course, at Easter, when, along with the women at the tomb, the reader encounters the decisive amazement: "Do not be alarmed; you are looking for Jesus of Nazareth, who was crucified. He has been raised; he is not here. Look, there is the place they laid him. But go, tell his disciples and Peter that he is going ahead of you to Galilee; there you will see him, just as he told you" (16:6–7).

This is the flabbergasting bumper crop, the ultimate surprise ending, an event so outlandishly unexpected it leads, on the part of the women and the reader too, to the ultimate "Huh?": "So they went out and fled from the tomb, for terror and amazement had seized them; and they said nothing to anyone, for they were afraid" (16:8).

We are now very close to the "secret [or mystery] of the kingdom of God" (4:11). God is at work in the world to bring forth a head-spinning Easter harvest of abundance. Not in spite of the cross, but through it. Not apart from the land littered with the hard, rocky, and thorny ground of history and humanity, but in it. Eventually this mystery will send us out as Jesus' disciples, preaching, teaching, healing, reconciling, and even raising the dead.

But not before and until this mystery has overwhelmed us, leaving us, like the women at the tomb, silent and afraid in the presence of the power of God. To even think for a second "What kind of soil am I?" is to completely miss the moment. This is not about us, at least at first. It is about what God has done and is doing in the world, a mighty act so unprecedented and improbable and astonishing as to leave us in voiceless awe.

Why Parables?

Before Jesus gives the explanation of the Parable of the Sower, he responds to a question from the disciples about the parables more generally (4:10). We are not told exactly what the disciples asked Jesus, but based on his reply, it must have been something like, "Why all the riddles, puzzles, and mysteries? Why don't you teach straight up? Why speak to the crowd in parables?"

Good question, but Jesus' answer is confounding. You disciples "have been given the secret of the kingdom of God," he says, but to all those on the outside I speak in parables "in order that" (ἵνα) they would look but not get it, listen but not understand, so that they won't repent and be forgiven (4:11–12). That statement has caused generations of commentators to become pretzel makers, twisting these words into all manner of contortions in an effort to keep Jesus from really saying what these words clearly mean.

The notion of a Jesus who divides people into insiders and outsiders, those who know the secret of the kingdom and those who don't, and then uses parables to block those outsiders from understanding and forgiveness runs against the grain of the inclusive, welcoming, forgiving Jesus who appears in most pulpits every week. Even Matthew is bothered, and he makes his own pretzel when he tells the same story in his Gospel. He replaces Mark's word ἵνα (in order that) with ὅτι (because), to the effect that, instead of Jesus saying, "I speak in parables in order that they won't get what I'm talking about," the Matthean Jesus speaks in parables "*because* they don't understand me." Ah, that's better.

But we're in Mark here. What sense can we make of a Jesus who speaks in parables so that the people will listen to them but not really hear and understand them? It is crucial to keep in mind that Jesus is quoting Isaiah 6 in his reply to the disciples. In a terrifying scene in the temple, Isaiah finds himself gathered up into a vision of the heavenly court. Six-winged seraphs fly above the enthroned Lord, singing "Holy, Holy, Holy" as the temple thresholds shake and the room fills with smoke.

Overwhelmed, Isaiah cries out, "Woe is me!"

But the Lord is not aiming to obliterate Isaiah. Instead, God desires to call a messenger. "Whom shall I send?" God says. "Who will go for us?"

Isaiah undoubtedly surveyed the room. Seeing no other candidate for the ministry standing there, he timidly raises his hand. "Here I am," he whispers. "Send me."

Now comes the really odd part. God says to Isaiah, "Go, and this is what I want you to say to the people:

> "Keep listening, but do not comprehend;
> keep looking, but do not understand."
> Make the mind of this people dull,
>   and stop their ears,
>   and shut their eyes,
> so that they may not look with their eyes,
>   and listen with their ears,
> and comprehend with their minds,
>   and turn and be healed.
>
> Isa. 6:9b–10

"Isaiah's mission," writes Gene Tucker, "is clear: He is to prevent repentance and healing."[19]

Can you imagine a young pastor being ordained today being told at the commissioning service, "God calls you to go out into the world and to do everything you can to prevent repentance and healing"? No wonder Isaiah responded by asking God, "How long?" which is an Old Testament prophet's way of saying, "This sounds like miserable ministry to me. How many years until I can retire?"

Gene Tucker warns us not to pass over Isaiah's harsh mandate too quickly. "Is it ever possible," he asks, "that the Word of God, the truth for the present and future, is the proclamation of judgment? The Word of God is not a dogma, requiring the same proclamation in all times and places. Thus there is a time and an occasion not only for judgment, but also for salvation. We could miss the yes because we have not heard the no."[20]

For Mark, we cannot hear the yes of the gospel until we have endured a season of no. We cannot know God-in-Christ is in the world until we have walked the long journey with Jesus, who is the Christ, and have been with him as he experiences the sting of rejection and as he suffers and dies. In other words, until we truly grasp the mystery of the kingdom, we are, just like the crowds: "outsiders." Jesus later says that "there is nothing hidden, except to be disclosed; nor is anything secret except to come to light" (4:22), but it will take a cruel death on a cross to bring the secret of God's mystery to the light.

"To you has been given the secret of the kingdom," Jesus tells the disciples, but have they? Yes, they have been given the mystery of the kingdom in the Parable of the Sower itself, which is, to those who have ears to hear, the kingdom's secret in narrative form. But even though the disciples have been *given* the secret, they have not yet *grasped* it. They do not yet understand this parable, Jesus tells them. How could they? How could any human being understand that the life and ministry of Jesus, which spirals toward defeat, abandonment, rejection, and death, is but the prelude to a final scene so unexpected and astonishing as to leave us gasping in uncomprehending wonder, a resurrection bumper crop of life and hope?

So why does Jesus preach in parables? Because, says Jesus, the commission of Isaiah continues, to go to the people and allow them to look but not to perceive, to listen but not to understand, to keep people for the time being on the outside. The crowds are on the outside, the disciples are on the outside, and we, the readers of Mark, are on the outside too. Then suddenly there we all are, all of us outsiders, at the end of the journey standing there with the women at the cemetery on Easter, blinking uncomprehendingly through the early morning light at the young man dressed in white who tells us the blazing improbability, that the one we seek is not here but has been raised, that we should go to Galilee, where we will see him.

We have only two choices. We can remain outsiders, saying, "Huh?," shrugging our shoulders, and heading back to our everyday hardscrabble lives tilling hard, rocky, and thorny ground. Or we can flee in terror and amazement, only to realize, as we sprint away as fast as we can, that we are on the road to Galilee. When we arrive in Galilee we can start over, read the Gospel of Mark again, travel again with Jesus the road to the cross, this time with at least a fragile insider's grasp of the mystery of the kingdom. When we do, we will indeed see him, pouring out his life and casting the Word across the breadth of the world. We will once again experience the plots against him, the rejections, and the apparent failures, but this time we will see what, at first, only the demons recognized: that this Jesus is indeed the strong One of God, the Messiah who will surely preside over God's astonishing harvest.

When we get back to Galilee, we will find that we are no longer simply observers of Jesus' ministry. We are also followers and participants, and our ministry is now formed in the pattern of his. Perhaps we will also sow the seed in the same free and reckless ways, as Juel suggests, "speaking gracious words without carefully calculating the potential for success in the face of daunting challenges to growth."[21] As Paul Tillich said in a sermon,

> The history of [humankind] is the history of men and women who wasted themselves and were not afraid to do so. They did not fear the waste of themselves, of other [people], of things in the service of a new creation. They were justified, for they wasted all this out of the fullness of their hearts. They wasted as God does in nature and history, in creation and salvation.[22]

THE PARABLE OF THE SEED GROWING SECRETLY (MARK 4:26–29)

This little parable has had a hard time making friends. As brief as it is, this Zen-like story about an oblivious gardener is nevertheless a perplexing parable, difficult to understand. Jesus says the parable is about the kingdom of God ("The kingdom of God is as if . . . ," 4:26), but Bultmann throws up his hands and admits that it isn't easy to figure out what, if anything, this story has to do with the kingdom.[23] Matthew and Luke don't warm to it either; they gladly borrow the Parable of the Sower from Mark, but when they come across this one about a farmer who hasn't the foggiest idea how his crop grows, they both take a pass. C. H. Dodd, who rejects the use of allegory to interpret parables because, he says, in the New Testament parables "all is true to nature and life,"[24] is so nonplussed by this one that he churns out a full-blown allegorical rendering. God is the sower, the seed is "prevenient grace" sown into creation at the beginning, the stages of growth are the prophets and John the Baptist, the harvest is the culmination of God's kingdom activity, and Jesus is the one urging the reaper to "go in with his sickle because the harvest has come" (4:29).[25] Neatly done, to be sure, but that interpretation probably says more about Dodd's theology than Mark's.

Once again, if we are content to allow Mark to guide us through the flow of the parable, if we pay attention to its language, to its plot movements, to its twists and turns, this parable may turn out to be both simpler and, at the same time, deeper and more pertinent to the kingdom of God than we first expected.

As He Was Saying . . .

The parable is introduced with the connective phrase "he also said" (4:26) or, perhaps better, "as he was saying" (καὶ ἔλεγεν). Saying to whom? Jesus began this parables sermon of Mark 4 out by the sea, speaking to the multitude, but then, in 4:10, he pulled away from the crowd for a private conversation with the disciples and other insiders. Somewhere along the way we know that Jesus went back out to the crowd, because by the time we get to the end of the parables discourse, Jesus is clearly once more in public (4:33–34).

When does the shift take place? It could have been in the previous passage, 4:21–25, which also begins with καὶ ἔλεγεν, but the content of that passage, which is about hiddenness and disclosure, seems to connect best with the private conversation of 4:10–20. It's hard to read Mark's mind as a narrator, but it is probably here, at 4:26, where the move from "inside" back to "outside" takes place. The private conversation Mark has been reporting between Jesus and the disciples and other insiders seems now to be over, and we have been swept with Jesus back out to the boat on the sea, where Jesus resumes telling parables in public.

By the way, Mark has given us one example of Jesus telling a parable in public, the Parable of the Sower, followed by a private explanation to the disciples. Mark wants the readers to know that this public discourse–private explanation arrangement was the customary pattern. He says, "[Jesus] did not speak to them except in parables, but he explained everything in private to his disciples" (4:34).

Jesus has already told the crowd the Parable of the Sower, and now he follows that one with this second seed parable: the Seed Growing Secretly.

"The kingdom of God," he begins, "is as if someone would scatter seed on the ground" (4:26). As soon as the seed is cast, the parable imagines what might happen next by describing two parallel rhythm tracks. One track describes the sower, and the other describes the seed and the ground. The sower "would sleep and rise night and day" (4:27). In Mark's day, Jews measured days beginning with the evening, as in the Genesis creation story ("And there was evening and there was morning, the first day" [Gen. 1:5]), so the night-and-day language here simply underscores that the sower is going about his normal daily routines. As for the seed, it too pulses along with its normal rhythms; it "would sprout and grow" (Mark 4:27). The poetic rhythms apparent in the English translation—sleep and rise, night and day, sprout and grow—are there in the Greek as well. The point is that, after the sowing, the normal cadences of everyday life unfold, for both the sower and the seed.

So far, so good; the sower and the seed are rocking along as expected. But then the parable becomes a tad strange. It throws up a curtain of ignorance between the sower and the gestating seed. The seed cruises merrily along, doing its thing, sprouting and growing as seed does, but the parable flatly says that the sower "does not know how" this is happening (4:27). The sower and the seed are now on separate trajectories. This gardener is depicted as unknowing and uninvolved, and the parable swiftly shifts the focus away from the sower completely over to the seed and the earth in which it is planted. "The earth produces of itself, first the stalk, then the head, then the full grain in the head" (4:28). The Greek word for "of itself" is *automatē* (αὐτομάτη), from which we get the word "automatic." The growth of the seed, the parable insists, proceeds without the efforts of the sower. At the sowing, the sower and the seed were obviously together, but not now. Only when the harvest has come will the two tracks merge again and the sower reenter the picture: "But when the grain is ripe, at once he goes in with his sickle, because the harvest has come" (4:29).

Dodd may have claimed that in Jesus' parables "all is true to nature and life," but not in this one. As anyone who has ever planted peas, green peppers, or other vegetables knows, scattering seed and then going to sleep and forgetting it is a recipe for a garden disaster. This parable does not depict a "natural" farming situation, but a kingdom reality. Something about the kingdom is different from the average gardener's bed of tomato plants in the backyard. In the case of the parable, the seed "produces of itself," thank you very much. If real gardens actually grew automatically, without tilling, tending, and weeding, probably more people would be gardeners! The point in the parable is that, unlike any other garden we have known, this kingdom garden grows apart from the efforts or knowledge of the sower.

Who Is the Sower?

In our discussion of the first parable in Jesus' sermon, the Parable of the Sower, we discovered Mark ultimately wants the reader to recognize that Jesus himself is the sower. Read the whole Gospel of Mark, and we will see that Jesus is the one who sows the seed widely into all kinds of soils, the one who sows the word into the ears of those who hear, and the one who presides over the surprising bumper crop harvest. But what about here in the Parable of the Seed Growing Secretly? Does this identification carry through? Is Jesus still the sower, but this time, a sower who doesn't know how the seed he cast grows toward harvest? Although a clueless Messiah would be an odd christological image, it is nevertheless not entirely out of the question in Mark. He does let us know later that Jesus himself is ignorant of the "day or hour" of the kingdom's arrival (13:32). Only God knows the timing. Maybe Jesus is indeed the one who sows the seed of the word but doesn't know how that seed sprouts and grows.

It is far more likely, though, that Mark has shifted frames of reference in this parable. In the Parable of the Sower, the one who sows the seed is expressly called ὁ σπείρων, "a sower." This person has a role and an identity. But in this parable the one who casts the seed is merely described as *anthrōpos* (ἄνθρωπος), "a man," an anonymous "someone." Thus the parable begins in effect, "The kingdom of God is as if some guy (or woman) should cast seeds on the ground." The focus here is not on who is doing the sowing but on what happens afterwards.

The Sudden Harvest

There is, however, one theme that links the Parable of the Sower to the Parable of the Seed Growing Secretly: surprise. The Sower described the surprise of an outlandishly abundant harvest, especially given how much poor soil and resistance the seed encountered. The Seed Growing Secretly also describes a surprise, but here the surprise doesn't have to do with the size of the harvest, but with its timing. The seed was sprouting and growing out of sight, out of mind, when suddenly the grain becomes ripe, and now the alarm bells ring and the sower has to spring immediately into action with the sickle, "because the harvest has come" (4:29).

The swift appearance of the ripened grain is a kingdom surprise, God's surprise. The ripening of the grain comes from seed growing beyond human effort and knowledge. As we noted, when the parable says that the "earth produces of itself," the phrase "of itself" is a translation of the Greek word *automatē* (αὐτομάτη), literally "automatically." But we should exercise care here. Contemporary readers may assume that "automatically" refers to the normal biological process of germination—like first-graders who put a seed in a paper cup and wait for it spontaneously to sprout.

But this parable is about theology, not just biology. This parable is about God's surprise, not Mother Nature's. That same Greek term, αὐτομάτη, is also used in the Septuagint text of Leviticus (see Lev. 25:5, 11) in the description of the Jubilee Year. In that holy year, all human agricultural efforts are, by God's command, to cease—no sowing, no working the crops, "For it is a jubilee; it shall be holy to you: you shall eat only what the field itself produces" (Lev. 25:12). These Jubilee Year crops that grow "of themselves" and not by human toil are gifts and blessings from God. Markan scholar Joel Marcus notes that these freely available crops "display God's sovereign care for his people."[26] What our parable is describing is just such a reality. Human beings may sow the word, and when the harvest comes, they are called to be gatherers of the harvest, but the germination and growth of the seed and the appearance of the grain are finally God's work, God's timing, God's good gifts, not ours. God's kingdom is "at hand" but not "in hand."

A similar picture of God having charge over the seasons, a God whose timing of the appearance of the kingdom is hid from human knowledge, is expressed in *2 Baruch* 48:2, when Baruch, the legendary scribe and friend of Jeremiah, prays,

> O my Lord, you summon the advent of the times,
> And they stand before you;
> You cause the power of the ages to pass away,
> And they do not resist you;
> You arrange the method of the seasons,
> And they obey you.
> You alone know the duration of the generations,
> And you reveal not your mysteries to many.[27]

The obliviousness of the sower in this parable may not reflect real-world agriculture, but it does reflect kingdom realities. What is emerging to those who have eyes to see and ears to hear is not a utopian society hard wrought through human effort and savvy, but the gift of life given by God, a new Eden, a redeemed world in which God truly reigns.[28]

On Hand for the Kingdom

Where, then, is this parable taking us in regard to experiencing the kingdom of God, to participating in the inbreaking of the life of God into our world? The Parable of the Seed Growing Secretly has the ultimate harvest in view, the time when suddenly "they will see the Son of Man coming in clouds with great power and glory" (Mark 13:26), but it also points to those more proximate times of God's appearing that serve as an anticipation of the final harvest.

In his essay "Economy and Pleasure," Wendell Berry describes the tobacco harvest in his area of rural Kentucky: "This work usually occurs at some time between the last part of August and the first part of October. Usually the weather is hot; usually we are in a hurry. The work is extremely demanding, and often . . . it has the character of an emergency."[29]

A harvest emergency, a harvest so swift and urgent that it constitutes a crisis—this is the theme of the Parable of the Seed Growing Secretly. Like the sower in this parable, we go about life minding our own business, when suddenly the grain that has been growing out of mind and mostly out of sight is ripe, and the moment has come. The time for leisurely sleeping and rising, night and day, has come screeching to a halt. We don't know the hidden processes that generated the appearance of the harvest. All we know is there it is, the ripe grain of God's appearing, demanding our immediate action and response: "At once he goes in with his sickle, because the harvest has come" (4:29).

The Babylonian Talmud says, "There are three things that come by surprise: the Messiah, a found article, and a scorpion."[30] The prophet Joel, from whom Jesus borrows this parable's image of the sickle and the ripe harvest (see Joel 3:13), describes a surprise advent of God, but in Joel it is the scorpion of God's judgment that has burst forth like a surprise summer thunderstorm:

> Come quickly,
>   all you nations all around,
>   gather yourselves there.
> Bring down your warriors, O LORD.
> Let the nations rouse themselves,
>   and come up to the valley of Jehoshaphat;
> for there I will sit to judge
>   all the neighboring nations.
> Put in the sickle,
>   for the harvest is ripe.
> Go in, tread,
>   for the wine press is full.
> The vats overflow,
>   for their wickedness is great.
>
> Joel 3:11–13

Here the vats are overflowing with wickedness, and God is moving swiftly to judge the nations. In our parable, though, the harvest is messianic and ripe with joy, not the bitter grain of judgment. This glorious harvest is what the ancient rabbis had in mind when they recounted this tale: "It is told of Rabbi Hiyya and Rabbi Simeon that they walked in the valley of Arbela early in the morning and saw the dawn breaking on the horizon. Thereupon Rabbi Hiyya said, 'So too is Israel's redemption; at first it will be only very slightly visible, then it will shine forth more brightly, and only afterward will it break forth in all its glory.'"[31]

So too in the parable. There was the first glimpse as the stalk emerged, and then the head, and suddenly there it was in its fullness: the grain is ripe and the great harvest has come.

In Tennessee Williams's *A Streetcar Named Desire,* Mitch and Blanche, two lonely and broken people, suddenly find tenderness and love developing between them. Mitch says, "You need somebody. And I need somebody too. Could it be—you and me, Blanche?" With a soft cry, she falls into his embrace. He kisses her forehead, her eyes, and then her lips.

Blanche begins to sob, and then she says, "Sometimes—there's God—so quickly!"[32]

Indeed, God does appear so quickly, and the swift appearance of a harvest we did not produce and do not know how it came to be is the surprise to which this parable points.

In her memoir *Eat This Bread: A Radical Conversion*, Sara Miles describes a God-come-quickly moment, a sudden harvest, in her own life. Miles is the founder and director of the Food Pantry, which provides free groceries every Friday around the altar of St. Gregory of Nyssa Episcopal Church in San Francisco. She is the granddaughter of missionaries, but her mother, who "nursed a grudge against Christianity for more than fifty years,"[33] embraced atheism as a child. Miles's mother rejected "what she called 'the whole unbelievable, illogical concept' that her parents assumed was the obvious truth." Her mother finally escaped the religious home of her upbringing and married a man who shared her views. Miles writes, "My parents never went to church—not on Easter, not at Christmas. . . . Our Sundays were for reading the *New York Times*, listening to Vivaldi on the record player, eating artichokes and mussels, aioli and lemon ice."[34]

Raised, then, in a secular environment, Miles "soaked up experience: sex, travel, drugs, food, hard physical work—anything that would take us further into the sensual, immediate world that my parents insisted was the opposite of religion."[35] Moving into adulthood, Miles became a cook in a restaurant, a researcher and activist in war-torn Nicaragua, and, after moving to San Francisco, a reporter for a politically left-wing magazine. She became pregnant and gave birth to a daughter, Katie.

One winter morning, Miles, taking a walk, found herself in St. Gregory's Church. She writes,

> I had no earthly reason to be there. I'd never heard a Gospel reading, never said the Lord's Prayer. I was certainly not interested in becoming a Christian—or as I thought of it rather less politely, a religious nut. But on other long walks, I'd passed the beautiful wooden building, with its shingled steeple and plain windows, and this time I went in, on an impulse, with no more than a reporter's habitual curiosity.[36]

A service was in progress, and Miles participated in the standing up and sitting down, in the singing and the listening. "It crossed my mind," she says, "that this was ridiculous."[37]

But then suddenly, unexpectedly, the grain was ripe. "[S]omething outrageous and terrifying happened," she writes. "Jesus happened to me." It happened when she went to the communion table with the others in the congregation that day. Someone put a piece of bread in her hands, saying, "The body of Christ," and passed her a goblet of wine, saying, "The blood of Christ." Swiftly these elements were more to Miles than a morsel of bread and a sip of wine. They were the presence of God, for her.

Miles says, "What I knew was happening—God, named 'Christ' or 'Jesus,' was real, and in my mouth—utterly short-circuited my ability to do anything but cry."[38] Elsewhere she writes, "This was my first communion. It changed everything."[39] A seed sown somewhere, sometime by some unknown sower who hadn't a clue as to how the seed grows had suddenly come to fruition:

> I couldn't reconcile the experience with anything I knew or had been told. But neither could I go away: For some inexplicable reason, I wanted that bread again. I wanted it all the next day . . . and the next week, and the next. It was a sensation as urgent as physical hunger.[40]

Having seen the ripe grain, Miles put in the sickle. She became active at St. Gregory's, started a food ministry that gave away food around the very altar where she had herself been so surprisingly and graciously fed, learned about the blessings of the parish and some of its warts, and faced, as do all faithful people, her doubts.

At some point she had to confess her newfound faith to her atheist mother. It was in her mother's Vermont apartment. Miles cooked a supper for the two of them, and they sat at a table set with lamb, bread, and wine. "Ma, I have to tell you something," Miles said, raising a glass of wine as she fearfully told her secret. "I'm a Christian. I've started going to church."

"My mother was kinder than I deserved," she writes, and the fear evaporated. She told her mother everything she loved about Jesus.

Her mother listened and then replied, "I told my mother when I was ten I didn't believe in God and I haven't ever since." But then her mother surprisingly added, "I love the hymns, though. . . . I bet I still know all the verses." The two of them, mother and daughter, remembered together the words of the old hymns: "Time like an ever-flowing stream . . . changed from glory into glory, till in heaven we take our place . . . be Thou welcome, gentle King! Firmly stands Thy throne of peace."

"She poured me some more wine," Miles says. "It wasn't official Eucharist. It was real communion, with all the incomplete, stupid, and aching parts still there, . . . what the Russian mystics called 'a foretaste of the heavenly banquet, where none are left behind.'"[41]

THE PARABLE OF THE MUSTARD SEED (MARK 4:30–32)

The last of the three parables that Jesus tells in his seaside sermon is also a seed parable, this time about a tiny mustard seed that grows up into a great shrub with large branches, offering shade and nesting places for the birds of the air.

This parable is not overly complicated, even though it is expansive and powerful in meaning. In fact, the simplicity of this parable confounds a number of interpreters, who perhaps cannot believe that a parable of Jesus could be so clear and direct, and who have consequently worked overtime to find buried clues and hidden, elusive meanings. Amy-Jill Levine, in her refreshing treatment of this parable in *Short Stories by Jesus*, wryly observes, "The parable of the Mustard Seed has put forth so many branches of interpretation that the birds of heaven could build multiple nests and still have room for expansion."[42]

When we simply read this parable, the basic plot line is quite visible: something very small (a mustard seed) is planted and grows up to be something quite large (the greatest of all shrubs, with large branches), and that large shrub does something, namely, provides ample shade for the nesting of the birds of the air. Whatever we ultimately make of this parable, our interpretation will need to cohere to this main plot trajectory.

Red Herrings and Rabbit Trails

Beware, then, of the red herrings and rabbit trails that would take us off track and mislead us in our interpretation. Two stand out. First, there are some who suggest that the mustard seed or plant is somehow bad, unclean, even noxious and dangerous. Jesus, therefore, is featuring a wicked plant as part of a radical "outlaw" parable.

There are variations on this toxicity theme, but the main thread seems to go like this: In Deuteronomy, the Law forbids the mixing of two different kinds of seed in the same vineyard ("You shall not sow your vineyard with a second kind of seed, or the whole yield will have to be forfeited," Deut. 22:9). In other words, one field, one crop, that's the law. As agricultural methods changed and improved, however, this commandment, taken literally, probably turned out to be inconvenient, enforcing an inefficient way of crop management. This prompted the rabbis to give the commandment a closer look.

Some of the rabbis suggested a more nuanced reading by fashioning a distinction between plantings that were "seeds" and those that were "vegetables." The commandment in Deuteronomy, they opined, forbade seeds to be mixed in the same field, but not vegetables, and they even named some examples of what fell in each category. Mustard and small chickpeas, for example, were considered seeds, but large chickpeas were vegetables.[43] So a farmer could plant barley and large chickpeas in the same field, but not barley and mustard seeds.

Why do seeds in general, and mustard seeds in particular, get a bad rap here? Why is the planting of them alongside other plants considered a violation of the Torah, when large chickpeas are no problem? Almost surely because the plants that come from seeds like mustard are often hard to control. The plants grow prolifically and could even be called "invasive," like kudzu or honeysuckle, virtually impossible to keep in bounds. Mustard plants overrun fields and can crowd out other crops—in short, they can do harm to the life of other plants—and that, the rabbis deduced, is the underlying rationale of the commandment's prohibition.

Aha! The plot thickens. Jesus, the argument runs, is spinning a yarn not about figs or marigolds but about the sowing of dangerous, forbidden, and illegal mustard seed in order to depict the kingdom of God as invasive and outside the holy law—or, as one commentator put it, "illegitimate, tainted, unclean. . . . The kingdom is associated with uncleanness just as Jesus himself associates with the unclean, the outcast."[44]

Yes, Jesus and his movement were a threat to the religious establishment. But is that scandal at the heart of this parable? It is quite a stretch to think so. Levine is quick to point out that viewing the mustard as "unclean" treads perilously close to the vaguely (or not-so-vaguely) anti-Semitic interpretations that have dogged parables study for generations, namely, that one of the major purposes of Jesus' parables was to show "how bad the Jewish Law is."[45] For some interpreters, it is irresistible to see this Parable of the Mustard Seed and the bird-filled bush it produces as a poke in the eye of Judaism itself, a story symbolic of the kingdom's welcome to those wild nesting birds, namely, "unclean" Gentiles and outsiders over against self-righteous, purity-driven Jews. (Levine delightfully reminds her readers that mustard, as a matter of fact, is perfectly kosher and that anyone who has ever eaten a kosher hot dog slathered with the requisite mustard will have a hard time associating mustard with a violation of Jewish purity laws![46])

But perhaps even more pertinent is the fact that if Jesus had wanted to tell a parable that was an allusion to the commandment in Deuteronomy, one that turned on the mixture of "scandalous" and "clean" plants in the same field, he would have done so. In fact, he did: it is the Parable of the Weeds and the Wheat, and it appears in Matthew 13. The Parable of the Mustard Seed doesn't mention anything about mustard plants invading other plants or infecting a field. This is not because Jesus forgot to mention it or because the hearers are intuitively supposed to supply those missing details. Rather, it is because this isn't the point of the parable. This is a parable about one tiny seed that grows into an impressive bush, and if there is any importance to the fact that Jesus talks about a mustard plant rather than lilies of the valley or cymbidium orchids, it is because a mustard seed is tiny and the plants are common and ordinary.

Second, some search around for exotic meanings in this parable because of all the bad, triumphalistic sermons they have heard on this text. They worry that this parable, with its picture of a tiny seed growing into a huge plant, indulges preachers who are gripped by "a lust for big-time success,"[47] who chirp about visions of the church growing from humble beginnings to great size and power.

It is surely a worthy cause to oppose cheap and grandiose church-growth ambitions, but this doesn't justify distorting the parable, forcing it to say the opposite of what it wants to say. There is actually, as we shall see, plenty in this parable to undermine superficial, corporate visions of church growth. But to discern this, we don't need to turn a blind eye to the fact that this parable indeed presents a dramatic portrait of growth, a picture of a tiny seed that grows into "the greatest of all shrubs." There are no hidden codes here, no secret messages or murky symbols. Even in the parables, Levine again reminds us, "sometimes a seed is just a seed, a bird is just a bird, and a tree is just a tree."[48]

With What Can We Compare the Kingdom?

Essentially, then, this parable is an astounding growth story, like the story of Jack and the Beanstalk, where a small magic bean surprisingly produces an enormous stalk reaching into the clouds. Except in the parable, instead of a magic bean we have an ordinary mustard seed, and instead of a towering stalk we have a shrub measured by breadth rather than height.

The parable begins with a rhetorical question: "With what can we compare the kingdom of God, or what parable will we use for it?" (4:30). Good question. Here Jesus invites his hearers (and Mark's readers) to supply possible answers. What *would* you say would be a good comparison to use to describe God's kingdom? What parable would *we* tell? Be careful here. When Jesus poses an open question, it comes with a warning sign: "Caution! Surprise answer ahead!" Sure enough, when Jesus supplies his own answer, we shake our heads. The kingdom, he says, is not like the Roman Empire, or a massive army on the march, or the Magic Kingdom at Disney World, or Shangri-la. It "is like a mustard seed, which, when sown upon the ground, is the smallest of all the seeds on earth" (4:31). Comparing the kingdom of God to a flyspeck-sized mustard seed was probably way down on most people's list.

By the way, no need to lose sleep—as some interpreters have done—over the worry that mustard seeds are not, in biological fact, "the smallest of all the seeds on earth." Jesus is teaching the kingdom of God here, not botany, and we should yield to his storyteller's art. He is saying, in effect, "What's a good image to use to compare to the kingdom of God? I will compare it to a mustard seed. Can you imagine anything smaller than that?"

A number of commentators have pointed out that when the parable goes on to describe how this mustard seed is sown, the language becomes a bit clumsy. Jesus says that the mustard seed is sown upon the ground (γῆς) and is the smallest of the seeds on the ground (γῆς again, 4:31). Why mention the ground at all? And why mention it twice? Where else would one sow a seed, and if the parable says that the sower sowed the mustard seed on the ground, why repeat in the same sentence that the seed was on the ground?

We can see the editorial hand of Mark at work here, and this may be nothing more than a stylistic tic, a little Markan throat-clearing. On the other hand, we noted earlier that the ground, the land, is a major theme in this seaside sermon. The crowd listening to Jesus is on the land (4:1); in the Parable of the Sower, seed is sown on the land (4:5, 8, 20); and the same is true in the Parable of the Seed Growing Secretly (4:26, 28). The ground in Mark is not merely the soil under our feet. It is a symbol of the places in human life where the Word of God falls. The ground is human life, human history, the ears of those who listen. Perhaps Mark is risking a little syntactical infelicity to underscore the theological truth that this tiny mustard seed, like all the other seeds in this sermon, has fallen on the land, on the crowd, on history, on the world.

The rest of the parable resembles time-lapse photography. Watch as the mustard plant emerges from the earth and begins to grow and grow, large branches unfurling, extending wider and wider until what started as the barely visible speck of a seed has become "the greatest of all shrubs" (4:32). The shrub is so wide and inviting that the "birds of the air" (literally "the birds of heaven") nest in the shade afforded by its branches.

Echoes of Trees and Birds

Most commentators agree that parable's picture of birds nesting in the shade of the giant shrub is an allusion to imagery in the Old Testament. But where in the Old Testament? Daniel 4, Ezekiel 17, Ezekiel 31, and Psalm 104 are the passages most frequently suggested, but, as John Dominic Crossan says, "If one makes the mistake of actually looking up these references, one immediately senses a problem: the allusion is not very explicit and not very appropriate."[49]

Let's take a look for ourselves. We begin with Daniel 4. Here we find the image of a "great tree at the center of the earth" with beautiful foliage and abundant fruit, a tree so ample that "the animals of the field found shade under it, and the birds of the air nested in its branches" (Dan. 4:12). That certainly sounds a lot like our parable, but the problem is that Daniel's tree appears in King Nebuchadnezzar's bad dream. As the dream unfolds, the tree gets chopped down and its branches lopped off, forcing the birds and animals to flee. The tree "is you, O king" (Dan. 4:22), Daniel says to Nebuchadnezzar, turning his dream into a political nightmare that presages the fall of his kingdom.

Ezekiel 17 also talks about a growing cedar tree and about Nebuchadnezzar and the Babylonian Empire, but this time the king himself is a bird, not a gentle little nesting bird but a great and menacing eagle (Ezek. 17:3). Once again, though, this kingdom of Nebuchadnezzar is headed for doom, and only God's kingdom turns out to be a truly "noble cedar" (Ezek. 17:23).

We find yet another lofty cedar tree in Ezekiel 31, a tree with branches so large and long that "all the birds of the air made their nests in its boughs" (Ezek. 31:6). But this tree as well represents the haughty leader of a doomed empire, this time the Egyptian pharaoh, and here too the tree is eventually destroyed.

So we hear echoes of Daniel and Ezekiel in the Parable of the Mustard Seed, but would Jesus really compare the kingdom of God to a couple of ruined pagan empires? Crossan doubts it, but another commentator, Robert Funk, argues that this is precisely the point. Jesus, says Funk, is telling a joke here. Ezekiel uses the image of a towering cedar tree as the symbol of a kingdom; sometimes it's a doomed earthly kingdom and sometimes it's God's everlasting kingdom, but regardless, it's always a tall tree. Jesus' parable, argues Funk, with its lowly mustard bush standing in for the lofty and proud trees in the Old Testament, is really a parody, a send-up of Ezekiel, a burlesque satire of power:

> When the parable of Jesus is set alongside the vision of Ezekiel (17:22–24), the first impression one gains by the juxtaposition is that Jesus has created a light-hearted burlesque of Ezekiel's figure: The noble cedar, which provides a haven for the beasts and birds of the earth, is

> caricatured as a lowly mustard plant! And the first impression is not entirely wide of the mark. At second glance, however, the parable takes on the character of serious satire. Jesus appears to have grasped the final injunction of Ezekiel's oracle radically, "The Lord will bring the high tree low and make the low tree high"![50]

Funk's interpretation has stumbled across a grain of truth, but it is finally overly ornate. We do not have to imagine Jesus' seaside audience, or Mark's readers, being able to step nimbly through the complex metaphorical do-si-do of a "big tree/lowly plant," "pompous nonkingdom/humble real kingdom," "Ezekiel/Jesus" satire to get to the insight that Jesus' vision of God's kingdom is not the same as worldly kings and pharaohs. We shall arrive there soon enough and by a less circuitous route.

Much more likely is that these images—trees as symbols for kingdoms and nesting places for birds and animals as symbols of care and protection—were a part of a scriptural repertoire funding the Parable of the Mustard Seed. In particular, the parable seems to draw upon two parts of this repertoire: Ezekiel 17:22–26 and Psalm 104:10–17.

In Ezekiel 17:24–26, the prophet, who has described the fall of earthly domains, contrasts God's own kingdom to all of these failed empires. Amid the ruins of fallen sovereignties, God decides to act, to create, to plant:

> I myself will take a sprig
> from the lofty top of a cedar;
> I will set it out.
> I will break off a tender one
> from the topmost of its young twigs;
> I myself will plant it
> on a high and lofty mountain.
> Ezek. 17:22

When God plants, the results are different than when Nebuchadnezzar swaggers or pharaoh rages. God's tree produces branches that yield fruit and provide true and lasting care for the creatures of the earth:

> On the mountain height of Israel
> I will plant it,
> in order that it may produce boughs and bear fruit,
> and become a noble cedar.
> Under it every kind of bird will live;
> in the shade of its branches will nest
> winged creatures of every kind.
> Ezek. 17:23

At the heart of the passage is the idea of a God who humbles earthly ambitions and who lifts up the lowly and brings fruitfulness to arid places:

All the trees of the field shall know
  that I am the LORD.
I bring low the high tree,
  I make high the low tree;
I dry up the green tree
  and make the dry tree flourish.
I the LORD have spoken;
  I will accomplish it.
Ezek. 17:24

Psalm 104 employs similar imagery to describe God's creative power and care for creatures. God makes "springs gush forth in the valleys. . . . By the streams the birds of the air have their habitation; they sing among the branches" (Ps. 104:10, 12). As for God's trees, "they are watered abundantly. . . . In them the birds build their nests" (Ps. 104:16–17).

The Parable of the Mustard Seed, then, draws broadly on the repository of Old Testament images of trees growing and birds nesting. In particular, though, it draws on those places that proclaim that when God plants a kingdom, it grows from a tiny sprig into a huge plant full of care and protection for all God's creatures.

In the Old Testament, though, the kingdom of God is a tree. In the parable, it is a shrub (in Matthew's Mustard Seed parable, the seed becomes a shrub, but then turns into a tree; in Luke, it's a tree plain and simple; we will address these other versions of the parable in due course). We know that Mark's parable is clearly referencing the tree-and-birds imagery in the Old Testament, so why, in Mark, does the tall tree become a fat shrub?

There is irony here; Funk has a point. But it's irony with maybe a hint of wry comedy, not burlesque. Mark's parable does not poke fun at Ezekiel's picture of God's kingdom as a noble cedar. Rather, the parable translates that concept into Mark's theology. As we said in the last chapter, when we squint in Mark, we can see that Jesus is a tall tree. He is the Messiah, the strong one of God, the Son of Man, whose power will ultimately rule and whose glory will be all-in-all. But when we relax our vision, funny, it doesn't look that way. The kingdom of God as present in Jesus looks less like a tree and more like a humble mustard shrub, like a man whose ministry meets resistance and who hurtles toward an ignominious death on a cross. Mark joins Zechariah in the conviction that one day we will all sing "Thine Is the Glory," but Mark knows that the only way to get there is first to sing "When I Survey the Wondrous Cross."

When we put these images together, the Jesus whose tall-tree power is hidden in humility, we perceive the heart of this parable. "With what can we compare the kingdom of God?" Jesus asks. In contrast to expectations, God's kingdom as present in Jesus is impressive, not for its towering height or imposing power as the world defines power, but for its spreading breadth and ample branches, for its healing of the distressed, its cleansing of lepers, and its feeding of multitudes. The kingdom is not about military muscle, economic supremacy, or political manipulation, not about tall steeples, mushrooming membership rolls, or jaw-dropping church budgets. It displays its divine power by enlarging hospitality and care; the event of the kingdom creates places where the low are brought high, where the drought-plagued land is irrigated by mercy, and where all of the birds of heaven and all of the children of God can find restful shade and place to dwell.

As is the case with all of Jesus' parables, the Parable of the Mustard Seed has both present and future implications. Ultimately the parable envisions a time when the kingdom will extend its branches of welcome wide and the whole of creation will be gathered into the motherly embrace of God. But the parable also fastens our gaze on places and moments in the present where God's kingdom is breaking in.

On Hand for the Kingdom

As I was writing about this parable and pondering where in everyday life it trains our vision to see the advent of the kingdom, I took a short break to pick up a few things at the grocery store. In the produce section, I ran across a friend and colleague in ministry. My friend is not the pastor of a traditional church but instead runs a multifaceted, social service ministry out of an old gas station in the center of our town. He and volunteers converted the building into a coffee shop and lunchtime café, where they serve lunch daily at nearly giveaway prices in order to serve a low-income clientele. Customers who cannot pay are fed at no charge. A hand-lettered sign at the counter reads: "We basically want to feed people so we are asking folks to pay what they want to. Our base cost is $8 per meal. If you've got it, great. If not, no worries. If you've got a little more and want to help us feed those who don't have it, then so much the better." The cooks, servers, and other staff are all drawn from those in town experiencing homelessness or recovering from addiction. They are learning on the job and when the inevitable mistakes and stumbles happen, the staff are not scolded or fired but gently taught, the goal being the development of lasting work skills.

It took a moment for my friend and me to recognize each other in the grocery aisle, since this was in the middle of the COVID-19 health crisis and both of us were wearing masks. He was talking with a woman, also masked, whom I did not know, and my friend introduced her to me.

I asked him how the café had been doing during the health crisis, and he shook his head. "The first month we lost 75 percent of our business. As you know, we operate on a shoestring anyway, and common sense would have dictated that we close the doors until this is over. But this is the worst time to stop feeding the hungry, so we decided to double down. In addition to lunch, we started serving a full dinner on a 'pay-what-you-can, pay-if-you-can' basis."

"How did you fund this?" I asked.

"Well, we didn't have the funds at all to support this, but folks needed the food, and we just did it on faith. People around town started hearing about it. Lots of them were hurting, too, but a number of folks came in the café and signed over their coronavirus government stimulus checks so that we could feed the hungry. It wasn't a lot of money, but we made it work. Last month we fed 430 people."

"My husband and I help out at the café some," the woman chimed in, "but mostly we're really busy with our kids. We've raised twenty children."

I showed my surprise. "Twenty children! You're foster parents?"

"No," she replied. "We adopted the kids. My husband's retired military. We have his pension and lots of free time, and we just felt that God wanted us to take into our home and our family kids that nobody else would have. And that's what we've done. Twenty so far."

There I was, standing beside the potatoes and the onions in the Food Lion and watching that mustard plant grow and grow and the branches reach out farther and farther. According to Jesus, the kingdom doesn't look all that impressive at first, sort of like the smallest of seeds—an abandoned gas station or a couple on a military pension—but when all is said and done, it grows into a most welcoming plant that gathers into its embrace of care, love, and protection all of God's precious creatures.

The Parables in Action

With the Parable of the Mustard Seed, the written account of Jesus' seaside sermon comes to an end, but Mark is eager to let his readers know that the sermon kept going, and the parables kept coming: "With many such parables he spoke the word to them, as they were able to hear it; he did not speak to them except in parables, but he explained everything in private to his disciples" (Mark 4:33–34).

But then, strangely, Jesus' parabolic voice in Mark grows silent. Except for one short, proverb-like statement about defilement, which Mark calls a parable (7:14–23), we go eight chapters before Jesus speaks again in parables. However, it is not as though the parables have ceased. Instead they become embodied in the action of Jesus as he moves through Galilee, sowing the seed of the kingdom on the often-unpromising ground, confident of two conflicting certainties: his death and the coming abundant harvest. Jesus *is* the parable, and consequently he is still teaching "many things in parables." Just watch him.

THE PARABLE OF THE WICKED TENANTS (MARK 12:1–12)

After many chapters with no spoken parables, Mark abruptly announces, "Then he began to speak to them in parables" (12:1). Jesus has returned, after a long silence, to parabolic speech. Mark says that Jesus spoke "parables," plural, but here he records only one: the Parable of the Wicked Tenants. At this point in the narrative, Jesus has arrived in Jerusalem, and the cross, which back in Galilee was only a tiny dot on the horizon, now looms large and overshadows the whole narrative. The ministry of Jesus reached its apparent zenith at Caesarea Philippi with Peter's confession (8:27–30) and on the high mountain with Jesus' transfiguration (9:2–8); now we are on the long, downhill road to Golgotha. So it is fitting that Jesus here tells a parable about the murder of a beloved son.

Jesus speaks this parable in the temple, and the congregation that hears him includes an impressive array of religious leaders: the chief priests, the scribes, and the elders. In the previous passage (11:27–33), we were told that Jesus was simply walking around the temple grounds when these authorities jumped all over him, confronting him about his authority for doing what he was doing. A little verbal swordplay ensued, and Jesus prevailed—at least temporarily (11:29–33). But noses are out of joint, and for the whole time that Jesus is in the temple—that is to say, for Mark 11:27–12:44—the air is thick with tension and controversy.

The disputes in the temple are reminiscent of those in the early days of Jesus' ministry, when he was attacked by religious leaders (2:1–3:6). But back in Galilee the religious leaders were offended by what Jesus *did.* Here in the temple they are also offended by what he *said,*[51] and that offense continues with this parable.

Déjà Vu All Over Again

The parable begins with the description of a very busy man—he "planted a vineyard, put a fence around it, dug a pit for the wine press, and built a watchtower; then he leased it to tenants and went to another country" (12:1).

Planting, putting, digging, building, leasing, departing: the string of verbs leaves us breathless and exhausted.

What are we supposed to think of this man? He is industrious, that's for sure, and he is invested in the well-being of this vineyard. He works hard to see that the vineyard is amply equipped and, with that fence and watchtower, well protected. He also rings a memory bell. We have heard about this man before and seen him in action, in the Old Testament; he is the "beloved" of whom the prophet sings in Isaiah 5, and when we hear and see him anew in Mark, as Yogi Berra once said, "It's déjà vu all over again." Here is how Isaiah describes his beloved:

> Let me sing for my beloved
> my love-song concerning his vineyard:
> My beloved had a vineyard
> on a very fertile hill.
> He dug it and cleared it of stones,
> and planted it with choice vines;
> he built a watchtower in the midst of it,
> and hewed out a wine vat in it.
> Isa. 5:1–2

Planting, digging, building; a vineyard, a wine pit, a watchtower: it's all there, the same elements we find in the parable. The only thing missing is the erection of the fence, but if we read Isaiah 5 in the Septuagint, which would have been Mark's source, there is the fence, as advertised.

Now, if one text or one performance incorporates an earlier text or performance, it could be merely an allusion. If you ask a young woman how her first semester went at Vassar, and she replies, "It was the best of times, it was the worst of times," you don't need to consult Dickens's *A Tale of Two Cities* to know what she means. She is borrowing from Dickens, to be sure, but what she means to say about her college experience is fully contained in her words. But if the reader *needs* the earlier text to make sense out of the present one, indeed, if the aim of the text is to send the reader to a place outside where the full meaning is located, we are in a different literary environment. In the case of our parable, specifically we are in the world of allegory. Pieces of the parable correspond to bits outside of the parable, and we cannot understand what is happening inside the parable without possessing the outside key.

In this case, it's doubly complex, because this allegorical parable is linked to a song in Isaiah that is itself an allegory. One allegory (our parable) throws us into another allegory (Isaiah's love song). This could turn out to be a hall of mirrors, but fortunately Isaiah deciphers his allegory. He gives the reader the interpretive key. The beloved one, Isaiah tells us, is the Lord of hosts, and the vineyard is the people of Israel and Judah. The Lord expected the vineyard to yield grapes, that is, justice and righteousness, but instead the crop was wild grapes, that is, bloodshed and the cry of oppression (Isa. 5:7). When we line the parable in Mark 12 up to Isaiah 5, the tumblers fall into place. We discern that in Mark also the vineyard owner is a symbol for God, the vineyard a symbol for the people of God, and the tenants a symbol for those charged to tend and lead God's people. There's more to come, but already we are aware that we are deep into allegorical territory.

Allegory Allergy

But as soon as we say that this parable is an allegory, alarms go off all over the building.

As we said in chapter 1, some interpreters object to the very idea that Jesus had allegory in his repertoire and deny that any of Jesus' parables, including this one, could be allegories. Desperate to escape the world of allegory, they speculate that either this parable is a wholesale creation of the early church or that, if it is an authentic parable of Jesus, when Jesus originally told it, it was a straightforward story and not an allegory. As a smattering of evidence, they point to a somewhat less-allegorical version of the parable found in the *Gospel of Thomas* and wonder if Jesus' original parable was closer to this version: [Jesus] said,

> A usurer owned a vineyard. He gave it to some farmers so that they would work it and he might receive its fruit from them. He sent his servant so that the farmers might give him the fruit of the vineyard. They seized his servant, beat him, and almost killed him. The servant went back and told his master.
>
> His master said: "Perhaps they did not recognize him." He sent another servant, and the farmers beat that other one as well. Then the master sent his son and said: "Perhaps they will show respect for my son." But those farmers, since they knew that he was the heir of the vineyard, seized him and killed him.

Other interpreters don't want this parable to be an allegory because of how the parable, taken as allegory, has been interpreted by some Christians, namely, as expressing anti-Jewish supersessionism. This stained legacy goes back at least to the fourth century and to John Chrysostom, who preached that the end of the parable, where the tenants are destroyed and the vineyard is given to others, signifies "the calling of the Gentiles [and] the casting out of the Jews."[52]

Still others resist allegory because they see Jesus as essentially a social critic who spoke in direct prose about economic and political circumstances. Thus they understand this parable as embodying a realistic description of the social situation of tenants and landowners in ancient Palestine. For example, Luise Schottroff, in conversation with William Herzog, sets this parable into the sociological context of first-century Galilean tenant–absentee landlord relations. The tenants in the parable, she claims, are the victims of economic exploitation by the absentee landlord and who, as a consequence, become violent against the landlord's slaves "who are themselves already the victims of economic and physical violence."[53] Taken this way, what we have is a graphic and tragic story from Jesus of economically abused tenant farmers who, perhaps understandably but foolishly, express their rage by mauling and murdering the servants of their powerful Roman landlords and, as a result, get themselves killed in retaliation. Why Jesus would tell such a story or why the early church would remember it as a part of its sacred memory is anybody's guess.

The Parable of the Wicked Tenants that we have before us in Mark is clearly an allegory, a theological allegory at that, and should be interpreted allegorically. While this will involve some puzzle-solving, the parable is by no means impenetrable. There are clues all over the ground. As we have seen, the parable begins by importing, almost in its entirety, a scene from Isaiah 5, complete with its array of allegorical associations. A man (representing God) works tirelessly and carefully to prepare a vineyard (Israel and Judah, the people of God). The vineyard owner leases the vineyard to tenants (the leaders of the people) and goes to another country. The point is not to try to name this other country—Rome? heaven?—but to recognize that the owner is far away. The distance emphasizes that the tenants are on their own and have been entrusted with care of the vineyard. Similarly, in Mark 13:34 we will encounter another parabolic "man" who goes away and "puts his slaves in charge." By contrast, the Parable of the Laborers in the Vineyard in Matthew 20:1–16 features a vineyard owner who does not go far away but who is, rather, a hands-on, very present supervisor of the vineyard.

Trouble in the Vineyard

In due course, the harvest season arrives in the vineyard (12:2)—the Greek is *tō kairō* (τῷ καιρῷ), "at the right time"—and the owner sends a slave to collect a portion of the crop (12:2–3). Is this, as interpreters such as Schottroff and Herzog argue,[54] the all-too-common story of an elite but distant landowner sending an enforcer to the vineyard to extract outrageously greedy proceeds? Markan scholar Joel Marcus suggests just the opposite. He observes that the description of the owner's portion of the produce in Greek ("his share of the proceeds of the vineyard," NRSV) involves a grammatical construction (partitive genitive) that, far from implying ruthless exploitation, actually "emphasizes the kindness of the vineyard owner: he does not take all of the fruits, or even most of them, only some."[55]

The tenants seize this slave, beat him, and send him away empty-handed. Another slave is sent, and this one is beaten over the head and insulted. Yet another slave is sent, and this time the violence becomes murderous. The slave is killed. Many other slaves are sent, and all of them are either beaten or murdered (12:2–5).

In Isaiah, the vineyard produces the wrong crop. God, as the owner of the vineyard, wants grapes of righteousness but instead gets wild grapes of oppression. In the parable, however, the nature of the crop is not the issue, but instead the refusal of the tenants to give the owner a share. The crop is not bad; it is the spirit of the tenants that is evil, and the relationship with the vineyard owner that is broken. The series of slaves who arrive on the scene only to be rejected, brutalized, and killed undoubtedly represents the sequence of prophets sent to call God's people to justice, obedience, and fidelity. Some have speculated that the slave who was "beat over the head and insulted" (12:4) represents John the Baptist, who was beheaded (6:14–29), but probably the main thrust of this detail in the parable is to reflect an ever-increasing level of violence against God's messengers.

Finally, the owner is down to one remaining messenger, this time "a beloved son," who the owner is sure will earn the respect of the tenants (12:6). "Beloved son" is an unmistakable christological reference, and the arrival in the vineyard of this beloved son inspires not respect but a sinister plot on the part of the tenants. "This is the heir," the tenants mutter to one another. "Come, let us kill him, and the inheritance will be ours" (12:7). And that is precisely what they do, throwing his body out of the vineyard.

The parable comes to a close with a dramatic question: "What then will the owner of the vineyard do?" (Mark 12:9). In Isaiah, what the vineyard owner did was to destroy the vineyard itself (Isa. 5:5–6), but in the parable it is the tenants who are destroyed, and the vineyard is given to others (Mark 12:9). Jesus then quotes Psalm 118:22–23, a favorite text of the early church to describe how Jesus, rejected by his own people, nevertheless was glorified by God:

> The stone that the builders rejected
> has become the cornerstone;
> this was the Lord's doing,
> and it is amazing in our eyes.
> Mark 12:10–11

When we decipher all of the allegorical terms in this parable, we find that the parable throws us, as allegories are wont to do, into another text outside of the parable, and this text, as it turns out, is not just Isaiah 5 but also the

Gospel of Mark itself. This parable is an allegory of the story of Jesus, the story that the whole of Mark's Gospel tells. Jesus is the "beloved son" sent to the vineyard, and we will watch as Jesus, like the son in the parable, is seized, humiliated, and killed. Already in Mark, Jesus has predicted his death three times (8:31; 9:31; and 10:32–34), and here in 12:1–11, Mark has Jesus narrate an allegorical tale of his own death.

It is quite likely that this parable, as Mark records it, did not originate with Jesus but is mainly an early church sermon on the meaning of Jesus' death. But it is both poignant and powerful when Jesus, in the middle of the narrative, preaches this sermon himself. For Mark's church, this parable tells the long story of how God's prophets have been repeatedly rejected by those responsible for God's vineyard. Then Jesus, who was a prophet but more than a prophet—a "beloved son"—was likewise rejected by the leaders of his own people. But this rejection could not overcome God's will for the vineyard or for the son. The rejected one has been established by God as the cornerstone, and the vineyard has been turned over to new tenants.

On Hand for the Kingdom

The main referent, as we have seen, of the allegorical Parable of the Wicked Tenants is the story of Jesus itself. The story told in Mark is the narrative of God's coming to humanity in Jesus the Messiah, and it is in the telling, retelling, and trusting of this story that we continue to experience the kingdom.

Even though the parable primarily points to the meaning of the life and work of Jesus as depicted in Mark, it also goes beyond these strict christological bounds to reveal the ancient and repeated pattern of God's call and humanity's resistance. God the creator loves the vineyard and desires to be in covenant relationship with the people who live in it. God continually raises up prophets, from Nathan, who called King David to responsibility, to Martin Luther King Jr., and beyond. The earth is stained with their blood, and this parable is a narrative version of what Jesus says in Matthew: "Jerusalem, Jerusalem, the city that kills the prophets and stones those who are sent to it! How often have I desired to gather your children together as a hen gathers her brood under her wings, and you were not willing! See, your house is left to you, desolate. For I tell you, you will not see me again until you say, 'Blessed is the one who comes in the name of the Lord'" (Matt. 23:37–39). The "one who comes in the name of the Lord" is, of course, Jesus, the beloved son. As the risen Christ, he keeps coming to humanity, calling the world to life and hope. Despite the no of humanity, God keeps on saying yes, refusing to abandon the vineyard and those who live in it.

In Saul Bellow's novel *Mr. Sammler's Planet,* Elya Gruner, the dear friend of the book's protagonist, Artur Sammler, has died. Sammler, a scholar and Holocaust survivor who quests for wisdom, views the lifeless body of Elya. As he looks at his dead friend, he remembers Elya's many deeds of kindness and generosity ("much kinder than at my best I have ever been or could ever be"). In an insane world torn apart by evil and violence, Elya Gruner's life was well lived, a life of goodness and mercy, a life even of joy. Standing beside his now-dead friend, Sammler speaks—speaks to Elya, to God, to whoever will listen—part eulogy, part prayer. He asks God to remember Elya's soul, because

> He was aware that he must meet—and he did meet—through all the confusion and the degraded clowning of this life through which we are speeding—he did meet the terms of his contract. The terms which, in his inmost heart, each man knows. As I know mine. As all know. For that is the truth of it—that we all know, God, that we know, that we know, we know, we know.[56]

All of us as human beings, as tenants of God's vineyard, know in our inmost hearts the humanity and goodness required of us. And yet, and yet . . .

Shimmering beneath the specific elements of the allegory, therefore, is a kingdom drama that continues in every time and every place. The turning point of this drama is when the tenants of the vineyard mutter to one another: "This is the heir; come, let us kill him, and the inheritance will be ours" (Mark 12:7). This is the oldest story in human history, as old as Adam and Eve hiding from God in the first garden, and it is the newest story, the latest breaking news, as new as the flattened secularity of the West and the dreamy and empty, bourgeois spirituality of middle America, the endless quest to banish God, the living God, the demanding God, from the vineyard.

God keeps coming to us, the Beloved Son keeps adventing into our lives, coming in love and yearning; like the tenants in the parable, we are under the illusion that if we can only banish God, then the vineyard, the inheritance, will be ours. We can live as we please. No troubling thoughts about carrying a cross, or welcoming the stranger, or embracing the outcast. If there is no owner and no Beloved Son, then we are free to make our own choices and decisions and to live as the book of Judges says, "In those days there was no king in Israel; all the people did what was right in their own eyes" (Judg. 21:25).

Elya Gruner knew that he lived his life before God and that the quality of his life was a response to God's presence. By contrast, philosopher Michael Ruse and biologist Edward O. Wilson claim, "The basis of ethics does not lie in God's will. . . . Ethics as we understand it is an illusion fobbed off on us by our genes to get us to cooperate. . . . The way our biology enforces its ends is by making us think there is an objective higher code to which we are all subject."[57] In terms of sociobiology, what they claim makes an interesting argument.

Theologically, however, we must not be mistaken. Thinking that the call to "love one another" is not the voice of God, but merely our old genes acting up and fobbing off an illusion in an attempt to imagine a godless world, is yet another effort to kill the heir so that the vineyard will be ours. Ethically, once we have cast God out of the vineyard, there is no more Beloved Son, no more inconvenient will of God pressing in and demanding a share of the produce. As another biologist, Richard Dawkins, avers in his book *The God Delusion*, "I think God is very improbable, and I live my life on the assumption that he is not there."[58] Dawkins goes on to say that imagining a God, like the God who enters the vineyard and calls us to ethical responsibility, is "infantile": "There is something infantile in the presumption that somebody else has a responsibility to give your life meaning and point. . . . The truly adult view, by contrast, is that our life is as meaningful, as full and as wonderful as we choose to make it."[59]

To the contrary, in Christianity, as Terry Eagleton has said,

> [It] is our dependence on God that allows us to be self-determining, as it is our dependence on language or history or culture which allows us to come into our own as persons. God for Thomas Aquinas is the power that allows us to be ourselves, rather as the love of our parents allows us to be ourselves. We can fantasize like Oedipal children that we would be more free by breaking loose from the sources of our life, but this is self-deception. Instead our parents have to find a way of nourishing us which also contains the potential to let us go, so that their love can become the ground of our independence rather than the impediment to it.[60]

The good news of the parable is that all attempts to establish a godless world—whether these attempts be the crucifixion of the Beloved Son or the smug sneers of the "new atheists"—will ultimately fail. God will not abandon the vineyard, and the rejected Beloved Son will become raised up as the cornerstone of all of life.

In the parable, the owner gives the vineyard to "others," but the parable does not say who those others might be. The suggestion that the others are Gentiles, replacing Jews, is unjustified, despite its persistence in the tradition. The point of the parable's ending is that God will not abandon the vineyard but will always supply new tenants who will care for the vineyard and for God's people. This makes the parable similar to the prophecy against the "shepherds of Israel" in Ezekiel 34, where God denounces the leaders for their neglect of the people and promises to take the sheep away from them. "I myself will search for my sheep and will seek them out," God says (Ezek. 34:11). In the economy of the parable, being given the vineyard is not an indulgence but a responsibility to care well for God's people. The leaders who heard this parable spoken by Jesus recognized themselves in the story and resented what they heard so much they wanted to shout, "Lock him up!" But the crowd had heard the parable too, and sensed the good news at its core. So, fearing public disapproval, the leaders slinked away for the time being. They will, of course, be back.

In the end then, the Parable of the Wicked Tenants is a parable about the love of God and the failure of the worst instincts in humanity to overthrow that love. God prepares the vineyard with loving care and desires to share a relationship with those in the vineyard, even to the point of coming to the dangerous vineyard as a "beloved son." Even when human arrogance and greed rise up against God in murderous rage, God's love prevails. The vineyard is restored, new and responsive tenants provided, and the murdered and rejected son is established as the cornerstone of the redeemed community. "This was the Lord's doing, and it is amazing in our eyes" (Mark 12:11).

In his poem "At the Smithville Methodist Church,"[61] Stephen Dunn talks about a time when he and his wife decided to allow their young daughter to go to a week of vacation Bible school at the local Methodist church. Not believing people themselves, they were not too concerned that their daughter would be contaminated by faith. He and his wife had not been believers for a long time, Dunn says, and they considered Jesus "sufficiently dead, that our children would think of him like Lincoln or Thomas Jefferson."

But at the church their daughter heard the stories about Jesus, and the parents realized that they did not have a comparably good story to tell. "Evolution is magical but devoid of heroes. You can't say to your child 'Evolution loves you.'" On parents' night the children proudly displayed the arts and crafts they had done during the week. Driving home, their daughter was singing all the songs she had learned, every now and then standing up in the back seat of the car as she sang about the love of Jesus.

"The stone that the builders rejected has become the cornerstone; this was the Lord's doing, and it is amazing in our eyes."

THE PARABLE OF THE DOORKEEPER (MARK 13:32–37)

This is the last full parable in the Gospel of Mark, but it hardly looks like a full parable at all. The parable proper is only one verse long, and as a story it is quite incomplete. It just gets started when it ends abruptly with everything still hanging in suspense: "It is like a man going on a journey, when he leaves home and puts his slaves in charge, each with his work, and commands the doorkeeper to be on the watch" (13:34). At first, this brief parabolic statement seems like a simple repetition, in different imagery, of the "keep watch" lesson of the fig tree a few verses earlier: "From the fig tree learn its lesson: as soon as its branch becomes tender and puts forth its leaves, you know that summer is near. So also, when you see these things taking place, you know that he is near, at the very gates" (13:28–29). But, the doorkeeper, unlike the fig tree image, seems incomplete, prompting the curious hearer to ask, "What happened next?"—which may, in fact, be the very point of this parable.

It is significant that this parable is the culmination of a chapter-long discourse from Jesus to his disciples regarding the eschaton, the end of all things. Here is how Mark describes how that discourse gets going. Jesus engages in a series of disputes in the temple in which Jesus gets the best of the scribes and other religious leaders. A crowd is standing around, hearing these clashes, delighted that these religious bigwigs have at last met their match. Jesus then turns to address the crowd, and what he says throws even more shade on their religious leaders, the scribes in particular. "Beware of these guys," Jesus says. "They love their fancy vestments, having people bow to them in the marketplace, and occupying the VIP seats in the synagogues and at banquets. But the truth is they are frauds and hypocrites, and they take advantage of the most vulnerable among us. They devour widows' houses."

"They devour widows' houses" is a phrase to remember as we witness what unfolds next. Jesus sits down opposite the temple treasury, and Mark describes a scene that serves as many a preacher's favorite stewardship text: the story of the poor widow (12:32–37). Jesus watches as a parade of rich folk drop big offerings into the box. Then a poor widow appears to make her offering, which is only one penny. Then Jesus calls his disciples and gives them an analysis of what just happened. "That widow," he says, "has given the greatest contribution of them all. Those rich folk were basically tipping God out of their largesse, but she put everything she had into the treasury, her whole house, everything she had to live on."

What are the disciples supposed to discern here? The difference between fake sacrifice and the real thing? Yes, but they are also to perceive how the temple had become a theater of oppression, applauding the faux sacrifices of the rich while squeezing the life's blood out of that barely noticed widow. Do the disciples get it? Not in Mark; they never fully do. Indeed, to underscore the disciples' oblivion, Mark tells us that as they leave the temple, one of the disciples glances back and exclaims, "Wow, what a place! Large stones! Big buildings! How about that temple!"

In some of the best news in Mark's Gospel, Jesus then responds, "Do you see these great buildings? Not one stone will be left here upon another. All will be thrown down" (13:2). This is what happens to even the greatest of religious institutions—temples and churches alike—when they begin to flatter the rich and to suck the blood out of the poor and widows (now *that* would make a terrific stewardship sermon!).

Then Jesus, who has just sat "opposite" the temple treasury, goes to the Mount of Olives and sits "opposite" the whole temple (13:3). The disciples, their heads no doubt still reeling from the news that the seemingly impregnable temple will be destroyed, ask Jesus, "Tell us, when will this be?" (13:4a). If the temple is going to be knocked down, they want to know when this will happen. Jesus, however, has a bigger event in mind, and he answers the disciples with a long discourse on the end of the whole world and the coming of the day of the Son of Man.

Biblical scholar George B. Caird pondered the disjuncture here. Why, he wondered, does Mark have Jesus answer the disciples' question about the end of the temple with a discussion of the end of the world? The disciples ask when the temple will come down, but Jesus ups the ante and describes a time when the whole shebang will come down, the sun, the moon, the stars, all of it (13:24–25). Is Mark a fool? Caird wondered. Does Mark not realize that Jesus answers a question he wasn't asked? No, said Caird. Mark's readers already know that the temple was in fact knocked down, destroyed in 70 CE. That's history for them. Mark is asking his readers to see in that catastrophe an intimation of the end of all things and the triumph of the Son of Man.[62] Like the other Gospel writers, Mark believed that the world would one day come to a literal end, but, again like the other Gospel writers, Mark "used end-of-the-world language metaphorically to refer to that which they well know was not the end of the world,"[63] like the destruction of the temple.

This is an important theological insight. The eschaton, the end of the world, the advent of the kingdom of God, is both an ultimate event and a proximate one. It happens at the end of time and also in the middle of time. Like Vesuvius, there are tremors and earthquakes rattling through the land before the final catastrophic eruption. Ultimately, "the powers in the heavens will be shaken," and the Son of Man will come in ultimate glory and victory (13:25–26). In the meantime, signals and signs of that Great Day are all around us.

As Jesus ramps up from the destruction of the temple to the ultimate arrival of the kingdom of God, the disciples' question has ramped up as well. "When?" has become even larger and more urgent. But Jesus warns, "[A]bout that day or hour no one knows. . . . Beware, keep alert, for you do not know when the time will come" (13:32–33). Then he tells the Parable of the Doorkeeper. The coming day of the Son of Man, Jesus says, is like this: it is like a man who is going on a journey who, when he leaves, puts his slaves in charge of his house, each with assigned duties, and installs a doorkeeper at the door to await the man's return. On his way out, the man turns to this doorkeeper and says, "Be on the watch."

That's it. As we have noted, that is the way the parable proper ends. We who hear this parable are left standing watch with the doorkeeper, peering into the darkness of an unknown future, awaiting the return of the master, awaiting the irruption of the kingdom.

Then something odd happens. Jesus proceeds to apply the parable, to interpret it, just as he interpreted the Parable of the Sower earlier; but this time, as he applies the parable, Jesus actually extends the parable, adds to the plot of the story. The hearers had been left in suspense. The master was gone on a journey, the slaves were hard at work in the house, and the doorkeeper was gazing through the window keeping alert watch. What's going to happen next? Well, the master will eventually return, says Jesus, but God only knows when. It could happen at any moment, so the doorkeeper had best not relax vigilance. "Therefore keep awake," Jesus says, "for you do not know when the master of the house will come, in the evening, or at midnight, or at cockcrow, or at dawn, or else he may find you asleep when he comes suddenly" (13:35–36).

So far, the parable has given us a picture of the faithful community, a community that has two main assignments: to do the work of the master and to watch for the master's return. The two belong together. If the church does not expect God's advent in Christ, then the household chores become mere busy work. If the church stays up all night watching for Jesus but neglects the work of the master, it forfeits its mission.

When Charles Dickens died of a stroke in 1870, he was in the middle of working on a crime novel, *The Mystery of Edwin Drood.* In the novel Edwin Drood, a young man engaged to be married, is mysteriously murdered, but Dickens died midnovel, before revealing the identity of the murderer. Who killed Edwin Drood? It was anyone's guess. So, when the novel was adapted as a Broadway play, it was designed as an interactive play where the audience got to decide at each performance the guilty party. Late in the play, the action would be halted and the audience would be asked to vote on which character they thought had committed the crime. The play had several possible endings, and the actual ending of the play each night depended upon the choice made by the audience.

The Parable of the Doorkeeper, like *The Mystery of Edwin Drood*, has several possible endings. The master, we are told, might return "in the evening." Or he might return "at midnight." Then again, he might return in the waning hours of the night, "at cockcrow." Or come to think of it, the master might delay until sunrise, "at dawn" (13:35). One parable, multiple times, multiple endings.

The time designations—evening, midnight, cockcrow, dawn—are the four watches in the night, the time between 6:00 p.m. and 6:00 a.m., as Romans measured them (Jews generally divided the night into three watches).[64] So back to the disciple's original question: When? Evening? Midnight? Cockcrow? Dawn? Jesus does not answer; the parable is mute. Slowly the answer forms in the hearer's mind and conscience: any of the above and all of the above. The kingdom, like the returning master, comes "suddenly" (13:36), and we, like the doorkeeper, are to "keep awake" (13:35). The worst thing is to be asleep when the master returns, to miss the advent of the kingdom. This means not only standing on tiptoe looking over the horizon of history for the coming of the Son of Man, but also being alert to the comings of the kingdom that occur with every passing hour, every tick of the clock—at evening and at midnight and at cockcrow and at dawn.

As soon as this parable ends, Mark transitions to the story of Jesus' passion, and evening, late night, cockcrow, and morning become important punctuation marks in this story. One of the first episodes recorded is that of the Last Supper. This story begins—and we should stay alert here—"in the evening, he came with the twelve" (14:17). At the supper, it is the betrayer who is "asleep" to the arrival of the kingdom. Later that night, Jesus went to Gethsemane to pray. This time, it was all of the disciples who fell asleep. "Could you not keep awake one hour?" Jesus asked (14:37). He goes to pray again, and again the disciples fell asleep. "Are you still sleeping . . . ? Enough! The hour has come" (14:41). Jesus is arrested and taken to the high priest. Now it is Peter's turn to be comatose and to miss the kingdom. Warming himself at a fire outside, Peter was confronted by one of the servant girls of the high priest. "You also were with Jesus," she said, and Peter denied any knowledge of Jesus. "Then the cock crowed," Mark announces, yet another watch in the night, yet another stroke of the clock. Finally, the chief priests hand Jesus over to Pilate, who in turn hands Jesus over to the executioners. The whole world has fallen asleep as the kingdom advents before them. When did this happen? "As soon as it was morning," Mark says (15:1).[65]

Evening, midnight, cockcrow, morning—all through the passion the kingdom arrived, the life of God was made present and visible, and all of the doorkeepers were asleep. The warning is for us all. "And what I say to you," Jesus said, "I say to all; Keep awake" (13:37).

Alfred Nobel was a nineteenth-century inventor whose greatest engineering achievements were in the area of munitions and the weapons of war. He made a fortune from his inventions, which included not only dynamite but also a blasting cap that harnessed the destructive power of nitroglycerin. When his brother Ludwig died in France, the death was reported in the French press, but the news accounts confused the brothers and mistakenly declared that it was Alfred who had died. Alfred Nobel had the unsettling experience of opening the morning papers and reading his own obituary. One paper featured the headline "*Le marchand de la mort est mort*" ("The merchant of death is dead"). Nobel read what the world thought of him: not as a brilliant inventor but as "the dynamite king," as "the merchant of death" who has greedily accumulated wealth from the horrors of war.

In terms of our parable, Nobel had been morally and spiritually asleep, numb to the fact that his legacy was one of bloodshed and destruction. But also, in terms of our parable, reading his own obituary served as a wake-up call. It was as if the Spirit had spoken to him, saying, "Are you still sleeping? Enough! The hour has come." Nobel changed his will, devoting his fortune to the establishment of the world's most significant award for peace.[66]

5

Matthew's Parables

Background

Wisdom shouts in the street;
  in the public square she raises her voice.
Above the noisy crowd, she calls out.
  At the entrances of the city gates, she has her say:
"How long will you clueless people
  love your naïveté?"

—Proverbs 1:20–22 CEB

"Is that you, fool?"
—Russian novelist Mikhail Saltykov-Shchedrin,
when he felt death approaching

Matthew's Gospel is a magnificent mansion, set on a hill with a breathtaking view, but disconcertingly the mansion comes equipped with a dungeon. It's difficult to sit on the sofa upstairs in Matthew's great house, sipping tea, eating sweetmeats, and discussing meekness, mercy, purity of heart, and peacemaking (Matt. 5:5–9) when we can hear rising from the basement weeping and gnashing of teeth (25:30), the groans of the tortured (18:34), and the shrieks of those being cut into pieces (24:51). Especially in Matthew's parables, unfortunate wretches meet miserable fates, being dismembered, cast into outer darkness, or tossed into a fiery furnace. Compared to the urgent Jesus of Mark, the inclusive Jesus of Luke, and the comforting Jesus of John, Matthew's Jesus can sometimes come across to uninitiated readers as like a vindictive assistant principal at a hellish high school for delinquents, full of rage and bloodthirsty retribution.

Why the tough talk? Understanding Matthew's rough language, rather than turning away from it, is actually a crucial task for interpreters, especially interpreters of the parables. We cannot appreciate Matthew's broad theological vision unless we make sense of the dark places in his vocabulary and worldview. As strange as it may seem, Matthew's tough language is rooted in a confidence in God's justice and—dare we say it?—in the joy of God's promised future. What sounds at first so ominous and threatening, even repulsive, turns out, counterintuitively, to be very good news indeed.

This will not be an easy case to make, and exploring it will require a long walk up a steep ramp. But it is a trip worth taking.

WHAT IS MATTHEW AFTER?

The place to begin this journey is not with the nightmares found in some of Matthew's parables—we will eventually get to that—but with Matthew's overall goal in his Gospel. What is Matthew basically after? The reader does not have to wait long to find out. A good clue to Matthew's overarching vision comes in the very first story he tells, about the day a good man named Joseph got the unsettling news that his fiancée, Mary, was pregnant, and not by him (1:18–25).

Matthew describes Joseph as "a righteous man," which is not a throwaway line. It is more than a mere gratuitous nod to the fact that Joseph was a nice guy. He was, Matthew is saying, a *tzaddik*,[1] a truly righteous man in regard to the Torah, everything that Judaism seeks to form in a human being, a son of the commandments, one who so embodied the holy law as to shine in virtue before all who saw him.

In Chaim Potok's novel *The Chosen*, a teenaged boy named Reuven Malter, the son of a forward-thinking Brooklyn rabbi, becomes friends with Danny Saunders, the son of an ultraorthodox Hasidic rabbi. Danny's father, a silent and somewhat mysterious man, is considered by his community to be a *tzaddik*. One day, the two friends find themselves in Rabbi Saunders's study at the synagogue, and Reuven tells his friend's father that he intends to study to become a rabbi. Rabbi Saunders is silent for a while. He had once hoped that his own son, Danny, would become a rabbi and succeed him at the synagogue, but he has recently discovered that Danny secretly desires to become a psychologist instead. Now it is Danny's friend, Reuven, and not his own son, who has announced his intention to enter the rabbinate. Finally, Rabbi Saunders responds to Reuven, sharing some wisdom from his own life, wisdom that he says Reuven will not understand until he is much older. He tells Reuven how it happened that he became a *tzaddik*. He says that when he was very young, his father would wake him up in the middle of the night to tell him stories of the sufferings of the Jewish people. These stories would make his son cry. He goes on to tell Reuven that once his father took him to a hospital to witness firsthand the suffering of the sick, the poor, and the beggars. He said that his father rarely spoke in words, only with silence, teaching his son to look within, to find inner strength.

He goes on to tell Reuven that his father told him later, when he got to be old enough to understand, that a *tzaddik* must understand pain and suffering and must himself be ready to suffer for others. "He must take their pain from them and carry it on his own shoulders," his father said. "He must grow old before his years. He must cry, in his heart he must always cry. Even when he dances and sings, he must cry for the sufferings of his people."[2]

After describing how his own father formed him to be a *tzaddik*, Rabbi Saunders reveals to the two friends that he knows his son's secret; he knows that Danny desires to be a psychologist and not a rabbi. Rabbi Saunders is disappointed, but he has made a kind of peace with his son's desire. "Let my Daniel become a psychologist," the rabbi says. "All his life he will be a *tzaddik*. He will be a *tzaddik* for the world. And the world needs a *tzaddik*."[3]

Indeed, the world needs a *tzaddik*, a truly righteous person, and Joseph is a *tzaddik*. To be a *tzaddik* is more than strictly obeying the commandments. It is about a texture of morality and faith, about embodying the commandments with one's whole heart, about living the merciful and life-giving will of God that stands at the core of the law. "The tzaddik," writes Jewish author Tzvi Freeman, "is calibrated to the Manufacturer's original specifications, so that everything about him is just as his Creator meant it should be, and all he desires is what his Creator desires."[4]

So, when Joseph learns that his betrothed is pregnant, as a righteous man he intends to obey the law, which is clear on the face of it: Mary is to be divorced. In fact, going strictly by the book, a public trial and execution were not out of the question (see Deut. 22:20–21). But Joseph is a true *tzaddik*; his intent is to be obedient, not vengeful. So as not to disgrace Mary publicly, Joseph seeks no public shaming but plans to dismiss her quietly (Matt. 1:19).

But then something surprising happens that tests Joseph's righteousness and throws a searchlight on Matthew's central purpose. An angel visits Joseph in a dream with news from the Lord, news so unexpected, so unprecedented Joseph could never have imagined it on his own. There is, the angel says, more God in Mary's pregnancy than Joseph knows. "The child conceived in her is from the Holy Spirit" (1:20). To this stunning and startling announcement, the angel adds a double command: take Mary as your wife and name the baby Jesus (1:20–21).

Joseph is now thrown into profound moral crisis. What should he obey? The clear command of the Torah or the equally clear command of the angel, God's messenger? Marrying a woman whose virginity had been compromised would have been unthinkable for one whose whole life had been devoted to obedience to the command "You shall be holy, for I the LORD your God am holy" (Lev. 19:2). To take Mary as his wife would be to knowingly join himself with sin. But the unthinkable is exactly what the angel in the dream commanded him to do.

The angel had also said something else: "Joseph, son of David, do not be afraid to take Mary as your wife" (1:20). Afraid? What was Joseph afraid of? Some suggest that Joseph's fear was simply the fear of the Divine that is a standard element in biblical theophanies,[5] but the story does not say that Joseph was afraid of the angel. Rather it says that he was afraid to take Mary as his wife, in other words, afraid to violate the commandment, afraid to transgress the holiness of God. It is important then that the angel goes on to assure him that Mary's pregnancy is not the result of sin but is an act of the Holy Spirit. At this point, Matthew as narrator cannot resist chiming in and adding his own endorsement to the angel's message. What is happening to Mary and to Joseph, Matthew affirms, does not violate the ancient tradition. To the contrary, it fulfills it. "All this took place to fulfill what had been spoken by the Lord through the prophet [Isaiah in the Septuagint]: 'Look, the virgin shall conceive and bear a son, and they shall name him Emmanuel,' which means, 'God is with us'" (1:22–23).

A woman who is holy, and a virgin, and pregnant? And a woman who in her holiness, virginity, and pregnancy actually fulfills a prophecy of Isaiah in a way no one saw coming? This is a lot to swallow, a lot to trust, but when Joseph woke up from his dream, he had decided what he should do: "He did as the angel of the Lord commanded him; he took her as his wife, but had no marital relations with her until she had borne a son; and he named him Jesus" (1:24–25).

Gaze, then, upon Joseph. Right at the beginning of the Gospel, Matthew gives us, in the character of Joseph, a model of what the whole Gospel is after. Matthew wants his readers, his congregation, to become like Joseph, formed as *tzaddikim.* That means two essential things. First, they are to be righteous people, steeped in the traditions of Israel, whose lives are obedient to the law of God. "Do not think," Jesus says in Matthew,

> "that I have come to abolish the law or the prophets. I have come not to abolish but to fulfill. For truly I tell you, until heaven and earth pass away, not one letter, not one stroke of a letter, will pass from the law until all is accomplished. Therefore, whoever breaks one of the least of these commandments, and teaches others to do the same, will be called least in the kingdom of heaven; but whoever does them and teaches them will be called great in the kingdom of heaven." (5:17–19)

Jesus did not come to abolish the law or the prophets, and a *tzaddik* of the kingdom of heaven is going to do and to teach the commandments, the Law and the prophets, down to the smallest detail.

But there is a second essential way in which Matthew wants his readers to become like Joseph: to be open to serving a God who does not write always in straight lines, a God who fulfills the promises of the law and the prophets in new and unexpected ways, a God who is even now breaking forth before our eyes, a God who speaks not only in holy writ but also in the whispers of angels in the middle of the night.

Jesus came not simply to reiterate the law and the prophets but to *fulfill* the law and the prophets, that is, to bring them to completion, to reveal their deepest and truest intention. And there's the rub. The Jesus we see in Matthew fulfilled the Law and the prophets, but hardly in ways that could have been anticipated. From his birth to his resurrection to his final command to make disciples of all the nations, all the Gentiles, he was a stream of surprises. This is the added dimension to the story of Joseph as a righteous man. A *tzaddik* of the kingdom is going to have to be open to divine surprises, nimble as well as obedient, ready to adjust to the unexpected.

This is because the God of Jesus Christ fulfills the tradition in ways that forever overturn expectations. Check out that genealogy of Jesus by which the Gospel begins, the one with the five unexpected women in Jesus' lineage (1:1–17). Surprise! Or how about the story where the first people said to worship the newly born Jewish Messiah were not Jews from Bethlehem or Jerusalem but Gentile magi, astrologers and magicians, from God-knows-where out east. Surprise! No wonder Jesus says that he is trying to form his followers into "scribes trained for the kingdom of heaven" and that such scribes are "like the master of a household who brings out of his treasure what is new and what is old" (13:52).

Those who find God in what is new and what is old are the scribes trained for the kingdom of heaven, the *tzaddikim* of Christ, that Matthew wishes to develop—righteous people in the way of Joseph. Joseph knew the Law called for the purity of the marriage bed—that's old. But in his case this meant taking as his wife a pregnant virgin—that's new. He knew how to read the Torah—that's old. But he also knew to listen to angels who interrupt dreams with unconventional commands—that's new. You cannot be a *tzaddik* like Joseph simply by checking off the boxes. You have to be like a great shortstop in baseball who has a feel for the game. You have to be so steeped in the Law and prophets that the tradition becomes body knowledge. You have to be ready to handle the routine grounder but also to field the unpredictable short hop when an angel wakes you up in the wee hours of the morning. Joseph's anguished choice was not between good and evil but between being righteous and being *truly* righteous. Joseph's righteousness was an intensified righteousness. This is why Jesus said, "For I tell you, unless your righteousness exceeds that of the scribes and Pharisees, you will never enter the kingdom of heaven" (5:20).

In his book *A Community of Character*, ethicist Stanley Hauerwas writes, "My father is a good but simple man. He was born on the frontier and grew up herding cows. Living with a gun was and is as natural to him as living with an automobile is for me. He made his living, as his father and five brothers did, by laying brick. He spent his whole life working hard at honest labor."[6] Hauerwas had no doubt that his father loved him, but as is often the case with people who live on the rugged frontier, his father rarely expressed his love in words or gestures. Hauerwas writes, "Love meant working hard enough to give me the opportunity to go to college so that I might have more opportunity" than his father had.[7]

Hauerwas did go to college and began to study things like philosophy and theology and to discover things—the sin of racism, the insanity of American gun culture, the beauty of art and music—that had not been a part of life back home with his father in Texas. Hauerwas, by then married to a woman he says his parents never really fully understood, eventually made his way to Yale Divinity School, not to study to be a minister but to become a teacher, a theologian, and an ethicist. "The further I went," he says, "the more unlike my parents I became."[8]

Hauerwas and his father would talk occasionally by phone, and his father's news was almost always about the deer rifle he was painstakingly handcrafting. Hauerwas would listen, thinking to himself, "That's fine for you, but that's your life, not mine." But when Hauerwas and his wife visited his parents in the summer, they had hardly made their way through the door when his father brought out the handmade rifle and placed it into Hauerwas's hands, a gift. Hauerwas blurted out that the gun was beautifully made, but he didn't stop there. He writes, "Flushed with theories about the importance of truthfulness and the irrationality of our society 's gun policy I said, 'Of course you realize that it will not be long before we as a society are going to have to take all these things away from you people.'"[9]

Reflecting later on these harsh words spoken to his father, Hauerwas says,

> Morally what I said still seems to me to be exactly right as a social policy. But that I made such a statement in that context surely is one of the lowest points of my "moral development." . . . I was simply not morally mature enough or skillful enough to know how to respond properly when a precious gift was being made. For what my father was saying, of course, was someday this will be yours and it will be a sign of how much I cared about you. But all I could see was a gun, and in

> the name of moral righteousness, I callously rejected it. One hopes that now I would be able to say, "I recognize what this gun means and I admire the workmanship that has gone into it. I want you to know that I will always value it for that and I will see that it is cared for in a manner that others can appreciate its value."[10]

In other words, in moral choices, contexts matter and nimble discernment is required. All Hauerwas could see was the rifle and the abstract moral issue. He couldn't see his father or the gift he was being given. So he made a decision that was "right" as social policy but, in a fuller and deeper sense, morally harmful. If Joseph had demanded a public shaming of Mary and then divorced her, he would technically have been in line with provisions of the Law, but he would have been blind to the context and would have missed what God was doing right before his eyes. He would have been righteous in a way, but not in the way of a true *tzaddik*, a wise scribe alert to the movement of God and thus able to combine what is new and what is old.

HEARING AND DOING, WISDOM AND FOOLISHNESS

Matthew's goal in his Gospel is to form a community of *tzaddikim*, a righteous community, a church (*ekklēsia*, that is, a "called out" community), of wise scribes trained for the kingdom of heaven. But if the goal is forming wise scribes, that raises the question of wisdom. What is "wisdom" for Matthew? Joseph proved himself righteous in old and new ways. Are wise scribes also wise in ways old and new?

In the Old Testament wisdom tradition, emphasized especially in Proverbs, to be wise is not equivalent to being what we would call "spiritual" or otherworldly. Actually, wisdom in the Old Testament is, in its own way, quite worldly. To be wise is to tune one's moral life to the melody of the world, to calibrate one's whole way of being with the way the world works. What makes this theological and not merely expedient is the conviction that God made the world, that God inscribed wisdom into the text of reality, that wisdom is stamped into the very grain of creation. The central claim of wisdom is "stunning," writes biblical scholar Christine Yoder: "[W]isdom is how God made the world. Wisdom is woven into the fabric of creation, giving it shape, meaningful order, and a coherence that God continues to uphold."[11]

This does not mean that the way to become wise is to run out into the world and drink down goblets of experience. God ingrained wisdom into the structure of the world, but wisdom is hidden and not readily accessible to raw experience. It has to be learned and taught. Sages observe God's world with rare discernment and gather wisdom over the generations. "Ah," they are finally able to say, after years of observing and sharing what they have seen with other sages, "so God has shown us that *this* is the way the world works." This is why Proverbs insists that it is the Lord who gives wisdom (Prov. 2:6), that youth should listen to the teachings of those who are older and wiser (Prov. 2:1), and that those who seek wisdom must "trust in the LORD with all [their] heart, and . . . not rely on [their] own insight" (Prov. 3:5).

Wisdom is comprehensive, and the sages have proverbial advice to impart on every sort of practical matter, from work, to sex, to honesty in commerce, to managing households, and more. But the sages do not gather these insights piecemeal, do not ramble through life collecting proverbs like hidden Easter eggs. No, what the sages discern is the bigger frame, of which individual proverbs are component parts, the master narratives of life that together tell the story of how the world really is. Individual proverbs are cantilevered off these master narratives. Old Testament scholar Carol Newsom calls these "iconic narratives,"[12] oft-told stories that claim "to offer a window onto a fundamental structure of reality." God made the world a certain way, so the moral configuration of the world is stable and coherent, and the "iconic narratives" describe this morally constant world and how it works.[13]

Newsom suggests that a contemporary American version of an "iconic narrative" would be the story, "told over and over, of the individual who turns a creative idea into a flourishing business."[14] We have heard this story many times, of course. Someone has a fresh idea—a food truck serving Pakistani street food, an art shop featuring original works made of sea glass—and has the dream of turning this idea into a thriving business. Naysayers rise up to express doubts. Skeptical bankers refuse loans. Even close family members scoff. But the dreamer persists and works tirelessly to make the dream come true. And today—what do you know?—she is the owner of a multimillion-dollar corporation with successful franchises in twenty states.

What's the "iconic narrative" here? Those who dream big, never doubting the dream within, and who work hard, who add perspiration to their inspiration, will be rewarded with success. For those with wise discernment, that's the way the world is; that's the way the world works.

"Facts," however, as President John Adams once said, "are stubborn things." For every "iconic narrative," reality is full of counterexamples (the books of Job and Ecclesiastes could be seen as powerfully argued counternarratives to the main "iconic narratives" of biblical wisdom). Your Aunt Matilda may have turned her sea glass hobby into an arts and crafts empire listed on the New York Stock Exchange, but the cold truth is, most new businesses fail, no matter how hopefully people dream or how hard they work. Even so, no one makes a speech at the Rotary Club or the Junior Chamber of Commerce about the cruel lessons of failed dreams. No, the story that is inevitably told is the "iconic narrative" of the dream that flourished against all odds. The truthfulness of an "iconic narrative is," Newsom writes, "not an empirical truth but something like a mythic truth."[15] Every alert observer knows that the business landscape is littered with shuttered shops and failed ventures. Mistakes were made. Bad luck was encountered. But faith in the "iconic narrative" persists because of the conviction that, when all the clutter is cleared away, this really is the way the moral world is constructed. Exceptions notwithstanding, the world is designed to reward hard work and courageous faith in one's dreams. That's our story, and we're sticking to it.

In the biblical wisdom tradition, there are also "iconic narratives." Yoder says that the "iconic narrative" shimmering behind the book of Proverbs (at least the first section of that book), is that those who are able to gain wisdom, to glimpse the "divine handiwork" in the world around them, and who are able to align their practical lives with this moral structure, will prosper, and those who don't are destined for destruction: "The wise live well and long. They enjoy ease and abundance (3:10, 21–26; cf. 1:33), health and happiness (3:2, 8, 16, 18), riches and honor (3:4, 16, 35). In contrast, the foolish and wicked are "out of place" in the world (cf. 2:22), and are therefore expelled from it variously by calamity, disgrace, and premature death (e.g., 1:26–27, 32; 2:22; 3:25, 33)."[16]

How does Matthew's notion of the "wise scribe" line up with this view of wisdom in Proverbs? In some ways, Matthew walks hand-in-hand with Proverbs. For Matthew too, there are the wise, who travel the way that leads to life, and there are fools, who are on the road to destruction and oblivion. But in Matthew there is one very large, stunningly surprising, and quite embarrassing exception to this conventional view of wisdom, namely, the story of Jesus itself, the very story that Matthew is telling. Jesus' life is a massive counternarrative to the conventional wisdom story. Jesus, who was true righteousness and true wisdom, did not "live well and long," did not enjoy a life of "ease and abundance," received no "riches and honor," unless we count the riches of a scarlet death robe, the honor of a crown of twisted thorns, and a face full of spit given on the way to the cross (Matt. 27:27–31). It was Jesus who was expelled "by calamity, disgrace, and premature death."

Matthew's insight is that Jesus was wise, but unlike any wise person we have seen before and with a wisdom that it unlike anything we could have expected. Once again, as in the Joseph story, we find ourselves close to the surprising paradox of Matthew's theology. Joseph fulfilled the tradition of righteousness but was righteous in a surprising way, and Jesus embodied the wisdom tradition but was wise in surprising fashion. When Jesus taught in his hometown synagogue, the congregation was astonished at all his wisdom. They knew him as merely "the carpenter's son" and wondered out loud, "Where did this man get this wisdom?" (13:54–55). But Jesus did not simply express wisdom; he intensified it. He told the scribes and Pharisees that while the queen of Sheba may have traveled the ends of the earth to listen to the wisdom of Solomon, "something greater than Solomon is here!" (12:42).

Jesus embodies wisdom, but he reframes it. To be wise, we noted, is to tune one's life to the melody of the world, to calibrate one's whole way of being with the way the world works. But the question Jesus raises is this: *which* world? This world, or the world of the kingdom of heaven? In Matthew, two worlds lie uneasily side by side. There is the kingdom of this world, glistening, seductive, seemingly strong and permanent. It was to this reality that Satan pointed on the mount of temptation when he tried to entice Jesus with its lures and splendors: "All of this I will give you, if you will fall down and worship me" (4:9). Jesus left that mountain and became a preacher of the other kingdom: "Repent, for the kingdom of heaven has come near" (4:17).

In proverbial wisdom, the lessons of life lie around the house and right outside the window in the everyday practical world. Want to know the value of hard work? Look at the ants (Prov. 6:6). Want to know what it's like for someone to sing happy-clappy songs to someone in the depths of grief? Try putting vinegar on a wound (Prov. 25:20). Want to know what it's like to be a person who constantly seeks flattery? Eat a whole jar of honey in one sitting and see what happens (Prov. 25:27). Want to know what results when people elect a fool to high office? Watch some idiot tie a large stone snugly to a coiled catapult before setting it off (Prov. 26:8).

But Jesus invites his followers to look for wisdom not to the everyday world, but to the new world of God's kingdom, now breaking in all around us. Wisdom is no longer conforming to the world as it appears outside the window but instead being aligned to the new reality that is dawning—the way the world that belongs to God really is. In Proverbs, the sages comment on life's smallest everyday details, what we eat, what we drink, and what clothing we wear. But Jesus in Matthew, in the Sermon on the Mount, warns not to fret about what we eat or drink or wear. "But strive first for the kingdom of God and his righteousness, and all these things will be given to you as well" (Matt. 6:33). Proverbs asks us to look at the obvious, at ants for wisdom about work, but Jesus invites his hearers to look at the unexpected, at the birds and the lilies—and to look counterintuitively not at what *they* are doing but at what God is doing for them. No need to be anxious about the everyday concerns of life. The birds don't break their backs, Jesus says, toiling away for food and clothing, because God feeds them well and clothes them lavishly. That's the way it truly is in God's kingdom.

At first, Jesus' analogy seems to die the death of a thousand qualifications. Sure, birds and lilies don't sow or reap, toil or spin, but they also don't have mortgages, car payments, or college tuitions. The book of Proverbs would have wagged a stern finger at anyone who thought they could get away with spending the day like some blithe bird or flower. Proverbs' analogy of the ants seems shrewder, more realistic. Playing around as if you are a carefree bird or a lovely lily depending upon God to take care of you is nice poetry but also a certain path to poverty.

But not for the Jesus of the Sermon on the Mount. New Testament scholar Robert Tannehill observes that the Greek verbs in this passage—"*look* at the birds of the air . . . *consider* the lilies of the field"—are very strong.[17] The English translations—"look," "consider"—unfortunately are relatively weak. What Jesus is actually saying is, "*Look*, no, *really look. Look again*, hard!" When we really look with a steady gaze at the birds and lilies, there is a chance that we will have a perceptual breakthrough. Over against our anxiety-ridden world, we may for a flashing instant perceive in the birds and lilies a world of carefree providence. We have to return, of course, to the pressure-filled world of mortgages and demands, but, as Tannehill says,

> We begin to wonder which is the real world, the world of our anxiety, or this other world of which the birds and flowers are images. Thus the text induces a sense of strangeness about our life and a sense of the presence of something more, something deeper, which offers an alternative for action and makes finally unimportant our structures of care. We experience a heightened awareness and the disturbing impingement of another reality. This opens a new possibility for life, a possibility which the text describes as seeking the Kingdom (Matt 6:33).[18]

The wisdom that Matthew describes, the wisdom possessed by scribes trained for the kingdom of heaven, is not worldly wisdom but the wisdom of lives tuned to the frequency of this new and impinging reality that God is bringing into being in Jesus. This wisdom has to be alert and nimble. Like Joseph hearing the voice of the angel in the depth of the night, the truly wise listen for the voice of Jesus. The wise person, Jesus says, "hears these words of mine and acts on them" (7:24).

There are the wise in the way of the kingdom of heaven, then, and there are fools, who give themselves to that which is not the kingdom. A number of the parables unique to Matthew draw a sharp contrast between them. "Want to know the difference between wisdom and foolishness?" they seem to ask. "Well, just watch." There are those who come to the marriage feast of the Son and the fools who turn down the invitation; there are the wise who invest their God-given talents in the marketplace of righteousness, and there is the fool who buries his talent in the backyard; there are the wise bridesmaids who bring along enough oil for their lamps and the fools who are out shopping for lantern fuel at the 24-hour Walmart when the groom arrives and the party begins.

GATES, ROADS, WARNINGS, AND NIGHTMARES

The marked disparity between the life of the wise and the life of fools gives us a glimmer of understanding as to why Matthew's language and imagery are often so violent. Matthew isn't kidding around here. Wisdom or foolishness? He urgently beckons the church to be wise, and he is painfully aware that the temptation to foolishness lurks everywhere. The stakes are high, life or death actually. As the sages long ago knew, wisdom leads to a life that matters, and foolishness leads to catastrophe. Jesus in Matthew agrees. Using the images of gates and roads, he issues an urgent warning: "Enter through the narrow gate; for the gate is wide and the road is easy that leads to destruction, and there are many who take it. For the gate is narrow and the road is hard that leads to life, and there are few who find it" (7:13–14).

Matthew consistently places the reader at this fork in the road. In one direction is a narrow gate leading to a hard and rocky path. In the other direction, a broad gate leads to a smooth and easy path. Don't be fooled, he warns. Counterintuitively, it is the unpromising, difficult route that leads to life, and the well-lit, smooth highway that leads over the cliff, into the abyss and destruction. As one could guess, though, the world is deceived by surface perceptions, and the road to life is traveled by a precious few, while the expressway to death is thronged with fools speeding their merry way toward oblivion.

Matthew thinks of traveling the way to life as something like walking at night up a narrow and precipitous path carved into a steep mountainside. The only light we have comes from the words of Jesus, and for God's sake, he cautions, follow that light and don't step off the path into the darkness and the empty depths below! Matthew is like the mother of a teenage son who is about to take the family car out on his own for the first time. She hands him the keys, anxiety for his safety in her heart. She does not gently murmur, "Now, son, I really hope you will be careful tonight." No, she points her finger and says, "Now you listen to me. You drive carefully tonight. No speeding, no texting, no trying to impress your friends. You act carelessly for a minute, and you could wrap the car around a telephone pole and break everybody's heart! You hear me?" Likewise, Matthew does not pussyfoot around the dangers for those who act the fool and miss the life offered in the kingdom.

Matthew's theology, his view of life, borrows a theme from Psalm 1. This psalm, which serves to introduce the whole Psalter, also starkly contrasts the way of the wise with that of the wicked and foolish. The wise "delight . . . in the law of the LORD" (Ps. 1:2) and, as a consequence, "They are like trees planted by streams of water, which yield their fruit in its season, and their leaves do not wither. In all that they do, they prosper" (Ps 1:3).

But as for wicked fools, they are "like chaff that the wind drives away" (Ps. 1:4). The psalm closes with the warning that "the way of the wicked will perish" (Ps. 1:8). Commenting on this psalm, Patrick Miller notes that much is said in the psalm about the prospering tree, but the chaff gets only one short relative clause. "Of the chaff there is nothing to say except that the wind drives it away to nothingness. That's all there is to chaff."[19] The warning of the psalm is much more frightening, much worse, than the threat of active punishment. Rather it is that a life of foolishness simply doesn't matter, doesn't count. It is inconsequential. It just evaporates.

UNDERSTANDING MATTHEW'S PARABLES: RULES OF THE ROAD

Given Matthew's goal of forming a community of *tzaddikim* of the kingdom and his urgent call to life-giving wisdom, not the destruction of foolishness, it is possible to name a couple of rules of the road in interpreting the parables in Matthew:

1. *Let the characters in Matthew's parables be who they are.* When we read the parables in the Gospel of Luke, we encounter a number of characters we can empathize with. We feel it when the good Samaritan is "moved with pity" over the plight of the injured man on the road (Luke 10:33). We are right there emotionally when the prodigal son comes to himself out there in that pigsty (Luke 15:17), and we are touched when the father of the prodigal runs to his returning son and embraces and kisses him (Luke 15:20).

Matthew's parables are not like that. It is not a stretch to say that not one character in any of the parables in Matthew ever changes, grows, develops, repents, or moves emotionally.[20] The characters in Matthew's parables are largely what literary critics call "flat characters." Novelist E. M. Forster described "flat" characters as those who "are constructed round a single idea or quality," as opposed to "round characters," who are complex and capable of change and even of surprising the reader.[21] The characters in Matthew's parables are straightforward and uncomplicated example figures of virtues or faults. They are wise or foolish, good or evil, obedient or disobedient, and that's that. This does not mean that Matthew's parables are inferior to Luke's, just different. All of Jane Austen's characters are "round," notes Forster, while almost all of Dickens's characters are "flat."[22]

In a famous experiment in the 1940s, two Smith College psychologists showed a group of students a brief film in which geometric shapes—a circle, a small triangle, a larger triangle, and a rectangle—move around on the screen, sometimes bumping into each other. After the film, the students were asked to describe what they had seen. All they had actually seen was shapes moving on the screen, nothing more, but almost all of the students projected personalities, feelings, and motives to the shapes. For example, the small triangle was described as "heroic" and "courageous." The larger triangle was a "bully," "mean," "aggressive," and "warlike," while the circle was "shy" and "afraid" and relied on the small triangle for protection.[23]

A danger to interpreters of Matthew's parables is to treat the characters as the Smith students treated those triangles and the circle, by projecting onto them a complexity that is not there. Sometimes readers of Matthew's parables will say things like, "Gosh, sometimes I feel like I'm good soil, and other times I feel like rocky soil." That may be true about us, but it's irrelevant to Matthew. For him, good and bad soils are matters of obedience, not emotional intuition. Or we wonder, "Why didn't those wise bridesmaids with all that extra oil share some with the foolish bridesmaids who were running out?" Good question in Luke, but not in Matthew. Such speculation about characters in Matthew simply sends the interpreter off on a snipe hunt. For the most part, we are not supposed to empathize, sympathize, or psychoanalyze the characters in Matthew's parables. Rather, we are supposed to watch them. "Here is a wise person," Matthew implies, "watch him flourish. And, look, there is a kingdom fool. Watch his world come apart. Take notes."

2. *Hear both the warning and the deep hope in Matthew's tough talk.* We return now to the issue with which we began in this chapter: Jesus' rough talk in Matthew. How could the gentle and inviting Jesus, who says, "Come to me, all you that are weary and are carrying heavy burdens, and I will give you rest. Take my yoke upon you, and learn from me; for I am gentle and humble in heart, and you will find rest for your souls. For my yoke is easy, and my burden is light" (11:28–30), also be the Jesus who says, "The Son of Man will send his angels, and they will collect out of his kingdom all causes of sin and all evildoers, and they will throw them into the furnace of fire, where there will be weeping and gnashing of teeth" (13:41–42), and "And in anger his lord handed him over to be tortured until he would pay his entire debt. So my heavenly Father will also do to every one of you, if you do not forgive your brother or sister from your heart" (18:34–35)?

In thinking this challenge through, we should first recognize that, between Matthew's time and our own, massive changes have taken place in the understanding of such issues as the nature of the self and the character of divine agency. This is not the place to debate the relative virtues and defects of Matthew's theology and ours, but instead to point out how our theological perspective can cause us to misunderstand Matthew.

For example, when Matthew's Jesus begins a sentence about punishment in the Parable of the Unforgiving Slave (18:23–35) with the clause "so my heavenly Father will also do to every one of you," we reflexively translate that into contemporary terms and think that Matthew is speaking of a specific kind of divine agency. God, as we understand this language, is pictured as a decision-making force in the world, a force perhaps greater than other worldly forces, but like them. The human master in this parable gets angry at a servant and decides to hand the servant over to be tortured. Well, just so, Jesus seems to be saying, God gets angry at unforgiving people and does what the human master in the story does, just on a larger scale. We are left with the picture of a God who is like a prison warden prowling the blockhouse looking for misbehavior and, when he finds it, throwing the offender into solitary confinement, which will be accompanied by frequent beatings.

To read Matthew this way, though, is a disaster. What other reaction could such a reading provoke in us than an offended protest that the God of Jesus Christ could never be like that, and who wants to have anything to do with a vindictive and punitive God like that?

But Matthew's larger theology is different. For Matthew, God is not an agent combing the earth looking for do-gooders to reward and lawbreakers to punish. God is not a force in the world like other forces, only stronger. Rather, for Matthew, God is the author of reality. The world, as creation, is an expression of the life of God. Everything that has existence and that endures is enveloped in the life of God. Everything that is outside of the life of God is unreal. Matthew may call "evil" all that is counter to God or outside of God, but what he means is that it has no reality. It is nothing, nonexistent, zilch, death. The role of Jesus as the Messiah is to come to rescue a world that had fallen away from life and into nothingness. Matthew quotes Isaiah to name the role of Jesus: "the people who sat in darkness have seen a great light, and for those who sat in the region and shadow of death light has dawned" (Matt. 4:16, quoting Isa. 9:2).

So the choice is clear: "I have set before you life and death, blessings and curses. Choose life so that you and your descendants may live," Moses tells the children of Israel on the cusp of the promised land (Deut. 30:19). Likewise for Matthew, to listen to the words of Jesus and to do them is to choose what is real, to choose life, to choose to be in the life of God. To do so is to be wise, to calibrate one's life with the reality of God's kingdom. To choose otherwise is foolishness, a decision to step out of reality and into free fall, to throw oneself into the darkness, to walk in the shadow of death, and to become a part of that which has no existence.

How does a narrator describe this foolish option? A poet, like the composer of Psalm 1, might say it's like choosing to be chaff, inconsequential, of no account, simply blown away by the wind. A storyteller might say that it's like being thrown into outer darkness where there is weeping and gnashing of teeth, to experience the pain and loss of self-imposed torture, to discover that the wholeness of one's life had been cut into pieces. Our language today might be different. Perhaps we would say, "To live outside the orbit of the kingdom of heaven is to have one's life unfold into tragedy."

The same goes with Matthew's talk about persons. He often depicts people in sharp contrasts: wise or foolish, righteous or wicked, faithful or disobedient. We, on the other hand, as the heirs of modern psychological and existential views of humanity, tend to see ourselves and other people in more nuanced and complex ways. I am a blend. Part of me is faithful, I pray, but part of me is not. Whatever wisdom I may possess is surely marbled by deep streaks of foolishness. We have known of saints who radiate holiness, and we have known of history's villains, who seem to have given themselves almost completely to evil, but most of us bounce along somewhere in the middle as perplexing admixtures.

It makes us queasy then to hear Jesus say things like, "The Son of Man will send his angels, and they will collect out of his kingdom all causes of sin and all evildoers, and they will throw them into the furnace of fire." The "causes of sin" we are glad to see burned up, but the casting of "all evildoers" into the furnace gives us pause. What about the traces of goodness that run in the background of even the most distorted of personalities, and what of the spasms of malevolence that rise up even among the kindest of people?

Does Matthew ultimately see people monochromatically, as all evil or all good, all sinner or all saint? Surely not, even though, as we have seen, he tends to describe things via sharp contrasts. He knows, for example, that Peter, the rock upon which Jesus promises to build his church (16:18), could also be a stumbling block (16:23) and a denier of Jesus (26:69–75). And we also know from the announcement of the angel at the very beginning of Matthew that the purpose and mission of Jesus is not to be a destroyer but a savior, one who will "save his people from their sins" (1:21).

Perhaps the best way, then, to read the tough language in Matthew that all sin and all sinners will be burned up in the fire of God's judgment is to understand it as a graphic expression of what is ultimately a glad, confident, and hopeful promise that nothing that mars God's goodness will endure. There is no cancer, no killing virus, no Alzheimer's, no plague, no child abuse, no tyranny, no cruelty, no oppression, no lynching, no placing of children in cages, no homelessness, no tragic tears, no suffocating loneliness, no torture, no death in the kingdom of heaven. God and God's kingdom will be revealed to be all that truly exists, all-consuming, and nothing outside of it will have any reality at all. All that has destroyed and maimed and oppressed and polluted creation and the human prospect will be burned away like straw. Catching this vision allows us to voice a mature prayer: "O Lord, for all in me that is faithful and responsive to your kingdom, preserve this and let it prosper and endure. For all in me that is unfaithful and opposed to your kingdom, for all that separates me from your love and mercy, burn, baby, burn."

Matthew is finally not very far from Paul when he pictures the last day as a day of revealing and purifying fire:

> For no one can lay any foundation other than the one that has been laid; that foundation is Jesus Christ. Now if anyone builds on the foundation with gold, silver, precious stones, wood, hay, straw—the work of each builder will become visible, for the Day will disclose it, because it will be revealed with fire, and the fire will test what sort of work each has done. If what has been built on the foundation survives, the builder will receive a reward. If the work is burned up, the builder will suffer loss; the builder will be saved, but only as through fire. (1 Cor. 3:11–15)

Note that here what is being tested by fire, and potentially consumed by it, is one's work, what one has done with one's life. To build on the foundation of Christ with gold, silver, and precious stones is to have built a life that will prove worthy and abiding. To build with wood, hay, and straw ensures that the life one has crafted will not endure the raging fire of God's appearing. Even though those who build with dross will suffer tragic loss, the builders will themselves be saved, but only by going through the refining fire of God.

"What actually saves," writes Joseph Ratzinger, "is the full assent of faith." He continues:

> But in most of us that basic option is buried under a great deal of wood, hay, and straw. Only with difficulty can it peer out from behind the latticework of an egoism we are powerless to pull down with our own hands. [Humanity] is the recipient of the divine mercy, yet this does not exonerate [human beings] from the need to be transformed. Encounter with the Lord is this transformation. It is the fire that burns away our dross and re-forms us to be vessels of eternal joy. This insight would contradict the doctrine of grace only if penance were the antithesis of grace and not its form, the gift of a gracious possibility.[24]

In Charles Dickens's classic tale *A Christmas Carol,* Ebenezer Scrooge, a miserly businessman, a "tight-fisted hand at the grindstone, . . . a squeezing, wrenching, grasping, scraping, clutching, covetous, old sinner,"[25] is visited in the middle of the night on Christmas Eve by his long-deceased business partner, Jacob Marley. Scrooge is alarmed to see that Marley's ghostly body is bound in a chain made with cashboxes, the heavy weight of years of greed.

"I wear the chain I forged in life," Marley tells Scrooge, "the weight and length of the strong coil you bear yourself."[26]

"I am here tonight to warn you," Marley tells Scrooge, "that you have yet a chance and hope of escaping my fate."[27] Marley goes on to say that Scrooge will be haunted in the night by three spirits and that he must heed their warnings. Then Marley's apparition disappears, and, indeed, just as Marley said, Scrooge is haunted by the spirits. The first two, the ghost of Christmas past and the ghost of Christmas present, show Scrooge dreary scenes from his pinched life that reveal what a flinty, lonely, self-centered man he has become. The last spirit, the ghost of Christmas future, reveals Scrooge's funeral, letting him see the terrifying truth that, because he has lived a life unconcerned about anyone but himself, his death will be unmourned by anyone.

Scrooge's nightmares disclose the ugly truth about his life and the choices he has made. But then he awakens from these nightmares to a new day. His Christmas Eve ghostly visitations seem to have lasted many nights, but when he awakens he finds that they endured for only one night. Now it is finally Christmas morning, and everything is new. Scrooge wakes up a changed man. Having been shown the terrible truths about his life, Scrooge repents and spends Christmas Day out in the city doing good deeds and acts of generosity and vowing to remain a better man. "Scrooge was better than his word," says the narrator at the end of the tale. "He became as good a friend, as good a master, and as good a man, as the good old city knew."[28]

Some of the parables in Matthew are nightmare parables. They come to us in the night and showcase the ghosts of lives poorly lived, decisions badly made. But then we wake up, and it is Easter morning, and there is Jesus Christ, full of light and life, joy and glory, saying, "Do not be afraid" (28:10). Fools though we may have been, we are offered a new future, a profound mission, a great hope, and the promise that the Jesus who saves us will be with us always, "to the end of the age" (28:20).

6

Matthew

The Parables

There are two ways, one of life and one of death, and there is a great difference between the two ways.

—*Didache* 1.1

Without doubt, there is still a long way to go in order to understand or guess that the Wrath of God is only the sadness of love.

—Paul Ricoeur[1]

Jesus is a great teacher in Matthew—and a refreshingly clear one. The Jesus of Mark, we recall by contrast, comes across as a somewhat mysterious communicator, a whisperer of secrets, whose message remained obscure until the final act, when Jesus' death and resurrection jolted the careful reader into pulling together all the clues. In Mark, Jesus told his inner circle that he spoke in parables precisely so outsiders would "listen but not understand" (Mark 4:12), which makes sense in Mark, given the strong secrecy motif.

But Matthew is different. He presents Jesus "as a teacher who wants to be understood and who is understood."[2] In Matthew Jesus describes those who hear his words and do them as like the wise who build their houses on rock (7:24). So important is Jesus' teaching role in Matthew, he holds five intense seminars in which he presents significant clusters of teachings: (1) the Sermon on the Mount (chaps. 5–7), (2) the missionary discourse (chap. 10), (3) the sermon in parables (chap. 13), (4) teachings about the life and discipline of the church (chap. 18), and (5) teachings about the coming eschaton (chaps. 24–25). Every time Jesus finishes one of these teaching sessions, Matthew's narrator plainly marks the end of class by stepping up to the microphone and announcing, "When Jesus had finished saying all these things. . . ."

The parables in Matthew are teaching devices, and most of the major parables fall, naturally, in these teaching sections, namely, discourses 3, 4, and 5, each one a part of the theme of the discourse in which it appears. Four parables in Matthew do graze beyond the fences and appear in Matthew 20–22, outside the formal instructional circles—the Laborers in the Vineyard, the Two Sons, the Wicked Tenants, and the Marriage Feast—but even these parables seemed not to have wandered too far from the eschatological teaching cluster in chapters 24–25.

We turn now to explore each of the parables in Matthew. Three of Matthew's major parables were borrowed from Mark (the Sower, the Mustard Seed, and the Wicked Tenants); because we have already commented on these in detail in chapter 4, we will note mainly how Matthew's presentation of these parables differs from Mark's.

THE PARABLE OF THE SOWER (MATTHEW 13:1–23)

The Parable of the Sower is the first major parable in Matthew, and this is one of the parables Matthew borrows from Mark (see the treatment of Mark's version at pp. 56–72). At first, Matthew's version seems remarkably like Mark's:

- In both Gospels, this is the first parable in a sermon filled with parables.
- In both Gospels, this sermon is preached to a large crowd from a boat on the Sea of Galilee.
- The basic details of the parable are the same—a sower sows seed in four different kinds of soils with varying results, three crop failures followed by a success.
- Both Gospels include a detailed explanation of the parable that Jesus provides privately to the disciples.

But when we look more closely, we are surprised to see that with a few deft strokes of his pen, Matthew has set the Parable of the Sower sailing in a remarkably different direction than does Mark.

A Change of Depth

In Mark, Jesus just shows up at the seashore, gets into a boat, and starts teaching in parables. It's almost that way in Matthew too, except for one little detail: Matthew remarks that Jesus' sermon in parables was preached "that same day" (13:1). Unlike Mark, Matthew is eager for us to know that when Jesus started speaking in parables, it was a continuation of what had been happening earlier on "that same day."

What had been happening that day? It's hard to judge how far back to read in the previous material, but at the very least "that same day" links us to the immediately preceding story, Matthew 12:46–50. In that episode, Jesus is pictured as speaking to the crowds while members of his family, namely, his mother and brothers, wait around the edges for a chance to have a word with him. Someone lets Jesus know that his mother and brothers are outside, which prompts Jesus to ask, "Who is my mother, and who are my brothers?" Then, pointing to his disciples, Jesus says, "Here are my mother and brothers! For whoever does the will of my Father in heaven is my brother and sister and mother" (12:49).

This story makes us wince perhaps, but finally its thrust is less about rejecting one's own biological family—after all, Jesus later sharply condemns the Pharisees and scribes for breaking the commandment to "honor your father and mother" (15:1–9)—and more about defining a new kind of "family," one that transcends traditional blood relations and is defined by hearing and doing God's will (see also 10:34–39).

So Jesus starts preaching in parables on the very same day that he names the disciples as his true family. What difference does that make? A number of commentators have suggested that Matthew 13 marks a pivotal point in the ministry of Jesus, the time when he changes primary audiences. He now turns his attention toward the disciples as the real hearers of the word. But if Jesus turns toward the disciples, does that mean that at the moment he begins to speak in parables he explicitly turns away from others?

Some say yes, that in fact is exactly what Jesus does; precisely at this point in the Gospel, he turns *toward* the disciples and *away* from the Jewish people as a whole. Jack Dean Kingsbury, for example, in his influential *The Parables of Jesus in Matthew 13,* states that Jesus came as Messiah to the Jews, but "the Jews on all sides reject Jesus as the Messiah and inaugurator of God's eschatological kingdom (chaps. 11–12). When the Jews turn against Jesus," Kingsbury argues, "Jesus in reaction turns against the Jews."[3] In other words, what was happening on "that same day," according to Kingsbury, was that the Jews were making it plain that they had no use for Jesus as the Messiah, and Jesus is now about to make it plain that he is turning his back on them and turning his face toward his own disciples. For Kingsbury, this is the reason Jesus suddenly begins talking in parables at this point. From this point on, Jesus intends to make his teaching plain and understandable only for his true "family," for the disciples. For the Jews there will be only a string of inscrutable parables, intentionally dark and obscure language designed to be understood by the insider disciples but for the Jews, now outsiders, to cut them out.

Is Kingsbury right? His claim seems at best an overstatement. If Jesus turns away from the Jews here, why is it that, two chapters later, Jesus can still describe himself as one "sent only to the lost sheep of the house of Israel" (15:24); and when Jesus laments over Jerusalem as a prelude to the passion, he can still say of the city, "How often have I desired to gather your children together as a hen gathers her brood under her wings, and you were not willing!" (23:37). Moreover, when Jesus adds, "For I tell you, you will not see me again until you say, 'Blessed is the one who comes in the name of the Lord'" (23:39), is there not at least a hint of hope or, stronger perhaps, an expectation that when Jesus returns as the glorified Messiah, Jerusalem itself will lift its voice to him in blessing?

While Kingsbury is right that there is some kind of pivot in Matthew 13, it seems less a radical turn away from the Jews and more like an intensification of focus on those who are willing to hear Jesus' words: a turn from the surface and toward the depths, a turn away from superficial definitions of "hearers" and "family" toward more profound understandings of these relationships, a turn away from those who miss the claim of the kingdom and toward those who open their hearts to what Jesus is teaching. Matthew lets his readers know that Jesus' master class on wisdom is now at midsemester, and we are realizing that the students are dividing into two groups: the foolish crowds, who have their ears closed and their hearts hardened, and the wise disciples, who genuinely hear what Jesus teaches and do "the will of my Father in heaven" (12:50). As Birger Gerhardsson says,

> To understand the "parable chapter" of Matthew in its entirety we must realize that the tension is not between Jesus and the Pharisees or between church and synagogue: the contrasted groups are the spiritually inert crowds (ὁ ὄχλος) and the inquiring disciples (οἱ μαθηταί). The problem under review is not why some go to church and others to the synagogue, but why so few of the people are spiritually alive, and so reveal themselves to be true children of the heavenly kingdom.[4]

Every shrewd teacher knows the difference between students who listen to what is taught, take it in, and make it their own and the lazy, inattentive students for whom instruction is like dropping marbles onto a tile floor. This is why, in Matthew, Jesus suddenly starts speaking in parables. Parables expose the difference between wise students and foolish ones.

My first, and unforgettable, class as a new seminary student was with a professor who had a reputation as one of the most passionate and engaging teachers on the faculty. All of us first-year students in the course were excited when the class began, our notebooks open and our pens at the ready. But to our dismay, the professor delivered an absolutely impenetrable theological lecture. Virtually every word of what he said was a theological term we had never heard before and could not possibly have understood. He was, in a sense, speaking to us in parables, parables we did not grasp.

We left class that day shaken by the realization that, if this was the very first class, maybe theological education was too steep a mountain for us. Looking back on the experience, I think I see now what the professor was doing. He was intentionally pitching the ball too high for us to hit. The goal of that class was to knock the academic chips off our shoulders. What was important that day was not so much the specific content of the lecture as the message that, however much we thought of ourselves as accomplished students, learning theology was going to require a stronger effort, a deeper commitment, a more profound discernment than we had imagined. We were supposed to leave class that day both discouraged that our customary standards for learning were not sufficient, but also amazed at the world of new learning that was before us and that would require a greater openness and diligence. We were like Dorothy in Oz: "Toto, I have a feeling we're not in Kansas anymore."

What Jesus was doing in Matthew 13 when he suddenly started speaking parables is similar, but here is a key difference: Jesus was not giving a lecture with big fancy theological words that were over the hearers' heads. Rather he was preaching in *parables*, which are ways of teaching that require new ways of hearing and imagining. In other words, for Matthew Jesus' parables were not impossible to understand, but they did require a change of attitude, a change of heart, and a change of imagination.

Eugene Boring rightly observes that "Matthew's view of parables is akin to that of Jesus ben Sirach, who saw them as a teacher's method of distinguishing perceptive students from indolent ones."[5] How does a good teacher tantalize the alert students to move even deeper, signal to the lazy students that the boat is sailing without them, and perhaps encourage a few of the indolent to dare to open their eyes and ears? If you're a biblical teacher of wisdom, one good approach is to tease the imagination of the students with a *mashal*—a proverb or a parable. These Rubik's cubes of rhetoric are perfect for provoking the wise to dig even deeper to become wiser, while exposing the torpid folly of the chronically unwise.

In the early 1970s, Texas singer-songwriter Ray Wylie Hubbard wrote a song called "Up against the Wall Redneck Mother." The war in Vietnam was still claiming lives, hippies were camping out in San Francisco and other cities, social protests roiled the streets, feminism was on the rise, and Hubbard wrote "Redneck Mother" as a kind of protest song, an ironic parody of backward redneck life oblivious to the changing tides in society. In the song, he described the object of his scorn as clueless cowboys who are "thirty-four and drinkin' in a honky tonk, just kickin' hippies' asses and raisin' hell."[6]

The song was recorded by country artist Jerry Jeff Walker and became a runaway hit. Curiously, it became a favorite of the crowds in those very honky-tonks that Hubbard intended to satirize. An astounded Hubbard marveled that the people his song intended to lampoon had turned it into their own private anthem, requesting it to be played over and over in country dance halls. "You had these rednecks in cowboy hats and 'America—love it or leave it' T-shirts singing along with it," Hubbard said. "Jerry Jeff was playing at the Broken Spoke, and people are two-stepping to it."[7]

"That's the problem with irony," Hubbard later reflected. "Not everybody gets it."[8]

That's the thing about parables. Not everybody gets them. They divide the wise, who hear them, receive them, and form their lives around their truth, from the foolish, who simply skate along over the surface.

A Change of Emphasis

Matthew's version of the Parable of the Sower constitutes not only a change of depth, but also a change of emphasis. Mark's version of the Sower is mainly christological, about Jesus. Jesus himself is the sower, and the parable is the story of his life—one failure and defeat after another, but the great and surprising harvest his ministry brings at the end through the resurrection is nevertheless secure. As the Gospel of Mark unfolds, Jesus looks for all the world like a failed farmer of the kingdom, but in the Easter ending, his harvest is abundant, and the whole world will ultimately see his hidden identity as the victorious Son of Man.

Matthew changes the subject. Mark's parable is about the adventures of the sower; Matthew's is about the adventures of the soils. If any reader of the Parable of the Sower in Mark should ask, "What kind of soil am I? Good soil or bad soil?" Mark would rap their knuckles with a ruler and growl, "Wrong question! This is not about you. This is about Jesus and his harvest." But in Matthew, What kind of soil am I? is precisely the right question, indeed the main question. It's not that Matthew isn't interested in Jesus—of course he is; but he is interested in how hearers receive Jesus and his teaching. Are we good soil, that is, wise students who hear Jesus' words and do them, or bad soil, that is, foolish students who are closed to his teaching?

This wise/foolish distinction is at the heart of the exchange between Jesus and the disciples in response to the Parable of the Sower (13:10–17). The disciples, obviously noticing that Jesus has switched into parabolic gear, ask him why he speaks "to them"—meaning to the crowd—in parables (13:10). But Jesus responds first not about the crowd but about the disciples themselves. "I'll talk about 'them' in a minute," Jesus seems to be saying, "but first I want to talk about you, about why I speak in parables in your hearing as well."

The disciples, Jesus says, are extraordinary students. They have been gifted with "the secrets of the kingdom of heaven" (13:11). Because the disciples have these "secrets of the kingdom," even more will be given to them, to the point of abundance. Sadly, by contrast, there are foolish students "who have nothing" and who will find even what little they have will be taken away (13:12). Once again, there are two kinds of students: the wise ones, who "have it" and therefore get even more, and the foolish ones, who don't have it and consequently end up worse off than they were when they started. The disciples are the first kind and are among the "blessed" because their eyes truly see and their ears truly hear (13:16).

After answering a question the disciples did not ask (why do you speak to us in parables?), Jesus turns to the question they did ask: "Why do you speak to them in parables?" The reason, Jesus says, is that the crowds are dull and recalcitrant students. They see but they don't perceive; they hear but they don't listen or understand. Indeed, they are living fulfillments of Isaiah's prophecy about the people of God whose hearts have grown dull (the issue, we should be careful to note, is not raw intelligence, but openness of heart to the truths of the kingdom) and whose "ears are hard of hearing" (Matt. 13:13–15; see Isa. 6:10). The parables then shine light in two directions. They reveal the heart of the wise, and they expose the stubborn hard-heartedness of the resistant.

In the parallel text in Mark, Jesus tells the disciples they have been given "the secret [singular] of the kingdom" (Mark 4:11), but in Matthew it's plural: "the secrets of the kingdom" (Matt. 13:11), a subtle but important difference. Mark's singular "secret" points to what we described in chapter 1 as the master secret of that Gospel: that the strong and ultimately victorious Messiah is concealed under the rejected, weak, and crucified Jesus. Matthew's plural "secrets" points to something else altogether, namely, the specific teachings of Jesus. In Mark, the secret is christological, a secret about Jesus himself. In Matthew, the secrets are truths about wisdom in one's relationship to God and to the kingdom. In Matthew, the disciples have heard Jesus' words and taken them to heart. The disciples are, in other words, good soil, and the words of Jesus have taken root in them. By the way, the Greek term for "secret" in Mark is *mystērion* (μυστήριον). In Matthew it's the plural form of the same word, *mystēria* (μυστήρια). This word can mean either "secret" or "mystery," and in Mark the best translation is "secret," while in Matthew probably the better rendering is "mysteries." Secrets are to be kept; mysteries are to be probed and explored.

In Mark, Jesus says he speaks in parables "in order that" the hearers not understand and not repent and be forgiven (Mark 4:12). Matthew changes that to say that Jesus speaks in parables "because" people don't understand, and he leaves out the part about not being forgiven. In Mark, failure to understand the parables is what Jesus intends. The Markan parables will open themselves up to full understanding only when the whole story of Jesus has been told. A parable in Mark is a way of keeping the secret until the time is ripe for that which is concealed to be revealed. But in Matthew failure to understand is not what Jesus wants; it's the result of willful resistance on the part of the hearers (Matt. 13:13–15). It will be a challenge, to be sure, for these dull-hearted people to receive what Jesus teaches in the parables, but Jesus is still teaching them and hoping for a response. Every parable told to the crowds is, in effect, Jesus tossing them an oyster and a knife: I challenge you to open this, if you can. If they should "understand with their heart and turn," Jesus promises, "I would heal them" (13:15).

Putting all of this together, we can see Matthew borrowing this conversation from Mark and then dramatically rearranging the furniture. In Mark, the purpose of the parables is to conceal things, at least for the time being, but in Matthew the purpose of the parables is to reveal things—especially to the wise, but even to the resistant who are willing to open their ears and hearts—to disclose the mysteries of the kingdom, even if this disclosure comes in the very demanding pedagogical form of parables.

From Crescendo to Decrescendo

The third difference in Matthew's version of the Sower comes from a change at the end of the parable. In Mark, after seed fell uselessly on hard ground, rocky ground, and thorny ground, other seed fell into the good soil and produced grain "thirty, sixty, and a hundredfold" (Mark 4:8). Matthew reverses the numbers—"some a hundredfold, some sixty, some thirty" (Matt. 13:8)—turning Mark's crescendo into a decrescendo.

The reversal of the numbers describing the harvest comes, not because Matthew wants to temper expectations, but because Matthew and Mark are describing different realities. In Mark, the harvest describes the coming of God's kingdom as a sudden reversal and as a fullness beyond all expectation. It is, as we noted in chapter 4, a parable about a situation of utter hopelessness into which the abundant harvest of God arrives as a complete surprise, a moment of astonishment. "Can you believe the kingdom harvest," Mark exclaims. "Thirtyfold! No, look! Sixtyfold! Wait, oh, my, a hundredfold!"

Matthew's parable, by contrast, focuses on the kingdom happening in those times when people hear Jesus' words and do them. Mark describes the kingdom as a macro event, the reversal of all things in the arrival of the Son in glory. So it is perfectly appropriate for the harvest to come with a trumpet blast, an overflowing cornucopia of thirty-sixty-a hundredfold, and an exclamation point. Matthew expects that same macro event, but in this parable describes the signs of that kingdom in the microevents of disciples hearing and taking to heart Jesus' words. Disciples grow in different measures—some a hundredfold, but some sixtyfold and others thirtyfold. Matthew, in contrast to Mark, is absorbed by the question of what kind of soil a person is, and he recognizes that even people who are good soil grow in different ways and at different levels.

Neither Mark's version of the Sower nor Matthew's actually contains the word for "seed." In Greek there are only modifiers; for example, the sower sowed "some," the sower sowed "other." In Mark 4:4, 5, and 7, the modifiers are singular, and in each case Matthew changes them to plural. Matthew wants to underscore that the sower sowed seeds (plural), which again almost surely refers to the specific teachings of Jesus and which together form "the word of the kingdom" (Matt. 13:18). Those seeds get planted in the soil of the faithful, and they grow—some dramatically at a hundredfold rate, but some only thirtyfold. That is the way it is with disciples in the community of faith, but it is all growth nevertheless.

Four Ways of Hearing

The last difference between Matthew's Parable of the Sower and Mark's version has to do with the interpretation Jesus gives the disciples in private. In Mark the plot moved this way: failure, failure again, failure yet again, and then astonishing success. The thrust of the parable comes in the amazing climax of the overwhelming harvest, and the purpose of the repeated crop failures is mainly to set up the miraculous turnaround, the stunning bumper crop at the end.

Matthew makes it clear, though, that each of the four sowings is worth pondering on its own, because each one stands for a different kind of hearing. In each case, someone hears the "word of the kingdom," and then something happens as a result. The four places where the seeds land—the path, rocky ground, thorns, good soil—form a representative encyclopedia of the different ways people hear and understand the word, both foolish and wise.

The Path

In the case of the path (13:19), the "word of the kingdom" is sown in a person's heart, but this person fails to understand what has been heard. The word, consequently, just lies there on the hard surface of a stubborn heart, ready to be snatched away by "the evil one" (13:19). The church knows about this, knows how many times Jesus' words are superficially heard, and since they are not understood, they are then "snatched away" and disfigured beyond recognition. As Frederick, the reclusive artist in the movie *Hannah and Her Sisters,* says after watching a huckster evangelist on television, "If Jesus came back and saw what's going on in his name, he'd never stop throwing up."[9]

Letters to a Young Pastor is a collection of letters of wisdom, reflection, and advice that the pastor-theologian Eugene Peterson wrote to his son Eric when Eric was a young pastor. In one of these letters, the father bemoans the current fascination of the church and its clergy with what Peterson considers to be a disfigured concept of "leadership." He writes that he had a sense that

> one of the primary seductions to pastoral faithfulness and integrity these days is this drumbeat of emphasis—throughout church and society—on leadership. All these books and conferences and tapes on leadership—how to be an effective leader, a successful leader, a powerful leader. Leadership distilled to technique and strategy and method. And much of it—maybe most—good and useful. But so much of it has little to do with what it means to be a pastor.[10]

These understandings of leadership, Peterson wrote, are not taken from Jesus but borrowed from the corporate world. Pastoral leadership, however, is radically different:

> [Pastors] get out of bed each morning and pray, "Lord Jesus Christ, I follow you. I deny myself. I take up my cross, and I follow you." Our basic identity is not leader but follower. Jesus never tells us to lead; he invites us to follow. Followership is previous to and more comprehensive than leadership.[11]

Peterson was saying, in essence, that the word of Jesus to "take up the cross and follow me" (10:38) has fallen often on the hard path and become distorted into "pick up your portfolio and manage the people."

The Rocky Ground

The seeds that withered away on rocky ground, Jesus explains, represent "the one who hears the word and immediately receives it with joy; yet such a person has no root, but endures only for a while, and when trouble or persecution arises on account of the word, that person immediately falls away" (13:20–21).

The point here is what Christians have discovered through the centuries: authentic commitment to the way of Jesus carries a cost. The way of the kingdom is not well received when it is practiced in a world where the way of darkness is in charge (how many pastors, white and Black, had crosses burned in their yards in the 1950s and '60s because they preached the gospel of God's love for all?). Christians can expect resistance and opposition. The question is, "When trouble or persecution arises," what then?

The southern writer Flannery O'Connor explores the cost of commitment to Jesus in dramatic fashion in her short story "A Good Man Is Hard to Find." In this story, a family, including a pious grandmother, are on an automobile trip in rural Georgia. The countryside is full of rumors that a notorious prison escapee, called "the Misfit," is loose in the land. As misfortune would have it, on a deserted road in a remote place the family experiences an automobile accident and must wait for help to come along. Unfortunately, the Misfit and his gang are the ones who come along, and the family immediately recognizes that their lives are in danger.

The grandmother engages the Misfit in an unctuous and pious conversation, trying even to coax the Misfit into praying, but the fugitive will have none of it. Senselessly, ruthlessly, and without provocation, the outlaws begin to shoot the members of the family one by one. The terrified grandmother attempts to use her religious language to flatter and appease the Misfit and save herself. Crying out to Jesus, she tells the Misfit that she knows he must come from good "blood," from a good family and that he would surely not shoot a lady.

In response to her cries, the Misfit ironically snarls out a truth about the radical nature of following Jesus:

> "Jesus was the only One that ever raised the dead," The Misfit continued, "and He shouldn't have done it. He thrown everything off balance. If He did what He said, then it's nothing for you to do but throw away everything and follow Him, and if He didn't, then it's nothing for you to do but enjoy the few minutes you got left by killing somebody or burning down his house or doing some other meanness to him. No pleasure but meanness."[12]

His words and his menacing threat expose the rootlessness of the old woman's faith, and, as the parable warned, she falls weakly away: "'Maybe He didn't raise the dead,' the old lady mumbled, not knowing what she was saying and feeling so dizzy that she sank down in the ditch with her legs twisted under her."[13]

The Thorns

If the rocky soil represents those who lose grip on the gospel because of negative forces—trouble and persecution—the thorns represent those who are seduced away by something that seems more attractive, most notably the lure of wealth.

The North American church knows firsthand the dangerous lure of wealth. Many of our congregations are, in fact, built in the thorn patch, constantly overwhelmed by the lures of prosperity. "God wants us to prosper financially, to have plenty of money, to fulfill the destiny He has laid out for us," Joel Osteen, senior pastor of one of the largest churches in the United States, wrote in a 2005 pastoral letter to his congregation.[14] In his best-selling book

Your Best Life Now, Osteen speaks with contempt of his father, an old-style evangelist, who was raised with what his son calls "a poverty mentality."[15] Osteen tells of the time when his father's church hosted a visiting evangelist for a several-night-long series of services. This clergyman stayed with the Osteens in their home. The Sunday after these special services, a businessman in the congregation told Osteen's father that he knew how hard it must be to bear the expense of this guest and handed him a check for a thousand dollars. That was "tantamount," writes Osteen, "to ten thousand dollars today!"

Osteen's father refused the check, indicating that it should be put instead in the offering plate. Osteen writes:

> God was trying to increase my dad. He was trying to prosper him, but because of my Daddy's deeply imbedded poverty mentality, he couldn't receive it. What was Daddy doing? He was eating more cheese and crackers. God was trying to get him to step up to the banquet, but because of Daddy's limited mind-set he couldn't see himself having an extra thousand dollars.[16]

It is easy, of course, to see the superficiality of Osteen's view of God and the gospel. But, of course, Osteen is but the most obvious and ugly edge of a more widespread notion of entitlement that chokes out the commitment to carry a cross. The seeds of the kingdom are proclaimed and sowed, but the thorns of selfishness and greed grow up, and the result: "it yields nothing" (13:22)

The Good Soil

There are times, of course, when the gospel is proclaimed, the words of Jesus are heard, understood, and taken to heart, and the result is the bearing of fruit in the life of a disciple, sometimes a hundredfold, sometimes less—but bearing fruit nonetheless.

One of the main leaders in Black South Africa's struggle against apartheid in the 1980s and '90s was Bishop Desmond Tutu. A deeply committed Christian, Tutu was constantly the subject of persecution by the government. The government seized his passport twice, to forbid Tutu traveling overseas to spread information about his country. On two occasions, Tutu was attacked by judicial commissions in South Africa, and his life was always being threatened.

But it was not only the government and white society that mounted opposition to Tutu. Because of his commitment to nonviolence and to the love and forgiveness of Christ's kingdom, Tutu was often seen by Black South Africans as too moderate and timid. For example, Buti Thlagale, a young Roman Catholic priest connected to South Africa's Black Consciousness movement, had a love-hate relationship with Tutu. He both adored Tutu and criticized him.

When others called for more aggressive action, Tutu always responded, "Love your enemy." Thlagale complained. "At his age, he should hate a little bit more. There's this problem with Tutu—he believes in the Gospel literally."[17]

It was, of course, Tutu's unshakable belief in the gospel—his believing the gospel literally—that kept him going, and it was love, not hate, and peace, not violence, that ultimately brought justice to South Africa. The seeds of the gospel landed in good soil in Tutu, and bore fruit a hundredfold.

THE PARABLE OF THE WHEAT AND THE WEEDS (MATTHEW 13:24–30, 36–43)

The Wheat and the Weeds is another sowing parable, but this time the parable is unique to Matthew. If the Parable of the Sower was all about the "good soil," this time the parable focuses not on good soil but on "good seed." The owner of a field, we are told at the very beginning, "sowed good seed in his field" (13:24).

One would expect, of course, that good seed would result in a good crop. But the plot of the parable takes a sinister turn. At night, when everybody at the farm was asleep, an "enemy" crept out into the field and performed some nighttime sowing, this time weeds. Naturally, when the first shoots of the wheat crop appeared, the weeds also appeared.

The slaves who worked the farm noticed immediately the mixed crop, and they responded in two ways. First, they challenged the owner of the field: "Master, did you not sow good seed in your field? Where then did these weeds come from?" The master indicates that the weeds were not sown by him, but by a foe. "An enemy has done this," he says (13:28).

Second, they volunteer to try to fix the problem: "Then do you want us to go and gather them?" The master turns them down. "No, for in gathering the weeds you would uproot the wheat along with them," he says. "Let both of them grow together until the harvest; and at harvest time I will tell the reapers, Collect the weeds first and bind them in bundles to be burned, but gather the wheat into my barn" (13:29–30).

We can dispense quickly with the idea, one that has grown up in the popular interpretation of this parable, that there is a variety of weed in ancient Palestine that, when it first sprouts, looks just like a young wheat plant. Only when it matures can one tell that it is a weed. According to this view, no wonder the master refused to let the slaves get rid of the weeds. At this point in the growth, one cannot tell the difference between the wheat and the weeds, and if they look the same, then surely the slaves would "uproot the wheat along with [the weeds]" (13:29).

Even if there was such a wheat-masquerading weed in the botany of the ancient Mideast, so what? The parable clearly indicates that the slaves can, in fact, tell the difference between the wheat and the weeds. That's what gets them concerned about the situation. This is a story, the storyteller gets to set the terms, and the plot turns on this very realization: there are both weeds and wheat out there in the field, and the slaves are not confused about which is which. So we can put aside monographs on "Weed Species in Ancient Palestine" and pay attention to the storyteller's art. The slaves can discriminate between weeds and wheat in this parable, no question. So now what?

According to the parable, the reason the master puts up his hand to halt the slaves from dashing into the field to do weeding isn't because they can't tell the difference between weed plants and wheat, but rather because of timing. "Don't do it now," the master indicates. "For in gathering the weeds you would uproot the wheat along with them." The weeds and the wheat will eventually be separated, the master tells them, but not now, only at the harvest: "[A]t harvest time I will tell the reapers, Collect the weeds first and bind them in bundles to be burned, but gather the wheat into my barn" (13:30).

If we had not guessed it before, we can surely see it now: this parable is not a farming manual. It's an eschatological parable about the kingdom of heaven. While most gardeners would love it if savvy gardening meant not bothering about the weeds in the backyard vegetable patch until it's time to gather the fruits, to leave weeds growing all summer among the tomato plants would be madness. But in the kingdom of heaven, it's wisdom. The weeds and the wheat will eventually be separated, but not now. In the kingdom, the separation happens only at the end, at the harvest.

After Jesus tells the Parable of the Wheat and the Weeds, he tells the crowds two more parables, the Parable of the Mustard Seed and the Parable of the Woman and the Yeast (13:31–33). Then Jesus leaves the crowds and retreats "into the house" with his disciples. There, in private, the disciples ask for a tutorial: "Explain to us the parable of the weeds of the field" (13:36).

This raises the question, Why the delayed interpretation? When Jesus told the Parable of the Sower, the disciples got a private interpretation of that parable immediately, but here Jesus has told three parables before the disciples get an explanation of the first one. And why do the disciples ask only about the Wheat and the Weeds and not about all three parables?

Maybe the answers are simple. Perhaps Matthew simply wanted to depict Jesus preaching a sermon comprising several parables before having him leave the crowds to enter the house. Maybe the Parable of the Wheat and the Weeds is the hardest of the three parables, prompting the disciples' request for an explanation of that one and not the others. More likely, though, the three parables are linked in Matthew's scheme of things. The explanation of the Parable of the

Wheat and the Weeds depends somehow on the Parable of the Mustard Seed and the Parable of the Woman and the Yeast being told beforehand.

Decoding the Parable

When Jesus explains the Parable of the Wheat and the Weeds to the disciples (13:36–43), he begins by giving them a key to decode the parable: the sower of good seed is the Son of Man, the field is the world, the good seed are the children of the kingdom, the weeds are the children of the evil one, the enemy who sowed them is the devil, the harvest is the end of the age, and the reapers are angels (13:37–39). In other words, this is an allegory, and you need a scorecard to know the players. When we do know the players, the penny drops. We realize that not only is this parable not a farming manual; it's not even a purely this-worldly story. It is a story about cosmic conflict and the ultimate fate of humanity. The recognition allows us to take a closer look at the three essential questions embedded in the plot of the parable:

Question #1: "God, Did You Do This?"

In the parable, the slaves are shocked to see weeds growing and befouling the good crop of wheat. Now we know the cosmic scope of the story, that the sower is actually the Son of Man, God's own agent, the one who will ultimately stand in glory as judge over all the nations (see Matt. 25:31–46). We also know that the field is the world, and knowing these things, the question of the slaves—"Master, did you not sow good seed in your field? Where then did these seeds come from?" (13:27)—comes into dramatic focus. This is the theodicy question. They had been singing, "This is my Father's world: I rest me in the thought of rocks and trees, of skies and seas, God's hand the wonders wrought." Then they arose one morning to see that this world is infected with weeds, with evil. There may be anger in their voices: "We thought you sowed good seed? What's all this evil, master? Did you do this? Is this the world you created? Is this the world you want?"

"No," responds the master, "an enemy has done this" (13:28). We know from the scorecard that this "enemy" is not a jealous neighbor farmer—no, an enemy way bigger than that. This is a cosmic struggle, and the enemy is none other than the old snake, the ancient accuser, Satan himself.

The appearance of Satan in this parable presents a challenge to many contemporary readers. "The Devil made me do it!" was a satirical joke popularized by television comedian Flip Wilson in the 1970s, not a serious theological statement. Most people today look for the sources of evil in the baser human motives, such as greed or fearful bigotry, rather than in some murky devil wandering to and fro across the earth.

What this washes out, though, is the sheer mystery of evil. We know in our experience that evil cannot be reduced to merely human scale. Add the greed in me to the greed in you and the greed of all other humans, and we have still not accounted for the total force of greed in the world. Evil is more than the sum of its parts. As one of the soldiers who attempted to account for his participation in the massacre of innocent villagers in the Vietnamese village of My Lai, said, "Something came over me." Or ask almost anyone who has struggled with addiction, and they will honestly speak of being at the mercy of a power they cannot control on their own.

"Let's start with the devil," theologian William C. Placher wrote in a discussion about the saving work of Christ. He continues,

> Forget about pictures of horns and goat hooves. Simply face a reality to which Scripture and our own experience both testify: evil has its own kind of power. Whether it's the logic of warfare that seems to require murdering innocent people, or the sexual affair that gathers its own momentum, or the economic situation that forces a factory closure, or the history of abuse that goes down the generations in a family, there are countless situations in which the evil that surrounds us seems greater than the sum of the bad deeds of the human agents involved.
>
> We make free choices, but then we find ourselves entrapped. We can blame the military-industrial complex, or the media, or the corrupt politicians, and all that often contains a measure of truth, but beyond it lies a power that evil itself seems to exercise on all those who have fallen under its sway. Evil seems to have its own kind of cunning, as if it were plotting to entrap sinners yet further into the consequences of their sins. Whether or not there is someone named "Satan," we can certainly experience evil as a malevolent force beyond any of the human persons we confront.
>
> Therefore, if God is to rescue us from the mess we're in, it is not enough that we be comforted by the thought of God's solidarity with us, or even that we be reconciled to God. Something needs to be done about the power that evil has over us. Evil needs to be defeated.[18]

Regarding "the power evil has over us," we can see this in many places, including the fog of war. In a review of *Generation Kill*, the HBO miniseries that followed the activity of "First Recon," the First Reconnaissance Battalion of US Marines in the early days of the Iraq War, journalist Sue Halpern writes,

> First Recon could be freshmen on a spring-break road trip. . . . They drive along, mile after mile, shouting out insults to men in "man pajamas" and eating junk food and singing off-key, and it gets so tedious for the viewer as well as for the Marines that one begins to appreciate

> the whiny desire of the youngest of them, nineteen-year-old James Trombley, to "get some." His first "kill" comes during a skirmish, and he's as happy as a boy who has bagged his first deer. Then the rules of engagement change, and the higher-ups declare that all Iraqis are to be considered hostile, meaning that everyone is fair game, no matter if they're firing a gun or not, no matter if they're carrying a weapon or not, no matter if they're men or women or children or dogs. It's under these rules that Trombley pulls the trigger on two camel-herders walking in the distance, potential bad guys who turn out, in fact, to be unarmed boys. Later, this will earn him the nickname "Whopper," because Whoppers are sold at Burger King and the initials for Burger King, B.K., are the same as those for "baby killer." It's a term of endearment.[19]

How did nineteen- and twenty-year-old young men—boys in a way—from farms in Nebraska and small towns in Alabama and Ohio become "baby killers"? How do carefree American kids who look like they're on a spring-break road trip become heartless murderers? "Evil seems to have its own kind of cunning," says Placher. No wonder the slaves in our parable were shocked: "Did you do this, master? Where did these evil weeds come from? We thought you sowed good seed in your world."

"No," the master responds, "this is not the world I desire. This is the work of an enemy, the work of evil."

Question #2: Do You Want Us to Fix It?

When the master assures the slaves that it was not he, but an enemy, who has sowed evil in the world, they immediately rush to volunteer to go into the field and root out the noxious crop of weeds: "Then do you want us to go and gather them?" (13:28).

Now that we know that this parable is about the whole of creation and the massive sweep of cosmic time, as well as good and evil, we recognize immediately how foolish and arrogant these slaves are to think that eradicating the weeds is in their power. They are like a freshly graduated MD on the first day of her residency in the oncology ward, a wing of the hospital filled with seriously ill and dying cancer patients, saying to her supervisor, "Do you want me to go in there and take care of this?" Would that you could, but it is not in your power to "take care of it." I am reminded of a radio talk show I once heard in which the host and a scientist guest were discussing an eclipse of the sun that was to occur the next day. The scientist described safe ways to view the eclipse and warned sternly against the dangerous practice of viewing a solar eclipse with the naked eye. A caller to the show foolishly asked, "Well, if this eclipse is so dangerous, why are they having it?" Some things are not in our control.

Indeed, it is the issue of control that is front and center. The chief role of Satan, as God's adversary, is not merely to tempt people to cheat on history exams or drink too much wine, but to usurp the role of God altogether. Already in Matthew we have seen Satan take Jesus to a high mountain, where Jesus could get a good view of "all the kingdoms of the world and their splendor." Then Satan purrs, "All of these I will give you, if you will fall down and worship me" (4:8–9). Talk about an eclipse of the sun! That's what Satan does—that's what evil does: attempts to come between us and the living God, to usurp God's place, to beckon us to let all that we are revolve around the dark moon of evil rather than the brightness of God's glory. "So, God thinks God can sow good seed and that God is the one power in this field," shrieks the satanic power of evil. "I'll show God who's in charge!" And he—the anti-creator—sneaks in by night to scatter his vile spawn in the world.

The irony is that the offer of the slaves—"Do you want us to go and gather them?"—on the surface looks innocent, even cooperative, but down deep it is the mirror image of the enemy's vain attempt to control what is not in their power to control. If God was foolish enough to allow an enemy to sow destruction, then we'll have to take matters into our own hands and repair the damage.

In the 1920s, American business tycoon John D. Rockefeller Jr. advocated bringing business techniques into the work and mission of the church. In an article for *New Era Magazine*, arrogantly titled "Efficiency in the Lord's Business," Rockefeller trumpeted, "I see the church molding the thought of the world as it has never done before, leading in all great movements as it should, I see it literally establishing the Kingdom of God on earth."[20] In other words, are there weeds mixed in with the wheat in the field? No problem, let us out there with business methods, and we'll literally establish the kingdom of God on earth! We know how to run Standard Oil; running the kingdom of heaven is not a challenge, really.

The master knocks such presumption off its pedestal: "No, for in gathering the weeds you would uproot the wheat along with them" (13:29). In other words, you don't have the discernment, you don't have the wisdom, you don't have the finely tuned power to do the job of rooting out the weeds, of eliminating evil from the world.

This refusal leads to the next question, this one implied in the plot of the parable:

Question #3: Will It Always Be This Way?

If the enemy has spoiled God's world with evil mixed in among the fruit of good seed, and God has exposed our fist-pumping pledges to pluck out the weeds as vain and shortsighted, then what? Do we have to live for all time with a polluted creation?

No, says the master. The harvest is coming. "Let both of them grow together until the harvest; and at harvest time I will tell the reapers, Collect the weeds first and bind them in bundles to be burned, but gather the wheat into my barn" (13:30). In other words, at God's great harvest, all evil will be destroyed, and the goodness in creation will be preserved in God's storehouse.

At first, it may seem that this parable is teaching quietism. Good and evil lying side by side in the world? Don't worry about it. Leave it alone and let the angels sort it out at the end. The possibility that the parable counsels followers of Jesus to simply sit on their hands, awaiting judgment day, so alarmed one parables interpreter, Herman Hendrickx, that he leapt over the details of the parable and raced to the battlements to issue a counterorder: "So, for the love of all humankind we will have to attack the tares, leaving it, however, to the Father to decide who will ultimately sit at his right and left hand (Mt. 20:23)."[21]

But Hendrickx needn't have worried. To understand this parable as encouragement to relax moral action would be a misunderstanding of the Gospel of Matthew and consequently a misunderstanding of the parable itself. Matthew, after all, is the Gospel that shines the light on disciples who hear Jesus' words and do them, that urges us to be peacemakers, that advocates being so zealous in efforts for justice that we risk being persecuted for righteousness' sake.

No, to the contrary, the purpose of this parable is not to tamp down faithful service in the world but to describe the environment in which that service inevitably happens. We live in an ambiguous world where wheat and weeds, light and shadow, good and evil are constantly in a confusing and tangled mixture. The parable doesn't discourage ethical action. Rather, it discourages the notion that human efforts can achieve purification of the world.

We have one more step to take in understanding this complex parable, but we cannot take that step until we have explored the two parables that Jesus tells between the Parable of the Wheat and the Weeds and its interpretation: the Parable of the Mustard Seed and the Parable of the Woman and the Yeast.

THE PARABLE OF THE MUSTARD SEED (MATTHEW 13:31–32)

Once again, we have a parable that also appears in Mark (see the treatment of Mark's version at pp. 80–89). There are only two significant differences between Mark's version and Matthew's. For Mark, as we noted in chapter 4, it is important that the little mustard seed be sown on the earth, the ground, *gēs* (γῆς), while in Matthew the mustard seed is sowed in the planter's field, *agrō* (ἀγρῷ). The Greek word for field is the same one used in the Parable of the Wheat and the Weeds, and provides a link between the two parables.[22] The "field," we will soon be told, is "the world" (13:38). The second difference is that, in Mark, the mustard seed grows into a great shrub with large branches, affording shelter to the birds of the air, while in Matthew the seed grows into a great shrub that "becomes a tree, so that the birds of the air come and make nests in its branches" (13:32). For Mark, the emphasis falls on hospitality, the welcoming and expansive branches of the shrub, while in Matthew the emphasis falls on the contrast between the tiny mustard seed and the impressive greatness of the tree that ultimately grows up.

The key insight to take away from this parable in Matthew is that the presence of the kingdom of heaven is like someone sowing the smallest of all seeds in the field, that is, the world. That world is fully compromised, as we saw in the previous parable, with wheat but also vexatious weeds growing all over the place. The contrast in this parable is not only that of a small seed compared to the tree that it eventually produces but also in the ways of the kingdom contrasted to the ways of the world. In a world dominated by Roman imperialists with a big army, the solution might seem to be to send in a bigger army. But in the kingdom, the response is to plant a mustard seed. As Klyne Snodgrass suggests, this parable conveys the truth that "the kingdom, which has already begun with Jesus, does not come with a glorious bang and the defeat of Rome; rather it comes unexpectedly, almost unnoticed."[23]

THE PARABLE OF THE WOMAN AND THE YEAST (MATTHEW 13:33)

This parable seems so gentle and inoffensive. What could be disturbing about a woman mixing bread dough? But it has jagged edges all around. To begin, there is the woman herself. Comparing the kingdom of heaven to anything in the life of a woman was bound to be unexpected at least. It unsettled the paternalistic, nationalistic, and even militaristic expectations of some of Jesus' hearers. Just saying the words "the kingdom of heaven" was, to some hearers, certain to conjure up the sound of clanging swords and the clatter of horses and chariots. No, said Jesus, the kingdom is more like a woman, a woman making bread dough, to be precise. Kneading and baking bread was, in the ancient world, largely "women's work," and Jesus suddenly whisks his hearers from the parade grounds to the clay oven and the woman working the dough, from militancy to domesticity.

Corrupting the Corruption

Then there is the business of the yeast. In the vast majority of instances in Scripture, yeast is a negative image. "Beware of the yeast of the Sadducees and Pharisees," Jesus will tell his disciples later (16:6). "Seven days you shall eat unleavened bread," Exodus instructs, regarding observance of the Passover. "On the first day you shall remove leaven from your houses, for whoever eats leavened bread from the first day until the seventh day shall be cut off from Israel" (Exod. 12:15). Paul, speaking about the corrupting teaching inflecting the Galatian congregation, warns, "A little yeast leavens the whole batch of dough" (Gal. 5:9), meaning essentially, "One rotten apple spoils the whole barrel."[24]

The Platonist philosopher Plutarch, roughly a contemporary of Matthew, also issued warnings about yeast. Asked, Why was it not permitted for the priest of Jupiter to touch yeast? he says, "Yeast is . . . the product of corruption, and produces corruption in the dough with which it is mixed; for the dough becomes flabby and inert, and altogether the process of leavening seems to be one of putrefaction; at any rate if it goes too far, it completely sours and spoils the flour."[25]

We catch a whiff of this dangerous quality of yeast in the language of the parable. The woman did not merely "mix" the yeast in with all that flour (as the NRSV suggests). The Greek word is *enekrypsen* (ἐνέκρυψεν), from which we get the English word "encrypted." She encrypted the yeast into the flour.

This encryption has two implications. First, the yeast was hidden. The woman doesn't just stir in the yeast; she conceals it in the flour. This idea of hiddenness is a theme in Matthew. Earlier Jesus prayed, "I thank you, Father, Lord of heaven and earth, because you have hidden these things from the wise and the intelligent and have revealed them to infants; yes, Father, for such was your gracious will" (11:25–26). The things of God are hidden from the eyes of the elite, those who believe themselves to be discerning and all-knowing, and yet are perceived by the little ones, the children of faith. God's kingdom makes "wise the simple" (Ps. 19:7). The very next parable Jesus will speak in Matthew announces that the kingdom itself is like "treasure hidden in a field" (Matt. 13:44). In Matthew, God and God's kingdom are already present and at work, but hidden to ordinary eyes, out of sight. As Günter Bornkamm said, "God's reign is hidden from us, and must be believed and understood in its hiddenness. Not in the way the apocalypticists thought, beyond the heavens, in the bosom of a mysterious future, but here, hidden in the everyday world of the present time, where no one is aware of what is already taking place."[26]

There are two realms of activity: the surface, the visible, where human activity reigns, and the hidden deep, where God is working out of sight, ultimately to transform all things. Matthew says that the very reason Jesus speaks in parables is to announce to the visible surface prophetic news of what is taking place out of sight, to bring to speech what has been hidden from the beginning of the world. Right after speaking the Parable of the Woman and the Yeast, Matthew makes this connection clear by saying that Jesus fulfills these words of "the prophet" (Matthew may think of David as a "prophet" because the words he cites are from Ps. 78:2):

> "I will open my mouth to speak in parables;
> I will proclaim what has been hidden from the foundation of the world."
> Matt. 13:35

But, second, there is more in the woman's action than hiddenness. The woman's encryption of the yeast into the flour also conveys a hint of stealth. The woman is secreting, even smuggling, yeast into a whole heap of flour and transforming it through a process that smacks of corruption. The woman is not innocently working away at a batch of sourdough but, symbolically, committing an act of sabotage.

What is being sabotaged? Some commentators have suggested that the flour represents the temple cult, and the corrupting effect of the yeast on the flour represents Jesus' "attack on temple and cult, an attack that comports with Jesus' displacement of the righteous and pious in Israel with the poor and destitute, the tax collectors and harlots: 'The tax collectors and prostitutes go into the kingdom, but you (the Pharisees) do not (Matt. 21:31).'"[27] Jesus did have a reputation, according to Matthew, for claiming that he would destroy the temple and rebuild it in three days (26:61; 27:40), and perhaps the parable of the yeast is a foreshadowing of Jesus' at first hidden but finally thoroughgoing undermining of the cultus.

But such a view is too narrow here. The Parable of the Woman and the Yeast comes in the middle of a swatch of parables that have the whole world in view, and the hidden, fermenting yeast of God's kingdom is undermining not just the Jerusalem cult in the religious situation of Jesus' day but all of the powers and kingdoms of this world, always and everywhere. The kingdom of heaven destroys the old world as it creates a new reality. Again, as Bornkamm said, "To make the reality of God present: this is the essential mystery of Jesus. This making-present of the reality of God signifies the end of the world in which it takes place."[28] Bornkamm is right. The woman in our parable looks as if she is preparing to bake bread, but if she is smuggling kingdom yeast into the flour of the world, she is bringing about the end of that world.

In the Parable of the Mustard Seed, the tiny seed, representing the seemingly insignificant reality of the kingdom, is sowed in a field, which represents the world. Here the kingdom, symbolized by yeast, is covert. The flour, symbolizing the world, is, by contrast visible and vast. Scholars are uncertain what "three measures of flour" (13:33) adds up to, but everyone recognizes it is an enormous amount. In his book about breadmaking, *Bake and Be Blessed,* Father Dominic Garramone, who is also known as "the bread monk," writes that three measures of flour constitute "a ridiculously large amount of flour—you'd need a 100-quart Hobart mixer with a dough hook as big as your leg to knead it!"[29] Jeremias guesses that we are talking about fifty pounds of flour here, which would make enough bread for at least a hundred people.[30] Ulrich Luz ups the ante, calculating that three measures of flour would produce about 110 pounds of bread.[31]

So the first characteristic of the flour that jumps out at us is the sheer volume of it. Three measures are three measures, and that's a lot of flour, no matter how one measures it. Looking more closely, we see that three is not a number plucked out of thin air but in fact has biblical precedent. Robert Funk has noted three occasions in the Old Testament when three measures of flour are mentioned.[32] First, in Genesis 18, when Abraham was visited by God, in the form of three strangers, by the oaks of Mamre, Abraham said to the visitors, "Let me bring a little bread, that you may refresh yourselves" (Gen. 18:5). He then ducked into the tent and said to Sarah, "Make ready quickly three measures of choice flour, knead it, and make cakes" (Gen. 18:6). Likewise, when the angel of the Lord visited Gideon under the oak at Ophrah, Gideon prepared for his visitor "a kid, and unleavened cakes from an ephah [that is, three measures] of flour" (Judg. 6:19). The point in both of these stories is that cakes made from three measures of flour is an extraordinary overflowing of hospitality. As Funk notes, "[T]he amount is suitable for the celebration of the epiphany."

This theme is continued in the third instance in the Old Testament of the use of three measures of flour. When Hannah dedicates her son Samuel to the Lord at Shiloh, she takes with her as an added offering "a three-year-old bull, an ephah of flour [again, three measures], and a skin of wine" (1 Sam. 1:24). It is hard to imagine that the enormity of the "three measures of flour" in the parable would not at least rhyme with these earlier biblical examples. The flour is ordinary, but there are three measures of it, and the bells go off. The three measures represent not only just a large amount of flour, but what the flour could become when transformed by the kingdom yeast, how it could be used, as an offering, a sign of God's presence, a sacramental element. As Funk says, "The everyday realism of the parable of the leaven appears to be shattered, then, on the gross amount of dough—about as much as a woman could knead at one time—and the specific amount is intended to suggest that the occasion is no ordinary one, perhaps even an epiphany."[33]

The End Game

It is important to notice not only the yeast, the woman's stealth, and the significant amount of flour, but also how the parable ends. We might expect it to end with the woman taking beautifully baked bread, and a lot of it, out of the oven. In a similar parable in the *Gospel of Thomas*, that is indeed what happens. A woman takes a small amount of yeast, hides it in dough, and the result was "large loaves" (*Gos. Thom.* 96). But in our parable in Matthew, the end result is not sizable loaves or even, as we might expect, a huge quantity of bread. In fact, the main focus of this parable is, perhaps surprisingly, not on bread at all (no bread is baked here) but on the leavening, the transformation of the flour. The parable ends with all of that flour completely leavened. Some may say that this parable is about a woman baking bread, but it's not really. It's about a woman doing what it takes to *leaven* the flour by "corrupting" the huge amount of flour with hidden yeast. If the flour were pure and good, that corruption would be a travesty, but the flour is the world—a world, like the field in the Parable of the Wheat and the Weeds, inextricably corrupted itself. So here is the primary equation: the woman is corrupting the corruption. The yeast smuggled in by the woman is, like the kingdom of heaven, corrupting the corruption of the world, until the whole world is leavened by the kingdom.

Snodgrass downplays all of this, discounting the odd features of this parable, preferring to see it as a fraternal (but not identical) twin of the Parable of the Mustard Seed. The aim of both of these parables is to "portray the surprisingly large effect of something small."[34] After all, everyday breadmaking involves yeast, no need to make much of that. If the Parable of the Woman and the Yeast adds anything to the Mustard Seed, it is the idea that the working of the kingdom is concealed. In the kingdom, "[a] hidden power, hardly discernable to some, is already and irresistibly working."[35]

But, while it is true that, practically speaking, the amount of yeast implied in the parable is small relative to the flour, the parable in fact says nothing explicitly about smallness. If Jesus wanted to underscore how small the yeast was over against the large amount of flour, as he did about the tiny mustard seed, he forgot to mention it. What he does mention is the jarring symbols—the woman, the yeast, the encryption, the three measures, the leavening—and they begin to pile up, hinting that this parable is more complex than Snodgrass would suggest.

Luz lists how many unexpected and peculiar details are packed into this brief parable. For example, where we might expect to get a story about the world of males, we get the picture of a woman at work, which, Luz says, Jesus' hearers would have found "a great surprise." Where a reader might expect "kneading" we get "hiding." We get the unsettling element of yeast, and, Luz continues, "[l]eaven is not one of the metaphors that demonstrates a relationship to the Kingdom of God." If the parable were simply about how something small could change a huge amount of flour, Luz suggests, the image of salt would have worked better than the more ambiguous leaven. Putting all this together, Luz notes, in a wry understatement, that this parable "does not describe what a farmer's wife ordinarily does."[36] This parable is not the *Good Housekeeping Cookbook*; it's more like *Lord of the Rings.* If Matthew had wanted to include a simple confidence-instilling story about a concealed kingdom force steadily growing to a surprising result, he had Mark's Parable of the Seed Growing Secretly (Mark 4:26–29) right in front of him ready to use. No, this parable contains hiddenness, stealthiness, and extravagance.

Where do we see in our history the kind of God-event pointed to in this parable? Where do we find the kingdom to be "at hand" in the ways of this parable? Not far from where I am writing these words, in rural Maryland along the Chesapeake Bay, is the birthplace of Harriet Tubman. She was enslaved on a small farm nearby, on land rich with corn, wheat, oats, and timber. But Harriet, a small and somewhat frail woman, no more than five feet tall, a woman who could neither read nor write, boldly escaped to freedom in the North and then became a "Moses" figure, repeatedly risking her life by returning to Maryland helping to liberate scores of enslaved people.

In 1854, Harriet was living in freedom in Philadelphia, but she heard that her brothers, still on the farm in Maryland, were going to be sold by the slaveowner over the Christmas holiday. A sale meant almost surely that her brothers would be torn from their families and sent to larger, and even harsher, plantations in the South.[37]

Harriet asked a literate friend in Philadelphia to write a letter to Jacob Jackson, who lived near the farm where her brothers were enslaved. Jackson was a free Black who owned land and, more important to this case, was literate. Harriet, knowing that the letter would almost surely be intercepted by white postal inspectors and carefully read before passing it on to its rightful recipient, dictated the letter in a kind of code. After going on for a few sentences about mundane matters, the letter read, "Read my letter to the old folks, and give my love to them, and tell my brothers to be always watching unto prayer, and when the good old ship of Zion comes along, to be ready to step aboard."

The letter was from Tubman, of course, but it was signed "William Henry Jackson," Jacob Jackson's adopted son, at the time living in Canada. The white postal officials who screened the letter were completely puzzled. As Tubman biographer Sarah H. Bradford writes, "[The postal inspectors] . . . got together, wiped their glasses, and got them on, and proceeded to a careful perusal of this mysterious document. What it meant, they could not imagine, William Henry Jackson had no parents or brothers, and the letter was incomprehensible."[38]

So the inspectors thrust the letter in front of Jacob Jackson and demanded to know what it meant. Jacob read it and decoded it instantly. But he feigned ignorance, telling the officials that this letter "can't be meant for me, no how. I can't make head nor tail of it." But as soon as the investigators were out of sight, Jacob swiftly went to Harriet's brothers to tell them that their sister was on her way, that the "old ship of Zion" was soon to arrive, and that "they should be ready to start at a moment's notice for the North."[39]

The "old ship of Zion" is a phrase with double meaning from a spiritual. The old ship signifies the ultimate arrival of God's kingdom. In the spiritual, the old ship of Zion has Jesus as the captain and angels as the crew, and it's "making for the promised land." But the old ship of Zion also represents the arrival of God's liberating power at work close at hand, in the present circumstances of life. On Christmas Day, the old ship of Zion sailed as Harriet Tubman led her three brothers and two others out of slavery and into freedom.

To this day, some of the old-timers along the Chesapeake Bay say that Harriet Tubman was corrupt, "a thief who stole other people's property." But, of course, it was the massive system of enslavement that was truly corrupt, and like the woman in the parable, Tubman was smuggling some dangerous yeast into the huge load of flour, the flour of oppression, confident of the day when it would all be leavened. She was, in the name of God, corrupting the corruption of the world.

Putting the Puzzle Pieces Together

So, in this swath of Matthew 13, Jesus tells the crowd a parable, the Parable of the Wheat and the Weeds, and then goes inside "the house" and privately explains that parable to the disciples. But, as we have seen, before he performs this private instruction, he speaks two more parables publicly, the Mustard Seed and the Woman and the Yeast, accompanied by Matthew's observation of Jesus' speaking in parables being a fulfillment of the prophecy that what is hidden will be proclaimed publicly.

These three parables form an ensemble, and we are now in position to hear Jesus' explanation of the Parable of the Wheat and the Weeds as the interpretation of *that* parable, but an explanation nuanced by the other two parables as well.

The Parable of the Wheat and the Weeds shows us what not to do. This is a parable about what God does and what is happening on the cosmic plane.

The sower of the good seed is the Son of Man, the sower of the weeds is the devil, the reapers are the angels, and the harvest is the end of the age and the dawn of God's kingdom. In the meantime, do not expect in the present set of circumstances to experience the kingdom in pristine purity. Don't go looking for the kingdom in some unsullied desert sanctuary uncorrupted by the world. The field to be worked is this world; the kingdom is germinating in this world, this real and compromised world where good and evil so clearly coexist. And do not think you have the power to purify the world; you do not. Therefore, do not be tempted to think that human cooperation with the kingdom is purification, draining the swamp, clearing out the dive bar, plucking out all the weeds.

According to Matthew, a disciple of Jesus will later succumb to that temptation when he will try to stop Jesus' arrest by pulling out a sword and slicing off the ear of the slave of the high priest (26:51); talk about plucking out the weeds! Jesus will tell that disciple then what he is telling the disciples now: put away the sword; that is the world's way, not the kingdom's. Jesus will tell them that he could, if he desired, cry out to God and a hundred thousand angels would swarm to the rescue and put an abrupt halt to these evil schemes. But Jesus will go on to say that is not the way it is with God. "[H]ow then would the scriptures be fulfilled," Jesus will tell them, "which say it must happen in this way?" (26:54).

If the Parable of the Wheat and the Weeds tells the big, cosmic story of what *God* is doing—not what *we* are doing—to bring in the ultimate kingdom at the end of the age, then what role do we play? What are the followers of Jesus to do now? The other two parables—the Mustard Seed and the Woman and the Yeast—speak to these questions: the followers of Jesus should work for the kingdom in humility and hope. The work of God's people is done in humility because, over against the vastness and complexity of the field that is the world, our efforts are but a speck, as tiny as a mustard seed. All of the work of God's people—laboring for righteousness, for the meek, for the poor, for mercy and peace—is like the smallest of all seeds. You have to squint to see them. Kingdom work is mostly not prominent or powerful in the ways the world measures, but more like a barely noticed and uncelebrated woman putting yeast into bread flour. But such work is done in hope, because the promise is that mustard seed grows into a great tree of welcome and that yeast ultimately leavens the whole world.

This is a challenging message to receive. Can it be true that the ministry of the kingdom is a mustard seed, a dash of yeast, none of it very visible? What is that, in the face of the cruel realities of this world? We are not blind; we can see that the field is now rife with malevolent weeds, and we know the dire prospect that poses for the fate of the precious wheat. Are you sure, Jesus, you don't want us to form a well-financed task force to go out there and pluck up every single one of those damned weeds? "No," we hear from our Lord, "the total elimination of evil from the world is God's work, not yours. One day the angels will purify the field, one day the weeds will be collected and burned, the tiny seed will be a tree, the vast amount of flour will be fully leavened, and righteousness will shine like the sun, but for the time being, it's mustard seeds and yeast."

These parables are talking about hope, not progress. Jesus is not saying that, if we plant those mustard seeds and keep mixing in that yeast, inexorably the world will get better and better until everything is perfect. In the first parable, the field does not gradually become less weed infested. The reaping in the parable does not come at the end of the growing season but at the eschatological "end of the age" (13:39). The harvest comes as a surprise, not as the inevitable outcome of nature; it is a messianic disruption of the world and not the foreseeable unfolding of history toward improvement.

According to Matthew, the promise of the gospel is that the omega point of history is the reign of the glorified Christ. "For the Son of Man is to come with his angels in the glory of his Father," Jesus later tells his disciples (16:27). The dawn of Christ's reign means the toppling of all the kingdoms of this world. Righteousness will shine like the sun, and the ancient curse of evil will be destroyed. In the meantime, the role of disciples is neither disengagement from the world—climbing a mountain with a robe and a hymnbook to await Christ's coming. It is not overconfident action in the world—storming the citadels of the present age with scythes and swords, as if we could establish God's reign by our own wisdom and might. Disciples are, rather, to be about humble and hopeful kingdom work, planting mustard seeds and slipping yeast into the flour of the world.

But what is the relationship between God's actions and ours, between our little kingdom seeds and yeast and the ultimate disruption of history that occurs in Christ's reign? Our actions do not by any means cause Christ's kingdom to come, at least not in the ordinary meaning of "cause." Despite our misguided prayers, "O God, help us to bring in your kingdom" (as if *we* were the ones bringing in God's kingdom, with God in the role of helper), the kingdom arrives by God's initiative and by God's power. Rather, God takes our efforts for love, mercy, and peace and weaves those threads into the great tapestry of God's coming reign. Our kingdom ministries—small, often hidden, and to all appearances weak—anticipate the messianic age, indeed discern what God is already doing in the world to bring that age to fruition, and they join in that work of God and gain their meaning and energy from what God is doing.

To have Christian faith is to participate in two large narratives. One is the world's story, and we can be candid about the main plot: there are always weeds in the wheat, and the wheat's prospects don't look good. Many try to avoid this grim story by concocting false optimism or the power of positive thinking, by numbing themselves with fleeting pleasures, or by investing themselves in weeds, a growth stock, and thereby appearing for a season to be savvy worldly successes.

But Christians can face the world's story head-on because we also discern that another story, a counterstory, is at work, one that is hidden to the world but perceived by the eyes of faith and one that runs against the plot of the dominant narrative. The counterstory is the gospel, God's story, and though we pray an urgent and heartfelt "Come, Lord Jesus!" (Rev. 22:20), the timing of this story is not ours to decide. We don't get to hasten it or to force a premature conclusion by plunging ahead to pluck out the weeds. What we do get to do is to plant mustard seeds and mix gospel yeast into the world's flour, which means that by the grace of God we become characters in God's counterstory. We are confident that our small breaths on behalf of the kingdom will be gathered into the great hurricane God is bringing at the end of the age. Because we know, trust, and live God's story, we also know a secret the world does not yet know: the weeds do not prevail after all, and righteousness will shine like the sun.

So we await the end of the age, the time when the Son of Man will reign in glory and righteousness will triumph; but as another parable will say, "the bridegroom is delayed" (Matt. 25:5). The end of the age is not yet, and we continue to live and work during the delay and in a field filled with weeds as well as wheat. The Messiah's delay means, as Terry Eagleton has said, that "it falls to each generation to exercise a small portion of [Christ's] power on behalf of the oppressed. . . . In this sense, the Messiah's absence is not contingent but determinate: it clears a space in which the task of redeeming history is placed in the hands of humanity."[40] And the task that is placed in our hands, as we await the delayed Messiah, is the planting of mustard seed and the mixing in of yeast.

Where do these three interconnected parables—the Wheat and the Weeds, the Mustard Seed, and the Yeast—beckon us in order to be "on hand for that which is at hand," in order to see small, smuggled-in signs of the kingdom? In an essay titled "The Man Who Changed My Life," Archbishop Desmond Tutu recalled the agonizing experiences that were a part of daily life for Blacks in apartheid-era South Africa: "One of the earliest and most painful memories of my childhood is accompanying my father, a school principal, to the shop—I think it was in Ventersdorp—and witnessing him being humiliated by a young white shop assistant . . . being addressed, 'Ja, boy?' by one much younger than himself, and being forced to swallow his pride."[41]

But Tutu also remembered a different sort of experience. When he was quite young, he and his mother encountered Trevor Huddleston, a white Anglican priest whose fierce antiapartheid stance cut deeply against the grain of most whites in South Africa, even against many in his own church. But when Desmond Tutu met Huddleston, he did not know who he was, was not aware of his prominence or his outspoken views. For Tutu, Huddleston was just a man walking down the street, but the experience of meeting him was life-changing. Tutu said,

> I believe the most defining moment of my life occurred when I was about nine years old, outside the Blind Institute in Roodepoort where my mother was a domestic worker. We were standing on the stoep when this tall white man in a black cassock, and a hat, swept by. I did not know that it was Trevor Huddleston. He doffed his hat in greeting my mother.
>
> I was relatively stunned at the time, but only later came to realize the extent to which it had blown my mind that a white man would doff his hat to my mother. It was something I could never have imagined. The impossible was possible.[42]

A simple gesture—the doffing of a hat in respect—and yet it was a gesture that defied both the law of South Africa and the prevailing culture of racial hatred, a gesture so outside the norm that Tutu calls it "impossible." Tutu was so shocked by this action that he asked his mother why the man had done it. "Because he is an Anglican priest," his mother told him. "He is a man of God,"

"When she told me that he was an Anglican priest I decided there and then that I wanted to be an Anglican priest too. And what is more, I wanted to be a man of God," said Tutu.[43]

To realize that this small gesture by a follower of Jesus was pivotal for Desmond Tutu's life and vocation is to witness "the smallest of all seeds" transformed into a tree and a little bit of countercultural yeast leavening a whole nation.

THE PARABLE OF THE TREASURE HIDDEN IN A FIELD (MATTHEW 13:44)

This parable is only one verse long, but it is packed with action. In the space of a single compound sentence, a person finds a treasure hidden in a field, conceals it again, joyfully goes and sells all that he has, and then buys that field. It is this plot sequence—finding, selling, and buying—that led John Dominic Crossan, in his early work on the parables, to call this story one of three "paradigmatic" parables (the other two are the Parable of the Pearl of Great Value, which is the very next parable in Matthew, and the Parable of the Great Fish, which is found only in the *Gospel of Thomas*).[44]

Crossan argued that most of Jesus' parables emphasize a single kind of activity. They are either parables of *advent*, in which something unexpected appears that "opens up a new world and unforeseen possibilities"; parables of *reversal*, in which the kingdom turns the status quo upside down; or parables of *action*, in which a character in the parable engages in some kind of activity that wasn't available before and could not have been programmed by the actor.[45] "Paradigmatic" parables, by contrast, contain all three kinds of activity: *advent*, *reversal*, and *action*. In our Parable of the Treasure Hidden in a Field, the *advent* is the finding of the hidden treasure, the *reversal* is the willingness to sell everything the finder had, and the *action* is the buying of the field.

We will soon enough part company with Crossan on the meaning of this parable, but at this point we can agree with him, at least to the extent that he has rightly identified the essential threefold-plot structure of this parable (and, as we shall explore later, the similar plot in the subsequent Pearl of Great Value parable).

The Advent

"The kingdom of heaven," begins the parable, "is like treasure hidden in a field, which someone found and hid." What advents in this story is a treasure. It was hidden, and then it was there, visible and found.

We know almost nothing about the details of this finding of the treasure. We are told that "someone"—in Greek "a man," *anthrōpos* (ἄνθρωπος)—was the finder, but we don't know whether this "someone" was a farmer, a vineyard owner, a merchant, a king, a beggar, a lucky bloke taking a walk, or a treasure hunter; he was just "someone," an everyperson. We might imagine that he was plowing in the field, since that would be a likely way to unearth buried treasure, but that would be a guess. Some commentators fret about the fact that people in the first century who did menial work like plowing would be unlikely to have the worldly goods to raise enough money to buy the field. But such interpreters need to keep their eye on the ball. This is not a sociological anecdote; it's a parable, and wondrous things happen in parables. We have just heard about a mustard seed that grows into a tree and about a woman hiding yeast in enough flour to feed a Roman legion, so we can relax about how the guy who found the treasure raised the money to buy the field. We're in a parable here. The point is that Jesus doesn't say, and what this silence signals is that it doesn't matter much, not to the meaning of the parable at least. What matters is that a treasure that the man couldn't see a minute ago is now suddenly visible, and he has found it. The fact that the treasure is described as "hidden" does tend to emphasize the surprise of the discovery.

The Reversal

The finding of the hidden treasure sets in motion a string of dramatic events. The finder rehides the treasure, goes out and "sells all that he has," and then purchases the field, thus making the hidden treasure his own. Our imaginations can supply a number of possible emotions as the man performs these actions—self-congratulation, greed, an adrenaline rush, panic, anxiety—but again Jesus holds up a stop sign to all of our speculations. According to Jesus' telling of the story, the man had one and only one important emotion: joy. It was "in his joy" that he swapped all his possessions for a deed.

Here then is the reversal: at the beginning of the parable the man owns some stuff and not the field; at the end of the parable the guy doesn't own any of the stuff but does own the field, with its concealed treasure. Everything the man previously owned and valued has become expendable in the light of the found treasure. A day before, the man had no idea there was a treasure hidden in that field, but on this day, nothing is more important to him. A new world of value has replaced the old.

The Action

There are many actions in this brief parable, but the one toward which the whole story moves is the purchase of the field. One helpful way to analyze a story is to divide it into the beginning, the middle, and the end, and then to ask, "What is present at the end of the story that was not present at the beginning, and how did what happened in the middle cause this to be?" What we have at the end is that the man is now in possession of the field and the treasure. What happened in the middle was his selling all he owned in order that he might purchase the treasure-rich field.

We can see now how the springs and gears that operate this parable work together. Before the man went into the field, his life was stable (at least narratively), but then the advent of the hidden treasure turned his world upside down. Would he act on this new reality or not? He did. He sold all of the goods of his old life in order to enter into a future, breathtakingly new one that he could scarcely have imagined only hours before.

But there is a dark cloud in the sky we need to acknowledge. Many readers of this parable have been rubbed the wrong way by its ethical implications. This "someone" finds a treasure in a field and covers it up to keep anyone else from finding it. Then he runs out and raises enough cash to buy the field from the unsuspecting owner. Isn't this a deception? Is it even legal? It's hard to say. A number of commentators on this parable have rehearsed in minute detail various rabbinic regulations regarding the legality of keeping a treasure found in another's field. It turns out that the laws are complex and confusing. But perhaps the law isn't the main question. Was what the man did moral?

Several years ago, a "candid camera" type television show pulled a practical joke called "The One Millionth Customer" on a number of people. An actor for the show would pose as a customer at a supermarket. Carrying just one grocery item in his hand, he would approach the first person in line at the cash register and say in an urgent voice, "Sorry, I just have this one thing, and I left my dog in the car. Do you mind?" Of course, the person at the head of the line, wanting to be accommodating, would allow this fellow to break into line. But then, as soon as the cashier rang up his one item, lights would flash, sirens would sound, and confetti and balloons would fall from the ceiling. The store manager, carrying a huge mockup of a $1,000,000 check, would rush to the register, loudly announcing, "You are our one millionth customer, and you are the lucky winner of one million dollars!" The looks on the faces of those customers who had given up their places in line moved predictably from shock to dismay to anger as they realized that, had they not given away their place in line, they would have won the jackpot. Almost every one of them eventually voiced some version of protest: "Hey, this isn't right! That was supposed to be mine!"

Wouldn't the original owner of the field feel the same way if he ever discovered what the new buyer had done, covering up the treasure like that and then buying the field out from under him? In a later monograph devoted to this parable, *Finding Is the First Act: Trove Folktales and Jesus' Treasure Parable*, Crossan argues that the man in the parable is indeed immoral and, ironically, his immorality is the point.

Many years ago, a service of worship in the chapel at Princeton Theological Seminary included Martin Luther's hymn "A Mighty Fortress Is Our God." For the convenience of the worshipers, the words of the hymn were printed in the service bulletin. However, the printed lyrics contained an unfortunate typographical error. The soaring final verse, which is supposed to be, "Let goods and kindred go, this mortal life also," actually read, "Let goods and kindred go, this *moral* life also."

That wayward line provoked laughter among the congregation, but if Crossan's view is correct, the congregation was unwittingly singing an astute interpretation of the Parable of the Treasure Hidden in a Field. To Crossan, abandoning the moral life is precisely the import of this parable. The man who covered up the treasure and bought the field, says Crossan, "abandons, explicitly, his *goods*, and, implicitly, his *morals* to obtain the treasure."[46] Crossan sees the kingdom challenge of this parable operating across three concentric circles of abandoning. In the innermost circle, the kingdom demands all of our goods, "and one thinks," says Crossan, "of a range from almsgiving to martyrdom." Moving out to the second circle, the kingdom challenge "threatens to consume our morals as well." If that were not strange enough, there is a third outermost circle in which one is challenged to abandon not only one's goods and morals but also "the very parable itself."[47]

Once he has started this line of thinking, Crossan, like the highwire daredevils the Flying Wallendas, cannot turn back but must keep advancing. He writes,

> The Kingdom demands our "all," demands the abandonment not only of our *goods* and our *morals*, but, finally, of our *parables* as well. The ultimate, most difficult and most paradoxical demand of the Kingdom is for the abandonment of abandonment itself. . . . The finder gives up everything, and does so with joy, to obtain the treasure. And that, says Jesus, is what the Kingdom is like. One gives up everything to obtain the gift of God. But here a dark shadow appears. If one gives up everything—gives up "all"—and if this "all" be taken seriously, then *one must give up this parable itself.* One must give up even the advice to give up everything. We have walked, we have been led, straight into a paradox like that of the sign, which reads "Do not read this sign."[48]

At this point, we realize that we have been lured into a nightmare hall of mirrors from which there is no exit. What could it possibly mean to abandon abandonment itself?[49] More important, could this nest of wormholes possibly be what Jesus is talking about? Fortunately, we wake up from this bad dream by reminding ourselves that Matthew's Jesus is not Kafka. If we return to the parable itself, located in Matthew's literary and theological world, we see this parable, however complex and unsettling, as coming from the same world of meaning as the other parables in Matthew.

First a "someone," a man, finds a hidden treasure. This is a parable, and the ethics and legality of the man's actions in response to the discovery are no more pertinent than whether Goldilocks violated nineteenth-century British trespassing laws when she entered the forest home of the three bears. It's just the way this tale gets going.

When the man finds the treasure, his response is joy, and in that joy he willingly gives up all that he had to have this treasure. We have seen this kind of joy before in Matthew, when the wise men following the star realized that it had stopped over the place where the child Jesus was: "[T]hey were overwhelmed with joy" at what they had found (Matt. 2:10). We will encounter it again later in the Parable of the Talents, when the faithful slaves are invited to "enter into the joy of your master" (25:21, 23).

The joy in this parable comes from both finding and possessing the treasure. The parable evokes Proverbs, where the quest for wisdom is compared to searching for hidden treasure:

My child, if you accept my words
  and treasure up my commandments within you,
making your ear attentive to wisdom
  and inclining your heart to understanding;
if you indeed cry out for insight,
  and raise your voice for understanding;
if you seek it like silver,
  and search for it as for hidden treasures—
then you will understand the fear of the LORD
  and find the knowledge of God.
Proverbs 2:1–5

Here, wisdom itself is the hidden treasure, a treasure that, when found, entails being drawn into the life and knowledge of God. That is the deepest joy.

Essentially this parable is a narrative version of a major theme in Matthew, namely, that true wisdom consists of hearing Jesus' words and doing them. The first move is to hear Jesus' words and to receive them with joy. But reception—even joyful reception—is not enough. We learned earlier in the interpretation of the Parable of the Sower about the "rocky ground" kind of hearer, "the one who hears the word and immediately receives it with joy; yet such a person has no root, but endures only for a while, and when trouble or persecution arises on account of the word, that person immediately falls away" (13:20–21). No, the real joy comes to those who both receive God's treasure *and* possess it. There must be both joyful reception and action, hearing and doing. What the parable adds is motivation. The reason why true hearers of Jesus' words put them into action is because they discern that they have found a treasure, one that makes all other so-called treasures pale by contrast. In other words, how fortunate and joyful are those who have discovered the wisdom Jesus teaches and who therefore have a powerful future opened up before them.

If a wealthy person were asked, "What is your most prized possession, the Rembrandt that hangs on the wall of your drawing room or the rubber raft in your pool house?" the obvious answer is the Rembrandt. But actually, the true answer would depend on whether or not the dam on the reservoir up the hill from the house has broken. When the dam breaks and one is about to be swept away, the art can go. It's the life raft that one urgently needs. The advent of the kingdom of heaven is like finding a treasure hidden in a field; it is also like the dam breaking. Both cases are life-changing and deeply clarifying: one discerns what really counts.

The celebrated New Testament scholar and preacher Fred Craddock once told a story about discerning what matters. Craddock said,

> Glenn Adsit, a schoolmate from years ago, ministered mostly in China. He was under house arrest in China when the soldiers came one day and said, "You can return to America."
>
> They were celebrating, and the soldiers said, "You can take two hundred pounds with you."
>
> Well, they'd been there for years. Two hundred pounds. They got the scales out and started the arguments: two children, wife, husband. Must have this vase. Well, this is a new typewriter. What about my books? What about this? And they weighed everything and took it off and weighed this and took it off and weighed this and, finally, right on the dot, two hundred pounds.
>
> The soldiers asked, "Ready to go?"
>
> "Yes,"
>
> "Did you weigh everything?"
>
> "Yes."
>
> "You weighed the kids?"
>
> "No, we didn't."
>
> "Weigh the kids."
>
> And in a moment, typewriter and vase and all became trash. Trash. It happens.[50]

If we desire to let this Parable of the Treasure Hidden in a Field take us to those places where the kingdom is happening, where we can be "on hand for that which is at hand," we will look for places in life where someone has found the gospel to be so joyfully transformative that a new future has been created and a life is set in a new direction.

Candler School of Theology, where I taught for many years, has a relationship with a state women's prison a little over an hour from the campus. Candler offers a theological certificate program for the women incarcerated at the prison; the program involves the serious study of Scripture, theology, and ethics.

One day, while visiting the prison, I was standing in the main prison yard with the prison chaplain. A small group of prisoners walked past us, on their way from theology class back to their cellblocks. The women were obviously in a good mood, laughing and talking among themselves. They greeted us cheerily. I happened to notice that one of them was carrying her theology textbook, a volume written by a Candler colleague.

"Looks like you're reading some good material," I said to her, pointing at her book.

She pulled the book to herself in an embrace. "Oh yes!" she exclaimed. "We're learning about agape love." She paused a moment to assess my reaction, and then she asked, "Do you know what agape love is?"

"Why don't you tell me?" I replied.

She broke into a broad smile and said, "Agape love is the kind of love God has for us. It is love that is given without any conditions; it doesn't have any strings attached. It's completely free." She held her book up for me to see and continued, "I have learned that we can participate in agape love right here in the prison."

She hesitated a few seconds, and then said, "I used to do terrible things to myself." She then showed me her wrists, deeply scarred with knife wounds. "But I don't do this anymore," she said. Again, the smile, full of joy. "Now I get up every day and pray, 'God, how can I be a part of agape love, how can I show agape love to other people today?"

I was looking at a woman, a prisoner, who had obviously found a treasure hidden in a field and who had, in great joy, let go of her old life and eagerly embraced the new life and future that treasure offered.

THE PARABLE OF THE PEARL OF GREAT VALUE (MATTHEW 13:45–46)

This parable is, in many ways, quite similar to the previous Parable of the Treasure Hidden in a Field. Both parables have the *advent-reversal-action* plot structure identified by Crossan (see the comments on p. 151). The two parables also share a central meaning: the experience of the kingdom is like finding something valuable that revolutionizes a person's basic values and opens the possibility of a life of action and response.

But there are differences. The hidden treasure parable has a mood of unexpected discovery, surprise, and spontaneous joy. The camera zeros in on the experience of serendipitous discovery and what that prompted. In the pearl parable, though, the camera focuses as much on the discoverer as it does on the discovery, on the merchant who is actively seeking fine pearls as much as it does on the pearl. The treasure parable is sudden; the pearl parable is a quest story that involves a search that takes some time.

In the parable, it is "a merchant" who is doing the questing. He is searching for fine pearls, which, in the ancient world, meant that he was working the top shelf, seeking the most prized of precious objects. The Roman naturalist Pliny, not too many years before Matthew, in his *Natural History* wrote, "The first rank . . . , and the very highest position among all valuables, belongs to the pearl."[51] In our day, we might have a story about someone searching for gold or diamonds, but in the first century pearls were the best prize.

This merchant finds not only what he was looking for, a fine pearl, but even better, a "pearl of great value." It was as if he set out looking for Ferraris and found a 1962 GTO 250 in mint condition, or was seeking good wines and came across an 1869 Chateau Lafite Rothschild. The Greek word for "great value" in this parable is the same term used to describe the "very expensive" perfume that Mary used to anoint Jesus' feet (John 12:1–8 CEB). The best of the best.

The finding of this extraordinary pearl prompts the merchant to do almost word for word what the man who found the treasure did: "he went and sold all that he had and bought it" (Matt. 13:46). But again, there is a difference. In the treasure parable, the man does this with "joy," but joy is not mentioned in this parable. Why? It is hard to imagine that this is a joyless experience. Who gives up everything he owns in order to acquire a superlative pearl without thinking that the pearl would bring some joy?

The mention of joy in the first parable but not in the second comes because the two parables focus on different experiences of the kingdom of heaven. Sometimes the kingdom of heaven is like a sudden discovery of that which was hidden. You can hardly believe what you have found. It feels like an unexpected gift, so you thank heaven and joyfully race away to rearrange your life. That's the Parable of the Treasure. But here, in the Parable of the Pearl, the experience of the kingdom of heaven is like arriving at a powerful and satisfying conclusion to a strategic and intentional quest. This is what Jesus was talking about in the Sermon on the Mount when he described the lifelong and urgent searching of a disciple: "But seek first his kingdom and his righteousness" (6:33 RSV).

We saw in the discussion of the Parable of the Treasure Hidden in a Field that Proverbs compared seeking wisdom to finding hidden treasure. Proverbs also describes finding wisdom as even more precious than silver, gold, and jewels, and promises that finding wisdom leads to blessedness:

> Blessed are those who find wisdom,
> those who gain understanding,
> for she is more profitable than silver
> and yields better returns than gold.
> She is more precious than rubies;
> nothing you desire can compare with her.
> Long life is in her right hand;
> in her left hand are riches and honor.
> Her ways are pleasant ways,
> and all her paths are peace.
> She is a tree of life to those who take hold of her;
> those who hold her fast will be blessed.
>
> Prov. 3:13–18 NIV

Where do we see this event of the kingdom breaking into life? When he was in his fifties, Leo Tolstoy experienced what many today would call a midlife crisis. He was a successful author, having already published such works as *War and Peace*, but in his inner life he was at war and had no peace. The crisis had been a long time in the making. "I was baptized and brought up in the Orthodox Christian faith," he wrote. "I was taught it in childhood and throughout my boyhood and youth. But when I abandoned the second course of the university at the age of eighteen, I no longer believed any of the things I had been taught."[52]

At first, his lack of belief was of little consequence to Tolstoy. He built his reputation as a writer and, after a season of sowing wild oats as a young man, married, had children, and settled down into his life of fame and brilliant reputation.[53] "So I lived," Tolstoy writes in 1879, "but five years ago something very strange began to happen to me. At first, I experienced moments of perplexity and arrest of life, and though I did not know what to do or how to live; and I felt lost and became dejected. But this passed and I went on living as before. Then these moments of perplexity began to recur oftener and oftener, and always in the same form. They were always expressed by the questions: What is it for? What does it lead to?"[54]

Tolstoy remembered an old fable that seemed to describe his life. A man is attacked by a wild beast. He runs to an old well, and climbs into the well for safety, clinging to a tree branch growing out of a crack in the well, only to discover that a ravenous dragon lies at the bottom of the well. The man is caught between two perils. He cannot drop to the bottom of the well. The jaws of the dragon lie waiting. He cannot climb out of the well. The beast will devour him. He can only hover at the top of the well, clutching the branch.

Then two things happen to the branch to which the man is clinging. First, two mice begin to gnaw away at the branch, threatening to sever it. But ironically, drops of honey appear on the branch, and the man in danger licks the drops of its sweetness. For Tolstoy, this was a symbol of his plight. He was surely doomed, and all attempts to distract himself from his plight with the sweet things of life failed. "The two drops of honey which diverted my eyes from the cruel truth longer than the rest: my love of family and of writing—art as I called it—were no longer sweet to me."[55]

Tolstoy was narrowly averted from suicide. He decided instead to go on a quest for some meaning in life that would give him purpose. He was, like the merchant in the parable, "in search of fine pearls." He looked for meaning, first in the physical sciences, then in psychology and philosophy, but he did not find there what he was looking for. Then he turned to great teachers, to the preacher of Ecclesiastes, to the philosopher Arthur Schopenhauer, to Buddha, but he found each of them as confused about life as he was.[56] "I sought everywhere," Tolstoy wrote, "and thanks to a life spent in learning, and thanks also to my relations with the scholarly world, I had access to scientists and scholars in all branches of knowledge, and they readily showed me all their knowledge, not only in books but also in conversation, so that I had at my disposal all that science has to say on this question of life."

He began to look to Christianity, but this too was a disappointment. Whether they were Orthodox or evangelical, Christians seemed to Tolstoy insincere in their beliefs. But then his gaze fell upon poor Christians, and there he observed a crucial difference. Tolstoy saw that these Christians, who seemed to lack everything in life, possessed all, especially a freedom of the fear of death. "And I learnt to love these people," Tolstoy said. "The more I came to know their life, the life of those who are living and of others who are dead of whom I read and heard, the more I loved them and the easier it became for me to live."[57]

Observing the faith of the poor and feeling love for them allowed Tolstoy to find the pearl of great price: a God whom he could trust and serve. He said that he felt as though he had been placed in a boat and pointed toward a distant shore. "That shore was God," he wrote. "That direction was tradition; the oars were the freedom given me to pull for the shore and unite with God. And so, the force of life was renewed in me and I again began to live."[58]

THE PARABLE OF THE NET (MATTHEW 13:47–50)

At the very beginning of his ministry, Jesus saw two brothers, Peter and Andrew, both fishermen, casting a net into the Sea of Galilee. "Follow me," Jesus said, "and I will make you fish for people." Immediately the brothers left their nets of rope and took up the nets of the kingdom. As he walked a little farther down the shoreline, Jesus saw two other fishermen brothers, James and John, in their boat mending a net. He called them as well, and they too joined the kingdom fishing crew (Matt. 4:18–22).

The very first image of ministry that Jesus gives to his newly called disciples is that of fishing. To follow Jesus means doing the same job they had been doing—casting nets, mending nets—but in a new way. And now we get a fishing parable, the Parable of the Net, which begins with an everyday scene from the life of fishermen, one that old salts like Peter, Andrew, James, and John would have well remembered. A net has been cast into the sea, and when it filled up with fish, the fishermen put their backs into drawing the heavy net ashore. What's in that net? What is almost always in the net: everything in the sea. Big fish and small ones, beautiful fish and trash fish, good and bad, and, in Jewish context, clean and unclean. So the fishermen sit around the net and sort the fish, putting the good fish into baskets and tossing the bad ones away—an ordinary conclusion to the day for fishermen in Galilee.

Suddenly the film lurches; the screen goes dark, then is quickly illuminated again, this time by an apocalyptic light, and the scene has changed dramatically. We are no longer at seaside at the close of an ordinary fishing day but instead on the edge of time, at "the end of the age." Now the ones doing the sorting are not fishermen but angels, and what is being sorted are no longer sea creatures but people, evil ones and righteous ones.

What is this parable about? Some interpreters see here mainly a repetition of the theme of the Parable of the Wheat and the Weeds (13:24–30, 36–43). There too we ended up with good and evil all mixed together, and there too the angels show up at the "end of the age" to sort things out.[59] But even though the two parables share much, there are clear differences. When the servants in the Parable of the Wheat and the Weeds discover that weeds were growing up among the wheat, the field owner tells them plainly, "An enemy has done this" (13:28). Later, when Jesus interprets that parable to the disciples, he lets them know that the field represents the world, and the malevolent weed sower is "the devil" (13:38–39). But in the Parable of the Net, there is no enemy. The fact that bad fish are mixed in with the good ones is not the result of malevolence but of normal fishing. Put theologically, if Jesus has turned the disciples into fishermen casting nets to gather in people, the results of their ministry will be, frankly, impure and compromised. They will draw in some good people and some not-so-good people, serious and faithful followers of Jesus and others who just somehow got caught in the net. It's not the fault of some satanic enemy; it's what happens when they do ministry and practice evangelism.

That, in fact, is the nub of this parable. The ministry of the disciples—and subsequently of the church, a ministry that will call them to "make disciples of all nations" (28:19)—will inevitably produce mixed, and sometimes alarming, results. "If Christianity were judged entirely by the quality of Christians," writes Michael Gerson in a *Washington Post* op-ed, "it would be a tough sell."[60] In another place, Gerson expressed horror at the sight of armed and barbaric people attacking the US Capitol on January 6, 2021, more than a few wearing shirts and carrying banners that proclaimed their love of and fidelity to Jesus.

Someone, somewhere, somehow evangelized these people. Sometime earlier someone preached the love of God to them and called them to a faithful life, a life, says Gerson, that includes "concern for the weak and vulnerable in our society, including the poor, immigrants and refugees. A passion for racial reconciliation and criminal justice reform, rooted in the nonnegotiable demands of human dignity. A deep commitment to public and global health, reflecting the priorities of Christ's healing ministry. . . . An insistence on public honesty and a belief in the transforming power of unarmed truth."[61]

But there they were, with their sticks, bear spray, and baseball bats, clashing violently with peace officers, while waving a banner that proclaims "Jesus

Saves." The Parable of the Net is utterly realistic about this. Sometimes those who fish for Christ will be surprised and dismayed by what the net brings in.

Some months after the January 6, 2021, insurrection at the US Capitol, the nation was rocked by another deranged act of violence. A twenty-one-year-old man, Robert Aaron Long, walked calmly into three massage parlors in the Atlanta area and shot and killed eight people, six of them of Asian descent. The citizens of Atlanta, indeed people everywhere, were shocked by this brutal massacre, but no group was more scandalized and grief-stricken than the congregation of the Baptist church where Long was a member. An anguished statement posted on the church's website read:

> We were absolutely distraught when we found out that the shooter was a member of our congregation. The Long family have been members of our church for many years. We watched Aaron grow up and accepted him into church membership when he made his own profession of faith in Jesus Christ. These unthinkable and egregious murders directly contradict his own confession of faith in Jesus and the gospel.
>
> We want to be clear that this extreme and wicked act is nothing less than rebellion against our Holy God and His Word. Aaron's actions are antithetical to everything that we believe and teach as a church. In the strongest possible terms, we condemn the actions of Aaron Long as well as his stated reasons for carrying out this wicked plan. The shootings were a total repudiation of our faith and practice, and such actions are completely unacceptable and contrary to the gospel.[62]

It can lead to despair to recognize that the proclamation of the gospel and the efforts to gather a faithful church do not always lead to a community of righteousness but instead to a morally compromised gathering of people seemingly as riddled with evil as any other group.

That brings us to the closing scene of the parable, where the angels "separate the evil from the righteous and throw them into the furnace of fire, where there will be weeping and gnashing of teeth" (13:49–50). We must tread carefully here; there are so many ways to stumble over this part of the parable.

First, this ending, like that of the Parable of the Wheat and the Weeds, takes the ultimate judgment of people out of human hands. Who people truly are can be known only by God and can be seen only in the light of God's great day; no deacons' board, synod, presbytery, or diocese may claim the role of final judge. This is the task of the angels, and it is performed not today in snap judgment but at "the end of the age."

Beyond this, some interpreters can see only gloom in this parable. The parable seems to them lopsided toward darkness. In the Parable of the Wheat and the Weeds, there was at least a contrast: evil was thrown into the fire, but "the righteous will shine like the sun" (13:43); in this parable; the spotlight falls exclusively on the destruction of the wicked. "The parable serves as a warning to those who profess to be disciples of Jesus," writes Arland Hultgren. "Since the judgment is certain and the evil ones will be taken from the fellowship of the righteous, it is essential for each member of the community to remain faithful."[63]

However, this take on the parable's ending overlooks the fact that, for Matthew, God's judgment is a positive category. The announcement that God will ultimately banish the wicked is a promise, not a threat. When the English physician Edward Jenner declared in 1801 the goal of eventually annihilating smallpox, no one mistook that for bad news. Just so, this parable declares God's intention of eradicating evil. In God's reign, goodness and righteousness win! That's good news. Judgment is not about a stern, offended God getting revenge on the wicked, but about God setting things right, validating goodness, and preserving it from evil's contamination.

The primary function of the Parable of the Net is not to scare Christians into being righteous, but to reassure those who cast out and haul in missional nets that their labors are not senseless or in vain. The ultimate end of ministry in the name of Jesus, however befuddling and confusing it may sometimes appear in the middle of things, is a community of righteousness. Outsiders may look at the church and cry, "Hypocrites!" Insiders may look at their always morally ambiguous congregations and sigh, "Look at what the net just dragged in!"

"Yes," says the parable, "you're right, but the day is not done. Don't forget, just as earthly fishermen put the good fish in baskets and toss the bad fish at the end of the day, so will the angels do at the end of the age."

There is, however, a troubling loose end here. Matthew, as we have seen, tends to think in clear, crisp categories. As seems the case for the author of Psalm 1, there are for Matthew two kinds of people, period: the righteous and sinners, wheat and weeds, good fish and bad fish. This turns Matthew's picture of sinners being destroyed at the end of time into a puzzling and thorny moral and theological issue. It is all but impossible for contemporary readers, steeped as our era is in psychological self-awareness, to enter completely into Matthew's view. We are fully aware that no human being is pure good or pure evil but an inextricable mixture. Even the Mother Teresas of this world have their shadow side.

It is possible, however, to step back from Matthew's sharp and unambiguous categories—sinners and righteous—and still find encouragement in the underlying theology, namely, that it is God's good pleasure to establish a kingdom where righteousness shines like the sun. Very soon, Matthew's Jesus will tell parables about the need for forgiveness and compassion toward wayward

Christians, showing that Matthew knows quite well the frailties and failings that occur even inside Christian community. But in this parable, he looks at the cosmos—not philosophically or psychologically but apocalyptically. Under the apocalyptic gaze, all subtleties vanish, and the world appears as a pitched battle between God's righteousness and the powers of evil. To ally oneself with evil, Matthew wants us to know, is not only ultimately to lose the battle but to lose oneself as well.

With this parable, Jesus ends his long seaside sermon filled with parables. "Have you understood all this?" Jesus asks the disciples, and they say, "Yes." They are good students, ready for the next lesson.

THE PARABLE OF THE SHEEP GONE ASTRAY (MATTHEW 18:10–14)

Both Matthew and Luke include this parable about a sheep that gets separated from the flock, but the settings are strikingly different. In Luke, Jesus is under fire from the scribes and Pharisees, and he is defending his ministry against the charge that he eats and drinks with sinners (Luke 15:1–2). In Matthew, the context is far friendlier. Jesus is not in conflict with his opponents but is instructing his disciples. Indeed, the whole of Matthew 18 is a conversation and teaching session between Jesus and the disciples about the nature of life together in the Christian community, the church. As this chapter was read aloud in Matthew's church, we can imagine the leaders and others in the congregation leaning forward and listening intently, because it addresses very practical matters in the life of the community, in their day and indeed in every day, such as leadership, pastoral care, and mending broken relationships in the church.

Caring for the "Little Ones"

One of those practical matters concerned how leaders should care for the "little ones" in the community. The term "little ones" probably covers several different sorts of persons: new Christians who are like tender shoots not yet having deep roots in the gospel, those who faith is weak and wandering, those who are suffering doubt provoked by illness or other trouble. Every pastor knows whom Jesus is talking about when he names "the little ones": the vulnerable ones in the congregation.

Jesus introduces the parable with a word of encouragement to the disciples (and by extension to all church leaders and, beyond this, to the whole community) to pay special attention to the "little ones." "Be careful that you don't look down on one of these little ones. I say to you that their angels in heaven are always looking into the face of my Father who is in heaven" (18:10 CEB).

Jesus uses here the image of guardian angels to underscore the importance of these "little ones," who are always needy, sometimes demanding. Pastors might be tempted to neglect or avoid them, but Jesus says that the greatest of the angels, those who are closest to God's throne and who "continually see God's face," are the very ones assigned as guardian angels of the vulnerable. "The point," says Eugene Boring, "is clear: Heaven does not give up on the marginal, the lapsed, or the strayed, and what heaven values so dearly cannot be disdained by the 'big people' in the church on earth."[64]

The parable proper involves a shepherd with a flock of a hundred sheep, and one of them goes "astray," *planēthē* (πλανηθῇ). In Luke, the sheep is "lost" (Luke 15:4, ἀπολέσας), a term that serves Luke's theological concern, but the picture of a sheep gone astray is more congruent with Matthew's emphasis on the pastoral care of wandering "little ones."

"What do you think?" Jesus asks the disciples (Matt. 18:12). This question not only gathers the hearers more deeply into the situation; it also implies that the disciples will think rightly, that is, that they will guess accurately what this shepherd will do, namely, "he [will] leave the ninety-nine on the mountains and go in search of the one that went astray."

Abandoned Sheep, Fat Sheep, and the Urgency of Searching

Several aspects of this picture deserve consideration. First, there is probably no hidden symbolic meaning in the size of the flock, one hundred sheep, except that it is large enough that the wandering of a solitary sheep would not, based on numbers alone, represent a major crisis.[65] Some shepherds, with so many sheep to care for, might well shrug their shoulders over one wandering sheep, but not this shepherd. Good shepherds, and good pastors, do not shrug off the straying of even one little one.

Second, some interpreters have wondered what to make of a shepherd who leaves ninety-nine sheep on the mountainside to go chasing after one that has wandered away. Is this willful neglect, and if so, is it exegetically and theologically significant? Or perhaps we have some missing information. Shepherds in the ancient world often worked in teams, and maybe Jesus simply assumed his hearers would know that the searching shepherd left the ninety-nine under the care of another shepherd. One scholar has even suggested that when Jesus told this story in Aramaic, he said that the shepherd left the ninety-nine sheep in the *dura*, "the sheepfold," but that his Galilean followers had trouble making the *d* sound, and inadvertently changed the word to the more easily pronounced *tura,* "the mountains."[66] So in Jesus' original parable, the shepherd left the flock not in the rugged hills but in the safety of the fold.

The *Gospel of Thomas*, which recounts a version of this parable, solves the problem another way. There the shepherd does in fact abandon the ninety-nine because the sheep that went astray was "the largest" in the flock and the one that the shepherd loved "more than the ninety-nine" (*Gos. Thom.* 107). This undoubtedly reflects gnostic elitism. This fat sheep represents the person who is truly enlightened, engorged with gnosis and more worthy than those ninety-nine oblivious ones; so, who cares where they were left?

As interesting as all this speculation may be, in Matthew there is no mention of a crew of shepherds or a protective sheepfold, and the wandering sheep is not fat, desirable, and best loved; the wandering sheep has simply strayed from the flock. That is the point. The parable is entirely absorbed with pastoral responses to wandering "little ones," and in the story the shepherd immediately goes out to search. The question of the flock left behind is not where our attention should be drawn, except perhaps to highlight the shepherd's urgency to recover the wandering sheep.

The Precariousness and the Joy of Pastoral Care

"And if he finds it," Jesus says, as the parable moves toward its conclusion (18:13). In Luke, there is no question about finding the sheep ("*When* he has found it," Luke 15:5), but Matthew is discussing pastoral care, and there is always an "if." Sometimes a wandering sheep is restored to the flock and sometimes, despite the most intense searching and best pastoral efforts of the shepherd, the recovery effort fails.

But "if" the straying sheep is restored to the community, the shepherd "rejoices over it more than over the ninety-nine that never went astray" (Matt. 18:13). This extra measure of joy over the one restored comes not because this sheep is more valued than the others. It comes because restoration is joyful to God and is therefore joyful in Christian fellowship. If a child who has wandered off into a dark forest is found by a search team and returned to his anxious and desperate parents, their joy will naturally overflow toward the child who was missing, not because they love this child more than their other children safely at home in their beds, but because the child they feared they would never see again is once again in their embrace.

Jesus raises this joyful response to an even higher theological level when he says, "So it is not the will of your Father in heaven that one of these little ones should be lost" (18:14). This is much stronger than merely saying, "God doesn't want the vulnerable 'little ones' in the community to be lost." The phrase "will of your Father" appears, in various forms, several times in Matthew (7:21; 12:50; 21:31; 26:42), and while it does entail obeying God's commandments and doing what God desires, it is rooted in the petition of the Lord's Prayer, "Your will be done on earth as it is in heaven" (6:10). In other words, the "will of your Father" is when our lives become congruent with the very life of God. Restoration of the "little ones" who have wandered is at the heart of God, and the joy of the shepherd if the wandering sheep is found is but the reverberation of heaven's jubilee.

Vigilance and the Kingdom

This parable points us to events of the kingdom that sometimes involve sheep wandering into danger. During the "joys and concerns" part of worship at a large church, a member of the congregation enthusiastically announced that another member of the church had just been named president and CEO of a large and influential bank. The congregation applauded vigorously, and the new bank president stood to receive their recognition. The next day, however, the wise pastor of the congregation went to the man's office at the bank, closed the door behind him, pulled his chair close to the president's desk, and said, "I came to warn you, your soul is in peril." He then had a frank and loving pastoral conversation about the dangers of power, status, and wealth and how, in this new and prestigious position, he would have to be all the more vigilant to be the kind of faithful person God called him to be.

Mostly, though, this parable points to events of the kingdom that are quiet and hidden. A sponsor in Alcoholics Anonymous climbs an apartment stairway late at night to provide support for a man who has slipped back into alcohol use. A pastor prays with a mother whose faith has been shaken by her child's accidental death. A church provides a summer arts and recreation program for restless kids in the neighborhood. The many places where "little ones" are brought into the embrace of God's love are not merely social service but eruptions of the kingdom of God.

Once, when I was doing research for a book on vital worship, I worshiped in a city congregation located a few blocks from a state-run special education school for children with Down syndrome. Some members of this congregation regularly volunteer as tutors and teachers' assistants at the school, but they also desire, like a shepherd seeking out the "little ones," to gather these children into the Christian community. With the permission of the school and the parents, they invite the children to Sunday worship and provide transportation for those who wish to come, usually a few dozen children. At worship in this church, one can hear the distinctive voices of these children as they join in the hymns and the prayers. It is the practice of this church for the whole congregation to form a large circle, holding hands, around the communion table each Sunday. "This is not our table," the pastor says each week. "This is God's table."

And one can hear the children with Down syndrome joining with the others in the congregation, indeed with the whole host of heaven, as they practically shout the joyful response: "*Everyone* is welcome at God's table!"

THE PARABLE OF THE UNFORGIVING SLAVE (MATTHEW 18:23–35)

Like the Parable of the Sheep Gone Astray, this parable is also a part of the cluster of teachings in Matthew 18 about leadership and life together in the church. Specifically, the parable comes as the third and concluding passage in a short sequence of three texts about forgiveness. In the first of these three texts, Matthew 18:15–20, Jesus describes a step-by-step process for dealing with broken relationships in the community. The process begins with a very particular situation—namely, "If another member of the church sins against you"—and then outlines the remedial steps to be taken: first, go to the person privately to restore the relationship; if that doesn't work, take one or two others with you to reopen the dialogue; and so on.

In the second text, Peter comes to Jesus with a question for clarification (18:21–22). He begins with words very similar to the first passage: "If another member of the church sins against me." Peter is clearly asking a follow-up question about the same situation. He wants to know the duration of the process Jesus has given. "How often should I forgive? As many as seven times?"

Jesus' response is hard to translate. It could be "Not seven times, but I tell you seventy-seven times," or it could also be "Not seven times, but I tell you seventy times seven" (18:22); but it hardly matters. Both renderings convey the same meaning. Jesus is saying that forgiveness in the church is not a matter of counting out some required number of times; forgiveness is a constant mode. Peter's question assumes that forgiveness and the work of restoring relationships is the exception to the rule, a process buried somewhere in the church's book of discipline that gets trotted out when things go awry. The assumption is that relationships normally run quite smoothly and cordially in the church, but every now and then some rabid dog in the budget committee loses it and insults you and your mother. What then? And what if he goes off at the next meeting, and the next as well? How often do you have to take time out of your life to go through the laborious process of trying to restore relationship with this fellow? How often do you need to travel the difficult path of this peculiar reconciliation process?

Jesus' response—whether it's translated "seventy-seven times" or "seventy times seven"—reveals that forgiveness and reconciliation are not the occasional exceptions to the rule in the church; they *are* the rule. In the life of the church, forgiveness is not a limited task; it's the weather. Peter might as well have asked, "When I am driving in Chicago, how often do I have to drive on the right side of the road?" The answer, of course, is always; that's the way we do things in Chicago. Perhaps better, Peter's question is like asking, "How often do I need to obey the law of gravity?" The kingdom of heaven—and the church participates in that kingdom—operates by forgiveness and reconciliation, as surely as the physical world operates by gravity and thermodynamics. It's the way it is, constantly. In the beloved community, forgiveness and reconciliation aren't pieces of equipment stored behind glass, to be broken out in an emergency; they are the water in the aquarium.

The Parable of the Unforgiving Slave, which forms the third and final text of this sequence about forgiveness, deepens and amplifies this truth.

Wham! Sock! Pow!

It is important to loosen our grip on this parable a bit. It will turn somber and serious at the end, to be sure, but most of this parable is intentionally cartoon-like. It will eventually make us wince and perhaps cry, but at first it makes us chuckle.

In the parable, there is a king who decides one day that it is time to settle up financial accounts with his slaves (18:23–25). No reason is given; kings don't need reasons. Anyway, as a part of this reckoning, one of his debtor slaves is brought before him, a slave who owed the king ten thousand talents. Again, we should relax here and enjoy the ride. No need to take out the calculator and say, "Now, let's see, one talent was worth about fifteen to twenty years wages for a daily worker, and so we have 10,000 talents at. . . ."

What the parable is saying is that this slave owed the king a bazillion bucks! The figure is so large it provokes a chortle. This slave owed the king something like the gross national product of the whole Mediterranean world. We will become dizzy if we try to guess why in heaven's name a king would lend a bazillion bucks to a slave, or what in the world the slave would have done anyway with a two-hundred-thousand-year advance on his wages, or what he was thinking when he put his "X" on that note. The point is that we have a ridiculous situation—amusing in its own way—of a slave who owes his king more money than King Croesus and the queen of Sheba could imagine.

The slave cannot, of course, pay the debt (really?), so the king proposes to cut his losses in the only way possible: by selling the slave, his family, and his possessions for whatever they will bring. Not much compared to the debt—the discount bin at Goodwill really—but something. End of story? No, the story improbably keeps unfolding. In the next panel of this cartoon the slave falls to his knees and begs, "Have patience with me, and I will pay you everything" (18:26). The slave does not describe how he intends to scrape up a bazillion bucks. GoFundMe? Any such scheme would be absurd. He might as well be promising to meet his debt from the proceeds of his marigold farms on the moon. But the next panel in this cartoon carries a big surprise: the king, seeing his slave on his knees in the posture of worship, and hearing him beg for patience, astonishingly has pity on this slave and forgives the whole debt; the entire bazillion is wiped off the books, and the slave is free to go (18:27).

As this unbelievably fortunate slave leaves the king's throne room—no doubt skipping as he went—he chances to pass a fellow slave who happens to owe him some money, and the whole story goes into a repeat loop. Like the king earlier, slave #1 says to slave #2, "Pay up." Same exchange as before, but two things are different. The size of the debt here is not a bazillion bucks but a hundred denarii—not a pittance by any means, but certainly something more on the human scale, more imaginable, more manageable, and extremely small potatoes compared to what slave #1 owed the king. The second difference is that physical cruelty has entered the picture. Slave #1 has slave #2 by the throat (18:28).

Slave #2 cannot pay his debt either, so he does what slave #1 did before the king: he begs for patience and promises to find the money eventually (18:29). But instead of forgiving the debt, as had been done previously for him, slave #1 mercilessly throws slave #2 into prison until such time as the debt would be repaid (18:30). Fellow slaves, who have been watching all of this unfold, cannot believe their eyes. Slave #1, who received such lavish mercy from the king, hasn't one second of patience with his own debtor, not one drop of mercy. Scandalized, the fellow slaves run and tell the master what is going on. The master summons slave #1 and confronts him with the obvious moral point. "I forgave you a bazillion bucks because you begged for mercy, and yet you, after receiving all this lavish forgiveness, couldn't show any mercy to your fellow slave?" With that he sends him to the torture chamber to work off his entire debt, which, given the enormity of balance, sounds pretty much like a hundred thousand life sentences tacked end to end.

Thus far, we have a cartoon parable with a clueless and morally vacant villain who gets, in the way of comic justice, what he deserves. The recipient of debt forgiveness beyond all imagining turns right around and throws one of his own small-potato debtors into prison. So, the king throws him into the chamber. Live by the sword, die by the sword.

But then the parable turns solemn, dark. In what is surely the voice of Jesus, the parable concludes: "So my heavenly Father will also do to every one of you, if you do not forgive your brother or sister from your heart" (18:35). Contemporary readers flinch at this point. God, the "heavenly Father," as torturer? Matthean scholar Warren Carter at first tries to rescue the parable from any notion that the king in the story could represent God. That would be "unsettling," he writes, and "the imperial scenario of exploitative and oppressive reign which the parable evokes . . . indicates that this figure cannot be God."[67] But then he trips over this "so my heavenly Father will also do" saying and has to come to terms with the fact that maybe the parable itself does make some kind of connection between this king and God:

> The king's final act does represent something God will do! Drawing on this cultural image, the ending shows that God will act as a tyrant king if God's will to extend forgiveness is not done. As much as the parable rejects the king's bullying ways, it resorts to them to bully readers/hearers into compliance with God's will. Failure to enact God's will, failure to forgive and to sustain the community of disciples, means eschatological consequences from God's wrath.[68]

There is, however, another way to read Matthew on this theological point and, therefore, a different way to understand this parable than as a picture of a divine bully patrolling the middle-school playground, ready to commit torture.

Panning for Gold

A parable about mercy that teaches the importance of forgiveness by threatening torture requires, I admit, some sorting out. We will have to pan for gold here, and there is a lot of silt to swirl away to find the nuggets. Let's begin clearing out some of the silt by saying what this parable is not.

First, this is not a realistic parable about slave-master relationships in the ancient world. Attempts, as some have made, to identify the king as a Gentile overlord, or to see this parable as set in the ancient Hellenistic tax system in which the slaves in the parable are actually revenue agents,[69] miss the point and are like trying to decipher "Goldilocks and the Three Bears" as a sociological analysis of Victorian British family structures. Such efforts finally are blind to the art of storytelling and the obvious hyperbole of the parable, the fact that the parable is a tale, as John Drury observes, "about people unsubtly characterized, [with] sharp contrast, vivid exaggeration, and hell."[70]

In short, the main story in the parable is burlesque, a slapstick depiction of an ethical numbskull. Slave #1 in the parable is like Wile E. Coyote, who has purchased a case of TNT from Acme Explosive Company to blow up his nemesis, the Roadrunner, only to accidentally flick a lighted match into the dynamite and blow himself up. Desert justice, and remember it's a cartoon.

Or the final scene of the parable is like the old James Bond movie *Goldfinger* (another slapstick cartoon), in which the completely scurrilous villain, Auric Goldfinger, tries to kill Bond as they fly on a private jet. Bond and Goldfinger wrestle over a gun, which fires, puncturing a window in the pressurized plane, and Goldfinger is sucked, wiggling as he goes, through the window to his doom. Yes! A most satisfying ending to a fable, meant to be enjoyed as the hero triumphs over the really bad guy, not to be taken literally. If this were a real news story, it would be a tragedy, even if the man sucked through the window was morally compromised. No real human being deserves such a terrible death, and the National Transportation Safety Board would mount an investigation. But *Goldfinger* is a playful movie, and this parable is a piece of fictional hyperbole. Given that slave #1 lacks even an ounce of moral awareness and is one nasty and cruel dude to boot, the fact that the story ends with him being tossed into a chamber of horrors seems, when we reflect on it, about right.

Second, even though the parable falls in Matthew 18 as the concluding episode in a three-part sequence about forgiveness, it is not in any way a practical illustration of how to put the process of forgiveness (18:15–20) into effect. Nobody in the parable follows the process Jesus has just provided. No one goes to an offending party in private to try to work things out, as the process demands, or follows up by taking one or two members of the community to a session aimed at reconciliation. In fact, almost every attempt, and there have been many, to wrest some pragmatic method-to-be-followed from the parable ends up wrecked on the shoals.[71]

Choosing Worlds

No, this is a "Can You Imagine?" parable. Can you imagine anyone who experiences the spacious world of unbounded forgiveness choosing to reenter the cramped and bitter world of selfishness and servitude? Of course not! This exercise in moral imagination is what lies behind the troubling last words of the parable, when Jesus says, "And in anger his lord handed him over to be tortured until he would pay his entire debt. So my heavenly Father will also do to every one of you, if you do not forgive your brother or sister from your heart" (18:34–35).

In chapter 5, we discussed how to interpret Matthew's frequently employed fearsome language. To cut to the chase, the best way for contemporary people to understand the ending of this parable is to realize that it confronts the hearer with this urgent question: You have before you two worlds, on the one hand, the kingdom of heaven where a vast and unlimited forgiveness is the very air you breathe and, on the other, the dog-eat-dog world where, in order to survive, you need to grab others viciously by the throat before they grab you. Which one do you choose? If you choose the latter, then that is the world you will get: a world of self-inflicted torture, where you will slave away forever, trying to do the impossible, pay off your own debts.

We may like it in the movies when villains get what they deserve and are sucked out of airplane windows, so long as we don't let it touch reality and raise the issue of what it is that we deserve. What if *we* received what we deserve? What then? That is the torture chamber of guilt and blame, and who would choose to live there if they knew there was a choice?

How does this parable enable us to perceive the kingdom breaking into life? We look for those places where people—here and there, now and then—realize that the unseen wind of God's mercy and forgiveness is blowing all around us and, in response, turn their boat windward and unfurl full sail.

In May 1981, as Pope John Paul II festively greeted crowds of the faithful in St. Peter's Square, a flurry of gunshots shattered the celebration. The bullets came from the gun of Mehmet Ali Agca, a Turkish nationalist, who had been plotting for weeks to assassinate the pope. The attempt failed, even though several bullets struck the pope, one passing perilously close to his heart, and only emergency surgery saved his life. From his hospital bed, the pope said in a faint voice, "I pray for the brother who struck me, whom I have sincerely forgiven. United to Christ, Priest and Victim, I offer my sufferings for the Church and for the world."[72]

A few days after Christmas two years later, John Paul II made his way down a dim cellblock in Rebibbia prison in Rome to meet his attacker face-to-face. The pope entered Agca's cell, sat down next to him, and talked to him. Then the pope prayed with him and told him, "I forgive you."

This act of forgiveness was so out of place, so unexpected in the arena of customary human relations, that many refused to accept it at face value. The pope, said some, was a "professional forgiver" and was just checking off a box on his job duties. Others sneered that this was a photo op, the pope posturing for the cameras. Still others suggested that John Paul II, if he was serious about this act of forgiveness, was a fool to have done it. After all, they said, Agca, an unrepentant criminal, had not requested the visit, expressed no remorse for what he had done, and if he had possessed the means, might well have taken another shot at the pope.[73] But the pope was simply putting into action the life of the kingdom of God disclosed in this parable, the way of forgiveness that lies at the heart of the Christian faith.

How many times do we need to drag ourselves down to some cellblock to say, "I forgive you"? It's not the right question. Forgiveness already bathes all of the world's cellblocks with mercy. Forgiveness is the native tongue of God's reign, the lingua franca of God's people.

Did you see that king simply forgive the slave's impossibly large debt? Unimaginable! Well, imagine it, the parable declares. This unimaginable forgiveness is an ordinary day in the kingdom of heaven. It's not about duty, means and ends, or personal rights. It's just the way it is in the kingdom. As theologian Lewis B. Smedes says, "There is no such thing as a right to be forgiven. Forgiving flows always and only from what theologians call grace—unearned, undeserved favor. Grace that is earned is not grace at all. In an odd way, if we deserve to be forgiven, we would not need to be."[74]

When one discerns the kingdom's forgiveness flowing free and wild through the desert of recrimination and revenge, one leaps joyfully into its cleansing water. Not to do so would be utter foolishness, and that's the point of the parable. As Smedes again says, "When we forgive, we set a prisoner free and discover that the prisoner we set free is us."[75]

THE PARABLE OF THE LABORERS IN THE VINEYARD (MATTHEW 20:1–16)

A common mistake in parables interpretation is to see the parables as only nuggets of theological truth, spiritual wisdom remote from the hard demands of ethics. This is not true, of course. The parables of Jesus are indeed theological, but like all expressions of good theology, they ultimately make claims not only on how we believe, but also on the way we live.

An equally serious mistake, though, one that infects some contemporary approaches to the parables, is to see the parables as the reverse, as exclusively moral example stories, scenes of good behavior to be imitated, having only, or primarily, direct and straightforward ethical implications. But the parables do their ethical work indirectly. They first point to God's kingdom, that is, to the event of God erupting in, interrupting, and disrupting the world; only then do they illuminate the ethical path to follow. They allow us to witness where God is present and what God is doing before they invite us to pick up our feet and respond. The ethics implied in the parables are derivative of the disclosure of God. Thus, the parables are not to be imitated deed for deed, but once they have shone their light, they disclose opportunities to improvise ethically, based on what is seen.

This Parable of the Laborers in the Vineyard is a particularly tempting trap for those who want to cut cross-country to ethics. This story of a landowner who hires workers throughout the day and then at closing time pays everyone the same wage, regardless of how long they have worked, has generated reams of sober-faced balderdash about such topics as alternative economic systems and distributive justice. It is amazing how many interpreters finally want to turn this tale into a moral lesson about employer-employee labor practices. It has been viewed as revolutionary because the landowner acts counter to any known economic scheme and undermines all conventional notions of justice in the workplace. And that's right. If anyone should take this parable seriously as a prescription for the structure of an economy or a labor market, it would indeed prove revolutionary, because it would blow all economic systems out of the water. Capitalism would collapse, as would Marxism, socialism, agrarianism, feudalism, barter economy, and all other known economic schemes.

This parable is not Karl Marx's *Das Kapital*, nor is it Adam Smith's *The Wealth of Nations.* It's a parable—in this case a story with a bizarre surprise ending. Attempts to treat it as a moral example of economic life simply overlook how weird it is. Any employers who actually behaved like the landowner in this parable—making multiple runs out to the labor pool, paying everybody the same regardless of how long they worked, and dramatically paying the one-hour workers first in a move guaranteed to tick off the others—would soon find themselves short of labor. Who would put in a full day's work when one gets paid the same whether one grinds away all day under the broiling sun or shows up an hour before quitting time? To do so would be as foolish as the relative comic Jack Handey satirized in one of his *Saturday Night Live* "Deep Thoughts": "The whole town laughed at my great-grandfather, just because he worked hard and saved his money. True, working at the hardware store didn't pay much, but he felt it was better than what everybody else did, which was go up to the volcano and collect the gold nuggets it shot out every day."[76]

Despite the futility of turning this parable into an economic template, some nevertheless plunge ahead. In his book *Jesus the Radical: The Parables and Modern Morality,* Raymond Angelo Bellitoti winds a tortured path through wage-labor contracts and worker rights, before saying this about the parable:

> *Again, my analysis understands the parable only at the level of human economics.* Those who insist plausibly that we should analyze the story only in terms of Jesus' need to soften the growing pretensions of the apostles or of Jesus' efforts to defend his associations with and acceptance of sinners or of Jesus' message that God's grace of salvation is a gift that is not subject to human expectations will be unmoved.[77]

If we don't agree that this parable operates only at the level of economics, Bellitoti insists, we will be unmoved by his analysis. Well, yes, I am indeed unmoved by Bellitoti's interpretation. In fact, all of his options, economic and theological, miss the thrust of this parable. This is not a story mainly about economic structures, pompous disciples, the mission to sinners, or even the dynamics of salvation. It is in fact even more radical than that; it is about the very character of God and the ethical responses that flow from that. This parable has implications for all of life, including economic justice, but they are far more sweeping than any of the moral examples interpreters have imagined. It speaks to the way we view the world, including economics, but only after it has done its main work of disclosing a God with unpredictable and uncomfortable ways in the world.

Cutting Deals

The parable begins with a vineyard owner going out early in the morning to hire workers. There is nothing unusual about this. The typical workday for agricultural laborers in Jesus' day was from sunrise to sunset, so we can picture this landowner recruiting workers at the labor pool just before dawn.

But then things become strange, and as is often the case in parables, the very strangeness proves to be pay dirt. The landowner goes back to the labor pool at about nine o'clock, sees other laborers without work, and hires them. He does the same thing about noon, about three o'clock, and about five o'clock, and immediately we are provoked to wonder why. Most vineyard owners would have known from the beginning how many workers were needed for the day. It's not as if his vineyard got bigger or the job expanded unexpectedly during the day. We could jump to the conclusion that we just have a missing detail here. For some reason that Jesus chooses not to disclose in the parable, the landowner realized throughout the day that he needed more workers, so he kept going to the labor pool to get them. It just goes with the flow of the story.

But actually the story itself flows in another direction. The parable is not driven by the landowner's need for workers, but by the laborers' need for work. "When [the landowner] went out about nine o'clock, he saw others standing idle in marketplace, and he said to them, 'You also go into the vineyard'" (20:3–4). The landowner sees people not working and puts them to work. Who are these people "standing idle in the marketplace"? Amy-Jill Levine helpfully points out that the NRSV translation "standing idle" can be misleading, since it could give the impression that these were idle slackers. The Greek, however, says they were *argous* (ἀργούς), literally "without work."[78] So the workers aren't goof-offs; they are simply those who had no work, no way to earn their daily bread. The parable does not say that the landowner needed more workers. It says he saw people in the marketplace who were without work, and he hired them. At about noon and three o'clock "he did the same" (20:5). At about five o'clock, he saw others standing in the marketplace, and he asks them, "Why are you standing here idle [i.e., 'without work'] all day?"

"Because no one has hired us," they replied.

"You also go into the vineyard," said the landowner (20:6–7).

The focus, then, is not on the vineyard owner's need, but on the needs of the laborers who are out of work.

A second dynamic energizes these hiring scenes: the different agreements made with each group of workers. Notice that the first group of workers strikes a negotiated deal with the landowner, coming to an agreement with him for "the usual daily wage" (20:2), for a denarius. The workers hired about nine o'clock don't cut a bargain. Rather, they simply receive a promise from the landowner that he will pay them "whatever is right" (20:4). The Greek term used here, *dikaion* (δίκαιον), means more than merely what is fair; it means what is "righteous." The landowner is promising to pay them what is righteous in the moral but also in the theological sense of that word. Presumably, the same arrangement applies to the workers hired about noon and three o'clock, since the landowner "did the same" (20:5). When we get to the last workers hired, at about five o'clock, there is something new. No terms of payment are mentioned at all. The landowner simply sends them into the vineyard, and they go.

These differing terms may reflect levels of trust, or perhaps levels of desperation. The first-hired workers evidently feel as though they are in a position to negotiate a contract, the middle workers rely only on a promise, and the last-hired just go when summoned.

These details become important when we get to the payment of wages at the end of the day. It is worth observing that paying the workers at the end of a day is not merely a matter of custom or convenience but a matter of righteousness. Poor workers lived day to day on their wages, and God's law demanded they be paid at the close of each workday: "You shall not withhold the wages of poor and needy laborers, whether other Israelites or aliens who reside in your land in one of your towns. You shall pay them their wages daily before sunset, because they are poor and their livelihood depends on them; otherwise they might cry to the LORD against you, and you would incur guilt" (Deut. 24:14–15).

Sunset Surprises

It is at sundown, pay time, that this parable discloses its breathtaking kingdom surprises. The end of the workday arrives, and the landowner tells his manager to gather the workers to receive their pay. What the landowner actually says is, "Call the laborers and give them their *misthon* (μισθόν)," a word that can mean ordinary wages, but this everyday meaning is not likely in Matthew. It can also be translated as "reward," and that term, which appears prominently in Matthew, is used to describe the summation or fulfillment of the way one lives one's life. Those who live as children of the kingdom of heaven receive a heavenly reward; perhaps more accurately, living as God's child, participating therefore in the very life and will of God, *is* heaven's reward. On the other hand, for those who serve something lesser than the kingdom of heaven, their reward is a humanly constructed prize. Those who live for God get the reward of a life in God, and those who live for acclaim or self-importance . . . well, that's the reward they get.

The word appears six times in the Sermon on the Mount alone:

> "Blessed are you when people revile you and persecute you and utter all kinds of evil against you falsely on my account. Rejoice and be glad, for your reward [μισθὸς] is great in heaven." (5:11–12)

> "But I say to you, Love your enemies and pray for those who persecute you. . . . For if you love those who love you, what reward [μισθὸν] do you have?" (5:43, 46)

> "Beware of practicing your piety before others in order to be seen by them; for then you have no reward [μισθὸν] from your Father in heaven." (6:1)

> "So whenever you give alms, do not sound a trumpet before you, as the hypocrites do in the synagogues and in the streets, so that they may be praised by others. Truly I tell you, they have received their reward [μισθὸν]." (6:2)

> "And whenever you pray, do not be like the hypocrites; for they love to stand and pray in the synagogues and at the street corners, so that they may be seen by others. Truly I tell you, they have received their reward [μισθὸν]." (6:5).

> "And whenever you fast, do not look dismal, like the hypocrites, for they disfigure their faces so as to show others that they are fasting. Truly I tell you, they have received their reward [μισθὸν]." (6:16)

In Matthew 10, when Jesus sends the twelve disciples out to preach the gospel and to proclaim the nearness of the kingdom, they too are promised kingdom rewards:

> "Whoever welcomes you welcomes me, and whoever welcomes me welcomes the one who sent me. Whoever welcomes a prophet in the name of a prophet will receive a prophet's reward [μισθὸν]; and whoever welcomes a righteous person in the name of a righteous person will receive the reward [μισθὸν] of the righteous; and whoever gives even a cup of cold water to one of these little ones in the name of a disciple—truly I tell you, none of these will lose their reward [μισθὸν]." (10:40–42)

So the theological themes in this story are jutting out, and the parable is beginning to glimmer even more brightly, not as a manual of labor rights but as an eschatological kingdom story. The vineyard owner promises to do what is *righteous*, not just what is fair. The workers don't get merely wages; they receive *rewards*. As Jesus told us at the beginning of the parable, this is not about vineyard economics; this is about the kingdom.

One more odd detail: the order of payment. The vineyard owner instructs the manager to pay the workers in the reverse order of their hiring, "beginning with the last and then going to the first" (20:8). This gives mild reinforcement to the "last will be first, and the first will be last" saying that Matthew uses to bracket the parable (19:30 and 20:16), but it is primarily a narrative device to set up the drama of the story, which requires that the all-day workers be present and accounted for in order to witness how much the one-hour workers get paid.

At this point, the midday workers, the ones hired at 9:00 a.m., noon, and 3:00 p.m., fade from view. The parable is interested only in the stark contrast between the last and the first: the last hired, who have come on trust alone and who have worked but an hour, and the first hired workers, who have forged an agreement for a denarius and who have labored all day. When the five o'clock workers are paid, surprise! They are each given a denarius—a whole day's wage for an hour's work. This naturally leads the early-bird workers, who have seen what the latecomers were paid, to assume that their pay would be more, much more. We can almost hear the wheels of their internal calculators whirring: "If those guys got a denarius for one hour's work, and I worked twelve hours, then. . . ." But to their shock and disappointment, they receive only a denarius as well.

These first-hired workers understandably begin to grouse, aiming their grievances toward the landowner: "These last worked only one hour, and you have made them equal to us who have borne the burdens of the day and the scorching heat" (20:12). At this point, the parable is raising the issue of justice in the sense that most people would understand it, as a matter of fair play. In fact, most hearers of the parable would probably agree with these first-hired workers. If laborers hired late in the day, who worked but a single hour, get a full denarius, how fair is it to give the same amount to workers who labored all day and broiled in the sun's heat? Bernard Brandon Scott even goes so far as to suggest that the parable is designed to evoke our sympathies with and for these all-day workers and so to deliberately poke us in the eye by offending our intuitive sense of justice.[79] The parable, in other words, is intentionally constructed to tick us off as strongly as the situation angered the first-hired workers, to violate our sense of fair play, to generate outrage over the injustice done to these all-day workers. Equal pay for equal work!

But beware, the parable is about to tilt the world on its axis.

Lady Justice or the God Who Sees?

The sense of fairness and unfairness that wells up, both for the all-day workers and for us, at the end of this parable is well represented by Lady Justice, an allegorical figure for fairness in the legal system. Everyone has seen her statue. She is blindfolded, and she holds in her hand a balance scale. Because she cannot see who is coming to the court for justice, she treats all appellants equally, and her scale weighs the two sides of every case with equitability.

It's a good image, since most people naturally desire impartiality and fairness in life. At our best, we want, for both ourselves and others, equal pay for equal work; we support "fair trade" coffee that does not involve exploitation of workers; we want our professors to grade the test papers without bias. Parents want to treat their children evenhandedly, and the best law courts provide access and equal justice for all. Maintaining ideals of fairness is the best human beings have learned to do to provide for the dignity and worth of all.

But the scandal of this parable is that God is not Lady Justice. God is not blindfolded but sees the plight of the needy and hears the cries of the oppressed. God is not sightlessly impartial, but alert and responsive to the specific conditions of the human situation. "For human ways are under the eyes of the LORD, and he examines all their paths" (Prov. 5:21).

In Psalm 10, the psalmist complains that God seems indifferent to oppression:

> Why, O LORD, do you stand far off?
> Why do you hide yourself in times of trouble?
> In arrogance the wicked persecute the poor—
> let them be caught in the schemes they have devised.
> Ps. 10:1–2

He prays urgently for God to do something, "Rise up, O LORD; O God lift up your hand; do not forget the oppressed" (Ps. 10:12). And then the psalmist arrives at a stunning discovery and proclamation; God is not blind or indifferent at all, but vigilant and all-seeing:

> But you do see! Indeed you note trouble and grief,
> that you may take it into your hands;
> the helpless commit themselves to you;
> you have been the helper of the orphan.
> Ps. 10:14

The parable has deftly summoned our allegiance to blind Lady Justice, only to call it into question in the face of the all-seeing God. The parable provokes and evokes our intuitive sense of fair play and justice. We have known since we were children that if my sister gets a candy bar for being well behaved, then, if I am well behaved, I should get one too. If George gets an A on his math test for solving all of the problems correctly, then Tiana deserves an A as well if she got them all right. If a guy who works an hour in the vineyard gets a denarius for that hour, then those of us who worked all day should get a denarius per hour as well. Widows, orphans, workers, students, people of all colors, statuses, and economic means should be treated on an equal basis, measure for measure. This is blind justice, and it is the best basis of rights that human beings have been able to devise.

But here is the disturbing possibility that the parable raises: What if the kingdom does not operate this way? What if God is not like Lady Justice and does not conform to our carefully calculated sense of fair play? The landowner singles out one of the grumblers and makes five responses, each one theologically provocative:

1. "Friend, I am doing you no wrong; did you not agree with me for the usual daily wage?" (20:13)

The Gospel of Matthew uses the word "friend" as a form of address three times (the other two are at 22:12 and 26:50), and each time it has a negative connotation, something like "Buster." The effect of this statement by the landowner then is, "OK, Buster, you worked the system, you bargained for a denarius, and then you got a denarius. No harm, no foul."

This statement throws the spotlight on the character of the all-day workers. They are like most of us. They operate in a Lady Justice world—fair is fair—but they don't quite trust the system to operate on its own, don't quite have confidence in the landowner to obey the rules of fair play. So they negotiate up front to make sure that the terms of justice are met. "We will work all day, and you will pay us the customary day's wage of a denarius. Agreed?" In short, these workers are bargainers, and in order to ensure that they get their fair share of what's coming to them, they relate to the landowner in a wholly transactional way.

The well-known business and statistics professor W. Edwards Deming once quipped, "In God we trust, all others must bring data,"[80] meaning that in the business world no one should be trusted unless they have the goods to back up their claims: the data, the receipts, the signed contracts. These all-day workers, shrewdly by the world's standards, do not trust the landowner without a deal in place, and since, in the parable, the landowner represents God, these workers can't even say, "In God we trust"!

We recognize these characters from earlier in Matthew. They show up in the Sermon on the Mount, relating to God transactionally. They bargain for a certain religious outcome and, guess what? They get what they bargained for. For example, if your goal is to have other people be impressed by your piety, then go ahead, blow a trumpet to get their attention when you put some money in the alms box. Such people, Jesus says, "have received their reward" (6:2). You get what you bargain for.

When these transactional plea bargainers saw, however, that the last hired workers also got a denarius, they quickly and unhappily tried, like a covetous NFL quarterback who sees another quarterback getting a fatter deal, to renegotiate their contract. Appealing to the higher virtues of Lady Justice, they say in effect, "Now that we see that these latecomers got a whole day's pay for an hour's work, we want to rest on blind justice and put our case on the balance scales to decide what's fair for us. If they got a denarius for an hour, we want what blind justice says is rightfully ours."

But the parable shocks with God's declaration, "First of all, if you are plea bargainers in life, then go ahead and live that way. Turn everything into a negotiation and live transactionally. Make prayer a transaction, let your faith be deals cut with your little deal-making gods. Plea bargain for a reward, and at the end of the day, you will receive a plea-bargainer's reward. And second, I am not Lady Justice. Your humanly constructed commonsense rules of justice are just that—humanly constructed. I am the all-seeing, living God, and that makes all the difference."

At first, this parable seems to be about the question, Is the landowner fair or not? But this discovery that the landowner represents the all-seeing God, who transcends human standards of justice, raises a third option. But it must wait until the parable discloses more of its revelations.

2. "Take what belongs to you and go" (20:14)

The import of the landowner's statement is, "Here is the denarius you transactional deal-cutters wangled to receive. Now take your money and go. The terms of our transaction have been fulfilled, and we have no other relationship." A similar expression of nonrelationship over money and transaction is found later in the Parable of the Talents (25:25).

3. "I choose to give to this last the same as I give to you." (20:14)

The denarius given to each of the last-hour workers did not come from negotiation, transaction, or obligation, but from the sheer freedom of the landowner ("I choose to give . . .").

Actually, the word translated "choose," *thelō* (θέλω), is used elsewhere in Matthew to express not mere choice or whim but the desire of God, the will of God. When a man with leprosy knelt before Jesus, he said, "Lord, if you are willing (θέλῃς), you can make me clean." Jesus reached out, touched him, and said, "I am willing (Θέλω). . . . Be clean!" (8:2–3 NIV). When the Pharisees were puzzled by Jesus' association with tax collectors and sinners, Jesus told them, "Go and learn what this means, 'I desire (Θέλω) mercy, not sacrifice'" (9:13; see also 12:7). When Jesus prayed in Gethsemane for his cup of suffering and death to pass, he said, "Yet not what I want (Θέλω) but what you want" (26:39). So when the landowner, who represents God, indicates, "I choose to give," he means it is his will to give. The gift is not an arbitrary choice but a deep expression of God's will and desire.

Notice, also, that earlier the landowner told the manager to "pay," *apodos* (ἀπόδος), the workers (20:8), but here the landowner says, "I choose to *give dounai* (δοῦναι)." This lifts the offering of the denarius to the one-hour workers out of the scheme of payroll transaction and renders it as a gift. The same idea of giving will appear later in this chapter when Jesus says, "[T]he Son of Man came not to be served but to serve, and to give (δοῦναι) his life a ransom for many" (20:28).[81] No one obligated Jesus to die, no one took Jesus' life. Jesus *gave* his life. No obligation or transaction forced the landowner to pay a day's wage to these one-hour workers. It was his will to give it.

4. "Am I not allowed to do what I choose with what belongs to me?" (20:15)

This rhetorical question is translated in the NRSV as "Am I not allowed . . . ?" but the Greek is stronger: "Is it not lawful . . . ?"

In Matthew, the question of lawfulness, as an expression of God's Law, is a recurring and significant issue. John the Baptist doesn't simply challenge the morality of Herod's marriage. He pointedly questions its lawfulness (14:4), that is, its acceptability to God, and the stakes are high. This dispute over lawfulness ultimately costs John his life (14:10). Jesus defends the lawfulness of his ministry in ways that display his radical departure from conventional religious practice. The Pharisees say that "it is not lawful" for Jesus' disciples to pluck grain on the Sabbath, but Jesus argues that it is indeed lawful, because "the Son of Man is lord of the sabbath" (12:1–8). When Jesus is in the synagogue and a man with a withered hand is present, the leaders bait Jesus with a question, hoping to snare him: "Is it lawful to cure on the sabbath?" (12:10). Jesus replies that "it is lawful to do good on the sabbath," and he restores the man's hand (12:12). Jesus is an embodiment of the heart of the Law, the heart of the Torah, the heart of God's intention for humanity and all creation, and the stakes remain high. Jesus' new understanding of what is "lawful" ultimately costs him his life as well (12:14).

So, when the landowner raises the issue of lawfulness, he is saying more than "I have the right to give these people a full denarius." He is saying that his action fulfills the divine Law, performs God's will for humanity and all creation.

"Or are you envious because I am generous?" (20:15). Here the NRSV, along with most other contemporary translations, smooths out a rough patch of Greek, which literally reads, "Is your eye evil because I am good?" It is, however, worth leaving the smooth translations behind and paying attention to the original Greek wording, odd as it is. The notion of an evil eye hearkens back to Jesus' word in the Sermon on the Mount: "The eye is the lamp of the body. So, if your eye is clear, your whole body will be full of light. But if your eye is evil, your entire body will be dark. If, therefore, the light in you is darkness, how great is the darkness!" (6:22, author's trans.).

In this saying, the eye is a symbol for the inner life. The eye is more than a bodily organ; it symbolizes the way one sees everything—God, the world, life, other people, oneself. If one's "eye" is clear and true, then one's inner being is flooded with light. But if one's "eye" is distorted, clouded, darkened, evil, then life itself is dark, and how deep is that darkness. In the parable, therefore, the landowner is saying to the grumbling worker, "Everything depends on your eye, depends on how you view life, how you view me, how you view our relationship."

A healthy eye will see the landowner, that is, will see God, as "good," *agathos* (ἀγαθός, 20:15). The NRSV translates this as "generous," and that's not far off the mark, but "good" is to be preferred for two reasons. First, "good" is a description of character prior to any expression of that character in deeds. If the *Godfather* movies are to be believed, even mafia dons can be generous and perform acts of generosity, but they do so out of calculated power and a desire to control, not out of any intrinsic goodness. Yes, the landowner is generous, and he performed a generous act toward the late-arriving workers,[82] but the parable insists on a more basic truth: this generosity comes because the landowner is intrinsically "good." Second, in the previous chapter, Jesus told the rich young man that the term "good" should be reserved for God alone (19:17). The landowner, then, is not merely a good guy, he is a symbol for God and is "good" in the way God alone is good.

The grumbling worker, however, does not have a healthy eye but an "evil eye." What caused that? Was he mistreated as a child? Did he have tragic experiences that soured him on life? No, the parable indicates that, surprisingly, it is the very goodness of the landowner that has poisoned his vision.

Here is the question at the nub of this parable. What is it about the goodness of the landowner—or, in kingdom terms, the goodness of God—that causes some people to have a darkened and evil vision of life? The grumbling landowner prefers that the world rest on a universally agreed-upon contract of fairness. We all know what fairness is: you get your fair share and I get mine. Just to be doubly sure that everyone is on the same page about this contract, these early workers negotiate the terms with the landowner. "OK, we give you one day's work, and you will give us one day's pay. Fair is fair. Agreed?"

If we put this in religious terms, it means that standing between human beings and God—indeed shielding humanity from God—is the fairness contract. We like this kind of religion, because it binds God to our negotiated agreement. God is not allowed to do anything that violates this contract, which means, of course, that God is not ultimate; the contract is ultimate, our little notions of fairness and justice are ultimate, and God must keep to the deal. Human relations to God can then be transactional. "OK, God, you said if I keep your commandments, then you will bless me. I have kept all of your commandments, so where's my blessing?"

But what if God is not bound by anything outside of God's own self, not even something as noble as impartial justice? What if God is pure and perfect freedom? What if God is not inalterably evenhanded? What if, more powerfully and more dangerously, God is *good*? This is terrifying to some, because God is then unpredictable, and therefore unmanageable. God is free to receive Abel's offering and refuse Cain's (is that fair?). God can throw a party for the prodigal son while the older son grumbles in resentment, and God can pay a whole denarius to people who worked only a short shift at the end of the day.

The God who is free and good generates in human beings both attraction and fear. Attraction, because we sense our need for the good and merciful God, but fear because this God cannot be managed or controlled, even by our most pious gestures or reasonable bargains. "It is no wonder," writes Walter Brueggemann, "that the Priestly interpreters in ancient Israel and in the ancient world generally attempted to corral holiness into manageable administrable categories." But many of the narratives in the Old Testament, Brueggemann argues, "attest an awareness that the holiness of God cannot be presumed upon. That dangerous holiness of God defies the domesticating efforts of the ancient priests even as it escapes the efforts of modern science." He continues, "The outcome of this trajectory concerning God's holiness is the recognition that God will not be entrapped in our best efforts. God may and will do wild things beyond our hopes or expectations. Thus the 'wonders' that God performs in creation and in history are beyond expectation or administration."[83]

But this God who is free and good, the God who does "wild things," not only frightens people. This God also ticks some people off, because they prefer a transactional faith lived in relation to a transactional God. The parable makes two big claims: one wonderful and the other terrifying. The wonderful claim is that God is good, free, and generous, beyond all human categories of fairness to imagine or contain. The terrifying claim is that people who don't want that God, who want instead to live transactionally, get just what they want. They live pinched little lives serving a transactional idol of their own making. Their eye is evil, and they have their reward. Although it is perhaps a bit too contemporary to say it this way, slightly anachronistic psychologically perhaps, it is nevertheless not far from the mark: In the Gospel of Matthew, the god you see is the god you get. If in a world bathed in the light of God's freely given goodness, you prefer to guard your interests, try to cut deals for your own protection and advantage, so be it. That is your god, you have your reward, and "how great is the darkness!"

5. "So the last will be first, and the first will be last" (20:16)

This phrase is uttered by Jesus twice in Matthew: right before he tells this parable (19:30) and here at the end of the parable, forming bookends around the story. Therefore, this is obviously the frame in which Matthew wants us to understand the parable. Most scholars, though, are persuaded that this "first and last" business is something Matthew inserted himself. Indeed, the saying seems forced and fits the parable only clumsily, since "first" and "last" refer only to the order of hiring and paying and not to the heart of the parable. But Matthew gets first dibs on how we read this parable. So what sense can we make of his first and last language? In Matthew's mind, the parable speaks directly to some who would usually be considered "first" but who are actually "last," and vice versa. But whom is he talking about?

Some have suggested that Matthew is thinking of Jews and Gentiles. The Gentiles are "the last" to be invited into the kingdom, the latecomers; the Jews, who were "the first," grumble in the parable just as they did in the wilderness of Sinai. "How long will this wicked community grumble against me? I have heard the complaints of these grumbling Israelites" (Num. 14:27 NIV).[84] Others think Matthew has the Pharisees and the disciples in mind as the first and the last. Perhaps better, if Matthew's church is composed mainly of Jews, formerly of the synagogue, who have come to believe that Jesus is the Messiah and who in the end are sent out as missionaries to "make disciples of all nations, baptizing them in the name of the Father and of the Son and of the Holy Spirit" (28:19), then it seems most plausible that the "first" are the Christians in Matthew's own congregation, and the "last" are the people from "all nations" whom they are evangelizing.

In the deepest sense, however, it matters little whom Matthew specifically means by "first" and "last" in his own context. The larger point is that the goodness of God is revolutionary in every context, overturning much about all humanly constructed values and assumptions about who deserves to be "first" and who gets relegated to "last." In the parable's own terms, the "last" workers are those who are still out of work near the close of day and who, in their need, immediately respond to the call of the landowner to come into the vineyard. They strike no bargains, cut no deals. Out of their need, they simply come at the sound of the landowner's appeal. These are the "little ones" whom the disciples are told to seek like a shepherd, the least ones who turn out to be the prized ones, the ones who bring the most joy to the shepherd when they are found and restored to the community (see 18:10–14). These latecomers are like the child Jesus places in the midst of the disciples and about whom he says, "Whoever becomes humble like this child is the greatest in the kingdom of heaven" (18:4).

The Disturbing and Joyful Goodness of God

The late Christopher Hitchens, one of the so-called new atheists who made a splash in the early 2000s, wrote a book titled *God Is Not Great*, in which he dismissed religion on the grounds that science had rendered it obsolete and unnecessary. "Religion has run out of justifications," he wrote. "Thanks to the telescope and the microscope, it no longer offers an explanation of anything important."[85]

Philosopher Terry Eagleton countered Hitchens's idea that it is the responsibility of religion to offer justifications. Those are Hitchens's rules and requirements, not God's. "Christianity," Eagleton wrote, "was never meant to be an *explanation* of anything in the first place. [What Hitchens said] is rather like saying that thanks to the electric toaster we can forget about Chekov." Eagleton sniffs out that Hitchens is operating with a straw figure view of God, looking with an "evil eye," to use the parable's language, seeing a God who created some elaborate machine-like creation that has rules and principles that can be explained and need to be justified. To the contrary, argued Eagleton, God, like the vineyard owner in the parable, does not operate out of need but instead formed the creation out of freedom and for the sheer love of it:

> God for Christian theology is not a mega-manufacturer. . . . Creation is not about getting things off the ground. Rather, God is the reason why there is something rather than nothing, the condition of possibility of any entity whatsoever. . . . God the Creator is not a celestial engineer at work on a superbly rational design that will impress his research grant body no end, but an artist, and an aesthete to boot, who made the world with no functional end in view but simply for the love and delight of it. . . . He created it out of love, not need. There was nothing in it for him. The Creation is the original *acte gratuit*.[86]

Artist and theologian Makoto Fujimura agrees:

> God exists outside of time and space, not needing to create this world. . . . So why did God create? . . . God created out of love. God created because it is in God's nature to make and create. . . . God created out of abundance and exuberance, and the universe (and we) exist because God loves to create. Some will misunderstand what I just stated and ask, "But isn't there a purpose behind creation, or purpose in the cosmos? Yes, but this purposefulness goes far deeper than in the industrial sense.[87]

The Parable of the Laborers in the Vineyard cuts deep to the question of how we view God and God's creation. Do we view God as the megamanufacturer, a dutiful, purposeful God bound to rules and set protocols, a boring and bureaucratic administrator of tit-for-tat justice? If so, we will go into the vineyard expecting predictable evenhanded outcomes, even negotiating a deal to make sure things go by the book. But if the kingdom's vineyard belongs to the God who is good and free, exuberant and abundant in love, then who can predict what grace and generosity will overflow at the end of the day?

If our eye is clear and healthy, and we see God as God truly is, we see that God is good, and God's free and unpredictable goodness is at the core of life. Goodness is the way things are, the way reality is made, and we can see it if our eye is healthy. We are able each day to bend the knee, open our arms, and pray, "Give us this day our daily bread" (6:11). But if our eye is distorted and we prefer the world to be run by our rules and God to be the transactional deity of deals we cut, then we pray a bargainer's prayer: "All right, God, if I put in a day's work, I get a day's worth of bread, right?" When we suddenly realize that God is a good giver of life on God's own terms, then we will grumble in resentment. The judgment we receive is one of our own making: "Stop whining, Buster. You cut a deal with reality, and that deal is what you got as your reward. Now leave!"

Where does this parable take us to experience the breaking in of God's kingdom? Garrison Keillor, who clings to his faith, even as he admits it wavers, wrote of his own experiences of the God of love and joy: "My elders tried to make Scripture be clear, rational, inevitable, irrefutable, but it actually is miraculous. Ancient tribes wandering the desert discovered that they were dearly loved by their Creator who allowed them to suffer in hopes it would draw them closer to Him. I don't get it but I go for it. And the choir was glorious on Sunday. Oh my God in heaven, what a joyful noise."[88]

He then points to places where his own eye sees the goodness of God breaking into life:

> I know two women who recently gave birth to their first babies and are joyful and so are their men and that is real news. A grandson is starting college. A daughter is moving. A friend has finished a novel. A widowed friend, marrying again at 84, writes to say he is well and adds, "And it's none of your business but the sex is great." A cousin attended a graduation ceremony at a school for intellectually disabled children and one poor graduate stammered through a speech of which little could be understood and the crowd clapped all the harder for him.[89]

Where else do we see God's goodness breaking in? Before dawn every workday morning, vans pull into the parking lot of the Border Agriculture Workers Center in El Paso. Crowded into the lot are dozens of migrant workers, who have spent the night in the Center apart from their families and who are now, like the laborers in the parable, eager to be chosen to work in the fields. The vans will travel to New Mexico, where the workers will pick chili peppers all day.

The Center was founded by Carlos Marentes, a Catholic layman who was himself once a worker in the fields. "For a long time, I didn't see the connection between my faith and striving for justice," Marentes said. "Being Catholic was just what I was, like being Mexican."[90] But then Marentes watched news reports of Brazilian garbage workers struggling for decent wages. At first, this worker action simply seemed to be laborers demanding fair treatment, but looking more closely, Marentes saw that something more, another source of daily bread, was at work. "I realized that the struggle is not about organizing the collective action of workers, it represents another kind of strength. Their main power was coming from their faith, faith in God and faith the situation would get better. . . . We cannot solve our problems without strength in our faith. We need power that doesn't come from ourselves."[91] Beyond mere questions of economic justice, Marentes saw the goodness of God offering life and hope.

So, when the vans return to the Center in the evening, the workers will be fed a hot meal, there will be showers and fresh towels, and at the end of the day welcome beds where the workers will rest before beginning all over again the next morning. But Carlos Marentes also provides one other gift. Some evenings, he leads the workers in a study of Pope Benedict's encyclical letter regarding economic development, *Caritas in Veritate.* These workers, their faces deeply browned from the glaring sun and their hands worn from the labor of picking, are nevertheless deeply engaged when they learn and discuss ideas such as that true economic justice

> requires a transcendent vision of the person, it needs God: without him, development is either denied, or entrusted exclusively to man, who falls into the trap of thinking he can bring about his own salvation,

> and ends up promoting a dehumanized form of development. Only through an encounter with God are we able to see in the other something more than just another creature, to recognize the divine image in the other, thus truly coming to discover him or her and to mature in a love that becomes concern and care for the other. . . .
>
> *Development needs Christians with their arms raised towards God* in prayer, Christians moved by the knowledge that truth-filled love, *caritas in veritate*, from which authentic development proceeds, is not produced by us, but given to us. For this reason, even in the most difficult and complex times, besides recognizing what is happening, we must above all else turn to God's love. Development requires attention to the spiritual life, a serious consideration of the experiences of trust in God, spiritual fellowship in Christ, reliance upon God's providence and mercy, love and forgiveness, self-denial, acceptance of others, justice and peace. All this is essential if "hearts of stone" are to be transformed into "hearts of flesh" (Ezek. 36:26), rendering life on earth "divine" and thus more worthy of humanity.[92]

Presbyterian pastor Joanna Adams faced a wrenching tragedy in her ministry. A sixty-five-year-old leader in her congregation, Jim, panicked when he discovered that his adult son, Mark, suffering for years from schizophrenia, had stopped taking his medication, was refusing to see his psychiatrist, and had begun to act erratically. Deeply fearful that his son might do harm to others, the father, in his desperation, killed his son and then took his own life. Adams was to preach at the memorial service for both father and son. What can one say in the midst of such perplexity and grief?

In the funeral sermon, she named the questions on the hearts of many present:

> *Why* did it happen? *Why* did Mark get so sick? *Why* did Jim sink into such despair? They are the questions one asks late at night when sleep won't come, and our psyches are demanding an explanation.
>
> . . . Because we are human, we want to know why; because we are only human we cannot know why. The Scripture promises that someday we will know why, but that day is not today. . . . God knows that beneath all our whys is the only question that matters: Can God be trusted with the deaths of those we love?[93]

As the sermon came to its conclusion, Adams told this experience:

> I met somebody yesterday I had not met before. Her name is Lauren. She is three years old, Jim and Carolyn's granddaughter, a bright and happy blond-headed little girl. She wore a bib with a duck on it, and a ready smile as she sat on Carolyn's knee and met the preacher. "Tell Joanna what you say before you have your supper," Carolyn

said. Lauren looked at me, a perfect stranger, and spoke as if she was sharing with me the most wonderful news you could imagine. "God is great," Lauren said. "God is good," she said, and suddenly I could not wait to come to church today, so that I could tell you what Lauren said and what the scripture promises and what faith knows even when the pain is piercing and the shadows fall. God is still great. God is still good. It is true![94]

THE PARABLE OF THE TWO SONS (MATTHEW 21:28–32)

This parable is spoken by Jesus in the middle of a testy exchange with the temple authorities. In fact, this jagged-edged conversation unleashes a barrage of three barbed parables from Jesus, all aimed at the chief priests and the elders. Understanding this parable, and the two that follow, requires paying attention not only to the parable itself but also to the context, especially to the flow of the debate.

By Whose Authority?

At the point where the parable appears in Matthew, the story of Jesus is coming to its denouement. Jesus "the Messiah, the Son of David, the Son of Abraham" (1:1) is now drawing near to Jerusalem, close to the time of his passion, through which he will become Jesus the crucified and risen Lord. Jesus enters the city on the road from the Mount of Olives, and Matthew views this event entirely through a theological lens. His report of Jesus' entrance is not merely an account of a noteworthy Galilean preacher arriving in Jerusalem. It is a vivid piece of eschatological theater.

Messianic themes abound. The crowd greets Jesus with excited shouts that hint dangerously of regime change: "Hosanna to the Son of David!" The entire city, Matthew says, was thrown into "turmoil" (21:10), and Jesus keeps the pot boiling by entering the temple grounds and not only overturning the tables of the money changers but also overthrowing the powers holding the lame and the blind captive (21:12–14). Children begin to echo the messianic cry heard on the road, "Hosanna to the Son of David!" All of this activity upsets the chief priests and the scribes, who, perhaps dimly aware that the wheel of God's kingdom is about to roll over them, angrily reprimand Jesus, saying, "Do you hear what these [children] are saying?" (21:12–15).

Yes, Jesus does hear what the children are saying, and he answers his accusers wryly, "Don't you know what the Scripture says? 'Out of the mouths of infants'" (from 21:16). The time is ripe, the Messiah has arrived in Jerusalem, and the world is about to turn.

Leaving this uproar behind, Jesus withdraws to Bethany for the night (21:17). The next day, when he returns to the temple and begins to teach, the chief priests and the elders are no doubt still smarting from the exchange the day before (later we learn that this group included some Pharisees, 21:45). So again they confront him, demanding to know this time, "By what authority are you doing these things, and who gave you this authority?" (21:23).

Jesus, ever the clever teacher and debater, proposes a trade: "I'll ask you a question. If you answer my question, then I'll answer yours." The question Jesus asks is a perfect wedge, cleaving the group of temple leaders in two: "Did the baptism of John come from heaven, or was it of human origin?" (21:25). This sets the leaders immediately squabbling among themselves about how to respond. On the one hand, they could say that John had heavenly authority. That was the popular view, and saying so would score some points with the crowd. But they quickly realized that, if they said John had divine authority, the people would shoot back, "Well, then, why didn't you believe what John preached?" On the other hand, the leaders could say what they really thought, that John was merely a troublemaker, an irritating eccentric out in the Judean wilderness raving about repentance on his own misguided authority. But they couldn't say that either, because the people were convinced that John was a true prophet.

Finally, realizing they're damned if they do and damned if they don't, the leaders decide on a safe and sheepish shrug: "We don't know," they reply. Well, then, counters Jesus, "Neither will I tell you by what authority I am doing these things" (21:27).

With this riddle about John the Baptist, Jesus has deftly tilted the playing field against his challengers in two ways. First, he has powerfully redefined the question of authority. When the temple leaders ask him by what authority he has created disruption on the temple grounds, they mean bureaucratic authority, specifically *their* authority. They didn't give Jesus permission to turn over tables or get children into an excited state. Then who did provide Jesus with the authority to do these things? Let's see your license and registration. By raising the authority connected with John and his baptism, Jesus has redefined authority not as human rules but as what God is doing in the world, as God's will, as the unregulated authority of the kingdom movement that John inaugurated and that Jesus himself embodies.

Many years ago, a theological seminary in the South hired as a professor a young theologian from Europe, unfamiliar with the ways of America, much less of the South. It was the custom at this school for every faculty member, once a school year, to lead chapel worship, preaching and presiding at the Lord's Supper. When it came time for this new faculty member to take his turn, he preached his sermon and then stood behind the table to lead communion. He lifted the top off of the tray of communion cups, and the aroma of red wine wafted through the chapel. How could he have known the strict but unwritten rule at this school that no real wine was to be served at communion, only grape juice?

When the unmistakable fragrance of alcohol filled the chapel, an electric alarm jolted the congregation. Every eye quickly fixed on the president of the school, sitting in the front pew. To no one's surprise, his face was reddened and his jaw locked in silent fury. When the service ended, the president bolted forward to the chancel to confront the unsuspecting presider. "Who authorized you to serve this wine!" demanded the president, his voice trembling with rage.

Stunned, the young professor lifted his hands in bewilderment. "Jesus Christ," he replied innocently.

The exchange about authority between the temple leaders and Jesus operates out of the same shift in categories. The leaders are thinking of the authority of the rules, and Jesus counters with the authority of the kingdom, the authority of God, an authority he himself carried.

The second way Jesus tilts the playing field is by turning his interrogators into the interrogated. The leaders thought they had asked Jesus a "gotcha question" that would silence him, but Jesus countered with his own "gotcha" that put the leaders on the hot seat and left them whimpering, "I don't know."

It is worth noting here that our picture of the religious leaders, especially of the Pharisees, can easily slip into caricature. Because the Pharisees are the opponents that Jesus most vigorously engages, it is tempting to view them as mustache-twisting villains, sinister figures who are the antithesis of all that Jesus represents. Later in Matthew, Jesus, it will seem, joins in the Pharisee bashing, calling them "blind guides," "hypocrites," "snakes," and "brood of vipers" (chap. 23).

The truth of the matter, though, is that Matthew's Jesus erupts into fierce controversy with the Pharisees not because they are so distant but because they are so close. The Pharisees sought to transform the nation into the faithful and obedient people of God. So did Matthew. The Pharisees advocated purity and righteousness in daily life. So did Matthew. "The scribes and the Pharisees sit on Moses' seat" (23:2); in Matthew's theological world, that means their teachings are worthy of attention. Luz goes so far as to say, "Jesus is quite similar to the Pharisees, explaining why the controversy between Jesus' disciples and the . . . Pharisees is so prominent in the NT. What we have in the NT is in the widest sense of the word an inner-Pharisaic controversy."[95]

The conflict with the Pharisees, then, is tragic. The Pharisees are not cardboard villains; they are people of faith who were playing the right game and who had everything going for them but fumbled the ball at the goal line. God sent them John with the message of true righteousness, and they missed it. God sent them Jesus, the very embodiment of the kingdom, and they rejected him. God will send preachers to them in the name of Christ who will proclaim the gospel of peace and forgiveness, and they will flog them in their synagogues (23:34). The Pharisees are people who see clearly that the prophets of old were truly God's messengers and who say, "If we had lived in the days of our ancestors, we would not have taken part with them in shedding the blood of the prophets" (23:30), but they were deaf to the prophecy being announced in their own ears and blind to what God was doing right before their own eyes. The lesson of Jesus' conflict with the Pharisees is not that the "bad guys" got what they deserved, but a sad and urgent warning to all people of faith in all times that blindness and hypocrisy lie ever close at hand and that God's people must be always vigilant, keeping eyes open to the new thing that God is doing now.

In this particular encounter with the authorities, Jesus, with the momentum now going in his direction, adds another question to the exchange. He says, in effect, "You couldn't answer the first question, well here's a question that perhaps you can answer," and then the parable is spoken. "What do you think?" Jesus begins (21:28), making it clear that the leaders are still on the answering end of things. He then poses a case: A man with two sons[96] said to both of them, "Son, go and work in the vineyard today" (21:28). The first son said, "I will not," but later he changed his mind and went to the vineyard to work (21:29). The second did exactly the opposite. He said he would go, but then he failed to show up for work (21:30).

Jesus then asks the leaders the definitive question: "Which of the two did the will of his father?" (21:31). This time Jesus' question is so clear,[97] the leaders cannot hide behind an ambiguous "I don't know." They have to spit it out. "They said, 'The first'" (21:31).

They are correct, of course. It is the son who actually went to work in the vineyard who did his father's will.

Hypocrisy or Repentance?

But now things take a curious turn. Jesus provides his own application of this parable, and it's not what we expect. When we look just at the parable itself, it appears to be a fairly straightforward story about saying versus doing, talk versus action. One son talked a good game, but didn't act on his word. The other son, despite his refusal at first, actually went to work. The parable looks very much like a narrative expression of what Jesus said earlier in the Sermon on the Mount: "Not everyone who says to me, 'Lord, Lord,' will enter the kingdom of heaven, but only the one who does the will of my Father in heaven" (7:21).[98] Talk is cheap; it's action that counts.

But when Jesus gives his own application of the parable, he seems to take it in a different direction. His emphasis falls not so much on the contrast between words and deeds but on whether the chief priests and scribes believed John the Baptist: "Jesus said to them, 'Truly I tell you, the tax collectors and the prostitutes are going into the kingdom of God ahead of you. For John came to you in the way of righteousness and you did not believe him, but the tax collectors and the prostitutes believed him; and even after you saw it, you did not change your minds and believe him'" (21:31–32).

With this saying, Jesus appears to have looped back to that earlier exchange about John's authority, the one in which the chief priests and elders mumbled that they didn't know whether John had divine authority (21:23–27). When Jesus says, "For John came to you in the way of righteousness and you did not believe him," this sounds more like a conclusion to that dispute than it does an interpretation of the parable per se. In fact, we begin to wonder if the parable is out of place, an interruption in the flow of the debate between Jesus and the leaders about John.

But if we put the parable under a microscope, we begin to see more clearly how the parable and Jesus' interpretation of it fit. A closer look reveals that the story is not actually a simple story about words versus deeds. If it were, then the story would be about two sons who *both say* they will go into the vineyard, but then only one keeps his word. This story, however, is more complex, involving two different kinds of responses to the father's command: a son who says no but then, after a change of heart, acts out a yes, and a son who says yes only to default on his word and act out a no.

We note that the father does more than simply speak to his two sons, commanding them to work in the vineyard. Before he speaks, he travels, that is, he goes from where he is to the places where they are. He "went to the first son" (21:28) and he "went to the second" (21:30). The word translated "went to," *proselthōn* (προσελθὼν), is a characteristic Matthean expression often serving to emphasize the dramatic quality of what follows. In Luke, when the devil tempts Jesus, he just starts speaking (Luke 4:3), but in Matthew the tempter *comes to* Jesus and speaks (Matt. 4:3). When Peter wants to know how often a member of the church should be forgiven, he doesn't simply ask the question, he *goes to* Jesus and asks it (18:21). When the risen Christ appears to the eleven disciples in Galilee, he *comes to* them and says, "All authority in heaven and on earth has been given to me" (28:18).

So the father's words to the two sons to go and work in the vineyard aren't just commands; they are disruptive visits. The father *comes to* them, enters into their zones, and summons them to leave where they are and to go to a new place of work and service. The key insight here is that this is exactly what John the Baptist did. "John came to you in the way of righteousness," Jesus tells the leaders (21:32).

When the father goes to the first son, he receives no respect. The first son blows him off, responding bluntly, "I will not," to his father's command to go and work in the vineyard (21:29). Fathers today may not be so surprised when their adolescent children mouth off at them and go back to their smart phones, but in Jewish families in Jesus' day this reply of the first son is shocking. He hasn't merely refused his father; he has insulted him, shamed him, dishonored him.[99] But then he changes his mind, repents, and goes into the vineyard.

Or does he repent? The parable says that he "changed his mind" (21:29), which in Greek is *metamelētheis* (μεταμεληθεὶς). Earlier in Matthew, when Jesus calls on people to repent (4:17), another Greek word is used: μετανοεῖτε. J. Ramsey Michaels thinks this difference in terminology is important and claims that what the first son does is to express regret, not repentance. True repentance is stronger, Michaels argues, "a total conversion, a change in the whole orientation of one's life. . . . Futile regret is a long way from saving repentance."[100]

When it comes to Matthew's theological world, though, Michaels exaggerates the difference between repentance and a change of mind that leads to obedience. To use the language of "saving repentance," as Michaels does, edges away from Matthew and moves closer perhaps to Lukan theology (or maybe even contemporary evangelical views). Matthew is far more interested in whether people travel the path of righteousness, in whether they truly hear Jesus' words and act on them, than he is in whatever inner emotional gymnastics people perform to get there. For Matthew, working in God's vineyard is the very definition of true life; not working in the vineyard is itself outer darkness. He requires no tear-stained walk down the sawdust trail. Instead, Matthew wants us, when the call of God comes, to get up, roll up our sleeves, and go into the vineyard. Luke will tell a story about a prodigal son who has a dramatic inner experience of change, who comes to himself, and who rushes home to his father with "I have sinned" on his lips (Luke 15:17–19). But in Matthew, when those who have refused to work in the vineyard change their minds and go to work, that counts for a turnaround, for repentance.

When the father goes to the second son, this son, in contrast to the first, speaks very respectfully to his father. He says, "I go, sir" (21:30). In Greek what the son says, *Egō, kyrie* ('Εγώ, κύριε), points theologically: "I will, Lord." But this son does not do what he says he will do. At this point, the second son is an easily identifiable theological type: the hypocrite, the one who says, "Lord, Lord," but who does not do the will of God. Earlier in Matthew, Jesus, using imagery from Isaiah, scolded the religious leaders, the scribes and Pharisees, as people who, like this second son, give lip service to God but not their hearts (15:7–9).

Now the parable is coming into focus. This parable begins with an urgent summons: a father intrudes into the closed worlds of his two sons with a call to leave the way of life they now have and to take up a new vocation, work in the vineyard. The father is a symbol for God, of course, his arrival corresponds to the breaking in of God's kingdom, and the call to work in the vineyard is the call to live as children of the kingdom of heaven. The kingdom keeps coming to humanity, keeps adventing and calling for a response, keeps calling people to go to work in God's vineyard. That call came from John the Baptist: "Repent, for the kingdom of heaven has come near" (3:2). It also came from Jesus, who joined John in proclaiming, "Repent, for the kingdom of heaven has come near" (4:17). It keeps coming because God, as the Parable of the Laborers disclosed, is like a landowner who goes out over and over to call laborers for the vineyard (20:1).

Once the parable issues its urgent kingdom summons, it divides into two branches. Matthew is fond of displaying parabolic contrasts—the wheat and the weeds, the wise and foolish bridesmaids, the wise and wicked servants, the sheep and the goats—and these two sons express another contrast. Just as Jesus' entry into Jerusalem created turmoil and divided the city, just so, the call of this parabolic father divides his two sons.

On one side of the contrast, one of the parable's two branches, is the second son, who, we have noted, is a hypocrite, a person who coos, "Lord, Lord," but doesn't produce obedience. What is particularly interesting about this son is the *reason* he is disobedient. It is not merely because he is a rebellious guy; it's that he is numb to what is happening around him. His father has intruded into his life, the kingdom of heaven has drawn near with its summons, and he sits there as if nothing has happened. That's why Jesus, in applying this parable to the religious leaders, says, "For John came to you in the way of righteousness and you did not believe him" (21:32). The term "believe" here implies not just fact-based belief, but perception, recognition, awareness of what is happening. In short, Jesus is saying that John came to them with heavenly authority, the very kingdom of heaven was knocking on their front doors, and they were clueless. Even when others finally heard the knocking, "got it," and responded with changed lives, the religious leaders remained oblivious. "[T]he tax collectors and the prostitutes," said Jesus, "believed him; and even after you saw it, you did not change your minds and believe him" (21:32).

By contrast, the first son is the one who finally hears the cry in the wilderness, the shout in the night, the invitation to the party, the summons of the father, and at last responds. He is like the tax collectors and the prostitutes, and beyond them are those who are closed, in whatever time and for whatever reason, to the summons of the kingdom, but who, again in whatever time and for whatever reason, finally listen and respond. This responsiveness to the kingdom's call, not the respectful but empty "Yes, Lord" language of the pious, is what takes precedence in the economy of God. "Truly I tell you," Jesus said to the priests and elders, "the tax collectors and the prostitutes are going into the kingdom of God ahead of you" (21:31).

Some commentators argue, more narrowly, that this parable is only about how the religious leaders responded to John. It doesn't encompass, they argue, how people responded to Jesus or, beyond him, to the gospel message proclaimed by the church.[101] This parable, they say, is about the religious establishment's response to John the Baptist, period. But Matthew sees John the Baptist, Jesus, the disciples, and all the preachers who go out later to proclaim the gospel as part of one incoming kingdom tide, wave after wave. "Elijah came," Jesus said (meaning John the Baptist), and they did not recognize him, but they did to him whatever they pleased." Just so, "the Son of Man" (meaning Jesus himself) came and received the same treatment (based on 17:12–13). The disciples came to the people, sent out "like sheep into the midst of wolves" (10:16) "to proclaim the good news, 'The kingdom of heaven has come near.'" (10:7). The call of the kingdom keeps arriving, and people respond—some in obedience and others in indifference.

The tax collectors and prostitutes, by their very ways of living, are those who said no to God, no to God's will, "no to working in the vineyard, that is, no to living "the way of righteousness." But then something happened. John happened, Jesus happened, the kingdom of heaven happened, and the tax collectors and prostitutes became alert to the inbreaking of God, changed their minds, and began to walk in the way of God. But the chief priests and elders, whose very vocation announced that they were laborers in God's vineyard, that they had said yes to God's call, heard and experienced John and then ignored him. They heard and experienced Jesus and rebuffed his authority. Even when they felt the wind of the Spirit blowing in the lives of those who previously had turned away from righteousness, even when they saw with their own eyes the kingdom changing the lives of sinners, they still refused to go to work in the vineyard (21:32). They refused to acknowledge that the time had come, that the kingdom was at hand. They had always said they would, but when the time came to enter the vineyard, they didn't show up.

Two Kingdom Signs: Obedience and Repentance

As a compass of the kingdom, this parable points in two directions, not just one. We can perceive the event of God breaking in around us, first, when people, as Jesus taught in the Sermon on the Mount, hear Jesus' words and act on them (7:24). In his study on the Sermon on the Mount, Dietrich Bonhoeffer wrote: "Humanly speaking, it is possible to understand the Sermon on the Mount in a thousand different ways. But Jesus knows only one possibility: simple surrender and obedience—not interpreting or applying it, but doing and obeying it. That is the only way to hear his words. He does not mean for us to discuss it as an ideal. He really means for us to get on with it."[102]

This parable serves as a barometer of the kingdom breaking through around us by evoking a character who appears in the parable only indirectly: the "third son," the one who says yes and acts out this yes; the one who perceives a summons to the way of righteousness and responds obediently; the one who, in Bonhoeffer's words, "gets on with it." The second son, the one who said yes but then did not go, is a portrait of the *via negativa*, the one whose disobedience exposes where the fullness of the kingdom is not present. By implication, the parable effectively discloses where the fullness is actually present, where God's people both hear Jesus' words and act. Obedience here is not begrudging submission but, rather, participation in the fullness of God's life. Willful disobedience, by contrast, is the zone of death, an oxygen-starved expanse in life's sea.

In 1965, when Martin Luther King Jr. asked for volunteers to join the march from Selma to Montgomery and to assist the efforts to secure universal voting rights, one person who responded was Viola Liuzzo, a wife and mother from Detroit. When her husband tried to dissuade her from going to Alabama and joining the march, telling Viola, "It's not your fight," she responded, "It's everybody's fight. There are too many people who just stand around talking."[103] That is why Viola Liuzzo went to work in that part of God's vineyard known as the civil rights struggle in Alabama.

After the march, Viola was giving a young man, a civil rights worker, a ride back to Selma. A car full of Klansmen, who were enraged by the sight of a white woman in a car with a black man, sped up beside them and fired a flurry of bullets into their car. The man survived, but Viola, thirty-nine years old, was killed instantly. When Mary Lilleboe, one of Viola's daughters, was in her seventies, she remembered her mother: "She actually believed it when Christ said that the suffering and needy are our people. Mom saw all other human beings as her people."[104]

In the obedience of Viola Liuzzo, we perceive the kingdom of heaven drawn near. In her suffering and death are fulfilled the words of Jesus, "Your reward is great in heaven, for in the same way they persecuted the prophets who were before you" (5:12).

The parable also points to the kingdom in another way, through the picture of the first son, who said no at first but then repented. The kingdom, the event of God breaking in, can be perceived in the lives of those who are stubbornly opposed to the call of God, but who, in the end, change their minds and repent. One person who truly changed his mind and went to work in God's vineyard was C. S. Lewis, an Oxford and Cambridge academic whose countless radio speeches, lectures, and books (including *Mere Christianity, The Screwtape Letters,* and *The Chronicles of Narnia*) have encouraged Christian faith in millions of listeners and readers.

Lewis was raised as a child in the Church of Ireland, but soon fell away from the faith and became a firm and vigorous atheist. He was the son who was told to go and work in the vineyard and who, without hesitation, said, "I will not!" But, as the parable shows, God is one who goes to human beings and pursues them. In *Surprised by Joy,* Lewis describes God's relentless pursuit of him, how he felt almost stalked by the mystery of God's call. It came to a head one night when Lewis was a fellow at Oxford's Magdalen College, when he yielded to that divine pursuit and, like the son in the parable, had a change of mind that gradually led him to work in the vineyard:

> Amiable agnostics will talk cheerfully about "man's search for God." To me, as I then was, they might as well have talked about the mouse's search for the cat.
>
> . . . You must picture me alone in that room in Magdalen, night after night, feeling, whenever my mind lifted even for a second from my work, the steady, unrelenting approach of Him whom I so earnestly desired not to meet. That which I greatly feared had at last come upon me. In the Trinity Term of 1929 I gave in, and admitted that God was God, and knelt and prayed: perhaps, that night, the most dejected and reluctant convert in all England. I did not then see what is now the most shining and obvious thing: the Divine humility which will accept a convert even on such terms. The Prodigal Son at least walked home on his own feet. But who can duly adore that Love which will open the high gates to a prodigal who is brought in kicking, struggling, resentful, and darting his eyes in every direction for a chance of escape? The words *compelle intrare*, compel them to come in, have been so abused by wicked men that we shudder at them; but, properly understood, they plumb the depth of the Divine mercy. The hardness of God is kinder than the softness of men, and His compulsion is our liberation.[105]

Another child of God who said a vigorous no before he said an astonishing yes was Josh Bishop. When Bishop was nineteen years old, he and a companion, both under the sway of alcohol and cocaine, tried to hijack a car. When the owner refused to hand over the keys, the two men beat him to death. After he was arrested, Bishop readily confessed to the crime and volunteered the information that he had earlier killed another person, a man he believed had assaulted his mother. In 1996, a jury in Georgia convicted Bishop, and he received a death sentence.

A year later, Diana Shertenlieb, a lifelong Catholic and a member of a parish in the Atlanta suburbs, began posting messages about her faith on the internet. A priest who was connected to a prison ministry of the Archdiocese of Atlanta read these posts and asked Diana if she would be willing to correspond with an inmate on death row. When she agreed, the priest gave her a list of Georgia's condemned prisoners. Shertenlieb selected the youngest person on the list, twenty-two-year-old Josh Bishop.

She sent her first tentative letter, and Bishop responded quickly and gratefully with a letter of his own. An increasingly frequent exchange of letters followed, the relationship grew, and eventually Shertenlieb decided that she wanted to visit Bishop in prison. She presented herself at the gate and was escorted through the check points. "I was very intimidated by the guards. They can smell a newbie," she said.[106]

Shertenlieb was surprised by the young man she found. "He just wasn't what I expected," she said. "He looked like a kid you'd see out fishing. He just seems to be one of my kids."[107] Shertenlieb discovered that Bishop had been abandoned by his father and neglected by a mother who became addicted to alcohol and drugs. As a child, Bishop slept under highway bridges, foraged for food in garbage cans, and cycled through a series of group and foster homes. Beneath the damaged human being, Shertenlieb sensed an underlying goodness, even a sweetness, in Bishop.

She began to tell him about her faith, told him about the wideness of God's mercy and the depth of God's love. She gave him books, some of them religious and others not, and he began to read ("Anne Frank blowed my mind!" he told her[108]). Bishop began to blossom. He took up painting and deepened his enjoyment of country music. Shertenlieb said that her goal was not overt evangelism but instead, "I just wanted him to have something to hold on to. . . . I wanted him to know that someone on the outside was thinking of him and praying for him."[109]

Like John the Baptist, Shertenlieb had come to Josh Bishop announcing the way of righteousness, and gradually Bishop's life turned from a no to a yes. "I had lost my trust in people," he said. "But she brought me back into the arms of God," he wrote. "I truly cannot say enough about [her]."[110]

Shertenlieb and her husband, Gary, made Bishop a part of their family. Others reached out to him as well, and all were amazed to see how fully he flourished. He started attending mass, and when he was twenty-three years old, he was baptized and confirmed by the Archbishop of Atlanta. Diana Shertenlieb and her husband, Gary, were named as godparents on Josh Bishop's baptismal certificate. He took up a life of service:

> In his last years, working with a clinic at Mercer Law School, he taught close to fifty students lessons about justice that they could never learn in a classroom. He offered abject apologies to the families of his victims, and was comforted in the grace offered by a number of those he had hurt. His heart bled for children who lived without hope for a better life, and he did what he could to encourage teenagers who struggled with bitterness or apathy. From his prison cell, Josh reached others with his kind and open heart. He bore others up. He made the world better.[111]

On March 31, 2016, speaking words of repentance and love to the end, Josh Bishop was executed by the state of Georgia. Who was the son who said yes but acted out a no? Perhaps it was the state itself. Jaded by so many prisoners who feign religious conversions simply to curry favor with the parole board, the state of Georgia, like the authorities of old, couldn't discern whether what was happening to Josh Bishop was the work of God or merely human posturing. So, like those chief priests and elders before them, the state authorities could say only they didn't know, and as Herod did to John, they executed Josh Bishop. The truest goal of incarceration is reform. Georgia says yes to that, but, when genuine reform occurs in a human being, when the "tax collectors and prostitutes believe," the system can only perform a no.

Bishop was buried in the cemetery of the Monastery of the Holy Spirt in Conyers, Georgia. One of those who had cared for Bishop in prison and loved him said,

> In his last hours, Josh comforted his friends, prayed with us, reminded us to take care of one another, and sang "Amazing Grace." He hoped that his death would "take away from the pain and add to the peace" of those he had hurt. His continued concern for the suffering of others while he faced the ultimate penalty showed that the evil the State wanted to stamp out was not there, and all that was lost was the potential of a redeemed soul to do good. If there is justice in heaven, if not on earth, he is painting with Rembrandt and humming along with Merle Haggard.[112]

One irony of Josh Bishop's story is that Diana Shertenlieb almost did not reach out to him. When the priest invited her to write to a death-row inmate, she was like the first son in the parable. She declined the priest's request, but then she changed her mind and walked in the path of righteousness. It is the way of the kingdom.

THE PARABLE OF THE WICKED TENANTS (MATTHEW 21:33–46)

This parable was obviously important to the early church. It is one of the few of Jesus' parables that appear in all three Synoptic Gospels as well as the *Gospel of Thomas*. It clearly spoke to the early generations of Christians, probably because it brought light on the vexing question of why Jesus, as God's Messiah, was rejected by his own people. Matthew's version is close to Mark's, and the majority of what was said about this parable in the commentary on Mark's parables (pp. 89–97) can be applied to the parable in Matthew's Gospel as well. There are, however, a few differences in the Matthean version of the parable that are worth consideration.

1. In both Mark and Matthew, the context of the parable is a dispute between Jesus and the Jewish authorities about John the Baptist, but in Mark, Jesus tells only this one parable. In Matthew, this is one of three parables hurled against the authorities (the others are the previous parable, the Two Sons, and the following one, the Wedding Banquet), serving to intensify the argument. It's as if Jesus keeps pummeling them, saying, "Take this, and while I'm at it, take that, and, to make this absolutely clear, here's another thing."

2. In Mark, the one who planted the vineyard is simply "a man," that is, some guy, some generic person. In Matthew, the planter is specifically an *oikodespotes* (οἰκοδεσπότης)—a "householder," "a landowner" (21:33). This is a favorite title in Matthew (used seven times), showing up in two other Matthean parables (the Wheat and the Weeds and the Laborers in the Vineyard); in each case, it is a stock character representing God.[113]

3. Mark and Matthew differ about when the slaves arrive to collect the owner's share of the produce. In Mark, the first slave is sent simply at the right or opportune time (καιρῷ). The NRSV does well to render this "when the season came" (12:2). But Matthew gives a fuller description. The first wave of slaves arrives *ho kairos tōn karpōn* (ὁ καιρὸς τῶν καρπῶν), that is, at harvest time or, more literally, at "the time of the fruits" (21:34). This both underscores the eschatological theme in Matthew's parable and connects it to two previous statements of Jesus: "[Y]ou will know them by their fruits" in the Sermon on the Mount (7:16, 20), and the curse of the barren fig tree earlier in this chapter: "May no fruit ever come from you again!" (21:19). In Matthew, this parable is not about just *any* harvest but about *God's* harvest; what gets emphasized is that the religious authorities are those who refuse to present the fruits of the harvest.

4. In Mark, the slaves are sent one at a time to collect the produce—the first slave, another slave, yet another, and so on. The slaves come like a steady drumbeat in the score of a thriller movie, and the effect is to create mounting

suspense until the denouement, when, at last, the owner sends his beloved son. By contrast, in Matthew, those sent to the vineyard come in three waves, each wave more significant and impressive than the previous one. First, there are simply "slaves" sent to the vineyard. When that goes badly, the landowner sends "other slaves, *more than the first*" (21:36, emphasis added). Finally, the landowner's very own son is sent. Mark's version of the parable gradually tightens the screw of suspense; what will happen next? Matthew's version ratchets up urgency; it is crucial to respond. The landowner earnestly wants a response from the tenants and keeps raising the level of the appeal.

5. In Mark, the vineyard owner sends at the last "a beloved son" (Mark 12:6), but in Matthew, he is called simply "my son" (Matt. 21:37). The difference is interesting but finally insignificant, since in both Gospels the son is quite clearly a christological reference. Snodgrass notes that there is no good reason for Matthew to have erased the term "beloved son"; he has already used it three times to refer to Jesus (3:17; 12:18; 17:5).[114] He wonders if perhaps Matthew, who usually follows Mark, was in fact employing a different source for this parable.[115]

6. In Matthew's telling of the parable, the tenants in the vineyard "saw the son" and then hatched their murderous plot. The tenants in Mark also kill the son, so logically they would also have seen him, but Mark doesn't explicitly say so. Matthew makes sure to note that the tenants *saw* the son, to strengthen the connection to the chief priests, the elders, and the Pharisees—the targets of this parable. They also had been those who saw but did not respond. They rejected John the Baptist and didn't respond, even when the kingdom was so clearly breaking in all around among the tax collectors and prostitutes. It wasn't because they were doing busywork and just missed it. No, they *saw* what was happening, and as Jesus charged, "Even after you saw it, you did not change your minds and believe him" (21:32).

7. In Mark, the tenants "seized [the son], killed him, and threw him out of the vineyard" (Mark 12:8), but in Matthew they killed the son *after* they threw him out of the vineyard. This sequence in Matthew probably represents an attempt to bring the details of the parable more in line with the story of Jesus, who, according to tradition, was killed outside the walls of Jerusalem (see John 19:20; Heb. 13:12).

8. In both Mark and Matthew, Jesus brings the parable to a close by asking what the vineyard owner will do in response to the killing of the son (Mark 12:9; Matt. 21:40). In Mark, the owner will "destroy the tenants and give the vineyard to others" (Mark 12:9). In Matthew, it's even more graphic. He will put the tenants to a "miserable death" and turn the vineyard over to tenants who will "give him the produce at harvest time" (Matt. 21:41). The "miserable death" may be a reference to the destruction of Jerusalem, but more broadly

it reflects Matthew's tendency to see evil as stirring up similar evil in response. In the Parable of the Unforgiving Slave (18:23–35), for example, the servant who chooses a world of unforgiveness ends up having to live in that world; here, the tenants who choose a world of violence will experience themselves the violence they have generated. The deeper point, though, has to do with God's care for the vineyard and expectation of the fruits. Despite the rebellion of those entrusted with the vineyard, God will summon tenants who will faithfully produce the produce of the vineyard, that is, will walk in the "way of righteousness" (21:32) proclaimed by John and by Jesus.

9. In both Mark and Matthew, Jesus concludes the parable by quoting a saying from Psalm 118:22–23: "The "stone that the builders rejected has become the cornerstone." In Mark, that's all it takes. The religious leaders recognize immediately that Jesus has told the parable "against them," and they would have arrested him if it weren't for their fear of the crowd. In Matthew, however, the uptake is slower, and Jesus has to add two additional statements before the religious leaders realize that they are standing in the center of the bulls-eye and that these parables were actually "about them" (21:45).

In the first statement, Jesus spells out directly that what one character in the parable, the landowner, will do to other characters in the parable, the tenants, will be precisely what will be done to the religious leaders as well: "Therefore I tell you, the kingdom of God will be taken away from you and given to a people that produces the fruits of the kingdom" (21:43).

The second statement appears at first to be a non sequitur: "The one who falls on this stone will be broken to pieces; and it will crush anyone on whom it falls" (21:44). What stone? Reading the passage as a whole, it becomes apparent that the "stone" is "the stone the builders rejected" (21:42), named in the previous verse, and the reading would have been smoother if verse 45 had appeared right after verse 43. Even though the inserting of verse 44 in the middle of a saying about the cornerstone is a little awkward,[116] the meaning is not obscured. In fact, the disrupted sequence may even make a certain sense. If the leaders reject all of those sent to collect the fruits of the harvest, especially the son, then they have rejected the "cornerstone" and fulfilled Psalm 118. In the short run, the vineyard will be taken from them and given to "a people that produces the fruits of the kingdom" (21:44). In the largest sense, though, once again the Matthean principle holds of reciprocal justice. Those who fall upon the stone of all that God is doing through Jesus and the kingdom are ultimately against the grain of the divine will, and the stone of God's history will roll over them and destroy.

It would be a stretch to argue that the earliest Christians did not read this parable allegorically and christologically. The ligaments between the parable and the Old Testament are too strong not to read the vineyard as a symbol for what it always has been in Scripture: Israel. The tenants are the leaders of Israel, the slaves are the prophets, and the son is, of course, Jesus.[117]

But we must not hold the allegory too tightly. To make the next move, as too many Christian preachers through the generations have done, and to turn this parable into a triumphalist cry of Gentile Christians taunting Jews, "You used to have the vineyard, but now it is ours!" would, ironically, be to mangle the parable itself. In the parable, the heart of the tenants' evil is the greedy thought that, by doing away with the son, they could make the vineyard their own (21:38).

No, the place to begin our understanding of the parable is with the fact that the vineyard belongs to *God*. To connect the vineyard to Israel is to see the vineyard as a symbol of God's stakehold in the world, the kingdom of heaven, the arena of the active and eventful presence of God. The vineyard does not belong to the tenants. It is entrusted to them, and the parable does not stop its sweep across history. Jews and Gentiles, those who belong to the church and those without, indeed all nations are offered a chance to work in the vineyard and to produce its fruits. Whenever we get within a hundred miles of shouting, "It's mine, and not yours!" we have missed the whole point.

Put all of this together, and we can say that, while the versions of the Parable of the Wicked Tenants in Mark and Matthew are quite similar in intent, the theological winds that blow through Matthew set the parable on a slightly different tack. If the parable has two main themes—the sure victory of what God intends for the son and for the vineyard, and the role of the tenants in the vineyard—Mark and Matthew include them both, but Mark puts a bit more weight on the first and Matthew on the second. Matthew emphasizes God's desire for a people who will live in the way of righteousness and thus produce the fruits of the kingdom.

It is important to recognize that Matthew knows almost nothing of the struggle between faith and works, between law and grace, that runs through Paul's thought and was a preoccupation of the Reformation.[118] Good works are not, for Matthew, vain attempts by human beings to earn God's favor. To the contrary, God has made it possible for human beings to live the way of righteousness, a way of faith, wisdom, forgiveness, joy, and light. To live in this way is to partake of life in its fullness; to refuse to walk in this way is to partake of darkness and death. Jesus lived this way, Jesus taught this way, and Jesus died and was raised that this way might be made available to all nations (28:19–20). The way of righteousness, the way constituted by hearing Jesus' words and doing them, is not in tension with grace. It *is* grace. The Westminster Shorter Catechism states that the chief goal of humanity is "to glorify God, and to enjoy him forever." Just so, when at the end of this parable Jesus says that God will take the kingdom from those who resist and reject the way of righteousness and give the vineyard to those who will produce fruits, the point is not that God resented not getting the fair share of the fruits. The point, rather, is that God desires a people who know and live and enjoy the life that is God's, the life that produces fruitfulness, and those who choose fruitlessness instead will not have the last word.

THE PARABLE OF THE WEDDING BANQUET (MATTHEW 22:1–14)

This complex parable, complete with scenes of violence, murder, and military carnage is, as Klyne Snodgrass said, "enough to make any interpreter go weak in the knees."[119] The parable not only has its disturbing moments of savagery but it also confounds readers with a gnarled plot. Matthew's heavy editorial hand is evident here, and the plot gets tangled because he's actually mashing up five different allegorical stories—a wedding banquet story; a retelling of portions of the Parable of the Wicked Tenants (the previous parable, itself an allegory); a military conquest story; a missionary tale; and a purification story.

The resulting labyrinth twists and turns improbably. Servants bringing banquet invitations not only are ignored and rebuffed; they are finally and inexplicably greeted with violence and murdered. This localized personal violence immediately escalates into extreme and widespread violence. Troops are mobilized, people are massacred, and a whole city is burned down. And all of that is just in the first half of the parable and in response to an invitation to come to a feast! Reading this parable is like walking through a house of horrors in an amusement park. Something often grisly, always shocking, and utterly unexpected lies around every turn.

Five Allegorical Tales, One Big Story

When we recognize that these five interlocked stories are actually working in the service of one larger master allegorical narrative, it may not offer much comfort, but it does bring a little clarity. This parable is the third of three parables of rebuke set in the context of a long argument Jesus has with the religious authorities (21:23–23:39). Each of these parables tells how the good news of God's kingdom repeatedly came to the religious leaders—through John, through Jesus, and through the preaching of missionaries—and each time they rejected it. As John Donahue has observed, the first of these three (the Parable of the Two Sons, 21:28–32) describes the rejection of John the Baptist, the second (the Parable of the Wicked Tenants, 21:33–46) the rejection of Jesus and his ministry, and this third parable reaches into the future to portray how the authorities will rebuff Christian missionaries who proclaim the good news of the risen Christ, who will return to reign.[120]

Here are how the allegorical pieces of this parable unfold:

The Wedding Banquet (22:1–4). First we have the allegory of the wedding banquet. God is the king, the son is Jesus, and the wedding banquet is the eschatological heavenly feast. As Luz states, "In Jewish tradition the image of a banquet is closely associated with the coming new age." The message of the gospel is that this victorious feast has "come near" (4:17), and in the parable the slaves, who represent Christian preachers, evangelists, and missionaries, are sent out by the king to tell those invited that the time has arrived to come to the feast: "everything is ready" (22:4). The long-awaited wedding feast has at last arrived, and the call is issued to come.

The Wicked Tenants Redux (22:5–6). But now, in the second allegorical piece, the story suddenly turns dark. The messenger slaves calling people to the wedding banquet are not well received, to say the least. At first, they are merely made light of and ignored. Those invited can't be bothered, preferring to keep on with their normal routines of farming and business. Others, however, are not content merely to turn away from the invitation. As in the previous parable, the Parable of the Wicked Tenants (21:33–46), the messenger slaves are "seized," brutalized, and murdered. Later Jesus will level a charge against the scribes and Pharisees that this is exactly what they will do to early Christian missionaries, preachers, and teachers: "I send you prophets, sages, and scribes, some of whom you will kill and crucify, and some you will flog in your synagogues and pursue from town to town" (23:34).

The Destruction of Jerusalem (22:7). The rejection and violence of those invited to the banquet triggers the third allegorical element, the sending of troops by an "enraged" king to destroy the murderers and to burn their city. This is an unmistakable representation of the destruction of Jerusalem in CE 70. In *The Jewish War*, Josephus describes the terror inflicted by the Roman invaders of Jerusalem, who brought both sword and fire. They "made the whole city run down with blood, to such a degree indeed that the fire of many of the houses was quenched with these men's blood. And truly so it happened, that though the slayers left off at the evening, yet did the fire greatly prevail in the night; and . . . all was burning."[121]

Josephus says that the city was warned about what was to befall them. He tells the story of a man, ironically also named Jesus (this Jesus was the son of Ananus), who, several years before Jerusalem's destruction, showed up at the feast of Tabernacles and began to cry out a warning against the city: "A voice from the east, a voice from the west, a voice from the four winds, a voice against Jerusalem and the holy house, a voice against the bridegrooms and the brides, and a voice against this whole people!" Every day for over seven years, Josephus says, this strange prophet wandered the streets crying, "Woe to Jerusalem!" The prominent citizens of the city were so indignant over this warning that they flogged the man. When that didn't silence him, they turned him over to Albinus, the Roman procurator, who had the man "whipped till his bones were laid bare." But nothing could stop the man's constant lament, and, Josephus adds a poignant note, "This cry of his was the loudest at the festivals."[122]

Mission Work (22:8–10). The fourth allegorical piece depicts what happened after the rejection of the missionaries by the scribes and Pharisees. The wedding banquet was ready, and the feast would go on, even when those invited were deemed "not worthy" by the king. We must allow this parable to proceed with its own logic. If we insist on making this parable march to the normal rules of storytelling, we will be caught up in questions such as those Luz imagines. A perplexed reader unacquainted with the exaggerations of Jewish allegory might ask, How was the grilled oxen still "ready" after a military excursion? Where exactly is this banquet to take place amid the ruins of a burned city?[123] But the smaller allegorical gears of this parable do not stand by themselves. They instead are about the turning of the larger wheel of the overarching narrative.

The king issues a new command: "Go therefore into the main streets, and invite everyone you find to the wedding banquet" (22:9). Therefore the slaves, the missionaries, began a street ministry, going "out into the streets and [gathering] all whom they found, both good and bad; so the wedding hall was filled with guests" (22:10). Where are the missionaries to proclaim the good news of the kingdom? The Greek phrase *diexodous tōn hodōn* (διεξόδους τῶν ὁδῶν) can mean crossroads or "main streets" (as the NRSV renders it), but it is probably better translated "the ends of the roads" or "the places where the roads cut through the borders of the kingdom." In other words, the missionaries are now sent everywhere, even to the uttermost edges of the kingdom. The inclusion of Gentiles and the broad mandate of the Great Commission (28:16–20) are already in view.[124]

And whom are they to invite? "Everyone you find" (22:9). If the job of the evangelist is to invite "everyone," then two things result. First, a crowd is gathered, and sure enough, "the wedding hall was filled with guests" (22:10). But a full house does not guarantee that the crowd is composed only of good people; indeed, the missionaries "gathered all whom they found, both good and bad" (22:10). This mixture of "good and bad" names a recurring theme in Matthew and reflects what was almost certainly a hotly debated issue in Matthew's church. It hovers over this parable and several other parables as well, for example, the Wheat and the Weeds, the Net, the Ten Bridesmaids, and the Sheep and the Goats. Purity is in tension with mission. If God's command is to offer the gospel to "everyone," then everyone is exactly whom the church will get—good and bad. What is to be done about a church that preaches purity but is not itself pure, that advocates righteousness but is not altogether righteous?

One thing this parable makes clear is that it is not the job of the missionaries to enforce purity by discriminating between the righteous and the unrighteous. They are to issue the gospel's invitation to everyone, and they are to open the doors of the banquet hall wide to receive all of the guests who stream to the banquet. Does that mean that God's beloved community is forever compromised? The last allegorical piece of this parable is addressed to that question.

At the End of Time (22:11–14). In the fifth and final scene of the parable, the king himself comes into the wedding hall to survey the gathered guests. Just reading the parable, we might get the impression that the king's entrance is only a few minutes after the banquet has begun, but actually we have changed time zones from the present to the eschatological future.

The beginning of this parable is about the present. In the NRSV, this parable opens with Jesus saying, "The kingdom of heaven may be compared to a king who gave a wedding banquet for his son" (22:2). However, the verb *Hōmoiōthē* (Ὡμοιώθη), which the NRSV renders "may be compared," is aorist passive and can better be translated "has become like."[125] In other words, the first part of this parable is speaking not about the future but about what the kingdom has already become like *here and now*.

In this final scene, though, the present tense melts away, and suddenly we are thrown into the future. The wedding hall is transformed into the final judgment hall. The king's arrival marks not just another moment in the festival but the consummation of the kingdom.

What happens causes one's head to spin. The king casts his eye over the gathered crowd and spots a man not wearing a wedding garment. "Friend, how did you get in here without a wedding robe?" asks the king (22:12), and we already know that being called "friend" in Matthew is not a good thing (see comments on 20:13). Earlier in the parable, when the slaves issued the call to come to the banquet, those who were invited were full of ridicule and lame excuses (20:5). Now, however, the time for excuses has clearly passed, and the man is "speechless" (22:12). The slaves are ordered to "bind him hand and foot, and throw him into the outer darkness, where there will be weeping and gnashing of teeth," classic Matthean language to describe the judgment of the unrighteous (see 8:12; 13:42; 13:50; 24:51; 25:30).

It is a waste of time to fret, as some commentators have done, over the illogical details in this scene. How could a man who was pressed into coming to the banquet off the streets be expected to have proper wedding clothes? Suggestions that the wedding hall would have had a closet full of extra wedding gowns that unprepared guests could have borrowed is simply a frail attempt to tidy up after Matthew's allegedly loose storytelling. The fact is, as Eugene Boring suggests, that for Matthew once again realism gets sacrificed on the altar of theology.[126] This is an overt theological allegory, and the place where Matthew wants us to make sense of this passage is in the decoding.

The man whom the king singles out is someone who has responded to the invitation of missionaries to come into God's banquet hall, that is, the church, but who has not recognized with due seriousness where he is. In Matthew's theology, responding to the call is only the beginning of the process of faith formation, not the end. Matthew thinks of the church as a school of righteousness where disciples are formed in faith and obedience, and the wedding garment represents the clothing of a mature disciple, one whose life is shaped in the "way of righteousness" (21:32). The parable's use of the wedding garment as a metaphor for deeds of righteousness is akin to the picture in Revelation where the church, as Christ's bride, clothes herself in good deeds of Christian saints for the wedding:

> "Hallelujah!
> For the Lord our God
> the Almighty reigns.
> Let us rejoice and exult
> and give him the glory,
> for the marriage of the Lamb has come,
> and his bride has made herself ready;
> to her it has been granted to be clothed
> with fine linen, bright and pure"—
> for the fine linen is the righteous deeds of the saints.
> Rev. 19:6–8

Putting the Pieces Together

Five smaller allegorical pieces have been woven together to tell the overarching story of salvation. God desires to bring God's people to the wedding feast of Jesus, the Son, and to make of them a righteous people. Through the prophets, through John the Baptist, and ultimately through Jesus, God over and over again called the people to the feast, but their leaders were hypocrites and blind guides, and the "people's heart [had] grown dull, and their ears were hard of hearing" (Matt. 13:15). The destruction of Jerusalem by Gentiles in CE 70 was a judgment upon them for their refusal to respond to God's invitation and their rejection of the way of righteousness.

But God did not weary of the desire to gather the people into the banquet hall. So missionaries were sent out once again with the invitation to come, and God's house, now the church, was filled with people drawn from near and far.

Those gathered into the church were not pure, but in fact were "both good and bad," creating tensions in the community. But ultimate judgment is God's business, not the church's. Only at the end of time, when the king appears in glory, will the unrighteous be revealed as inconsequential and the righteous shine like the sun. There is a difference between being called into the church ("many are called") and being revealed as having grown in faith and obedience ("few are chosen," 22:14).

This parable was surely quite useful to Matthew's church. Not only did it describe God's intention to form a saving community. It made theological sense out of some troubling facts. For one, Jesus was rejected by his own people. Also, the memory of Jerusalem's destruction would still have been fresh in the minds of Matthew's readers, and the parable puts that challenging event into a theological frame. The parable also made clear that the inevitable ethical tension within the church (with people "both good and bad") was not evidence of the failure of the gospel. It was, rather, the way Jesus said it would be until the end of time. By telling and retelling this parable, Matthew's church could see how all the parts of their experience—rejection of Jesus by his own people, the destruction of Jerusalem, the mission of the church, the conflicted life of the church, the hope for a righteous future—fit together.

The Urgent Moment and the City of No

To read this parable strictly in its primary Matthean context, that is, as an allegory of the history of salvation, carries for many readers today a nest of problems. First, has Matthew forgotten that he is composing the story of "Jesus the Messiah" (Matt. 1:1)? Except for the detail —that the wedding banquet in this parable was for the "son," the son does not appear and plays no active role in the parable. It is an odd omission for a Christian rendering of the story of salvation to give so little place to Jesus Christ.

Second, although we are accustomed by now to rough talk from Matthew (see the discussion of this in chapter 5), the notion of an angry God destroying people and burning Jerusalem as an act of revenge is, to say the least, theologically troubling. To put it another way, one can agree with Matthew's perspective that God is involved in cataclysmic events of history, such as the fall of Jerusalem, even as judge, without adopting Matthew's instrumental notion of divine agency and heavy-handed depiction of *how* God was involved.

The parable describes God's banquet hall filled with guests who are "both good and bad," but Matthew scholar Warren Carter is disturbed by the good and bad in Matthew's own rhetoric. On the good side, Matthew summons his readers to deeply mistrust human empires and rulers and to trust God's empire instead. But on the negative side, Matthew sometimes describes God acting much like some Roman despot and depicts God's reign in imperial language:

> But there's the rub. Finally, as much as the gospel re-describes "empire" and counters the imperial paradigm, it employs this same paradigm to image God's work, present and future. As we have observed [in the Parables of the Unforgiving Slave and the Wedding Banquet] the borrowing is not restricted to a few words. Rather, the gospel embraces the whole paradigm, its structures, practices, and commitments. Applying the entire paradigm to God, it renders the things of Caesar to God.[127]

And then there's the business of that guy in the banquet hall without a wedding garment. Since the garment is, for Matthew, righteous deeds, the old debate about good deeds versus faith gets raised anew. Is salvation for Matthew altogether a matter of doing good deeds? This view may be particularly worrisome to Protestants who wear T-shirts emblazoned with Ephesians 2:8–9: "For by grace you have been saved through faith, and this is not your own doing; it is the gift of God—not the result of works, so that no one may boast."

Luz is wise to suggest that the New Testament contains a diversity of views of the role of faith and of good works and that perhaps the chief value of Matthew is to tug an exaggerated Protestantism back to the center:

> Perhaps we can understand Matthew's meaning and the traditional Protestant interpretation as complementary accents of the gospel, both of which are covered by the Jesus tradition. The danger of the Matthean theology is that in the final analysis at the judgment everything depends only on the demonstration of one's own achievement. The danger in the Protestant tradition is that works will be reduced to something that no longer has anything to do with a person's identity.[128]

Beyond these theological thorns, though, it is important to realize that, however much the Parable of the Wedding Banquet functioned in Matthew's community as a master allegory of the mysterious twists of salvation history, for contemporary readers it should not be limited to this purpose. The parable is more than merely an explanatory device. It continues to function as a dynamic parable, that is, as an active pointer to the places where the kingdom, the life of God, is breaking into our experience. Jesus does not begin the parable by saying, "The plan of salvation may be compared . . ." but "The kingdom of heaven may be compared . . ." to this story (22:2). But how?

One theme that runs through this parable is that the invitation of God is urgent and provokes a crisis. The feast is prepared, "everything is ready," the invitation is to come immediately, a decision must be made. There is not a moment to waste. This is an eschatological parable, and the urgency is generated by God's coming kingdom, but it flows into the present. G. R. Beasley-Murray says that this "parable appears to be one of those utterances of Jesus wherein distinctions of time seem out of place, where [people] are confronted with the ultimate issues of grace and judgment, and a decision is demanded of them."[129]

The Catholic theologian Richard John Neuhaus tells of a dramatic experience he had while recuperating from nearly fatal surgery to remove a tumor from his colon. During the surgery, Neuhaus's blood pressure collapsed, and his other vital signs began to drop. The surgeon sent word to the immediate family that Neuhaus would probably not make it through the night. But he rallied, and after a few days in intensive care, he was moved to a regular bed. "It was a couple of days after leaving intensive care, and it was night," Neuhaus writes,

> I could hear patients in adjoining rooms moaning and mumbling and occasionally calling out; the surrounding medical machines were pumping and sucking and bleeping as usual. Then, all of a sudden, I was jerked into an utterly lucid state of awareness. I was sitting up in the bed staring intently into the darkness, although in fact I knew my body was lying flat. What I was staring at was a color like blue and purple, and vaguely in the form of hanging drapery. By the drapery were two presences. I saw them and yet did not see them, and I cannot explain that. But they were there, and I knew that I was not tied to the bed. I was able and prepared to get up and go somewhere. And then the presences—one or both of them, I do not know—spoke. This I heard clearly. Not in an ordinary way, for I cannot remember anything about the voice. But the message was beyond mistaking: Everything is ready now.
>
> That was it.[130]

To make sure he was not dreaming, Neuhaus pinched himself hard, recited the multiplication tables, and named to himself the birth dates of all seven of his siblings. He was wide awake and fully alert. "I resolved at that moment," he said, "that I would never, never let anything dissuade me from the reality of what had happened."[131] Theologically oriented, Neuhaus knew immediately who had visited him in the night. "They were angels, of course. *Angelos* simply means 'messenger.' There were no white robes or wings or anything of that sort. . . . I did not see them in any ordinary sense. But there was a message."

As was the case with the slaves in the Parable of the Wedding Banquet, the message was "Everything is ready." Neuhaus recognized the ethical imperative implicit in this message. "Clearly, the message was that I could go somewhere with them. . . . But where? To God, or so it seemed. I understood that they were ready to get me ready to see God. It was obvious enough to me that I was not prepared, in my physical and spiritual condition, for the beatific vision, for seeing God face to face."[132]

For Neuhaus, the urgent word, "Everything is ready," was more than an invitation to enter the banquet hall. It was a summons to be ready, spiritually and ethically, to enter into God's presence. He desired, in other words, to face God not merely as an interloper at the feast but wearing the robe of righteousness.

Standing over this parable, then, is the final scene where God comes to see those gathered. The time is coming when God will see us face to face, which should not evoke fear but a striving "first for the kingdom of God and his righteousness" (6:33).

What happens, though, when the call of God, the invitation of the gospel, comes to human beings and social structures time and again, only to be met with ridicule, resistance, and violent rejection. What happens, in other words, when the city keeps saying no and repeatedly refuses the calls to peace, justice, and love? The news of the parable is severe, but it is good news nonetheless. God intends to bring the whole creation to a just and righteous end, and no human resistance, however strong or stubborn, can endure. Matthew may describe this divine action in military terms—God sends troops to destroy the city—but this can better be reframed as the futility of evil over against God's sure redemptive purposes. When "the city" says no over and over to God's call, no to honest and fair lawcourts, no to caring for those in need, no to healthcare for all, no to racial justice, those rejections of God's invitation to righteousness, no matter how seemingly permanent, invincible, and immovable, will not forever stand.

In the summer of 1963, the Rev. Dr. Martin Luther King Jr. was in a Birmingham jail, having been arrested for participating in a nonviolent protest against racial segregation. While he was jailed, King wrote a famous document, "Letter from the Birmingham Jail," in response to a statement issued earlier that year by eight prominent white clergy. The group of eight had criticized the methods of protest and direct action used by King and other civil rights leaders in Alabama, urging patience, negotiation, and recourse to the lawcourts.

In his own letter, which King wrote longhand and began "My Dear Fellow Clergymen," he responded by pointing out that the city of Birmingham had been repeatedly the city of no to racial justice:

> Birmingham is probably the most thoroughly segregated city in the United States. Its ugly record of police brutality is known in every section of this country. Its unjust treatment of Negroes in the courts

> is a notorious reality. There have been more unsolved bombings of Negro homes and churches in Birmingham than in any other city in this nation. These are the hard, brutal, and unbelievable facts. On the basis of them, Negro leaders sought to negotiate with the city fathers. But the political leaders consistently refused to engage in good-faith negotiation.[133]

King knew that patience and more appeals for negotiation would be in vain. "We know through painful experience," he wrote, "that freedom is never voluntarily given by the oppressor; it must be demanded by the oppressed." So, like the messengers in the parable, King and his followers decided to make the urgent appeal for God's justice at the risk of their own lives. "[W]e would present our very bodies as a means of laying our case before the conscience of the local and national community."[134]

The work of racial reconciliation is not finished, of course, but much of the intransigent world of Bull Connor, the vicious police dogs of Selma's Edmund Pettus Bridge, and the city of the stubborn and persistent no has crumbled.

THE PARABLE OF THE TEN BRIDESMAIDS (MATTHEW 25:1–13)

In the previous parable in Matthew, readers were taken to a wedding banquet (22:1–14), and things went badly off course. The invited guests spit on the invitations, the messengers delivering the invitations were assaulted, shock troops were dispatched in retaliation, blood flowed in the streets, the city was burned, and once the wedding banquet finally got going, an improperly dressed fellow found himself bounced into outer darkness. So in this story about another wedding banquet, complete with bridesmaids, a tardy bridegroom, and a banquet hall with an ominously shut door, we can be forgiven if we wince and brace ourselves for trouble.

Wedding Woes

Sure enough, there is trouble ahead. There is distress *in* the parable but also *around it* in the history of interpretation. Just as actual weddings often conceal underlying crevices of tension and conflict, this bridesmaids' parable has over the years proved to have an uncommon capacity to tick off many interpreters.

Some are bothered by how difficult Matthew makes it just to keep the logistical details of the story straight. The wedding in this parable sounds sort of like a wedding in the time of Jesus, but some of the details seem oddly off. While weddings then, like weddings today, were not completely uniform in practice, typically, the bridegroom would go to fetch the bride at the home of her parents. Sometime after sundown, the groom and the veiled bride, in a torchlit procession that includes companions of both the bride and the groom, would leave the bride's house to travel to the home of the groom's parents. When they arrived, the wedding festivities, including a banquet, would begin.

But in this parable, some of the key details get blurred or twisted. The bridesmaids aren't accompanying the bride; they are waiting for the groom. Where? Presumably at the groom's house, but the parable doesn't say. The bridegroom arrives at midnight, apparently alone, which is also odd. A pesky detail, but this wedding story never mentions the bride. And then there's that plot twist in the middle of the story, when the groom arrives at last, deep into the night, and half of the bridesmaids discover that their lamps are running short on oil. The other half advise them to go to the dealers to buy some more. But this advice seems ludicrous. This wedding is not in a bustling modern city like London or Istanbul but in ancient Palestine. Good luck finding an oil shop open at midnight.[135]

Eventually it dawns on us that Matthew's Jesus is not really telling a wedding story, at least not a perfectly coherent one. The parable evokes the idea of a wedding, but the wedding is symbolic, allegorical actually, a setting for telling a stylized story about expecting, waiting for, and being prepared to welcome the bridegroom. This is an eschatological tale bolted to the chassis of a wedding story, a tale about waiting for Jesus to come at the end of all time, which is what Jesus earlier told his disciples to expect (24:29–31). The details of a typical wedding have been stretched to depict this event.

Some feminist scholars have been particularly negative toward this parable, beginning with Josephine Massyngbaerde Ford's observation in 1967 that this parable is "the only place in the Gospels where Jesus utters any criticism either direct or in metaphorical language against women."[136] While feminist interpreters zero in on themes they don't like in the parable itself, the parable has a strong Matthean agenda, and it is actually Matthew's theological program that they find objectionable.

Vicky Balabanski's assessment of the parable, one that takes the side of the losing team in the parable by seeking "to stand with the 'foolish' young women as those who find themselves marginalized and excluded from the feast,"[137] is representative of some feminist critique. Balabanski imagines that the origins of this parable were in something like a crude guys' joke, an ancient version of a coarse locker-room jest at the country club. It was, she writes, "a man's story told to men"[138] that makes sporting fun of the "foolish" women in the story.

She points out that there were several Greek terms that could have been used to describe young women, but the parable chooses to sexualize them, calling them "virgins," *parthenois* (παρθένοις), which "gives prominence to their nubility, and thus their sexual availability."[139] There are other language problems. Half of the virgins are called "wise," but Balabanski points out that the Greek for "wise" in this parable is not related to *sophia*, wisdom that is "always relational," but is *phronimos,* closer to calculated shrewdness aimed at self-preservation. So the telling of this parable is like saying, "Did you hear the one about these ten virgins, five of 'em were shrewd and savvy, but the other five were dunces." Get ready for the punchline as the story recounts how these foolish women, as foolish women do, inevitably messed up.

But women, then or now, are unlikely, Balabanski argues, to appreciate the humor in this story. Women in the ancient world valued and depended upon mutual cooperation simply to navigate the demands of daily life, but the so-called wise women in this story violate that ethic by callously refusing to share what they have with others. The man at the center of this story, the bridegroom, is also a bad actor. Men held the power in ancient society, and frankly the bridegroom abuses his power at the expense of the so-called foolish women. The women go out trying to find oil, which makes them late to the festivities. The bridegroom harshly and without compassion enforces a rigid rule of punctuality instead of showing hospitality and kindness. He heartlessly shuts the door to them, keeping them out and informing them cruelly that he doesn't even know them. "The actions of the 'wise' young women and the actions of the bridegroom," Balabanski states, "are unjustified and wrong and we need to name them as such." Matthew may think the bridegroom represents the coming Christ, but the groom acts in un-Christlike ways. "Feminist readers," Balabanski says with irony, "would be justified in replying to this Jesus, 'I do not know you.'"[140]

Thus, from Balabanski's perspective, the whole parable is infected with patriarchy. As it appears in Matthew, the story reinforces patriarchal views and the static empowerment of elites. Even if the parable is read as a purely eschatological allegory, it cannot escape Balabanski's withering critique:

> Along with other theologies of liberation, feminist theology is not content to look to the righting of wrongs in the end times, but seeks to expose, critique and change current evils via a feminist political hermeneutic. Simply to reiterate first-century eschatology, as though the intervening twenty centuries had not taken place, would be to validate and hallow a system of meaning which has served patriarchy well. . . . One of the prime functions which eschatology has performed over the centuries is to relativize the demand for justice in the here and now.[141]

Others, too, have been offended by the ways this parable seems to push against the values of the gospel. Jan Lambrecht has raised the possibility that we might be better off to drop this parable altogether from the church's lectionary.[142] Novelist Nikos Kazantzakis found the harshness of the story so distasteful he went as far as creating a new and better ending for the parable. In Kazantzakis's version, Jesus tells the story to the point that the foolish virgins return, only to find the door shut. The foolish virgins weep and plead to be let in. "Open the door! Open the door!" they beg, while the wise virgins inside laugh and gloat, "It serves you right." Then Jesus pauses the story and addresses his disciple Nathaniel, "What would you have done if you had been the bridegroom?" Nathaniel is hesitant to answer, but finally whispers, "I would have opened the door." It turned out to be the right answer. Kazantzakis writes:

> "Congratulations, friend Nathanael," said Jesus happily, and he stretched forth his hand as though blessing him. "This moment, though you are still alive, you enter Paradise. The bridegroom did exactly as you said: he called to the servants to open the door. 'This is a wedding,' he cried. 'Let everyone eat, drink and be merry. Open the door for the foolish virgins and wash and refresh their feet, for they have run much.'"[143]

Giving the Parable a Second Chance

So critics, feminist and others, have knocked the vase of this parable off the mantle, leaving it shattered in pieces on the floor. Can it be glued back together? Is there a way of discovering value here?

Yes, and we should begin by reaffirming the obvious, that this is a parable, a folktale. Like all parables, all folktales, it borrows cultural artifacts, and this one happens to borrow from first-century wedding customs. The extent to which the patriarchy embedded in those customs affects the details of the parable is a worthy matter of discussion and debate, but the primary theme of this parable is not the social import of weddings or of marriage in a particular cultural moment. A wedding is the *setting*; the *theme* is wisdom and foolishness in the light of the kingdom of heaven.[144] The parable is about ten young women at a wedding. It could have just as well have been about ten firefighters at the station, ten night nurses at the hospital, or ten air traffic controllers in the tower—any group whose social role involves faithful watching and waiting, which is the main focus of this story.

Next, we should retrieve Matthew's reputation as a preacher of kindness. Matthew and Matthew's Jesus value mercy as much as any of Matthew's critics (see 5:7; 9:13). But as we have seen before, Matthew is convinced that there is a great difference between a life that is shaped around Jesus' mercy and forgiveness, and one that is not. Reading this story in an overly literal way may cause the reader to be puzzled or even offended by some of the characters' behavior, but reading the parable as a theological allegory allows the reader to see it in a different light. As the *Didache*, a Christian manual of practice that possibly dates from Matthew's time, says in its first verse, "There are two ways, one of life and one of death, and there is a great difference between the two ways" (*Didache* 1.1). The main purpose of the Parable of the Ten Bridesmaids is to allow the hearer to experience the "great difference between the two ways," the consequences of living out each of these two ways.

God's Future Impinging upon the Present

The parable is spoken in the middle of a long discourse (24:1–25:46) about the eschaton, the end of the age, which will be consummated by the coming of the Son of Man. In the midst of life's travails, people in every age have sometimes thrown up their hands and cried out, "Where is this world headed?" The answer to that question, Matthew is convinced, is that the world is headed toward an omega point in the triumph of Christ. Jesus promises his disciples that at the end of all things, he will come to this troubled world in power and glory: "Then the sign of the Son of Man will appear in heaven, and then all the tribes of the earth will mourn, and they will see 'the Son of Man coming on the clouds of heaven' with power and great glory. And he will send out his angels with a loud trumpet call, and they will gather his elect from the four winds, from one end of heaven to the other" (24:30–31).

This is, of course, apocalyptic, not literal, imagery, and it invites the reader to imagine the unimaginable. The inconceivable promise is that fragmented and often tragic history, seemingly "one damned thing after another," is ultimately arcing toward justice, not out of any sunny optimism that progress is woven into the fabric of things, but because the victorious Son is arcing toward the world. The Messiah, who is Christ, is calling the creation toward himself, even as he is coming to the creation as savior and redeemer. "Tell us when this will be?" the disciples understandably ask, "and what will be the sign of your coming and of the end of the age?" (24:3).

No one knows the answer to that, Jesus responds, not the angels, not even the Son, "only the Father" (24:36). The task of the faithful is not to pull out charts, sift through obscure Bible verses, and scan the stars in a vain attempt to calculate the end times, but instead to be steady in place—vigilant, awake, waiting, and watching. "Therefore you also must be ready, for the Son of Man is coming at an unexpected hour" (24:44).

But the years have gone by, and the world and the church have creaked along. Matthew's community lived about a half century after the years of Jesus' ministry. They were told to stay awake, to watch and to be ready, but even the watchman in the tower grows drowsy so deep into the night. Sunday after Sunday of worship. Year after year of mission. Decade after decade of trying to be church, of striving after peacemaking and hungering for justice in a world that seems more broken than ever. And still the trumpet has not sounded. The sky remains empty. The question the disciples urgently asked so long ago takes on a cynical, world-weary edge, "When will this be?"

This was a question for Matthew's day as well as our own. The question hangs in the air through this entire swath of Matthew. Just before our parable, Matthew inserts two teachings of Jesus that are warnings against going slack, even as the kingdom seems delayed. In the first (24:36–44), Jesus compares the coming of the kingdom to the flood in Noah's time, a severe and drastic image, to be sure, but that is part of the point. People were minding their own business, going about the routine activities of life—eating, drinking, family life—when the flood suddenly and unexpectedly rushed upon them. "[T]hey knew nothing until the flood came and swept them all away, so, too, will be the coming of the Son of Man" (24:39).

The South Fork dam forming Lake Conemaugh above Johnstown, Pennsylvania, had been springing leaks for years, but it was always dutifully patched. Some people downstream looked warily toward the hills and raised concerned questions about the dam's long-term stability. But for the most part, daily life in Johnstown moved along normally, and people mostly didn't give a thought to the South Fork dam—until May 31, 1889, when the dam failed, unleashing devastation upon the unsuspecting town of Johnstown below. Jesus uses the story of Noah to issue a similar warning. Those who allow the passage of time to cause them to forget about the kingdom and to push its urgency to the edges of life will be surprised and unprepared. The coming of the Son of Man will be just as swift, just as unexpected, and just as devastating as Noah's flood, as the Johnstown catastrophe.

In the second teaching (24:45–51), Jesus describes a master who goes away, leaving his household in the charge of his slaves. These "slaves" are, of course, Christians in the church. The "faithful slave" does his work, waiting patiently for his master to return. By contrast, the "wicked slave" tells himself, "[M]y master is delayed." Confident no one is coming to see what he's up to, the slave forgets his work and disintegrates into violent treatment of others and drunkenness. Jesus warns, "[T]he master of that slave will come on a day when he does not expect him and at an hour that he does not know" (24:50).

So the theological issue on the table for Matthew is the need for the Christian community to be always on the watch for the arrival of God's kingdom. Matthew knew that a church without an active eschatological expectation is essentially a church of functional atheism. When the church no longer expects God to act and ceases to watch for the inbreaking of God, it ceases to hope and dissolves into intramural squabbles and a flaccid, numb, and drowsy faithlessness. As the advertising slogan of an app that provides soothing Bible readings as a remedy for insomnia puts it, "Fall asleep to the Word of the Lord." When the church does fall asleep theologically to the Word of the Lord, it stops expecting the advent of God and stops waiting for anything outside of itself to happen. That's when the infighting, the political jockeying, the institutional rot, and the pompous claims for this or that agenda begin.

So that's how we get this parable about ten bridesmaids. What happens when Christians forget how to wait? "I wait for the LORD, my soul waits, and in his word I hope; my soul waits for the LORD more than those who watch for the morning," sings the psalmist (Ps. 130:5–6). It is a mark of discipleship never to flag in watching and waiting for the advent of God. But what happens when zeal diminishes?

Right at the beginning, we are told that five of these ten bridesmaids were wise and five were fools, no question about it. As is usual in the parables in Matthew, these people are fixed and representative types. There is not going to be any change, any transformation. The wise aren't going to devolve into foolishness, and the foolish are not going to fall on their knees in repentance and suddenly become wise. No, the wise ones are going to be wise to the core and act that way, and the fools will play their part. Our job is to watch this contrast unfold.

The bridegroom is expected any minute but delayed, which is exactly the case with Jesus, the coming Son of Man, whom the bridegroom allegorically represents. This is the theological situation for followers of Jesus in all generations. Jesus doesn't arrive on our schedule but on his. In the midst of life's struggles and crises, we want to shout into the skies, "O that you would tear open the heavens and come down" (Isa. 64:1), but God comes in God's good time, not ours. The one job of the bridesmaids in this parable is to wait for the coming of the groom and, when he does come, to meet him with torches,[145] festive lights to illumine his way to the wedding banquet. But, as we would expect of fools, the five foolish bridesmaids fail at their one task, and the reason they fail is that, unprepared for the groom's delay, they don't have enough oil to keep their torches lit.

Although there is abundant literature debating what "oil" stands for here, the clear consensus is that, for Matthew, oil stands for works of righteousness, that is, for following the teachings of Jesus in the Sermon on the Mount. It would be a mistake, however, to think of "oil" as simply deeds, righteous actions. For Matthew, to possess "oil" is not only to do certain kinds of things but, even more, to be a certain kind of person. A greedy corporate executive who exploits his workers may also drop a dollar into the Salvation Army

Christmas kettle. A good deed? Yes. A good person? Not so much. Matthew's focus is on those who are disciples of Jesus, who hunger and thirst for righteousness, who "strive first for the kingdom of God and [God's] righteousness" (Matt. 6:33). The oil of good works comes from them because they are formed in faith, because they are vessels filled up with oil.

When the shout goes out, "Look! Here is the bridegroom! Come out to meet him" (25:6), the foolish bridesmaids are exposed by the moment, caught in unreadiness; they become desperate and try to get some oil from the wise bridesmaids. Once the symbolism in the parable is allowed to work, we can see that only fools would make such a request. The day of the test has arrived unexpectedly, and the unprepared students whisper to the prepared, "Mind if we look on your paper? We're in a pinch here. Have any oil for us?" It's what fools do.

The wise bridesmaids reply, "No! There will not be enough for you and for us. You had better go to the dealers and buy some for yourselves" (25:9). To frown and wag a disapproving finger at the wise bridesmaids for not sharing is to badly misread the parable. If this were a parable in Luke, the theme might well be empathy and benevolence in relationships; therefore, it might provide a warm moment of compassionate sharing. But this is a parable in Matthew, who has a different but equally important theological agenda, and it should be read on its own grounds. The issue in this particular parable is not to generate a compassionate and transformational twist in the plot (we'll get to Luke soon enough). The issue in this parable has been fixed from the beginning. There are wise disciples, who live out the righteousness that Jesus taught, and there are fools who do not, and this parable allows us to see the consequences of these two ways of life.

The foolish bridesmaids have allowed their lives to go slack, and they are not prepared for the sudden appearance of the kingdom. That alone is the point here. No need to speculate about how the wise bridesmaids couldn't have shared the oil of good works even if they had wanted to do so. The exit of the foolish bridesmaids to make a midnight run to the oil dealers is both a fool's errand and a plot device to set up the last scene in the parable.

While the foolish bridesmaids are offstage, the bridegroom arrives. Those "who were ready" (25:10) accompany him into the banquet hall, and the door is shut. When the foolish bridesmaids return from their midnight ramble, a tragic scene unfolds. They pull back the curtain on the allegory by calling the bridegroom "*Kyrie*" (Κύριε), that is, "Lord," and they plead, "Lord, lord, open to us," only to be told that the groom does not recognize them: "Truly, I tell you, I do not know you" (25:12).

This groom's rebuff is, of course, an echo of Jesus' words in the Sermon on the Mount:

> "Not everyone who says to me, 'Lord, Lord,' will enter the kingdom of heaven, but only the one who does the will of my Father in heaven. On that day many will say to me, 'Lord, Lord, did we not prophesy in your name, and cast out demons in your name, and do many deeds of power in your name?' Then I will declare to them, 'I never knew you; go away from me, you evildoers.'" (7:21–23)

In fact, the Parable of the Ten Bridesmaids is a narration of Jesus' contrast between wisdom and foolishness that concludes the Sermon on the Mount, where the personae have been changed from bridesmaids to house builders:

> "Everyone then who hears these words of mine and acts on them will be like a wise man who built his house on rock. The rain fell, the floods came, and the winds blew and beat on that house, but it did not fall, because it had been founded on rock. And everyone who hears these words of mine and does not act on them will be like a foolish man who built his house on sand. The rain fell, and the floods came, and the winds blew and beat against that house, and it fell—and great was its fall!"

The underlying theology of the Parable of the Ten Bridesmaids is a theme that runs like a ribbon throughout Matthew's Gospel: a life and a community of faith dedicated to the way of righteousness that Jesus taught is a life and a community that matter eternally. Reciprocally, a life and community that are focused on eternity, that is, a life and a faith community alive with the expectation of God's coming kingdom, are a life and community shaped in the ways of righteousness. Again, Psalm 1 reverberates in Matthew's theology. The righteous are "like trees planted by streams of water," but the wicked are inconsequential, "like chaff that the wind drive away" (Ps. 1:3, 4). To be formed in the way of righteousness is to be formed in the likeness of Jesus, that is, to be recognizable to Christ: "I know you."

The Shout of the Bridegroom Continues

What to make of this parable today? This parable can stimulate our theological imagination in at least three ways:

First, the life of faith formed around Jesus' teaching is always watchful and alert, focused on hope and ready at every moment for the inbreaking of the life of God, whether that comes in the ultimate sense at the end of all things or on some seemingly ordinary Thursday afternoon. In other words, Christian faith is an eschatologically oriented faith. That's why the parable ends, "Keep awake therefore, for you know neither the day nor the hour" (25:12).

This is, of course, contrary to the nervousness of commentators such as Balabanski that "one of the prime functions which eschatology has performed over the centuries is to relativize the demand for justice in the here and now."[146] Quite to the contrary, deeds of righteousness here and now—that is, working tirelessly for justice in the present moment—depend upon the hope provided by the promise of God's coming reign of justice. If God is not coming to validate our efforts and to establish the promised beloved community, then all of our little efforts to establish justice will be tossed about by the unyielding waves of injustice and shattered against the rocks of an unyielding world of greed and oppression. Our frail programs for social improvement will run out of steam or, to use the parable's imagery, will run out of oil. We cannot continue to be wise bridesmaids if there is no bridegroom for whom to wait, no advent about to erupt around the next bend in the road, and no one will ever come. As theologian and historian Justo González has written:

> I would emphasize the importance of eschatology not just as something for which we wait but also as the future from which we live. Eschatology, precisely because it is the expectation of the reign of God, means that our engagement in the present social, political, and economic order must be shaped by our knowledge of that other coming order, out of which we live and which we seek to proclaim.[147]

In May 2020, in an event that would rivet the attention of the nation, an unemployed security guard named George Floyd was detained by Minneapolis police, who suspected Floyd of trying to use a counterfeit $20 bill in a store. He was handcuffed and placed face-down on the street, where one of the officers callously pressed a knee on his neck for over nine minutes. Floyd, who several times pleaded in a choked voice, "I can't breathe," died in the street, while the whole horrifying experience was captured on a cell-phone camera. The officer who placed his knee on Floyd's neck was eventually tried and convicted for murder.

The cruel death of George Floyd sparked protests around the country, sometimes erupting in violence. The issue of unjust, sometimes brutal, police enforcement, particularly in African American communities, was placed once again in the spotlight by the death of Floyd, and "Defund the Police!" became a controversial rallying cry. Video of police in a number of communities clashing with protesters was a steady diet on cable news, and these conflicts between police and protesters further exacerbated an already bitterly divided political landscape.

Although not a fact widely reported, George Floyd was born in the southern military town of Fayetteville, North Carolina. Fayettevile residents knew, however, and a number of protests in tribute to Floyd sprung up in his native town. Most of these were peaceful, but not all of them. Some buildings were damaged, fires were set, windows were broken, and a few stores were looted. Even though these acts of violence were the exception, they ratcheted up the political and racial tensions in Fayetteville.

Things came to a head on Monday, June 1, 2020, when more than two hundred protesters gathered in Fayetteville's Bronco Square near historically Black Fayetteville State University and marched down Murchison Road toward downtown. Waiting for them, and blocking the road, were more than sixty Fayetteville police officers in riot gear. When the crowd drew near, the police ordered the protesters to stop and to step back, angering many of the marchers. But the crowd did stop, glowering at the armed enemy in blue facing them. It was a familiar scene in a very old story: protesters, many of them Black, seeking justice and facing off against a heavily armed and largely White police force.

As the television news cameras recorded the event, hardly anyone was prepared for what happened next. All sixty-plus police officers laid their weapons aside and knelt in the street, a sign of peace and solidarity with the protesters. "As a show of understanding the pain that is in our community and our nation regarding equality," a police department representative said later, "the Fayetteville police department took a knee to show that we also stand for justice for everyone."[148]

Astonished protesters could hardly believe their eyes. One by one, they too knelt. One of the protesters wrote on social media, "Men and women alike started crying and then cautiously came toward the police officers to shake their hands. These are moments that will go down into history and will be taught to future generations."[149]

How did such a thing happen? It turns out that one of Fayetteville's police officers regularly played pickup basketball in a group that included one of the protesters, and the two men had discussed the protests. This officer went to his supervisor and said, "All they want from us is some empathy." This message made its way to Fayetteville police chief Gina Hawkins, who replied, "Why are we waiting?" So a gesture of peace was born. "When it happened," Chief Hawkins said later, "my officers were emotional just as the community was emotional. That showed a sign for our community to share who we are." She added that "there is some change and movement coming."[150]

Change and movement are coming. What the police chief said can be expressed in faith language, in parabolic terms, as well: the sudden cry sometimes goes out, when you least expect it, that the advent of God has come. A police officer with some oil in his lamp recognized that "all they want is some empathy" and perceived that the moment had arrived to be a peacemaker. A police chief with some oil in her lamp recognized that the time was ripe: "Why are we waiting?" They were prepared and ready.

Second, the parable recognizes that waiting for the advent of God can wear away at the willingness and capacity of disciples to live faithfully. It is one thing to have a torch ablaze for righteousness when the times are full and excitement is at a fever pitch. It is quite another thing to have the kind of faith formation that can withstand the long and empty night, when it seems that redemption will never come.

Jane Bernstein, who wrote in *The Sun* magazine about her difficult life as a mother of an emotionally and physically challenged daughter, tolerates no euphemisms. While Bernstein says that she could come up with plenty of acronyms and medical names of disabilities describing her daughter's conditions, the facts are that her thirteen-year-old daughter, Rachel, spends her days following Jane around the house, constantly calling her names, but resisting being hugged or held, always needy but never satisfied.

When Rachael was very young, Bernstein wrote a book about the experience of raising her, which is why she appeared on a television talk show alongside the father of a twenty-two-year-old autistic son. At the time, Bernstein was bothered by what she saw as this father's callous attitude. When asked if he regretted the birth of his son, he said that he was realistic about the life his son would be forced to live and that he would never wish such a life on anyone. Everybody loved his son when he was a toddler and a cute little boy, but "It's hard," the father said, "when they lose their kittenness."[151]

Bernstein was offended by what this father said, but now, nearly a decade later, she began to see things differently, realizing now that the father was warning her of what it would be like to give love and care not just for a day, or a week, or a year, but for year after year. This awareness was sharpened one day when Bernstein was giving a seminar and a middle-aged woman from Ohio with a saccharine smile leaned over to her as people were gathering and said, "Did you see that adorable little crippled girl? You know she was adopted? Why, I think that's the most wonderful thing!"

Bernstein said, "The heat rose in my cheeks." "You like that cute girl? I wanted to say. Take her, please! Not just for an hour—for a year. For five years! Change her diapers! Find her friends! Figure out what to do with her when the two of you are home alone!"[152]

Despite being sobered by her reality and stripped of easy optimism, Bernstein still works with all the energy she has for her daughter and her future. She remembers one very special summer, when a dedicated social worker helped her find the funds to send Rachel to a residential camp for special-needs kids. While Rachel was at camp, the family had a welcome time of refreshment. They had Sunday lunch together and sat on the porch relaxing. A family doing regular family things. Rachel "swam, went horseback riding, painted pictures, rehearsed songs from *Cats* for the camp show on visiting day. She had friends, bunkmates, and counselors from around the world.[153] Bernstein has a photograph of Rachel taken that summer. "My daughter cannot share her memories with me, but in the picture I have, there is a huge smile on her face, the kind of joy she rarely displays at home."[154]

Bernstein puts one foot in front of the other, day after day, as Rachel's mother. "My daughter is not just flesh and blood," she writes, "but heart and soul, too. She is thirteen years old, no longer a cuddly, adorable poster child [and] . . . she knows pain, just as she knows boredom and happiness."[155] "Once in a while," Bernstein writes in conclusion, "weary from struggling on her behalf, I let myself dream about her future. . . . If she were your child, you would think, *Please, let there be someone to care for her.*"[156]

Bernstein's story is a vivid account of the demanding challenge of forming a life with enough oil for delay and disappointments, enough oil for the wait in the night. What keeps her watchful and hopeful is the possibility that her daughter may have a future with someone to care for her. Pious reassurances that God can "turn bad things to good," "turn lemons into lemonade," are empty. What the parable depicts is the gritty reality of staying up through the long night with no divine epiphany in sight, of having the kind of faith that is resilient and built for the long haul. What the parable also depicts is the sure hope that God will come, the bridegroom is surely on the way, coming into a real world of pain. No bland sentiment here, for even "the powers of heaven will be shaken" (24:29). The photograph Bernstein treasures of Rachel smiling and joyful is not just a snapshot from a blissful summer day but a glimpse of the great joy to come. We have known from his birth that Jesus "will save his people from their sins" (1:21), and we are promised that all the heaving, gasping, suffering of human history is moving toward that banquet of unending joy in which Rachel will find herself cared for by the infinite love of God.

Third, there is that troubling scene where the foolish bridesmaids are pounding on the closed door of the banquet hall, pleading, "Lord, lord, open to us," only to hear the voice of the Lord of all time saying, "I don't know you." This is one more of Matthew's "nightmare parables"; that is, we look anxiously at those bridesmaids cut off from the joyful banquet, scanning to see if our face is among them. And then we wake up, relieved. It was but a dream, and the sun is shining through the window. We get up to the new day that is fresh with possibilities of trusting and obeying Jesus so fully that we are formed in wisdom, ready to endure the long night of kingdom service, ready to receive the bridegroom when he comes.

In other words, Matthew places this parable in his Gospel in part to provoke his readers inside the community of faith (note that all of the women, wise and foolish, were insiders, bridesmaids) to deep and searching ethical introspection. In 2022 American society was embroiled in a great and complex debate about race. In the midst of that debate, a decades-old academic idea called "critical race theory," once confined to the lecture halls of universities, suddenly emerged as a hot-button political issue. Critical race theory, simply put, is about the largely noncontroversial notion that racism is not simply a matter of personal attitudes and prejudices, but also of systems and structures. Racism becomes embedded in the policies, laws, and institutions of a society.[157]

One achievement of critical race theory was, like Matthew, to invite people to engage in deep ethical introspection. Those who had benefited from racially constructed systems of domination were challenged to realize that, even if they personally were open-minded on matters of race, they were still the beneficiaries of a racist inheritance.

However, one ultraconservative white member of the Florida legislature, disturbed that critical race theory might affect education, proposed a bill making it illegal for public school teachers to teach critical race theory or anything else that would cause students to "feel discomfort, guilt, anguish, or any other form of psychological distress."[158]

The following Sunday, the pastor leading the prayer of confession in our congregation referred to the proposed Florida law and noted how very different this impulse was from a Christian understanding of guilt and sin. The prayer of confession, she said, is an invitation always to scrutinize ourselves, and "If we say that we have no sin, we deceive ourselves, and the truth is not in us" (1 John 1:8).

Indeed, Christians do not engage in moral self-examination out of fear but out of confidence in the forgiveness of God. As Saint Sophronius of Jerusalem said in a sermon, "Let us be shining ourselves as we go together to meet the light whose brilliance is eternal."[159] The parable puts us all momentarily in the position of the bridesmaids out in the cold, begging to be admitted to the feast. By doing so, it enables us to search ourselves to see if our faith has gone slack, our hope diminished.

In the movie *Places in the Heart*, a widow with two children struggles desperately to save the family farm in the depths of the Great Depression. To raise some money, she agrees to provide a room for a man named Will, who is blind. Will brings with him a windup Victrola with a collection of recordings for the blind. One afternoon, when Will is out of his room, the children sneak in and put one of the records on the machine. It begins, "Recordings for the Blind presents: Trent's Last Case, by E. C. Bentley. Chapter one, 'Bad News.' Between what matters and what seems to matter . . . how should the world we know judge wisely?"[160]

Right at that moment, the children hear Will coming back to his room. Not wanting to be caught snooping, they quickly pull the record off the Victrola, managing to scratch it, so that from then on it skips at this point: "Between what matters and what seems to matter (skip) . . . between what matters and what seems to matter (skip). . . ." This is, of course, a moral theme in the movie: How to tell the difference between what matters and what seems to matter.

So too in the Parable of the Ten Bridesmaids we see the theme—how to tell the difference between what matters and what seems to matter. Discernment is urgent for, again, as the *Didache* puts it, "There are two ways, one of life and one of death, and there is a great difference between the two ways." To live a life of faith, one foot in front of the other, day after day, is not just to be a doer of good deeds, but also to be in the process of formation, to become like Christ. When the final victory of God comes, the injustices, oppressions, and disfigurements that have marred human history will not be recognizable in the light of God's glory. "I do not know you." Followers of Christ who have endured through it all and who have grown ever more in Christ's likeness are recognizable to him.

Describing some examples of everyday saints, people who have let their lamps shine, Richard Lischer writes,

> When you stop and think about it . . . many of the saints . . . made 180-degree detours from one life to another. But instead of reinventing *themselves*, they were reinvented by God. In the fourth century, Martin of Tours was a soldier in the Roman army. One day he saw a beggar at the city gate of Amiens and he impulsively cut in two his *cappa*, his cloak, and covered the man with half of it. He proceeded to devote the rest of his life to being a *capalein*, a chaplain, to those in need.
>
> In the late nineteenth century, Thérèse of Lisieux was a French teenager who became convinced that God's love is best practiced in "the little way" of everyday acts of kindness and mercy toward others. She once said, "Sufferings gladly borne for others convert more people than sermons"! By the time she gets around to writing her autobiography at the ripe old age of twenty-three, she has already dived so deeply into the ocean of God that she hardly mentions that she's dying of tuberculosis.
>
> . . . After medical school [Paul Farmer] founded an organization that brings free health care to the people of Haiti and other impoverished nations. Several years ago, on All Saints' Day, a priest in Boston—and one of Paul's old fraternity brothers—said, "I know it embarrasses him when I say it, but Paul's a saint. . . . He models for us how to be a Christian, how to be human in these inhumane times."[161]

When Jesus disciples are so formed, they are formed in ways that resemble Christ. "I know you," the bridegroom will say.

THE PARABLE OF THE TALENTS (MATTHEW 25:14–30)

Matthew depicts Jesus as on a roll here. He began the previous parable, the Ten Bridesmaids, by announcing his topic: "Then the kingdom of heaven will be like this" (25:1). But here he hardly takes a breath before telling another parable. He opens this next parable with a mere *hōsper* (ὥσπερ), which simply means "as." He is then off and running about this story of a man going on a journey who needs to stash his fortune somewhere.

The translators hardly know what to do with this abrupt transition. The NRSV expands that naked "as" into "it is as," which is smoother perhaps but fails to say what the "it" is that Jesus is talking about. The King James translators try to help out Jesus, or at least the reader, by supplying the missing subject: "*For the kingdom of heaven is* as a man travelling into a far country." Actually, the unadorned "as" serves a purpose. It connects this parable with the bridesmaids parable and has the effect of having Jesus say, without skipping a beat, "And here's another way to see it." In other words, "I'm talking about the same theme, and here's yet another angle." The NIV gets closer by rendering the opening line, "Again, it will be like a man going on a journey" (25:14 NIV).

The theme is important to Jesus and to Matthew too. Jesus is talking about the kingdom of heaven, of course, but not the kingdom in only general terms. The particular emphasis of this whole section of Matthew is on eschatology, the kingdom that could arrive unexpectedly at any moment. "The Son of Man is coming at an unexpected hour" (24:44), and the faithful are called to watchfulness, readiness, wakefulness. In short, the mysterious arrival of God's kingdom precipitates a crisis not only for the cosmos, but also for the faithful. In the Parable of the Ten Bridesmaids, the crisis concerns readiness, and here in the Parable of the Talents, the crisis is accountability. The arrival of the kingdom will be a day of reckoning, and it involves a settling of accounts.

A Train Wreck in Slow Motion

The parable gets going when "a man" sets out on a journey (25:14), a trip that we find out later in the parable will take "a long time" (25:19). As the man departs, the question is, What should he do with his "property" (in this case, his possessions, specifically, his money) while he's gone? The man decides to entrust his fortune to three of his slaves. A number of commentators have worked up a lather over whether this would have been likely, whether a wealthy man would transgress social strata to trust slaves with a massive amount of money, whether slaves would even have the authority to make financial transactions in the ancient world, whether perhaps these "slaves" were actually "servants," and so on. None of it matters much. As we will see, the slaves or servants are symbols for disciples of Jesus, so beyond the fact that they are not on equal footing with the master, their exact economic and social status is mostly irrelevant. The parable says the man parceled out his treasure to these folks, and that's the way the story goes.

What is staggering is the amount of money the man places under the slaves' supervision. In this parable, a talent is an amount of money, period, and not the kind of attribute that will get someone on *America's Got Talent.* In fact, the use of the word "talent" to mean natural endowment or aptitude is a later development derived *from* this parable, not a term used *by* the parable. A talent is an amount of money worth fifteen to twenty years of wages of a daily worker. So when the man gives one slave five talents, another two talents, and a third one talent, we're looking at a lot of money. It isn't necessary to calculate the exact value to the dollar to get the point; even the one-talent slave was entrusted with a fortune. It's as if Jeff Bezos showed up in the mailroom of Amazon, called three clerks and said, "I'm getting ready to take another Blue Origin trip into space, and while I'm gone, I'm divvying up my stock portfolio among you."

But as the man divides his money, he does not do so equally. The three slaves receive different amounts of money, "to each according to his ability" (25:25). This is very telling. We have seen this plot technique before, in fact in the Bridesmaids parable. There we were told from the outset that five of the bridesmaids were wise and five were foolish, and we watched as the story unfolded, and the wise did their predictable thing and the foolish theirs. As we have noted before, characters in Matthew's parables do not change or grow; they just act according to type. Now in this parable we already know that, whatever counts for "ability" here, the one-talent person is running short on it, and we can expect his performance to reflect this limitation. We already sense that events will go badly for him, and, of course, they do. This is not an open-ended story full of possibilities for surprise. This a slow train wreck. This is not *Let's Make a Deal,* where anyone can come out on top. This is *Hamlet,* a moral tragedy about to be played out before our eyes.

The man hands over the talents to the three slaves, and then he "went away" (25:15). In Matthew's parabolic world, this man represents God or, more probably and specifically, Jesus. He has gone away, only to return "after a long time." In Jesus' parables, and in other rabbinical parables, as David Flusser has stated, "The departure of the Master . . . was a technical means to describe how human beings would behave if they believed that God is not present."[162]

And how do these slaves behave when the man is away, when Jesus is not present? The first two dash to the marketplace and somehow make deals to double the man's money. Five talents are now ten, two talents now four. It is not possible or necessary to determine how these slaves managed this near-miraculous yield. This is a parable, after all, and the plot simply invites us to marvel at the way they magnified what they had been given.

But now the stage grows dark. Enter the one-talent man, the one with the lowest level of "ability." We expect him to behave differently, and, of course, he does. He digs a hole in the ground and hides the money. Burying money in the ground is not in itself imprudent and was, in fact, an accepted way to provide safekeeping for one's possessions. The historian Josephus reported that when the Romans destroyed Jerusalem in 70 CE, they found gold, silver, and other valuables buried in numerous hiding places all over the ruined city.[163] The key to this parable is not *that* the man buried the talent. It is *why* he did so, as the parable will eventually reveal.

The Reckoning

Eventually the man who owned the talents returns. It takes a "long time," which no doubt reflects the same sense of the kingdom's delay that we found in the bridegroom's tardiness in the previous parable. The return of the master means the time has come for a reckoning. His arrival calls for a settling of accounts (25:19).

What follows is that the slaves come forward and present themselves in respective order: the five-talent slave, the two-talent slave, and finally the one-talent slave. The first two make almost exactly the same speech: "Master, you handed over to me X talents; see, I have made X more talents" (25:20, 22). The master in turn makes the very same speech in reply: "Well done, good and trustworthy slave; you have been trustworthy in a few things, I will put you in charge of many things; enter into the joy of your master" (25:21, 23).

Any worship leader who has read this parable out loud to a congregation is aware how excruciatingly slow and repetitive the story is at this point. A simple "and the same happened with the servant who had received two talents" would keep things moving expeditiously, but, no, the parable grinds away, laying out the full details and repeating the very same plot development, the very same dialogue word for word. However, there's genius here, because we are kept waiting for the inevitable other shoe to drop. We know that the one-talent fellow, as the outlier, is in for a different reckoning, and the parable makes us wait for it, building anticipation.

At last, the story turns in his direction, and the one-talent fellow knows he's in trouble. He steps forward, however, not with sheepishness but with defiance: "Master, I knew that you were a harsh man, reaping where you did not sow, and gathering where you did not scatter seed; so I was afraid, and

I went and hid your talent in the ground. Here you have what is yours." In other words, "Yeah, I hid the talent in the ground, and I did it because you are a jerk and I'm afraid of you. Here's the talent. Take it, it's yours" (based on 25:24–25).

Parsing this speech, we remember that we have heard a small part of it before. In the Parable of the Laborers in the Vineyard, when the all-day workers grumble that they were treated unfairly, the vineyard owner snaps back, "Did you not agree with me for the usual daily wage? Take what belongs to you [in Greek *to son* (τὸ σὸν)] and go" (20:13–14). Now, in this parable, the one-talent man says: "Here you have what is yours [*to son* (τὸ σόν)]" (25:25). In both cases, the import is, "Here's your stuff. Take it. I want no relationship with you."

Also, let's look at the accusations of the one-talent slave against the character of the master. He calls the master harsh, cruel and demanding beyond reason, and scary. Is this so? Some commentators would answer yes and argue that this is, in fact, the point. William Herzog, for example, pours into his interpretation a heap of external social analysis to argue that this parable, sociologically, is about a familiar first-century villain: the master of the parable is an absentee landlord who has no compassion or conscience where profits are concerned and who bleeds the life out of peasant workers. In this light, the one-talent guy, who is a whistle-blower, is the hero of the story. What he boldly says to the master, Herzog claims, "has unmasked the 'joy of the master' for what it is, the profits of exploitation squandered in wasteful excess, and he has demystified 'good' and 'trustworthy' by exposing the merciless oppression they define."[164]

This view of the parable runs completely counter, of course, to its presentation in Matthew. What Herzog and others who take similar approaches overlook is that Jesus' parables are parables, not transcripts of first-century social situations.[165] Yes, real kings often oppress and actual landlords sometimes scheme, but to see the referent of this parable as the oppressive economic system inflicted by absentee landlords is like demanding that Bing Crosby's sentimental 1945 movie about a Catholic school, *The Bells of St. Mary*, be interpreted as a *film à clef* of the child abuse scandals in the Catholic Church. People who have lived under the thumb of tyrants still have the ability to enter into the environment of and to enjoy tales like "The Princess and the Pea" or "The Snow Queen" without immediately rushing to a political denunciation of Catherine de' Medici. It is possible to enjoy "Jack and the Beanstalk" without seeing it as a corrupt attempt to reestablish the power of European elites over against the heroic anticolonialist giant who can "smell the blood of an Englishman." There is plenty of room for dissertations on the hidden social and psychological realities reverberating through the folk and fairy tales we tell, and there have been many such treatises, but doing so, as interesting a blood sport as it might be, can be a distraction to hearing the parable on its own ground.

If we examine the master within the confines of the story itself, we encounter a man who entrusts his fortune to his slaves, who praises them lavishly when they do well ("well done, good and trustworthy slave"), who empowers them ("you have been trustworthy in a few things, I will put you in charge of many things"), and who even invites them into the intimacy of his own life ("enter into the joy of your master"). This is a trusting, blessing, welcoming master. This master who has gone away for a long time and is returning is, after all, Jesus, who said earlier in Matthew's Gospel, "I am gentle and humble in heart, and you will find rest for your souls. For my yoke is easy, and my burden is light" (11:29–30). But not for the one-talent guy: "I know who you are. You're a harsh man. You expect to reap even where you did not sow. You want to gather crops where you did not even scatter any seed. I'm afraid of you, so I hid your miserable talent in the ground. Here, take your money and leave me alone."

At this point we can begin to see what this parable is not, as well as what it truly is. This is not a parable about doing good deeds to earn God's favor. This is not even a parable about stewardship, as it is often treated in the pulpit ("Hey, everybody has at least one talent. God wants you to get out there and use your talents!"). No, this is a parable about the collision of two different worlds: the kingdom of heaven and not-the-kingdom. Those who "strive first for the kingdom of God and his righteousness" (6:33) see life as full and abundant. They see God as disclosed in the face of Jesus, and therefore they live in freedom and are empowered to receive the gifts entrusted to them by God and take the kind of risks possible for those who know God's abundance. "For to all those who have, more will be given, and they will have an abundance" (25:29).

But for those who have a pinched and punitive view of God, life is full of fear and resentment. "I know who you are," they cry to God, "and I'm afraid of you." The tragedy is that they lose the very gospel they have been given in trust, for "from those who have nothing, even what they have will be taken away" (25:29). The one-talent servant is called "wicked and lazy," but this may better be translated as "worthless and dithering." Fear has rendered him impotent.

Writing in the *New York Review of Books* about the Eastern Roman Empire that ruled from Constantinople from the fourth through the eighth centuries, Peter Brown observed that the newly Christianized elites still shared the basic worldview of their pagan past. So they

> needed to be sure that God Himself was not distant from them. This was no small concern. Modern people tend to worry about whether or not God exists. East Romans worried about the exact opposite: Did God know that *they* existed? A Being as majestic and remote as any emperor, God might turn away entirely from the human race. In 614, as a Persian army closed in on Jerusalem, a monk in the Judean Desert had a vision of Christ turning His Face away from those who prayed to Him as He bled on the Cross at Golgotha. God had made Himself distant. Now they were on their own.[166]

Being on one's own, apart from God, is the deep tragedy of this parable and of Matthew's Gospel. Like the foolish bridesmaids on the outside as the banquet of joy inside proceeds in full abundance, the one-talent man ends up alone.

One aspect of this parable that bothers contemporary readers perhaps more than Matthew's original audience has to do with the seeming tendency of the parable to undermine its own theological point. If the main idea of the parable is that God is not the fearful ogre depicted by the faithless servant in his speech, then why does the master's subsequent behavior appear to confirm the one-talent slave's worst fears? "As for this worthless slave," the master declares somberly in the final sentence of the parable, "throw him into the outer darkness, where there will be weeping and gnashing of teeth" (25:30). Sounds like plenty to fear there.

For Matthew, though, God is sovereign over all. Matthew has no neat partitions between God on the one side, and the natural order or human volition on the other. Nothing that happens, happens outside of God, in Matthew's view. This causes Matthew to use instrumental language when today we might use consequential language. For example, a theologian today might say that God created the world in such a way that a major force in the creation is gravity. If someone jumps off the roof of his house, gravity will take him tumbling into his yard. Matthew might describe the same event, "God cast him to the earth."

The parable speaks causally: the master commands that the one-talent slave be thrown into outer darkness. A better way for contemporary people to understand this is that the man who said, "Here is your talent. I don't want it, and I don't want you," indeed lives in the world he has chosen, outside the realm of God's blessing. He chose outer darkness, and that is where he lives. Again, this is Matthew's Jesus expressing parabolically the theology of Psalm 1: those who delight in the trustworthiness of God flourish and bear fruit; those who do not, choose to be of no consequence, like the chaff the wind drives away.

Where does this parable take one to experience the kingdom? To places where those who know and trust the love and mercy of God share that in ways that create an abundance of grace. We can see one such place in the life of Japanese Christian Toyohiko Kagama. Kagama was born in 1888 in Kobe to a wealthy father and his mistress. When he was four, both of his parents died, and he was sent to live with his maternal grandmother in a home "where he was tolerated but not loved."[167]

When Kagama was fifteen, he decided to learn English and found an opportunity to do so at a school run by Christian missionaries. His uncle warned him, "Toyohiko, you may study English with that American missionary, but don't believe in Christianity. It is a bad religion."[168]

Kagama's English textbook was the Bible. He began by memorizing the Sermon on the Mount, and when he did, he made a joyful discovery. "When I began to study these wonderful verses from the Sermon on the Mount, I discovered that the Creator of the universe is my Father," he wrote later. "Being an orphan, I discovered that God is my Father. . . . [L]ife began to take on new meaning, and the flowers everywhere seemed to blossom."

Kagama soon felt a call to ministry, and he began to preach in the slums of Kobe. Once he preached on the streets every day for forty days. On the fortieth day, it began to rain as he was preaching, and he felt his voice begin to fail and his body grew weak with chills. He would soon find out that he had life-threatening tuberculosis, but in that moment he was determined to finish his sermon. "I tell you, God is love, and I will affirm God's love till I fall. Where there is love, God and life reveal themselves."[169]

Kagama recuperated from his illness in a sparse fishing cottage where he had no bed and slept on straw. People feared catching his tuberculosis and avoided visiting him. "I was very lonesome," he wrote. One day, Kagama was surprised to find that one of the missionaries in the school came to visit and care for him. "Aren't you afraid of me?" Kagama asked him. "Your disease is contagious," the missionary friend said, "but love is more contagious." Kagama recalls, "At that moment I realized more truly than ever what love really means: that love can have no fear; that love can have no limits; that love encompasses everything—the people sick like me, and the people sick in spirit and mind. I thought I must love everybody, too. . . . I told God that if He would let me live, I would serve His children in the slums."[170]

And serve people in the slums, he did. He moved into Shinkawa, Kobe's most desperately poor neighborhood, and cared for the physical and spiritual needs of thousands of people. After receiving a theological education in the United States, Kagama returned to Kobe, where he became involved in labor movements and in efforts to improve the lives of peasants. He organized the Friends of Jesus, modeled on the life of Saint Francis, a group that was committed to spiritual discipline, witness, and compassion for the poor. When a severe earthquake damaged Tokyo, he moved to that city to aid those who had suffered losses.[171] Before World War II, he put himself at risk by becoming an advocate for peace, efforts he continued after the war. He had already been jailed in the 1920s for leading a dock workers' strike, and in 1940 he was jailed again for his outspoken views on peace.[172]

When Kagama died in 1960, he left behind a legacy of courageous and compassionate ministry. He had personally helped many thousands of people in the name of Christ. He had written over 150 books and was awarded the Nobel Prize for literature. He was also awarded the Nobel Peace Prize. The Episcopal Church recognizes his service for the gospel through a feast day for Kagama on its liturgical calendar. It is said that on the day he died, he suddenly woke from a coma, smiled at those around his bed, and uttered his last words, "Please do your best for world peace and the church in Japan."[173]

In his life we see the kingdom breaking in, as we are aware that Kagama could have said, like the servants in the parable, "Lord, you entrusted to me the gospel. I have done all I could to magnify it."

THE PARABLE OF THE SHEEP AND THE GOATS (MATTHEW 25:31–46)

This parable has been one of the most influential in Jesus' repertoire. Christians have been attracted to its ethical clarity and challenge throughout the centuries. The eloquent fourth-century preacher John Chrysostom couldn't get enough of it, quoting this parable in his sermons nearly two hundred times and finding in this parable motivation for his commitment to social justice.[174] At Mother Teresa's funeral in Calcutta in 1997, she was eulogized as one who truly embodied Jesus' word in this parable, "What you do for the least of these my brothers, you do for me."[175] Joe Scarborough, who was raised as a Southern Baptist and who is the host of the television show *Morning Joe*, has said on the air more than once, to contrast his views with Christians unconcerned about the plight of the poor and needy, "I am a Matthew 25 kind of Christian." Verses from this parable adorn posters, coffee mugs, bookmarks, and T-shirts.

It is perhaps unbecoming to complain about the popularity of any parable of Jesus', but at least some of the enthusiasm for the Parable of the Sheep and the Goats is misplaced. First, some are drawn to this parable because, taken in isolation, it seems to make an end run around all doctrinal understandings of the Christian faith. The parable appears to have a cut-to-the-chase emphasis on acts of mercy as the only important element of faithful living. All that doctrinal folderol, all that fussing around about such notions as incarnation, resurrection, sin, and salvation is fine for theologians, the argument goes, but it's the practical stuff, like feeding the hungry and caring for the stranger, that really counts.

To be sure, the world needs all the compassionate and merciful people it can get, but to understand this parable as an invitation to clear away the clutter of theological thought, in favor of practical ethics alone, is to ignore its context. It appears, after all, in the Gospel of Matthew, in which all of the parables are wound into the latticework of the whole Gospel, which includes a full array of essential theological and christological claims and concepts. In fact, this very parable is grounded in Christology and in the theological concept of eschatology, and it serves as the gateway to the passion story in Matthew, a christologically saturated account of key events in the Christian story.

Second, the parable appeals to some others because it seems to provide a clear, simple, and powerful motivation for acts of social justice, namely, that Christ is identified with the poor, hungry, and imprisoned. After all, the glorified Christ does say in the parable, "I was hungry and you gave me food, I was thirsty and you gave me something to drink, I was a stranger and you welcomed me, I was naked and you gave me clothing, I was sick and you took care of me, I was in prison and you visited me" (25:35). Consequently, many sermons have been preached around the theme that when we see the faces of those in need, we should see in them the face of Christ and should care for them, because doing so is to care for Christ himself.

It's a worthy thought, but the problem in interpreting the parable this way is that it runs against the grain of the story as given. The parable turns on the discovery that not one person in the parable—not the sheep, not the goats, not the righteous, not the unrighteous—is aware of the presence of Christ among people in need. Everyone, righteous or not, is oblivious to Christ's presence. "When was it that we saw you?" (25:37, 39) is the question on everyone's lips, and no one in the parable is motivated to serve the needy because doing so would be service to Christ. Indeed, they are all surprised to know that serving the needy was tantamount to serving Christ; this fact may be a key to understanding the parable's meaning.

It should be noted that some major scholars of parables do not consider this text to be a parable at all. The text comes at the end of a long teaching session by Jesus about the future coming of the Son of Man to reign in glory, instruction that was set in motion by the disciples' question, "Tell us, when will this be, and what will be the sign of your coming and of the end of the age?" (24:3). Jesus concludes this teaching with this image of the Son of Man dividing the people into two groups, as a shepherd divides the sheep from the goats. But what is this text exactly? Is it a parable or is it simply an apocalyptically drawn scene of what will happen when that time comes? Bultmann decided the latter and called it "an apocalyptic prediction."[176]

It is true that this story doesn't involve the indirection of setting, like the Parable of the Ten Bridesmaids and the Parable of the Talents, which compare the kingdom to a wedding or a transaction between a wealthy man and his servants, everyday events that are not themselves the kingdom. This story doesn't say the kingdom is *like* something. It takes the hearer right into the future, into the kingdom event itself, and makes a picturesque but fairly straightforward announcement of what will take place "[w]hen the Son of Man comes in his glory" (25:31).

On the other hand, there is something about the rhetorical character of this text that invites readers to receive it as one of the parables. John Donahue uses the phrase "parabolic narrative" to describe texts, such as the story of Mary and Martha in Luke, that may not technically be parables but work on the imagination of readers in ways similar to a parable.[177] Yes, the Parable of the Sheep and the Goats is somewhat different from other parables, and some want to say that it's not a true parable. However, it is still similar enough to the other parables to qualify as a "parabolic narrative." The story is built around a powerful central metaphor, the image of a shepherd with sheep and goats, and it includes some surprising dialogue and plot twists. In short, the story has enough of the furniture of a parable for us to treat it as such.[178]

How should we understand this scene involving a shepherd dividing his flocks? The parable is placed strategically as the final teaching of Jesus in the Gospel of Matthew. It can be argued that it functions as the climax, or perhaps as a summation, of Jesus' teaching. The Jesus we have encountered all through the pages of Matthew, as one who calls and teaches and heals and prays and feeds, now appears at the end of all things, as the long-expected messianic Son of Man reigning in glory, complete with angelic host (see 24:29–31). The NRSV says that "all the nations" are gathered before him (25:32). While it is possible for the Greek here *panta ta ethnē* (πάντα τὰ ἔθνη) to be translated "all the Gentiles," the NRSV rendering is better. There is no reason to limit the scene to Gentiles. All humanity, Jew and Gentile alike, is present before the throne of Christ's glory.

Like a shepherd separating his flock into the sheep and goats, Christ now separates people, one from the other. The sheep are placed at his right hand, indicating favor, and the goats are placed at the left, indicating a lack of favor (see Ezek. 34:17–22). Speaking to the sheep, Christ proclaims, "Come, you that are blessed by my Father, inherit the kingdom prepared for you from the foundation of the world" (25:34). The goats receive, by contrast, a dire word: "You that are accursed, depart from me into the eternal fire prepared for the devil and his angels" (25:41). The difference between the two groups is that the sheep performed acts of mercy on behalf of "the least of these who are members of my family," and the goats did not.

Who are "the least of these who are members of my family"? The strongest possibility is that the phrase refers to the whole human family, and that "the least of these" are simply human beings in need. There is, however, a long tradition of interpretation that sees "the least of these" as members of the church, either vulnerable members of the church or Christian missionaries. To see that parable this way narrows the parable's impact dramatically. The parable would mean either that Christians are called to treat other Christians, especially the weaker members, in merciful ways, or that the peoples of the world will be judged according to how they have treated Christian missionaries. Arland Hultgren has a long and convincing argument putting forth a dozen reasons why this is *not* what the parable is about.[179] A particularly strong reason he gives is that the parable sounds very much like other classic texts in both Greco-Roman and Jewish literature that express a universal ethic.[180] For example, the Jewish document *2 Enoch*, which was probably written just before 70 CE (and therefore before Matthew), says, in language similar to the parable,

> This place, O Enoch, is prepared for the righteous, who endure all manner of offence from those that exasperate their souls, who avert their eyes from iniquity, and make righteous judgment, and give bread to the hungering, and cover the naked with clothing, and raise up the fallen, and help injured orphans, and who walk without fault before the face of the Lord, and serve him alone, and for them is prepared this place for eternal inheritance. (*2 Enoch* 9:1)

In other words, the Parable of the Sheep and the Goats can best be seen as a Christianized version of a widespread ethical trope found in both Jewish and Greco-Roman sources about the need for God's people to show mercy to their fellow human beings. This is also the simplest interpretation of the parable. Adding weight to this view is the sheer rhetorical power of the passage. While the story could be read narrowly, as a warning about mistreating Christian missionaries, the story's own internal power seems to push in another direction, toward a great vision of compassion to all people in need. Whenever it is read, those who hear this story sense it as a broad challenge, a description of the way Christians are to respond to the needy of the world, whoever and wherever they are.

This parable could well be yet another of Matthew's "nightmare parables." It takes the hearers imaginatively to the place where they contemplate a final, solemn, and terrible decree from the reigning Christ: "Depart from me into the eternal fire prepared for the devil and his angels." Then the hearers wake from the dream, shaken but resolved not to live the parable in reality. So they gird up their loins to be about the works of compassion, mercy, and justice commanded by Jesus.

But to see this parable as mainly a word of warning or as a fearful motivation to do good deeds to others misses a major point of the story. The righteous ones in the parable, the ones who hear a word of blessing from Christ, "Come, you that are blessed by my Father, inherit the kingdom prepared for you from the foundation of the world," are not motivated by fear of damnation, not even motivated by seeing Jesus in the face of the poor. They feed the hungry and thirsty, they welcome the stranger, they clothe the naked, they care for the sick, and they visit those in prison purely because people are in need. What they do comes not from what they *fear*, but instead from who they *are*, who they have become.

The sheep in this parable are those who have become "righteous." They are those who have heard Jesus' words and done them, done them so often and so long that their very character has been shaped by those words. They have performed works of righteousness, but even more, in doing so, they have become "righteous." We have come full circle to Jesus' first complete parable in Matthew, the Parable of the Sower. The righteous are those sown on good soil. They hear the word and take it in. They understand it in the depth of their lives, and they bear fruit and yield a bountiful harvest (see 13:23). To hear Jesus' words and do them is not only to be obedient; it is also to be formed, to live Jesus' words so faithfully that one's life is molded according to the pattern of Jesus.

To live such a life is to be of consequence—both now and, as the parable insists, eternally. Robert Wuthnow, who was a sociologist and the director of the University Center for the Study of Religion at Princeton, engaged in a study of how people come to make the ethical decisions they do. He found that people who are generous and merciful to others have often had in their past transformative experiences of people being merciful to them. He tells the story of Jack Casey, a firefighter and rescue worker. One day, Casey was called to an accident on the highway. A man was pinned in his overturned pickup truck. Gasoline was dripping on him as the rescuers used power tools to try and free him. A single spark could have turned the scene into an inferno.

Jack was taken back in his memory to his childhood, when he had to have several teeth pulled surgically under general anesthesia. "I remember the nurse standing there and just saying, 'Don't worry, I'll be here right beside you no matter what happens.' And when I woke up again, she was still there."

The man in the pickup was crying out in fear, saying how scared he was of dying. Guided by his childhood memory, Jack kept saying to him, "Look, don't worry, I'm right here with you, I'm not going anywhere." And he stayed with him. "When I said that," Jack said later, "I was reminded of how that nurse said the same thing and she never left me."

Later, in the hospital, the injured man said to Jack, "You were an idiot, you know that the thing could have exploded and we'd have both been burned up!" Jack told him he had to stay with him that day because it was the thing to do, the thing he *had* to do. Jack Casey wasn't acting out of fear, nor was he trying to earn a reward. He was acting instead out of his character formed over the years by the promise of that operating nurse years before and other experiences of mercy.[181]

This is why the Parable of the Sheep and the Goats can be seen as the culmination of Jesus' teaching. Disciples absorb all that Jesus taught, all the words he spoke, all the stories Jesus told, all the stories told about Jesus, and from all of this are formed into people who, as the psalmist says, "are like trees planted by streams of water, which yield their fruit in its season, and their leaves do not wither" (Ps. 1:3). The unrighteous are not so. They live lives that evaporate into nothingness, "like chaff that the wind drives away" (Ps. 1:4).

Having explored how character gets formed, Wuthnow asked, "What then is the role of Christianity in all this?"

> An ethic of love and compassion is of course central to the Christian gospel. The stories of caring that we experience in our own lives are epiphanies. They become part of the gospel message. When they are related to the biblical tradition, they take on a larger meaning, an added historical and sacred significance. When they are told in community, their power is amplified. Other people hear them and are encouraged to love by identifying with the characters in the story.[182]

Saint Pachomius was a fourth-century desert father and a pioneer in the monastic movement. He was not always inclined, however, toward the faith. As a young man, he was conscripted against his will into the Roman army, which meant basically that he was placed under arrest and sent down the Nile River to a camp in Egypt with other recruits awaiting assignment. While he was in the camp, discouraged and disoriented, some eccentric people showed up and began to distribute food and fresh clothes and to show kindness. "Why are they doing this?" Pachomius asked. "They're not our cousins or uncles or aunts."

Someone at the camp told him, "Oh, they're a crowd called Christians, and they do this sort of thing because they think it's the right thing to do."

Overwhelmed by this, Pachomius thought, "If I get out of the army alive, I will explore this."[183] When he eventually did explore the faith, it became his own way of life.

They do this sort of thing because they think it's the right thing to do. They feed the hungry and thirsty, they welcome the stranger, they clothe the naked, they care for the sick, and visit those in prison. That's what they do because that is *who they are*.

7

Luke's Parables

Background

"You can't talk to God while flying commercial."

—Televangelist Kenneth Copeland, on why he needs a luxury private jet to do his ministry[1]

The heart of the Christian Gospel is precisely that God is the all holy One; the all powerful One is also the One full of mercy and compassion. He is not a neutral God inhabiting some inaccessible Mount Olympus. He is a God who cares about His children and cares enormously for the weak, the poor, the naked, the downtrodden, the despised. He takes their side not because they are good, since many of them are demonstrably not so. He takes their side because He is that kind of God, and they have no one else to champion them.

Desmond Tutu[2]

IS THERE A DOCTOR IN THE HOUSE?

It is well known that Luke and Acts are a two-volume work written by the same author,[3] and since the late second century, strands of Christian tradition have identified that author as Luke "the beloved physician," the traveling companion of Paul (see Col. 4:14; 2 Tim. 4:11). Contemporary scholars, however, are not so confident about this. In his 1919 doctoral dissertation at Harvard, H. J. Cadbury took on the assumption that Luke was a physician, arguing that Luke's use of medical language was not the vocabulary of a medical specialist but was just the way educated writers of his day typically spoke. People at Harvard quipped that Cadbury "won his doctor's degree by taking Luke's away from him."[4]

On the one hand, as Lukan commentator David L. Tiede has claimed in his lucid discussion of the Lukan authorship question,[5] it does not matter much whether the author of Luke was a cherished doctor or not, Paul's fellow traveler or not. First, we know few hard facts about him at all. Virtually every question about the authorship of the Gospel of Luke is vexed. Was Luke a physician or not, was he a Jew or a Gentile, did he travel with Paul or not? Arguments can and have been made for each of these views, but all are highly speculative.[6] Tiede goes on to say, Even if we could substantiate a few facts about Luke, say that he was in fact a Gentile physician, so what? It would be difficult to draw much of value from these isolated facts.

On the other hand, the notion that Luke was written by "the beloved physician" has indeed mattered to some interpreters, and not always in a good way. When the pious imagination pictures some "romanticized portrait of 'the beloved physician,'" a worldly-wise clinician, a kind of Albert Schweitzer of the first century, this tends to cast the Gospel of Luke as the work of a compassionate humanistic scientist who freed the gospel from the grip of rigid Jewish legalism. Such a view, Tiede maintains, inevitably leads to "thoroughly anti-Semitic readings of [Luke] on both a popular and academic level."[7]

Interpreters stand on firmer ground, Tiede says, when they take the view that "both 'Luke' and 'Acts' are anonymous narratives, as are all of the Gospels."[8] The important author of Luke is not the one fabricated out of a few contested historical details but instead the "implied author," the one whose voice and views can be derived from the Gospel itself. "The documents themselves must bear the weight of interpretation, and the author they indirectly reveal is the only author worth discussing."[9]

REASSURING A SHAKY THEOPHILUS

So who is this "implied author," that is, the author we encounter in the literary fabric of the Gospel itself, and what is he up to? The "implied author," unlike the historical author about whom we know little, leaves his fingerprints all over the text.

One of the first clues he drops concerns why it was that he wrote this Gospel. In the opening verses of Luke, the author names his intended reader, "Theophilus" (Luke 1:3), which means "lover of God" and may refer to an actual person or may be a generic term that refers to Luke's faithful readers generally. Why did Luke write to this "Theophilus"? He says that he has crafted the Gospel "so that you may know the truth concerning the things about which you have been instructed" (1:4). But truth here is more than simply facts. The word the NRSV translates as "truth" is *asphaleian* (ἀσφάλειαν), which carries with it the idea of reassurance. Luke wants to reassure Theophilus, whoever that may be, to make him feel secure about what he has been taught, about the truthfulness of the gospel but also about the trustworthiness of the faith.

This implies, of course, that Theophilus (and others among Luke's readers) are a little shaky about their faith and need reassurance. But why? What has unsettled them? Perhaps it was simply the fading confidence that can affect any believer. Or maybe it was the nagging theological questions that inevitably arise when one thinks through the complexities of the faith.

Eugene Boring suggests a third possibility. One concern almost surely nagging at "Theophilus," he proposes, is the delay of the Parousia, that is, the fact that the ultimate consummation of God's victory at the end of all things has not arrived. "The earliest Christians," Boring writes, "saw themselves living in the eschatological times of fulfillment, between the resurrection of Jesus . . . and the final triumph of God that would occur before very long, in their own lifetimes."[10] By the time the Gospel of Luke was written, a lot of history had flowed under the bridge, and the end had not come. It is hard to stay alert, expectant, and confident that the kingdom is soon to break forth when the days simply march on.

It wasn't as if nothing dramatic ever happened. No, as Boring notes, a lot of significant events had occurred that perhaps made Christians wonder if the end was nigh, but all of them fizzled out in disappointment. For example, there was a seemingly portentous drama involving gross imperial sacrilege. Around 40 CE, the megalomaniacal Roman emperor Caligula started playing dress-up as a god, began referring to himself blasphemously as "divine," and hatched an outrageous and potentially disastrous plan to sully the temple in Jerusalem with a statue of himself, a scheme narrowly aborted. Maybe, some people thought, Caligula was the "anti-Christ" whose appearance would trigger the arrival of God's kingdom. But Caligula was ultimately assassinated by his own bodyguards, the empire moved on to a new emperor, and no divine kingdom came.

A decade later, there was another ominous upheaval and possible sign of the end times when Nero blamed Christians for a major fire in Rome and launched a program of persecutions. Then, in 70 CE, the Romans destroyed the temple and much of the Holy City. Was this the trigger, as some suspected, for the arrival of God's kingdom? A few years later, nature provided yet another possible omen when the volcanic Mount Vesuvius erupted with 100,000 times the destructive power of the first atomic bomb. Each time one of these momentous events happened, Boring says, the hope of Christians flamed up that surely this was the sign that the end was at hand and that Jesus would soon return. "Yet Jesus did not come back. History moved on."[11]

Luke's readers were not the only early Christians troubled by the kingdom's delay. Several parables in Matthew specifically addressed this problem, such as the Faithful and Unfaithful Slaves (Matt. 24:45–51) and the Ten Bridesmaids (Matt. 25:1–13). But Luke's response to the crisis of the kingdom's delay is quite different from Matthew's. For Matthew, the timing of the kingdom is God's business alone, and the church is simply to bear any delay with patience, faith, and unflagging zeal. Christians are to be formed so fully by the words of Jesus that they can remain faithfully at work, with enough oil for their lamps, in spite of the delay.

Luke's response, on the other hand, was more radical. According to Boring, he rethought the whole meaning of the Christ event and the advent of God's kingdom: *"The Christ comes into the midst of ongoing history, not at its end."*[12] In other words, Luke calls his readers to stop standing on their tiptoes looking for Christ to come in some cataclysmic apocalypse at the end of time. *Now* is the time of salvation. Look around you, every day, where Christ is already and always present.

THE "TODAY" SHOW

Boring's claim that Luke draws our attention to the present as the time of salvation, rather than to some apocalyptic future hope, is well taken, but this does not mean that Luke abandons entirely the machinery of a future apocalypse. Jesus still points to an eschatological future with "the Son of Man coming in a cloud with power and glory" (Luke 21:27). Luke 's emphasis may fall on the present tense, but, for Luke, the Christ event occurs in both time frames, present and future, in the midst of ongoing history and at its ultimate end. Even so, Boring is right to observe that Luke shines the spotlight less on future speculation and more on the present activity of God, away from some apocalypse transcending ordinary time to "the ongoing course of history."[13]

This is a dramatic theological move, and as Joseph Fitzmeyer has noted, "Admittedly, Luke has . . . dulled the eschatological edge of some of the sayings of Jesus to make of them a hortatory device for everyday Christian living."[14] As Ernst Käsemann famously said, noting that Luke wrote not only a Gospel but also the book of Acts, "You do not write the history of the Church, if you are expecting the world to end any day."[15]

One indication of Luke's emphasis on God's saving action here and now is his heavy use of the word "today." Luke uses *sēmeron* (σήμερον), meaning "today," twenty times in his Gospel and in Acts, as many as in all the rest of the New Testament, and in most of these occurrences Luke describes "today" as the time of God's saving activity.[16] For example, the angels who appear to the shepherds near Bethlehem tell them that in the city of David a savior, the Messiah, was born "today" (2:11). When Jesus preached his inaugural sermon to his hometown synagogue in Nazareth, he read from the Isaiah scroll and announced, "Today this scripture has been fulfilled in your hearing" (4:21). When Jesus made a life-changing visit to the tax collector Zacchaeus, he declared, "Today salvation has come to this house" (19:9).

If salvation in Luke takes place "today," then it follows that discipleship is to be practiced "daily." In both Matthew and Mark, Jesus calls on his disciples to take up a cross (Matt. 16:24; Mark 8:34), but in Luke, followers of Jesus are urged to "take up their cross daily" (Luke 9:23), and the community formed on Pentecost worshiped, praised God, and ate their meals with gratitude every day (Acts 2:46–47). For Luke, the Christian faith shapes and is woven into the rhythms of everyday life.

This present-tense theological perspective of Luke has profound implications for understanding Luke's parables. It is no accident that Luke tells parables such as the Good Samaritan and the Prodigal Son, which emphasize everyday life, and that he does not include parables like Matthew's Parable of the Sheep and the Goats or the Parable of the Ten Bridesmaids, which cast readers forward toward an eschatological future. In fact, one danger we will face when we get around to exploring the parables in Luke is the temptation (to which many interpreters and preachers fall) to treat Luke's parables simply as "example stories," practical advice on how to behave in everyday moral situations, rather than as parables. Example stories are ethical illustrations (e.g., you should be compassionate like the good Samaritan or humble like the publican), whereas parables, while they surely have ethical import, do more. They disclose not merely good human behavior but the places where the agency of God is breaking into life. Parables are about how God is adventing into our life and history, and all ethical implications of the parables spring from that activity of God.

IS THAT ALL THERE IS?

There is a strong possibility that Theophilus and others among Luke's readers are troubled, like many other Christians of that time, by the delay in the arrival of the kingdom. Luke counters this disappointment by drawing their attention away from the future and focusing on the realities of the present. God is already powerfully at work today, Luke announces, in the unfolding of history.

There is, however, another possibility (not necessarily a mutually exclusive one) about what is troubling Theophilus. What if Luke's readers already had a strong present-tense theology, already expected God to come in the here-and-now of everyday history? What if Luke's community had been taught well not to focus on the "big bang" of Christ's return at the end of time, but instead to look for the Christ who appears in a thousand ways and places in everyday life? Ironically, that could be what has shaken Theophilus's confidence. Perhaps Theophilus is now looking around at present history, at everyday life, and saying, "God is at work now, every day? Really? Where?"

We can see how this problem may have occurred when we consider a major theological theme that runs through all of Luke: the "great reversal." This is Luke's theological claim that God is step by step, piece by piece, turning the world upside down, lifting up the weak, the poor, and the oppressed and bringing down the rich and the haughty. We hear of the "great reversal" from Jesus' own lips in his Sermon on the Plain:

> "Blessed are you who are poor,
> for yours is the kingdom of God.
> "Blessed are you who are hungry now,
> for you will be filled.
> "Blessed are you who weep now,
> for you will laugh.
>
> "Blessed are you when people hate you and when they exclude you, revile you, and defame you on account of the Son of Man. Rejoice on that day and leap for joy, for surely your reward is great in heaven, for that is how their ancestors treated the prophets.
>
> "But woe to you who are rich,
> for you have received your consolation.
> "Woe to you who are full now,
> for you will be hungry.
> "Woe to you who are laughing now,
> for you will mourn and weep."
> Luke 6:20–25

At the close of Justo González's commentary on Luke, he reflects on the surprise he experienced as he studied that Gospel when he discovered how much the "great reversal" theme permeates Luke's whole Gospel:

> As I began my study for this commentary, I knew—because many others had told me—that this great reversal was an important element in the Gospel of Luke. I expected to find it here and there: in Mary's Magnificat, in some of the parables, in the words of Jesus when his disciples debate their own greatness. But I have found that this theme is so pervasive that without it the entire Gospel of Luke is unintelligible. Were we to delete from Luke all the passages that speak of such a reversal, we would have very little left indeed![17]

But, for all of Luke's fanfare about a world being turned upside down, perhaps Theophilus was beginning to wonder if such promises were, to quote Macbeth, but "sound and fury, signifying nothing." In the Magnificat, Mary sings, in "great reversal" terms, that God "has brought down the powerful from their thrones and lifted up the lowly; he has filled the hungry with good things and sent the rich away empty" (1:52–53). But Jesus lived and died. Easter has come and gone, and, as Matthew Skinner observes, "When the Gospel narrative ends, the powerful remain on their thrones and the rich still enjoy full stomachs."[18] Maybe Theophilus, living in a time when the Roman Empire still has its vise grip on the world, and the poor are still on the short end of the stick, sees no signs at all of any "great reversal." Maybe he can hear his own voice echoing the sad lament of the two followers of Jesus on the Emmaus road: "We had hoped that he was the one to redeem Israel."

There is evidence that Luke responds to the struggle to perceive God's saving power already at work by training the reader to perform what might be called a "knight's move" kind of thinking. In chess, the knight does not move in a straight line like the other pieces but in an L-shaped path. The knight moves two squares in one direction and then abruptly moves one square at a right angle. Just so, Luke sometimes takes his readers along a path in one direction, only suddenly to veer off that path and move in another, unexpected direction. Take, for example, Luke's introduction of the ministry of John the Baptist: "In the fifteenth year of the reign of Emperor Tiberius, when Pontius Pilate was governor of Judea, and Herod was ruler of Galilee, and his brother Philip ruler of the region of Ituraea and Trachonitis, and Lysanias ruler of Abilene, during the high priesthood of Annas and Caiaphas, the word of God came to John son of Zechariah in the wilderness" (3:1–2).

There's the knight's move. Luke first heads out like a typical historian, naming all the big names and usual places. Here's the emperor, there's the governor, and then there are the rulers and the powerful clergy—the kind of people in the kind of places of power that CNN would feature. But then Luke veers off at a sharp angle: "the word of God came to John son of Zechariah in the wilderness." In other words, here are the important places on the map populated with the powerful people, but, wait, don't look in that direction. Instead, cast your eyes where you normally would not look, out into the wilderness, in an out-of-the-way place, where you'll see God at work in a man named John. *There* is where the real action is. The effect of this now-you-see-it, now-you-don't approach to history is to say that God is at work in real history, the history of kings and rulers, but that work is often hidden, invisible. If one wishes to see God at work, then one needs to look not where historians usually focus, but at the edges and margins.

This theological idea, namely, that God is working in history, but visible in the out-of-the-way and overlooked places, may be a key part of the reassurance Luke wishes to provide his shaky readers. The point is not that God works *only* at the margins, leaving the main arena under the sway of corrupt powers. No, Luke is confident that ultimately the powerful will be pulled from their thrones and that the weak, poor, and lowly will finally be lifted up in God's kingdom. But what God is doing now to turn the world upside down, this great reversal, can be seen only with a side glance at the borders and peripheries. Want to see what God will ultimately do in Washington, Beijing, and all palaces of power? Then look now at what God is doing to give life and to bring hope in overnight shelters, soup kitchens, and hospice rooms. As the hymn "Canticle of the Turning" says, "the world is about to turn," but the first visible signs of that turning are perceived in the small, local, and wilderness places.

We will observe this knight's-move theology in a number of Luke's parables. Where can we see God's kingdom breaking in? Don't look toward the proud priest or the liturgically trained Levite, but toward a despised Samaritan bending in compassion over the bloodied body of a wounded traveler. Don't expect to see it in the magnificent palaces of the nobility, but in a father's embrace of a disgraced son stumbling down a dusty road on his remorseful way home. Look not in the corridors of power but rather at a panic-struck middle manager tossed out of his job for corruption and desperately grasping for a place to land. As Skinner observes:

> Preachers and teachers do well, therefore, to follow Luke's lead and to see themselves as leaders trying to help others navigate a persistently unjust system. They should expect big things. But they should do so fully aware that Luke shows interest in shining a light on God's salvation spilling into settings that are at the edges of the arena. Those are the settings where Jesus devotes most of his attention and where he calls his followers to take up the same work. Instead of looking solely at the level of nations, lawmakers, and militaries, preachers and teachers should look locally. Look at the kind of people and activities that animate Jesus' parables. Look for them in your settings. Look at dinner tables and conference tables and see who might be invited and empowered there. Look into families, businesses, neighborhoods, community groups, clubs, and villages.[19]

PRAYERS AND TABLES

Praying and eating. Hardly a page goes by in Luke without Jesus doing one of those things. More than in any of the other Gospels, Jesus in Luke is in frequent prayer, and he enjoys table fellowship to the point that he gets a reputation for gluttony (7:34). In Luke, one commentator quipped, "Jesus is either going to a meal, at a meal, or coming from a meal."[20] But there is an ominous cloud over these meals. "In Luke's Gospel," Lukan scholar Robert J. Karris claims, "Jesus got himself crucified by the way he ate."[21] Karris elaborates: "To the religious leaders Jesus' promiscuous table fellowship is apostasy and an act of perverting the people."[22]

Nine times in Luke, Jesus is described at prayer, and seven of those prayers are unique to Luke. Jesus prays at his baptism (3:21), after a hard day of ministry (5:15–16), before choosing his disciples (6:12), at the time of Peter's confession (9:18), on the Mount of Transfiguration (9:29), when the seventy missionaries return (10:21–22), before he teaches his disciples how to pray (11:1), on the Mount of Olives (22:39–46), and on the cross (23:34–46).[23]

The cumulative effect of these prayers is that we do not see a Jesus who is following some predetermined script or doing ministry simply in response to his inner moral compass, but, instead, one who lives in the immediacy of God's presence and who serves and obeys in continual communion and communication with God. The scribes say "long prayers" to look devout (20:47), but Jesus prays, often out of sight on a mountain or in the wilderness, in responsiveness to God's direction.

Just as Jesus' ministry is guided by prayer, so is the life of disciples and of the church. "If following Jesus in Luke means doing as Jesus does," notes R. Alan Culpepper, "then prayer is a vital part of being a follower of Jesus."[24] On the cross, Jesus prayed that his crucifiers would be forgiven and that God would receive his spirit as he died (23:34, 46). Stephen, following Jesus' example, prayed the same two prayers as he was being stoned to death (Acts 7:59–60). At least three of the parables in Luke are explicitly focused on prayer (the Friend at Midnight, 11:5–8; the Widow and the Judge, 18:1–8; and the Pharisee and the Publican, 18:9–14), and others have implications for prayer.

There are nineteen mentions of meals in Luke, thirteen of them peculiar to that Gospel.[25] There are ten scenes in Luke set at a meal that are major occasions for Jesus' teaching (5:27–39; 7:36–50; 9:10–17; 10:38–42; 11:37–54; 14:1–24; 19:1–10; 22:7–38; 24:13–35; 24:36–53). Markus Barth has noted, "In approximately one-fifth of the sentences in Luke's Gospel and in Acts, meals play a conspicuous role."[26]

What is the significance of all this eating and drinking? I once heard Fred Craddock say in a sermon that "the measure of your faith is not who you will feed but who you will eat with." Jesus ate with . . . everybody: Pharisees and tax collectors, close friends and astonished disciples, life's leaders and life's losers. He told those who would listen that, when they gave a banquet, not to forget to "invite the poor, the crippled, the lame, and the blind" (14:13). This expansive guest list for banquets is about the radical inclusivity of the gospel, of course, but it is also about the kind of community the kingdom of God creates and the nearness of God's reign to our daily routines, to our tables, and to our everyday relationships.

In Luke, what happens at tables is not just about full stomachs but about the greater fullness brought by the inbreaking of God's reign. When the Pharisees and scribes, not so delicately, pointed out the contrast between John's disciples, who were austere and sober, given to much prayer and fasting, and Jesus' disciples, who were constantly gathered happily around the welcome table with chalices held high, Jesus responded by letting his interrogators know that, so long as he was around, the long-awaited bridegroom was present, and life was a joyful wedding feast. "You cannot make wedding guests fast while the bridegroom is with them, can you?" he asked provocatively (5:33–34).

Jesus promised his followers that they would "eat and drink at my table in my kingdom" (22:30) and that people would come "from east and west, from north and south" to gather at table in the kingdom of God (13:29). True to Luke's theology about the kingdom happening in daily life, the two followers of Jesus who walked with the risen Christ on the road to Emmaus do not have to wait long before being gathered at the kingdom table. They recognized the risen Christ that very evening "in the breaking of bread" (24:30–31). Since this is no doubt an allusion to the experience of the Lord's Supper in Luke's community, Luke's readers are alerted to the fact that they too in their worship "eat and drink at my table in my kingdom."

Small wonder, then, that several of the major parables in Luke, for example, the Great Dinner (14:15–24) and the Prodigal Son (15:11–32), focus on meals, and that two tragic parables in Luke, the Rich Fool (12:13–21) and the Rich Man and Lazarus (16:19–31), feature feasting all right, but sad, lonely meals consumed by self-centered narcissists who always eat alone.

MONEY TALK

In *Lost in the Cosmos: The Last Self-Help Book*, Walker Percy quotes an unintentionally funny "Dear Abby" letter written to popular advice columnist Abigail Van Buren:

> Dear Abby,
> I am a twenty-three-year-old liberated woman who has been on the pill for two years. It's getting pretty expensive and I think my boyfriend should share half the cost, but I don't know him well enough to discuss money with him.[27]

Money is, indeed, a touchy topic, touchier perhaps than sex, but Luke is bold enough to talk straight about money. In Luke, how one views and handles money is a revealing "tell" of one's real convictions about life, faith, and God. The Pharisees, for example, talk a good game and look holy as choirboys; but scratch the surface, and underneath Luke's Jesus sees them as basically self-serving "lovers of money" (16:14). Luke uses the word "rich" or "riches" fifteen times, far more than any other book in the New Testament, and most of those times he speaks of the "rich," you can almost hear Luke snort with contempt. In the popular religion of the day, being rich was a sign of God's blessing, but in Luke, "Jesus turned popular theology on its head."[28] "Woe to you who are rich," Jesus preaches (6:24), and he tells the congregation at Nazareth that he is "anointed . . . to bring good news to the poor" (4:18).

In the parables in Luke, money often plays a prominent role. For example, in the Rich Fool (12:13–21), an arrogant and wealthy man pompously congratulates himself that his wealth has secured a life of pleasure and contentment, only to hear a voice from heaven thunder, "You fool!" In the Rich Man and Lazarus (16:19–31), the rich man is a conspicuous consumer, wearing the purple designer clothing of the rich and powerful and feasting sumptuously, while ignoring the beggar on his porch. In the King James Version of the Parable of the Dishonest Manager (16:1–9), Jesus uses the phrase "unrighteous mammon" (16:11), by which is meant not drug money or mafia embezzlements but the money used by this unrighteous world—in other words, money, ordinary money.

Given Luke's conviction that all money is tainted by this unrighteous age, we might expect him to demand that followers of the way of Jesus wash their hands of such "filthy lucre." Fascinatingly, he does not. The goal in Luke is not to avoid money altogether but rather to use money as kingdom people with a kingdom perspective. "If you have not been faithful with the dishonest wealth," Jesus says in Luke, "who will entrust to you the true riches?" (16:11). The Dishonest Manager turns out to be very much about what possibilities emerge for the use of money when the kingdom happens in our midst.

THE CONSUMMATE STORYTELLER

Like the other Gospel writers, Luke exercises much literary control over his narrative. Of all the parables, the ones that Luke tells—the Good Samaritan, the Friend at Midnight, the Prodigal Son, and others—are perhaps the best-known and most loved. Partly this is because Luke gives texture and dramatic depth in his presentation of the parables. Many of the parables in Luke, with their poignant and affecting scenes, read as if they were crafted by a short-story writer today, and contemporary readers can readily identify with the characters. "Luke," writes Eugene Boring, "is a composer who creatively constructs a narrative to inform and persuade."[29]

Many people today see Luke as their favorite Gospel. Luke's winsome spirit is attractive, especially over against Matthew, who can sometimes sound like an aggrieved schoolmaster. Luke has an inclusive vision and a theology that undergirds appeals for social justice. He is openly positive toward women, often moving back and forth between male and female figures in his narrative (including in some of the parables). He presents the Christian faith as something lived and experienced every day and in the familiar places of our lives.

Luke is so irenic it is important to guard against being lulled to complacency by his gentleness. As interpreters, we should remind ourselves not to allow his tenderness to conceal the steel rod that runs through the entire Gospel: the "great reversal" that we described above. Even Luke's touching stories, like the Parable of the Lost Coin (15:8–10), where an unnamed woman lights a lamp in her house and sweeps the floor clean in search of a single lost coin, are built on the conviction that God is turning the world upside down. When the top becomes the bottom and the bottom the top, this is good news for the poor, the hungry, and the mournful—but hard news for those previously on top of the world. As Jesus says in Luke, "Woe to those who are rich and full and consoled and laughing now, for you will mourn and weep" (see 6:20–25).

8

Luke

The Parables

> Preachers and teachers do well, therefore, to follow Luke's lead and to see themselves as leaders trying to help others navigate a persistently unjust system. They should expect big things. But they should do so fully aware that Luke shows interest in shining a light on God's salvation spilling into settings that are at the edges of the arena.
>
> —Matthew Skinner[1]

Imagine that a long-dormant volcano has begun ominously to rumble and spew smoke, threatening an imminent explosion of fire and destruction, and those living in the valley below are watching warily, preparing to flee at any moment. But at the mouth of this upheaval-in-the-making, we find the author of the Gospel of Luke, smiling graciously, cheerfully calling for a crowd to gather, setting up folding chairs and a lavish buffet and handing out ringside tickets for the eruption.

That is the contradiction inherent to Luke. On the one hand, Luke is the gentlest, the most attractive and irenic of the Synoptic Gospel writers. Luke describes a Jesus who seeks to save all humanity, Jew and Greek alike. Unlike Matthew's Jesus, who thunders about a kingdom on the distant horizon of history, Luke's Jesus brings God's kingdom home to everyday life, to the neighborhood and the dinner table. Unlike Mark's enigmatic Jesus, Luke's Jesus talks clearly about how God has drawn close and is at work today in the here and now. Accordingly, Luke's parables are the most congenial in the New Testament, full of familiar, down-to-earth, emotionally rich scenes. As John Drury has noted, with Luke we leave the bizarre world of historical allegory and covert meanings in the parables of Mark and Matthew. "With Luke," he says, "we meet this—and something different: unallegorical, realistic stories which are rich in homely detail and characterization."[2] Luke is a gifted storyteller, and the stories he tells of Jesus are filled with festive meals and with tales of the sick healed and the poor and outcast invited to the welcome table.

What is more, Luke is a joyful Gospel. Joyful good news arrives in the midst of real, everyday life. When Jesus sends out seventy mission workers to do ministry, they return to Jesus "with joy" (Luke 10:17) over the ways their work overcomes the forces of evil. After Jesus ascends into heaven at Bethany, the disciples return to Jerusalem "with great joy," eager for the next chapter in ministry to begin. Jesus' message has universal appeal, and Luke himself can hardly wait to get down to composing the book of Acts, in which the gospel spreads "in Jerusalem, in all Judea and Samaria, and to the ends of the earth" (Acts 1:8).

On the other hand, all of this gentleness and joyfulness in Luke rests on the foundation of a theology of upheaval and disruption. Luke is persuaded that God is turning the established order upside down, stripping the power from tyrants and lifting up the poor and the weak. The kingdom comes close in Luke, but it has sharp edges. It is a revolutionary message that threatens the prevailing powers. The mood of the Gospel of Luke is much like the contemporary hymn "Canticle of the Turning," which borrows language and images from Luke. Set to the jubilant dance tune "Star of the County Down," the hymn begins "My soul cries out with a joyful shout," but the reason for this joy is that "the world is about to turn," disrupting the powers that be:

> From the halls of power to the fortress tower
> Not a stone will be left on stone
> Let the king beware for your
> Justice tears ev'ry tyrant from his throne.[3]

God's kingdom is far more than simply a spiritual realm, and when that kingdom arrives, earthly kings take it on the chin (see the discussion of the "great reversal" in the previous chapter). Any who draw near to Jesus soon find themselves, oddly, feasting lavishly at the table of joy but also sitting on the rim of an active volcano of social disruption. No sooner does one put on party clothes to attend the feast than one realizes that the theme of the party is a line from Paul: "God chose what is low and despised in the world, things that are not, to abolish things that are" (1 Cor. 1:28). The joy in Luke is the elation of those on the underside of life who are about to be magnified. God is even now throwing the orders of society into upheaval, with the rich, the smug, the proud, and the amused, self-satisfied power elite about to be cast to the bottom, in favor of the poor, the hungry, and the mournful. This is the theme of Jesus' Sermon on the Plain in Luke (see esp. Luke 6:20–26).

No wonder the Lukan Jesus throws nearly everyone into confusion. Who is this seemingly nice, welcoming guy who is turning the world upside down? In the first third of the Gospel, Jesus provokes a stream of questions about his identity. "Who is this who is speaking blasphemies?" sputter the scribes and Pharisees (5:21). John the Baptist sends two disciples to inquire, "Are you the one who is to come, or are we to wait for another?" (7:20). The guests at Simon the Pharisee's dinner party wonder, "Who is this who even forgives sins?" (7:49). Even his disciples have a hard time figuring out exactly whom they are following: "Who then is this?" (8:25). Herod gets drawn into the confusion and mutters, "John I beheaded; but who is this about whom I hear such things?" (9:9). Finally, Jesus acknowledges that he is a public puzzle: "Who do the crowds say that I am?" he asks his disciples (9:18).[4] Is he a prophet, a troublemaker, an apocalyptic portent, a revolutionary, a gentle Mr. Rogers who wants to be everyone's neighbor? Who indeed? He is a gentle and imaginative storyteller who extends a banquet invitation with one hand while waving a revolutionary flag in the other. He is hard to classify.

In Luke, God's coming kingdom doesn't have to be waited for; it can already be seen in the here and now. It arrives in the person of Jesus, and keeps poking out at dinner tables and in the decisions people make every day. From the birth stories onwards, the Gospel of Luke talks in dramatic terms: this world is passing away; the rich are doomed, the poor and weak will be lifted up, and the mighty will be thrown down from their power perches. But for the moment, Caesar and the rich folks are doing just fine, thank you, and it takes a discerning eye to spot the kingdom emerging through the lattice work of this world's power grid. At present, the kingdom is like a tiny sprig of an oak growing in the crack of a sidewalk, beautiful and harmless, unless, of course, you are the one in charge of maintaining the sidewalk. If the oak sapling is not resisted and promptly removed, the roots will grow, the seemingly permanent concrete will give way, and the sidewalk is doomed. So it is with the kingdom fermenting amidst the seemingly stable world of the powerful and the rich.

This double intentionality of gentleness and revolution in Luke will be felt in many of the Lukan parables. They are quite like contemporary tales in their emotional character development and their settings in the familiar trappings of highway travel, family tensions, and table etiquette. Some sophisticated readers of Luke, say urbane first-century Hellenistic readers, would be forgiven for seeing these parables as rather conventional tales of acceptance, humane attitudes, and inclusivity, lovely but benign. To them, the parables could convey that the Christian movement, as Luke Johnson observed, is "a philosophically enlightened, politically harmless, socially benevolent and philanthropic fellowship."[5] But do not be deceived. When the merciful, accepting, and inclusive prophet Jesus arrives in town, he brings with him the announcement of the great reversal. The smiling crowd of power brokers soon begins to clench their teeth. As Johnson goes on to say,

> Those who are powerful, rich, and "have consolation" within society and who seek on that basis to "justify themselves" respond to this prophet with "testing" and rejection. They themselves are "cast down" or "lowered" and in the end "cut off from people." In contrast, those ordinarily deemed unworthy, lowly, marginal, or even outcast, are accepted by God. They are "raised up" and become part of the restored people of God.[6]

It is no accident, then, that many of the parables in Luke have a characteristic plot feature that reflects this interplay between everyday life and the revolutionary implications of God's kingdom. In several major Lukan parables, a crisis happens in the middle of the story.[7] In Matthew, if there is a crisis in a parable, it usually occurs at the *end* of the story: the bridegroom shows up at midnight, the king rolls into the banquet hall after all are wining and dining, the landowner pays the servants wages at the close of day. But Luke is all about midlife crises.

In Luke, things are cruising along fine until, in the middle of the story, the engines flame out on the plane and the cockpit goes into crisis mode: there is surprisingly an injured man right there on the road to Jericho; a friend needs groceries, not tomorrow but now, in the middle of the night; a middle manager loses his job and has to figure out his options on the spot; a rich man finds himself suddenly dead and in Hades while the unspeakable and insignificant beggar at his gate is nestled for eternity in the bosom of Abraham.

For the powerful, the message becomes clear: the "safe" world of privileged life can suddenly fall apart in the middle of things, leaving the once complacent frantically scrambling to cope with the sudden crisis. In Matthew, the issue is cast in stark and apocalyptic terms: the ultimate end of all things is looming on the horizon, calling everything into judgment. In Luke, the crisis occurs halfway down the road, and there is time to scramble, to respond now, to repent and live in the light of God's kingdom appearing here, there, and everywhere.

We turn now to explore each of the parables in Luke. Seven of Luke's major parables appear also in Mark, Matthew, or both (the Sower, the Mustard Seed, the Woman and the Yeast, the Banquet, the Lost Sheep, the Minas or Pounds [i.e., the Talents], and the Wicked Tenants), and because we have already commented on these in detail in Chapters 4 and 6, we will note mainly how Luke's presentations of these parables is different and how Luke's version discloses his Gospel's particular slant on things.

THE PARABLE OF THE SOWER (LUKE 8:4–15)

This parable and the subsequent explanation of the parable to the disciples also appears in Mark (4:1–20) and Matthew (13:1–23), but Luke's version is shorter, simpler, and more direct than either of the other versions. There are some obvious differences in Luke's version. In Mark and Matthew, Jesus teaches by the sea, but in Luke he is teaching out in the Galilean landscape. Clearly there is no need for a boat, no distinction to be made in Luke's rendition between the sea and the land.

In Mark, as we saw, Jesus is actually living out the action in the parable. He is in a boat casting his word toward the crowd on the land, just like the sower in the parable, who casts seed on the ground. But not in Luke. Here the emphasis falls not on the crowd's location "on the land" (Mark 4:1) but on where they came from. They have gathered from "town after town" (Luke 8:4). In Mark, the parable hints that seed is being sown onto the crowd itself. In Luke, Jesus, the parables teacher, has drawn a crowd, a multitude formed from people all around Galilee.

In Luke and in the companion volume, Acts, we see both diastolic and systolic action, a drawing in and a sending out. Jesus diastolically draws people to him, creating a new community of followers, and then he sends them out to live and to proclaim the kingdom. In the introduction to this parable, we see a "drawing in" moment, as people gather from the whole countryside to hear Jesus preach. In the next chapters, the energy will move in the other direction, systolically, as Jesus sends out the twelve "to proclaim the kingdom of God and to heal" (9:2), and then the seventy "as laborers into [the Lord's] harvest" (10:2). All of this gathering and sending builds ultimately toward the sending out of missionaries in Acts. The Gospel of Luke ends with Jesus ascending into heaven, leaving his newly gathered community together in Jerusalem in joy and in anticipation that they will receive the power needed to go out on Jesus' great mission to the "ends of the earth" (Luke 24:50–53; Acts 1:8).

Theologically, Luke's version of the Sower also takes a different angle than Mark or Matthew. In Mark, we recall, the point of the parable is the amazing and yet inevitable kingdom harvest. Prospects for God's work in the world don't at first look promising, but in the end, despite every obstacle and discouragement, God's kingdom yields a miraculous bumper crop. In Matthew, the emphasis falls on moral introspection. The four different soils described in the parable represent four different kinds of hearers of the word, some bad soil and some good. Luke shares some of Matthew's emphasis; the four soils describe the differing experiences of people who hear the word. But in Luke, the light falls more on endurance.

What is it that either thwarts or enables people to hear the word of God and to hold on to what they have heard?

1. The first bunch of seeds lands on a path (Luke 8:5). In Mark and Matthew, this seed just sat there, propped up on the path's surface. This made the seed an easy meal for the birds, who, sure enough, "came and ate it up" (Mark 4:4, see Matt. 13:4). But events are more sinister in Luke. The birds do indeed come along to eat up this seed, but before they do, the seed on the path gets "trampled on" (Luke 8:5). Seed being trampled on a path seems, at first, to be unsurprising. It's a path, after all. Presumably people travel to and fro on the path, so maybe this trampling is simply a picturesque but ordinary detail.

Actually, probably not. The term translated "trample," *katepatēthē* (κατεπατήθη), was also employed as a term for "disdain,"[8] and it is the experience of scorn that seems highlighted in this first round of sowing. Some hearers of the word, however much they may be drawn to the word, are nonetheless vulnerable to the ridicule of others. Whatever chance they may have had for a saving experience of trusting the word falls away before the world's contempt (8:12).

Several years ago, Michael Gerson, an evangelical Christian, *Washington Post* columnist, and a senior adviser at a group called "One," a bipartisan organization fighting poverty and preventable disease, was troubled by the way that Christian faith, especially the views of evangelicals, was increasingly connected in public opinion to racist and nationalist political views. So he decided to go public with his concern. He wrote a bold and forthright opinion essay in the *Post* in which he attempted to contrast authentic Christian faith over against these cruel and nationalistic distortions. Among other things, he said, in words that echo many of the themes in Luke,

> Jesus welcomed social outcasts whom polite society rejected—people with leprosy, prostitutes, the mentally disabled, tax collectors and those in the catch-all category of "sinners." He elevated the status of women, who traveled with Him throughout Galilee. And He commended religious and ethnic outsiders—Romans, Samaritans, Canaanites—who displayed genuine faith. . . . This was not only the announcement of a new age but of a new order, in which the last shall be first. And the reverse.[9]

Gerson's essay, lucid, touching, and persuasive, was a superb public presentation of what Christianity is, over against what it is not and how some self-proclaimed Christians have warped the faith. Some readers were simply not familiar with this kind of open-minded, accepting, justice-seeking form of Christianity. In the online responses, Gerson received much praise, such as, "Wow! This is one of the best sermons I've ever heard about the nature of Christianity."[10]

His essay sat out there in full view, vulnerable, like a seed on a path, and soon the disdainful trampling began. "Shame on WP for publishing such rampant nonsense," wrote one offended reader, adding, "The fact this passes for scholarship in the US just goes to show how corrupted the thinking of even the elites is."[11] "Religion is only a banner people use to empower themselves," wrote another. "Absolutely nobody knows god. The fight has always been between 'my belief' against the other belief. What a bankruptcy of human intelligence."[12] "Has anyone determined if Christianity (all religion) is a mental illness?" chirped a smug reader. "Obviously it's not sane to believe in an imaginary sky daddy and his zombie son."[13]

These acidic responses were all slung, of course, from a contemporary skeptical, antireligion vantage point, but Jesus' parable in Luke reveals that this kind of disdain for the faithful has always been there, in fact, ought to be expected by those who hear Jesus' word. Luke is aware that these are not only attacks on the truth claims of the faith but assaults on the heart, on the inner convictions of those who believe. That is why the parable describes this experience in dramatic and cosmic language that doesn't appear in Mark: "the devil comes and takes away the word from their hearts" (8:12). In other words, attempting to hold onto the word of God's kingdom will be opposed by more than a few huffy readers of the *Washington Post.* It rouses up the very forces of evil.

Fortunately, Gerson's faith was strong, but with some of those who believe the gospel, the sheer vulnerability of faith takes them down. They are vulnerable to these stabs to the heart. "Heart" is an important theme in Luke. The heart is where deep theological truths are pondered and treasured (1:66; 2:19; 2:51; 12:34). The downcast followers of Jesus on the Emmaus road were "slow of heart to believe" (24:25), until Jesus caused their hearts to burn within them (24:32). When the risen Jesus appeared to his rattled and anxious disciples, he asked them, "Why are you frightened, and why do doubts arise in your hearts?" (24:38). A successful attack on the heart can slip a scalpel between the follower and the word of Jesus and can cut the lifeline of faith (8:12). On the other hand, as we see at the end of the parable, the faithful can endure and hold the gospel "fast in an honest and good heart" (8:15).

2. In the second wave of sowing, the seed fell on rock, and it "withered for lack of moisture" (8:6). The scene is tragic because at first everything is so promising. The people described in this second wave of sowing don't merely receive the word; they receive it "with joy" (8:13). But when there is no root to give it nurture, no source of sustenance to give growth, the life of faith is on borrowed time, and the joy eventually turns to despair. At first, the gospel

looks full of hope and joy, but when those trying to live the gospel are cut off from their supply lines, the faith becomes hard to live over the long haul. The power of consumerism, the acids of a cynical culture, the temptations to exercise revenge and violence lie all around, and faith gets put to the test every day. The Christian life turns out to be harder, riskier, costlier, and more fraught than it seemed at first. The promising beginning withers under a "time of testing" (8:13), and with no roots in place to withstand the trials, those whose faith is lived out on rocky terrain "fall away" (8:13).

The "testing" presented in the parable is, in Greek, *peirasmou* (πειρασμοῦ), and it encompasses the daily temptations and trials Christians experience. But this testing is ultimately larger than the routine rough-and-tumble of living the life of faith. It is finally a test of one's willingness to bear a cross, and it corresponds to Jesus' own testing in his passion. At the Last Supper in Luke, Jesus describes his disciples as those "who have stood by me in my trials" (22:28, πειρασμοῖς), that is, in his own time of testing. Just before Jesus was arrested, he withdrew from his disciples to pray on the Mount of Olives. As he left them to wrestle with his own distress, he said, "Pray that you may not come into the time of trial" (πειρασμόν, 22:40). All alone then, he prayed the agonizing prayer, "Not my will but yours be done." When he returned to the disciples, he repeated, "Pray that you may not come into the time of trial" (πειρασμόν again, 22:46). In the prayer Jesus taught his disciples to pray, he told them to pray, "Do not bring us to the time of trial" (also πειρασμόν, 11:4). Trials will come, everyone's faith is tested, but it is not an experience to be sought. Even for Jesus, the time of testing was a life-sapping, faith-threatening assault, and without a source of strength, a rootedness, no one's faith could stand, not even his. Jesus' faith was rooted in prayer and in a relationship with God, whom he called "Father" (22:42). While he prayed and sweated, "an angel from heaven appeared to him and gave him strength" (22:43).

3. In the third wave of sowing, the seed fell among thorns, and the thorns choked out any possible growth. In Mark and Matthew, the thorns are the anxieties of this age and the deceit of wealth (Mark 4:19; Matt. 13:22). Luke gives this language a more positive accent; the thorns are now "the cares and riches and pleasures of life" (Luke 8:14). For Mark and Matthew, the world is full of anxiety and deception, and therein lies the danger to the faithful. In Luke, the world is full of abundance and pleasure, and therein lies the danger. It's not always the bad things that threaten, but sometimes the charms.[14]

Luke's version of the parable makes another interesting addition: the experience of having growth choked out by thorns happens to hearers of the word "as they go on their way" (8:14). In other words, the daily journey of the Christian life inevitably takes one through treacherous patches, which can cause a life intended to blossom and flourish to turn into "fruit [that] does not mature" (8:14).

In John Bunyan's *Pilgrim's Progress*, there is a scene depicting how "the cares and riches and pleasures of life" can tempt and distract the faithful as they go on their way. Christian, a pilgrim traveling to the Celestial City, is accompanied by Hopeful, a fellow traveler. They come to a place called the Plain of Ease, and on the far side of this plain is a silver mine.

> Now at the other side of this plain was a small hill called Lucre, and within it a silver mine; and because of the rarity of this place, some pilgrims having gone this way had turned aside to investigate it. However, drawing too near to the edge of the shaft, and because of the treacherous nature of the ground which broke under their feet, they were destroyed. Other pilgrims were known to have been maimed there, and for the rest of their lives were never free from the mine's wounding influence.[15]

Standing at the mouth of the mine is a man named Demas (modeled on the Demas in the New Testament who was Paul's coworker, but who deserted Paul because he was "in love with this present world" (2 Tim. 4:10). Demas tempts the travelers to depart from their pilgrim path:

> Then I saw in my dream that a little off the side of the road, and right next to the silver mine, stood Demas. Standing like a gentleman, he would invite passing pilgrims to step aside and investigate the sight; so, he hailed Christian and his companion. "Hello there friends; come over here and I will show you something quite remarkable."
>
> CHRISTIAN: What could be so deserving of our attention as to draw us out of the way?
>
> DEMAS: Here is a silver mine, and right now some are digging in it for treasure. If you also would come here, with only a little effort you will be able to richly enhance yourselves.
>
> HOPEFUL: If this be true, then let us go and investigate.
>
> CHRISTIAN: Not I! I have previously heard of the reputation of this place and how many have been destroyed here; and besides this, the treasure being promoted is in fact a snare for those who seek it because it hinders them in their pilgrimage.[16]

Andrew Kirtzman's biography of Rudy Giuliani tells the tragic story of how Giuliani, who had once been respected as a tough and ethical public prosecutor and an inspiring leader as New York City mayor, ended up a broken man, his law license suspended for ethical violations, his mind befuddled by conspiracy theories, and his hands soiled in corrupt politics. "What happened to

Rudy Giuliani?" Kirtzman asks, and his answer echoes the warning of Jesus' parable about the thorns encountered along life's way:

> His descent was the result of a series of moral compromises made over the years as the temptations of power and money grew. There were any number of opportunities to do the right thing when he did the opposite. By the time he reached an advanced age all those compromises left him an empty vessel, filled with a desire for power and little more.[17]

4. Finally, there is good news in the garden: seed that falls into good soil, producing a hundredfold harvest. In Matthew, this good soil is made up of disciples who hear Jesus' word and understand it (Matt. 13:23). In other words, the good soil is made up of the truly wise, who are attentive and alert disciples, over against the foolish, who lose everything because they understand nothing of what Jesus teaches.

In Luke, however, the good soil consists not of good students of the word but, instead, of the tenacious—those who "hold [the word] fast in an honest and good heart" (8:15). The abundant harvest of the kingdom can be seen in those people of faith who hold onto the gospel as a treasure and put one foot in front of the other down the long path of obedience. As Nietzsche said in *Beyond Good and Evil,* "I will say it again: what seems to be essential 'in heaven and on earth' is that there be obedience in one direction for a long time. In the long term, this always brings and has brought about something that makes life on earth worth living."[18]

In his book inspired by that quotation from Nietzsche, *A Long Obedience in the Same Direction,* Eugene Peterson complained about today's religious inclinations:

> Religion in our time has been captured by the tourist mindset. Religion is understood as a visit to an attractive site to be made when we have adequate leisure. For some it is a weekly jaunt to church. For others, occasional visits to special services. Some, with a bent for religious entertainment and sacred diversion, plan their lives around special events like retreats, rallies and conferences. We go to see a new personality, to hear a new truth, to get a new experience and so, somehow, expand our otherwise humdrum lives. The religious life is defined as the latest and the newest: Zen, faith-healing, human potential, parapsychology, successful living, choreography in the chancel, Armageddon. We'll try anything—until something else comes along.[19]

In order to resist this instant culture view of faith, Peterson calls on faithful people to embrace two old titles for themselves: disciple and pilgrim: "Disciple . . . says we are people who spend our lives apprenticed to our master,

Jesus Christ. We are in a growing-learning relationship, always." Pilgrim, on the other hand, reminds us that "we are people who spend our lives going someplace, going to God, and whose path for getting there is the Way, Jesus Christ."[20] The thrust of the Parable of the Sower in Luke is that the kingdom flourishes in the lives of those who are both disciples, hearers of Jesus' word, and pilgrims, those who hold this word fast in their hearts throughout the long journey of faith.

Ivan Rusyn is a pastor and seminary educator in Ukraine. During the 2022 Russian invasion of Ukraine, Rusyn found himself not in a seminary classroom but out on the battlefields with the Ukrainian troops. He wrote:

> We have been serving communion for our soldiers in the open air. We say, "Thank you for your service." They say, "No, thank you for *your* service." The church is present; we haven't fled to somewhere else. And I think that after this war, many Christians, as well as secular people, will ask, "Where were you when we were being killed?" And Christian leaders will be able to say, "I was with you. I was here. I was in Kyiv." And it will be very powerful.[21]

What Rusyn was saying was that the power of the church's witness in the terrible ordeal of war was in the willingness of the faithful to stay on the ground with those suffering, not simply to speak the gospel but to stay the course. In the words of the parable, the good soil is "the ones who, when they hear the word, hold it fast . . . with endurance" (8:15). Rusyn added,

> If we are Christians, we have to have an impact. Yes, we are not of this world, but we are in this world for the sake of this world. So we always have to be in the midst of everything. We have to be engaged if we want to be a true church. For me it was very important that I remain here with my people. If I evacuate before everybody else, what kind of pastor am I?[22]

In the face of the atrocities of the war in Ukraine, the cruel violence and the death of so many, someone asked Rusyn if he still believed in God. "I may have had some thoughts before the war," he replied, "but now I have no doubts."[23]

THE PARABLE OF THE GOOD SAMARITAN (LUKE 10:25–37)

Even though this parable has a lot of complex drama going on, the meaning of it seems at first to be quite obvious and simple. Jesus himself summed it up: "Go and do likewise" (10:37). In other words, be like the Samaritan in the story, who has justifiably become known as the "Good Samaritan" by showing mercy to others, with no boundaries. When we put the parable under the microscope, though, this deceptive simplicity evaporates, and we discover that this parable is far more complex and revolutionary than we perhaps imagined.

Two On-Ramps to the Jericho Road

Before Jesus tells the parable proper, Luke provides two prefaces, two ramps onto the story. *The first preface* is a series of statements by Jesus about hiddenness and revelation, seeing and not seeing. The seventy missionaries that Jesus sent out to do kingdom work (10:1–12) have returned with a joyful report on their ministry. Jesus rejoices as well, and then prays, thanking God that "these things" (that is, the manifestation of God's kingdom[24]) have been "hidden from the wise and the intelligent" and "revealed . . . to infants" (10:21). Then Jesus turns to the disciples privately and makes it clear that they are among those he has been praying about, that they are, in their own way, the "infants" to whom much has been revealed, that their eyes have seen things that powerful, wise, and discerning people longed to see but did not. "Blessed are the eyes that see what you see! For I tell you that many prophets and kings desired to see what you see but did not see it, and to hear what you hear, but did not hear it" (10:23–24).

In the middle of this, and almost as an interruption in the stream of Jesus' words, a lawyer stands up and begins to interrogate Jesus about eternal life. The NRSV introduces this exchange with the words "just then a lawyer stood up to test Jesus" (10:25). The Greek, however, is more intense. It's *Kai idou* (Καὶ ἰδοὺ), which means not merely "just then" but "look!" or "behold!" Here it carries the impact of "Well, well, look at this!" Jesus has just been saying how wise, intelligent, and important people wanted to see God's truth but did not see it. So take a look at this lawyer who stands up on cue. Watch carefully, because you're getting ready to see what Jesus has been describing here: an actual "wise" person who nevertheless misses the point.

The second preface to the parable involves the first layer of conversation between the lawyer and Jesus. The lawyer is not an attorney in the contemporary sense but, rather, one who is schooled in, and presumably wise about, God's Law, the Torah, the commandments. "Teacher," he asks, "what must I do to inherit eternal life?" (10:25). Is that a good question? Amy-Jill Levine thinks not. She claims Jesus ends up reproaching the lawyer for speculating about eternal life. "Do this, and you will live," Jesus instructs him, echoing Leviticus 18:5 and Deuteronomy 30:19–20, indicating, as Levine puts it, "The point is to 'live now' and not be focused on 'eternal life.'"[25]

In the context of Luke, though, the lawyer's question is actually quite apt. If the lawyer were merely asking, in the sense of popular piety, "What shall I do to go to heaven when I die?" then Levine's point would be well taken. But for Luke, "eternal life" is a positive theological concept. Later, in an exchange similar to this one with the lawyer, a rich ruler will also ask about inheriting eternal life (18:18), and after that Jesus will assure Peter that those who sacrificed for the kingdom of God will both be rewarded in the present and receive "in the age to come eternal life" (18:30; see also positive references to "eternal life" in Acts 13:46, 48).

As we noted in chapter 7, it is characteristic of Luke to narrow the distance between the present age and the age to come. In Luke the eternal spills over into "today," and to emphasize one is to emphasize the other as well. Those who perceive what God is doing in Jesus can begin to live now the life that is eternally validated in the age to come.

The question "What must I do to inherit eternal life?" is on target. The lawyer's motive in asking it is a different matter. Luke indicates that the lawyer was trying to "test Jesus" (10:25), and while some have suggested that he simply wanted to test out Jesus' depth of knowledge of the Law to see whether Jesus was a faithful and authentic teacher, the lawyer's intentions are surely more sinister. He's putting Jesus on trial. In Luke, as soon as Jesus is baptized, the devil shows up in the desert full of tests, trials, and temptations. The original tester of Jesus (4:1–13) is the devil, and the lawyer here is picking up where the devil left off.

Jesus turns the barbed question back on the interrogator. "You're the lawyer. What does the Law say? How do you read the Torah?" The lawyer gives the answer that lies at the heart of the Law and the heart of Judaism: "You shall love the Lord your God with all your heart, and with all your soul, and with all your strength, and with all your mind; and your neighbor as yourself" (10:27). This response combines Deuteronomy 6:5 and Leviticus 19:18 (along with an extra clause, "and with all your mind," that Luke may have taken from Mark 12:30).[26] Jesus approves: "You have given the right answer; do this, and you will live" (Luke 10:28).

Game, set, match—except that the lawyer is not done with Jesus and decides to pick at the scab. The lawyer can't let the exchange drop, and Luke once again pulls back the curtain on his motive, saying that the lawyer now sought "to justify himself." Any pretense of lawyerly innocence is now lost, because, in Luke's world, attempting to justify oneself is more than merely trying to prove oneself right. It is an attempt to create one's own righteousness before others and God, which in Luke is a serious theological no-no. Self-justification is an illusion—Jesus says it's one of the flaws of the Pharisees (16:15)—because true justification is something God grants only as a gift. When a character in another Lukan parable, the tax collector in Luke 18, is described as going to his house justified, the grammar makes it clear that this is not something he has done for himself, but that he goes home "having been justified" by God (see comments on 18:14).

The lawyer is attempting the impossible, to justify himself, and the question he poses in order to do so seems so positive: "And who is my neighbor?" (10:29). There was a long and complex discussion, both within Scripture and in tradition, about that very question and about the reach of responsibility of Jews toward bordering peoples and foreigners. But in the context of this story, as Levine points out, the question "Who is my neighbor?" is all about limits, "a polite way of asking, 'Who is *not* my neighbor?' or 'who does not deserve my love?' . . . or even 'Whom can I hate?'"[27]

Strangely, the next word in the Greek text, *Hypolabōn* (Ὑπολαβὼν) is omitted in the NRSV translation. It means "on that point,"[28] and it introduces the parable proper. Jesus is saying, "OK, you raise the question of 'neighbor.' *On that very point*, listen to this story."

The Rule of Three, with Strange Math

The parable itself gets going when "a man going down from Jerusalem to Jericho" gets robbed, stripped, beaten, and abandoned half-dead (10:30). This "going down from Jerusalem" is both geographical and theological. Jerusalem is literally higher than Jericho, some 1300 feet more above sea level,[29] but the city is spiritually elevated too. A Jew always goes "up" to the Holy City and never "down" to it.

The traveler who was mugged is *Anthrōpos tis* (Ἄνθρωπός τις), that is, "a certain man," or "some fellow." In other words, the guy who was robbed could have been anybody or, more pertinently, everybody. As Robert Funk stated, "The victim is faceless and nameless, perhaps intentionally so, since every listener finds himself in the ditch."[30] In a story, especially a good and dramatic story like this one, hearers or readers enter imaginatively into the experiences of the characters by an act of the imagination similar to what Irving Singer says of theatergoers:

> Think of yourself as a spectator in the theater, watching an engrossing drama. The hero dies, and you begin to weep. Now for whom are you crying? Surely not for the actor: you know that as soon as the curtain falls, he will scramble to his feet and prepare for a great ovation. Is it then the character in the play? But there is no such person. You are fully aware that Hamlet (at least Shakespeare's Hamlet) never existed. How can his death, which is purely fictional, sadden you? Yet it does, more so perhaps than the death of real people you may have

> known. What happens, I think, is that you respond *as if* the actor were really Hamlet and *as if* Hamlet really existed. The "as if" signifies that although you *know* the actor is only acting and Hamlet only fictitious, your imaginative involvement causes you to express feelings appropriate to real people. At no point are you deluded. The "illusion of the theater" is not an illusion at all. It is an act of imagination.[31]

So, the lawyer questioning Jesus hears immediately about a man, a certain fellow, a guy like him, who gets robbed on the road and left for dead. It's just a story, but the lawyer surely feels for this man, empathizes with the man's plight. He started out as a regular guy traveling down the road, but now he has tragically lost all standing. He has no money, he is naked, and he is beaten to the point he hovers between life and death. The lawyer can no doubt imagine himself making that same journey down from Jerusalem to Jericho, can imagine the sudden and fierce attack by robbers, can imagine the blunt force of their clubs on his own head, can imagine lying naked, half-dead, and desperate. This story has quickly become more than a suspenseful tale of misfortune on the highway. It has left the lawyer, and all others who listen with empathy, beside the road with the victim, indeed imaginatively *as* the victim. As Funk says, "The future which the parable discloses is the future of every hearer who grasps and is grasped by his position in the ditch."[32]

Now that the lawyer, by identifying with the character of the traveler, is lying half dead on the road, his pressing need is to somehow get out of that predicament, and there are several possibilities. (1) He could get up on his own and continue his journey, but that is hardly likely. He's naked and half-dead, remember. (2) He could find someone willing to help him out. (3) As a last resort, since identification with character is basically a matter of self-interest, he could search around for a more sympathetic character in the story to identify with and switch identities—this is a story after all. So far, though, the only other characters are the robbers. They aren't going to help the man off the road. They put him there in the first place. Who wants to identify with a vicious robber? So, if #2 or #3 is to happen, we'll need some new characters, and we will quickly get some, three of them: a priest, a Levite, and a Samaritan.

The appearance of these three new characters fits a familiar folklore formula called the "rule of three." In many folk tales, such as "Goldilocks and the Three Bears" and "The Three Little Pigs and the Big Bad Wolf," three characters appear, or a sequence of three plot actions occurs, and the first two establish a pattern that the third breaks. For example, in "Goldilocks" an ill-behaved little girl breaks into the cottage of three bears—Papa, Mama, and Baby—while they are out. She samples their porridge, which they have left on the table. Papa Bear's porridge is too hot for Goldilocks, and Mama's porridge is too cold. But Baby Bear's porridge is just right. The same sequence occurs with the Bears' chairs. Papa's chair is too hard, and Mama's is too soft. but Baby's chair is just right. Again, the pattern occurs when Goldilocks tries to take a nap in the Bears' beds. This is a classic expression of the "rule of three": bad experience, bad experience, but then a "just right" good one to break the pattern.

In the Good Samaritan, the "rule of three" kicks in as the three characters come down the Jericho road, three different possibilities for the lawyer to be rescued. The first is a priest, who Jesus says was traveling the same road "by chance" (10:31). The priest is not intentionally coming to rescue the wounded man. This is simply the random intersection of two lives. But the priest does see the injured man lying there, and now coincidence becomes opportunity. But he passes by on the other side of the road (10:31), and the opportunity is lost.

Now a second character comes down the road, a Levite, a temple official who is "entrusted with minor services related to the temple cult and rites."[33] When he gets to the scene of the crime, he too sees the injured man and passes by on the other side of the road (10:32), another opportunity lost.

The pattern has now been set: two experiences of seeing, passing by, and an opportunity lost. According to the rule of three, the hearers now expect a third character and something different. The wounded man's fortune is about to change. Whom do the hearers expect this time? We have had a priest, and we've had a Levite. Now, according to Amy-Jill Levine, the hearers are definitely expecting a layman. "Mention a priest and a Levite," she says, "and any person who knows anything about Judaism will know that the third person is an Israelite."[34] (See Ezra 10:5 and Neh. 11:3 for examples of this conventional threesome: priests, Levites, and Israelites.) It's automatic, Levine observes, just as "Father, Son, and . . ." calls for "Holy Spirit," and "Larry, Moe, and . . ." calls for "Curly," say, "'priest, Levite, and . . .' and everyone knows what's next: 'an Israelite.'"[35]

But there's a surprise, and what happens is so startling, so outlandish that the plot becomes distorted and barely comprehensible. The third character isn't an Israelite at all, but a despised enemy: a Samaritan. Instead of Larry, Moe, and Curly, Levine says it goes "from Larry and Moe to Osama bin Laden."[36]

It isn't necessary to know all of the complex historical, cultural, and racial reasons why Jews and Samaritans were bitter enemies. It must simply be acknowledged that the unexpected Samaritan is, as John Donahue has said, definitely "the enemy and religious apostate."[37] In the epilogue of Sirach, the Samaritans are not even considered worthy to be called a people:

> Two nations my soul detests,
> and the third is not even a people:
> those who live in Seir [the Edomites] and the Philistines,
> and the foolish people that live in Shechem [the Samaritans].
> Sirach 50:25–26

A contemporary of Luke, Rabbi Eliezer ben Hyrcanus, scoffed, "Whoever eats bread baked by Samaritans is like one who eats the flesh of a pig."[38] When Jesus encountered a Samaritan woman in John 4, the woman was surprised that Jesus, a Jew, would ask her, a Samaritan, for a drink of water. John explains this to his readers by saying, "Jews do not share things in common with Samaritans" (John 4:9). Eugene Peterson's translation in *The Message* probably gets closer to the emotional truth: "Jews in those days wouldn't be caught dead talking to Samaritans."[39] Today we talk of the *good* Samaritan," but the story didn't sound that way to Jesus' hearers. The third man coming down the Jericho Road was the *bad* Samaritan before he was anything else.

The Samaritan performed to a different tune than the other travelers. He too saw the wounded man, but unlike the priest and the Levite, he was moved with compassion, and then he put that compassion into action through a string of merciful deeds. Surely at great risk to himself, he took care of the wounded man, dressing his wounds, taking the man to an inn where someone could further care for him, then paying the innkeeper to provide more care, and promising to return.

Samaritans were obligated to obey the commandments in the Torah, as were Jews, but the difference here is that this Samaritan actually did it, putting the commandment to "love your neighbor as yourself" into practice. Even the lawyer in this episode had to admit that when Jesus asked him, "Which of these three was a neighbor to the man who fell into the hands of the robbers?" Even though he couldn't quite bring himself to name the despised Samaritan, he begrudgingly acknowledged, "The one who showed him mercy" (Luke 10:36–37).

Incidentally, the Samaritan's actions—he saw, he had compassion, and he acted with mercy—are part of a larger motif in Luke. The father in the Parable of the Prodigal Son did the same when his wayward son came home: he "saw him and was filled with compassion; he ran and put his arms around him and kissed him" (15:20). Jesus himself exhibits these actions when, in the village of Nain, he comes across a widow in a funeral procession for her son. "When the Lord saw her, he was moved with compassion for her and said to her, 'Do not weep' (7:13). One witty New Testament critic said that perhaps what we call Luke–Acts could be equally be called "look-acts."[40]

Beyond a Good Example

What does the Parable of the Good Samaritan mean? Given the way it has settled into a cultural convention, with our Good Samaritan laws, Good Samaritan hospitals, Good Samaritan roadside assistance trucks, and Good Samaritan thrift stores, it is important to begin by saying what the parable does *not* mean. As John Dominic Crossan has persuasively argued, several popular interpretations of this parable simply do not take full account of the actual details of the story.[41]

Perhaps the most popular interpretation of the parable treats it as an "example story."[42] The Samaritan does the right thing, and therefore he is a good example for others to follow. That seems to be what Jesus means when he says, "Go and do likewise." But as Crossan observed, if Jesus had simply wanted to describe a good example, it would have been better to have the third man, the good example, simply be another guy (presumably a third Jew, the Israelite expected by the hearers).[43] Why complicate things with an offensive reference to a Samaritan? As Ruben Zimmerman noted, the parable is unnecessarily complex to be merely an example story. He writes, "If the parable ultimately makes only such a simple point [i.e., imitate the Samaritan's good behavior], what is the point of the artistic structure and the carefully designed narrative form?"[44]

Other people think this is an anticlergy story or an antitemple tale, but that's wrong too. If the point is that the religious officials, the priest and the Levite, lacked compassion and were hypocrites, but that the layman in the story got it right, why not a Jewish layperson? No need to fuzz up the story by making the layman a Samaritan.[45] Some suggest that the reason the priest and the Levite would not care for the man on the road was that, by touching a corpse, they, as officials connected to the temple cult, would have become ritually contaminated according to the purity code. The Samaritan, on the other hand, outside the system, is free to do the ethical thing.

But the wounded man is "half dead," not dead, so he is no threat to purity. In fact, saving his life is the highest obligation of the law, higher even than keeping the Sabbath.[46] Even if the priest and the Levite *thought* the man was dead, that didn't let them off the hook either. Burying an unattended corpse is demanded by the law.[47] The priest and the Levite didn't pass by the wounded man because they were clerics or because they were obsessive about purity. No, they avoided the wounded man probably for the most human of reasons: they knew the commandments, but regardless of what the commandments say, when the chips are down, it's just easier and safer not to get involved.

Others say that the reason the hero of the story is a Samaritan, an enemy, is because loving one's enemy is precisely the point of the parable. But if that were the case, then the story would have been more effective if it had been the

Samaritan who was robbed and left half-dead on the road. It would have been a truly remarkable ethical lesson to tell a story about a Jew who sees a Samaritan in trouble, is moved with compassion, and acts with mercy.

The true revolutionary power of this story swings into view only when we realize that the appearance of the merciful Samaritan on the Jericho road is not simply the arrival of another traveler, a despised enemy, or even a good example. It is, rather, the arrival of another world, an unexpected and life-changing reality in which mercy overcomes alienation.

In Dostoevsky's *The Brothers Karamazov,* Ivan Karamazov is the brother most tortured and consumed by religious doubt. In one scene, Ivan says, "If God really exists and if he really has created the world, then, as we all know, he created it in accordance with the Euclidean geometry, and he created the human mind with the conception of only the three dimensions of space."[48]

In Euclidean geometry, two parallel lines can never intersect, but Ivan goes on to say that there are some who

> even dare to dream that two parallel lines which, according to Euclid can never meet on earth, may meet somewhere in infinity. I, my dear chap, have come to the conclusion that if I can't understand even that, then how can I be expected to understand about God? I acknowledge humbly that I have no faculty for settling such questions, I have a Euclidian earthly mind, and how could I solve problems that are not of this world?[49]

In the Parable of the Good Samaritan, Euclidian geometry has suddenly been transformed into non-Euclidian geometry. In the figure of the Samaritan, infinity has arced toward the earthly and touched on the Jericho road. The lawyer, like Ivan, like most of us, has a Euclidian earthly mind, and there is no way in this world that the heart of the Torah could find fulfillment in and through a Samaritan. Two parallel lines have met in eternity, and what comes down the Jericho road is not merely a Samaritan but the surprise of God's kingdom, eternal life itself drawn near in the form of an enemy-turned-neighbor whose compassion and action are considered humanly impossible.

When the lawyer spits out the unavoidable admission that the Samaritan is the one who acted as neighbor, one wonders what his next thought might be. Either, "Yeah, right, no way is *that* going to happen in the real world," or—if his eyes suddenly see what "prophets and kings desired to see"—"The world is not what I imagined, and now everything must be rethought, everything."

A young pastor once told me that two men in his small congregation had experienced a bitter falling out over some matter in the past; almost no one else could remember what. The division between the two men, we'll call them Jim and Robert, had hardened into a stony and hostile silence, a hatred that had endured for years. Every week at worship, they sat doggedly on opposite sides of the church, careful never to make eye contact. When each Sunday service ended, these two foes assiduously planned their exits so that their paths never crossed.

The congregation observed the Lord's Supper on the first Sunday of each month, and the pastor of this small flock had made a schedule of laypersons to assist at the table and to serve the bread and wine to the people in the pews—two persons for each communion service. It happened that one Sunday Jim was scheduled to serve communion, along with Mary, another church member, but when the pastor took his place behind the table only Jim was standing there to help. As it turned out, Mary was out of town, and it had slipped her mind to let the pastor know she would be absent. Needing a second helper on the spot, the pastor quickly scanned the congregation and, without thinking, said, "It looks like Mary is not here this morning. I wonder if I could get you to help serve today, Robert."

The pastor realized he had made an error when he saw a stricken look cross Robert's face, and heard Robert, before he could censor himself, blurt out loudly, "Oh sh**!"

But there was no respectable way for Robert to decline, so grudgingly he came forward and stood beside Jim at the communion table. The two men exchanged a darting glance. But then the power of the Lord's Supper and the power of the Spirit began to be felt as Jim and Robert gave bread to each other and passed the cup, looking each other in the eye as they said, "The bread of life" and "The cup of salvation," and as the pastor prayed, "By your Spirit make us one with Christ, one with each other, and one in ministry to all the world, until Christ comes in final victory and we feast at his heavenly banquet."

It would be too much to say that, when the service ended, the two men rushed to embrace each other in forgiveness. That would come much later. But they did stay to do what they had been unable and unwilling to do for years: to begin talking to each other and to allow the oil and wine of healing to begin to be poured over the old wounds. Two stubbornly parallel lines, lines that would never have intersected by the rules of this world, had been curved by the force of eternal life and, at the table of mercy, touched each other.

THE PARABLE OF THE FRIEND AT MIDNIGHT (LUKE 11:5–8)

This passage stretches the category of "parable" as we have been employing it. Even though not every text called "parable" in the New Testament is a story, we have been focusing here on the longer, narrative parables. The Parable of the Friend at Midnight feels a little like a narrative, but it's not (although many people, using a little overimagination, have tried to turn it into one). Nothing actually happens in this parable. It's just a brain teaser about something that might happen, and in fact the parable turns on the absurdity of it ever actually happening. The parable consists of two parts: a question Jesus asks his disciples about a hypothetical and ridiculous social situation, and the answer Jesus gives to his own question. Then the parable, both question and answer, is applied to the practice of prayer (11:9–13), which is the theme of this section of Luke (our parable follows and flows out of the occasion where Jesus himself prays and then teaches his disciples how to pray, 11:1–4).

Can You Possibly Imagine?

The Greek of this parable is often awkward or just plain ambiguous, setting many interpreters, as we shall see, running down rabbit trails trying to explain things. For example, in the NRSV, Jesus begins the parable, "Suppose one of you . . ." (11:5). That "suppose" is good for getting at the hypothetical nature of the situation to follow. But it misses one other important element, namely, that what follows is an adynaton, a rhetorical device involving hyperbole pushed to the point of implausibility—a "when pigs fly" kind of mind-stretching exaggeration. "Suppose one of you . . . ," *Tis ex hymōn* (Τίς ἐξ ὑμῶν), can better be rendered, "Who among you?" or, even better, "Who in the world among you?" or perhaps best of all, "Can you possibly in your wildest dreams imagine?"[50]

What follows, then, is a situation the disciples, in fact, cannot imagine. Jesus asks them if they could by any stretch picture a circumstance where a friend has arrived to visit them unexpectedly in the middle of the night, and having nothing to feed this guest, they go in desperation to another friend asking to borrow some bread, only to be refused? Can you imagine that? Jesus piles on a bit by role-playing how impossibly mean and grumpy the friend locked in his house would have to be to say no: "Do not bother me; the door has already been locked, and my children are with me in bed; I cannot get up and give you anything" (11:7). Can you imagine that?

Part of what makes this scene impossible to contemplate is the cultural context of the ancient Middle East, the customs regarding the obligation of providing hospitality, and the duties of friendship assumed in Jesus' setting. In our day, customs and values are different. When Harvey Greene was the public relations director for the New York Yankees, he worked for the team's owner, the gruff and unrealistically demanding George Steinbrenner, who was described in the *New York Times* as "an overbearing jerk."[51] Greene once described his own midnight interruptions: "The phone would ring in the middle of the night and you knew it was either Mr. Steinbrenner or a death in the family. After a while you started to root for a death in the family."[52] But Greene liked his job, so he tolerated the intrusions. It would be unimaginable not to do so.

In Jesus' day, refusal of a friend in that kind of need would be unthinkable, not because of financial pressures or job obligations, but because of concepts of humanity, honor, and shame. Perhaps a contemporary version of this scene would be parents whose young daughter has awakened in the middle of the night with an attack of appendicitis. She needs to go quickly to the hospital, but to her father's alarm, he finds that the family car has a flat tire and the jack needed to change it is missing. So he runs in a panic next door to his friend's house and bangs on the door. "Ruth is very sick," he shouts. "I need to rush her to the ER, but I have a flat tire, and I have no jack. Can I borrow your jack?" But from inside he hears his neighbor say, "Nah. It's late. Everybody's in bed. It's not a good time to be dealing with a jack. See you in the morning."

Can you imagine that? Absolutely not. That's exactly the response Jesus expects from his disciples as well.

Persistence or Shamelessness?

Then Jesus closes the episode by saying, "I tell you, even though he will not get up and give him anything out of friendship, at least because of his persistence he will get up and give him whatever he needs" (11:8). The point is that, even if the guy inside won't stir himself up out of the loyalty of friendship, he will give his friend what he needs because of his persistent entreaties for help.

But right here we have two new occasions of uncertainty. The word the NRSV translates as "persistence" is *anaideian* (ἀναίδειαν), but there is ambiguity about both what that word really means and to which character it applies. As for meaning, Snodgrass argues persuasively that *anaideian* in this context does not mean "persistence" at all, but the altogether negative quality of "shamelessness." He notes that the *Thesaurus Linguae Graecae*, a digital database of ancient Greek literature, lists at least 258 instances of *anaideia* up to the fourth century CE, and, virtually without exception, they describe a bad character trait, "people who have no proper sense of shame."[53]

So the word should be "shameless," but who is it who is shameless? The parable simply says "his" *anaideian*, "his shamelessness," and, in English at least, "his" could refer either to the man outside or the man inside. Snodgrass insists that it's the one outside, the man seeking the bread, not the friend inside the house. Some interpreters want to have it the other way, seeing the man inside as the one with *anaideian* and then translating the term as "avoiding shame." What Jesus means, then, is that, even though the guy inside might not respond out of friendship, he will ultimately do the right thing in order to avoid shame.[54] But to turn "shamelessness" into "avoiding shame" involves the linguistic alchemy of turning a historically negative term into a positive one, which Snodgrass rightly finds unacceptable. Fitzmyer adds weight to Snodgrass's position by claiming that the syntax of the Greek text demands that the "his" can satisfactorily apply only to the begging neighbor, the man outside.[55]

In a recent interview, Joanie Demer, founder of a shopping website, commented on the generous returns policies of some retailers, saying, "Petco takes back dead fish. Home Depot and Lowe's let you return dead plants, for a year. You just have to be shameless enough to stand in line with the thing you killed."[56] That's the kind of open shamelessness depicted in the parable. In our individualistic society, if we go into Petco and see someone at the customer service desk with the gall to be returning a bowl of dead goldfish, we probably would roll our eyes and keep shopping. Not so in the ancient world. In an honor-shame society, if a friend were standing outside another friend's house in the middle of the night, vulnerable, needy, and begging for food, it would be a shameful public display that the friend inside could not allow to continue.

Putting all this together, the parable reads something like this: Jesus said to his disciples, "Can you possibly imagine a situation in which you go to a friend of yours at midnight and say, 'I need some help here. Another friend just arrived unexpectedly and I'm caught unprepared. I have no food to serve him. I'm embarrassed, ashamed, and desperate. Can I borrow some bread?' and his friend inside the house would answer, 'No. Leave me alone. The door is locked and we're all down for the night. I can't help you'? No. I guarantee you, even if the guy in bed won't get up out of friendship, he will get up to give you what you ask simply to end the public display of your acting in such an embarrassing and shameful way."

How Much More

If Snodgrass is right, and I believe he is, then why do so many significant translations and interpreters take the path of seeing the man outside as "persistent" or seeing the man inside as acting to "avoid shame." It's because we all know that this parable is about prayer, and we are searching around for some indication of prayer virtues in the parable. We want to draw the cords tight between the parable and what Jesus says next about prayer:

> "So I say to you, Ask, and it will be given to you; search, and you will find; knock, and the door will be opened for you. For everyone who asks receives, and everyone who searches finds, and for everyone who knocks, the door will be opened. Is there anyone among you who, if

> your child asked for a fish, would give a snake instead of a fish? Or if the child asked for an egg, would give a scorpion? If you, then, who are evil, know how to give good gifts to your children, how much more will the heavenly Father give the Holy Spirit to those who ask him!" (11:9–10)

Jesus seems to be speaking of persistence in prayer, and one of the metaphors he uses is to compare praying to knocking at a door. Our interpretive imaginations spring to life, and we say, "Ah, yes, the man in the parable who knocks at the door at midnight is being persistent, and because of his persistence, the door will be opened and he will receive what he needs." Or, "The man who is asking and searching and knocking in the parable will get what he needs because the man inside is a symbol for God, and God acts in response to our prayers with honor, avoiding shame."

Alarms go off all over these interpretations of the parable. To begin with, the parable doesn't actually describe the man outside as knocking on the door. That's imposed on this passage by overly imaginative interpreters, who usually add to the knocking another detail, namely, that the man inside refused to get out of bed to help only to relent later, also not a detail in the parable. Whatever the man asking for bread is doing outside his friend's house, Jesus calls it *anaideian*, and that's not a good thing. It is a term universally associated in the ancient world with "rashness, insolence, disorder, coarse behavior, and recklessness."[57]

And there is no God character in this parable. Some parables do have God-like characters, the father in the Parable of the Prodigal Son, for example, but this is not one of those parables. This parable is Jesus describing, probably with some measure of wit, an implausible test case, an imagined thoroughly human situation that has gone, as human situations often do, completely off the rails. It was one of those nights; all was calm, all was bright, and then, bam! We have unexpected company saying, "Surprise! We were in the area," an unprepared friend, a bare pantry, a suddenly panicky would-be host, a rudely interrupted neighbor, and chaos. Yet, even with all this, it is simply unimaginable that the man wouldn't get what he asks for and needs, if not out of friendship, then because he risked making himself into a shameless jackass to get it.

Here is where this parable segues into Jesus' words about the practice of prayer. If a shameless guy with nothing going for him but desperation manages to finagle a few loaves of bread in the middle of the night from a friend rudely roused from sleep, then "how much more" will the God who is a benevolent parent "give the Holy Spirit to those who ask him?" (11:13). This is a "how much more" parable. If in a scene of almost burlesque miscalculations, with human beings mucking it up right and left, needed gifts are nonetheless given and received, then how much more will the God who loves us respond to our needs. So ask, search, and knock. Human parents don't give snakes to their children when they ask for fish, or scorpions when they ask for eggs. No, they give the best gifts they can, and if broken human beings give good gifts to their children, how much more can come from the hand of God (11:11–13)?

THE PARABLE OF THE RICH FOOL (LUKE 12:13–22)

This parable is the first of five parables in Luke that could be called the "what in the world am I going to do?" parables. In each of these parables, one of the characters gets into a crisis and wonders, usually in a formal soliloquy, how to get out of the mess (the others are the Prodigal Son, the Unjust Steward, the Unjust Judge, and the Wicked Tenants). These parables are particularly engaging for hearers, since we join existentially with the interior life of the characters as they struggle to break out of their troubles.

Prodigal Son: The Prequel

When we look at the full narrative setting of the Parable of the Rich Fool, it suddenly hits us that this is a kind of prequel to the Parable of the Prodigal Son, which will come along three chapters later in Luke (15:11–32). The two parables have similar plot structures, except that the Prodigal reverses all the values of the Rich Man.

In the Prodigal a man has two sons, and the younger asks his father to advance him his share of the family inheritance (15:12). The Rich Fool also gets going with an inheritance request, when someone in the crowd says to Jesus, "Teacher, tell my brother to divide the family inheritance with me" (12:13). In the Prodigal, though, the implied answer is yes, and the inheritance is divided (15:12). In this parable, the answer is no (12:14), leading Jesus not only to reject the role of being an arbitrator in a family dispute about money but also to warn about the dangers generally of greed and overvaluing possessions (12:14–15).

Then the two parables become stories of crisis. In the Prodigal, the crisis is scarcity, as the younger son, far away from home and having blown through his inheritance, now faces poverty and famine (15:13–16). In the Rich Fool, the crisis, conversely, is abundance, a super crop that causes the rich man to run out of room to store his produce (12:16–17).

Now comes the "what in the world am I going to do?" moment in each parable as the reality of crisis prompts the characters into a time of introspection and decision-making. In the Prodigal, the younger son, presumably after a season of reflection, comes "to himself," and knows what his decision will be. He will go home and throw himself on the mercy of his father, asking to be treated like a hireling (15:17–19). In the Rich Man, the man soliloquizes about how to solve his problem: "What should I do, for I have no place to store my crops?" The decision the rich man makes is to hold fast to his possessions by pulling down his barns and building larger ones (12:17–18).

Then each of the two parables has a time of blessing and merrymaking. In the Prodigal, the blessing is given by the younger son's father, who orders a robe, a ring, sandals, and a feast for his son, followed by a celebration of eating, music, and dancing (15:22–25). But in this Rich Fool parable, the rich man pronounces his own blessing, "Soul, you have ample goods laid up for many years," which is followed by a party with only one guest, as the rich man coos to himself to "relax, eat, drink, be merry" (12:19, probably using a well-known phrase, see Ecclesiastes 8:15; Tobit 7:10). In the Prodigal, the father gives the party, but in this parable the rich man, to put it theologically, gives his own damned party.

Each of these two parables concludes with a statement of judgment about what has happened in the story. In the Prodigal, the judgment statement comes in the context of a tense discussion between the father and the disapproving older brother. "But we had to celebrate and rejoice," the father says, "because this brother of yours was dead and has come to life; he was lost and has been found" (15:32). In the Rich Fool, the judgment statement is made by none other than God, who, in the only occasion when God speaks in all of the New Testament parables, says to the rich man, "You fool! This very night your life is being demanded of you. And the things you have prepared, whose will they be?" Jesus affirms this judgment on the rich man, winding up the parable by announcing, "So it is with those who store up treasures for themselves but are not rich toward God" (12:20–21).

Investment Counsel

Sadly, this parable tends to get underplayed, and the challenge for interpreters is to save it from interpretations that border on the conventional, even the banal. The reason for underestimating this parable's power is familiar, the same issue we saw in the interpretation of the Good Samaritan: the constricting idea that some Lukan parables are merely "example stories," parables that aim toward moral instruction by portraying a really good or a really bad character and then summoning the hearers to imitate (or to avoid) that character's behavior.[58]

Admittedly, it's an easy mistake to make here. On the surface this parable seems to be a prima facie case of an "example story," since it presents a really distasteful character, a rich man who talks to himself, hoards possessions for himself, and then congratulates himself heartily for being so prudent. We almost do a fist pump when God suddenly interrupts the man's self-absorbed monologue and reduces him to ash with a withering, "You fool!" What else could this be but a warning to those who hear? Don't be that guy. Sure enough, Hultgren takes this view, saying, "This parable provides an example of what one ought not to be like."[59] Fitzmyer agrees as well. He too sees the parable an "example" and says, "The message of the episode is simple." It creates an example story out of Jesus' statement, "What good is it for someone to gain the whole world, and yet lose or forfeit their very self?" (Luke 9:25 NIV).[60]

But is this really only the story of a bad example, and is the message so simple? The problem taking the parable as a straightforward example story is that it fails to take account of the eschatological context in Luke's Gospel. Stripped of eschatology, the parable operates within a single frame—ordinary life as we know it—and is merely a lesson in everyday moral choices. It seems to say, look, there are two basic ways to live. Some people out there live a life of selfishness and greed, like that wretched narcissist in this story. But that's not really living. There is a second and better way to live. Even though the parable doesn't portray the alternative, it can be inferred: live generously toward others. So the moral of the parable seems to be, as Fitzmyer argues, that when a person concentrates on amassing wealth, it distracts "that person from what life is all about."[61] A number of Greek and Roman philosophers would concur, the Kiwanis Club would agree, and so would Rotary, with its "Service above self" motto. Fitzmyer goes on to admit that the moral lesson of the parable "may sound like bourgeois piety; but it is part of the message of the Lucan Jesus."[62]

Really? Actually, Luke has no "bourgeois piety." Even though Luke's eschatology may be different from, say, Matthew's stress on the future judgment, Luke still has a strong eschatological emphasis. The whole Gospel is built around the eschatological idea that human life and history are being surrounded and revolutionized by the breaking in of a second frame, God's new and eternal reality. As Gabriel tells the peasant girl Mary, her life and the life of God are about to intersect:

> "Do not be afraid, Mary, for you have found favor with God. And now, you will conceive in your womb and bear a son, and you will name him Jesus. He will be great, and will be called the Son of the Most High, and the Lord God will give to him the throne of his ancestor David. He will reign over the house of Jacob forever, and of his kingdom there will be no end." (1:30–33)

What is God doing in human history? When his miracle son, John, was born to him and Elizabeth, the aged priest Zechariah sang out the essence of Luke's theology of God's activity: "By the tender mercy of our God, the dawn from on high will break upon us, to give light to those who sit in darkness and in the shadows of death, to guide our feet into the way of peace" (1:78–79). Jesus, the new king, has come, and the kingdoms of this world are being transformed into the kingdom of Christ. Eventually the world "will see the Son of Man coming in a cloud with power and great glory," but this new reality is even now breaking through. The fig tree is already sprouting green leaves (21:29–33), and the arrival of this kingdom in Jesus is "good news of great joy for all the people" (2:10). For those who recognize the kingdom proclaimed by Jesus, everything has changed. The jubilee year has arrived, and the poor have good news preached to them, the captives are released, the blind are given sight, and freedom comes to the oppressed (4:18).

Although the redemption of the world is not yet fully accomplished, it has begun, and among the many places where this new reality can be seen even now is in the peculiar behavior of those who respond to Jesus and his word. Among other things, they act counterculturally regarding their possessions. They freely share their food and belongings (3:11; Acts 2:45; 4:32–35), sell assets and cheerfully turn over the proceeds to the movement (Acts 4:36–37), and invite the poor and needy to dinner, not hoping for a return invitation. They act this way not because of customary charity but because doing so is to give and receive a blessing and reflects a way of life revealed in the light of the resurrection (14:13–14).

Even though Snodgrass (along with others) dismisses the idea that this parable is eschatological ("I see nothing to support the idea the parable was originally about the approaching eschatological catastrophe"[63]), what else could a story about possessions be in Luke but eschatological? The world needs, goodness knows, generous people, but the truth is that kingdom people do not share their possessions merely because they are good-hearted and nice or because they adhere to high civic virtues, such as Aristotle's axiom that "the best user of riches will be the person who has the virtue concerned with wealth; and this is the generous person."[64] They do so because they are loyal to a different king and are citizens of the new sovereignty inaugurated by Jesus. That citizenship loosens the bonds of this world and gives them the freedom to travel light when it comes to possessions. Unlike most of the rest of humanity, Jesus' followers are growing in their trust that ultimate security and freedom are gifts from a loving God and not products of stockpiling assets. They hear Jesus assure them,

> "Do not be afraid, little flock, for it is your Father's good pleasure to give you the kingdom. Sell your possessions and give alms. Make purses for yourselves that do not wear out, an unfailing treasure in heaven, where no thief comes near and no moth destroys. For where your treasure is, there your heart will be also." (12:32–34)

Yes, the parable generates changed behavior regarding possessions, but it does so not primarily by giving us a good example to imitate or a bad one to avoid. Instead, it changes our behavior by first changing our vision. It takes us into a scene of routine human life. A man has somehow become wealthy, and according to the prevailing values, lucky him. His good fortune continues when his land produces a bumper crop. He is forced to make a happy decision about what he will do with his newly increased abundance, and he makes a pretty good and logical choice: he builds barns large enough to store the big crop. Why not? Doing so affords him the benefits most human beings desire out of life, namely, leisure, security, and pleasure. As Snodgrass admits, most of us would kind of like to be in this man's position. "We want to say to ourselves, 'I have many good things (or a lot of money) laid up for many years: eat, drink, and celebrate.'"[65]

A wise pastoral counselor once told me, "I think most people do the best they can with what they see. So, the crucial issue is, what do they see?" The rich man sees the world the way most people do. From his perspective, the crisis he faces is that he has too much of a good thing, too much stuff to store, and he does the best he can with what he sees: he builds more storage. But what if there is another way to see?

In the UK, they enjoy telling an amusing story about the Irish soccer player George Best. In the 1960s, Best, who played for the legendary team Manchester United, was considered the greatest soccer player in the world. The dashingly handsome and wildly celebrated Best was known not only for his athleticism on the pitch but also for his playboy lifestyle outside the game. He once said, "I spent a lot of money on booze, birds [women], and fast cars. The rest I just squandered."

One evening Best and his date, who happened to be the reigning Miss World, were gambling in a Spanish casino. Like the rich man in the parable, Best hit a lucky streak and had an abundant harvest; he won thousands of dollars at the tables that night. He and Miss World retired to their hotel room to celebrate with champagne and caviar. When their supplies ran low, Best called room service to order more. When the bellman arrived with the food and drink, he entered the room to see the famous George Best on the bed, entwined with a scantily clad beauty queen, a glass of champagne in his hand and the bed strewn with thousands of dollars of newly won cash. Placing the champagne and caviar on a table, the bellman looked over at Best and said, "Mr. Best, when did it all go wrong?"

Years later, an older and more reflective Best observed, "Perhaps he saw something in me that I didn't."[66]

As the counselor said, "People do the best they can with what they see." The bellman saw something different from what George Best saw, different from what most people would see. The bellman saw a reality in which a fabulously wealthy, famous, and fortunate man who, according to the accepted rules, had everything going right, actually had gone all wrong.

Jesus came to bring in a radical new reality, one that reverses all the rules of play and changes the way we see. Not fortunate are the rich and well-fed, but, "Blessed are you who are poor. . . . Blessed are you who are hungry now. . . . Woe to you who are rich. . . . Woe to you who are full now" (6:20–21, 24–25). If people don't see that new reality, then they will keep investing in the only world they can see and keep congratulating themselves for the illusory security they supposedly have created by building bigger barns.

The parable got going when a man in the crowd around Jesus requested that Jesus instruct his brother to split the family inheritance. Jesus refused to do so, saying, "Friend, who set me to be a judge or arbitrator over you?" (12:14). In other words, "Don't try to make me your umpire, judging things according to the rules of the world as it is. Instead, I will tell you a story about how that very world is coming to an end."

At the end of the parable, as we have noted, God makes a cameo appearance. He calls the man a "fool," which echoes the psalmist, "Fools say in their hearts, 'There is no God'" (Ps. 14:1). The psalmist is not saying that fools are atheists, which is a modern category, but that fools have a heedless way of living, as if God were not present and made no difference. Luke's readers know that God is indeed present, and in Jesus is turning the world upside down. Luke's readers know that the hoped-for time of redemption has come and that, as Zechariah sang, even now God's dawn is breaking in "from on high" (Luke 1:78). But for the rich man of this parable, God is doing nothing. That makes him a "fool," because it causes him to assume the world is unchanging and will keep rocking along forever.

But it won't. This is the import of God's second word to the rich man: "This very night your life is being demanded of you. And the things you have prepared, whose will they be?" (12:20). The parable is not speaking here about the traditional view that at death people will face the judgment of God over how they lived their lives.[67] Rather, the issue is the impermanence of owning possessions. Purses wear out, thieves steal, moths destroy (12:33), and eventually death peels our fingers away from the possessions we once grasped so firmly. But to employ one's goods and wealth according to the way Jesus proclaims, to ride loose with them and to share them generously, because possessions do not provide the security and joy we yearn for, is to build up "an unfailing treasure in heaven" (12:33). Kingdom people do not "spend like there's no tomorrow," but instead spend as those who know that tomorrow belongs to God and God's kingdom. The rich man is a fool, not only sinful but also stupid. He invests in a world that he believes to be permanent, when in God's economy that world is actually passing away. He is like an investor who put all his assets into Studebaker, Pan Am, and Blockbuster Video, and then patted himself on the back, saying, "Relax, old man, you've got it made, so eat, drink, and be merry."[68]

THE PARABLE OF THE BARREN FIG TREE (LUKE 13:6–9)

Understanding this parable requires that we take one step back, so that we can see the parable as it fits into the sweep of this section of Luke, and then to take several more steps back, in order to see this parable in the context of the whole Gospel of Luke.

Baptism, Fire, and Stormy Weather

This parable is spoken at a particular moment in a long and winding conversation Jesus is having with the crowds following him. The particular phase of that conversation in which our parable appears gets going when Jesus seems to turn from a private sidebar with Peter and the other disciples and resumes speaking to the crowds generally (12:49). At this juncture in Luke, Jesus has arrived at the midpoint in his ministry, and what he says to the crowds not only serves as a kind of midcourse reminder of the nature of his ministry; it also moves step by step toward the parable.

Step 1. First, Jesus reminds the crowds of the overall *purpose* of his ministry, employing dramatic images: fire and baptism. "I came to bring fire to the earth, and how I wish it were already kindled! I have a baptism with which to be baptized, and what stress I am under until it is completed!" (12:49–50).

Fire for the earth and baptism for himself—the symbols here are rich and complex, pointing both backward and forward, to the past and to the future. Back when Jesus was baptized (3:21), John the Baptist spoke of both baptism and fire. Baptism for John was about "repentance for the forgiveness of sins" (3:3), and he warned of a time of fire that would burn up the fruitless trees of nonrepentance. The moment was urgent: "Even now the ax is lying at the root of the trees; every tree therefore that does not bear good fruit will be cut down and thrown into the fire" (3:9).

John also promised that one was coming who would bring a new and more powerful kind of baptism and fire: "I baptize you with water; but one who is more powerful than I is coming; I am not worthy to untie the thong of his sandals. He will baptize you with the Holy Spirit and fire" (3:16). Luke's readers recognize this coming one as, of course, Jesus.

Looking forward, we also find baptism and fire, but in a new key. Jesus will be baptized again, but this time not in the waters of the Jordan but in the "baptism" of his death on the cross. And when his baptism is complete, the fire that John said burns up the dead wood of nonrepentance, the fire that destroys, will be transformed, on Pentecost, into the fire that empowers by the Holy Spirit (Acts 2:1–4).

So Jesus is continuing the emphasis of John, announcing that this is an urgent moment. The old world—the world dominated by sin, oppression, and death—is passing away, just so much chaff to be burned up, and the new world of mercy and hope and Spirit is being born. The turning of the ages will occur through the passion of Jesus' baptism, that is, through his death. The time has come for people to repent, to discern what God is doing in and through Jesus, to leave their ties with the old world behind and to become a part of the world coming to be. Jesus expresses the urgency of finishing his work: "What stress I am under until it is completed!" (12:50).

No earthly power, not even Herod, can stop Jesus from finishing the course. Some Pharisees, out of whatever motive, will soon warn Jesus that he should immediately leave the area, because Herod was plotting to have him killed. "Go and tell that fox for me," Jesus responds to the Pharisees, "'Listen, I am casting out demons and performing cures today and tomorrow, and on the third day [i.e., the resurrection] I finish my work'" (13:32).

Step 2. Having spoken of the purpose of his ministry, Jesus now tells the crowds about the *effect* of that ministry: his ministry precipitates a crisis that causes division. "Do you think that I have come to bring peace to the earth?" he tells the crowds. "No, I tell you, but rather division!" (12:51). This surprises us. Readers of Luke have been told from the beginning that Jesus was born to bring peace (1:79; 2:14, 29). In Acts, Peter gives a summary of the gospel, saying, "You know the message [God] sent to the people of Israel, preaching peace by Jesus Christ—he is Lord of all" (Acts 10:36).[69] Why now is Jesus saying that he has come to bring *not* peace but division?

The fact is that here in the middle of things and because of human resistance, the true and lasting peace Jesus brings generates rejection and hostility, and the gospel of reconciliation, ironically, divides the house—sometimes literally, father against son and mother against daughter (12:52–53).

When an angel told the shepherds outside Bethlehem about Jesus' birth, the news was good: "Do not be afraid; for see—I am bringing you good news of great joy for all the people: to you is born this day in the city of David a Savior, who is the Messiah, the Lord" (2:10–11). But Jesus' own mother knew that the good news of the new world God is bringing into being is considered bad news by those who are content with the world as it is. Jesus would do God's will and "lift up the lowly," but this would mean toppling "the powerful from their thrones" (1:52). He would fill "the hungry with good things," but he would also send "the rich away empty" (1:53). When Jesus was taken as an infant by his parents to the temple in Jerusalem, Simeon, a righteous man who was guided to the temple by the Holy Spirit (2:27), cradled the young Jesus in his arms, praising God and saying, "[M]y eyes have seen your salvation" (2:30). But then he turned toward Mary and warned of division, "This child is destined for the falling and rising of many in Israel and to be a sign that will be opposed" (2:34).

Step 3. The question now is, Do people perceive what God is doing in this moment? Can they read the true signs of the time? Do they see that the world is turning and the time to repent is at hand? Jesus presses the issue of discerning the signs of the times by talking about the weather, in particular the crowd's ability to do local weather forecasting. When a cloud rises in the west, Jesus notes, folks know by experience that the weather is changing and rain is on the way, and when the wind starts blowing in from the south, people sense with certainty that it's going to turn into a scorcher of a day. The people, Jesus says, are quite good at deciphering the signs of changing weather.

But then Jesus himself begins to cloud up and storm: "You hypocrites! You know how to interpret the appearance of earth and sky, but why do you not know how to interpret the present time?" (12:56). In other words, Jesus tells them they are good at meteorology, but terrible at theology. They put their fingers in the air and know when a rainstorm is coming, but they completely miss what God is doing right now, right before their very eyes.

If they could see what God was doing, they would repent. If they could see the new world inaugurated by Jesus, they would freely and joyfully repent and change citizenship, leaving the old world behind and giving themselves to the new. But no, they resist. Jesus says this blind stubbornness is like people who are on the losing end of a lawsuit who nevertheless foolishly stride into court as if they have it made in the shade. "Can't you see?" Jesus tells them, "I have come to show you that God is trying to settle with you out of court, reaching out with forgiveness and mercy?" But they rely instead on the most unfortunate of all human inclinations: trusting in their own presumed righteousness (see 18:9). If you insist on smugly going to court, Jesus says, the results will be dramatic and unpleasant: "[Y]ou may be dragged before the judge, and the judge hand you over to the officer, and the officer throw you in prison. I tell you, you will never get out until you have paid the very last penny" (12:58–59). For God's sake, Jesus urges them, read the signs of the times!

Step 4. The crowd is not going to take Jesus' scold lying down. When Jesus scoffed that they did "not know how to interpret the present time" (12:56), some in the crowd objected, saying in essence, "Oh yes we do!" They then describe a bloody act of violence Pilate committed against Galilean Jews in the midst of their worship. You want a sign that will make you repent? Well, take that!

No, replied Jesus, that's not the sign. Do you for a minute think those suffering Galileans were "worse sinners than all other Galileans?" (13:2). And don't bother to tell me, Jesus goes on to say, about those eighteen people who were crushed when the tower of Siloam fell on them.[70] You think that tragic accident is a sign calling you to repent? No, those people didn't deserve what happened to them any more than anyone else in Jerusalem. But there *is* a sign calling you to repent right in front of your eyes, and discerning it is a matter of life and death (13:5).

So what is the true sign? If it isn't the slaughter of those Galileans, or the terrible day the tower fell leaving eighteen dead, or the Indian Ocean tsunami that took thousands of lives, or 9/11, or the hurricane that destroyed a coastal city, then what is the sign?

That's when Jesus tells the parable.

Give It One More Year

Taken just on its own, the details of the parable (13:6–9) are fairly simple. A man owns a fig tree in a garden. He comes year after year to see if the tree has any fruit, but it never does. So he decides the tree is "wasting the soil," and he orders the gardener, "Cut it down." But the gardener suggests they give the tree one more year. He will dig around the tree and put fertilizer on it. "If it bears fruit next year, well and good," the gardener says, "but if not, you can cut it down."

A simple scene, but when we pull back and hear this parable in the context of Luke's Gospel as a whole, what we have here is theologically fascinating—almost as if this were an imagined conversation between John the Baptist and Jesus. Like the owner of the fig tree in the parable, John knows what to do with fruitless trees: cut them down immediately and burn them. John's statement, "Even now the ax is lying at the root of the tree; every tree that does not bear good fruit is cut down and thrown into the fire" (3:9), uses the same root word for "cut down" as the parable (13:7).

So there is John, staring in disgust at this fruitless fig tree, saying, "Cut it down! It's a waste!" But Jesus, the gardener, wants to give the fruitless tree "one more year" (13:8), and readers of Luke's Gospel know about that year. They remember what Jesus preached at the inauguration of his ministry,

> "The Spirit of the Lord is upon me,
> because he has anointed me
> to bring good news to the poor.
> He has sent me to proclaim release to the captives
> and recovery of sight to the blind,
> to let the oppressed go free,
> *to proclaim the year of the Lord's favor."*
> 4:18–19, emphasis added

Jesus' ministry is "the year of the Lord's favor," the "one more year" in which people are called to repentance and fruitfulness. Now we see what the true sign is. Jesus' ministry of preaching good news to the poor, release to the captives, recovery of sight to the blind, and freeing the oppressed is the sign that summons people to repentance. Not bloody massacres or falling towers, but healing the sick and giving hope to the hopeless. The time is indeed urgent, and the stakes are high, but there is patience and mercy in Jesus. That's the sign that leads to the fruit of repentance.

The parable contains great promise. Jesus' ministry is one of patience with the fruitless tree, tenderly encouraging it to fruitfulness, bringing it back to life. But the parable also implies a warning. Those who insist on remaining fruitless, those who are content to cling to the world as it is, rather than turning in repentance toward the new world breaking in through Jesus, will find that their old world—the world where the rich prosper and the poor are ignored, the world where the self-righteous pat themselves on the back while the oppressed and the captives languish without hope, that world they love so well—is passing away into death. "Unless you repent," said Jesus, you pass away with it (13:5).

Where does this parable take us to be on hand for God at hand? We could hardly do better than Luke himself, who immediately after this parable recounts the story of a woman who was crippled for eighteen years, twisted cruelly, bent over and "unable to stand up straight" (13:11). Undoubtedly, those around her considered her condition uncurable and viewed her as a barren and fruitless fig tree, wasting the soil she occupied. But Jesus, the gardener, tended to her with mercy. "When Jesus saw her, he called her over and said, 'Woman, you are set free from your ailment.' When he laid his hands on her, immediately she stood up straight and began praising God" (13:12–13). There is the sign we've been straining to see, the sign of God's new world overcoming the old. As Luke Johnson says, "[H]er standing to glorify God will remind us of the saying about the return of the Son of Man (21:28): 'when these things begin to happen, stand up straight, lift up your heads, for your time of liberation has come.'"[71]

THE PARABLE OF THE MUSTARD SEED (LUKE 13:18–19) AND THE PARABLE OF THE WOMAN AND THE YEAST (LUKE 13:20–21)

Luke is just about to remind his readers that Jesus is on his way to Jerusalem, going through towns and villages as he travels (13:22). But before he does, he reports that Jesus tells two short parables: the Mustard Seed and the Woman and the Yeast. The Mustard Seed appears in all three Synoptic Gospels (Mark 4:30–32; Matt. 13:31–32), and Matthew also has a version of the Woman and the Yeast (Matt. 13:33).

The parables are similar across the Gospels, but Luke has a few interesting differences:

1. Mark and Matthew place these parables along with several others in a long teaching section in which Jesus proclaims the kingdom. Luke, by contrast, records these two parables by themselves and places them after the story of the healing of the crippled woman in the synagogue on the Sabbath (Luke 13:10–17). He introduces the first parable with the words "He said therefore . . ." (13:18) and the second parable with, "And again he said . . ." (13:20), clear indications that the parables are to be understood as commentaries on the healing story.

2. The placement of these parables tends to underscore that Luke understood the parables to illustrate a dynamic in the healing story: something small and hidden becomes large and visible. In Matthew, the fact that a woman mixes the yeast is probably an image of the disruptiveness of the kingdom, but Luke seems simply to be following his often-repeated pattern of pairing an account of a man with that of a woman. The mustard seed is planted by a man; the yeast is placed in the flour by a woman.

3. In regard to the Parable of the Mustard Seed, in Mark and Matthew, the seed is "sown," but here in Luke the seed is *ebalen* (ἔβαλεν), better translated "cast" than "sown." Fitzmyer renders this as "tossed" and suggests that "the Lucan phrase sounds as if the man's action were less deliberate that the Matthean . . . 'sowed in his field.'"[72] However, Luke later uses the same word to describe the poor woman who "cast" two small coins into the temple treasury. The issue, then, may not be whether the man was deliberate in what he did but, rather, that Luke's version is set in a garden rather than a field. It is more about horticulture and planting than farming and sowing.

4. Indeed, in Luke's version the mustard seed is cast "in the garden," while in Mark the seed is "sown on the ground," and in Matthew "sown in the field." It is likely that Luke's "garden" is in the original source of this parable and that Mark has changed it to "ground" for theological reasons, to fit into his picture of Jesus teaching (sowing the seed) to the crowd "beside the sea on the land"

(literally "on the ground"). Matthew has the mustard seed sown in a "field" to square up the imagery with his preceding Parable of the Wheat and the Weeds, and perhaps to share in the eschatological imagery of fields and harvest.

After the healing story, Jesus asks, "What is the kingdom of God like?" His parabolic answer makes it clear that the kingdom is like what has just been experienced in that synagogue. A man casts the smallest of all seeds into a garden, and it grows straight and tall, just like that bent-over woman who just stood up straight by the mercy of Jesus. The little seed grew into a tree, and just like the birds of the air making nests in the branches, the entire crowd in the synagogue, having seen a daughter of Abraham set free, sang out with joy "at all the wonderful things that [Jesus] was doing" (13:17).

Then Jesus added another parable to the set. Placing the Parable of the Woman and the Yeast here says that what had happened to that one crippled woman in one synagogue somewhere along the road to Jerusalem is a sign of the power and glory of God that will one day fill all of creation. If the Parable of the Mustard Seed announces the good news of the healing of the crippled woman, the Parable of the Woman and the Yeast says that the good news of God's healing mercy spreads to all who are in need. The kingdom that was glimpsed in that woman's healing is like yeast that a woman mixed in with an enormous amount of flour. Not much at first, but the promise is that this kingdom activity will be at work until everything and everyone undergoes its leavening (13:20).

THE PARABLE OF THE GREAT FEAST (LUKE 14:15–24)

This parable is spoken in the midst of a lengthy story about a Sabbath dinner party at the home of one of the leaders of the Pharisees (14:1–24). Jesus was one of the guests, and Luke's readers have already had enough experiences of Jesus dining with Pharisees to expect that this meal is going to erupt in conflict (see 5:29–32; 7:36–50; 11:37–54).[73] The other guests, alert to trouble in the air, watch Jesus with suspicion (14:1). Sure enough, before the dinner is over, Jesus has offended his hosts and the other guests by healing a man on the Sabbath (14:2–4), shut them down in a theological argument (14:5–6), disparaged their self-centered table manners in scrambling for the seats of honor (14:7–11), and then criticized the makeup of the guest list itself (14:12–14). Taking Luke's depiction of the dinner party at face value, by the time the lamb was served, the host must have been wondering what he had been thinking when he invited Jesus.

But this Sabbath dinner narrative is not actually a story about Jesus as a rude guest. Luke is using the framework of this dinner party to underscore some of his significant themes: that Jesus is himself the "Lord of the Sabbath" (6:5) and healer of the sick (4:40); that in the light of the kingdom "all who exalt themselves will be humbled, and those who humble themselves will be exalted" (14:11; 18:14); and that Jesus came with good news to the poor, the blind, and oppressed (4:18).

One of Luke's theological views that has particular significance for this parable (and, as we shall see, also the Parable of the Dishonest Manager, 16:1–9) is contained in Jesus' statement, "When you give a luncheon or a dinner, do not invite your friends or your brothers or your relatives or rich neighbors, in case they may invite you in return, and you would be repaid. But when you give a banquet, invite the poor, the crippled, the lame, and the blind. And you will be blessed, because they cannot repay you, for you will be repaid at the resurrection of the righteous" (14:13–14).

The idea here of being "repaid at the resurrection" is not some crude form of heavenly reward: be nice to poor people and God will reward you with a Rolls Royce in the afterlife. Rather, behind this statement stands a collision of social values: the patron-client system with its elaborate rules of exchange that prevailed in Jesus' day, over against resurrection values, the values of God's kingdom. Under the patron-client system, if someone provides something of value to someone else, like an invitation to a meal, this puts the other person in social debt. They are now obliged to reciprocate by giving back something of equal value, such as a return dinner invitation. Why then would anyone ever invite the poor to a meal? They can't reciprocate; they can't play by the rules of the game. However, Jesus tells the dinner guest, that may be the way this society operates, but there is another society, another kingdom, God's kingdom, where the values are reversed. Inviting the poor, the crippled, the lame, and the blind to a meal may appear foolish by the present world's standards, but the goal is for table manners now to reflect the table manners of the heavenly banquet. Anyone who behaves this way is participating even now in God's righteous way, which will be disclosed, honored, and valued in the life of the resurrection (see also 6:27–36).

Two Sabbath Meals

The Sabbath meal, which serves as the occasion for this parable, is among Jews a meal of special religious significance. The gathering was, in the NRSV, "to eat a meal on the sabbath" (14:1), but the Greek is more richly symbolic: "to eat bread on the sabbath." In Jesus' day, such meals were customarily held as a part of the larger Sabbath ritual, either on Friday evening, just before the

Sabbath began at sundown, or the next day, after the synagogue service ended around midday.[74] Sabbath meals were often family affairs, but sometimes, as is the case here, they included a wider circle of guests.

These Sabbath meals were not ordinary meals but were intended to be enactments of the meanings of the Sabbath and a celebration of its blessings. Like the observance of the Sabbath as a whole, these meals pointed back to creation (Exod. 20:8–11) and to the liberation of Israel from slavery (Deut. 5:12–15). They celebrated the goodness of God in blessing the earth with bread. An early Palestinian table blessing says, "Blessed are you, Lord our God, ruler of the universe, who feed the whole world with goodness, with grace, and with mercy. Blessed are you, Lord, who feed all."[75] In addition to the past and the present, these meals also looked forward toward the great feast on Mount Zion anticipated by Isaiah:

> On this mountain the LORD of hosts will make for all peoples
> a feast of rich food, a feast of well-aged wines,
> of rich food filled with marrow, of well-aged wines strained clear.
> And he will destroy on this mountain
> the shroud that is cast over all peoples,
> the sheet that is spread over all nations;
> he will swallow up death forever.
> Then the Lord GOD will wipe away the tears from all faces,
> and the disgrace of his people he will take away from all the earth,
> for the LORD has spoken.
> It will be said on that day,
> Lo, this is our God; we have waited for him, so that he might save us.
> This is the LORD for whom we have waited;
> let us be glad and rejoice in his salvation.
>
> Isa. 25:6–9

In other words, this Sabbath dinner, the one where Jesus is a guest, is, like all Sabbath meals, a taste of the messianic banquet set, like the Sabbath itself, as a timeless gift of shalom into ordinary time. As Jesus himself, on the road to Jerusalem, has just said about the kingdom banquet, "Then people will come from east and west, from north and south, and will eat in the kingdom of God" (13:29).

When Jesus talked about "the resurrection of the righteous," one of the other guests responded, "Blessed is anyone who will eat bread in the kingdom of God!" It is hard to know whether that guest was being astute or simply trying to sound pious while changing the subject, but either way his words get to the heart of the matter. The very meal they are now eating, *this* eating of bread on this Sabbath, points toward that time when people will come from the four corners of the earth to feast on bread in the kingdom of God.

But the problem is that the link between the actual Sabbath meal they are now eating and the vision of joyful Sabbath feasting in the kingdom of God is badly broken, and the choreography is all wrong. Instead of reflecting the coming kingdom feast, the guests have acted out the worldly mores of the day by being offended by the presence of a man with dropsy, scrambling over each other in a desperate grab for seats of honor, and luxuriating in the company only of those who have, according to the customs of this world, the means to repay social obligations. In other words, this meal was supposed to be a sacred theater of Sabbath righteousness. Instead, it is really only a carnival of the prevailing culture's prejudices, ambitions, and social barriers.

So, when the other guest said, "Blessed is anyone who will eat bread in the kingdom of God!" Jesus immediately told him the parable about another dinner, a great feast that contrasted with the corrupted meal going on in his presence, a story that ends in a way that discloses what eating bread in the kingdom of God is really like.

Empty Excuses and a Full House

The Parable of the Great Feast also appears, as we have seen, in Matthew 22:1–14, but the parable in Matthew is remarkably different from Luke's version. There the meal is a wedding banquet given by a king for his son. Things go badly awry, and violence erupts. Slaves are killed, troops are deployed, a city is burned, a man off the street is bounced from the wedding banquet for not having a proper wedding garment.

In Luke, though, the story is much simpler and, by contrast, gentler. There is no king, no son, no wedding. The parable is just about a fellow who wants to have a great feast and what happened to those who were invited, period. The differences between Matthew and Luke are so many and so stark that some scholars think they are not telling the same story at all, but different stories obtained from different sources.[76] I think it likeliest, though, that Matthew has taken from the tradition something like the parable that Luke tells and harnessed it to his own theology of salvation history. In Matthew's editorial hands, the parable becomes an elaborate allegory. The feast becomes a wedding banquet, the man becomes a king (who symbolizes God), and the king has a son (who is Christ), all the better to allude to the messianic wedding feast. The parable then gets stretched to include allusions to the destruction of Jerusalem, the missionary work of the church, and the ethical reckoning in the eschaton. At this point, Matthew has pinched and squeezed the clay of this parable sufficiently so that it looks like a different story than Luke's.

In Luke, though, this parable is not about the history of salvation in terms of chronology (although some interpreters have tried to make it so[77]). It is instead about the *texture* of salvation. It provides a glimpse into two opposing ways of perceiving reality, a contrast between being numb to the ways of God and being alert to what God is doing in the world.

Here is how the parable unfolds. A certain man planned a great dinner and "invited many" (14:16). This will evidently be a large feast with many guests. The Greek for "invited" is *ekalesen* (ἐκάλεσεν), a variant of *kaleō* (καλέω), meaning "to call, to summon, to invite." This is clearly an important term in this section of Luke, because some variation of *kaleō* appears twelve times in 14:7–24.[78]

The man sends out a servant "at the time for the dinner" (literally, "at the hour of the supper") to all the invitees, who tells them, "Come, for everything is ready now" (14:17). Unlike contemporary dinner parties, where the guests are typically invited for a specific day and time, hosts in Jesus' day often would issue double invitations. The first invitation would invite guests to dinner on a certain day but leave the precise time of the dinner unspecified. A second invitation would go out when the food and other arrangements were ready.[79] The guests who accepted the first invitation would be expected to be waiting for the second invitation and to respond promptly when it was issued. Notice in Matthew's version of this parable the words of the exasperated king when the guests did not respond to the second invitation, "Tell those who have been invited: Look, I have prepared my dinner, my oxen and my fat calves have been slaughtered, and everything is ready; come to the wedding banquet" (Matt. 22:4).

The guests don't respond in Luke's version either, at least not positively. To the anger of the host, the word that all was ready was rebuffed by every one of the invited guests. They made excuses as to why they could not come to the feast, and Jesus cites three examples. One guest said that he had bought some land and needed to inspect it; another said he had bought some oxen and wanted to try them out; a third said that he had just gotten married and would need to be excused (14:18–20).

Some readers of this parable have noted the similarity between the excuses in the parables and the exemptions stipulated for going to battle in Deuteronomy 20:5–8. There men who have just built new houses, who just planted vineyards, or who are engaged but not yet married are excused from fighting, lest they die and never enjoy the pleasures of their homes, the fruits of their vineyards, or the joys of marriage. Is the dinner party in the parable being compared in some way to war?[80]

Probably not. This story is about a dinner, not a war, and the excuses in the parable are only vaguely similar to the war exemptions in Deuteronomy. If the point were for the parable to evoke Deuteronomy, the excuses could well have been aligned more closely. And why, if the guests were simply following the provisions of the Torah in asking to be absent, would the host be angry? No, all of these excuses, "Hey, I can't come to dinner now. I've got new land, new oxen, a new wife," are examples of people being preoccupied with the routine business of life, caught up in mundane concerns. "I know I once said I would come, and I realize you think your dinner is urgent and important, but I can't come; I've got other stuff to do."

The angry host now gives new instructions to the servant: "Go out at once into the streets and lanes of the town and bring in the poor, the crippled, the blind, and the lame" (14:21). This is, of course, exactly the list of people who Jesus just told his dinner host should be invited to a meal (14:13). When the servant told the man that the new invitations had been issued but there was still room for more at the dinner, the man told the servant, "Go out into the roads and lanes, and compel people to come in, so that my house may be filled" (14:23).

There are several things to notice here. First, the way Jesus describes the host is evolving. In 14:16 he is *Anthrōpos tis* (Ἄνθρωπός τις), that is, "someone," "a certain fellow." By 14:21, he is *oikodespotēs* (οἰκοδεσπότης), "the owner of the house," "the head of the household" and *tō kyriō autou* (τῷ κυρίῳ αὐτοῦ), "his [i.e., the servant's] master." At the end of the parable, in 14:23), he is called *ho kyrios* (ὁ κύριος), "the master" or "the Lord." Second, when the house was not filled, the host ordered his servant to "into the roads and lanes" (14:23). This refers, as David Garland says, to "the areas outside the city [that] would have been inhabited by outcast groups (ethnic groups, tanners, traders, beggars, prostitutes), who required access to the city but were not allowed to live within it."[81] Luke Johnson says, "The servant is literally sent out to fetch the 'street people' without discrimination."[82] Third, the command to the servant to "compel people to come in" (14:23) should not be understood in the sense of force or coercion but rather as an instruction to the servant to strongly urge, to insist, that these folk come to the dinner. In the background may be the social convention of the time that a person unexpectedly given a dinner invitation should politely resist ("Oh, you shouldn't. I couldn't."), to which a diligent host presses the invitation more firmly: "Oh, I insist that you come!"[83] The point then is that "compel people to come in" is not an order to force them to come but a sign of how much the host desires them to come and wants his house to be filled.

We can tell, by the formulaic phrase "I tell you" and by the fact that the "you" here is plural, that the last verse of the episode (14:24) is probably Jesus speaking to the group at dinner *about* the parable, not something spoken *in* the parable by the host to his lone servant. Another possibility is that, using a storyteller's freedom, Jesus has allowed the host in the story both to speak to his servant and simultaneously to step outside of the story and address those at the Pharisee's table. If the latter, as Snodgrass indicates, "Probably the voice of Jesus and the host merge at this point, and, if so, the Christological implications are significant."[84] Jesus is speaking not merely about the dinner in the parable but of "my dinner," the kingdom feast.

Regardless of who says it, the words "For I tell you, none of those who were invited will taste my dinner" (14:24) are an indictment of those, like the Pharisees and lawyers, who have rejected Jesus and his message. It is not clear whether Jesus speaks in anger or in sadness: "Alas, they have chosen not to come when invited, and, therefore, they will miss my dinner." Probably Jesus is speaking with both, the prophetic anger and sadness of Isaiah:

> . . . [W]hen I called, you did not answer,
>   when I spoke, you did not listen,
> but you did what was evil in my sight,
>   and chose what I did not delight in.
> Therefore thus says the Lord GOD:
> My servants shall eat,
>   but you shall be hungry;
> my servants shall drink,
>   but you shall be thirsty;
> my servants shall rejoice,
>   but you shall be put to shame;
> my servants shall sing for gladness of heart,
>   but you shall cry out for pain of heart,
>   and shall wail for anguish of spirit.
> Isa. 65:12–14

The Host of the Dinner: Repentant Sinner or Lord of the Feast?

The first inclination of some interpreters is to treat this parable as a full and consistent allegory. The host of the dinner is God, the dinner is the eschatological banquet, the ones who made excuses not to come to the banquet are those first invited (Israel? the Pharisees?), and so on. But this interpretation soon gets tripped up. Some of the guests who made excuses appear to be people of means; at least they can buy land and oxen. So that puts the host in a questionable light. He seems unworthy to be a symbol for God, since it appears that the dinner party he originally planned had a guest list of "rich neighbors," just like the one Jesus puts down in 14:12.

Some try to rescue the narrative integrity of this parable by arguing that the host in the parable is not a symbol for God at all but, to the contrary, an example of a repentant sinner.[85] The parable is not allegorical, and it's not eschatological either. It's chiefly a this-worldly ethical story, they say, about a rich dinner host who gets burned by the system he once propped up, repents of his previous attitudes, and, in a dramatic turnaround, invites the poor and homeless to his table. Seen this way, the parable is an example story with a moral lesson: this guy in the parable wised up, repented, and learned righteous behavior, and we should too.

But this interpretation is strained. There is actually no sign of any repentance in this parable. Jesus will tell some repentance parables in the next chapter of Luke, but this parable is not one of them. It would also be difficult, at this point in Luke, to hear a parable about a great dinner and not to hear eschatological overtones. This whole incident—the Pharisee's dinner, the teaching of Jesus, the parable, all of it—is placed in Luke, as Donahue says, "in the context of sayings dealing with the eschatological banquet."[86] And the parable is specifically spoken in response to a statement about the blessing of eating bread in the kingdom of God, clearly an eschatological lead-in. It's not as if Jesus snapped back, "Cut out the pious talk about bread in the kingdom. Let's get real and talk about feeding people here and now."

It seems far more likely that any internal stress we feel in the plot of the parable is due to Luke's desire to address two related, but different, theological issues: the new reality breaking in through Jesus, and the rejection of that new reality by those who should have recognized it. The parable expresses both.

The parable first describes a great feast to which many are invited. This image evokes the great eschatological banquet, the eating of "bread in the kingdom of God" (Luke 14:15). The host, through his servant, issues the urgent invitation, "Come for everything is ready!" (14:17). At this point, the parable is a picture of what is happening in and through the ministry of Jesus: the proclamation of and the invitation to the kingdom, The time is now, the kingdom is at hand, come! Even though the relationship of God to Jesus is Father to Son and not master to servant, the role of issuing the pressing invitation is evocative of Jesus' ministry. As Jesus said, early on in his ministry when the people of Capernaum wanted him to stay in their town, "I must proclaim the good news of the kingdom of God to the other cities also, for I was sent for this purpose" (4:43).

But the proclamation of Jesus, the invitation to the kingdom, was resisted and rejected by the very people who should have been expecting it. To put it in terms of the parable, many of those called by Jesus to the new world of God's kingdom preferred to remain in the old world, the world of acquiring property, trying out oxen, and conventional family life, rather than coming to the joyful and welcoming heavenly feast.

In another parable in Luke, the Parable of the Rich Man and Lazarus, Abraham appears as a character in the story and makes an ironic statement: "[The people] have Moses and the prophets; they should listen to them. . . .

[But if] they do not listen to Moses and the prophets, neither will they be convinced even if someone rises from the dead" (16:31). Who are those who have Moses and the prophets but don't listen to them and do not respond even to the one who will indeed rise from the dead? Not Jews in general. Luke's Gospel talks about both those who say no to Jesus and those who say yes, and almost all of them are Jews. The Parable of the Rich Man and Lazarus has in its sights certainly the religious leaders, the Pharisees and lawyers, just like the one who has invited Jesus to dinner. They are the ones who resist Jesus throughout his ministry and who will scoff at Jesus on the cross, "He saved others; let him save himself if he is the Messiah of God, his chosen one!" (23:35).

But in Luke, the Pharisees are depicted as rejecting Jesus because they are hypocrites (12:1). In the parable, though, the invitation to the feast is declined for more mundane reasons, "the cares and riches and pleasures of life," as they were named in Luke's version of the Parable of the Sower (8:14). The time for the feast arrived and the call to come went out, but those invited were preoccupied with land, livestock, and domestic life. They are much like the people Jesus will later describe, those who lived in Noah's time, who were distracted by the humdrum routines of life, "eating, and drinking, and marrying and being given in marriage" (17:27), and who were caught unaware by the flood waters.

So beyond targeting just the religious leaders, this Parable of the Great Feast probably has in view a broader group, namely, all who have experienced Jesus' invitation to the kingdom and refused, preferring in the moment the values and comforts of this world to the world proclaimed by Jesus. In the previous chapter of Luke, Jesus has described an eschatological scene in which the kingdom door is shut. There will be "many," Jesus says, who "stand outside and . . . knock at the door, saying, 'Lord, open to us.'" But the Lord does not recognize them. So, they plead, "We ate and drank with you, and you taught in our streets." But they are still not recognizable. "I do not know where you come from," the Lord says. "[G]o away from me, all you evildoers!" (13:24–27).

The first word of the Parable of the Great Feast, then, is a warning: Don't miss it! The kingdom is breaking in, even now; the feast is ready and this is "the year of the Lord's favor" (4:19). Don't miss it! The parable exposes the tragedy of those who are so enmeshed in the world as it is that they miss the great banquet of the world to come. "I tell you. None of those who were invited will taste my dinner" (14:24).

But if the parable's first word is a warning, the second word concerns the good news about God's kingdom, the character of the new reality breaking in through Jesus. This is the kingdom of a God who is generous, who wishes that God's "house may be filled" (14:23). At the Last Supper in Luke, Jesus will say to his disciples, "I have eagerly desired to eat this Passover with you"

(22:15). At the heart of this parable is that same voice, that of a host who eagerly desires to feast with humanity. The whole passage is saturated with the language of invitation and calling. As Pope Francis said in a pastoral letter, "The world still does not know it, but everyone is *invited to the supper of the wedding of the Lamb* (Rev 19:9). . . . Before our response to his invitation—well before!—there is his desire for us."[87]

God's feast is different from the dinner parties of the world. When God's house is filled, the guest list at the party looks like nothing the leader of the Pharisees would countenance. God is a host who sees those the world has relegated to the lowest places and says to them, "Friend, move up higher" (14:10). The "poor, the crippled, the blind, and the lame" are all there, and still "there is room" (14:21–22).

Where does this parable take us to experience the inbreaking of the kingdom? It takes us first, *via negativa,* to experience the kingdom by contrast, by witnessing the tragic impoverishment of those who reject it, who cling to the values of this world over the way of God.

I went to college and seminary in a small town in South Carolina. One day, when I was a seminary student, I was sitting alone in the school's coffee lounge, where students and faculty often hung out between classes. While I was there, the elderly pastor of the town's African Methodist Episcopal church, who had just finished a meeting in the office of the seminary dean, came in to pour a cup of coffee and pulled up a chair at the table. He and I knew one another, and we began a friendly conversation.

Eventually the conversation turned to racial relations in that southern town. The pastor had served his congregation for many years, and he told me several stories from the town's past, including one about a funeral that was held in his church in the early 1950s. It was for a woman who had worked as a maid and a cook in the homes of several white families in town. The pastor said, "I did what I usually do at funerals. I asked if there was anyone in the congregation who would like to say a word about her. Several people spoke, but no white people said anything, even though there were a number of white folks present. I thought that wasn't right, and I finally said, 'Is there someone from the white community who would like to speak?'"

There was an awkward moment of silence, the pastor told me, but finally a respected minister and educator in the town stood and came to the pulpit. He named the deceased and said, "We all loved her, and her loss makes us sad. But I am sure that right now she is in heaven's kitchen baking biscuits."

I looked at the floor, embarrassed beyond measure. Finally, I mumbled weakly, "He didn't know. He was a man of his time."

The pastor turned toward me in fury. "No!" he said, slamming his fist on the table. "That man had everything. He had standing, he had education, and he had the gospel! He had everything, but it turned out that he had nothing! Nothing!"

Indeed, the man who pictured the deceased baking biscuits in a heavenly kitchen disclosed by his comments that he envisioned the heavenly banquet as merely an extension of the unjust structures of this world and the privileged meals of the present age, with everybody in their proper place. The Jesus of this parable might well say to him, "You were invited to eat bread in the kingdom, but if what you described is the kind of meal you prefer, then you will never taste my dinner."

On the positive side, the parable takes us to places of hospitality and justice where the heavenly banquet is reflected already. The narrator of Hugh Nissenson's short story "Charity" is Jacob, a twelve-year-old boy who lives with his family in a cold-water flat on the Lower East Side in Manhattan. The year is 1912, and the family is quite poor, making ten dollars a week from piecework in the garment industry. They eat very meagerly most of the week, saving carefully for a more lavish meal, a feast by their standards, for their Friday night Sabbath dinner.

It was the father's custom, in the hours before the Sabbath meal, to find a "guest," a poor Jewish beggar on the streets of the city to invite to share their Sabbath dinner and to stay with the family that night. "They were almost always old men smelling of snuff," the young son said, "who wore ragged beards, earlocks, and had dirty fingernails." But when the boy would complain that the street people his father brought home for the night disturbed him with their snoring, his father would shush him and quote the book of Proverbs, "Remember," he would say, "Charity saves from death."

That winter, Jacob's mother became seriously ill. On a cold Friday afternoon, the mother's condition having grown dire, the doctor was called to her bedside. He said that she should be taken right away to the hospital, that she was on the brink of a crisis. Either her fever would break and she would recover, or she would not.

By this point, the mother was coughing up blood into her handkerchief. An ambulance was summoned, and as the family waited, the boy was shocked to hear his father say, "Jacob, go do the shopping."

"For what?"

"For the Sabbath, what do you think?"

"Tonight?"

"The Sabbath is the Sabbath."

"I'm not hungry."

"But our guest will be."

Jacob could hardly believe that this was to be a normal Sabbath when his mother was to be hospitalized on the edge of death. At the market, as he shopped, he suddenly felt, though, that he understood. His father was performing a mitzvah, a good deed, an act of charity. With his mother so ill, this was a matter of life and death. "My father's charity would not go unrewarded," Jacob thought. Charity, after all, saves from death.

When Jacob returned from the market, his mother had already been taken to the hospital, but his father was standing in their apartment with a stooped man wearing tattered clothing, a poor guest invited to share the Sabbath meal, this time an elderly, withered, and destitute rabbi and teacher of Hebrew.

Later, after the Sabbath meal, the old teacher goes to sleep on the sofa, snoring loudly. Even so, the young boy tells his father that he feels better about his mother now because he now knows she will get well.

"How can you be so sure?" his father asks.

"You said so yourself. . . . You said that charity saves from death."

His father becomes angry. "Is that what you think a mitzvah is? A bribe offered the Almighty?"

"But you said so," his son replied. "You said that charity saves from death."

That very moment, the old man groans in his sleep, and the father says, "No, not Mama. Him."[88]

Jesus told his dinner host not to invite people to his table who could repay him, but to invite the poor, the crippled, the lame, and the blind, not as a good deed to bribe God, but to eat today as the family of God will eat in the kingdom, to allow our meals, indeed our whole lives, to be an expression here and now of the kingdom banquet and the resurrection of the righteous. Whenever kindness, hospitality, and grace break the rules of reciprocity and flow freely, we are on hand for the kingdom of mercy that is at hand.

THE PARABLE OF THE LOST SHEEP (LUKE 15:3–7)

This parable also appears in Matthew 18:10–14, but in a markedly different context. In Matthew the parable is told to the disciples as a guide to pastoral care: take care of the "little ones." Here in Luke, Jesus is in a vigorous debate with the religious leaders about his ministry, and the parable is a rhetorical grenade rolled at the feet of the Pharisees and scribes.

Of all the aspects of Jesus' ministry that offended the religious leaders, none was more odious to them than Jesus' table fellowship with sinners. Speak to sinners? If you have to. Feed sinners who are hungry? Perhaps, as an act of mercy. But *welcome* sinners and *eat with* them? Never! Luke says that when the Pharisees and scribes leveled this charge against Jesus, it was accompanied by "grumbling" (15:2, see also 19:7). This was not merely a quiet inner harumph but an audible public protest of disgust and disapproval, reminiscent of the grumblings of the Hebrew people in the wilderness against Moses and Aaron.[89]

The contrast here between the sinners and the religious leaders couldn't be any clearer. Luke 14 ended with Jesus saying, "Let anyone with ears to hear listen!" (14:35), and those words are still hanging in the air when Luke lets us know "all the tax collectors and sinners were coming near to listen" (15:1). They are doing what Jesus said. They are listening, they have ears to hear and are responding to the good news, while the Pharisees and scribes are grumbling, once again rejecting "God's purpose for themselves" (7:30).

When the Pharisees and scribes inundate Jesus with a hailstorm of grumbling over his associating with sinners, including tax collectors, Jesus responds with this barbed Parable of the Lost Sheep. It begins with Jesus posing a scenario to his opponents and making it personal: "Which one of you," he says, "having a hundred sheep and losing one of them, does not leave the ninety-nine in the wilderness and go after the one that is lost until he finds it?" (15:4). Jesus' question may well be ironic, since being a shepherd was considered an unclean profession by some strict Jews, and associating with unclean sinners was the Pharisees' and scribes' charge against Jesus.[90] So they may have done a double take at being asked to think of themselves as shepherds, but the logic and grammar of the question nevertheless assume that the correct answer will be, "Well, yeah, we agree. *If* we were that shepherd, we all would go after the lost sheep."

What does the lost sheep symbolize? In Matthew, the wayward sheep represents the wandering "little ones" in the church, sheep who have "gone astray," as drifting believers tend to do. But in Luke, the one wayward sheep represents sinners, and this sheep is "lost," and lost in the perilous environment of "the wilderness." The parable does not ask us to do the math, to calculate the wisdom of leaving ninety-nine sheep in the wilderness. It simply presents the urgency of a sheep that is lost.

In Matthew the shepherd who goes in search of the straying sheep represents the leaders of the church who are charged with pastoral care. Such ministry isn't always successful, so the parable says "if" the shepherd finds the sheep (Matt. 18:13). But in Luke, the shepherd figure points toward Jesus, the one who is doing the work of God, and Jesus will find the lost. So it's "*When* he has found it. . . ."

Luke's version adds a detail not found in Matthew, a tender image: the shepherd places the sheep, now found, on his shoulders. The shepherd in both versions rejoices over recovering the sheep, but in Luke, the shepherd invites the community to rejoice with him.

Jesus himself provides the meaning of the parable. Here in Luke, it's about joy over sinners repenting. "Just so, I tell you," Jesus says, "there will be more joy in heaven over one sinner who repents than over ninety-nine righteous persons who need no repentance" (Luke 15:7). The parable leaves the Pharisees, and the reader, with a choice. On stage right there is grumbling, and on stage left there is a compassionate shepherd with a found sheep on his shoulders and a call to rejoice. Where would you rather be?

Some fret unnecessarily over a seeming incongruity between the parable and the ending, where Jesus speaks of "one sinner who repents" (15:7). But the sheep in the parable didn't repent, they protest, it just got found by the shepherd. Not to worry; the parable is not a tight allegory, but a powerful image of zeal in searching and joy in finding. The joy a shepherd would feel over searching for and ultimately recovering a lost and imperiled sheep mirrors the joy in heaven when Jesus searches for lost sinners, associates tenderly with them, and calls them to repentance and restoration.

Others worry, for doctrinal reasons, about those "ninety-nine righteous people who need no repentance" (15:7), agreeing with Paul that "there is no one who is righteous, not even one" (Rom. 3:10, see also Eccles. 7:20). Some of them argue, therefore, that Jesus must be sarcastic, mocking the smug Pharisees and scribes as "you so-called 'righteous people' who think you don't need to repent."[91] Perhaps; it is certainly clear that the need for all to repent is an important theme in Luke, and that the mission of the church involves proclaiming in Jesus' name "repentance and forgiveness of sins . . . to all nations" (24:47).

Another possibility is that the parable is not trying to be an expression of precise Pauline theology but is instead addressed to the insider-outsider mentality of Jesus' critics. For the scribes and Pharisees, there are those inside the fold, who do their best to follow the Torah and to obey the commandments, and then there are outsiders, tax collectors and sinners, who do not. In their view, those inside should avoid interaction with those outside, and Jesus has offended them because he "welcomes sinners and eats with them." But the heart of God is to search out those who are outside, and the mission of Jesus is to "seek out and to save the lost" (19:10). When the mission is accomplished, it generates abundant joy.

In 2018, twelve young soccer players and their coach were on a cave-exploring expedition in Thailand when a sudden and unexpected rainfall flooded the access to the cave and left them trapped deep under the earth. For over two weeks, more than 10,000 people were involved in an attempt to rescue them. Because the trapped boys were running out of food, and monsoon rains would arrive any day and make rescue impossible, the rescue team was under intense time pressure. The plight of those trapped was worldwide news day after anxious day, and their terrified families kept vigil at the mouth of the cave. Finally, an international team of divers, at serious risk to their own lives, managed to accomplish a miracle, rescuing all of them. As they were brought out of the cave one by one, the children were greeted by their relieved parents with loving embraces and tears of joy. It is probably fair to say that, when they were rescued, there was more joy over them than over all the children in Thailand who were safe at home. Not more love or care, but when rescue is the mission, more joy.

Where does this parable take us to experience the inbreaking of the life of God? It guides us to all of those places where true repentance occurs, to places where people who are broken and who feel lost and endangered are summoned back to wholeness and restoration.

Many years ago, the Harvard theologian Harvey Cox wrote on the opinion page of the *New York Times* about a strange situation at the little Baptist church he attended near campus. The congregation had, as one of its ministries, been helping refugees from the civil war then raging in El Salvador. At Christmastime, the church had received a Salvadoran widow whose husband had been murdered by a death squad. They raised money for her children, who were still in El Salvador.

Word got around that churches with such ministries were covertly being investigated by the FBI, so the congregation requested, under the Freedom of Information Act, any files the government might be keeping on the church. But the government refused to give up the files, saying that to do so could "reveal the identity of an individual who has furnished information to the FBI under confidential circumstances."

That's how the little church discovered they had a spy in the pews.

They were surprised. After all, Cox wrote, "We are Baptists and therefore maybe a little on the zealous side, we are more often accused of telling people too much." The last place in the world one would try to keep a secret, he said, was in their Baptist church with its coffee hours, Bible studies, and prayer circles.

After the word got out that the church had a spy planted in their midst, the congregation joked with each other at a potluck family supper. What tactic would their spy use? Was she perhaps "a contralto Mata Hari in the choir"? Or maybe a gumshoe snooping around after prayer meeting "to dust the floor for knee prints"? Even so, the congregation became wary and fearful. They were being watched. Conversations became more guarded, relationships more restrained.

One Sunday, Cox reports, the pastor of the church, during the pastoral prayer, along with the usual prayers for the sick and the shut-ins, added an unexpected petition. She asked God to give a special blessing on "our informer." Cox writes that he was glad she prayed for God to bless the informer:

> In fact, we all secretly hope our infiltrator does not get tired and quit. If he stays around long enough, he'll learn that when we say our church is a "sanctuary," we don't mean just for Salvadoran refugees. Churches are sanctuaries for homeless, lost and confused people of all kinds, including secret agents. They, too, are welcome to come and pray, listen to the Gospel reading and belt out 'Beulah Land" with us. Who knows, they might even end up getting saved. It wouldn't be the first time.[92]

"There will," said Jesus, "be more joy in heaven over one sinner who repents than over ninety-nine righteous people who need no repentance."

THE PARABLE OF THE LOST COIN (LUKE 15:8–10)

We have noted the recurrent pattern in Luke to pair a story about a man with a story about a woman, and we find that pattern here. The parable just before this one, about a male shepherd searching for a lost sheep, is now followed by this parable about a woman searching for a lost coin.

Jesus barely takes a breath between ending the first parable and beginning this one. The parable is joined to the Parable of the Lost Sheep by a single word, the little particle *ē* (ἤ), which the NRSV translates simply "Or," as in, "Or, consider this other situation." As he did in the Parable of the Lost Sheep, Jesus presents a hypothetical scenario to his audience, the Pharisees and scribes who have been grumbling about his association with sinners (15:1–2; see the discussion of this context in the previous parable). "Or what woman," Jesus begins, "having ten silver coins, if she loses one of them, does not light a lamp, sweep the house, and search carefully until she finds it?" (15:8). The question assumes that the Pharisees and scribes would agree that Jesus' picture of the situation rings true and would say, at least to themselves, "Oh, yeah, that's what she would do. If she lost a coin, searching diligently is exactly what would happen."

The NRSV says she lost a "silver coin," but the Greek says more specifically that she lost a drachma, a Greek silver coin worth about the same as a Roman denarius, that is, about a day's wage.[93] She lost a coin, the shepherd in the previous parable lost a sheep; but neither parable seems to imply any culpability or negligence. The important thing is not why the sheep and the coin are lost, or how they got lost, but instead *that* they are lost.

We aren't told precisely what the woman's economic situation was, but we can make a good guess when Jesus says that she possessed ten drachmas. She had, then, a nest egg of about ten days' wages. She is not a beggar, but her resources are modest enough to make the loss of one of those coins, if not an emergency, at least an urgency. A drachma is a small coin, and it weighed slightly less than a current US nickel, tiny enough that Jesus' hearers could easily imagine it being lost in a house.

Some interpreters see this parable as basically a twin of the Parable of the Lost Sheep. Once again something is lost, something is found, and joy abounds. But what makes the Lost Coin parable different is the rhetorically intensified way the woman's search is described. The woman's actions are rhythmic and purposive. She lights a lamp, sweeps the house, and searches carefully. The parable pictures her moving with focus and diligence about the task of searching.

Just as there was communal joy when the shepherd found the lost sheep (15:6), there is joy in the Lost Coin parable as well. When the woman finally finds the lost coin, she calls "her friends and neighbors" together, saying, "Rejoice with me, for I have found the coin that I had lost" (15:9). The words for "friends and neighbors" in the Lost Sheep (15:6) are both masculine, but in this parable they are both feminine. The two parables probably assume the same-gender social gatherings that were customary in that day.

Some years ago, the New Testament scholar Carol LaHurd read this parable to a group of women in the Middle East and asked them to relate the parable to their own experiences of village life. One of the women commented on how realistic the picture was of the woman lighting a lamp before sweeping the floor, a practice "she too had experienced . . . in a pre electric, arid climate." LaHurd said, "All the women agreed that her celebration with female friends and neighbors was completely normal, as women act as a support network and their homes serve as the same type of gathering place as coffee shops do for men."[94]

The woman in this parable may be realistically portrayed, but she is also more than simply a woman in a village who has lost a coin. She is also a rich theological symbol. Hultgren says, "The parable is quite remarkable, for it portrays a woman as a metaphor for God. No other parable does so."[95] Snodgrass seems to disagree, at least objecting to the idea that the woman might serve as a symbol for Christ or divine Wisdom. The woman, he says, is compared to God, but "[a] comparison is not the same as a symbol."[96] He argues instead that this parable is a "how much more?" analogy. In other words, the parable asserts that, if we perceive in the human drama depicted here that a woman will search this diligently for one small lost coin, by comparison, we can understand how much more God will diligently search for sinners who are lost.[97]

But the idea that the parable is a "how much more?" story does not seem quite right. Yes, Luke is not a stranger to "how much more?" parables. As we saw earlier, he includes just such a parable in the Friend at Midnight (11:5–8), and he will add another in the Widow and the Judge (18:1–18). But usually "how much more?" parables display some rhetorical clue that the story is changing keys, moving higher. In the Friend at Midnight, for example, Jesus keeps stepping up the register, moving from describing the interaction between an insistent man and his somewhat irritated neighbor, to the caring relationship between parents and children, to finally saying, "If you then, who are evil, know how to give good gifts to your children, *how much more* will the heavenly father give the Holy Spirit to those who ask him!" (11:13, emphasis added). In other words, that parable sends out a clear signal that to understand it fully, we must begin with the strictly human situation in the parable and then step up higher. But there is no such clue of a key change in the Parable of the Lost Coin. Instead, this parable is a "just so" analogy (15:10). Do you see this in the life of the woman? Just so, then, you can see that in the life of heaven. The Parable of the Prodigal Son, which follows this parable, is more complex and more richly textured than this story, but the woman in this parable represents God as surely as the loving father does in that one.

What do we see in the life of the woman? She has lost something of value, and she gets to work, not stopping until she has found the lost coin. The parable presents an image of resolute searching and the shared joy of finding. If the critics of Jesus can understand that this would of necessity be the case—that the woman, having lost the coin, would search for it, would search hard until she found it, and then would gather with others to rejoice—they can understand the joyful mission of Jesus to associate with sinners in order to seek and save the lost.

Once again, we run into trouble if we try to press the parable beyond its limits. Some argue, for instance, that the statement at the end of the parable—"Just so, I tell you, there is joy in the presence of the angels of God over one sinner who repents" (15:10)—must be a Lukan editorial patch, and a clumsy one at that, because it seems to go in a different direction than the parable. Coins, after all, don't repent, so Luke's coda about repentance misses the point of his own parable. But it is actually this objection that misses the point. Regardless of whether Luke created this final verse or not, the claim of the verse is not a distortion of the parable but a focusing of it. Human repentance is a dynamic process, of course, but this parable is not about the inner workings of repentance. It's about the intentionality of God to recover the lost and about the contrast between the grim grumbling of Jesus' critics and the joy in the presence of the angels, the joy in the life of God generated by that recovery.

As Richard Lischer said,

> In Jesus's ministry the kingdom is breaking out of the circle, outside the amoeba, and moving toward tax collectors, prostitutes, sinners, and "foreigners." "This fellow welcomes sinners and eats with them,"

> say his perceptive critics. The church's move into gentile territory does not simply represent the extension of the organization, like adding a few more Starbucks franchises. It signals a change of age in which God is claiming us all as beloved children.[98]

One of the most moving examples in the history of the church of the diligent searching found in the parable is Monica, the mother of Augustine. For Monica, it was not a coin that was lost, but her son. Augustine was an exceedingly bright and ambitious young man, intellectually curious but spiritually restless and sexually indulgent. Monica was eager that Augustine share her devout Christian faith, but he resisted her and the Christian faith. Particularly distressing to Monica was the fact that, as a young man, Augustine drifted into the Manichean sect, a gnostic heresy. She prayed for him ceaselessly, talked to him endlessly, even cajoled him, all to no avail. Like the woman in the parable, she lit a lamp, swept the floor, and searched for her son's soul.

When she repeatedly sought counsel from a bishop about how to reach her son for the faith, he became irritated by her dogged persistence. He told Monica to leave Augustine alone and said that Augustine "was still unteachable, . . . full of hot air due to the heresy's exciting novelty."[99] He warned Monica not to drive her son away. Instead of talking to Augustine about God, he counseled, she should talk to God about Augustine.[100] "Get out of here," the bishop finally said, but then added a word of encouragement: "It's impossible that the son of these tears of yours will perish."[101]

As is well known, Monica's tearful prayers were eventually answered. One day, caught in an inner spiritual struggle, Augustine went from the place where he was staying to a garden outside. He threw himself on the ground and cried out, "How long, O Lord? Will you always be angry with me? Remember not my past sins." Augustine describes what happened next: "I was saying these things and weeping, with agonizing anguish in my heart, and then I heard a voice from the household next door, the voice of someone—a little boy or girl, I don't know which—incessantly and insistently chanting, 'Pick it up! Read it! Pick it up! Read it!'"

Augustine went back inside and found a copy of the Bible. He opened it at random, and his eyes fell on a passage from Romans: "Let us then lay aside the works of darkness and put on the armor of light; let us live honorably as in the day, not in reveling and drunkenness, not in debauchery and licentiousness, not in quarrelling and jealousy. Instead, put on the Lord Jesus Christ, and make no provision for the flesh, to gratify its desires" (Rom. 13:12–13).

"I didn't want to read further," he wrote, "and there was no need. The instance I finished this sentence, my heart was virtually flooded with a light of relief and certitude, and all the darkness of my hesitation scattered away."[102]

When Augustine told Monica what had happened, she was filled with joy. "You had turned her mourning into a joy much more fertile than she had wished for."[103]

Augustine was baptized on Easter Sunday in 387. Later, when Augustine remembered his turn to the faith and his mother's role in it, he associated it with the Parable of the Lost Coin: "The drachma is returned to your treasury [my good God], while the neighbors celebrate with the woman who found it."[104]

THE PARABLE OF THE PRODIGAL SON (LUKE 15:11–32)

Many people treasure this as the crown jewel of Jesus' parables, and, since the parable shows strong evidence of the Gospel writer's literary hand, it has also been called "Luke's *pièce de résistance*."[105] The story it tells has beauty, power, and emotional appeal. "Luke is at his best here," writes Drury, "deploying all his favorite themes and techniques with a freshness and vigor which survive endless readings and interpretations."[106]

The parable is the longest of Jesus' parables and more complex than the others ("virtually a novella"[107]). The themes it expresses and the family dynamics it describes are so universal that contemporary readers can imagine the story unfolding in their own family or among the neighbors down the street. It is also theologically luxuriant, and more than one commentator has called this parable "the gospel in miniature."

But this parable is also very seductive. The characters are so richly drawn, the narrative so close to the heart, the emotions so identifiable, that it is almost irresistible to project oneself personally into the story. In one sense, of course, this is a great part of the parable's power, but in another sense, this is the wellspring of many misconceptions as readers view the parable as a Rorschach blot on which are imposed endless projections. This one parable has grown, for good and for ill, into a great tree, and all the interpreters of the air make nests in its branches.

Introducing the Cast

The parable begins in characteristic Lukan fashion, "A certain man had two sons," or as Amy-Jill Levine has translated it, "Some man had two sons" (15:11). The universality of the story already has begun; this is a tale about some father, any father, who had a couple of boys. We know this family. We know a hundred families like this. Perhaps our family is one of them.

Already, though, the possibility of misinterpretation, or at least overinterpretation, creeps in. Precisely because the parable goes on to describe so vividly the interactions of this father and his sons, and because the reader can ride the wings of imagination into this family constellation, the question quickly arises, "Where is the mother? Why does she not appear at all in this dramatic story of family reunion and conflict?" Some have gone so far as to speculate that she is absent because she is ill, or maybe dead. Bernard Brandon Scott, in what seems to me to be an especially unfortunate move, even presses the father into playing both parental roles. Pointing to the scene that comes later in the parable when the returning younger son is kissed by his father, Scott writes,

> When the son returns home, the father returns immediately to him and kisses him. Many have objected to this because running offends the dignity of an Oriental man. . . . The Greek word, *katephilesen*, has overtones of an affectionate kiss of the type exchanged by husbands and wives. Many try to avoid this connotation, but the father here behaves like a mother. The father abandons male honor for female shame.[108]

Really? Despite the realism of this parable, we should remember it is fiction. Fiction is fiction, and the mother is absent because the mother does not exist. Nor is the addition of a maternal character essential to what Luke desires to do with this story and to the efficient unfolding of the parable's plot. We might wish that the mother would make an appearance, to enhance our sense of drama, or perhaps to strike a blow against biblical patriarchy, but the teller of the parable wanted to tell a parable about a man and his two sons. This is a contrast parable; the two sons represent contrasting views and attitudes, with the father mediating between them, and these are all the dramatis personae the story demands. As Snodgrass states, "Parables are marked by focus and brevity and do not care about unnecessary issues."[109] To exercise the imagination and to add a mother to the parable can be homiletically creative, perhaps enjoyable, maybe even in rare cases enriching, but it is hermeneutical embroidering.

The fact that the parable introduces the reader in the very first verse to all three of the key characters raises another issue: the name of this parable. I have allowed the traditional title to stand, the Parable of the Prodigal Son, only because that has endured for many centuries and is the most recognizable title, but it has for a long time been recognized as inadequate. There are two sons in the story, not one, and both play major roles. However, to call this "The Parable of the Two Sons" confuses it with the parable of the same name in Matthew 21:28–32.[110] There is also, of course, the father, and some have argued that he is actually the central character and that the parable should be called something like the Parable of the Loving Father to shine the light on him. In the final analysis, the parable has a trio of significant characters, and a title like the one suggested by Snodgrass, "The Compassionate Father and His Two Lost Sons,"[111] seems more apt.

Off to the Distant Country

As soon as the main cast of characters in the parable has been introduced, the action starts rolling. One of the sons, the older one, exits stage right and doesn't reappear until Act 3. That leaves the father and the younger son under the lights, and the interaction between them becomes immediately intense. The boy asks for money: "Father, give me the share of the property that will belong to me" (15:12). He is asking, of course, for his share of the father's estate in advance, and the father grants his request.

Because the story has two sons, younger and older, alert readers may wonder if the parable is playing off a familiar biblical trope where a younger brother gets favored over his older sibling. Abel's offering was accepted by God when older brother Cain's was not (Gen. 4:3–5). Younger Jacob obtains, albeit by trickery, his father Isaac's blessing over slightly older twin brother Esau (Gen. 27). God chose the youngest son, David, to be king and not any of his older brothers (1 Sam. 16:1–13). And so on.[112] But the parable actually doesn't work well as an expression of this younger brother–older brother trope. As we will see, the father in the parable doesn't favor or bless the younger son over the older. Both sons are embraced.

It may be that the sons are called "younger" and "elder" simply to identify them without manufacturing names for them, or at most, since this is an inheritance story, to pluck the strings of the Torah provisions regarding inheritance. The law stipulated that, if there were two sons, the father's possessions were to be apportioned two-thirds to the older son and one-third to the younger. Even if the sons were by two different wives and the father happened to like the mother of the younger son and dislike the mother of the older one, still the older son was to receive a double portion of the inheritance (Deut. 21:15–17). So in the parable, the younger son asks for his "share," presumably one-third of his father's possessions.

When the NRSV indicates that the father "divided his property between them," it doesn't mean that he split his possessions down the middle but instead "distributed" them, giving the younger son his designated portion. There is an interesting noun shift, however, between the request and the bequest. The younger son asks for his share of the *ousias* (οὐσίας), which means "possessions" or "wealth," but the father is said to give his son his *bion* (βίον), which means "life" or "living." The same word is used later in Luke when Jesus describes the two copper coins the poor widow contributed to the temple treasury as "all that she had to live [*bion*] on" (21:4). The use of *bion* in the parable underscores that this is not merely a financial transaction but a giving of "a living," of "life," to the younger son by the father.

Many sermons have mistakenly claimed the younger son's request for his inheritance while his father is still alive is the deepest of all possible insults, tantamount to saying, "I wish you were dead." This notion probably originated with Kenneth Bailey, who makes much of it in *The Cross and the Prodigal*[113] and again in *Poet and Peasant*.[114] Bailey claims that the request the younger son made is and was "unthinkable":

> Every Middle Eastern peasant understands this instinctively. With endless village groups all across the Middle East I have tested this thesis. The answer has always been the same. Again and again, I have engaged in some form of the following conversation:
> "Has anyone ever made such a request in your village?"
> "Never!"
> "Could anyone ever make such a request?"
> "Impossible!"
> "If anyone ever did, what would happen?"
> "His father would become very angry and refuse!"
> "Why?"
> "This request means *he wants his father to die!*"[115]

There are at least two problems with Bailey's view. First, there is a methodological difficulty. Bailey gets his main data about family attitudes in the first century from conversations with villagers in the Mideast in the latter half of the twentieth century, which is a little like trying to find out the political views of blacksmiths in Massachusetts in 1770 by interviewing ironworkers in a Foxborough bar after a Patriots game last fall. Jewish law scholar Bernard S. Jackson says that Bailey rode a "methodologically questionable premise" to a false conclusion. What Bailey was actually hearing was not first-century social reality in Jewish Palestine but cultural views "heavily informed by medieval Arab Christian interpretation and contemporary Arab custom."[116] In fact, Jackson argues, "Jewish sources give no support to a major plank in Bailey's interpretation of the parable, that the prodigal, in seeking the advance, wishes his father dead."[117]

For example, Sirach 33:20–24 discusses the possibility that a man might distribute his inheritance before his death but advises against it on the practical ground that one could run out of money and then end up asking for help from your children. "For it is better that your children should ask from you than that you should look to the hand of your children" (Sir. 33:22). The very fact that Sirach counsels against the practice, claims T. W. Manson, is evidence "that parents could and actually did hand over their property to their heirs."[118]

Bailey's second problem is theological. Seemingly the main reason he finds it so important to see the younger son's request as a death wish for his father is because of what it means theologically. "The request itself," argues Bailey, "is a form of mutiny. The prodigal is impatient for his father to die. Theologically, Jesus is affirming that humankind in their rebellion against God really wants him dead!"[119] Bailey seems to want this younger son to be portrayed as a complete and utter sinner from the beginning of the story so that the rest of the parable can be seen as Jesus' narration of an evangelical set piece of dramatic life turnaround and divine grace. Also, if we take Bailey's words with utter seriousness, that this parable is about humankind wishing God dead, it is not at all clear what imagining God as dead could mean in the context of first-century Judaism. Disobey God? Yes. Blaspheme God? Yes. But the death of God? That will need to wait for Blake, Hegel, and Nietzsche, and Bailey's idea that Jesus crafted the younger son as a symbol of humanity's desire for God to be dead probably grafts Bailey's own contemporary theological anxiety onto the parable.

How then should we understand the younger son's request for an advance on his inheritance? It is not a desire that anybody be dead but a desire on the part of the son to live in a different place and in a different way. As it turns out, the request for his inheritance was the means for him to leave his family and to go far away, where he could live on his own terms. The fact that he asked for the money and that his father gave it to him may have been unwise, may even have been worthy of frowns from those who heard about it, but it was not illegal and was by no means a murderous wish toward the father.[120] The prodigal's gravest sin was not how he got the money but, as his older brother will angrily point out later, how he spent it.

Soon, the younger son "gathered all he had," which Fitzmyer says probably means that he converted all his possessions into cash,[121] and "traveled to a distant country" (15:13). Trouble, however, lies ahead.

Waste, Famine, Poverty, and Hunger

Once we have traveled narratively with the younger son to the far country, we don't have long to wait for the wheels to come off his life. The parable includes no scenes of exciting adventures in the distant country, no accounts of pleasant dinners with newfound friends. No, as soon as the parable gets the boy to his new location, he unraveled and "squandered his property in dissolute living" (15:13). The description of the younger son's trip and his dissolution come so close together they form two clauses in the same sentence. We don't know what kind of dissolute living the son engaged in—the term can imply a number of forms of unworthy living—but the older brother suggests that his younger brother's money was wasted "on prostitutes" (15:30).

Once the younger son was out of money, things quickly went from bad to worse. As misfortune would have it, a famine swept the land—not an uncommon occurrence in the ancient world—just as the younger son was running out of cash. So he hired himself out to a local citizen. It is not clear whether or not the younger son is portrayed here as having freely gotten a job or as having become an indentured servant, one of several forms of dependent labor in the ancient world. J. Albert Harrell argues that the picture of the son's labor in the parable is indeed consistent with indentured servanthood and, therefore, translates the corresponding phrase in Luke 15:15 "he was indentured to one of the citizens of that country."[122]

More important, though, than the exact nature of his employment is the portrait in the parable of a life falling completely apart. His job is a menial one, feeding pigs, and the boy is so hungry "he would gladly have filled himself with the pods that the pigs were eating" (15:16). Many commentators make a case that the son is portrayed in disgraceful terms for a Jew, working in what is obviously Gentile territory, for a Gentile, and becoming unclean by associating with swine. Levine, though, argues that connecting purity issues to this parable is just one more example of an anti-Semitic bias in much New Testament interpretation (rigid Jewish purity laws versus more open-minded Christian views). Leviticus does declare pigs unclean, saying, "The pig . . . is unclean for you. Of their flesh you shall not eat, and their carcasses you shall not touch; they are unclean for you" (Lev. 11:7–8). True, Levine says, but "the son ate no ham hocks or pigs' knuckles; if he did, he would not be starving. . . . He was sent to feed the pigs, not to butcher them."[123] The son's problem is not that he is unclean; it's that he is starving.

Indeed, the main effect of this portion of the parable is to paint a picture of abject misery. The son's desperation seems more pertinent than the status of pigs in the Torah. The phrase "he would gladly have filled himself" with the pig food is virtually repeated in the Parable of the Rich Man and Lazarus, when poor Lazarus is said to have "longed to satisfy his hunger" with the scraps that fell from the wealthy man's table. In both parables, the language points to the depth of hunger involved. The boy has hit bottom. He is flat broke, starving to death, and with no friendships or solid relationships; "no one gave him anything" (15:16).

The Long Journey Home

The story of the younger son begins to pivot when "he came to himself" (15:17), meaning "he came to his senses."[124] At this point in the story, the younger son engages in a soliloquy, making this the second of the five "what am I going to do?" parables in Luke. In each of these parables, a character is in crisis and wonders, in a soliloquy, how to get out of it (the others, as we have noted, are the Rich Fool, the Unjust Steward, the Unjust Judge, and the Wicked Tenants). In his soliloquy, the younger son, now back to himself, first describes his plight, "How many of my father's hired hands have bread enough and to spare, but here I am dying of hunger!" (15:17), and then he makes his decision: "I will get up and go to my father, and I will say to him, 'Father, I have sinned against heaven and before you; I am no longer worthy to be called your son; treat me like one of your hired hands'" (15:18–19).

This parable is another story about "one sinner who repents," the third such parable in a row in Luke 15, and this scene captures the beginning of that season of repentance in the life of the younger son. Strangely, a significant number of contemporary interpreters have come to the counterconclusion that the younger son doesn't repent at all, that the parable, contrary to the traditional understanding of it, portrays the younger son as faking repentance as a tactic to get out of trouble and to reingratiate himself to his father.

Why do they think this? Some believe that the narrator of the parable himself tips off the reader that the younger son is insincere, mainly because he pictures the son rehearsing in advance the speech he will give to his father when he gets home.[125] But this rehearsal aloud of an anticipated action belongs more to the Lukan formula for a soliloquy than to any implied duplicity on the part of the speaker. Some others point out that these soliloquies in Luke's parables are spoken by shady characters, such as the dishonest manager (16:1–8) or the unjust judge (18:1–8), and the fact that this younger son now speaks one is evidence that he belongs in this suspect company.[126] But that doesn't quite work either. In the Parable of the Wicked Tenants (20:9–18), it is the vineyard owner, the God figure, who speaks the soliloquy.

Others among those who doubt the younger son's repentance don't find the boy sufficiently remorseful. Peter Hawkins, for example, reserves repentance to "those who are truly and earnestly sorry for their sins," and asks,

> Is this what we find in the parable? Does the prodigal give any indication of such interiority or, indeed, any hint of a "slain" heart? I think not. He comes home; he realizes that he cannot rightly hope for much. But rather than highlight the depth of the younger son's contrition, the storyteller gives us every reason to see his "coming to himself," at

> least initially, as a manifestation of enlightened self-interest. . . . [T]he prodigal's return looks more like a strategy than a wholehearted conversion; less a desperate measure than a calculation.[127]

Homiletician David Buttrick agrees. "Although the boy seems to have voiced repentance," he writes, "his supposed conversion may be mostly a 'soup kitchen conversion'—he's hungry."[128] Buttrick has somehow figured out that the younger son, a character in fiction, "has a shrewd, canny, calculating mind," and now, in trouble and desperately hungry, the boy comes to a conniving decision. "I know what I'll do. I'll go to Daddy and sound religious: I've sinned against heaven and in your sight. . . . Please pass the mashed potatoes!"[129]

I find this perspective deeply misleading. In chapter 15, Luke has already told two parables about repentance and rejoicing, the Lost Sheep and the Lost Coin, both of which proclaim how much joy there is in the life of God over one sinner who repents. Is it seriously imaginable that Luke would cap off this sequence with an elaborate story of a manipulative con artist who feigned repentance? Talk about anticlimactic.

Part of the problem is that Luke is such a fine storyteller that he has crafted what literary critics call "round characters," that is, characters so richly presented that readers imaginatively fill in the gaps and complete in their own minds the portrait of the character. When some contemporary readers round out this younger son character, they fill the gaps with negative features generated out of their own imaginations and then don't like what they see.

"In reading the story of the prodigal son," writes New Testament scholar Donald Juel, "I choose to play the younger son as a classic manipulator."[130] Why would Juel see the younger son this way?

> That interpretation had occurred to me when I read a letter a parishioner sent to his pastor after hearing the parable read in church. As an older, responsible child from a family of irresponsible siblings, the letter writer objected strenuously to the usual reading according to which the older brother is the villain. He had himself kept the family farm afloat despite the best efforts of his siblings to sink it, largely without any expressions of appreciation from his parents. They were endlessly preoccupied with his siblings and the crises they precipitated. He argued that the older brother was really taken for granted, was not appreciated, and that the father had no right to forgive the younger son and bring him back into the family.[131]

It's not difficult to see what has occurred. The parishioner rounded out the characters by reading himself and his family into the parable. He rounded off the older son with his own autobiography and rounded off the younger son with his experiences of irresponsible and manipulative siblings, causing him to see the younger son as a classic manipulator and leading Juel to do the same. Levine, a Jewish New Testament scholar, also rounds out the younger son as "an irresponsible, self-indulgent, and probably indulged child, whom" she quips, "I would not, despite his being Jewish, be pleased to have my daughter date."[132]

These contemporary readers take the line sketch given of the younger son and color in repulsive traits. As for the possibility that this bad actor repented, the younger son doesn't seem to them to show genuine repentance. I am not sure what truly repentant people are supposed to do—weep remorsefully through the night maybe, engage in a public display of self-loathing? As Mick Jagger of the Rolling Stones sings in "It's Only Rock and Roll, But I Like It,"[133] "If I could stick my pen in my heart and spill it all over the stage, would it satisfy ya?" But it is clear the prodigal doesn't measure up.

The truth is that the younger son has been overly psychoanalyzed by many contemporary readers (the older brother, by the way, is sitting in the psychiatrist's waiting room. He's next). The prodigal son is a fictitious character in a parable told by Jesus in the Gospel of Luke, but when he is placed on the psychiatric couch and interrogated, he turns for some into a whiny manipulator.

The important question, of course, is who is the prodigal *to Luke*? How does the parable on its face present him? First, he's a sinner, which he admits (15:18), and the theme of this whole section in Luke is sinners who repent. Second, a major sin in Luke's encyclopedia of sins is when people trust in themselves that they are righteous (18:9), which makes it significant that the prodigal acknowledges his unworthiness (15:19). He has decided to ask his father to receive him back into the family, but as a hired hand, not a son (15:19). Given Luke's palette, what he paints is clearly a portrait of a repentant sinner. If some contemporary interpreters see the younger son as an insincere manipulator, attribute it to Luke's strong skill to create round characters, or perhaps his failure to round out the prodigal in a way that convinces Dr. Phil.

Some of the confusion may result from the supposition that this parable is about an old-fashioned, mourners' bench, walk-the-sawdust-trail, Billy Graham revival-style "conversion story." But this is a repentance story, and there is a difference. In Hebrew, the word for repentance is *teshuvah* (תשובה), which literally means returning. God tells the prophet Jeremiah, "Have you seen what she did, that faithless one, Israel, how she went up on every high hill and under every green tree and played the whore there?" (Jer. 3:6). Then God told Jeremiah what to preach: "Return, faithless Israel, says the LORD. I will not look on you in anger, for I am merciful, says the LORD; I will not be angry forever" (Jer. 3:12). Likewise, Hosea issues a call for repentance: "Come, let us return to the LORD, for it is he who has torn, and he will heal us; he has struck down, and he will bind us up. After two days he will revive us; on the third day he will raise us up, that we may live before him" (Hos. 6:1–2).

This returning to God is a matter of the heart, of course, but repentance is manifested in a changed life. Repentance is like a change of citizenship, a change of location, a returning from the "distant country," from the idolatrous ways of other peoples, to the ways of God. In the Old Testament, repentance, writes Joseph P. Healey "is defined by clear actions that lead to justice, mercy, and fidelity."[134]

Luke continues this theme of repentance as a returning to the ways of God. "Bear fruits worthy of repentance," thunders John the Baptist (3:8). Peter preached to the people at Solomon's Porch in the temple: "Change your hearts and lives! Turn back to God so that your sins may be wiped away" (Acts 3:19 CEB), and Paul attempted to explain the substance of his whole ministry by saying that he "declared first to those in Damascus, then in Jerusalem and throughout the countryside of Judea, and also to the Gentiles, that they should repent and turn to God and do deeds consistent with repentance" (Acts 26:20).

So far, the Parable of the Prodigal Son has depicted two places: the home of the father and the distant country. The younger son left the first and went to the second, which meant not just a change of residence but a change in how he lived. His repentance was an act of returning, of being restored to the family of his father, which in theological terms is the family of God.

More Joy in Heaven

The younger son sets off for home, but when his father sees him coming, he doesn't wait with arms folded for him to arrive at the doorstep. "[W]hile he was still far off, his father saw him and was filled with compassion; he ran and put his arms around him and kissed him" (Luke 15:20).[135]

This scene is packed with significance. First, the word for "far" is *makran* (μακρὰν) and related terms appear several times in Luke and Acts. In the Parable of the Pharisee and the Tax Collector, the tax collector stands "far off" (*makrothen*) when he prays "God be merciful to me a sinner" (18:13). Peter, on the brink of betraying Jesus, is described as following Jesus from afar (22:54, *makrothen*). The followers of Jesus watch him being crucified "at a distance" (23:49, *makrothen*). Most significantly, when Peter has finished his sermon at Pentecost by calling on the people to "repent and be baptized" (Acts 2:38), Peter then adds that the promise of God "is for you, for your children, and for all who are far away [*makran*], everyone whom the Lord our God calls to him" (Acts 2:39). For Luke, humanity is at a great distance, "far off," from God, and Luke's story is about sinners who do an about-face and return, but even more about a God who, like the father in the parable, runs toward humanity to close the gap, to forgive and to save.

Second, the parable includes the Lukan pattern of seeing and having compassion. In the town of Nain, when Jesus encountered a widow whose only son had just died, he saw her and had compassion (Luke 7:13), and when the good Samaritan came upon the wounded man on the road, he saw him and was moved with compassion (10:33). Now the father of the prodigal shows how heaven responds to sinners who return. He saw his son while he was still far away and was filled, not with rage or resentment, but with compassion (15:20).

Finally, there is the father's embrace and kiss, in Greek literally "fell on his neck and kissed him" (15:20). The scene is reminiscent of two events in Genesis: the reconciliation of Jacob and Esau, where "Esau ran to meet [Jacob], and fell on his neck, and kissed him, and they wept" (Gen. 33:4) and the reconciliation of Joseph and his brothers, where Joseph "fell upon his brother Benjamin's neck" and "kissed all of his brothers and wept upon them" (Gen. 45:14–15). The embrace and the kiss of the prodigal's father symbolize forgiveness and reconciliation.

The parables of the Lost Sheep and the Lost Coin, which precede the Prodigal Son, both emphasize the great joy in heaven "over one sinner who repents." Now in this parable the sinner is home and the rejoicing begins. The younger son cannot even finish the speech he prepared before the father has lavished gifts on him—the best robe, a ring, sandals—all signs of honor. The father calls for a festive meal featuring "the fatted calf," which, in Greek, is literally "the grain-fed calf." As Johnson points out, "In contrast to the cattle left to graze on grass, the beast designed for special feasts is stuffed with grain to put on extra weight and tenderness."[136] When he was starving in the distant country, "no one gave him anything" (15:16), but now his father "gives him everything."[137]

The father makes a declaration to his household that expresses the theological core of this parable: "Let us eat and celebrate, for this son of mine was dead and is alive again; he was lost and is found!" (15:23). The "lost and . . . found" language connects this parable with the Lost Sheep and the Lost Coin. All three are parables of joy over the repentance of sinners. We hear also echoes of Luke's understanding of the church, a community of redeemed sinners, saved by Jesus, turning from the ways of death to the ways of life in the power of the resurrection, eating together "with glad and generous hearts" (Acts 2:46), the Lord "adding to their number those . . . being saved" (Acts 2:47).

The Parable's Third Location

So far, the parable has described two places: the distant country where the younger son hit bottom and the house of the father, which is now filled with music and dancing (Luke 15:25) because the son who was lost has returned and is now found. But there is a third place depicted in the parable: the field (15:25). As the plot of the parable develops, it too becomes a "distant country," even though it is walking distance from the house. It too is a place of contrast to the joyful celebration unfolding inside. Out in the field is the older brother. We met him in the first sentence of the parable, but only now does he reenter the drama.

Drawing close to the house, he hears the sound of celebration coming from within. He summons a servant to find out what's happening, and he receives the news: "'Your brother has come, and your father has killed the fatted calf because he has got him back safe and sound'" (15:27). This makes the older brother angry, and he refuses to go into the celebration in the house.

In a touching scene, the father, who had run out to meet the younger son, now goes out to his other son. The NRSV says that the father "began to plead with him" to come into the celebration, which is accurate enough. But it is worth noting that the word rendered "plead," *parekalei* (παρεκάλει), carries the sense of comforting and encouragement. This is an appeal by a loving, comforting father, not a harangue. The father's pleading, however, runs into a buzz saw,[138] as the older son explodes with a litany of complaints: "Listen! For all these years I have been working like a slave for you, and I have never disobeyed your command, yet you have never given me even a young goat so that I might celebrate with my friends. But when this son of yours came back, who has devoured your assets with prostitutes, you killed the fatted calf for him!"

At this point, we have, of course, come back around to how this all started. This necklace of three repentance parables in Luke was stimulated by the grumbling of the Pharisees and the scribes, who complained of Jesus, "This fellow welcomes sinners and eats with them" (15:2). And here we are in this parable, a sinner welcomed home by the father and a feast under way, complete with fatted calf, music, and dancing. The older son is physically, emotionally, and theologically separated, grumbling angrily to his father that you have welcomed this sinner and are now eating with him.

The customary interpretation of the older son and his angry speech is sharply negative. He has broken with his father, not even able to address him as "Father," but just with a disrespectful, "Listen!" He describes his relation to the father as slavery, and he has nothing but contempt for his brother ("this son of *yours*"). He's a self-righteous little jerk and a prickly rule-keeper ("I have never disobeyed your command").

There is, however, another way to understand this older son and his speech. The NRSV has the older son say, "I have been working like a slave for you," as if the word "slave" were a noun. But in Greek it's actually a verb, *douleuō* (δουλεύω), which, as Garland notes, is "the verb used in Acts 20:19 to refer to Paul's humble service to the gospel."[139] When we listen to Paul's speech to the elders of the church at Ephesus, we can perhaps hear echoes of the older son's speech: "You yourselves know how I lived among you the entire time from the first day that I set foot in Asia, serving [*douleuōn* , δουλεύων] the Lord with all humility and with tears, enduring the trials that came to me. . . . I did not shrink from doing anything helpful" (Acts 20:18–20). It's all there in what the older son says too, which could be paraphrased as, "I've been living here the whole time, serving you and never shrinking from doing what is helpful."

Karl Rengstorf states that in the Septuagint *douleuein,* which is a form of our verb *douleuō,* "is the most common term for the service of God . . . [in the sense of] total commitment to the Godhead."[140] It seems likely that the parable does not present the older brother as a self-righteous prude worthy of contempt, but instead as a son of the commandments, one who faithfully serves the father and one who is shocked and angered by this latest development in the life of the family.

Soon in Luke's Gospel, Jesus will meet another man, a rich ruler, who says that he has never disobeyed the commandments, that he has kept them all "since my youth" (Luke 18:21). Jesus tells him, "There is still one thing lacking" (18:22). Just so, there is still "one thing lacking" for this older son as well, a lack that keeps him outside the house, paralyzes him in his own "distant country," separated from the feast, the music, the dancing, and, most of all, from his brother, from his family. What the older son lacks is a religious worldview that makes room for the possibility that God might have joy over repentant sinners as well as joy over keepers of the commandments. To be even more theological, what he lacks is an understanding that God not only honors the children of Abraham who stay home in the house of God, faithfully keeping the commandments, but also rejoices over the sinner who repents and comes home from the far country. As Jesus will soon say about another repentant sinner, Zacchaeus, "He, too, is a son of Abraham. For the Son of Man came to seek out and to save the lost" (19:9–10).

The father's next words to the older son are tender. He addresses him as *Teknon* (Τέκνον), an affectionate term meaning "child," the same word Mary used to address the twelve-year-old Jesus (2:48). "Son [Child], you are always with me, and all that is mine is yours" (15:32). Some interpret this statement in light of the inheritance laws, but that misses the point. The father is not merely reassuring his older son that his property rights are intact. Rather he is assuring him that he is fully his son and that he shares completely in his life. Theologically, the parable is saying that he is still a son of Abraham, a child of God, in the family.

We noted that the theological core of this parable was already stated by the father when he began the celebration of the younger son's return: "Let us eat and celebrate, for this son of mine was dead and is alive again; he was lost and is found!" (15:23). In the parable's final words, the father reiterates this theme, that the celebration now underway is happening "because this brother of yours was dead and has come to life; he was lost and has been found" (15:32).

But two elements have been added to the earlier announcement. First, "this son of mine" has now become "this brother of yours," which is not just a biological fact but an eschatological hope. The love of God and the gospel proclaimed by Jesus offer the hope that all humanity will become sisters and brothers, children of the one God.

The second addition is that the father's statement employs one of Luke's favorite words, *edei* (ἔδει), meaning "necessary." It was, says the father to the older son, necessary "to celebrate and rejoice" (15:32), not just a nice thing to do, but *necessary*. Luke uses this term throughout his Gospel and Acts to describe events that are not just happenstance but are fulfillments of God's saving purpose.[141] Jesus stays at Zacchaeus's house, not merely because he wants a pleasant visit, but because it was necessary to do so (19:5), and the risen Jesus tells the travelers on the Emmaus road that it was "necessary that the Messiah should suffer these things and enter into his glory" (24:26). Here it was necessary to celebrate and rejoice when a sinner repents. Celebrating over the return of sinners is what all heaven does (15:7), it's what the angels do (15:10), and because God is who God is, it is also what God does. It isn't mere chance, it's necessary, because rejoicing over sinners who come home lies at the very heart of God. "With Easter," Moltmann said, "[begins] the laughter of the redeemed, the dance of the liberated."[142]

So the parable ends, but it doesn't really end. The stage goes dark with the father still outside the house, pleading with the older son to come inside, to join in the celebration. The open-endedness of the parable signals that this appeal is still going on. This is the appeal that Jesus made to the Pharisees and scribes who are grumbling over his welcome to sinners (15:2), it is the appeal that the risen Jesus tells the disciples that they will make: repentance and forgiveness of sins is to be proclaimed in his name to all nations, beginning from Jerusalem. You are witnesses of these things (24:47–48), and it is the invitation given by the church in Acts and by the church ever since: there is joy in the house of God. Leave the distant country, wherever that may be, come home, enter into the celebration of all heaven and the joy of God.

Like the Parable of the Prodigal Son, Arthur Miller's play *The Price* is about two brothers. One of the brothers, Walter, walked out on his family to focus on his own success. He got an education, became a famous physician, but then had an emotional breakdown. The other brother, Victor, is a policeman, a man who sacrificed his chance to get an education in order to stay at home and care for his father. After their father's death, the two brothers, who haven't communicated in years, meet in the attic of their father's home to make decisions about what will happen to their late father's possessions. Victor's wife Esther is there too to help out. But things go badly, and the brothers quickly descend into their old pattern of anger and recrimination. When Walter abruptly leaves, Esther says to Victor,

> I was nineteen years old when I first walked up those stairs—if that's believable. And he had a brother, who was the cleverest, most wonderful young doctor . . . in the world. . . . So many times I thought—the one thing he wanted most was to talk to his brother, and that if they could— But he's come and he's gone. And I still feel it—isn't that terrible? It always seems to me that one little step more and some crazy kind of forgiveness will come and lift up everyone. When do you stop being so . . . foolish?[143]

The parable proclaims just such "foolishness," that "some crazy kind of forgiveness" has indeed come and now offers to lift up everyone.

The Parable of the Prodigal Son swings for the fences. It pictures a God so loving and merciful that God goes out of the house in two directions: to welcome those whose ruined lives have generated self-loathing and to welcome those whose lives of obedience have generated other loathing. There is joy, music, and dancing inside God's house for both sons, for all sons and daughters who respond to God's beckoning, "Come home."

United Church of Christ minister Matt Fitzgerald serves a church near the Moody Bible Institute in Chicago. In 2017, the president of Moody signed the "Nashville Statement," a document that proclaims "it is sinful to approve of homosexual immorality or transgenderism and that such approval constitutes an essential departure from Christian faithfulness and witness." The statement goes on to insist that this view is the unambiguous Christian position and not one "about which otherwise faithful Christians should agree to disagree."[144]

Fitzgerald and some others organized a protest in front of the Moody president's office, and about fifty protestors showed up. They preached, prayed, sang hymns about Jesus, and carried signs with messages like "God made me gay" and "Moody, Repent of Your Homophobia!"

But even though he had helped put the protest together, Fitzgerald was not entirely at ease. "I've always been suspicious," he wrote, "of the self-righteous warmth protesting fuels. I felt out of place and I thought, 'What am I doing here?'"[145]

That feeling intensified when a young man "with a confused look on his face" approached Fitzgerald and asked him, "What are you doing here?" Fitzgerald started to explain, but the young man interrupted him: "I'm gay.

I graduated from Moody three years ago." I asked him if he was out as a student. He said, "No! Of course not. I came out at my graduation party and moved to California the next morning. I haven't been back since. But for some reason I decided to walk past the school today. And I see . . . this." He broke into a gigantic smile. "The *timing* is amazing. This is *amazing*."

Thinking later about what happened, Fitzgerald recognized the presence of a God whose mercy radiates out 360 degrees, whose compassion goes out every door of God's house in every direction toward humanity, calling all to the joyful feast inside. He said, "I might not have known why we organized that protest, but God knew. That young man might not have understood why he felt compelled to walk past his old school that afternoon, but God knew. The authors of the Nashville statement may never know what real church looks like, but God knows. Christ's hand is on them as well. I pray it turns them toward the light."

THE PARABLE OF THE UNJUST STEWARD (LUKE 16:1–8)

This parable is the third of the five Lukan parables that can be described as "what in the world am I going to do?" parables.[146] In each of these parables, a character gets thrown into a midlife crisis and wonders, usually in a soliloquy, how to get out of the mess. This is the murkiest of the four, and in fact is perhaps the most difficult of all of Jesus' parables to understand. Not only have many preachers foundered on its treacherous shoals; it is both amusing and discouraging to prowl through the academic history of interpretation of this text and to count the hermeneutical shipwrecks.

The interpretive problems with this parable tend to cluster around three thorny questions:[147]

The Moral Question

The challenge here is that the hero of this parable is a crafty, small-time crook. Fired by his master for mismanagement, he runs to his master's creditors and allows them to falsify their indebtedness in order to ingratiate himself to them. Sure, he proves himself resourceful when the pistol was cocked against his head, but, as Crossan said, "one has a picture of laziness organizing itself under crisis."[148]

Some interpreters, rattled by this perverse "when good things happen to bad people" story, have gone to great lengths to argue that at the end of the day the unjust steward was not really all that unjust. This is often accomplished either through the culturally biased argument that shady deals are routine in the Middle East, so the steward was only doing business as usual,[149] or by suggesting that, when the steward ordered the creditors to mark down their bills, he was finally doing the right thing by trimming away his own inflated share of the profits. Such attempts to clean up the reputation of the steward have to reckon with the fact that the parable itself calls the man "dishonest" (16:8), employing the same Greek word, *adikias* (ἀδικίας), that is translated "evildoers" in Luke 13:27.

The Closure Questions

There are two questions of closure: *where* does the parable end and *how* does the parable end?

As to where the parable ends, the question hinges on the identity of the speaker in 16:8a, which reads, "And his master commended the dishonest manager because he had acted shrewdly." Which master? The phrase translated "master" is *ho kyrios* (ὁ κύριος), which can also be translated "the Lord." If the master who speaks here is the rich man who was the employer of the steward, and he is the one who is impressed by the steward's shrewdness, then we are still inside the parable proper. However, if it is "the Lord," that is Jesus, who is speaking, then the parable proper ends at 16:7 and Jesus himself, standing outside the parable, is commending the con artist.

Technical arguments can be (and have been) mounted for both views, but when the dust settles, there is little reason to think *ho kyrios* here refers to Jesus. The most persuasive point is in many ways the most obvious: strictly on literary grounds, if the parable ends at 16:7, it's a poor ending, abrupt and unsatisfying. Read only 16:1–7 to a class of third-graders, and they will surely say, "Huh? Then what happened?"

As to the how of the ending, if the parable proper concludes with 16:8a, then Jesus seems to keep on talking about the parable, spinning out a series of moral lessons. The first (16:8b–9) compares the shrewdness of "the children of this age" with that of "the children of light," and calls upon the hearers to "make friends for yourselves by means of dishonest wealth." The second (16:10–12) is a statement about being faithful with "dishonest wealth." The third (16:13) is a saying about the impossibility of serving both God and wealth.

Many interpreters are puzzled not only by the sheer number of statements appended to the parable but also that they seem to be non sequiturs. They are all about wealth, but other than that, are they connected in any way? C. H. Dodd thought not, saying, "We can almost see here notes for the three separate sermons on the parable as text."[150] Fitzmyer agrees, arguing that the early church attached three different sayings of Jesus to this parable, reflecting the multiple ways the church employed this parable as a moral story in different settings.[151] David Buttrick is more negative, claiming that the early church was as befuddled by this parable as contemporary interpreters, and 16:8b–13 simply reflects "later attempts to find a redeeming message in the story."[152]

The Meaning Question

The most vexing question about this parable is finally what to make of it as a kingdom parable. Is there any way to understand this parable as somehow fitting into what we know about Jesus and his proclamation of the kingdom in Luke?

One interpreter, Dan Via, basically throws up his hands and admits that this parable is irretrievably odd, that it doesn't fit; but, ironically, that is the point. This is Jesus telling a picaresque story about a rascal, a rare joke told for comic relief in the midst of the otherwise serious business of proclaiming the kingdom. For Via the most profound theological insight of this parable may be "that our well-being does not rest ultimately on our dead seriousness."[153] In other words, the moral of this weird parable is "lighten up."

While being grateful for Via's insight that the Unjust Steward is an example of the picaresque folk genre, I find it nevertheless quite unlikely that Jesus would have told a story with no other purpose than to give a cheery jostle to the theological ribs or that Luke would have included such a story in an otherwise serious section of his Gospel about wealth.

Another intriguing approach was proposed by Kenneth Bailey[154] (an approach followed in part by Donahue).[155] Correctly noting the many literary parallels between the Parable of the Unjust Steward and the Parable of the Prodigal Son, Bailey sees the Unjust Steward making a similar theological point. In the Prodigal Son the son's life is thrown into crisis as a result of his foolish, wasteful behavior. In a soliloquy the son decides to throw himself on the mercy of his father, a mercy that proves, likes God's mercy, trustworthy in the end.

In the Unjust Steward, Bailey argues, this pattern is repeated. Through his own fault, the steward's life is plunged into crisis. In a soliloquy he too decides what to do: he will go to his master's creditors and tell them to trim their bills. Bailey claims that this action is tantamount to throwing himself on his master's mercy because of what will inevitably happen next. The astounded creditors, thinking that this was the master's idea, will immediately begin celebrating in the village, singing the praises of their master, who is "the most noble and most generous man that ever rented land in their district."[156] With these cheers ringing in his ears, the master now has a decision of his own to make. Does he run down to the village shouting that the steward is a crook and this whole discount plan was a fraud, thus turning the villagers' hosannas into disappointed curses? Or does he remain silent, accepting the accolades being showered on him by the creditors? The rich man would certainly choose the latter, of course. If the creditors think he is unbelievably generous, then so be it; he will play the part and act generously. As Bailey says, "In a backhanded way the actions of the steward are a compliment to the master. The steward knew the master was generous and merciful. He risked everything on this aspect of his master's nature. He won. Because the master was indeed generous and merciful, he chose to pay the full price for his steward's salvation."[157]

So, in Bailey's version, at the close of the parable the master is revealed to be merciful and the steward is shown to be a wise and decisive man. When the steward gets praised at the end of the story, Bailey says, "He is praised for his wisdom in knowing where his salvation lay, not for his dishonesty."[158]

Bailey's "solution" to the parable has been enormously attractive to many preachers. It solves the moral problem entirely—everybody turns out to be good in the end and it enables the preacher to hit the theological nail of the Prodigal Son yet again, assuring their congregations that we have a generous and loving God who takes on the full price for our redemption.

Bailey's view, however, is a bridge too far literarily and theologically. The main problem is that the actual parable as it appears in Luke is strained to the breaking point. Bailey's interpretation depends upon a festive celebration of the master's generosity breaking out among the debtors, but the parable mentions no such moment. Bailey describes a crucial inner debate on the part of the master over whether to unmask the manager's fraud or to accept the praise of the grateful creditors. But even though the parable does include an inner debate on the part of the steward, there is no mention of one by the master.

Such omissions are no problem for Bailey, since much of his interpretation depends upon his own experience as a teacher in the Middle East and his assessment of how this story would have been heard by Middle Eastern peasants. They would have guessed these events intuitively, Bailey assumes, and supplied the missing details in their imaginations. While it is true that almost all narratives have gaps—things unsaid, subtle winks to the context that say, "You know what this means"—would the central turning point of the narrative be elided as Bailey proposes? I think not. If it were, then we do not really have a parable in Luke at all, just a set of prompts to stimulate responses by listeners already in the know.

A Story of Wealth and Shrewdness

The Parable of the Unjust Steward has been a Sargasso Sea for interpreters. However, I believe that viewing the parable in its Lukan context and allowing it and the statements attached to it to unfold in sequence brings clarity and the possibility of hearing a kingdom word in it.

Understanding this parable begins by taking seriously its first words: "there was a rich man who had a manager" (16:1). For Luke, "rich" is by no means a neutral term. God has "sent the rich away empty," sings Mary (1:53). Jesus proclaims "good news to the poor" (4:18) and "woe to you who are rich" (6:24). Whenever a person appears in Luke who is specifically called "rich," the chances are excellent this is one who lives outside the sphere of the kingdom of God. "How hard it is," Jesus said, "for those who have wealth to enter the kingdom of God!" (18:24). So when this parable begins as the story of a "rich man," we aren't merely being introduced to a character; we are being invited to enter his world, a world alien to the kingdom.

The rich man has a manager, a man who works in the same environment of wealth and is responsible to it and for it. Luke's readers know that this world of wealth is passing away in light of the irruption of the kingdom of God. God is turning the world upside down and reversing its values. The rich fool encountered earlier in Luke deceived himself into thinking that his wealth gave his world permanence: "And I will say to my soul, Soul, you have ample goods laid up for many years; relax, eat, drink, be merry" (12:19). It is this statement, of course, that causes heaven to thunder, "You fool!" (12:20). His world was ending that very night.

Eventually the kingdom of God will overturn the kingdom of the rich, and the realm of wealthy privilege will come to nothing. The rich man's manager gets a foretaste of this coming cataclysm when his little corner of that world comes crashing down. He is brought up on charges of "squandering [the rich man's] property," and he is swiftly dismissed from his position. The act of squandering property rings a bell for Luke's readers, because that is exactly the terminology employed to describe the prodigal son in the parable that appeared right before this one. The son "squandered his property in dissolute living" (15:13). In the Prodigal Son story, the father, despite the son's squandering, welcomed the profligate son home, but that is the way of God's kingdom. By contrast, in this world's kingdom of wealth, if you eat into the bottom line, you're gone.

So the manager gets fired for squandering property. Some interpreters have debated unnecessarily whether the firing is immediate or whether it takes effect at some point in the near future. The fact is we simply have a storytelling device at work to convey two realities: the man is definitely fired and in crisis, and he still has a narrow window of crisis time when he can make decisions and act meaningfully. This creates narrative suspense. The man is out, he's thrown into a crisis. What will he do about it?

This suspense is underscored by the fired manager's soliloquy. He says to himself, "What will I do, now that the master is taking the position away from me?" (16:3). His options are limited. He doesn't consider himself strong enough to do manual labor, and he is too proud to beg. But suddenly a light bulb turns on, and he knows what to do: "I have decided what to do so that, when I am dismissed as manager, people may welcome me into their homes" (16:5).

Notice that the manager is quite clear about his objective. He has decided on a course of action that will ingratiate himself to people who have resources so that they will repay him by taking him into their homes. This "I scratch your back, and you'll scratch mine" notion of reciprocity is the way Hellenistic society operates,[159] indeed the way most societies operate; it is the way of the world. But in Luke, Jesus teaches that this way is by no means God's way:

> If you love those who love you, what credit is that to you? For even sinners love those who love them. If you do good to those who do good to you, what credit is that to you? For even sinners do the same. If you lend to those from whom you hope to receive, what credit is that to you? Even sinners lend to sinners, to receive as much again. But love your enemies, do good, and lend, expecting nothing in return. Your reward will be great, and you will be children of the Most High; for he is kind to the ungrateful and the wicked. Be merciful, just as your Father is merciful. (6:32–35, see also 14:12–14)

The manager uses the bargaining power of money to make a place for himself. He goes one by one to his master's creditors and reduces their obligations. He employs a money scheme to create a future community of hospitality, so that the homes and tables of these creditors will be open to him, pulling him back from the brink of homelessness. Say what you will about the man, he makes the one move available to him that allows him to wriggle off the hook of total ruin.

There remains but one more scene, a provocative twist at the end. The rich man, now twice conned by his dishonest manager, reappears, surveys the scene, and, probably begrudgingly, hands out an accolade to his dismissed manager: "Well, I have to hand it to you, Buster. That was pretty shrewd."

At this point, the parable concludes, and Jesus begins to comment on the parable, drawing several insights from it. His first teaching from the parable is a bit of a surprise, a parabolic left hook: "For the children of this age are more shrewd in dealing with their own generation than are the children of light" (16:8). In other words, there is one way that Jesus wishes that the "children of light" were like the manager in the parable: shrewdness. The parable is populated entirely with characters who are typical "children of this age." The rich man, the dishonest manager, and even the creditors all live in the present age and play by its rules. Working as a child of that age and as a part of that system, the manager proved to be shrewdest of all by how he responded to the crisis of his world coming apart. Jesus wants a similar shrewdness from the "children of light," the citizens of the age to come.

But by naming the "children of light," Jesus rachets up the parable into a kingdom of God story. The shrewdness that kingdom people will need is not merely that of a manager whose little employment world comes apart, but the shrewdness demanded of those who know the whole present age is coming apart. The crisis at hand is not the little job crisis of the manager but the ultimate crisis precipitated by the breaking in of the kingdom of God. How does one act shrewdly when it is the entire old world that is being invaded and replaced by God's new creation? Jesus lays it out: "And I tell you, make friends for yourselves by means of dishonest wealth so that when it is gone, they may welcome you into the eternal homes" (16:9).

Now we are getting close to the heart of this parable. The goal for God's people is a kingdom-oriented shrewdness, a shrewdness analogous to the shrewdness displayed by the manager in the parable but played out in the ways of the kingdom. The manager used dishonest wealth to make friends for himself; just so, the children of light should use dishonest wealth to create kingdom friendships. The term "dishonest wealth" in Greek is *mamōna tēs adikias* (μαμωνᾶ τῆς ἀδικίας), that is, "the mammon of unrighteousness," or better, "the money of this unrighteous age." Calling it "the money of this unrighteous age" makes it clearer that Jesus isn't merely talking about filthy lucre, drug proceeds, embezzled stock, laundered cash, and other ill-gotten gains. He's talking about money period, all of the money of this present age.

How does one use this world's money to make kingdom friends? The topic has already come up earlier in Luke. When Jesus is invited to dinner in the home of a Pharisee, he tells his host that when he gives a dinner party, he should not invite the "rich," who can easily reciprocate, but "the poor, the crippled, the lame, and the blind. And you will be blessed, because they cannot repay you, for you will be repaid at the resurrection of the righteous" (14:13–14). That earlier teaching is echoed here when Jesus instructs his followers to use the money of this world to make kingdom friends, not those who can reciprocate in this world, but those who will provide welcome in "eternal homes." The manager in the parable shrewdly made sure he had homes open to him in this world, but the children of light are to exercise a higher form of shrewdness by putting their hope in a new community in the next world, the banquet table filled in the house of God and the resurrection of the righteous in the world to come.

It is interesting to see that Jesus uses this parable not to tell his followers to avoid money but, instead, to see money for what it is in the light of God's kingdom. The money of this world, which seems so permanent and powerful, is, from a kingdom perspective, like Confederate bonds in 1862. It is the temporarily negotiable currency of a doomed and corrupted sovereignty, bound eventually to fail. The truly shrewd thing is not to use it to invest in the world that minted it—that world is passing away—but to use it now for something lasting, because it is a part of the life of God. Use the money of this unrighteous age to make kingdom friendships, so that "when it is gone," as it surely will be, what remains is eternal.

In his next comment on the parable, Jesus says, "Whoever is faithful in a very little is faithful also in much; and whoever is dishonest in a very little is dishonest also in much. If then you have not been faithful with the dishonest wealth, who will entrust to you the true riches? And if you have not been faithful with what belongs to another, who will give you what is your own?" (16:10–12).

In essence, Jesus is here continuing the theme of his first comment on the parable by saying that the way one treats money in the little theater of this present moment is reflective of the life to come. People who use money in kingdom ways now are revealed by the light of heaven to be faithful and trustworthy in the eternal life of God. The phrase "what belongs to another" is a matter of debate among interpreters, but it probably signals Luke's theology that people do not really own possessions in the sense of "This is *mine!*" Worldly possessions are but temporary trusts, and we are stewards of those trusts. Faithful trustees are then worthy of receiving treasure in heaven.

Finally, Jesus makes one last comment on the parable: "You cannot have it both ways." "No slave," Jesus says, "can serve two masters; for a slave will either hate the one and love the other or be devoted to the one and despise the other. You cannot serve God and wealth" (16:13). People are either managers of money who serve this world, or managers of money who serve the world that God is bringing in. There is no way to hedge bets and do both.

The Pharisees are, to Luke's eye, "lovers of money" (16:14), but they are fools to be so. They love what seems potent but will soon be obsolete, what is even now crumbling in their hands, and "they have their consolation" (6:24; see also 16:25). What are kingdom people to do with money? Avoid it? No. They are to do what the steward did, spend it with abandon to make kingdom friends.

Not too many years ago, the officers of a large urban church were considering a proposal to do a major remodeling of their building, including new lighting, a rebuild of their massive pipe organ, new furnishings, a significant redecoration, stonework repairs, and a roof replacement. The price tag was a staggering ten million dollars, but the remodeling was needed and long overdue, and the church had a large enough endowment to cover the cost. One of the officers, a man named George, said in the meeting that he was in favor of the proposal but that he thought they also should raise ten million dollars to build a facility to care for the large number of homeless folks who lived on the streets around the church.

Another man at the table looked at him incredulously. "Come on, George," he said. "Sure, we should do what we can for the homeless, but ten million dollars?"

"Yes," George said. "Ten million."

"No disrespect, George," said the other man, "but that's nuts!"

"You remember that woman who broke open the jar of very expensive perfume and poured it on Jesus' head?" George said. "We'll that's what we'd be doing. We need to do that."

After a long silence, a third officer raised his hand, "I vote to pour that perfume. Ten million for the homeless." One by one, the other officers raised their hands, and it was done. "And I tell you," Jesus said, "make friends for yourselves by means of the money of this world so that when it is gone, they may welcome you into the eternal homes."

THE PARABLE OF THE RICH MAN AND LAZARUS (LUKE 16:19–31)

This parable begins just like the previous one: "There was a rich man" (16:19). In effect Jesus is saying, "OK, here's yet another story about a rich guy," with all the negative connotations that the word "rich" carries in Luke (see the discussion of "rich" in the commentary on the previous parable). We ready ourselves for yet another tale of a person who displays, as the hymn puts it, "wanton, selfish gladness, rich in things and poor in soul."[160]

The parable is not only a "rich man" story. It is also a familiar trope in folklore: the story of situation reversals in the afterlife. There are numerous examples in many cultures (including rabbinical literature) about two people with contrasting lifestyles in this world, who die and find their situations inverted in the next world. Some commentators have even pointed to this or that specific pre-Christian folktale about the afterlife and claimed that this parable is adapted from it, but the arguments are inconclusive. This story is more like common and familiar tales today that begin "So a man dies on the golf course and finds himself standing before St. Peter at the pearly gates." There are a thousand such afterlife stories, and the Lukan Jesus is telling one more—perhaps original, perhaps borrowed.

Although it is a somewhat arbitrary division to make, the parable can perhaps best be analyzed by dividing it into a sequence of three scenes:

Scene One: Fine Linen and Desperate Hunger

Scene one takes place in the present world, where we are introduced to two starkly contrasting characters. The first is a "rich man," and with just a few deft strokes, the parable paints a revealing picture of this man. He is "dressed in purple and fine linen," and "he feasted sumptuously every day" (16:19). We should remember that we are in story world here, and the purpose of this description of the rich man is not subtle but overdrawn to magnify his wealthy status. It would be as if a story today began, "So, there was this rich man. How rich was he? He was so rich he wore only Armani suits, even to play tennis, and he had caviar and Dom Perignon champagne every day for a snack." His purple outer clothing is suggestive of royalty and wealth,[161] and even his undergarments add to his gilded image. They are made of "fine linen," the word for which is *bysson* (βύσσον), meaning both a kind of Egyptian flax and the linen cloth made from it. Garland states that *bysson* was "the most expensive fabric known to the ancient world."[162]

Then there was the man's table. Most people living in Jesus' day lived on a modest diet, feasting only on very special occasions, if ever. This rich man feasts every single day. Gildas Hamel reports that stories are told about King Agrippa II, before whom Paul appeared in Acts 25–26, that he ate only one meal a day, but it was of legendary proportions, with numerous side dishes and desserts brought out one by one to prolong the indulgent feast.[163] The rich man in this parable is described as living like a king, literally.

The word the NRSV translates as "feasted," *euphrainomenos* (εὐφραινόμενος), means "celebrating" or "making merry," and it is an important theme in Luke's parables. Variations of this word are used in Luke to describe two very different kinds of feast. They are employed four times in the Parable of the Prodigal Son (15:23, 24, 29, 32) to describe the very special celebration fitting to mark the return of the younger son (and the celebration the older brother resents not having). It also appears once in the Parable of the Rich Fool (12:19), closer in meaning to the present parable, to describe the nonstop indulgent merrymaking the rich man of that story naively believes will be his perpetual lifestyle.

Contrasted to this first man is a desperately poor man at the gate of the rich man's house (16:20). The NRSV says that he "lay" at the gate, but the Greek is the pluperfect passive *ebeblētо* (ἐβέβλητο), "had been laid," perhaps implying that the man had been placed at the gate by others. Sometimes a passive form of this word is used to describe someone who is crippled or bedridden.[164] Regardless of how this term is translated, though, the poor man is pictured as vulnerable.

His name is Lazarus, the Greek form of the Hebrew name Eliezer, which means "God has helped." None of Jesus' parables has named characters, except this one,[165] which has two named characters: Lazarus and Abraham (we will discuss the possible significance of this naming below). Lazarus is sickly, "covered with sores," and "even the dogs would come and lick his sores" (16:21). What to make of these licking dogs? Levine sees them positively, citing a second-century Greek story about a dog licking a wound to heal it, part of her argument that "the dogs provided [Lazarus] his only comfort."[166] But this is unlikely. The parable is staking out a sharp contrast between the rich man and the poor man, a portrait of unbridled luxury on the one hand and desperate need on the other. A tender picture of the dogs around Lazarus comforting him is almost surely not what is intended but, instead, scruffy street curs licking Lazarus, dogs like vultures circling the poor and vulnerable man.

Lazarus, the parable says, "longed to satisfy his hunger" with the rich man's table scraps (16:21), and the words "longed to satisfy his hunger," *epithymōn chortasthēnai* (ἐπιθυμῶν χορτασθῆναι), constitute the very same Greek phrase used to describe the prodigal son at his low point, when he would gladly have eaten his fill of pig food (15:16).

No sooner have we been introduced to these two contrasting characters than they both die. Opposites in life, they become opposites in death as well. The poor man, unexpectedly, makes a beautiful and dramatic departure from this world, carried by God's angels "to be with Abraham" (16:22). The Greek actually says, "to the bosom [or lap] of Abraham," a term conveying intimacy and "signifying the abode of bliss in the other world."[167] The poor man, who probably never once in his life was invited inside the home of a rich man, is now taken to the home of God by an angelic escort. As for the rich man, the parable simply reports that he "was buried" (16:22). Then, without missing a beat, the parable has him show up in Hades (16:23).

Scene Two: Bad News from Father Abraham

In scene one, we saw two men, the rich man and Lazarus, who lived only a few feet apart from each other but who were in completely different worlds. Now in scene two, the two men are literally in different worlds.

The rich man is in the nether world of Hades, the Greek term for the realm of the dead. Some commentators equate Hades here with Sheol, the Jewish land of the dead, but the Hades in this parable seems more to be a folkloric creation designed to form a terrifying contrast with the heavenly abode, where Lazarus is in Abraham's bosom. Lazarus is in a very different place, in a place of honor now, comforted (16:25), while the rich man is in a place of fiery torment (16:23–24).

Out of his anguish, the rich man looks up toward the heavenly world and sees Abraham with Lazarus at his side. He recognizes that he is not there with them but cast down into a place of anguish. Readers of Luke will remember that Jesus, speaking earlier to the crowd of people following him as he traveled, warned that this viewing of the kingdom from the outside was sure to happen:

> "Strive to enter through the narrow door; for many, I tell you, will try to enter and will not be able. When once the owner of the house has got up and shut the door, and you begin to stand outside and to knock at the door, saying, 'Lord, open to us,' then in reply he will say to you, 'I do not know where you come from.' Then you will begin to say, 'We ate and drank with you, and you taught in our streets.' But he will say, 'I do not know where you come from; go away from me, all you evildoers!' There will be weeping and gnashing of teeth when you see Abraham and Isaac and Jacob and all the prophets in the kingdom of God, and you yourselves thrown out. Then people will come from east and west, from north and south, and will eat in the kingdom of God. Indeed, some are last who will be first, and some are first who will be last." (13:24–30)

This anguished eschatological scene is being replicated in the parable. The rich man appeals across the vast gap to Abraham, "Father Abraham, have mercy on me, and send Lazarus to dip the tip of his finger in water and cool my tongue; for I am in agony in these flames" (16:24). Some hear these words of the rich man as presumptuous and condescending. They view him as trying still to play the insider "Father Abraham" card, still trying to pull rank and get waited on by poor Lazarus. But probably his words are less about presumption and condescension and more a sign of desperation and irony. The man who showed no mercy to a suffering poor man on his front porch now begs for mercy in his own time of suffering.[168]

Abraham replies to the rich man and begins with a term of intimacy, "Child" (16:25). This term, *teknon* (τέκνον), is the same word of affection used by the father of the prodigal son to address his angry older son (15:31) and by Mary to speak to the twelve-year-old Jesus when she and Joseph lost track of their son on a Passover trip to Jerusalem (2:48). The rich man is still a child of Abraham, but the bad news is that it is now too late to be gathered with the family. "A great chasm has been fixed" between the heavenly places and the rich man, Abraham tells him, and "those who might want to pass from here to you cannot do so, and no one can cross from there to us" (16:26).

As Jesus warned, the door is now shut, the chasm yawns, vast and unbridgeable. The rich man now sees the situation, but it's too late. He chose to receive his consolation in this world, but now that world has ended, and it is the poor man Lazarus who is consoled (16:25). Jesus spoke prophetically about this, too, when he preached, "Blessed are you who are poor, for yours is the kingdom of God. . . . But woe to you who are rich, for you have received your consolation" (6:20, 24).

Scene Three: Plea Bargaining

We have seen that many of Luke's parables are about crises that happen to people in the middle of life. A manager plays loose with his boss's portfolio and loses his job, a young man blows through his inheritance and ends up feeding pigs and starving, a wealthy farmer ends up with more crop than his present barns can store, a corrupt judge has an insistent and annoying woman in his court demanding justice. These crises come when there is still time to act and decide, to be righteous and faithful with the things of this life . . . or not. These parables are vignettes showing in small ways what Jesus is causing to happen in the largest possible way. He is the prophet who brings a crisis to the whole world in the middle of things. The breaking in of the kingdom is a call to repent, an opportunity to turn away from the old world and to turn toward God's kingdom. There is still time to act and to decide, to choose this day whom you will serve (see Josh. 24:15).

But this parable is about a midlife crisis that led to paralysis, not decisive action. In scene one of this parable, we watched a rich man miss his chance to act. The crisis came in the form of an impoverished and hungry man at his gate. The rich man is a child of Abraham, and he has the Scripture, Moses, and the prophets to guide him. He knows what to do, but the rich man chose self-indulgence over mercy. In scene two, he is pushed hard up against the reality that time has now run out for him.

However, he has five brothers, still living, so he engages in some special pleading for them. He begs Father Abraham to send Lazarus to his brothers to warn them before it's too late for them as well, "so that they will not also come into this place of torment." Abraham's reply is telling: "They have Moses and the prophets; they should listen to them" (16:29). In other words, any child of Abraham who pays attention to the Law and the prophets would already know about the responsibility to care for the poor and the weak. It's all there in Scripture. The encouragement to "listen to them" implies both hearing and obeying, listening to the Scriptures and also taking them to heart. Jesus said as much earlier in Luke, when a woman attempted to flatter him by saying, in essence, "Your mother is certainly blessed to have a son as wonderful as you!" Jesus countered by saying, "Blessed rather are those who hear the word of God and obey it!" (11:27–28). Father Abraham is saying to the rich man, "Your brothers already have the invitation to hear and obey the Torah and the prophets; they should do so."

The rich man, however, does not consider Moses and the prophets to be sufficiently persuasive to change his brothers. "No, father Abraham," the rich man continues to plead, "but if someone goes to them from the dead, they will repent" (16:30). Interestingly, the man's use of the word "repent" shows that he gets the true issue at hand. This is down deep a repentance story, not merely a folktale, one of many, where everyone's status is automatically reversed in the afterlife.

Abraham, though, will have nothing to do with this line of reasoning: "If they do not listen to Moses and the prophets, neither will they be convinced even if someone rises from the dead" (16:31).

This closing scene with its reference to rising from the dead can be understood at several levels. First, it can be a rather matter-of-fact and realistic statement about the likelihood of repentance. As A. M. Hunter said of this parable, "If a [person] cannot be humane with the Old Testament in his hand and Lazarus on his doorstep, nothing—neither a visitant from the other world nor a revelation of the horrors of Hell—will teach him otherwise."[169] After all, some accounts indicate that Herod thought Jesus was John the Baptist come back from the dead (Matt. 14:1–2), and that didn't prompt Herod to run down the aisle to the altar and fall on his knees in repentance.

At a second level, though, this closing scene is almost surely christological. Luke's community knows that one person did, in fact, rise from the dead, namely, Jesus himself, and the world did not suddenly repent. Luke's readers may even smile knowingly at the irony of Abraham telling the rich man that even a resurrected messenger wouldn't change his brothers' hearts.

At a third and more complex level, this section may show the work of Luke's editorial hand to anticipate the story of the church that will be told in Acts. The vocabulary of this scene is suggestive. The rich man wants Lazarus to "warn" his brothers, as the NRSV has it, but the verb is *diamartyrētai* (διαμαρτύρηται), which means "thoroughly witness," and variants of that term are used throughout Acts to describe the testimony of Peter, John, and Paul (Acts 2:40; 8:25; 10:42; 18:5; 20:21; 20:24; 28:23). Abraham said that the brothers would not be "convinced" or "persuaded," *peisthēsontai* (πεισθήσονται), even if someone were to rise from the dead. Variants of that same Greek word are used several times in Acts to describe the effects of the missionary preaching. Sometimes people were "convinced," sometimes not (see Acts 13:43; 17:4; 18:4; 19:8; 19:26; 26:28; 28:23; and 28:24). Of course, the message of the missionaries in Acts was "this Jesus God raised up, and of that all of us are witnesses" (Acts 2:32). The closing scene in this parable is not a strict allegory of the missionary work in Acts, but it does rhyme.

What's in a Name?

We noted above that this is the only parable of Jesus where characters are named, and they are, of course, Lazarus and Abraham. This is both odd and possibly significant. Before looking at what may be afoot in these names, we need first to say what is not true.

The Lazarus in this parable is not the Lazarus of Bethany who, in John's Gospel, is the beloved friend of Jesus, the brother of Mary and Martha, and who was raised from the dead by Jesus (John 11–12). Nothing connects these two Lazaruses other than their name, which was a common name in Jesus' day.

The rich man does not have a name in the parable, despite several attempts early on to give him one. Some later scribes, aware that the other two main characters are named, considered the rich man's namelessness an awkward omission that should be remedied, and they supplied a name. In some manuscripts of Luke he is "Ninevah," in another manuscript he is "Phineas," and in still another he is "Amonofis."[170] In popular usage, he is called Dives. This is not a name at all, but simply the Latin word for "rich" used in the parable as it appeared in the Vulgate Bible. Calling this parable "Dives and Lazarus" got reinforced by an old English Christmas carol of the same name, and then by a twentieth-century orchestral work, "Five Variations on Dives and Lazarus," by Ralph Vaughan Williams. In the original Lukan parable, though, the rich man is nameless, period.

The fact that we have a parable that names two of its characters, Lazarus and Abraham, is such an anomaly that it leads us to pay attention to an unusual and often overlooked suggestion about why those two names are present. This suggestion was perhaps first advanced by the seventeenth-century English churchman John Lightfoot, who argued that this parable is an "Abraham and Eliezer" story, one of several such tales found told in the rabbinic haggadic tradition.

Eliezer shows up only once by name in the Old Testament. In Genesis 15:2–3, Abraham (then Abram) complains to God that he remains childless, and unless God gives him a child, Eliezer of Damascus, "a slave born in my house," will be "the heir of my house." The Hebrew of that verse is difficult, but the probable meaning is that Abram has a slave named Eliezer, maybe from Damascus, who is a high-ranking member of his household, and that Eliezer is in line to inherit Abram's property unless God gives Abram a biological heir. God reassures Abram, "This man shall not be your heir; no one but your very own issue shall be your heir" (Gen. 15:4).

That's it. There are no more mentions of Eliezer by name in the Old Testament. But that did not stop rabbis from crafting stories about him. In fact, Eliezer has a colorful profile in later midrash. To begin with, the rabbinical commentators are virtually unanimous that Abraham's "servant, the oldest of his house, who had charge of all he had" (Gen. 24:2) was none other than Eliezer, and this is the servant who was sent by Abraham to find a wife for his son Isaac (Gen. 24:1–67).[171]

They told other Abraham and Eliezer stories as well. London University New Testament Professor J. Duncan Martin Derrett, taking a cue from John

Lightfoot, found in the midrashic literature a number of stories in which Eliezer, sent by Abraham (or, on at least one occasion, by Sarah), would travel the earth in disguise "and report back to Abraham on how his children observed the Torah, especially regarding the treatment of the poor and hospitality to strangers."[172] That makes a bit of sense of the request that the rich man made to Abraham that he send Lazarus to his father's house to witness to and warn his brothers. That's just the kind of job Eliezer performs in these legends.

These Eliezer tales are fanciful, and sometimes humorous. In one midrashic story, Eliezer, roaming the earth as usual, crashes a wedding banquet in Sodom. One of the rules of wedding hospitality was that, if you invited a person to a wedding banquet and the person arrived without a proper garment, the person who did the inviting must provide a garment, even if it means giving the person one's own garment. So Eliezer, testing the hospitality in Sodom, arrives without a garment. He took his place at the end of the table, the most humble spot. The man next to him asks, "Who invited you here?" and Eliezer replies, "You did." This throws the man into a panic. If people think that he invited this guest without a garment, they will expect him to give Eliezer his own garment. So he jumps up and flees the banquet.

Eliezer then slides over to the next guest, who also asks, "Who invited you?" Eliezer gives the same response, "You did," and that guest also flees, for the same reason. Eliezer keeps moving up the line, with the same results each time. Finally, all of the inhospitable Sodomites have fled the banquet, and Eliezer has the feast all to himself.[173]

Yet another midrashic document, the *Tractate Derekh Eretz Zuta*, says that Eliezer was among the "nine who entered the Garden of Eden [i.e., the heavenly paradise] alive."[174] In the Abraham and Eliezer stories, Eliezer is sometimes accompanied and protected by angels as he travels.[175] We are not surprised, then, to find in our parable that he was carried by the angels to Abraham's bosom.

Once we realize that Lazarus is the Greek version of the Hebrew name Eliezer, this parable looks for all the world like yet another midrashic tale of Eliezer, sent by his master, Father Abraham, to test how well people show hospitality to the poor. Two realities stand in the way of this view. First, the talmudic tales that we have of Eliezer all postdate the New Testament. Would Jesus, or Luke, have known of such an Abraham and Eliezer tale? Maybe, but we lack hard evidence, Second, Lightfoot, and to some extent Derrett, take this hypothesis to looney conclusions. Lightfoot saw the poor beggar Lazarus as Eliezer, "one born in Damascus, a Gentile by birth . . . the heir of Abraham, but shut out of the inheritance by the birth of Isaac . . . yet restored here into Abraham's bosom. . . . [Might it] not hint the calling of the Gentiles into the faith of Abraham?"[176]

No, it doesn't. This parable is not a story about Gentiles being incorporated into the Abrahamic faith and certainly not a story about the Gentile going to heaven while the Jew ends up in Hades. The most we can say is that maybe this parable is a midrashic tale of Abraham and his servant Eliezer, retold and adapted by the Lukan Jesus. Claiming such a lineage for the parable would change the meaning only slightly. At the rich man's gate was a poor and hungry man, but not just that. He was also an envoy from Father Abraham, whose presence was not just a challenge to obey the commandments of God but a potential blessing for the rich man. The beggar at the rich man's gate was God's own envoy in disguise. The rich man needed Lazarus far more than Lazarus needed the rich man, but he missed it.

Open Windows

Snodgrass helpfully observes "that parables are vignettes, not systems, and certainly not systematic theologies."[177] Even though some Christian groups have tried to derive elaborate ideas about the afterlife from this parable, that is not the purpose of the story. This is a story about repentance, focused on the issue of wealth and poverty, not a guided tour of heaven and hell.

When Jesus said that he had come "to bring good news to the poor" (Luke 4:18), this was good news but it wasn't novelty. He was saying that words spoken long before by Isaiah (61:1–2) were coming to fulfillment in him and his ministry. When Jesus proclaimed that God was turning the world upside down and that it was the poor who are blessed and the rich who were to be bewailed, he was recalling the words of the prophets.

For Luke, this turning of the world is happening "today" in the event of Jesus. For those with ears to hear and eyes to see, the old world was being replaced by the kingdom of God as Jesus walked from town to village on his way to Jerusalem. The time was at hand to decide to which world one was loyal, the old and dying world or the new world that God was bringing to be. Repentance was a change of citizenship, and the time to repent is now.

Here comes this Parable of the Rich Man and Lazarus giving us a snapshot of the real world, the world as it is. The characters are exaggerated—a man rich to the point of vulgarity on the same parabolic stage with a man poor to the point of utter despair—not to make it farcical but to make the issue clear. We indeed inhabit a world where rich and poor live side by side with only a gate to divide them. For the rich, of course, this leads to complacency. "Some are well off, and some are not," they (we) say. "That's the way the cookie crumbles. The world has always been this way; always will be." The best-intentioned among the rich give generously to charity, then sit down to yet another dinner table laden with whatever delights they desire.

But Jesus does not come calling for stronger charities. He came, rather, proclaiming good news to the poor, that God was reversing the way things are, breaking into history with a new kingdom, which belongs to the poor and oppressed. So the parable pictures two men, a rich man whose world is doomed and a poor man whose promised world of hope is being born. The parable screams, "Here's your chance. The window is open. Choose your world! The time is now!"

But, of course, the rich man, who has the power to choose, chooses nothing. Why would he choose to change anything? He loves the world he has, and he has the illusion that the rich always have behind the gates: that this world can be fortified and will go on forever. "Servant, bring me another serving of chateaubriand." Therefore, the rich man, who is able to choose, chooses nothing, but the poor man, whose destitution robs him of the power to choose, instead gets chosen. The angels carry him right into the heart of God's family of blessing.

The pictures in the parable of the rich man in Hades and Lazarus in a place of blessing are folklore staples, and it would be a distortion to see in them some literalistic message like "all rich people go to Hades while all poor people go to heaven." In Luke, as we have said, the focus is not on a distant afterlife but on this life. The kingdom of God is already present and active in and through the ministry of Jesus. Jesus' message is not, "This world is an oppressive place, but one day God will arrive in a chariot and bring in a new kingdom. So let's go to the mountaintop to pray and wait." No. Jesus is preaching good news to the poor today, healing the sick today, liberating the oppressed today.

El Salvadoran theologian Jon Sobrino states that the kingdom that arrived in Jesus "is liberating since it arrives in the midst of the oppression of the anti-kingdom." He goes on to say that the kingdom of God "generates a hope that is also liberating" because it unmasks the dispiriting lie "built up in history that what triumphs in history is the anti-kingdom."[178]

The pictures of the rich man in Hades and Lazarus in a place of blessing serve, first of all, to reassure that the antikingdom does not prevail, despite having to all appearances the vast predominance of evidence on its side. The good news to the poor proclaimed by Jesus is more than mere wishful thinking; it is God's promise and can be trusted. It is the antikingdom that ends up in darkness and oblivion.

The picture of poor Lazarus at the heart of Abraham's family also issues a sharp and urgent ethical challenge about wealth and possessions. The world of indulgent wealth blind to the needs of the poor and hungry is doomed, and the time has come for the rich to repent, not out of fear, but to come to the joyous feast of justice that God is preparing. The window is open, but the time to turn around is now. Jesus has come to our village today, the music is playing, the dancing has begun, and the life of the kingdom is available now. But this is no time to hesitate, no time to try to get some Lazarus to come and preach to us one more time. It's all there in Moses and the prophets. It's all there in Jesus too. As one of those prophets, Elijah, preached, "How long will you go limping with two different opinions? If the LORD is God, follow him; but if Baal, then follow him" (1 Kgs. 18:21). This very moment is a kingdom moment, but soon the window will close, the door will be shut, a great chasm will be fixed that cannot be crossed, and we will have missed it.

When Lazarus Comes to Our Town

Where does this parable take us to see and experience the kingdom? It takes us first to those places where hope for the poor breaks through the crust. In 1993, I spent part of a sabbatical leave in South Africa. That nation was in ferment, on the brink of the transformative April 1994 election of Nelson Mandela as president and the breaking of the back of the cruel apartheid system. But the forces of resistance to these changes was energized, and violence would occasionally break out.

Late one Sunday afternoon, I was driving on a freeway into the capital city of Pretoria. My eyes ranged across Pretoria's impressive skyline, composed both of imposing government buildings and glass and steel corporate offices. Pretoria was constructed with the vast wealth generated by the country's gold and diamond mines. Pretoria was the powerful ruling seat of the apartheid regime.

I then saw an amazing sight. In a green circle of grass formed by a curved freeway exit, there was an indigenous African church at worship. There must have been fifty Christians dancing, singing, and lifting their hands in praise. They had no pipe organ or piano, only handmade drums. They had no building, just the grass of the cloverleaf. Each of them wore a makeshift robe made from flour sacks and other scraps of cloth, decorated with crosses, stars, rainbows, and angels.

It was a stunning contrast. On the one hand, there was Pretoria, the gleaming city of wealth, power, and legislative oppression. On the other side, poor Christians singing and rejoicing in the freedom and power of the Spirit. Suddenly it came to me with blazing clarity: the promises of God belong to them, the future belongs to them, not with the seemingly invincible Pretoria of glass, steel, and iron fist, but with those dancing and praising, because Jesus has said to them, "Blessed are you who are poor, for yours is the kingdom of God."

The parable also invites us to perceive the kingdom in those places where the static picture in the first part of the parable—poor Lazarus suffering on his side of the gate while the rich man indulges himself on the other side—breaks apart and a new practice emerges regarding the use of wealth and possessions.

In 1981, Luke Johnson published *Sharing Possessions*, a fine and important book about biblical ethics and material possessions. Johnson was well prepared for the task of writing this book. His PhD dissertation, completed five years earlier, had been a thorough investigation of the very same issue: possessions in Luke and Acts. But in those five years between the dissertation and the book, Johnson had experienced some dramatic life changes. "When I wrote this book," he said,

> I was in a period of difficult personal adjustment with respect to possessions. I had been a Benedictine monk living within a community of possessions. But now I was married with seven children (six of them inherited), and responsible for acquiring and disposing of possessions in a manner I had never anticipated while living as a monk. I was learning that the meaning of "being" and "having" was much more complicated than I had earlier thought.[179]

The realities of life made Johnson even more alert to the ambiguities of life and to the fact that Scripture does not provide any one inalterable model for using money and possessions, not even Luke–Acts. Instead of strict rules to act this or that way with possessions, the Bible provides instead a way of thinking about possessions and ourselves that becomes action in different ways, depending upon the circumstances. "This way of thinking begins," Johnson says,

> with an acknowledgment of our own "poverty" before God: To accept our worth from God as a gift, then, means to dwell in continual nakedness before him, in the most radical form of poverty. We stand before him always as ones who know what he knows: that our being and worth come from him alone, for by ourselves we fall into nothingness at every moment.
>
> . . . If we stand before God with the poverty that is faith, then we need not cling to any of our possessions as a means of self-definition and self-justification. The consequences of this should be clear. We can, for the first time, use things freely. We can also, for the first time, share possessions with others in a variety of ways, without being existentially threatened. But this sharing moves, not out of a desire to possess in another form, but as a gesture of freedom.[180]

The parable then exposes the nightmare existence of those who do not know that their worth comes from God alone. They are like the rich man in the story, trapped in a bubble of self-indulgence. The best reading of the parable longs for this man, and all like him, to understand the "radical poverty" of those who stand before God and thus be able to open himself to the "good news to the poor" that is the kingdom of God.

If he heard this word, what would the rich man do? Would he sell all that he has and give it to the poor? Would he go out to the gate with a basket of food? Would he invite Lazarus to his table? Would he start a movement to found a hospital to care for a city full of Lazaruses?

We don't know, and the parable does not prescribe his, or our, behavior. What the parable does help us imagine, though, is a life that trusts the gospel, a life that doesn't need to "own" anything to be worthy, a life where the spell of fearful possession of riches is broken and a freedom is created to share joyfully. This is not the same as traditional charity, as an "I'll share some with the poor and the rest is mine" attitude. That's nothing more than letting the poor have "what fell from the rich man's table" (16:21). The gospel alleviates the need for anyone to act like an "owner" and frees all who listen to the possibility of being a "steward" of what ultimately belongs to God alone.

A seminary student in one of my classes went home for the Christmas break one year. He lived in a large city, where his father was the pastor of a downtown church. One afternoon, father and son got into a conversation about the need for the church in the United States to become much more alert to issues of social and economic justice. In the middle of the conversation, the two decided to take a walk in a nearby park and to continue their discussion as they walked. After walking and talking for a while, my student's father said, "Hey, it's getting late and we need to be heading home. I've got an idea. Let's order a pizza. By the time we get home, it won't be too much longer before it's delivered."

This was in the day when there were few mobile phones, but pay phones were available on almost every corner. So they headed toward the nearest phone to call the pizzeria. As they did, though, a man who lived on the streets stepped in front of them, held out his hand, and said, "Can you spare any change?" Father and son had just spent a couple of hours talking about the church and economic justice, so they could hardly turn away. "Sure," the father said to the man, and he and his son combined all of the change they had in their pockets. The father held the coins in both of his hands and extended it toward the man. "Here, take what you need," he said.

The man's eyes widened, and he said, "I'll take it all," as he scooped the change into his own hands and walked away. He had only gotten a few steps, though, when the father realized that he and his son now had no coin left to make their phone call. "Sir," the father called out to the man. "I was on my way to make a phone call. Could I possibly have a quarter?"

The man turned around and came back to the father. He held out his hands, full of change, and said, "Sure. Here, take what you need."

I think Father Abraham would rejoice to see Lazarus and the rich man together like that, not enacting one-way charity from the powerful toward the vulnerable, but instead their hands extended toward each other in mutual generosity, free to share what they had. "Here, take what you need." A glimpse of the kingdom.

THE PARABLE OF THE WIDOW AND THE JUDGE (LUKE 18:1–8)

This parable is so much like the Parable of the Friend at Midnight (11:5–13) that the two parables have been called twins.[181] True, they have much in common. Both are about prayer, both have a character in need of something from another character, and in both stories the character in need gets what is asked for only by becoming a bother. The two parables may be fraternal (or sororal) twins, but they are not identical. The Friend at Midnight is told in the context of Jesus teaching his disciples to pray by giving them the Lord's Prayer (11:1–4). The parable that follows is about God's children praying for the good gifts they need every day. The Parable of the Widow and the Judge is told in a quite different context, after Jesus teaches about the coming of the kingdom. If the Friend at Midnight is about praying for our needs every day, this parable is about praying for the kingdom to come in dramatic fashion in the midst of distress.

The Parable of the Widow and the Judge is one of the five "what am I going to do?" parables in Luke (the others are the Prodigal Son, the Unjust Steward, the Unjust Judge, and the Wicked Tenants). In each of these parables, a character gets into a crisis in the middle of the story and wonders, usually in a formal soliloquy, about how to get out of it. In this case, the crisis happens to the judge.

The Kingdom of God: When, Where, and How?

Even though this parable begins a new chapter in the Gospel of Luke, it actually flows directly from the material at the end of the previous chapter. There Jesus responds to three questions about the kingdom of God: When will it come? Where will it come? How will it come?

The "when question" is posed by the Pharisees, and Jesus responds by waving the question away. "The kingdom of God," he says, "is not coming with things that can be observed; nor will they say, 'Look, here it is!' or 'There it is!' For, in fact, the kingdom of God is among you" (17:20–21). There will be no portents to signal that the kingdom is about to arrive. No albino camels will strangely appear in the desert; the stars will not suddenly rearrange themselves into a celestial billboard reading, "It's about to happen!" Nor will there be any cataclysmic political developments to signal the kingdom's arrival.

Jesus redirects his questioners' focus. Instead of scanning the skies for comets, look right in front of you. The Pharisees had been watching Jesus closely (14:1), but they had missed the kingdom already happening in his person and ministry. "The kingdom of God is among you," Jesus told them. Some want to translate "among you" as "within you," as if the kingdom were simply a matter of inner spirituality, which it is not. It is an event out in public in which God's reign is manifest. We should remember that Jesus is talking here to the Pharisees. In Luke, they would be the last people to be spiritual virtuosi and to have God's kingdom within.

When Jesus said, "The kingdom of God is among you," he means just what he told John's disciples, "Go and tell John what you have seen and heard: the blind receive their sight, the lame walk, the lepers are cleansed, the deaf hear, the dead are raised, the poor have good news brought to them" (7:22). The Pharisees saw all that but didn't really see. They are standing there soaking wet and asking Jesus, "When is it going to rain?"

But for the next two questions—where? and how?—Jesus changes audiences. He is now talking to his disciples (17:22–37). This is surely because these are questions posed by the early church, by Luke's community. They believed that the kingdom had appeared in Jesus, and they also knew that the kingdom's full coming was in the future. Jesus had said that ultimately the nations "will see the Son of Man coming in a cloud with power and great glory" (21:27). But that day had not yet come, and the church lived its life in the "in between" times. Jesus had also said that these times were coming, the times when "the bridegroom will be taken away from them, and they will fast in those days" (5:35). In Acts, Paul and Barnabas on their missionary journeys "strengthened the souls of the disciples [the new Christians] and encouraged them to continue in the faith, saying, 'It is through many persecutions that we must enter the kingdom of God'" (Acts 14:22).

So Luke's community was living in the time of fasting and many persecutions. They had wagered their lives on the truth that Jesus, not Caesar and not Herod, was Lord and that possessions were to be shared not hoarded, that the meal shared in common was more important than a private feast in luxury, that love is stronger than death, and that the lowly will be lifted up and the hungry fed. To live this way invited scorn, opposition, and occasional persecution. One day, though, amid the distress and confusion of life, Christ would come in power and glory, and they would be able to stand up and raise their heads because their redemption would be drawing near (Luke 21:28). But where? And how?

Jesus begins his word to the disciples by acknowledging their situation, that there will be days ahead in which they long to see the Son of Man, but the fullness of time has not yet come (17:22). The church, of course, is living in those days, and Jesus warns that they must be careful. There are people who will tell them that the kingdom has come over here or over there. "There's a preacher in Chicago who has the whole truth!" or "There's a commune in New Delhi where paradise has arrived!" Jesus said, "Do not go, do not set off in pursuit." When the fullness of God's kingdom arrives, Jesus said, it will be like lightning streaking across the sky, visible to everyone, everywhere.

As to how it will come, Jesus says it will arrive suddenly, unexpectedly, like the flood that came in the time of Noah and the fire and sulfur that fell in the time of Lot. The words Jesus speaks here are artfully constructed. He describes the days of Noah. What were people doing? They were "eating and drinking, and marrying and being given in marriage" (17:27). These are ordinary and everyday human activities. Luke Johnson points out that eating and drinking are evidence of eschatological heedlessness in Luke 12:19, 29, and 45, and in Luke 20:35 "marrying and being given in marriage" are earthly activities that will not occur in the resurrection life.[182]

The conjunctions "and . . . and . . . and" aren't present in the Greek, just the four imperfect tense verbs: eating, drinking, marrying, being given in marriage. Moreover, the verbs are rhythmical and they are near rhymes, so to speak them out loud conveys the repetitive, familiar rhythms, maybe even the boring and oblivious patterns, of everyday life. What were they doing in Noah's day? They were eating, drinking, marrying, being given in marriage, ba-bada, ba-bada, ba-bada, ba-bada—or maybe better, yada, yada, yada—and then wham! The flood came and wiped them out.

Then Jesus adds a description of the days of Lot (17:28–29). What were they doing? They were "eating . . . drinking. . . ." Wait a minute. We've heard this list before, and we know that it ends in catastrophe! But the list keeps going: "buying . . . selling . . . planting . . . building." The list is getting longer, naming more activities of ordinary life. We lean forward, tense, expectant, waiting for the inevitable crisis. Then it comes: "but on that day that Lot left Sodom, it rained fire and sulfur from heaven and destroyed them all."[183]

In other words, Jesus is saying that "the day that the Son of Man is revealed" (17:30) will come suddenly, swiftly, unexpectedly, and while the world rocks along in the numbing rhythms of life as usual, like a sales executive at a two-martini lunch. People of faith, on the other hand, lean forward in eager anticipation, expecting Christ to arrive at any moment. One day their wager on the gospel will be shown to be not foolishness but eternal wisdom. Paul wrote to the Christian community in Rome that he was convinced that his commitment to the gospel would not finally put him to shame because "in it the righteousness of God is revealed through faith for faith" (Rom. 1:16–17). Luke's community lives in the same hope.

Boxing Match

The first readers and hearers of Luke's Gospel were living in the in-between times, between Jesus, whom they loved and served as Lord, and the promised time when everyone, everywhere will know that he is Lord of all and "will see the Son of Man coming in a cloud with power and great glory" (Luke 21:27). The in-between times can often be times of discouragement and the loss of hope, and the church today is still in those times.

What congregation has not sung Mary's song of praise that God "has shown strength with his arm—scattered the proud in the imagination of their hearts—brought down the powerful from their thrones and lifted up the lowly—filled the hungry with good things and sent the rich away empty" (1:51–53), only to fall back with the realization that the prideful, the powerful, and the rich are still apparently in charge. What community of faithful Christians has not prayed, "When, Lord? Where, Lord? How, Lord?" People of hope have their patience tested and join in with Isaiah's cry to God,

> O that you would tear open the heavens and come down,
> so that the mountains would quake at your presence—
> as when fire kindles brushwood
> and the fire causes water to boil—
> to make your name known to your adversaries,
> so that the nations might tremble at your presence!
> Isa. 64:1–2

In *Holy the Firm*, Annie Dillard describes her experiences when she was living for two years on an island in Puget Sound. She tells about a moment in a worship service at a small church she attended:

> There is one church here, so I go to it. On Sunday mornings I quit the house and wander down the hill to the white frame church in the firs. On a big Sunday there might be twenty of us there; often I am the only person under sixty, and feel as though I'm on an archaeological tour of Soviet Russia. The members are of mixed denominations; the minister is a Congregationalist, and wears a white shirt. The man knows God. Once, in the middle of the long pastoral prayer of intercession for the whole world—for the gift of wisdom to its leaders, for hope and mercy to the grieving and pained, succor to the oppressed, and God's grace to all—in the middle of this he stopped, and burst out, "Lord, we bring you these same petitions every week." After a shocked pause, he continued reading the prayer. Because of this, I like him very much.[184]

"Lord, we bring you these petitions every week," the pastor prayed. Christians sometimes wonder if our prayers for wisdom, hope, mercy, succor to the oppressed, and God's grace will ever be answered; this, Luke tells his readers, is why Jesus told the Parable of the Widow and the Judge, so that they would keep on praying and not lose heart, not give up (18:1).

There are two characters in this parable. Like the characters in the Rich Man and Lazarus, they are sharply drawn, to the point of being stock characters: a really bad judge and a really desperate and needy widow. The judge "neither feared God nor had respect for people" (18:1). "As a city judge," writes Garland, "this man would be a member of the urban elite and would hold a position of honor."[185] But this judge is not religious and has no regard for other people. He doesn't go to synagogue, and he doesn't give to the United Way. He's the kind of judge for whom the title "your honor" is a mockery. He lacks the qualities needed in a judge in any culture, but particularly in a Jewish setting, where even children are taught to "fear God" and keep God's commandments (Deut. 6:2). Human judges are to imitate the virtues of divine justice, not ignoring "the supplication of the orphan, or the widow when she pours out her complaint" (Sir. 35:17). But as the parable soon reveals, this judge turns a deaf ear to supplications.

Appearing before this judge is a widow, and while widows in the ancient world varied in status, generally widows were vulnerable socially and economically. Most women in ancient society were supported and defended by their husbands, so widows were, by definition, cut off from that provision. God, however, is described as one who "executes justice for the orphan and the widow" (Deut. 10:18), and the prophet Isaiah said that doing good was to "seek justice, rescue the oppressed, defend the orphan, plead for the widow" (Isa. 1:17).

So it is bad news indeed that this widow's case has fallen to a judge who couldn't care less about the commandments of God or the needs of widows. We don't know the exact nature of her case, but she has an adversary, an "opponent" in a lawsuit, and she is persuaded that she is the victim of an injustice (18:3).

Probably this widow has no money and no status, so she uses the only weapon she possesses: the capacity to be a bother and to stay in the judge's face. According to the well-known phrase, "Well-behaved women seldom make history,"[186] this widow decided to make history. She "kept coming to him and saying, 'Grant me justice against my opponent'" (18:3). Finally, the judge, exhausted by her repeated appeals, engages in a characteristic Lukan "what am I going to do?" inner dialogue. And he makes his decision: "Though I have no fear of God and no respect for anyone, yet because this widow keeps bothering me, I will grant her justice, so that she may not wear me out by continually coming" (18:4–5). This sentence employs language borrowed from the world of boxing, and a more literal translation would be, "Though I have no fear of God and no respect for anyone, yet because this widow keeps punching me, I will grant her justice, so that she won't give me a black eye." This could reflect a literal black eye from the feisty widow, or it could be metaphorical: a black eye in the sense of a bad reputation. For whatever reason, the judge ends up giving the widow what she asks for and vindicating her.

God the Good Judge

When we try to make sense of this parable, it is tempting to zero in on the widow. Though she makes only a brief appearance in Scripture, her spunkiness and bold willingness to take on the ruthless judge make her one of the most attractive figures in the Bible. Even so, the real focus of this parable is the judge. As Jesus, directing our attention, says, "Listen to what the unjust judge says . . ." (18:6). It is the judge who is thrown into the crisis at the heart of the parable, and it is the judge who makes the critical decision to grant justice after all.

Several commentators have made the convincing case that this parable forms a contrast to a passage in Sirach in which God is described as a just judge:

Luke 18:1–8	**Sirach 35:15–25**
"In a certain city there was a judge who neither feared God nor had respect for people. In that city there was a widow who kept coming to him and saying, 'Grant me justice against my opponent.' For a while he refused; but later he said to himself, 'Though I have no fear of God and no respect for anyone, yet because this widow keeps bothering me, I will grant her justice, so that she may not wear me out by continually coming.'"	The Lord is the judge, and with him there is no partiality. He will not show partiality to the poor; but he will listen to the prayer of one who is wronged. He will not ignore the supplication of the orphan, or the widow when she pours out her complaint. Do not the tears of the widow run down her cheek as she cries out against the one who causes them to fall? The one whose service is pleasing to the Lord will be accepted, and his prayer will reach to the clouds. The prayer of the humble pierces the clouds, and it will not rest until it reaches its goal; it will not desist until the Most High responds and does justice for the righteous, and executes judgment.

Luke 18:1–8 *(continued)*

And the Lord said, "Listen to what the unjust judge says. And will not God grant justice to his chosen ones who cry to him day and night? Will he delay long in helping them? I tell you, he will quickly grant justice to them."

Sirach 35:15–25 *(continued)*

Indeed, the Lord will not delay, and like a warrior will not be patient until he crushes the loins of the unmerciful and repays vengeance on the nations; until he destroys the multitude of the insolent, and breaks the scepters of the unrighteous; until he repays mortals according to their deeds, and the works of all according to their thoughts; until he judges the case of his people and makes them rejoice in his mercy.

The parable, then, contrasts a corrupt judge with the God of justice. In Sirach, God is a judge who is impartial and who is open to hearing the pleas of those who have been wronged, no matter who they are. God as a judge, therefore, does not ignore the cries of orphans and widows. God as a judge does justice for the righteous without delay. In the parable, though, the judge himself is "unjust" and at first is completely unresponsive to the pleas of the widow. Only when this judge is worn down by the widow's badgering does he, as a means of self-protection, give justice to the widow.

This parable, then, is a perfect case of a "how much more" parable. What the parable says is that, if a widow with no standing can finally at the end of the day get justice from a judge with no honor, how much more will the faithful, God's "chosen ones," have their prayers for vindication answered by God, who is a just judge. As C. E. B. Cranfield states:

> The eschatological teaching of these eight verses as they stand in Luke is, I suggest, as follows: If an unrighteous judge will heed the persistence of a widow's plea, how much more will the righteous and merciful God heed the cries of His servants who cry to Him continually, day and night! It is true that He is patient with regard to them—i.e. He is patient and longsuffering toward their persecutors, in mercy. But He will assuredly vindicate His servants soon. The Parousia is near![187]

The parable is not about *how* to pray—God does not need to be badgered as the widow goes after the unjust judge—but about confidence that God will surely answer prayer. It is an encouragement to the faithful not to lose heart, even during the long and seemingly endless night of oppression and injustice through which we are living.

Verse 7 presents a translation issue concerning the word *makrothymei* (μακροθυμεῖ), which can mean both delay and patience. The NRSV chooses "delay" and renders the verse as a question, to the effect, "Will God delay long in helping God's chosen ones?" When *makrothymei* is read as "patience," the verse becomes something like, "God will grant justice to his chosen ones and will show patience to them," implying that, if God seems to delay in providing justice, it's not a matter of indifference but God patiently bringing justice to fruition.[188] Either way, God's time is not always our sense of time. As Snodgrass observes, "Delay and quick vindication frequently stand as parallel themes in biblical and Jewish eschatology. Possible Hab 2:3 is most instructive: 'For there is still a vision for the appointed time; it speaks of the end, and does not lie. If it seems to tarry, wait for it.'"[189]

This parable is particularly challenging to us today because it takes us into the middle of one of the most vexing problems for faith, the seeming silence of God in the face of prayers for justice and vindication. As Lukan scholar John Carroll says,

> Yet even if the divine sovereign lacks the defiant disdain of the parabolic judge, we do still wait for justice on this planet, and we do still need—without giving in to despair—to continue resisting tenacious violent forces that produce injustice in the humanly constructed world. Indeed, one might recount innumerable tales of crushing oppression, brutal injustice, for which persistent petition and resistant action have been both necessary and, to all appearances, met with silence (or worse). In such moments, when history deals unrelenting, unjust suffering and when God has seemed distant and silent, why go on believing in God? This is the challenge to persevering faith that Jesus' parable invites readers to consider.[190]

The parable does not so much take us to a place where we can see its promise breaking through, because this parable, unlike the Friend at Midnight, is not speaking about everyday prayers but about prayers that Jesus will come, as he promised, with power and great glory, bringing ultimate justice and vindication. It takes us then to a place of hope that is not yet fulfilled. The parable wants us to keep praying and not to lose heart. It is a difficult challenge, which is why the parable wonders at the end if the faithful can hang on to prayer and hope: "And yet, when the Son of Man comes, will he find faith on the earth?" (18:8).

But every now and then we can taste, or perhaps foretaste, the promise made by this parable. Several years ago, I led a group of pastors on a trip to the southern border of the US at El Paso/Juarez. We visited a child resettlement facility, a place where unaccompanied children who had crossed the border to escape the dangers of their homelands could find care and help in finding new homes in the US.

In the vestibule of this facility, there was a painting done by a little girl, one of the resettlement children. The painting was of herself sleeping peacefully, all alone on the desert sand, while the moon shone brightly in the night sky above her. The director of the facility told us her story. She was orphaned in the drug wars in Guatemala and traveled through Mexico with a group of refugees hoping to receive asylum in the US. One night, when the "coyotes" who were leading the group thought she was asleep, she overheard them plotting to sell her into prostitution. Terrified, she fled into the desert, where she wandered without food or water.

Finally, her energy spent, she lay down on the sand to pray her last prayers and to die. She was not aware that she had managed to cross the border and was in Arizona. The night patrol found her, rescued her, and took her to the resettlement facility. She was soon placed safely and joyfully with a foster family in the Midwest. Before she left the facility, she painted the picture of herself sleeping in the Arizona desert and added the moon as a symbol of God's care over all those in desperate need. "And will not God grant justice to his chosen ones who cry to him day and night?" (18:7).

THE PARABLE OF THE PHARISEE AND THE TAX COLLECTOR (LUKE 18:9–14)

This is a tricky little parable which presents at least two potential pitfalls to contemporary interpreters. The first pitfall involves the way this parable can trap readers into a kind of circular moral reasoning. The story seems to pit two figures against each other: a Pharisee and a tax collector, who both show up at the temple to pray. We already know from prior exposure that the Pharisee is the obvious bad guy, sanctimonious, crowing to God in prayer about his many virtues and self-righteously congratulating himself that he is not like other people, especially that disreputable tax collector across the way. The tax collector, by contrast, is the true hero of the story, humble, confessing his sinfulness to God and begging for mercy. Many a preacher has concluded that the moral of the story is a call to the congregation to imitate the tax collector and get rid of any hint of Pharisaical haughtiness, to avoid the Pharisee's smug piety and puffed-up pride, and to assume the humility of the tax collector. Ironically, of course, this results in all the newly minted "tax collectors" in the congregation having effectively switched positions with the Pharisee. Now we are the ones praying, "God, I thank you I am not like other people. I am humble and self-effacing, not like that pompous Pharisee over there."

The second pitfall is to turn the tax collector into a kind of proto-Protestant, as if what makes him the hero of the parable is that he alone cuts through the ritualistic bombast of the temple and prays out of the sincere anguish of his heart. He gets the Christian definition of grace, preachers sometimes say, while the Pharisee is all about legalistic self-justification. One almost gets the impression that when this grace-saturated tax collector leaves the temple grounds he goes home not only "justified," as the parable states, but probably also ready to found a Baptist or a Lutheran church. Augustine may have started this. In his often-imitated sermons on this parable, he sometimes unfortunately identified the Pharisee as the Jew and the tax collector as the Gentile, that is as the Christian.[191] In the parable itself, though, both men are Jews, and both go to the temple for their prayers. Later in Luke, Jesus, quoting Isaiah, will say about the temple, "My house shall be a house of prayer" (19:46), and that is precisely what it is for both the Pharisee and the tax collector. The parable is not an attack on Jewish piety generally, the temple system, or Judaism as a whole, in favor of a more enlightened Christian or Protestant understanding of grace alone. Something else is at issue in this story.

So a Pharisee and a Tax Collector Walk into a House of Worship (Luke 18:9–14)

The parable begins like the setup for a "two guys walk into a bar" joke, except that it's "two guys walk into the temple to pray, a Pharisee and a tax collector." Both are typecast: the stereotypical religious guy and the quintessential sinner, the last person in the world we would expect to darken the door of a house of worship. At the outset, then, this story is "a deacon and a Hell's Angels biker show up at church" kind of story.

Amy-Jill Levine rightly observes, "Were Jesus to have told this parable to a group of Jews, they would have begun with the impression that the Pharisee was pious and righteous and the tax collector was sinful and self-interested." But what about readers of the Gospel of Luke? What would they have assumed? We are now eighteen chapters into Luke, and careful readers of that Gospel already have some experience with both Pharisees and tax collectors. For their part, the Pharisees have opposed Jesus at every turn and carped constantly about the unconventional behavior of Jesus and his followers. The picture of the Pharisees in Luke can aptly be summed up with the words of Jesus' own rebuke of them earlier in Luke:

> "But woe to you Pharisees! For you tithe mint and rue and herbs of all kinds and neglect justice and the love of God; it is these you ought to have practiced, without neglecting the others. Woe to you Pharisees! For you love to have the seat of honor in the synagogues and to be greeted with respect in the marketplaces. Woe to you! For you are like unmarked graves and people walk over them without realizing it." (11:42–44)

Tax collectors, on the other hand, all through Luke's Gospel have unexpectedly responded favorably to the gospel (3:12; 5:27–30; 7:29; 7:34; 15:1).

But, even if Luke's readers have already formed some negative thoughts about Pharisees, and some positive ones about tax collectors, that doesn't spoil the joke of this parable. Pharisees are famous advocates for righteousness, and tax collectors are well-known practitioners of unrighteousness. Those are the roles they play at the beginning of the parable. The Pharisees are still the "churchy" types, in contrast to the "nonchurchy" and sinful tax collectors. This is a story about a religious guy and a nonreligious guy showing up at the same time for a prayer meeting. The fact that Luke's readers have encountered some hypocritical Pharisees and some tax collectors who are attracted to Jesus simply heightens their expectation that "this is probably going to be a very good story" and makes the punch line, that the tax collector "went down to his home justified rather than the other" (18:14), both unexpected and ironically satisfying.

Incidentally, sometimes preachers get sentimental about the tax collector in this parable, mistakenly viewing him as a symbol of the people the church tends to marginalize, people who are unjustly shunned in worship by smug piety—the poor, the struggling, the homeless, the despised, the weak. But the tax collector is none of these things. He is almost surely rich, a traitor, and an extortioner, a Jew who collaborates for his own monetary benefit with the hated Roman occupiers. By every imaginable standard, the tax collector is a sinner. His style of life is clearly out of sync with the Torah, and he would be understood by other Jews to be powerful, greedy, corrupt, and merciless.

Standing Room Only

So we begin the parable with two men who have gone up to temple to pray: an assumed religious good guy, the Pharisee, and an assumed corrupt and irreligious tax collector. The facades crack a bit, though, when we observe their postures at prayer. The Pharisee prayed "standing by himself" (18:11),[192] and the tax collector prayed "standing far off" (18:13).

What's the difference? The Pharisee's "standing by himself" embodies self-sufficiency, the fact that he is not defined by relationships to others, that he is an island set apart. The "standing far off" of the tax collector is more complicated. The word for "far off" is *makrothen* (μακρόθεν), and that word (and related terms) appears in several significant places in Luke and Acts. As it is used, being "far off" is not a tape measure but a theological symbol of the distance between human need and divine response. When the prodigal son makes his way home, he is still "far off" (*makran*) when "his father saw him and was filled with compassion; he ran and put his arms around him and kissed him" (15:20). Peter, just before he betrays Jesus, is described as following Jesus from afar (22:54, *makrothen*). As Jesus is crucified, and the crowds return home beating their breasts, the companions of Jesus watch what is happening "at a distance" (23:28–49, *makrothen*). When Peter concludes his Pentecost sermon, the stunned crowd cries out, "Brothers, what should we do?" and Peter replies, "Repent and be baptized every one of you in the name of Jesus Christ so that your sins may be forgiven, and you will receive the gift of the Holy Spirit" (Acts 2:37–38). Peter, then, goes on to assure them, in language relevant to our parable, that God's promise of redemption was for them, their children, and *all who are far away* [*makran*], everyone whom the Lord our God calls to him" (Acts 2:39, emphasis added).

As we pointed out in the discussion of the Parable of the Prodigal Son (see pp. 312–27), this idea of distance is a key theological theme in Luke. Humanity is at a great distance, "far off," from God, and Luke's story is about God closing the gap, reaching across the distance separating God and humanity, in order to forgive sin and to save. God-in-Christ moves toward humanity "to give knowledge of salvation to his people by the forgiveness of their sins" (Luke 1:77). Luke agrees with Ephesians: "But now in Christ Jesus you who once were far off [*makran*] have been brought near by the blood of Christ. For he is our peace" (Eph. 2:13–14).

In sum, the big theological picture in Luke is of a compassionate God who moves savingly toward the world, who acts in Jesus to liberate a captive humanity. God's Spirit is upon Jesus, and as Jesus said in his inaugural sermon, God "has anointed me to bring good news to the poor . . . to proclaim release to the captives and recovery of sight to the blind, to let the oppressed go free" (Luke 4:18). The tax collector rightly perceives where he stands in this great arc of salvation, and therefore places himself at a distance to plead for God to move toward him in mercy. The Pharisee stands "by himself," apart from all others, in lonely isolation, outside of the loop of salvation.

Two Men, Two Prayers

Our insight into the two men at prayer deepens when we overhear the actual words of their prayers. We hear the Pharisee first: "God, I thank you that I am not like other people: thieves, rogues, adulterers, or even like this tax collector. I fast twice a week; I give a tenth of all my income" (18:11–12). Because we know this parable and its outcome, we are primed immediately to judge this prayer harshly. One commentator scoffs at the prayer, saying, "It is disingenuous, self-deceptive, and mean-spirited."[193]

But not so fast. Before we condemn this prayer, it deserves a second look. The Pharisee thanks God that he is not a thief, a rouge, or an adulterer, but instead he is one who fasts and tithes. One way to understand this prayer is in light of the holiness code in the Old Testament. God's people are called to be holy, because God is holy (Lev. 19:2). For Israel to be holy is to be different, even odd. Others may steal, lie, defraud their neighbors, or cheat their workers, but not God's people, those who fear God (Lev. 19:11–13). At face value, the Pharisee is simply thanking God that he has been superzealous in keeping the law of God, which by definition marks him as different from those who don't.

We provide even more context for the Pharisee's prayer when we look at a somewhat similar prayer in Deuteronomy. This is the prayer people were commanded to pray when they brought their agricultural tithes to God:

> When you have finished paying all the tithe of your produce in the third year (which is the year of the tithe), giving it to the Levites, the aliens, the orphans, and the widows, so that they may eat their fill within your towns, then you shall say before the LORD your God: "I have removed the sacred portion from the house, and I have given it to the Levites, the resident aliens, the orphans, and the widows, in accordance with your entire commandment that you commanded me; I have neither transgressed nor forgotten any of your commandments: I have not eaten of it while in mourning; I have not removed any of it while I was unclean; and I have not offered any of it to the dead. I have obeyed the LORD my God, doing just as you commanded me. Look down from your holy habitation, from heaven, and bless your people Israel and the ground that you have given us, as you swore to our ancestors—a land flowing with milk and honey." (Deut. 26:12–15)

Note that this prayer, much like that of the Pharisee, uses "I" language and says, in effect, "O God, I have tithed and given my offering to those in need. I am not like those people who have sinned or forgotten your commandments. I have obeyed you, O God."

So, what's wrong with the Pharisee's prayer? The problem is not that he is bragging about how good he is or that he is a legalistic Jew who fails to appreciate Christian grace and humility. The problem is even deeper. A primary goal of Judaism, and therefore of Christianity, is to increase the love of God and neighbor. Earlier in Luke, when a lawyer asked Jesus, "[W]hat must I do to inherit eternal life?" Jesus asked the lawyer how he himself understood the law on that question. The lawyer knew what to say. "You shall love the Lord your God with all your heart, and with all your soul, and with all your strength, and with all your mind, and your neighbor as yourself," he replied. Jesus said, "You have given the right answer; do this, and you will live" (Luke 10:25–28). The purpose of the law, the purpose of holy and righteous living, the purpose of temple worship, the purpose of prayer is to shape God's people into those who ever more deeply love God and neighbor.

The irony, however, is that those very rituals and practices can tilt one in the other direction, away from God and neighbor. Sadly, what often gets dropped out is that the whole life of faith is lived in grateful response to what God has done. God sounds the first words of love and justice; all human righteousness is but an echo. The Ten Commandments begin with an announcement of God's initial liberating act: "I am the LORD your God, who brought you out of the land of Egypt, out of the house of slavery" (Exod. 20:2). God makes the first move, and anyone who keeps the commandments that follow does so in response to what God has done.

The call to love the neighbor, to treat neighbors with compassion and justice, also comes as a response, because we have already been treated with compassion and justice by God (Exod. 22:21). When we lose sight of God's initiative in acting mercifully and savingly toward us, we begin to assume that our goodness is self-generated, and our righteousness becomes a way of one-upping our neighbor. There we see our Pharisee in the parable, standing by himself, isolated from everyone else, even from God, and condescending toward the tax collector on the other side of the room. That is why Luke primes the pump at the beginning of this parable, letting the cat out of the bag early that this is a story aimed at "some who trusted in themselves that they were righteous and regarded others with contempt" (18:9).

By contrast, the tax collector knows where he stands, literally and figuratively. He is "standing in the need of prayer," as the old spiritual puts it. He knows that there is a gulf separating him from God, and so he marks that reality by standing at a distance, not presuming that he has the power on his own to bridge the gap. He won't raise his eyes to look at heaven (see *1 Enoch* 13:5—"they did not raise their eyes to Heaven, out of shame for the sins, for which they had been condemned"[194]), he beats his breast in remorse, as the crowds will do later after seeing an innocent Jesus die on a cross (23:48), and he cries out for God to act in mercy toward him, a sinner (18:13). Jesus ends the parable by declaring that the tax collector "went down to his home justified rather than the other" (18:14).

The word translated "justified" is *dedikaiōmenos* (δεδικαιωμένος), from the root word for "righteous." It is significant that the Greek is a perfect passive participle, literally "having been justified."[195] In other words, the tax collector didn't go home after proving how right he was. No. Justification was something that happened to him; it was a gift given to him, an answer to the penitential prayer. He was declared and made righteous by God.[196] The closing moral of the story should be taken in the theological sense: those "who exalt themselves [that is, toward God and others] will be humbled, but all who humble themselves will be exalted" (18:14, see also 14:11). Those who believe that they can "stand by themselves" will find themselves standing all alone, but those who stand in humility far off, begging for mercy, will be given a new standing by God.

The point of this parable is not that the righteous life is rubbish and all posturing. It's a good thing that the Pharisee is not a thief, a rogue, or an adulterer. To care for the orphan and the widow, to fast and to bring one's offerings to the altar is to obey God. But all walking of the holy path is made possible only by God having opened up the way. We all come to the place of prayer as beggars in need of the mercy of God.

This parable allows us to see the kingdom of God in those places where people bow in awe toward God and reach out, in humility, need, and hope toward the mercy of God. In an essay by Joseph Holt, describing his alcohol addiction, his decade-long battle to maintain sobriety, and his experience of honest vulnerability at AA meetings, we can see some of the humility and the reaching out toward mercy that are at the heart of this parable:

> Sometimes I cry at meetings, and it's hard to explain why. I think it's because the people there are so candid and vulnerable. The newcomers, especially, fumble and repeat themselves and speak into their chests. They want their experience to make sense, but it won't, not yet. It's all confusion, no narrative. And the old guard, without fail, are wry and generous and perversely joyful. . . . These are people who have lived in darkness, lying flat under rocks and peering through sewer grates, and they are grateful for the light.[197]

THE PARABLE OF THE TEN MINAS (POUNDS) (LUKE 19:11–27)

It is hard to know what to call this parable. Most English translations call it the Parable of the Pounds, but this can be misleading. The best known monetary "pound" to many English readers is the British pound, which is a relatively small amount of money compared to the money unit being passed around in this parable, called in Greek a "mina." A mina amounts to about three month's wages for a typical laborer in Jesus' day. The NIV, to its credit, sticks with the Greek term, dubbing this "The Parable of the Ten Minas," and we will follow suit.

But even this title may miss the mark. The parable is not really mainly about the minas, the units of money in the story; that's more true about Matthew's Parable of the Talents (Matt. 25:24–30), which turns on the stewardship of talents, units of money. The reason why Luke's parable gets named after the money mentioned in it is because the parable sounds a lot like the Matthew parable, so it must be a stewardship story as well. As we shall see, though, the parable in Luke has a radically different emphasis from the parable in Matthew. The focus of Luke's parable is not on the minas, but on the sinister character of the nobleman who wants to be king.

Jeremias thought the parable in Luke was a fusion of the Parable of the Talents and another parable about a man who wanted to become king, a putting together of stories that would have occurred in the pre-Lukan tradition.[198] Jeremias is at least partly right; our parable does contain two smaller stories, but in my view, the joining of these two smaller stories into the Parable of the Minas makes the most sense as a piece of editorial artwork by Luke himself, since it fits nicely into the narrative flow of his Gospel. In Luke, Jesus tells the parable just as he is about to enter Jerusalem and when excited talk of a new kingdom is in the air. The questions in the air are, Is now the time when we get a new kingdom, and Is Jesus going to be the new king?

The mainframe in Luke's parable is not the part about the money, the minas, but the part about the king, in this case the story of a cruel nobleman who managed to get kingly power. New Testament scholar Alan Culpepper profitably suggests that the story be renamed the Parable of the Greedy and Vengeful King.[199] As such, it is the one parable in Jesus' repertoire that is not about what the kingdom of God is like but, instead, what the kingdom of God is *not* like.

Moving toward a Denouement

Jesus tells this parable in Jericho. His long journey to Jerusalem, which began at Luke 9:51, is nearing its end. Anticipation is building as Jesus has just told the twelve that the fulfillment of his purpose is near: "See, we are going up to Jerusalem, and everything that is written about the Son of Man by the prophets will be accomplished" (18:31). Immediately before he speaks the parable, Jesus has a dramatic encounter with a rich tax collector named Zacchaeus, which culminates in Jesus' announcement, "Today salvation has come to this house, because [Zacchaeus] too is a son of Abraham. For the Son of Man came to seek out and to save the lost." Seeing a rich and reviled tax collector beating his breast in repentance and pledging justice and generosity to the poor, while Jesus says that his main purpose is to seek and save the lost, and that salvation has come to this house "today" because even this man is a child of Abraham, seems about as full a climax imaginable to this part of Luke's Gospel.

Jesus then turns to move again toward Jerusalem, a relatively short distance from Jericho, and Luke's story of Jesus' ministry is clearly moving toward its denouement, a culminating chapter in the story of Jesus. Small wonder, then, that the disciples, and perhaps some others around Jesus, "supposed that the kingdom of God was to appear immediately" (19:11).

But before Jesus takes another step toward Jerusalem, he pauses to tell this parable. Why? Luke says it was because of this very view that the people around him held, the supposition that the kingdom was imminent. The implication is that what they were expecting—the kind of kingdom, the character of the king, the timing and meaning of its coming—was wrong, and that Jesus spoke the parable as a corrective. It should be noted, though, that there is some ambiguity in Luke's language, and a few maverick interpreters understand Luke to be saying the opposite, namely, that people were right in their presuppositions about the kingdom and that Jesus told this parable to confirm their expectation. But the parable has to be twisted and mangled out of shape to make it function this way, rendering this interpretation quite improbable.[200]

A Suspiciously Familiar Story

The people are expecting a new king and a new kingdom, and Jesus tells them a rough story about a king and a kingdom. The parable begins with a "nobleman" who desired a kingdom, or as the NRSV puts it, "royal power for himself" (19:12), so he went to a "distant country" to obtain it. The Greek for "distant country," *chōran makran* (χώραν μακρὰν), is the same term used to describe the place where the prodigal son wasted his money on a decadent lifestyle (15:13), and, as Culpepper says, "The Lukan reader knows that nothing good happens in a 'distant country.'"[201]

The nobleman's trip to get royal power was not untroubled. His fellow citizens back home hated this nobleman and were therefore disgusted by the possibility that he might come back home as their king. So they "sent a delegation after him, saying [presumably to the authority who could grant him kingship], 'We do not want this man to rule over us'" (19:14). Their appeal, however, fell on deaf ears, and the nobleman returned home as the newly designated king. Revenge was on his mind, and among his first actions is the command, "[A]s for these enemies of mine who did not want me to be king over them—bring them here and slaughter them in my presence" (19:27).

At this point, Jesus' hearers, and certainly Luke's readers, would likely hear echoes in their historical memory. "Wait a minute," they would probably say to themselves, "we *know* this story!" Indeed, they did know this story, both in a general and a particular sense. In the general sense, the story of a new king who uses power ruthlessly happens in history over and over. Culpepper calls this "a type scene," which is a scene in a story that "incorporates such familiar elements that the audience recognizes the pattern and anticipates the

five talents. When the first two servants report good stewardship, they are praised as "good and trustworthy," empowered by being placed in charge of "many things," and welcomed "into the joy of your master." The servant who chose to be paralyzed by fear of the master finds himself also described eschatologically, in "outer darkness, where there will be weeping and gnashing of teeth."

Luke's parable has none of these eschatological overtones. No one is given anything in trust, and no one is welcomed into the very heart and joy of the nobleman's life. Luke's version is an entirely this-worldly business narrative.

2. In Matthew's parable, the servants are entrusted with money, "each according to their ability." One is given five talents, one two talents, and the third one talent. No instructions are given to them about what to do with the money. This is a discipleship story, and disciples know what is expected of them.

In Luke's parable, on the other hand, the transaction between the nobleman and the servants seems much more like a straight business deal, or maybe even a test in a job interview. Each of the servants gets one mina. The ambiguity in verse Luke 19:13—"He summoned ten of his slaves and gave them ten pounds" (was that ten pounds each or one pound each?)—is cleared up by 19:16, 18, and 20; it was one pound each. A single pound is a relatively modest amount compared to the talents in Matthew's parable, and the servants are given clear instructions about what to do: "Do business with these until I come back" (19:13). When the nobleman comes back, now as a king, he interrogates the servants to see if they passed the test. "He ordered these slaves, to whom he had given the money, to be summoned so that he might find out what they had gained by trading" (19:15).

The first slave, having shown how capable he is by turning one mina into ten, is by the new king put in charge of ten cities. The second slave, having turned a mina into five, is made ruler of five cities. It's what kings do: find able and compliant people to put into positions of bureaucratic authority. The third, do-nothing, slave, is not punished like his counterpart in Matthew, even though he has spouted off at the king, calling him "a hard-boiled grasping predator."[209] This is not an eschatological story, as we said, and so the consequences for incompetence are relatively mundane. Being an enemy of the king in this parable, that is, being someone who actively opposed his becoming king, will get one slaughtered, but being an idiot at business means only that this servant flunks the interview, loses the mina he was given, is sharply criticized as "wicked" by the king, and loses out on the chance to have authority over anything.

How did Luke and Matthew both tell stories about money that are so similar and yet so radically different in how they employ those stories? It seems likely to me (but we'll probably never know for certain) that Matthew and

Luke found in their common source a parable about a wealthy man who gave money to three slaves and then asked for an accounting. Both Gospel writers had the same chess piece but placed it differently onto their very distinctive theological chessboards.

Matthew, with his well-developed eschatology, read this story about a master who entrusted his money to three slaves as an allegory of Christ, who entrusted the treasure of the kingdom to disciples and then went away for a long time, only to return for an accounting at the eschaton.

Luke, however, with his emphasis on the eschatological present, on "today," and with quite different views of power and wealth, read this same material very differently. He saw the wealthy man in the parable the way Luke tends to see all of the rich, as a typical example of a grasping power player, in this case trying to draw some of his slaves into his manipulations. When the third slave in the story says to the rich man, "I was afraid of you, because you are a harsh man; you take what you did not deposit, and reap what you did not sow," Matthew heard this as bad faith, but Luke took the opposite view: "Exactly! This fellow has nailed it." So Luke embedded this little parable of greed into a larger, and familiar, story of a nobleman performing a royal power grab, and the result is a complex parable-within-a-parable warning his readers not to confuse the machinations of earthly kings with the kingship of Jesus.

Battle of the Bands: Finding Meaning in the Parable

This strange and complicated parable sets interpreters running off into the forest in many different directions. Here are two of the more well-trod paths in the forest:

1. The Parable of the Minas, like Matthew's Parable of the Talents, is christological. An example of this view, a perspective that is perhaps the most frequent understanding of the parable, can be found in Fitzmyer. He sees, when the parable is taken in its Lukan context, the minas as allegorical representations of the "secrets of the kingdom of God" which have been graciously given to disciples (Luke 8:10). The parable "makes clear that a Christian disciple can respond to such graciousness either with obedience (as do the first two servants) or with disobedience (as does the third)."[210] As for the other part of the parable, the bit about the nobleman becoming a king, this too is an allegory. The nobleman, Fitzmyer argues, represents "Jesus the Son of God, who is about to begin his 'ascent' to the Father from the city of destiny." On his return, the kingly Son of Man will, according to the parable, take two actions: he will examine his servants to see how obedient they have been, and he will "take vengeance on his Palestinian compatriots" who rejected his kingship.[211]

This understanding of the parable, no matter how many times it has been stated, is simply overdetermined by the similarities to Matthew's Parable of the Talents, skewed by a desire to have Luke's parable focus on what is really Matthew's theme: how disciples use the treasure of the kingdom. But it isn't necessarily the case that Luke and Matthew are on the same page about this story; in fact, it is nearly certain they are *not.* There are clear tonal, contextual, and referential differences between Matthew's parable, with its invitation to "enter into the joy of your master," and this sinister tale in Luke.

Also, despite the claim of Fitzmyer and many others, the nobleman in Luke's parable who goes to a distant country seeking royal status actually makes a very poor allegorical stand-in for Jesus, the Son of Man. The nobleman, when he returns as a king, has his enemies slaughtered, and to make it even more cringeworthy, he wants to watch the carnage (19:27). The Jesus of Luke, on the other hand, says, "Love your enemies; do good to those who hate you; bless those who curse you; pray for those who mistreat you" (6:27–28).

The nobleman instructs his ten slaves to do business as usual with the minas given them, but Jesus in Luke has a contrary view of economics. "If you lend to those from whom you hope to receive," Jesus says, "what credit is that to you? Even sinners lend to sinners, to receive as much again. But love your enemies, do good, and lend, expecting nothing in return" (6:34–35).

The nobleman wants to seize kingly power for himself. Jesus wants to share it with his followers: "I confer on you, just as my Father has conferred on me, a kingdom," Jesus will soon tell his disciples at the Last Supper, "so that you may eat and drink at my table in my kingdom" (22:29–30). Surely Luke hasn't developed amnesia about who Jesus is and absentmindedly inserted a story in his Gospel in which a power-hungry, despotic mercenary symbolizes the Son of Man who "came to seek out and to save the lost" (19:10).

The Parable of the Minas is indeed christological, but only ironically. Other interpreters have recognized the inherent moral problems in understanding this parable christologically, but have still found ways to make the parable work as a christological analogy. Joel Green, for example, rightly acknowledges that seeing this parable as a straightforward allegory "would be highly problematic, since . . . it would portray Jesus in terms of harshness and exploitative practices."[212] On the other hand, he finds too many regal motifs in the Lukan narrative, both before this parable and after it, to ignore the kingly theme that hovers around this parable. Thus, for Green, the nobleman in the parable is "an analogy for Jesus" but "primarily in a parodic or ironic way."[213] How the nobleman in the parable became a king and how he enforced his rule is a kind of parody of "the construction of Jesus' kingship and kingdom in the Gospel of Luke."[214] What about the ghastly parts? Well, if the king in the parable seems harsh and arbitrary, Jesus' presentation of the kingdom of God "may seem harsh and arbitrary" as well, to those who have oriented their lives around the wrong values.[215]

This interpretation certainly addresses the ethical problems in seeing the parable christologically, but I am not persuaded that it solves them. It may even make them worse. It would take a very refined sense of parody indeed to see this story of a cruel king as an ironic depiction of Jesus and this merciless slaughter as an ironic depiction of divine judgment. That would be a very deep dish of irony to swallow. We can perhaps stretch and do that in Matthew, especially in the Parable of the Wedding Banquet, but not here in the theological world of Luke.

Rather than seeing this parable as directly christological, as an allegorical or an ironic depiction of Jesus' kingship, it is better understood as countertestimony, as a portrait of typical worldly kingship, in contrast to Jesus' kingship. The parable, as Luke implied, was spoken against what Jesus' followers thought was about to take place in Jerusalem. It is then a parabolic critique of their views of the kingdom, a story that says, "If you think I am going to Jerusalem to throw out Herod, get on his throne, and make Israel great again, then you misunderstand me and you misunderstand God's kingdom. In fact, let me tell you a story to remind you of what earthly kings have been like." Garland writes,

> As Jesus neared Jerusalem, his followers may have taken for granted that the same old human story of how one takes power and establishes a kingdom was in play. They may have anticipated that Jesus would restore the glory days of the kingdom of David (see Acts 1:6). They would gain supremacy through brute force to secure dominance over their enemies, and their supremacy would be obvious to all. But the reign of God is conducted on a totally different strategy.[216]

Culpepper concurs, rejecting any idea that this parable "represents either God or Jesus." To the contrary, "the parable establishes the common pattern of kingship so that the distinctive features of Jesus' kingship (and the kingdom of God) can stand in relief."[217]

The Third Parable

We have seen that Luke probably put together two little parables to make this one story. The first small parable is about a grasping and ruthless nobleman who traveled to a distant country to wrest even more power and status for himself. The second small parable is about that same man, now having gained royalty, coming home both to assess how his servants performed in a coldhearted financial test and to slaughter his political enemies. These two little parables have been knitted together to form the larger Parable of the Ten Minas, which puts on display earthly kingly power at its worst.

But there are really three parables operating here. The bifold Parable of the Minas is contrasted with a third parable, the story of Jesus' passion. Jesus' ministry is nearing its end. He is at the threshold of Jerusalem, and his very nearness to the city excites the crowd's expectations. Surely, they assume, he will charge into the city and seize kingly power. So the Parable of the Ten Minas addresses that expectation by saying, in essence, "You're imagining kingship in typically political ways. Well, this is a story of how earthly kings operate. Haven't we had enough of that? There is another way; watch me. There is another parable, my own life."

Then Jesus turns back to the road, enters the city, and enacts the third parable with his own suffering, the parable that reveals what kind of king he really is and what kind of kingdom he is bringing through the giving of his life. One of the criminals crucified beside Jesus rightly interpreted this living parable and recognized the true king and the true kingdom when he said, "Jesus, remember me when you come into your kingdom" (23:42). However, the two followers of Jesus who met the risen Christ on the Emmaus road missed the point. They told Jesus, whose identity was at this point hidden from them, of his own crucifixion, adding sadly, "We had hoped he was the one to redeem Israel" (24:21).

"We had hoped he was the one to redeem Israel" is an echo of the very misunderstanding expressed by the followers in Jericho, who "supposed that the kingdom of God was to appear immediately" (19:11), and it is a reverberation of what many around Jesus expected and hoped. In Jericho, Jesus counters that view with the two smaller parables woven into the Parable of the Ten Minas. On the Emmaus road, however, he responds to his confused and disappointed followers by underscoring the third parable, the parable of his own passion, by making it plain once more that God's path to glory is not the world's way: "Oh, how foolish you are, and how slow of heart to believe all that the prophets have declared! Was it not necessary that the Messiah should suffer these things and then enter into his glory?" (24:26).

THE PARABLE OF THE WICKED TENANTS (LUKE 20:9–19)

Malachi prophesied that "the Lord whom you seek will suddenly come to his temple" (Mal. 3:1). In Luke's story, this has now happened. Jesus has entered Jerusalem, and as he came down from the Mount of Olives, he was hailed as "the king who comes in the name of the Lord" (Luke 19:29–40). As his first act in the city, Jesus has suddenly come to the temple, driven out the sellers of animals for the sacrifices, and declared, "My house shall be a house of prayer, but you have made it a den of robbers" (19:45–46). By this, Jesus has, in effect, "taken possession" of the temple and reclaimed it as his Father's house.[218]

In the days that follow, Jesus teaches the people in the temple area, and all of his actions—the driving out of the sellers, the teaching, the preaching, the attention he draws from the people spellbound by his words, all of it—have set the religious leadership on edge. They would have preferred to kill Jesus and be done with it, but his popularity was too strong (19:48).

The authorities needed to gather some damning evidence against Jesus, or at least to find some wedge they could drive between Jesus and the people. So they confront Jesus in the temple in an attempt to entrap him. Soon enough the temple police will be involved in the arrest of Jesus (22:52), but for now it is the chief priests, scribes, and elders who try to get probable cause. They pose one of those loaded questions, one that sounds so innocent, so truth-seeking, but is really a cocked revolver. "Tell us," they asked, "by what authority are you doing these things? Who is it who gave you this authority?" (20:2). In other words, show us your credentials, since we know you have none. (The same exchange with the religious leaders is reported in both Mark and Matthew. See the discussion regarding Mark's version on pp. 89–97 and Matthew's version on pp. 203–7.)

Jesus responds, however, with a counter question, one which places the authorities in a lose-lose position: "Did the baptism of John come from heaven, or was it of human origin?" (20:4). Since these religious leaders had given John the back of their hand, they could hardly reply, "John's baptism was of heaven." But if they said, "All that baptism stuff John did was merely of human origin," they could soon expect the stones to fly in their direction, because the people were convinced that John was truly a prophet, and stoning was the prescribed punishment for blasphemy.[219] So they simply whimpered out an evasive, "We don't know" (20:5–7).

Since the leaders refused to give a clear answer to Jesus' question, Jesus refused to answer theirs: "Neither will I tell you by what authority I am doing these things" (20:8). Luke's readers, however, know the answers to both questions. As for John, his baptism and his authority were of heaven ("the word of God came to John son of Zechariah in the wilderness," 3:2), and as for Jesus' authority, Jesus is "the Son of God" (1:35). John himself said of Jesus, "[O]ne who is more powerful than I is coming; I am not worthy to untie the thong of his sandals" (3:16).

This verbal duel with the religious leaders flows into the Parable of the Wicked Tenants, which appears in all three Synoptic Gospels (here in Luke, in Mark 12:1–12, and in Matthew 21:33–46, where the Parable of the Two

Sons is inserted between the duel with the religious leaders and the parable). All three agree that Jesus directed the parable against those very leaders (Mark 12:12; Matt. 21:45; Luke 20:19).

Since we have already commented on the Markan and Matthean versions of the parable, we will confine our comments here to those features of Luke's parable that are different and that make it distinctive.

Two Audiences

Jesus has been, as we noted, in a testy exchange with the religious leaders, and in Mark and Matthew he keeps on talking to them when he tells this parable. In Luke, though, there is an interesting and significant shift of audience. Here Jesus directs the parable to the people (20:9), not the leaders, even though we find out at the end of the parable that the religious leaders have heard it too or, perhaps better, overheard it (20:19). So for Luke the parable has two audiences: the intended audience, who are the people, and the eavesdropping audience, who are the religious authorities. The religious authorities would love to have driven a wedge between Jesus and the people (see 20:26); instead, Jesus uses this parable to drive a wedge between the people and their leaders.

These two groups, the people and the leaders, have wound their way through the whole of Luke's narrative, the people representing a positive pole in the narrative and the religious leaders a negative pole. As for the people, angel Gabriel said of John the Baptist, "He will turn many of the people of Israel to the Lord their God," and he will "make ready a people prepared for the Lord" (1:16–17). Another angel announced Jesus' birth as "good news of great joy for all the people" (2:10). Simeon said of Jesus that he was "a light for revelation to the Gentiles and for glory to your people Israel" (2:32). When Jesus raised the widow's dead son at Nain, those who saw it said, "God has looked favorably on his people" (7:16). When Jesus restored sight to a man who was blind, "all the people, when they saw it, praised God" (18:43). When Jesus taught daily in the temple, "all the people would get up early in the morning to listen to him" (21:38).

As for the religious leaders, they are, in contrast to the people, consistently the opponents of Jesus. They operate in Luke in different combinations and configurations of scribes, Pharisees, chief priests, elders, and leaders, and while historically there were major differences between these groups, in Luke they are united in their antagonism to Jesus. As Jack Dean Kingsbury says of the religious authorities in Luke,

> While perceiving themselves to be righteous, the authorities nonetheless make themselves guilty of all of the following: They resort to betrayal

> to accomplish their aims; ally themselves with Satan; subject God's supreme agent to mockery and blasphemy; deny Jesus' true identity as the Messiah Son of God; lodge false accusations against Jesus before both Pilate and Herod Antipas; call for the release of a bona fide revolutionary and the crucifixion of the innocent Jesus; and ridicule God's chosen Messiah as he hangs upon the cross in the mistaken belief that his obedience unto death is merely a sign of helplessness.[220]

In one dramatic and exceptional moment in Luke, the distinction between the people and the religious leaders breaks down. When Pilate called a summit meeting of "the chief priests, the leaders, and the people" to tell them that he could not find Jesus guilty of any charges, they protested with one voice, "Crucify him!" (23:13–25). For the people, this enmity toward Jesus was short-lived. When the crowds actually saw Jesus dying on the cross, they were filled with remorse and returned to their homes beating their breasts in repentance (23:48). They were, observes Johnson, now "ready to respond to the call to conversion in Acts 2:37–41."

So in Luke, both the people and the religious leaders hear this parable, but the acoustical angles are not the same. Jesus speaks the parable *to* the people (20:9), but the religious authorities figure out that he has spoken the parable *against* them (20:19).[221] Therefore each audience gets hit by the parable in a different way and, as we shall soon see, responds differently.

Unmasking Rejection

Luke's version of the parable is distinctive in several important ways:

1. Luke softens the connection between the parable and Isaiah 5, a linkage that is very strong in Mark and Matthew. Isaiah 5 includes a narrative love song in which the prophet sings about "my beloved," who is the owner of a vineyard. This beloved owner is pictured as doing everything possible to care for his vineyard and to make it fruitful. He planted vines, put a fence around the vineyard, built a watchtower, and hewed a wine vat (Isa. 5:1–2 Septuagint). Despite all of these efforts, though, the vineyard produced a disappointing harvest, not the good grapes the owner expected, but wild grapes, so he destroyed the vineyard (Isa. 5:2–6). Isaiah soon announces that the vineyard owner in his song is none other than "the LORD of hosts," and the vineyard is "the house of Israel" (5:7).

In Mark and in Matthew, the Parable of the Wicked Tenants is elaborately connected to this Isaiah passage. The parable tells of a vineyard owner who, like the vineyard owner in Isaiah, plants vines, puts up a fence, builds a watchtower, and hews a wine vat. The point is plain: the parable is a mirror of Isaiah 5, a tale of divine disappointment over the disobedience of the house of Israel.

In Luke, however, Jesus begins the parable much more leanly, "A man planted a vineyard and leased it to tenants" (Luke 20:9). That's it, period; no fence, no watchtower, no wine vat. Luke's version still evokes the themes found in Isaiah's love poem. It would be almost impossible not to do so. A parable Jesus tells about a vineyard and a vineyard owner to a Jewish audience on the grounds of the temple cannot escape being an allegory for God and Israel. The imagery is too deep and long-standing to be anything else.

But Luke makes the connection to Isaiah 5 less comprehensive, probably because Luke does not see this parable as merely Isaiah 5 redux, yet another story of a disobedient Israel. Luke has a hawklike focus on the one particular moment of disobedience being described in his Gospel, namely, the rejection by the religious leaders of Jesus as the beloved son. Luke knows, of course, of the repeated history of killing the prophets, stoning those who are sent, and turning away from God (see 13:34), but for Luke the rejection of Jesus as Messiah by the religious leaders is not just one more example in a long history of disobedience, but the ultimate rejection, the final tilting, the turning point of all history. The owner of the vineyard is still God, and the vineyard is still Israel, but this time the vineyard has tenants, wicked tenants.

Luke uses his considerable skill as a storyteller to aim the parable not backward in history toward Isaiah's vineyard and Israel's past but, instead, on the present moment, on the vineyard that Jesus is presently standing in and on the treachery of the current tenants, the religious leaders, who are even now plotting to take his life. The result is a parable that is even more dramatic than the disappointed love song of Isaiah, because Luke's parable is, after all, a story of the plot to murder Jesus.

2. We see another distinctive of Luke's version of the parable, and an additional display of his narrative skill, in the main body of the parable. In Luke's version, the vineyard owner, having leased the vineyard to tenants, goes away "for a long time," not turning his attention to the vineyard again until the proper season, when the time is ripe.[222] In all three Synoptics, the owner sends servants to the vineyard to collect the owner's share of the produce, but in Mark and Matthew, the parable gets complicated over the details of how many of these servants are sent and what happens to them. Luke is again crisp. Only three individual servants are sent:

- The first the tenants beat and sent away empty-handed (20:10).
- The second the tenants beat, insulted and sent away empty-handed (20:11).
- The third the tenants wounded and threw out of the vineyard (20:12).

The plot in Luke's version moves swiftly and cleanly as the violence against these servants increases incrementally, tightening the violin string, creating suspense. Notice also that in Luke, unlike in the Markan and Matthean versions, none of the servants is killed. For Luke, only one killing matters: the killing that comes at the end of the parable, the murder of the beloved son, who is Jesus.

3. Perhaps the most significant change Luke makes is to insert a soliloquy into the parable, turning this into yet another of Luke's "what am I going to do?" parables. As we have noted, there are five such parables in Luke. The others are the Friend at Midnight (11:5–8), the Rich Fool (12:16–21), the Prodigal Son (15:11–32), and the Unjust Steward (16:1–8). In each of these parables, a character gets into a crisis in the middle of the parable. Then, usually in a soliloquy, the character ponders how to get out of trouble. Finally, the character makes a decision and acts accordingly.

This is the only one of the five in which the character representing God is the character in crisis, the only one in which the God character engages in a "what-am-I-going-to-do?" soliloquy. The God figure, the vineyard owner, has sent three servants to the vineyard, and each has met with an increasing level of violence and rejection. So the vineyard owner deliberates out loud to himself, "What shall I do?" Then he comes to a decision and acts, "I will send my beloved son; perhaps they will respect him'" (20:13). The imagery is clear. Luke's readers have known since Jesus' baptism that Jesus is the beloved son. The divine voice identified him: "You are my Son, the Beloved; with you I am well pleased" (3:22). The parable gathers the hearers into the mind and heart of God as God decides to send the beloved Son into a world of mounting disobedience and violence, a beloved Son who is worthy of respect (20:13).

When the vineyard owner sends his beloved son to the vineyard, the tenants see this as a golden opportunity. "This is the heir," they say, "let us kill him so that the inheritance may be ours" (20:14). The logic of their reasoning is completely clear, but how realistic this is or how the logistics would work are irrelevant. The point in the story is the tenants' desire to own and run the vineyard themselves, without interference from the owner or his son. The tenants accomplish their plan, and the murder is done: "So they threw him out of the vineyard and killed him" (20:15).[223]

It is this moment, this scene of rejection and murder, that serves as the focal point of the parable in Luke. For Luke, this is a story about the rejection, the suffering, and the killing of the beloved Son and the complicity of the religious authorities. For Luke, this vineyard story is a parabolic retelling of what Jesus told the disciples just before they set out on the journey to Jerusalem: "The Son of Man must undergo great suffering, and be rejected by the elders, chief priests, and scribes, and be killed" (9:22).

Luke has polished the parable into a taut narrative of escalating violence leading to the callous murder of the vineyard owner's beloved son. It is now time for the listeners to make a decision, and Jesus puts the question to them, "What then will the owner of the vineyard do to them?" Jesus answers his own question, "He will come and destroy those tenants and give the vineyard to others" (20:15–16).

What was the impact of this? It depends on who was listening.

Two Reactions

The people, who hear this parable in one way, and the religious authorities, who overhear it in another, have two very different reactions:

The People. The people recoil in horror, saying, "Heaven forbid!" (20:16, literally "May it not happen!"). Since only Luke depicts this parable as being directed to the people, he is the only one to include the people's response. Their reaction immediately raises the question, Heaven forbid what? What do the people hope will never happen?

One possibility is that the people are feeling sympathy for the tenants in the parable and responding to what Jesus says the owner will do to them, namely, destroy them and take the vineyard from them. But the idea that the people are feeling sympathy here is not likely. First, just staying within the economy of the narrative itself, the tenants have been presented as treacherous and murderous, and people rarely sympathize with the villains of a tale. Second, Luke, as we noted, has an overall pattern of distinguishing between the people, who respond positively to Jesus and the good news, and the leaders, who want him dead, and he has maintained that distinction in the circumstances around this parable. Luke would hardly report, at this point anyway, an incident in which the people take up the cause of the tenants, who represent, of course, the religious leaders.

Another possibility is that the people understand the vineyard imagery, that the vineyard is an age-old symbol for Israel, and what they are saying "Heaven forbid!" to is the handing over of Israel "to others." It would mean the end of their culture and their identity. But this interpretation hardly springs from the Lukan account and may well rest on a later and misguided supersessionist view that the giving of the vineyard "to others" implies the replacement of Jews with Gentiles or Judaism with Christianity. Not only is such an understanding bankrupt on theological grounds; there is no reason within the confines of the parable itself to hear the story this way. What Jesus is saying the owner will do is to destroy the violent and greedy tenants and give the vineyard to others, presumably other, more responsible tenants. This would not be about the destruction of Israel but, to the contrary, about God's continuing care of it.

What seems most likely is that the people are responding to the whole ugly story of tenants in a vineyard who respond to a perfectly routine arrangement between vineyard workers and the owner with violence, scheming, and finally homicide, a story that ends in tragedy for all. "Heaven forbid," the people blurt out, "that such a thing could ever happen!"[224] When they say this, the whole event takes on ironic overtones. Jesus, the beloved Son, is standing right there with the people, in the temple in Jerusalem, in the epicenter of the "vineyard," being encircled, as he speaks, by the religious leaders who are scheming how to throw him out of the vineyard and have him killed. "Heaven forbid!" say the people, unaware that the nasty story of deceit and slaughter they have just heard is being played out in real time all around them.

To grasp the irony of the whole scene helps us understand what happens next. After the people say, "Heaven forbid that this would ever happen!" Jesus gave them a penetrating, searching look. The NRSV simply says "he looked at them" (20:17), but that's too mild. The verb is *emblepsas* (ἐμβλέψας), and it is the same word Luke uses to describe how Jesus looked at Peter after the third denial and the crowing of the cock (22:61). Johnson translates this text as "he stared at them,"[225] and Garland renders it, "He looked them straight in the eye."[226]

Then Jesus quoted Scripture: "What then does this text mean: 'The stone that the builders rejected has become the cornerstone'?" (20:17, quoting Ps. 118:22). Psalm 118 is one patch in the quilt by which the early church understood Jesus' messiahship, including his death and resurrection, to be the fulfillment of what was foretold in Scripture. The implication is that Jesus is saying, "You responded to that parable by saying, 'May this never happen!' but Scripture says otherwise. It will happen. It has happened. The 'builders,' who are the leaders, have rejected the 'stone,' who is the Son.[227] Both Mark and Matthew go on to quote the next, more upbeat verse, Psalm 118:23, "This was the Lord's doing, and it is amazing in our eyes," but not Luke. He is laser focused on the theme of rejection.

Jesus is the rejected stone, but once this metaphor of Jesus as the stone has been introduced, it expands. The rejected stone will become "the cornerstone" (20:17), the stumbling block, and a stone that crushes (20:18). Fitzmyer observes that cornerstone here does not have the contemporary connotation of a stone at the base of a building, with a date and an inscription, but is rather "the stone used at a building's corner to bear the weight or stress of the two walls. . . . It was the stone that was essential or crucial to the whole structure."[228] The stumbling block image may come from Isaiah 8:14–15, where the prophet said that for those who fear God as holy, God would be a protective sanctuary, but for those who do not, God would be a stone causing them to fall. The stone that crushes may come from Daniel 2:34, 44–45, where God uses a stone to smash pagan empires.

The Religious Authorities

In Shakespeare's *Hamlet,* Prince Hamlet of Denmark suspects that his uncle, Claudius, murdered his father, the king, in order to take over the throne. So he arranges to have a play performed at the castle, a play that includes a murder by poisoning, similar to his father's murder. Hamlet plans to watch Claudius during the performance to see if his guilt will show. "The play's the thing," Hamlet famously says, "wherein I'll catch the conscience of the king." Sure enough, as he watches the play unfold, Claudius is visibly upset by the murder scene and storms from the room, exposing his guilt.

Here the parable's the thing wherein we catch the conscience of the religious leaders. As they hear Jesus tell this story of a vineyard, the religious leaders, knowing the plot brewing in their hearts to kill Jesus (19:47), immediately recognize themselves in the parable. They were unmistakably the wicked tenants, and they knew at once that the parable Jesus told *to* the people was told *against* them. To see themselves portrayed for the villains they were could have provoked sorrowful repentance, but instead it prompted them to double down on their plot. "They wanted to lay hands on him at that very hour, but they feared the people" (20:19).

The Stone That Was Rejected

The last parable Jesus told before entering Jerusalem was, as we discussed, the Parable of the Ten Minas. That parable was a story of earthly kings, a depiction of how the elite of the world seize power, enforce their will, and take revenge on their opponents.

The first parable, and the only parable, that Jesus tells in Luke after he enters Jerusalem is this Parable of the Wicked Tenants. This parable assures us that, in the midst of all the world's power plays, greed, and violence, God is anointing a very different kind of king and establishing a very different kind of kingdom. The vineyard has been infected with treachery and cruelty. What will the owner of the vineyard do? The owner of the vineyard has not abandoned it, the parable teaches, and he will act to save it. God will raise from death the crucified beloved Son and make him the keystone of redemption. The theological centerpiece of this story is the psalm Jesus quotes to interpret his own parable: "The stone that the builders rejected has become the cornerstone."

The people who heard this parable would have no way of knowing fully what Jesus meant by those words, but Luke's readers do. They have already heard Jesus tell his disciples that he "must" be rejected and killed (9:22), and several more times he will announce his coming passion (9:44; 12:50; 13:33–35; 17:25; 18:31–34). Luke "does not allow too much time to pass," observes Tannehill, "without a reminder of what Jesus faces in Jerusalem."[229] Later, after the resurrection, Jesus will tell two followers on the Emmaus road that his suffering was "necessary" (24:26), and in Acts, Paul will hold Scripture study sessions in the synagogue at Thessalonica for three Sabbath days "explaining and proving that it was necessary for the Messiah to suffer and rise from the dead" (Acts 17:1–3). The people, upon hearing the parable, cried out, "Heaven forbid!" but Jesus quotes the psalm to say, "No, this is what heaven is doing before your eyes. Haven't you read the Scripture? The builders are going to reject the stone. That's what the Scriptures say, but that's not all they say. The rejected stone will become the keystone."

We must tread carefully here. To say that Jesus' rejection, suffering, and death were necessary should not be understood in a mechanical, deterministic way, as if God somehow drew up a master plan that required the brutalization of Jesus. No. The necessity of Jesus' suffering is the inevitable consequence of the vulnerability of divine love interacting with human sinfulness. God's power is not like human power; God's ways are not like our ways, and when "love so amazing, so divine" enters the vineyard, suffering will result. Just as good parents soon learn that the love they try to give their own children is inevitably a suffering love, so much more is the love of God for God's children a suffering love.

When we seek to allow this Parable of the Wicked Tenants to take us to the place where we can be "on hand" for the kingdom that is "at hand," we can do no better than to read the rest of Luke's Gospel. Watch the beloved Son as he is betrayed with a kiss. Stay close to him as the "wicked tenants" arrest him, mock him, beat him, hand him over to the Gentiles, and finally kill him, as he told us they would. But do not leave, even though darkness has come over the whole land. Stay until dawn on the first day of the week, when we will know the joy of discovering what God's love was doing throughout the messiness of human history, taking the stone rejected by the builders and building a kingdom of peace and justice and love on that stone.

Nor does the story end there. Luke reports that the risen Jesus said to his astonished disciples, "Thus it is written, that the Messiah is to suffer and to rise from the dead on the third day, and that repentance and forgiveness of sins is to be proclaimed in his name to all nations, beginning from Jerusalem. You are witnesses of these things" (24:46–48). The story of the beloved Son continues in the preaching and witness of the disciples.

Sure enough, as Luke continues the narrative in Acts, Peter and John were heading to the temple to pray when they encountered a lame beggar who begged for money. Peter told him, "I have no silver or gold, but what I have I give you; in the name of Jesus Christ of Nazareth, stand up and walk" (Acts 3:6–8). The man, made strong, jumped up and went into the temple with Peter and John, praising God.

This naturally caused a stir among the people, who flocked around Peter and John in Solomon's portico in the temple. This soon attracted the attention of the "priests, the captain of the temple, and the Sadducees," who arrested Peter and John. The "wicked tenants" are still hanging around the vineyard, hassling the servants sent to them.

The next day the "rulers, elders, and scribes," along with the high priest Annas and some other priestly officials, confronted Peter and John, asking them about the healing of the lame man, "By what power or by what name did you do this?" (Acts 4:5–7). In other words, it is the same question they put to Jesus earlier: "By what authority are you doing these things?"

That must have seemed like déjà vu to Peter and John. When Jesus got challenged in the temple about his authority, he told the Parable of the Wicked Tenants. The Spirit also gave Peter a good word to speak. He told the religious leaders, "So you rulers and elders are questioning us because we did a good deed to a man who was sick, and now you want to know how he was healed. Well, I'll tell you. This man is standing before you in good health by the name of Jesus Christ of Nazareth, whom you crucified, whom God raised from the dead." While he was at it, Peter remembered a piece of Scripture he heard Jesus tell these leaders, so he added that this Jesus is "the stone that was rejected by you, the builders; it has become the cornerstone" (4:8–11, par.)

Because the rejected Son has been raised up by God, and because the vineyard has now been given to him as king, other rejected ones, like this lame beggar, now stand up straight and praise the God of Israel. Willie James Jennings observed this about what Peter said to the leaders who were challenging the source of his authority:

> Peter . . . has become like the great jazz master, Louis Armstrong. He states the melody and reveals the primordial blues structure that will become the home for endless variations, ever new but always familiar. "Jesus Christ of Nazareth, whom you crucified, whom God raised from the dead" (v. 10). The table is being turned over, an upside down world is being turned right side up in these words of Peter. Peter stands next to the man God has healed not by the power claimed

by the elites, by the judges of this world, but only through the Holy Spirit. The first word of judgment to the elites has come: You do not have the power to heal the broken. You cannot raise the dead, only Jesus can. There is a second word that comes from Peter: "This Jesus is 'the stone that was rejected by you, the builders; it has become the cornerstone'" (v. 11). What Jesus stated indirectly to the elites who persecuted him, Peter comes right at them. Peter comes correct![230]

Notes

Preface

1. Walter Benjamin, "Theses on the Philosophy of History," *Illuminations* (New York: Harcourt, Brace, and World, 1968), 264.
2. Augustine, *Sermons on Selected Lessons from the New Testament, Volume 2* (Oxford: James Parker and Co., 1875), 67:5. Translation modernized by the author.
3. 1 Thess. 5:2.
4. The quotation is actually a paraphrase of Jordan's words, one that is found on the back cover of his book about Jesus' parables. The full Jordan quotation is, "So he lit a stick of dynamite, covered it over with an interesting story, and presented it to them. By the time the 'good people' got these parables unwrapped, Jesus and his disciples were a few miles down the road." This is found at Clarence Jordan, *Cotton Patch Parables of Liberation* (Eugene, OR: Wipf & Stock, 2009), 59.
5. John R. Donahue, *The Gospel in Parable* (Minneapolis: Fortress Press, 1988), 11.

Chapter 1: Jesus' Parables on the Playground of the Scholars

1. Jean Luis Segundo, "Capitalism versus Socialism: Crux Theologica," in *Frontiers of Theology in Latin America*, ed. R. Gibellini (Maryknoll, NY: Orbis Books, 1979), 254.
2. Joel Marcus, "Entering into the Kingly Power of God," *Journal of Biblical Literature* 107, no. 4 (1988): 674.
3. Some have argued that this quip did not originate with Yogi, and, as the great Berra himself once said, "A lot of things I said, I didn't say."
4. My definition of a parable is different from but influenced by Arland Hultgren's definition: "A parable is a figure of speech in which a comparison is made between God's kingdom, actions, or expectations and something in this world, real or imagined" (Arland J. Hultgren, *The Parables of Jesus: A* Commentary [Grand Rapids: Eerdmans, 2000], 3).
5. C. H. Dodd, *The Parables of the Kingdom* (Glasgow: Collins Sons, 1978), 13.
6. Augustine, "Exposition on Psalm 126," https://www.newadvent.org/fathers/1801126.htm (altered for language and punctuation).
7. Mary Ford, "Toward the Restoration of Allegory: Christology, Epistemology and Narrative Structure," *St. Vladimir's Theological Quarterly* 34, no. 2–3 (1990): 189.
8. Ford, "Toward the Restoration of Allegory," 171.
9. Robert H. Stein, "The Parables of Jesus in Recent Study," *Word and World* 5. no. 3 (Summer 1985): 249.
10. Joachim Jeremias, *The Parables of Jesus*, rev. ed. (New York: Charles Scribner's Sons, 1963), 18.

11. "Proceedings, 1938," *Journal for Biblical Literature* 58, no. 1 (March 1939): iii.
12. Dennis C. Duling, "Norman Perrin and the Kingdom of God: Review and Response," *Journal of Religion* 64, no. 4 (October 1984): 468.
13. Aristotle, *Art of Rhetoric* (Chicago: University of Chicago Press, 2019), 167.
14. Stein, "The Parables of Jesus in Recent Study," 250. See also Jeremias, *The Parables of Jesus,* 19.
15. For a discussion of the generalized moral points Jülicher finds in Jesus' parables, see Jeremias, *The Parables of Jesus,* 19.
16. Ernst Fuchs, "The Essence of Language Event and Christology," in *Studies of the Historical Jesus* (London: SCM Press, 1964), 213–28. See also A. C. Thiselton, "The Parables as Language-Event: Some Comments on Fuchs's Hermeneutics in the Light of Linguistic Philosophy," *Scottish Journal of Theology* 23, no. 4 (November 1970): 438.
17. John Dominic Crossan, *In Parables: The Challenge of the Historical Jesus* (New York: Harper & Row, 1973), 32.
18. John Dominic Crossan. *The Dark Interval: Toward a Theology of Story* (Farmington, MN: Polebridge Press, 1994), 42, emphasis added.
19. Amos N. Wilder, *Early Christian Rhetoric: The Language of the Gospel,* rev. ed. (Cambridge: Harvard University Press, 1971), 84.
20. Sallie McFague, *Speaking in Parables* (Minneapolis: Fortress Press, 2007), 78–79.
21. Mary Ann Tolbert, *Perspectives on the Parables: An Approach to Multiple Interpretations* (Philadelphia: Fortress Press, 1979), 42–43.
22. Austin Farrar, "Revelation," in Basil Mitchell, ed., *Faith and Logic: Oxford Essays in Philosophical Theology* (London: George Allen & Unwin, 1957), 99.
23. Wilder, *Early Christian Rhetoric,* 82, as cited in Robert W. Funk, *Language, Hermeneutic, and the Word of God* (New York: Harper & Row, 1966), 155.
24. Funk, *Language, Hermeneutic, and the Word of God,* 155.
25. Funk, *Language, Hermeneutic, and the Word of God,* 156.
26. Funk, *Language, Hermeneutic, and the Word of God,* 155.
27. Peter S. Hawkins, "A Man Had Two Sons: The Question of Forgiveness in Luke 15," in Charles L. Griswold and David Konstan, eds., *Ancient Forgiveness: Classical, Judaic, and Christian* (Cambridge: Cambridge University Press, 2012), 175.
28. Funk, *Language, Hermeneutic, and the Word of God,* 161.
29. Funk, *Language, Hermeneutic, and the Word of God,* 161.
30. Paul Ricoeur, "Biblical Hermeneutics," *Semeia* 4 (1975): 32.
31. Funk, *Language, Hermeneutic, and the Word of God,* 162.
32. Funk, *Language, Hermeneutic, and the Word of God,* 161.
33. Frederick Buechner, "The End Is Life," in Thomas G. Long and Cornelius Plantinga Jr., *A Chorus of Witnesses: Model Sermons for Today's Preacher* (Grand Rapids: Eerdmans, 1994), 298.
34. Norman Perrin, *The Kingdom of God in the Teaching of Jesus* (Philadelphia: Westminster Press, 1963), esp. 157ff.
35. See Duling, "Norman Perrin and the Kingdom of God," 468–70.
36. Perrin, *The Kingdom of God in the Teaching of Jesus,* 167. See Duling, "Norman Perrin and the Kingdom of God," 469–70.
37. Perrin, *The Kingdom of God in the Teaching of Jesus*, 16.
38. Perrin, *The Kingdom of God in the Teaching of Jesus*, 16–23.
39. Perrin, *The Kingdom of God in the Teaching of Jesus*, 157.
40. Norman Perrin, *Jesus and the Language of the Kingdom: Symbol and Metaphor in New Testament Interpretation* (Philadelphia: Fortress Press, 1976), 197–98.

41. Perrin, *Jesus and the Language of the Kingdom*, 5.
42. Perrin, *Jesus and the Language of the Kingdom*, 30.
43. Perrin, *Jesus and the Language of the Kingdom*, 197.
44. Stephen Crites, "The Narrative Quality of Experience," *Journal of the American Academy of Religion* 39, no. 3 (September 1971): 291–311.
45. Crites, "The Narrative Quality of Experience," 294–97.
46. Crites, "The Narrative Quality of Experience," 202.
47. "Made into America: Immigrant Stories Archive," https://madeintoamerica.org/refugee-camp-and-then-a-new-life-in-the-us-vietnam/.
48. Norman Perrin, *Rediscovering the Teaching of Jesus* (New York: Harper & Row, 1967), 55.
49. Christopher Morse, *The Difference Heaven Makes: Rehearing the Gospel as News* (London: T. & T. Clark, 2010).
50. Morse, *The Difference Heaven Makes*, 10.
51. Morse, *The Difference Heaven Makes*, 75.
52. Morse, *The Difference Heaven Makes*, 23.
53. Morse, *The Difference Heaven Makes*, 60. See Karl Barth, *The Doctrine of the Word of God. Church Dogmatics* I/1 (Edinburgh: T. & T. Clark, 1936), 151.
54. Morse, *The Difference Heaven Makes*, 61.
55. Morse, *The Difference Heaven Makes*, 122.
56. "The Government as the Church Militant Is Always a Terrible Idea," Center for Religion in Public Life, Philips Theological Seminary, https://ptstulsa.edu/rpli/church-militant-terrible-idea/.
57. Karl Barth, *Church Dogmatics* III/3 (Edinburgh: T. & T. Clark, 1961), 485.

Chapter 2: Decisions Preachers Make

1. Harriet Tubman, "Letter to Jacob Jackson," as quoted in Kate Clifford Larsen, *Bound for the Promised Land: Harriet Tubman, Portrait of an American Hero* (New York: One World, 2004), 110.
2. Elizabeth Simonsen as quoted on Robert C. Walton's blog, https://www.rcwalton.com/wp-content/uploads/2016/08/Violent-Bear-It-Away-The.pdf.
3. Klyne Snodgrass, *Stories with Intent: A Comprehensive Guide to the Parables of Jesus* (Grand Rapids: Eerdmans. 2008), 8.
4. C. H. Dodd, *The Parables of the Kingdom*, rev. ed. (New York: Charles Scribner's Sons, 1961), 5.
5. Dodd, *The Parables of the Kingdom*, 96.
6. John Dominic Crossan, *In Parables: The Challenge of the Historical Jesus* (New York: Harper & Row, 1973), 10.
7. Crossan, *In Parables*, 13.
8. Crossan, *In Parables*, 13.
9. Crossan, *In Parables*, 13.
10. Joachim Jeremias, *The Parables of Jesus*, rev. ed. (New York: Charles Scribner's Sons, 1962), 113.
11. Jeremias, *The Parables of Jesus*, 28.
12. Jeremias, *The Parables of Jesus*, 48–63.
13. William R. Herzog II, *Parables as Subversive Speech: Jesus as Pedagogue of the Oppressed* (Louisville, KY: Westminster John Knox Press, 1994).
14. Herzog, *Parables as Subversive Speech*, 31.
15. Herzog, *Parables as Subversive Speech*, 15.
16. William R. Herzog, "Sowing Discord: The Parable of the Sower, Mark 4:1–9," *Review & Expositor* 109, no. 2 (Spring 2012): 187–98.

17. Herzog, "Sowing Discord," 194.
18. Herzog, "Sowing Discord," 194.
19. Herzog, "Sowing Discord," 194.
20. Dodd, *The Parables of the Kingdom*, 32.
21. Dodd, *The Parables of the Kingdom*, 164–65.
22. Craig Callender, "Is Time an Illusion?" *Scientific American*, June 1, 2010, https://www.scientificamerican.com/article/is-time-an-illusion/.
23. Callender, "Is Time an Illusion?"
24. Callender, "Is Time an Illusion?"
25. Brian Greene, *The Elegant Universe: Superstrings, Hidden Dimension, and the Quest for the Ultimate Theory* (New York: Vintage Books, 1999), 36.
26. Augustine, *Confessions*, 2nd ed. (Indianapolis: Hackett Publishing, 2006), 242.
27. Augustine, *Confessions*, 242.
28. Augustine, *Confessions*, 3.
29. Herbert McCabe, *God Matters* (London: Continuum, 2010), 48.
30. Adam Kirsch, "Faith Healing: A Poet Confronts Illness and God," *New Yorker* (May 6, 2013), 80.
31. Kirsch, "Faith Healing."
32. Christian Wiman, "I Will Love You in the Summertime," *American Scholar* 85, no. 2 (Spring 2016): 55–56.
33. Katherine Sonderegger, "Book Forum," *Theology Today* 68, no. 1 (April 2011): 65.
34. Markus Barth, "Introduction," in Leonhard Goppelt et al., *The Easter Message Today* (New York: Thomas Nelson & Sons, 1964), 10–11.

Chapter 3: Mark's Parables: Background

1. Martin Dibelius, *From Tradition to Gospel* (Cambridge: James Clarke & Co., 1971), 230.
2. Ched Myers, *Binding the Strong Man: A Political Reading of Mark's Story of Jesus* (Maryknoll, NY: Orbis Books, 2008), 384.
3. Adela Yarbro Collins, "Narrative, History, and Gospel," *Semeia* 43 (1988): 148.
4. David Rhoads, Joanna Dewey, and Donald Michie, *Mark as Story: An Introduction to the Narrative of a Gospel*, 3rd ed. (Minneapolis: Fortress Press, 2012), 106.
5. Myers, *Binding the Strong Man*, 102.
6. Adela Yarbro Collins, *Mark: A Commentary*, Hermeneia—A Critical and Historical Commentary on the Bible (Minneapolis: Fortress Press, 2007), 69.
7. A nice phrase suggested by Steven Kraftchick in personal communication.
8. Morna D. Hooker, *The Gospel according to Saint Mark* (London: A. & C. Black, 1991).
9. Collins, *Mark*, 70.
10. This and all other quotations from *1 Enoch* are taken from "The Book of Enoch," in *The Apocrypha and Pseudepigrapha of the Old Testament*, ed. R. H. Charles (Oxford: Clarendon Press, 1913), 163–281.
11. In the book of *Enoch*, the Son of Man turns out to be Enoch himself (*1 Enoch* 71:14).
12. Collins, *Mark*, 69.
13. Matthew L. Skinner, "Making a Life: A Tribute to Don Juel," *Inspire* 8, no. 1 (Summer/Fall 2003): 33.
14. Porter Anderson, "Review: Handel's 'Messiah' in Radiant Redux," CNN.com, December 22, 2005, http://www.cnn.com/2005/SHOWBIZ/Music/12/20/review.handel/index.html.
15. Hooker, *The Gospel according to Saint Mark*, 93.

Chapter 4: Mark: The Parables

1. Eberhard Arnold, "Jesus and the Future of the Earth," *Plough Quarterly* 32 (Summer 2022): 78.
2. There are several images, similitudes, and proverbial sayings in Mark, some of which are explicitly called parables (e.g., 7:14–17), but there are only five parables in Mark that approach being full narratives, the three in Mark 4, the Vineyard (12:1–10), and the Man on a Journey (13:32–37).
3. Klyne Snodgrass, *Stories with Intent; A Comprehensive Guide to the Parables of Jesus* (Grand Rapids: Eerdmans, 2008), 145.
4. Eugene LaVerdiere, *The Beginning of the Gospel: Introducing the Gospel according to Mark*, vol. 1 (Collegeville: MN: Liturgical Press, 1999), 117.
5. The boat has been ready since 3:9: "[Jesus] told his disciples to have a boat ready for him because of the crowd, so that they would not crush him." Some commentators see Jesus' ordering the disciples to have a boat ready so far in advance as not just foresight but foreknowledge and a nod to Jesus' role as the omniscient Son of God. Perhaps, but, if so, it is quite subtle.
6. M. Eugene Boring, *Mark: A Commentary*, New Testament Library (Louisville, KY: Westminster John Knox Press, 2006), 116.
7. The Greek text does not actually have the word "seed" or "seeds" in it. More literally translated, the parable states simply, if somewhat vaguely, "one fell" (v. 4), "another fell" (vv. 5, 7), "others fell" (v. 8). There is much scholarly conversation about whether the parable is talking about one seed in each case, or a portion of seeds—or seed at all, since the word is not mentioned—and whether the singular usage in vv. 4, 5, and 7 versus the plural in v. 8 is significant. Assuming that a person sowing something on the ground is usually sowing seed and not soap bubbles or gold coins, and that, when he gets to the interpretation of this parable later (4:13–20), Mark himself can't seem to keep the numbers straight, we can probably relax about the grammatical technicalities, go with the flow of the story, and take it as the farming tale it is.
8. Joachim Jeremias, *The Parables of Jesus* (New York: Scribner's, 1963), 12.
9. See, for example, W. D. Davies and Dale Allison, *A Critical and Exegetical Commentary on the Gospel according to Saint Matthew* (Edinburgh: T. & T. Clark, 1991), 2:385, and Eta Linnemann, *Parables of Jesus* (London: SPCK, 1966), 177.
10. Robert K. McIver, "One Hundred-Fold Yield—Miraculous or Mundane? Matthew 13:8, 23; Mark 4:8, 20; Luke 8:8," *New Testament Studies* 40 (1994): 606–8.
11. McIver, "One Hundred-Fold Yield—Miraculous or Mundane?," 607.
12. Frederick Buechner, *Beyond Words: Daily Readings in the ABC's of Faith* (San Francisco: HarperCollins, 2004), 41.
13. Donald H. Juel, "Encountering the Sower: Mark 4:1–20," *Interpretation* 56, no. 3 (July 2002): 277.
14. Georges Bernanos, *The Diary of a Country Priest* (New York: Carol & Graf, 1983), 53.
15. See Alexandra Rice, "East Lake Went from 'War Zone' to a National Model," in the online newsletter of Purpose Built Communities, October 1, 2012, https://purposebuiltcommunities.org/news-press/east-lake-in-atlanta/east-lake-went-from-war-zone-to-a-national-model/.
16. Mark, who was so explicit about the movements of Jesus and the crowd in 4:1–3, is exasperatingly vague here about when Jesus moves from inside with the disciples to back outside with the crowds. See the discussion of this in the treatment of the Parable of the Seed Growing Secretly below.

17. See, for example, Morna D. Hooker, *The Gospel according to Saint Mark* (London: A. C. Black, 1991), 129.
18. For a good discussion of the parallels between the interpretation of the Sower and the ministry of Jesus in the rest of Mark, see Mary Ann Tolbert, *Sowing the Gospel: Mark's World in Literary-Historical Perspective* (Minneapolis: Fortress Press, 1996), 124.
19. Gene M. Tucker, "The Book of Isaiah 1–39: Introduction, Commentary, and Reflections," in Leander E. Keck et al., eds., *The New Interpreter's Bible* (Nashville: Abingdon Press, 2001), 6:103.
20. Tucker, in *New Interpreter's Bible*, 6:105.
21. Juel, "Encountering the Sower," 277.
22. Paul Tillich, "Holy Waste," in *The New Being* (New York: Scribner, 1955), 48.
23. Rudolf Bultmann, *The History of the Synoptic Tradition* (New York: Harper & Row, 1963), 173.
24. C. H. Dodd, *The Parables of the Kingdom* (New York: Charles Scribner's Sons, 1961), 9.
25. Dodd, *The Parables of the Kingdom*, 143–44.
26. Joel Marcus, *Mark 1–8: A New Translation with Introduction and Commentary*, Anchor Bible (New York: Doubleday, 2000), 328.
27. *2 Baruch* 48:2 found at http://www.pseudepigrapha.com/pseudepigrapha/2Baruch.html.
28. *2 Baruch* 48:2.
29. Wendell Berry, "Economy and Pleasure," in *What Are People For? Essays by Wendell Berry* (Berkeley, CA: Counterpoint, 2010), 141.
30. *Sanhedrin* 97a, author's paraphrase.
31. *Midrash Shir ha-Shirim Raba*, VI, 10 as quoted in Gershom Scholem, *The Messianic Idea in Judaism: And Other Essays on Jewish Spirituality* (New York: Schocken Books, 1971), 10–11.
32. Tennessee Williams, *A Streetcar Named Desire* (New York: New Directions Books, 2004), 116.
33. Sara Miles, *Take This Bread: A Radical Conversion* (New York: Ballantine Books, 2007), 3.
34. Miles, *Take This Bread*, 9.
35. Miles, *Take This Bread*, 9.
36. Miles, *Take This Bread*, 57.
37. Miles, *Take This Bread*, 58.
38. Miles, *Take This Bread*, 59.
39. Miles, *Take This Bread*, xiii.
40. Miles, *Take This Bread*, 60.
41. Miles, *Take This Bread*, 277–78.
42. Amy-Jill Levine, *Short Stories by Jesus: The Enigmatic Parables of a Controversial Rabbi* (San Francisco: HarperOne, 2015), 166.
43. See *Mishnah Kil'ayim 3:2*, in Jacob Neusner, *Mishnah: A New Translation* (New Haven, CT: Yale University Press, 1988), 54.
44. Bernard Brandon Scott, *Hear Then the Parable: A Commentary on the Parables of Jesus* (Minneapolis: Fortress Press, 1989), 386–87.
45. Levine, *Short Stories by Jesus,* 186.
46. Levine, *Short Stories by Jesus,* 186.
47. David Buttrick, *Speaking Parables: A Homiletic Guide* (Louisville, KY: Westminster John Knox Press, 2000), 77.
48. Levine, *Short Stories by Jesus,* 180. Jesus was Jewish, of course, as were many of his opponents. He has so many collisions with the religious leaders over matters of purity and defilement, it is easy for Christian interpreters to see Jesus as opposed

to the whole Jewish concept of holiness, purity, and cleanliness. But a Jesus who teaches us to pray, "Father, hallowed be Your name," is not to be understood as rejecting Jewish understandings of holiness. They are at the center of God's own name and identity. In Mark, when Jesus engages the Pharisees and scribes in debate over cleanliness and defilement, the goal is not to reject cleanliness and holiness, but to retrieve the true understanding of God's commandments rather than the corruption of them in much "human tradition" (see Mark 7:1–23).

49. John Dominic Crossan, *In Parables: The Challenge of the Historical Jesus* (New York: Harper & Row, 1973), 47.
50. Robert Funk, "The Looting-Glass Tree Is for the Birds: Ezekiel 17:22–24; Mark 4:30–32," *Interpretation* 27, no. 1 (January 1973): 7.
51. Hooker, *The Gospel according to Saint Mark*, 273.
52. Chrysostom, "Homily LXVIII," in *The Homilies of S. John Chrysostom, Archbishop of Constantinople, on the Gospel of Matthew* (London: Oxford Press, 1851), 914.
53. Luise Schotroff, *The Parables of Jesus* (Minneapolis: Fortress Press, 2006), 21.
54. See, for example, William R. Herzog II, *Parables as Subversive Speech: Jesus as Pedagogue of the Oppressed* (Louisville, KY: Westminster John Knox Press, 1994), 105–10.
55. Joel Marcus, *Mark 8–16: A New Translation with Introduction and Commentary*, Yale Anchor Bible (New Haven, CT: Yale University Press, 2009), 802. See also A. T. A. Robertson, *Grammar of the Greek New Testament in the Light of Historical Research*, 3rd ed. (London: Hodder & Stoughton, 1919), 519.
56. Saul Bellow, *Mr. Sammler's Planet* (New York: Penguin, 1977), 260.
57. Michael Ruse and Edward O. Wilson, "The Evolution of Ethics," in James E. Huchingson, *Religion and the Natural Sciences: The Range of Engagement* (Eugene, OR: Wipf & Stock, 1993), 310–11.
58. Richard Dawkins, *The God Delusion* (Boston: Mariner Books, 2008), 73.
59. Dawkins, *The God Delusion*, 404.
60. Terry Eagleton, *Reason, Faith, and Revolution: Reflections on the God Debate* (New Haven, CT: Yale University Press, 2009), 16–17.
61. Stephen Dunn, "At the Smithville Methodist Church," in *New and Selected Poems: 1974–1994* (New York: W. W. Norton, 1994), 183–84.
62. George B. Caird, *The Language and Imagery of the Bible* (London: Duckworth, 1980), 266.
63. Caird, *The Language and Imagery of the Bible*, 256.
64. Arland J. Hultgren, *The Parables of Jesus: A Commentary* (Grand Rapids: Eerdmans, 2000), 267.
65. It was Bishop R. H. Lightfoot who most fully described these and other connections between Mark 13 and the subsequent passion narrative in Mark 14–15. See his *The Gospel Message of St. Mark* (Oxford: Clarendon Press, 1950), 48–59.
66. See "Alfred Nobel, Swedish Inventor," in *Britannica*, https://www.britannica.com/biography/Alfred-Nobel.

Chapter 5: Matthew's Parables: Background

1. The concept of a truly blameless, upright, and righteous person is rooted in the Old Testament (see Job 1:1; Ps.1), and the figure of the *tzaddik* is well-established in Judaism by the time of Maimonides.
2. Chaim Potok, *The Chosen* (New York: Random House, 1967), 284–85.
3. Potok, *The Chosen*, 287.
4. Tzvi Freeman, "What Is a Tzaddik? Being Human All the Way," at Chabad.org, https://www.chabad.org/library/article_cdo/aid/2367724/jewish/Tzaddik.htm.

5. Dale C. Allison, *Matthew: A Shorter Commentary* (London: T. & T. Clark, 2004), 14.
6. Stanley Hauerwas, *A Community of Character: Toward a Constructive Christian Social Ethic Book* (Notre Dame, IN: University of Notre Dame Press, 1981), 145.
7. Hauerwas, *A Community of Character,* 145.
8. Hauerwas, *A Community of Character,* 145.
9. Hauerwas, *A Community of Character,* 146.
10. Hauerwas, *A Community of Character*, 146.
11. Christine Roy Yoder, *Proverbs* (Nashville: Abingdon Press, 2009), 48.
12. Carol Newsom, *The Book of Job: A Contest of Moral Imaginations* (New York: Oxford University Press, 2009), 122.
13. Newsom, *The Book of Job*, 122.
14. Newsom, *The Book of Job*, 122.
15. Newsom, *The Book of Job*, 122.
16. Yoder, *Proverbs,* 48.
17. Robert C. Tannehill, *The Sword of His Mouth* (Philadelphia: Fortress Press, 1975), 62–63.
18. Tannehill, *The Sword of His Mouth*, 66.
19. Patrick D. Miller Jr., *Interpreting the Psalms* (Philadelphia: Fortress Press, 1986), 82.
20. An apparent exception is the Parable of the Two Sons (Matt. 21:28–32), in which one son refuses to work in the vineyard, but later changes his mind, and the other son says he will work but then doesn't. But even here, the characters are "flat" in that they are examples of two responses to the proclamation of the kingdom: the religious leaders, whose apparent yes to God is belied by their rejection of the gospel, and the sinners, who, even though their lives expressed an apparent no to God, were eager to hear Jesus.
21. E. M. Forster, *Aspects of the Novel* (New York: Harcourt, 1927), 67.
22. Forster, *Aspects of the Novel*, 71, 74.
23. Jason G. Goldman, "Animating Anthropomorphism: Giving Minds to Geometric Shapes," *Scientific American,* March 8, 2013, https://blogs.scientificamerican.com/thoughtful-animal/animating-anthropomorphism-giving-minds-to-geometric-shapes-video/.
24. Joseph Ratzinger, *Eschatology: Death and Eternal Life*, 2nd ed. (Washington, DC: Catholic University of America Press, 1988), 231.
25. Charles Dickens, *A Christmas Carol in Prose Being a Ghost Story of Christmas* (London: Bradbury & Evans, 1858), 2.
26. Dickens, *A Christmas Carol,* 18.
27. Dickens, *A Christmas Carol,* 21.
28. Dickens, *A Christmas Carol*, 99.

Chapter 6: Matthew: The Parables

1. Paul Ricoeur, *The Symbolism of Evil* (Boston: Beacon Press, 1967), 67.
2. M. Eugene Boring, *An Introduction to the New Testament: History, Literature, Theology* (Louisville, KY: Westminster John Knox Press, 2012), 545.
3. Jack Dean Kingsbury, *The Parables of Jesus in Matthew 13* (London: SPCK, 1969), 130.
4. Birger Gerhardsson, "The Parable of the Sower and Its Interpretation," *New Testament Studies* 14, no. 2 (January 1968), 173.
5. M. Eugene Boring, "The Gospel of Matthew: Introduction, Commentary, and Reflections," in Leander E. Keck et al., eds., *The New Interpreter's Bible* (Nashville: Abingdon Press, 1995), 8:304.
6. Ray Wylie Hubbard, "Up against the Wall Redneck Mother," copyright 1973 by Tennessee Swamp Fox/EMI Music.

7. Daniel Durchholz, "Singer-songwriter Ray Wylie Hubbard Confronts His Mortality on New Album," *St. Louis Post-Dispatch*, June 1, 2018, https://www.stltoday.com/entertainment/music/singer-songwriter-ray-wylie-hubbard-confronts-his-mortality-on-new-album/article_a75a157a-d2d2–5d76–a770–2e5559f5978f.html.
8. "Artist Interview: Ray Wylie Hubbard," *Texas Monthly*, January 2010, https://www.texasmonthly.com/articles/ray-wylie-hubbard/.
9. Woody Allen, *Hannah and Her Sisters: Shooting Script*, 1986, 116, https://indiegroundfilms.files.wordpress.com/2014/01/hannah-her-sisters-1986–shooting.pdf.
10. Eric E. Peterson and Eugene H. Peterson, *Letters to a Young Pastor: Timothy Conversations between Father and Son* (Colorado Springs, CO: NavPress, 2020), 7.
11. Peterson and Peterson, *Letters to a Young Pastor*, 8.
12. Flannery O'Connor, "A Good Man Is Hard to Find," *The Complete Stories* (New York: Farrar, Straus & Giroux, 1971), 132.
13. O'Connor, "A Good Man Is Hard to Find," 132.
14. Cathleen Falsani, "The Worst Ideas of the Decade: The Prosperity Gospel," *Washington Post*, https://www.washingtonpost.com/wp-srv/special/opinions/outlook/worst-ideas/prosperity-gospel.html.
15. Joel Osteen, *Your Best Life Now: 7 Steps to Living Your Full Potential*, rev. and expanded ed. (New York: Hachette, 2015), 85.
16. Osteen, *Your Best Life Now*, 86.
17. Joseph Lelyveld, "South Africa's Bishop Tutu," *New York Times Magazine*, March 14, 1982, section 6, 44, 102.
18. William C. Placher, *Jesus the Savior: The Meaning of Jesus Christ for Christian Faith* (Louisville, KY: Westminster John Knox Press, 2001), 147.
19. Sue Halpern, "The War We Don't Want to See," *New York Review of Books*, December 18, 2008, https://www.nybooks.com/articles/2008/12/18/the-war-we-dont-want-to-see/.
20. John D. Rockefeller Jr., "Efficiency in the Lord's Business," *New Era Magazine* 26 (June 1920), 418–19.
21. Herman Hendrickx, *The Parables of Jesus* (San Francisco: Harper and Row, 1986), 73.
22. Contra Klyne R. Snodgrass, see *Stories with Intent: A Comprehensive Guide to the Stories of Jesus* (Grand Rapids: Eerdmans, 2008), 241.
23. Snodgrass, *Stories with Intent*, 225.
24. Bernard Brandon Scott, *Hear Then the Parable: A Commentary on the Parables of Jesus* (Minneapolis: Fortress Press, 1989), 324.
25. Plutarch, *Moralia*, vol. 4 (Cambridge, MA: Harvard University Press, 1936), http://www.perseus.tufts.edu/hopper/text?doc=Perseus%3Atext%3A2008.01.0211%3Asection%3D109.
26. Günter Bornkamm, *Jesus of Nazareth* (Minneapolis: Fortress Press, 1995), 69.
27. Robert Funk, "Beyond Criticism in Quest of Literacy: The Parable of the Leaven," *Interpretation* 25, no. 2 (April 1971): 162.
28. Bornkamm, *Jesus of Nazareth*, 62.
29. Dominic Garramone, *Bake and Be Blessed*, 2nd ed. (Peru, IL: Saint Bede Abbey Press, 2008), http://breadmonk.com/my-bread-blog/three-measures-of-flour.
30. Joachim Jeremias, *The Parables of Jesus*, rev. ed. (New York: Charles Scribner's Sons, 1963), 147.
31. Ulrich Luz, *Matthew 8–20: A Commentary on the Gospel of Matthew* (Minneapolis: Augsburg Press, 1989), 262.
32. Robert Funk, *Jesus as Precursor* (Philadelphia: Fortress Press, 1975), 55–57.
33. Funk, *Jesus as Precursor*, 55.

34. Snodgrass, *Stories with Intent*, 233.
35. Snodgrass, *Stories with Intent*, 235.
36. Luz, *Matthew 8–20*, 262–63.
37. Kate Clifford Larson, *Bound for the Promised Land: Harriet Tubman, Portrait of an American Hero* (New York: One World, 2003), 110.
38. Sarah H. Bradford, *Scenes in the Life of Harriet Tubman* (Auburn, NY: W. J. Moses, 1869), 58.
39. Bradford, *Scenes in the Life of Harriet Tubman*, 58.
40. Terry Eagleton, *Hope without Optimism* (Charlottesville: University of Virginia Press, 2015), 27–28.
41. Desmond Tutu, "The Man Who Changed My Life," *Cape Times*, June 17, 2013, https://www.iol.co.za/capetimes/the-man-who-changed-my-life-1533199.
42. Tutu, "The Man Who Changed My Life."
43. Scott J. Higgins, "The Defining Moment in Desmond Tutu's Life," personal blog, December 5, 2012, https://scottjhiggins.com/the-defining-moment-in-desmond-tutus-life/.
44. John Dominic Crossan, *In Parables: The Challenge of the Historical Jesus* (New York: Harper & Row, 1973), 34.
45. Crossan, *In Parables*, 34.
46. John Dominic Crossan, *Finding Is the First Act: Trove Folktales and Jesus' Treasure Parable* (Philadelphia: Fortress Press, 1979), 93.
47. Crossan, *Finding Is the First Act*, 93.
48. Crossan, *Finding Is the First Act*, 93–94.
49. Equally confounding is Bernard Brandon Scott's riff on Crossan in which he endows the treasure with a personality, namely, as "lawless" and "narcissistic," which allows it to "be a sign of God's grace working outside the laws of the everyday." But the same lawless narcissism can lead to corruption, and that, says Scott, is what happens in this parable. The man in the parable turns out to be a tragic figure. "His joy has led him astray. So now the man has sold all, is impoverished, yet possesses a treasure he dare not dig up unless he wants to face the rather embarrassing question of whence it came" (Brandon Scott, *Hear Then the Parable*, 402).
50. Fred B. Craddock, *Craddock Stories* (St. Louis: Chalice Press, 2001), 22–23.
51. Pliny, *Natural History*, vol. 2, book 9:54 (London: Henry G. Bohn, 1855), 430.
52. Leo Tolstoy, *A Confession* (Scotts Valley, CA: CreateSpace Publishing, 2017), 1.
53. "A Confession: Study Guide," https://www.coursehero.com/lit/A-Confession/plot-summary/.
54. Tolstoy, *A Confession*, 11.
55. Tolstoy, *A Confession*, 16.
56. "A Confession Study Guide."
57. Tolstoy, *A Confession*, 20.
58. Tolstoy, *A Confession*, 56.
59. See, for example, John R. Donahue, *The Gospel in Parable* (Minneapolis: Fortress Press, 1988), 69. See also Snodgrass, *Stories with Intent*, 489.
60. Michael Gerson, "Opinion: Prominent Evangelicals Are Directing Trump's Sinking Ship. That Feeds Doubts about Religion," *Washington Post*, December 7, 2020, https://www.washingtonpost.com/opinions/prominent-evangelicals-are-directing-trumps-sinking-ship-that-feeds-doubts-about-religion/2020/12/07/5ad8eb0c-38c3–11eb-9276–ae0ca72729be_story.html.
61. Michael Gerson, "Opinion: Trump's Evangelicals Were Complicit in the Desecration of Our Democracy," *Washington Post*, January 7, 2021, https://www.wash

ingtonpost.com/opinions/trumps-evangelicals-were-complicit-in-the-desecration-of-our-democracy/2021/01/07/69a51402–5110–11eb-83e3–322644d82356_story.html.

62. Website of the Crabapple First Baptist Church, Milton, GA, https://www.crabapplefbc.org/
63. Arland J. Hultgren, *The Parables of Jesus: A Commentary* (Grand Rapids: Eerdmans, 2000), 307.
64. Boring, "The Gospel of Matthew," 375.
65. Boring, "The Gospel of Matthew," 375.
66. Frederick Bussby, "Did a Shepherd Leave Sheep upon the Mountains or in the Desert? A Note on Matthew 18:12 and Luke 15:4," *Anglican Theological Review* 45, no. 1 (1963): 93–94.
67. Warren Carter, *Matthew and the Margins: A Sociopolitical and Religious Reading* (Maryknoll, NY: Orbis Books, 2000), 370–371.
68. Carter, *Matthew and the Margins*, 374.
69. See J. Duncan M. Derrett, *Law in the New Testament* (Eugene, OR: Wipf and Stock, 2005), 32–47.
70. John Drury, *The Parables in the Gospels* (New York: Crossroad, 1985), 92.
71. For example, Robert W. Heimburger, Christopher M. Hays, and Guillermo Mejía-Castillo, in an otherwise worthy attempt to understand the Parable of the Unforgiving Slave in conversation with survivors of armed conflict in Colombia, conclude, "These conflict survivors tell us that forgiveness offered beyond one's religious community for all kinds of offenses, including financial and violent offenses, is the route to the peace. . . ." Readers can judge for themselves whether or not this parable advocates for public policy involving the cancellation of all debt and the release of every offender. Mainly, though, this seems like one more attempt to turn the parable exclusively into a moral example story and to squeeze some pragmatic juice out of a completely hyperbolic story. See Robert W. Heimburger, Christopher M. Hays, and Guillermo Mejía-Castillo, "Forgiveness and Politics: Reading Matthew 18:21–35 with Survivors of Armed Conflict in Colombia," *Hervormde Teologiese Studies* 75, no. 4 (2019): 1–9.
72. Andrea Tornielli, "Gunshots, Fear, Prayer, and Forgiveness," *Vatican News*, May 12, 2021, https://www.vaticannews.va/en/pope/news/2021–05/gun-shots-fear-prayer-and-forgiveness.html.
73. Lewis B. Smedes, *The Art of Forgiving: When You Need to Forgive and Don't Know How* (New York: Ballentine Books, 1996), 87.
74. Smedes, *The Art of Forgiving*, 91.
75. Smedes, *The Art of Forgiving*, 178.
76. "Deep Thoughts by Jack Handey," *SNL Transcripts Tonight*, https://snltranscripts.jt.org/94/94ldeep1.phtml.
77. Raymond Angelo Belliotti, *Jesus the Radical: The Parables and Modern Morality* (Lanham, MD: Lexington Books, 2013), 79, emphasis added.
78. Amy-Jill Levine, *Short Stories by Jesus: The Enigmatic Parables of a Controversial Rabbi* (New York: HarperCollins, 2014), 225.
79. Scott, *Hear Then the Parable*, 284.
80. https://medium.com/@adambreckler/in-god-we-trust-all-others-bring-data-96784d01e9be.
81. For being alerted to the importance of the concept of giving in this parable, I am indebted to Steven Kraftchick.
82. Bernard Brandon Scott, and he is not alone, insists the contrary. He believes, based on various historical calculations, that a denarius was but a subsistence

wage in first-century Galilee. This landowner, he decides, paid poverty wages and was patently unfair to the all-day workers. The only way, he says, that someone could see this stingy employer as "generous" is if they had decided in advance that the landowner is a symbol for God. If one does that, then one is obliged to switch sympathies from where they properly belong, with the wronged all-day laborers, to the divine landowner (Scott, *Hear Then the Parable*, 283–84). But Scott has forgotten that this is a parable, a story, a folk yarn, one that sets and follows its own interior terms. Right at the beginning, the parable indicates that the all-day workers negotiated for a denarius, which the NRSV accurately renders as "the usual daily wage." The parable contrasts the usual with God's unusual act in paying even the last workers enough to live on. What would one call an employer who did that? "Good," "generous," the parable's own terms, seem right. It seems that the problem of looking at things with an "evil eye" continues even to some contemporary interpreters.

83 Walter Brueggemann, "Reaping the Whirlwind," a special article from *Journal for Preachers*, March 2020, http://j4p.wncpresby.org/articles/2020/Reaping%20the%20Whirlwind.pdf.

84. See Amy-Jill Levine's witty takedown of this view in *Short Stories by Jesus*, esp. pp. 213–18.

85. Christopher Hitchens, *God Is Not Great: How Religion Poisons Everything* (New York: Hatchette Book Group, 2009), 282.

86. Terry Eagleton, *Reason, Faith, and Revolution: Reflections on the God Debate* (New Haven, CT: Yale University Press, 2009), 7–8.

87. Makoto Fujimura, *Art + Faith: A Theology of Making* (New Haven, CT: Yale University Press, 2020), 18.

88. Garrison Keillor, "A Man in a Back Pew, Thinking to Himself," *The Column*, June 4, 2021, https://garrisonkeillor.substack.com/p/a-man-in-a-back-pew-thinking-to-himself.

89. Keillor, "A Man in a Back Pew."

90. Elizabeth O'Hara, "El Paso Project Helps Farmworkers Recover 'Dignity of Their Lives,'" *National Catholic Reporter*, December 4, 2014, https://www.ncronline.org/news/parish/el-paso-project-helps-farmworkers-recover-dignity-their-lives.

91. O'Hara, "El Paso Project."

92. Benedict XVI, *Caritas in Veritate*, https://www.vatican.va/content/benedict-xvi/en/encyclicals/documents/hf_ben-xvi_enc_20090629_caritas-in-veritate.html.

93. Joanna Adams, "The Only Question," *Journal for Preachers* 28, no. 2 (Lent, 1985): 59.

94. Adams, "The Only Question," 60.

95. Ulrich Luz, *Matthew 21–28*, Hermeneia: A Critical and Historical Commentary on the Bible (Minneapolis: Augsburg Fortress, 2005), nn. 52, 146.

96. The Greek phrase used here is τέκνα δύο, technically "two children," but the grammar and sense of the whole parable indicate that these were male offspring, old enough to work in a vineyard. Thus the usual title of this story is "the Parable of the Two Sons."

97. The parable, as it appears in the NRSV and other major translations, is quite direct and clear. The only ambiguity comes from the fact that there are three major textual traditions, with competing versions of the parable.

The version that appears in the NRSV has good textual support. A second version is basically the same story, except that the order of the two sons is reversed. It is the second son who initially refuses his father's command and then changes his mind. It also has some support in ancient manuscripts, but not as extensive as version A.

A third version is the same as A, except that when Jesus asks the leaders which son did the father's will, they answer, improbably, that the second son is the obedient one. It has a lot of textual support.

The difference between versions A and B is hardly a concern. Maybe some early preacher, in telling the parable, simply got the order of the two sons backwards. One could argue that the story does flow slightly better narratively when it's the second son who refuses but then goes to work. Or maybe a scribe, noting that Jesus applies the parable to the leaders vs. the tax collectors and prostitutes, thought it made more sense chronologically to connect the leaders to the first son and the sinners to the second son, and so reversed the original order. It finally matters little. Jesus' question "Which of the two?" is a multiple-choice test, and it is of small consequence which is answer one and which answer two.

It's version C that creates consternation. It has solid textual attestation, and it is definitely the harder of the three versions. Often, when deciding on which textual variant is older and closer to the original, textual critics will give the nod to harder versions over smoother versions, on the theory that later scribes are more likely to smooth out problems than to create them. But most scholars have come to the conclusion that this "harder text" principle doesn't work well here, because version C results in a story that simply makes no sense. Jerome, who translated the Bible into Latin, was aware of version C and said that, if this version of the parable was the original, then Jesus' opponents were being obstinate and gave him an intentionally smart-alecky answer to his question.

The version that appears in the NRSV is the best, because it has two advantages: it had good textual backing, and it makes sense. See J. Ramsey Michaels, "The Parable of the Regretful Son," *Harvard Theological Review* 61 (1968): 15–26.

98. Michaels, "The Parable of the Regretful Son," 18–19.
99. See Scott, *Hear Then the Parable*, 84. Also, Hultgren, *The Parables of Jesus*, 220.
100. Michaels, "The Parable of the Regretful Son," 20.
101. See W. D. Davies and Dale C. Allison Jr., *A Critical and Exegetical Commentary on the Gospel according to Saint Matthew*, vol. 3 (London: T. & T. Clark, 1997), 172.
102. Dietrich Bonhoeffer, *The Cost of Discipleship* (New York: Touchstone, 1995), 196–97.
103. Robert Ellsberg, "Viola Liuzzo: Civil Rights Martyr (1925–1965)," *Give Us This Day*, March 25, 2021, https://blog.giveusthisday.org/2021/03/25/viola-liuzzo/.
104. Donna Britt, "A White Mother Went to Alabama to Fight for Civil Rights. The Klan Killed Her for It," *Washington Post*, December 15, 2017, https://www.washingtonpost.com/news/retropolis/wp/2017/12/15/a-white-mother-went-to-alabama-to-fight-for-civil-rights-the-klan-killed-her-for-it/.
105. C. S. Lewis, *Surprised by Joy* (New York: HarperCollins, 1955), 278–80.
106. Andrew Nelson, "Friendship between Catholic and Death Row Inmate Began with a Letter," *Georgia Bulletin*, October 16, 2014, https://georgiabulletin.org/news/2014/10/friendship-catholic-death-row-inmate-began-letter/.
107. Nelson, "Friendship between Catholic and Death Row Inmate."
108. Obituary of Joshua Bishop, died March 31, 2016, *Legacy.com*, https://www.legacy.com/obituaries/name/joshua-bishop-obituary?pid=179580627.
109. Nelson, "Friendship between Catholic and Death Row Inmate."
110. Nelson, "Friendship between Catholic and Death Row Inmate."
111. Obituary of Joshua Bishop.
112. Obituary of Joshua Bishop.

113. Hultgren, *The Parables of Jesus,* 371.
114. Snodgrass, *Stories with Intent*, 283.
115. Snodgrass, *Stories with Intent,* 288–89.
116. Luz, *Matthew 21–28,* 36.
117. This parable presents a special challenge to Amy-Jill Levine, who has, as one of her stated aims, to wrest the parables of Jesus away from the history of anti-Jewish interpretation in Christian teaching and preaching. In her *Short Stories by Jesus,* she treats this parable only briefly and ultimately resorts to questioning that the landowner is a symbol for God. For her, the landowner who keeps sending servant after servant to the vineyard is like military commanders who keep sending in more and more battalions, mistakenly thinking that the next wave of "shock and awe" will command the respect of the enemy. This is an understandable attempt to drag the donkey in a way he does not want to go. As I hope to show, we need no such undermining of Matthew's parable to keep the interpretation from being anti-Jewish.
118. See Snodgrass, *Stories with Intent,* 559 and Luz, *Matthew 21–28,* 60.
119. Snodgrass, *Stories with Intent*, 299.
120. Donahue, *The Gospel in Parable,* 94.
121. Flavius Josephus, *The Wars of the Jews*, book 6, chap. 8.5, https://www.gutenberg.org/files/2850/2850–h/2850–h.htm#link62HCH0008.
122. Josephus, *The Wars of the Jews*, book 6, chap. 5.3.
123. Luz, *Matthew 21–28,* 54.
124. Boring, "The Gospel of Matthew," 418.
125. Only Matthew among the authors of the New Testament uses the aorist passive of this verb, and it is always employed to introduce a parable (see also 13:24 and 18:23).
126. Boring, "The Gospel of Matthew," 418.
127. Warren Carter, "Resisting and Imitating the Empire: Imperial Paradigms in Two Matthean Parables," *Interpretation* 56, no. 3 (July 2002): 272.
128. Luz, *Matthew 21–28,* 60 and accompanying note.
129. G. R. Beasley-Murray, *Jesus and the Kingdom of God* (Grand Rapids: Eerdmans, 1986), 122.
130. Richard John Neuhaus, *The Eternal Pity: Reflections on Dying* (South Bend, IN: University of Notre Dame Press, 2000), 31.
131. Neuhaus, *The Eternal Pity*, 31–32.
132. Neuhaus, *The Eternal Pity,* 32.
133. Martin Luther King Jr., "Letter from Birmingham Jail," https://www.csuchico.edu/iege/_assets/documents/susi-letter-from-birmingham-jail.pdf.
134. King, "Letter from Birmingham Jail."
135. In his 1963 commentary on Matthew in the Cambridge Bible Commentary series, Oxford professor A. W. Argyle points out there is "the element of improbability" in some of the parable's details. Later, however, after "prolonged reflection and further reading," Argyle retracted that view. As for the shops being open at midnight, Argyle reasoned that getting a correct catering count for a wedding banquet was always difficult. Hosts could run out of food and wine, so "there probably would be catering shops open all night to meet such an emergency." What prompted Argyle's change of heart was additional research on Palestinian wedding customs but also a concern that his earlier view was insulting to both Jesus and Matthew. "[T]here is no need to regard any incident in the parable of Mt 25 1–13 as improbable," he wrote. "To do so is to do less than justice both to our Lord's skill in telling parables

and to the evangelist's fidelity in reporting them" (A. W. Argyle, "Short Comment: Wedding Customs at the Time of Jesus," *Expository Times* 86, no. 7 [April 1975]: 214–15).

Interestingly, *Tractate Semachot*, a rabbinical document generally dated around the end of the third century CE, includes a parable that makes mention of shops being open at night. Told by Rabbi Meir, the parable is about a king who gave a banquet. The king invited guests to the banquet, but failed to set a time when the party was over and the guests should leave. The shrewdest guests got up from the table "at the ninth hour" (that is, 3:00 p.m.). This allowed them wisely to get home and decently into bed before the sunset. Others waited until sundown to leave. A little risky, but "the shops were still open and the lamps burning," so they could see their way home. Still other guests waited until two or three hours after dark to leave. Some of the shops were still open and lit up, but others were closed, making it somewhat harder for these guests to make their way safely home. Some foolish guests didn't leave at all, and it didn't go well. "Those remaining at the banquet became intoxicated, and wounded and killed each other" (*Semachot 8:10,* https://www.sefaria.org/Tractate_Semachot.8.9?lang=bi&with=all&lang2=en). Matthew, it appears, is not the only one to tell tough wedding stories!

136. J. Massyngbaerde Ford, "The Parable of the Foolish Scholars: Matt. XXV 1–13," *Novum Testamentum* 9, no. 2 (April 1967): 107. Ford's statement seems wrong in two ways. First, if Ford means that this parable contains criticism made by Jesus against women *as* women, that falls when we realize that all of the bridesmaids were (obviously) women—the foolish ones and the wise ones. If, however, Ford means that this parable is the only place a critical word is uttered by Jesus about a character or person who is female, that also is wrong. See Jesus' comments about the Canaanite woman (Matt. 15:26) and the sharp word he speaks to his own mother at another wedding (John 2:4).
137. Vicky Balabanski, "Opening the Closed Door: A Feminist Reading of the 'Wise and Foolish Virgins' (Mt. 25:2–12)," in Mary Ann Beavis, ed., *The Lost Coin: Parables of Women, Work, and Wisdom* (London: Sheffield Academic Press, 2002), 75.
138. Balabanski, "Opening the Closed Door," 94.
139. Balabanski, "Opening the Closed Door," 84.
140. Balabanski, "Opening the Closed Door," 78.
141. Balabanski, "Opening the Closed Door," 93.
142. Jan Lambrecht, *Out of the Treasure: The Parables in the Gospel of Matthew* (Louvain: Peeters Press, 1991), 203.
143. Nikos Kazantzakis, *The Last Temptation* (London: Faber & Faber, 1961), 223.
144. I would maintain that "wisdom" in the sense pointed to in this parable entails a way of viewing self, life, and God that plays a part in challenging oppressive systems, such as patriarchy, sexism, and racism.
145. The parable says that the young women had *lampádas* (λαμπάδας). Ulrich Luz argues that, contrary to the way most people picture this story, no reader in Matthew's time would have pictured these lamps as small oil lanterns. They would think, rather, of torches which were soaked with oil and were commonly used to light wedding processionals. See Luz, *Matthew 21–28*, 227.
146. Balabanski, "Opening the Closed Door," 93.
147. Justo González, "Irrigating the Land: How My Mind Has Changed," *Christian Century* 137, no. 27 (Dec. 30, 2020): 31.
148. Mark Price, "Tense Protest Turns Emotional as 60 North Carolina Police Kneel before Demonstrators," *Charlotte Observer,* August 4, 2020, https://www

.charlotteobserver.com/news/state/north-carolina/article243193151.html#story link=cpy.

149. Price, "Tense Protest Turns Emotional."
150. Joshua Q. Nelson, "NC Police Chief Describes Moment Officers Knelt with Protesters: 'It Is Part of Building Trust,'" *Fox News Flash,* June 3, 2020, https://www.foxnews.com/media/gina-hawkins-fayetteville-nc-police-kneel-protesters.
151. Bernstein, "On Regret."
152. Bernstein, "On Regret," emphasis in the original.
153. Bernstein, "On Regret."
154. Bernstein, "On Regret."
155. Bernstein, "On Regret."
156. Bernstein, "On Regret," emphasis in the original.
157. See, for example, Steven Sawchuck, "What Is Critical Race Theory, and Why Is It under Attack?," *Education Week,* May 18, 2021, https://www.edweek.org/leadership/what-is-critical-race-theory-and-why-is-it-under-attack/2021/05.
158. The Florida Senate, "SB 148: Bill Analysis and Fiscal Impact Statement," January 14, 2022, https://www.flsenate.gov/Session/Bill/2022/148/Analyses/2022s00148.pre.ed.PDF.
159. St. Sophronius, *Orat. 3 de Hypaphante 6.7.* Portions of this sermon appear in the Roman Catholic office of readings for the Feast of Candlemas.
160. Robert Benton, *Places in the Heart,* Scripts.com, https://www.scripts.com/script-pdf/15947.
161. Richard Lischer, *Just Tell the Truth: A Call to Faith, Hope, and Courage* (Grand Rapids: Eerdmans, 2021), 163–64.
162. David Flusser, "Aesop's Miser and the Parable of the Talents," in Clemens Thoma and Michael Wyschogrod, *Parable and Story in Judaism and Christianity* (New York: Paulist Press, 1989), 22.
163. Josephus, *The Jewish War,* books 4–7, vol. 3 (London: William Heinemann, 1928), 539.
164. William R. Herzog II, *Parables as Subversive Speech: Jesus as Pedagogue of the Oppressed* (Louisville, KY: Westminster John Knox Press, 1994), 165.
165. Here I am placing my position over against Luise Schottroff, who would declare approaches to the parables like mine "dualistic," because an important distinction is made between the setting of parables and their theological intentionality. In other words, a parable set in a wedding banquet or a farm is not, in my view, a direct sociological commentary on marriage practices or a brief for agrarian reform. These are simply the kinds of settings that all folktales employ. They play a part in the meanings of the parables, of course, but they are not the focus of them. Schottroff, on the other hand, doggedly insists that the settings are key to the interpretation of the parables and that "parables really talk about people's lives in the Roman Empire, and these depictions contain their own immediate message that needs to be heard" (see Luise Schottroff, *The Parables of Jesus* [Minneapolis: Fortress Press, 2006], 2). This sometimes leads to quite forced interpretations that run counter to the literary and theological contexts.
166. Peter Brown, "The Other Rome," *New York Review of Books* 69, no. 2 (February 10, 2022): 35.
167. Keith Beasley-Topliffe, *Writings of Toyohiko Kagawa* (Nashville: Upper Room Press, 2017), n.p.
168. Beasley-Topliffe, *Writings of Toyohiko Kagawa,* n.p.
169. Beasley-Topliffe, *Writings of Toyohiko Kagawa,* n.p.

170. Beasley-Topliffe, *Writings of Toyohiko Kagawa*, n.p.
171. "Kagawa, Toyohiko (1888–1960): Japanese Evangelist and Social Movement Leader," Boston University School of Theology, History of Missiology, https://www.bu.edu/missiology/missionary-biography/i-k/kagawa-toyohiko-1888–1960/.
172. Beasley-Topliffe, *Writings of Toyohiko Kagawa*, n.p.
173. Toyohiko Kagawa, Wikipedia, https://en.wikipedia.org/wiki/Toyohiko_Kagawa.
174. Snodgrass, *Stories with Intent*, 562. See also Sherman W. Gray, *The Least of My Brothers, Matthew 25:31–46: A History of Interpretation* (Atlanta: Scholars Press, 1989), 50.
175. Kenneth W. Woodward, "Requiem for a Saint," *Newsweek*, September 21, 1997, https://www.newsweek.com/requiem-saint-172510.
176. Rudolf Bultmann, *The History of the Synoptic Tradition* (New York: Harper & Row, 1963), 120–23. See Snodgrass, *Stories with Intent*, 543, and Hultgren, *The Parables of Jesus*, 310.
177. Donahue, *The Gospel in Parable*, 134.
178. John Donahue states, "More accurately it can be called an 'apocalyptic parable' and should be interpreted from the horizon of apocalyptic" (*The Gospel in Parable*, 110).
179. Hultgren, *The Parables of Jesus*, 320–26.
180. Hultgren, *The Parables of Jesus*, 323.
181. Robert Wuthnow, "Stories to Live By," *Theology Today* 49, no. 3 (October 1992): 308.
182. Wuthnow, "Stories to Live By," 309.
183. Adapted from a transcript of a conversation among Maggie Fergusson, Sarah Coakley, and Erik Varden, https://coramfratribus.com/archive/conversation-with-sarah-coakley/.

Chapter 7: Luke's Parables: Background

1. Michael Brice-Saddler, "It's a Biblical Thing," *Washington Post*, June 3, 2019, https://www.washingtonpost.com/religion/2019/06/04/wealthy-televangelist-explains-his-fleet-private-jets-its-biblical-thing/#comments-wrapper.
2. Naomi Tutu, *The Words of Desmond Tutu* (New York: Newmarket Press, 1989), 26.
3. The view that Luke and Acts are two parts of a unified work has long and widespread support, but it is not unquestioned. See, for example, Patricia Walters, *The Assumed Authorial Unity of Luke and Acts: A Reassessment of the Evidence* (Cambridge: Cambridge University Press, 2008), and Mikeal Parsons and Richard I. Pervo, *Rethinking the Unity of Luke and Acts* (Philadelphia: Fortress/Augsburg Press, 1993).
4. Margaret Hope Bacon, *Let This Life Speak: The Legacy of Henry Joel Cadbury* (Philadelphia: University of Pennsylvania Press, 1987), 28.
5. David L. Tiede, *Luke*, Augsburg Commentary on the New Testament (Minneapolis: Augsburg Press, 1988), 17–21.
6. Tiede, *Luke*, 19.
7. Tiede, *Luke*, 19.
8. Tiede, *Luke*, 18.
9. Tiede, *Luke*, 18.
10. Eugene Boring, *An Introduction to the New Testament: History, Literature, Theology* (Louisville, KY: Westminster John Knox Press, 2012), 556.
11. Boring, *An Introduction to the New Testament*, 556.
12. Boring, *An Introduction to the New Testament*, 557.
13. Boring, *An Introduction to the New Testament*, 558.

14. Joseph Fitzmyer, *The Gospel according to Luke I–IX* (New York: Doubleday, 1970), 234.
15. Ernst Käsemann, "The Problem of the Historical Jesus," in *Essays on New Testament Themes* (London: SCM Press, 1960), 28.
16. Troy M. Troftgruben, "Salvation 'Today' in Luke's Gospel," *Currents in Theology and Mission* 45, no. 4 (October 2018): 6.
17. Justo L. González, *Luke* (Louisville, KY: Westminster John Knox Press, 2010), 286–87.
18. Matthew L. Skinner, "Looking High and Low for Salvation in Luke," *Currents in Theology and Mission* 45, no. 4 (October 2018): 24.
19. Skinner, "Looking High and Low," 28.
20. Robert J. Karris, *Luke: Artist and Theologian, Luke's Passion Account as Literature* (New York: Paulist Press, 1985), 47.
21. Karris, *Luke*, 47.
22. Karris, *Luke*, 59–60.
23. John Navone, *Themes of St. Luke* (Rome: Gregorian University Press, 1970), 115.
24. R. Alan Culpepper, "The Gospel of Luke: Introduction, Commentary, and Reflections," in Leander E. Keck et al., eds., *The New Interpreter's Bible* (Nashville: Abingdon Press, 1995), 9:28.
25. Mark Allan Powell, *Introducing the New Testament: A Historical, Literary, and Theological Survey* (Grand Rapids: Baker Academic, 2009), 158.
26. Marcus Barth, *Rediscovering the Lord's Supper: Communion with Israel, with Christ, and among the Guests* (Atlanta: John Knox Press, 1988), 71.
27. Abigail Van Buren, *The Best of Dear Abby* (New York: Andrews & McMeel, 1981), 242, as quoted by Walker Percy in *Lost in the Cosmos: The Last Self Help Book* (New York: Farrar, Straus & Giroux, 1983), 43.
28. Culpepper, "The Gospel of Luke," 25.
29. Boring, *An Introduction to the New Testament*, 565.

Chapter 8: Luke: The Parables

1. Matthew Skinner, "Looking High and Low for Salvation in Luke," *Currents in Theology and Mission* 45, no. 4 (October 2018): 28.
2. John Drury, *The Parables in the Gospels: History and Allegory* (New York: Crossroad, 1985), 111.
3. Rory Cooney, "My Soul Cries Out with a Joyful Shout: Canticle of the Turning," copyright 1990, GIA Publications, Inc.
4. The sequence of questions about Jesus is drawn from R. Alan Culpepper, "Luke," in Leander E. Keck et al., eds., *The New Interpreter's Bible* (Nashville: Abingdon Press, 1995), 9:13.
5. Luke Timothy Johnson, *The Gospel of Luke* (Collegeville, MN: Liturgical Press, 1991), 9.
6. Johnson, *The Gospel of Luke*, 22.
7. See Drury, *The Parables in the Gospels*, 112–14.
8. Arland J. Hultgren, *The Parables of Jesus: A Commentary* (Grand Rapids: Eerdmans, 2000), 197.
9. Michael Gerson, "Trump Should Fill Christians with Rage. How Come He Doesn't?," *Washington Post*, September 1, 2022, https://www.washingtonpost.com/opinions/2022/09/01/michael-gerson-evangelical-christian-maga-democracy/.
10. Gerson, "Trump Should Fill Christians with Rage," Comments.
11. Gerson, "Trump Should Fill Christians with Rage," Comments.
12. Gerson, "Trump Should Fill Christians with Rage," Comments.

13. Gerson, "Trump Should Fill Christians with Rage," Comments.
14. Johnson, *The Gospel of Luke*, 133.
15. John Bunyan, *The Pilgrim's Progress*, ed. Barry E. Horner (Lindenhurst, NY: Reformation Press, 1999), 130.
16. Bunyan, *The Pilgrim's Progress*, 130.
17. Andrew Kirtzman, *Giuliani: The Rise and Tragic Fall of America's Mayor* (New York: Simon & Schuster, 2022), 8.
18. Friedrich Nietzsche, *Beyond Good and Evil: Prelude to a Philosophy of the Future* (Cambridge: Cambridge University Press, 2002), 78.
19. Eugene Peterson, *A Long Obedience in the Same Direction: Discipleship in an Instant Society*, rev. and expanded ed. (Downers Grove, IL: InterVarsity Press, 2000), 16.
20. Peterson, *A Long Obedience*, 17.
21. Ivan Rusyn, "War and the Church in Ukraine," an interview by Susannah Black, *Plough*, May 6, 2022, https://www.plough.com/en/topics/faith/prayer/war-and-the-church-in-ukraine.
22. Rusyn, "War and the Church in Ukraine."
23. Rusyn, "War and the Church in Ukraine."
24. Joel Green, *The Gospel of Luke* (Grand Rapids: Eerdmans, 1997), 424.
25. Amy-Jill Levine, *Short Stories by Jesus: The Enigmatic Parables of a Controversial Rabbi* (New York: HarperCollins, 2014), 90.
26. The lawyer was not the first to combine these verses. That had already been done in Jewish thought and literature. The point is not that the lawyer is a religious virtuoso, but that he is giving a faithful and traditional answer to his own question. See Levine, *Short Stories by Jesus*, 89.
27. Levine, *Short Stories by Jesus*, 93.
28. Johnson, *The Gospel of Luke*, 172.
29. Johnson, *The Gospel of Luke*, 173.
30. Robert W. Funk, *Language, Hermeneutic, and the Word of God: The Problem of Language in the New Testament and Contemporary Theology* (New York: Harper & Row, 1966), 214.
31. Irving Singer, *The Nature of Love, Volume 1: Plato to Luther* (Cambridge, MA: MIT Press, 2009), 16–17.
32. Funk, *Language, Hermeneutic, and the Word of God*, 214.
33. Joseph A. Fitzmyer, *The Gospel according to Luke X–XXIV* (New York: Doubleday, 1985), 887.
34. Levine, *Short Stories by Jesus*, 103.
35. Levine, *Short Stories by Jesus*, 103.
36. Levine, *Short Stories by Jesus*, 103.
37. John Donahue, *The Gospel in Parable* (Minneapolis: Fortress Press, 1988), 131.
38. *Mishnah Sheviit*, 8:10.
39. John 4:9, in Eugene H. Peterson, *The Message: The Bible in Contemporary Language* (Carol Stream, IL: NavPress, 2005).
40. Stephen D. Moore, *Mark and Luke in Poststructuralist Perspectives: Jesus Begins to Write* (New Haven, CT: Yale University Press, 1992), chapter 6. Although Moore, an angular and eccentric critic, has a somewhat sinister take on Luke's fascination with "looking."
41. John Dominic Crossan, *In Parables: The Challenge of the Historical Jesus* (New York: Harper & Row, 1973), 63–64.
42. Adolf Jülicher called this parable along with three others (the Rich Fool, the Rich Man and Lazarus, and the Pharisee and the Tax Collector) "example stories," parables that present behavior that is either to be imitated or avoided. Klyne

Snodgrass presents a clear discussion of the category "example story" and then rejects the label as applicable to the Good Samaritan. See Klyne Snodgrass, *Stories with Intent: A Comprehensive Guide to the Parables of Jesus* (Grand Rapids: Eerdmans, 2008), 350–53.

43. Crossan, *In Parables*, 63.
44. Ruben Zimmermann, *Puzzling the Parables of Jesus: Methods and Interpretation* (Minneapolis: Fortress Press, 2015), 303.
45. Crossan, *In Parables*, 63.
46. Levine, *Short Stories by Jesus,* 102.
47. Levine, *Short Stories by Jesus*, 101–2.
48. Fyodor Dostoevsky, *The Brothers Karamazov* (New York: Alfred A. Knopf, 1992), 235.
49. Dostoevsky, *The Brothers Karamazov*, 235.
50. See Green, *The Gospel of Luke,* 446–47.
51. Gail Collins and David Brooks, "George Steinbrenner and His Ego," *New York Times,* July 13, 2010, https://archive.nytimes.com/opinionator.blogs.nytimes.com/2010/07/13/george-steinbrenner-and-his-ego/.
52. Collins and Brooks, "George Steinbrenner and His Ego."
53. Snodgrass, *Stories with Intent,* 443.
54. Snodgrass, *Stories with Intent,* 443–45.
55. Fitzmyer, *The Gospel according to Luke X–XXIV,* 912.
56. Joanie Demer, quoted in David Owen, "There and Back Again: How Product Return Became an Industry," *The New Yorker* (August 21, 2023): 20.
57. Snodgrass, *Stories with Intent,* 443.
58. See the discussion of Jülicher and example stories in note 42. More recently, Jülicher's categories have been strongly challenged, especially the "example story" label. See Jeffrey Tucker, *Example Stories: Perspectives on Four Parables in the Gospel of Luke* (Sheffield: Sheffield Academic Press, 1998).
59. Hultgren, *The Parables of Jesus*, 109.
60. Fitzmyer, *The Gospel according to Luke X–XXIV*, 971.
61. Fitzmyer, *The Gospel according to Luke X–XXIV*, 972.
62. Fitzmyer, *The Gospel according to Luke X–XXIV*, 972.
63. Snodgrass, *Stories with Intent,* 398.
64. Section 1120a in Aristotle, *Nicomachean Ethics* (Indianapolis: Hackett Publishing, 1999), 50.
65. Snodgrass, *Stories with Intent*, 400.
66. John May, "The Best and Worst of a Legend," *BBC Sport: Football*, November 25, 2005, http://news.bbc.co.uk/sport2/hi/football/4312792.stm.
67. Contra Fitzmyer, *The Gospel according to Luke X–XXIV,* 971.
68. Luke Johnson suggests that when the rich man addresses himself in 12:19, "Soul, you have ample goods laid up for many years; relax, eat, drink, be merry," the conversation with himself is so familiar "that one is tempted to render it 'old man.'" Johnson, *The Gospel of Luke*, 199.
69. See Robert C. Tannehill, *Luke* (Nashville: Abingdon Press, 1996), 214.
70. Nothing is known historically of either of these two tragedies. They are mentioned only here in Luke.
71. Johnson, *The Gospel of Luke*, 215.
72. Fitzmyer, *The Gospel according to Luke X–XXIV*, 1017.
73. Johnson, *The Gospel of Luke*, 223.
74. For a description of the Friday evening Sabbath meals see Paul F. Bradshaw and Maxwell E. Johnson, *The Eucharistic Liturgies: Their Evolution and Interpretation*

(Collegeville, MN: Liturgical Press, 2012), 5. See a reference to the midday Sabbath meals in Josephus, *Life of Josephus* (Boston: Brill Academic, 2003), 123.

75. The text of this prayer, constructed from early sources by Talmudic scholar Louis Finkelstein, is found in Bradshaw and Johnson, *The Eucharistic Liturgies*, 6–7.
76. See a good discussion of this issue in Snodgrass, who himself argues, "In Matthew and Luke we have two similar stories, not two versions of the same story" (Snodgrass, *Stories with Intent*, 310).
77. See Donahue, *The Gospel in Parable*, 145.
78. Snodgrass, *Stories with Intent*, 306.
79. David E. Garland, *Luke: Exegetical Commentary on the New Testament* (Grand Rapids: Zondervan, 2011), 586.
80. See James A. Sanders, "The Ethic of Election in Luke's Great Banquet Parable," in James L. Crenshaw and John T. Willis, eds., *Essays in Old Testament Ethics* (New York: Ktav, 1974), 245–71.
81. Garland, *Luke*, 590–91. See also Richard L. Rohrbaugh, "The Pre-Industrial City in Luke–Acts: Urban Social Relations," in Jerome H. Neyrey, ed., *The Social World of Luke–Acts: Models for Interpretation* (Peabody, MA: Hendrickson, 1991), 142–43.
82. Johnson, *The Gospel of Luke*, 229.
83. See Joachim Jeremias, *The Parables of Jesus* (New York: Charles Scribner's Sons, 1963), 177.
84. Snodgrass, *Stories with Intent*, 316.
85. See, e.g., Green, *The Gospel of Luke*, 557–63.
86. Donahue, *The Gospel in Parable*, 143.
87. *Desiderio Desideravi of The Holy Father Francis*, sections 5 and 6, https://www.vatican.va/content/francesco/en/apost_letters/documents/20220629-lettera-ap-desiderio-desideravi.html.
88. Hugh Nissenson, "Charity," *Esquire*, April 1970, 140–41.
89. Johnson, *The Gospel of Luke*, 235.
90. Joachim Jeremías, *Jerusalem in the Time of Jesus* (London: SCM Press, 1969), 303–12. See also Snodgrass, *Stories with Intent*, 102, and Donahue, *The Gospel in Parable*, 148. For a contrary view, see Green, *The Gospel of Luke*, n. 211, 573–74.
91. See, e.g., Hultgren, *The Parables of Jesus*, 60.
92. Harvey Cox, "The Spy in the Pew," *New York Times*, March 3, 1986, A15.
93. Suggestions that the lost coin was part of a necklace or a headdress have no basis in the parable and are misleading.
94. Carol Schersten LaHurd, "Rediscovering the Lost Women in Luke 15," *Biblical Theology Bulletin* 24, no. 2 (May 1994): 66.
95. Hultgren, *The Parables of Jesus*, 64.
96. Snodgrass, *Stories with Intent*, 114.
97. Snodgrass, *Stories with Intent*, 114. Another commentator, Alfred Plummer, writing in one of the most distinguished commentary series of the previous century, is also quite insistent that the woman in this parable can by no means be a symbol for God. Throttling the story with a cane until it collapses in the street, Plummer says that the sheep in the companion Parable of the Lost Sheep "could wander away of its own accord" but the woman in the Lost Coin "can blame herself for the loss of the coin." The shepherd [male] in the previous parable "might be moved by pity rather than self-interest to bring back the sheep," but "the woman must be moved by self-interest alone to recover the coin." Plummer's conclusion is that "we may infer that the woman represents the Church rather than Divine Wisdom, if she represents anything at all." I hope, if Plummer is the prosecuting attorney, that the woman gets

a good lawyer. See Alfred Plummer, *A Critical and Exegetical Commentary on the Gospel according to St. Luke*, 5th ed. (New York: Charles Scribner's Sons, 1902), 370.

98. Richard Lischer, *Just Tell the Truth: A Call to Faith, Hope, and Courage* (Grand Rapids: Eerdmans, 2021), 88–89.
99. Augustine, *Confessions*, book 3:21 (New York: Modern Library, 2017), 73–74.
100. Augustine, *Confessions*, 73.
101. Augustine, *Confessions*, 73.
102. Augustine, *Confessions*, 236–37.
103. Augustine, *Confessions*, 237.
104. Augustine, *Confessions*, 211.
105. Drury, *The Parables in the Gospels*, 139.
106. Drury, *The Parables in the Gospels*, 139, British spelling changed to American spelling.
107. Johnson, *The Gospel of Luke*, 236.
108. Bernard Brandon Scott, *Hollywood Dreams and Biblical Stories* (Minneapolis: Fortress Press, 1940), 64.
109. Snodgrass, *Stories with Intent*, 105.
110. I agree with Snodgrass that "evidence does not exist" for the idea that Luke created the Prodigal Son parable out of Matthew's Parable of the Two Sons (Snodgrass, *Stories with Intent*, 128–29).
111. Snodgrass, *Stories with Intent*, viii.
112. See Levine, *Short Stories by Jesus*, 50–51.
113. Kenneth E. Bailey, *The Cross and the Prodigal: Luke 15 through the Eyes of Middle Eastern Peasants*, 2nd ed. (Downers Grove, IL: InterVarsity Press, 2005), esp. chapter 2 ("The Death Wish").
114. Bailey, *Poet and Peasant*, 162–68.
115. Bailey, *The Cross and the Prodigal*, 41.
116. Bernard S. Jackson, *Essays on Halakhah in the New Testament* (Leiden: Brill, 2008), 116.
117. Jackson, *Essays on Halakhah*, 116.
118. T. W. Manson, *The Sayings of Jesus* (London: SCM, 1949), 287. Bailey is aware that Manson's statement is a problem for his theory, and counters with a more modern example. Bailey says that literature from the American South during the Civil War period admonishes readers not to trust "Yankees," and that, following Manson's logic, one would have to acknowledge that there must have been some Southerners who did trust Yankees, or there would have been no reason to warn against it. But, of course, Bailey says, no Southerners would ever trust Yankees, a claim that reveals that Bailey misunderstands the South as much as he misconstrues ancient Palestine. There was plenty of mistrust, for sure, but there are also many examples of relationships of trust between Southerners and Northerners even during the Civil War. In fact, in my native town, Atlanta, GA, several of the historic downtown churches were spared when the priest at the Catholic church negotiated a bond of trust with General Sherman not to destroy these churches when the city was burned. See Bailey, *Poet and Peasant*, 163.
119. Bailey, *The Cross and the Prodigal*, 42.
120. Getting an advance on one's inheritance may not even have been that uncommon in the culture in which the parable was told. Jeremias states Jewish Palestine had a population of a half million at the most, while an estimated eight times that many, four million Jews, lived in the commercial cities beyond Palestine. This was the result of a wave of migration stimulated by the hope of obtaining a higher standard of living. How many Jewish sons must there have been at the time who

asked their fathers for the means to move to Alexandria or somewhere else more promising? See Jeremias, *The Parables of Jesus*, 129.
121. Fitzmyer, *The Gospel according to Luke X–XXIV*, 1087.
122. J. Albert Harrell, "The Indentured Labor of the Prodigal Son (Luke 15:15)," *Journal of Biblical Literature* 115, no. 4 (Winter 1996): 717.
123. Levine, *Short Stories by Jesus,* 57.
124. Fitzmyer, *The Gospel according to Luke X–XXIV*, 1088.
125. See, e.g., Jackson, *Essays on Halakhah in the New Testament*, 134.
126. See, e.g., Levine, *Short Stories by Jesus*, 58.
127. Peter S. Hawkins, "A Man Had Two Sons: The Question of Forgiveness in Luke 15," in Charles L. Griswold and David Konstan, *Ancient Forgiveness: Classical, Judaic, and Christian* (Cambridge: Cambridge University Press, 2012), 168.
128. David Buttrick, *Speaking Parables: A Homiletic Guide* (Louisville, KY: Westminster John Knox Press, 2000), 202.
129. Buttrick, *Speaking Parables*, 43.
130. Donald Juel, "The Strange Silence of the Bible," *Interpretation* 51, no. 1 (January 1997): 10.
131. Juel, "The Strange Silence of the Bible," 10.
132. Levine, *Short Stories by Jesus,* 51.
133. The Rolling Stones, "It's Only Rock and Roll (But I Like It)," on the album *It's Only Rock and Roll* (Rolling Stones Records, 1974).
134. Joseph P. Healey, "Repentance, Old Testament," in David Noel Freedman, ed., *The Anchor Bible Dictionary* (New York: Doubleday, 1992), 5:672.
135. Some interpreters want to see in the father's running a loss of dignity. For example, Hultgren states, "The father *runs* to meet the son—an outlandish behavior. . . . [A] dignified man does not run. We must imagine here a prominent person wearing a long robe. In order to run, he must pull up the robe, exposing his legs, which would have been considered shameful in a Semitic culture" (Hultgren, *The Parables of Jesus,* 78). Maybe, but it seems far more likely that the detail of the father's running is meant simply to emphasize his joy over the return of his son.
136. Johnson, *The Gospel of Luke,* 238.
137. Garland, *Luke,* 629.
138. Garland, *Luke*, 631.
139. Garland, *Luke*, 631.
140. Karl Rengstorf, "δοῦλος," in Gerhard Kittel, ed., *Theological Dictionary of the New Testament* (Grand Rapids: Eerdmans, 1964), 2:267.
141. Fitzmyer, *The Gospel according to Luke I–IX* (Garden City, NY: Doubleday, 1981), 179–80.
142. Jürgen Moltmann, *The Church in the Power of the Spirit: A Contribution to Messianic Ecclesiology* (Minneapolis: Fortress Press, 1993), 110.
143. Arthur Miller, *The Price* (New York: Penguin, 1968), 112.
144. A Coalition for Biblical Sexuality, "The Nashville Statement" (2017), https://cbmw.org/wp-content/uploads/2017/08/The-Nashville-Statement.pdf.
145. Matthew Fitzgerald, "God's Hand," October 7, 2017, https://www.ucc.org/daily_devotional_gods_hand.
146. The others are the Rich Fool, the Prodigal Son, the Unjust Judge, and the Wicked Tenants.
147. Some of the discussion of this parable is an abbreviated and revised version of Thomas G. Long, "Getting By with a Little Help from My Friends: Preaching the

Parable of the Unjust Steward," *Sewanee Theological Review* 44, no. 2 (Easter 2001): 163–75, and is used by permission.

148. John Dominic Crossan, *In Parables: The Challenge of the Historical Jesus* (New York: Harper & Row, 1973), 109–10.
149. One of the earliest examples of this can be found in a comment by the Cambridge language scholar Margaret D. Gibson in the *Expository Times* 14, no. 7 (April 1903): 334: "I know that at the present time, wherever Orientals are left to their own methods, uncontrolled by any protectorate of Europeans, the plan is to farm out taxes or property of any description. The steward would therefore demand from the cultivators much more than he would pay to the overlord, perhaps even double, and pocket the difference himself. This is so usual in the East that those who were listening to our Lord, many of whom were themselves publicans, i.e., farmers of taxes, would understand the situation intuitively, and would not need any explanation." "Gibson," writes Kenneth Bailey, "shows the attitude of an imperialistic age in assuming the cultural superiority of Europeans" (*Poet and Peasant: A Literary-Cultural Approach to the Parables in Luke* [Grand Rapids: Eerdmans, 1976], 88).
150. C. H. Dodd, *The Parables of the Kingdom*, rev. ed. (Glasgow: Collins, 1978), 26.
151. Fitzmyer, *The Gospel according to Luke X–XXIV*, 1105.
152. Buttrick, *Speaking Parables*, 210.
153. Dan Otto Via, *The Parables* (Philadelphia: Fortress Press, 1974), 162.
154. Bailey, *Poet and Peasant*, 86–118.
155. Donahue, *The Gospel in Parable*, 162–69.
156. Bailey, *Poet and Peasant*, 101.
157. Bailey, *Poet and Peasant*, 102.
158. Bailey, *Poet and Peasant*, 107.
159. Johnson, *The Gospel of Luke,* 244.
160. "God of Grace and God of Glory," by Harry Emerson Fosdick, found in many hymnals.
161. Johnson, *The Gospel of Luke*, 245
162. Garland, *Luke*, 669.
163. Gildas Hamel, *Poverty and Charity in Roman Palestine,* 30, https://cpb-us-e1.wpmucdn.com/sites.ucsc.edu/dist/9/20/files/2015/06/poverty_charity.pdf.
164. Fitzmyer, *The Gospel according to Luke X–XXIV,* 1131.
165. Divine figures are named twice: the "Son of Man" in the Parable of the Sheep and the Goats and "God" in the Parable of the Rich Fool.
166. Levine, *Short Stories by Jesus*, 280.
167. Kaufmann Kohler, "Abraham's Bosom," *The Jewish Encyclopedia* (New York: Funk & Wagnalls, 1901), 1:92–93.
168. Johnson, *The Gospel of Luke,* 252.
169. Archibald M. Hunter, *Interpreting the Parables* (Philadelphia: Westminster Press, 1960), 84.
170. Bruce M. Metzger, *A Textual Commentary on the Greek New Testament* (New York: United Bible Societies, 1971), 165–66.
171. See L. I. Rabinowitz, "The Study of a Midrash," *Jewish Quarterly Review* 58, no. 2 (October 1967): 143–61.
172. Donahue, *The Gospel in Parable,* 170.
173. *Tractate Sanhedrin*, 109b.
174. *Tractate Derekh Eretz Zuta*, 1:9.
175. Louis Ginzberg, *The Legends of the Jews* (Philadelphia: Jewish Publication Society, 2003), 1:294.

176. John Lightfoot, in John Rogers Pitman, ed., *The Whole Works of the Rev. John Lightfoot, D.D., Volume XII, Horae Hebraicae et Talmudicae Upon the Gospels of St. Luke and St. John* (London: J. F. Dove, 1823), 158.
177. Snodgrass, *Stories with Intent*, 429.
178. Jon Sobrino, *Jesus the Liberator: A Historical-Theological View* (Maryknoll, NY: Orbis Books, 1993), 72.
179. Luke Timothy Johnson. *Sharing Possessions: What Faith Demands*, 2nd ed. (Grand Rapids: Eerdmans, 2006), vi.
180. Johnson, *Sharing Possessions*, 77.
181. Hultgren, *The Parables of Jesus*, 253.
182. Johnson, *The Gospel of Luke*, 264.
183. See a marvelous exegesis of this section of Luke, in Robert C. Tannehill, *The Sword of His Mouth* (Philadelphia: Fortress Press, 1975), 118–22.
184. Annie Dillard, *Holy the Firm* (New York: Harper & Row, 1977), 57–58.
185. Garland, *Luke*, 708.
186. From an essay by Harvard historian Laurel Thatcher Ulrich, "Vertuous Women Found: New England Ministerial Literature, 1668–1735," *American Quarterly* 28, no. 1 (1976): 20–40.
187. Charles E. B. Cranfield, "Parable of the Unjust Judge and the Eschatology of Luke–Acts," *Scottish Journal of Theology* 16, no. 3 (September 1963), 300.
188. John Carroll, *Luke: A Commentary* (Louisville, KY: Westminster John Knox Press, 2012), 355.
189. Snodgrass, *Stories with Intent*, 460.
190. Carroll, *Luke*, 357.
191. Snodgrass, *Stories with Intent*, 468. On the general theme of anti-Jewish stereotypes in Christian interpretation of this parable, see Levine, *Short Stories by Jesus*, 184–86.
192. The Greek behind this phrase is maddeningly ambiguous, and, making matters more complicated, this verse has several textual variants, all with some support. The text could say, as the NRSV would have it, that the Pharisee stood "by himself," but it could also mean that he stood and prayed "about himself," "within himself," or even "to himself." Good arguments can be made, and have been made, for all of these possibilities, and others, but, when we take the literary structure of the parable into account, the evidence tilts towards the NRSV rendering. The parable consists of a series of contrasts between the two men, and the first of these contrasts regards how they stand: the Pharisee is "standing by himself" while the tax collector is "standing far off."
193. Hultgren, *The Parables of Jesus*, 122.
194. See Fitzmyer, *The Gospel according to Luke X–XXIV*, 1188.
195. Fitzmyer, *The Gospel according to Luke X–XXIV*, 1188.
196. Fitzmyer, *The Gospel according to Luke X–XXIV*, 1188.
197. Joseph Holt, "Ten Years Sober," *The Sun* 559 (July 2022): 17.
198. Jeremias, *The Parables of Jesus*, 59.
199. R. Alan Culpepper, "The Gospel of Luke: Introduction, Commentary, and Reflections," in *The New Interpreter's Bible* (Nashville: Abingdon Press, 1995), 9:360.
200. Perhaps the most influential of those who think the parable was spoken as an affirmation of the listeners' supposition that the establishment of the kingdom of God was immediately at hand is Johnson, *The Gospel of Luke*, 288–95. For Johnson, the nobleman in the parable "is obviously Jesus himself," and the parable is "an authorial commentary" by Luke on the story he is about to tell, the narrative of Jesus entering Jerusalem, being hailed as king as he came down from the Mount of

Olives, and, as the risen Lord, continuing to exercise kingly authority. This interpretation of the parable, however, is a stretch. If Luke constructed this parable as a commentary on the ending of the Jesus story, why would he portray Jesus as a nobleman who is a violence-prone tyrant? Also, when Luke continues the story of Jesus in Acts, the disciples ask the risen Jesus, "Lord, is this the time when you will restore the kingdom to Israel?"—to which Jesus replies, "It is not for you to know the times or periods that the Father has set by his own authority" (Acts 1:6–7). In other words, the full establishment of the kingdom of God has not yet come, and the disciples are still guessing wrong about the timing.

201. Culpepper, "The Gospel of Luke," 362.
202. Culpepper, "The Gospel of Luke," 362.
203. Culpepper, "The Gospel of Luke," 363.
204. Josephus, *The Jewish Wars*, 2.3.6.
205. Jeremias, *The Parables of Jesus*, 59.
206. Richard Gottheil and Louis Ginzberg, "Archelaus," in *The Jewish Encyclopedia* (New York: Funk & Wagnalls, 1925), 2:79.
207. Culpepper, "The Gospel of Luke," 363.
208. Johnson, *The Gospel of Luke*, 173.
209. Garland, *Luke*, 761.
210. Fitzmyer, *The Gospel according to Luke X–XXIV*, 1232.
211. Fitzmyer, *The Gospel according to Luke X–XXIV*, 1233.
212. Green, *The Gospel of Luke*, 676.
213. Green, *The Gospel of Luke*, 676.
214. Green, *The Gospel of Luke*, 676.
215. Green, *The Gospel of Luke*, 677.
216. Garland, *Luke*, 764.
217. Culpepper, "The Gospel of Luke," 363.
218. Fitzmyer, *The Gospel according to Luke X–XXIV*, 1260. See also Luke 2:49.
219. Johnson, *The Gospel of Luke*, 218, 304.
220. Jack Dean Kingsbury, *Conflict in Luke: Jesus, Authorities, Disciples* (Minneapolis: Fortress Press, 1991), 103.
221. Actually, the Greek employs the same preposition for both groups, *pros* (πρὸς), which can mean, among other things, "to," "about" or "against," depending on context. The NRSV correctly reflects the context when it gives *pros* the sense of "to" in 20:9 ("He began to tell the people this parable . . .") and translates it as "against" in 20:19 ("he told this parable against them . . ."). It could be translated "about them," but since the parable is a negative one, being "about them" would carry the same force as being "against them."
222. The reason for the owner going away for a long time is not completely clear. It is not an allegorical reference to the Parousia, since the vineyard owner represents God, not Jesus. The Torah forbids eating fruit from a new planting for five years (see Lev. 19:23–25), and that may be in the background of the parable. Some suggest the "long time" is a theological reference to the patience of God (see David Tiede, *Luke*, 340), but that may add allegorical complexity where Luke intends none.
223. The killing of the beloved son outside the vineyard may "reflect the tradition concerning Jesus that he was killed 'outside the camp' (Heb. 13:12–13)" (Johnson, *The Gospel of Luke*, 306).
224. See John S. Kloppenborg, *The Tenants in the Vineyard: Ideology, Economics, and Agrarian Conflict in Jewish Palestine* (Tübingen: Mohr Siebeck, 2006), 212.

225. Johnson, *The Gospel of Luke*, 303.
226. Garland, *Luke*, 794.
227. Some commentators have noted that there may be a play on words involved in this Scripture. In Hebrew, the word for "stone" is *'eben*, and the word for son is close, *bēn*. However, the meaning of the passage in Luke doesn't depend on this pun.
228. Fitzmyer, *The Gospel according to Luke X–XXIV*, 1282.
229. Tannehill, *Luke*, 272.
230. Willie James Jennings, *Acts* (Louisville, KY: Westminster John Knox Press, 2017), 47.

Index of Ancient Sources

Index of Subjects